MORTGAGE RECEIVERSHIP:
LAW AND PRACTICE

MORTGAGE RECEIVERSHIP:
LAW AND PRACTICE

Stephanie Tozer
and
Cecily Crampin

Wildy, Simmonds & Hill Publishing

Contains public sector information licensed under the Open Government Licence v3.0

ISBN: 9780854902521

British Library Cataloguing in Publication Data

A catalogue record for this book is available from the British Library

First published in 2018 by

Wildy, Simmonds & Hill Publishing
Wildy & Sons Ltd
Lincoln's Inn Archway
Carey Street
London WC2A 2JD
www.wildy.com

Typeset by Heather Jones, North Petherton, Somerset.
Printed in Great Britain by CPI Antony Rowe, Chippenham, Wiltshire.

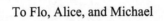

To Flo, Alice, and Michael

Foreword

As the title makes clear, this is a book on mortgage receivership. It deals with the law and practice in relation to receivers appointed by mortgagees out of court. The book therefore does not deal with receivers appointed by the court or with other types of receiver appointed out of court, such as a receiver of a company appointed pursuant to a debenture. The fact that there is this limit on the scope of the work will be of great assistance to practitioners. One of the difficulties in giving advice in this area is in trying to work out whether a decision in a particular case as to the powers and duties of a different type of receiver also applies to the specific case of a receiver appointed by a mortgagee out of court. The powers and duties of a receiver depend critically on what type of receiver one is dealing with; receivers are certainly not all the same.

There are other textbooks which deal with the law as to receivers, and those textbooks generally have a chapter on mortgage receivership. Indeed, there are textbooks dealing with the law of mortgages which also discuss the position of a receiver appointed by a mortgagee. However, the other works of this kind discuss mortgage receivership in much less depth than is the case with this new book. Such works tend to be reactive to cases which have been decided. If a particular point has been decided, then the textbook records that fact, but does not necessarily identify all of the questions which can arise and have not been decided. Further, books on mortgages tend to concentrate on what are called 'LPA receivers' appointed under section 109 of the Law of Property Act 1925. This book deals with 'mortgage receivers' rather than 'LPA receivers' because, these days, a standard form of mortgage contains express terms as to the appointment, and the powers, of a receiver which go beyond what is provided by the Law of Property Act 1925. Accordingly, a book which confined itself to LPA receivers would not deal with many matters which actually arise under today's standard forms of mortgage.

As the book explains, the fact that in law the receiver appointed by the mortgagee is deemed to be the agent of the mortgagor gives rise to considerable scope for misunderstanding. Indeed, the fact that the receiver is the agent of the mortgagor is counter-intuitive and is certainly not understood by many mortgagors. However, this deemed agency is fundamental to a resolution of the many issues which arise as to the powers, duties and responsibilities of the receiver and of the mortgagee who appointed the receiver. The deemed agency has a number of unusual features: the mortgagor cannot remove the deemed agent, the deemed agent can act contrary to the wishes of the mortgagor and the deemed agent does not owe to the mortgagor the usual duties owed by an agent to a principal. A practitioner needs a clear understanding of the nature of this agency in order to understand the various relationships – between the receiver and the mortgagor, between the receiver and the mortgagee, between the receiver and third parties and between the mortgagor and the mortgagee. The book also addresses an area which badly requires analysis and clear thinking: does the deemed agency extend to a power which the mortgagor does not have, but which is a mortgagee's power which the mortgagee has delegated to the receiver? This book provides a clear and reliable analysis to guide the practitioner towards a full understanding of the nature of the deemed agency.

Although there is a body of case law dealing with specific matters in relation to mortgage receivers, as the book points out, the case law is still relatively limited and often does not set out a detailed analysis of the nature of mortgage receivership. When reading cases in this area of the law, one constantly faces questions as to whether the ruling of the court contains a proposition of general application and how far the ruling extends.

Speaking generally, the four things which a practitioner needs a textbook to do are: (1) to identify the right questions for the practitioner to ask; (2) to provide answers to those questions; (3) to set out the reasons for those answers; and (4) to point out the practical implications of a possible step. Practitioners can get into real difficulty if they give advice or act without realising that certain questions arise and need to be addressed. Practitioners can also go wrong by failing to appreciate the consequences of certain steps which might be taken.

This book serves the needs of practitioners in these ways. It contains a thorough and robust analysis of the principles to be applied. It performs the vital task of identifying the questions which arise and need to be considered. Indeed, the book reveals that hitherto there have been questions which have not been addressed in the decided cases, but yet may be of great importance in particular cases. The book gives reasoned answers to the relevant questions and identifies the practical implications of various courses of action.

Although the scope of the book is confined to mortgage receivership, its length shows just how many issues potentially arise. Its length, as compared with the length of chapters in other less specialised works, also reveals how much needs to be said on particular points to give the practitioner the material needed to give sound advice.

Sir Paul Morgan
Judge of the High Court
July 2018

Preface

We are delighted to have had the opportunity to write a book about mortgage receivership. It is a subject which both of us realised was particularly interesting when we first encountered it in litigation. We have relished having the opportunity to address the subject comprehensively, rather than looking at the particular corners on which, from time to time, our cases have turned.

Although our two names appear on the title, a number of other people have contributed greatly to the content of this book. We thank, first, Tricia Hemans, who provided a detailed first draft of Chapter 3. We also thank Elizabeth Wilson who gave us guidance about some of the tax issues, Linda Williams who discussed with us Land Registry practice, and Philip Collis who, over what was no doubt for him a rather long coffee, discussed the practicalities of sales by receivers. We are grateful to all of them. Of course, any errors are our own.

On a personal level, we would also like thank our families for their support generally, and particularly during the writing of this book.

The law is as stated on 1 July 2018.

Stephanie Tozer
Cecily Crampin

Contents

Table of Cases

References are to paragraph numbers.

Table of Statutes

References are to paragraph numbers.

Table of Statutory Instruments

References are to paragraph numbers.

Table of European Material

References are to paragraph numbers.

Table of Non-Statutory Material

List of Abbreviations

2007 Act	Tribunals, Courts and Enforcement Act 2007
2013 Regulations	Taking Control of Goods Regulations 2013 (SI 2013/1894)
AGA	authorised guarantee agreement
CCA 1974	Consumer Credit Act 1974
CGT	capital gains tax
CONC	Consumer Credit Sourcebook
CPR	Civil Procedure Rules 1998 (SI 1998/3132)
CRAR	commercial rent arrears recovery
CVA	company voluntary arrangement
FCA	Financial Conduct Authority
FSMA 2000	Financial Services and Markets Act 2000
HMRC	HM Revenue & Customs
Insolvency Rules 2016	Insolvency (England and Wales) Rules 2016 (SI 2016/1024)
IPO	interim possession order
IVA	individual voluntary arrangement
LPA receiver	Law of Property Act 1925 receiver
MCD	Mortgage Credit Directive 2014/17/EU
MCD Order 2015	Mortgage Credit Directive Order 2015 (SI 2015/910)
MCOB	Mortgages and Home Finance: Conduct of Business Sourcebook
Protocol	Pre-Action Protocol for Possession Claims based on Mortgage or Home Purchase Plan Arrears in Respect of Residential Property (CPR)
RAO 2001	Financial Services and Markets Act 2000 (Regulated Activities) Order 2001 (SI 2001/544)
VAT	value added tax

Chapter 1

Introduction

1.1   The history of mortgage law in the 19th century could be seen as a battle between the rigours of the lender's powers and the fair hand of equity seeking to soften them.

1.2   Historically, mortgages were created by the borrower giving the lender his estate with a contractual right of redemption, and reconveyance, if the loan was repaid by the date agreed. If the agreed date passed without redemption, the land became the lender's. Equity intervened, giving the borrower the right to redeem after that date the equity of redemption.

1.3   Similarly, the lender had, by virtue of its estate, a right to possession of the mortgaged property, but equity intervened to impose various duties on a mortgagee in possession so as to prevent the lender from securing any advantage beyond securing repayment.

1.4   The lender in possession is under an equitable duty to be reasonably 'diligent in realizing the amount which is due, in order that it may restore the estate to the' borrower.[1] The lender must deal fairly and equitably with the borrower.[2] The lender in possession is held liable to account for rent and profits it would have received but for its wilful default.[3] He must keep the premises in repair and is liable for waste.[4]

1.5   Although those duties are not as great as a positive duty to the borrower to take reasonable care when dealing with the property, the duty on the lender when in possession to account to the borrower and those interested in the

---

[1]   *Lord Kensington v Bouverie* (1855) 7 De GM & G 134, distinguishing this from the position of the receiver, who is put in to repay the interest only. See also *Downsview Nominees Ltd v First City Corp Ltd* [1993] AC 295 at 315. See also *Gaskell v Gosling* [1897] AC 575; because of the onerous liabilities imposed on the lender in possession, the court is unwilling to decide it is in possession unless no other inference is possible on the evidence.

[2]   *Medforth v Blake* [2000] Ch 86 at 101H.

[3]   *White v City of London Brewery Company* (1889) 42 Ch D 237, for example. See *Medforth v Blake* [2000] Ch 86 at 93H. An account on the footing of wilful default is an equitable remedy. It requires the lender to set out its account of monies received into the mortgage account and monies spent, but the monies taken as received will include anything it should have received but for 'its wilful default', i.e. where lack of receipt is due to breach of the applicable duty, whether or not that breach was intentional. The lender will have to make good any such loss found under the account. The taking of an account on the basis of wilful default allows the court to undertake an extensive enquiry into its administration, and is hence something lenders would wish to avoid.

[4]   *Downsview Nominees Ltd v First City Corp Ltd* [1993] AC 295 at 315.

equity of redemption is strict[5] and particularly onerous[6] in the sense that that account imposes on the lender the burden of showing that the steps taken are within the duty.

1.6　　It was in order to avoid this potential liability, and the risk it imposes as to full recovery of the principal and interest under the loan, that mortgage receivership as a remedy of the lender was introduced.[7] Lenders began first to make it a contractual condition of the mortgage that the borrower would, at the lender's direction, appoint a receiver, as the borrower's agent. The role of the receiver was to collect the income and pay it to the lender to pay down the mortgage interest, holding the surplus for the borrower. Lenders then began to make it a contractual condition that the lender itself could appoint a receiver who would be the agent of the borrower.

1.7　　The purpose of the agency was to put the liability for any default of the receiver on the borrower, not the lender. That latter practice of receivership as deemed agent of the borrower was then enacted, the statutory version now in force being section 109 of the Law of Property Act 1925.[8]

1.8　　Thus, mortgage receivership arose precisely as a reaction by lenders to the imposition by equity of a liability on a lender in possession to account to the borrower for its wilful default. It is a reaction which has developed into a formidable power in the lender's armoury. Although the statutory receivership under section 109 of the Law of Property Act 1925 is limited to a receivership of income,[9] additional powers can be given expressly in the mortgage conditions: the right to take possession, the power of sale, and, where the borrower's business is charged, the power to run that business, all as deemed agent of the borrower.

1.9　　It is thus common for receivers to be appointed precisely to do what one might expect the lender to do: to obtain vacant possession of the mortgaged property and sell. By appointing receivers, the lender can avoid, or limit, its liability. The lender puts in charge of the property a receiver of its choosing, whose primary duty is to pay down the loan. Despite the direction of the receiver's interest and the borrower's lack of control over him, by the device of the deemed agency liability for the receiver is not on the lender but on the borrower.

1.10　　Despite the long history of receivership and its relatively common use, the case law on it is comparatively limited as against other areas of property law. In addition, many of the cases do not set out a detailed analysis of the

---

[5]　　*Yorkshire Bank v Hall* [1999] 1 WLR 1713 at 1728.

[6]　　*Medforth v Blake* [2000] Ch 86.

[7]　　Receivership is a device designed to insulate the lender from liability for the receiver's acts: *Edenwest Ltd v CMS Cameron McKenna (A Firm)* [2012] EWHC 1258 (Ch) at [61]–[62].

[8]　　See *Medforth v Blake* [2000] Ch 86 at 93H.

[9]　　With the lender's powers of leasing and accepting surrenders under Law of Property Act 1925, ss 99 and 100 delegable by it to the receiver.

nature of receivership and how that assists in answering the questions at issue. In that sense, this is an area of law which is little understood.

1.11 Traditionally, receivership was used more often in mortgages of commercial land. More recently, perhaps because of the prevalence of buy-to-let mortgages, receivership is being used increasingly often in the residential context. This has led to some recent case law testing the effect of the receivers' agency in residential landlord and tenant law, for example *The Keepers and Governors of the Possessions, Revenues and Goods of the Free Grammar School of John Lyon v Helman,*[10] in the context of a claim to acquire a freehold of a house in an enfranchisement under the Leasehold Reform Act 1967, and *McDonald v McDonald*[11] (appealed on other issues), which decided that receivers could serve a notice under section 21 of the Housing Act 1988 on a tenant of the mortgagor.

1.12 Despite this development, there remain crucial questions as yet unanswered, in part because the device of deemed agency is not easy to understand. What is the extent of the receivers' agency? Can receivers do what the mortgagor does not wish? Can receivers, for example, take possession against the mortgagor? These are not questions of academic interest only. Receivership is primarily practical. It is a practical means to ensure the payment of secured loans.

1.13 This book develops a detailed and coherent analysis of the nature of mortgage receivership, based on the history of the purpose of receivership and on the case law, from which answers to those important practical questions are proposed. Key to that analysis is the understanding that the receiver's powers come from the mortgage, not directly from the borrower, as would be usual in an agency situation. His powers 'are given by the disposition of the [borrower's] property which it made ... by the [mortgage] itself'.[12] The receivership is not best understood by a focus on agency, but on the powers given to the receiver, once appointed, by the statute and under the mortgage. That is why a receiver can do what the borrower does not want him to do. That is why receivership can survive an event which would end agency, such as borrower insolvency or death. It is the receiver's powers which determine what he can and cannot do, not necessarily what the borrower could do at the time the receiver exercises them.

1.14 Given the practical problems that receivers face in dealing with property issues which arise during receivership, this book also suggests answers to many issues in property law as they affect the receivership.

1.15 Whether or not a fear of liability as mortgagee in possession is today the true impetus for lenders' use of receivers, receivership remains a useful, often

---

[10] [2014] EWCA Civ 17, [2014] 1 WLR 2451.

[11] [2014] EWCA Civ 1049, [2015] Ch 357.

[12] *Sowman v David Samuel Trust Ltd* [1978] 1 WLR 22 at 20B, a case on the survival of receivership despite the winding up of the borrower.

cost-effective tool for readying a mortgaged property for sale or otherwise managing to pay down the debt. It allows property professionals into management of distressed property with a relative independence from both the lender and the borrower, and hence a potential for cost savings, since the need to incur the fees in taking instructions if a receiver were the lender's agent can be avoided.

1.16   A note on pronouns: in this book, borrowers, buyers and receivers have the pronoun 'he', and lenders have the pronoun 'it', on the basis that borrowers, buyers and receivers are often human, and lenders are most often companies, and to allow for easy differentiation between borrower and lender when they appear in the same paragraph. That convention is used unless from the context, for example when discussing a case, it is clear the borrower is a company or the lender is an individual. Unsurprisingly, the convention is not intended to suggest an absence of women. In addition, the singular 'he' is often used for receivers even though it is common for more than one receiver to be appointed by a lender over a mortgaged property.

Chapter 2

Mortgage Law

INTRODUCTION

2.1   A mortgage is security for the payment of a debt owed to a lender. It is a property interest, an estate in the land, which, by statute and by its express terms, allows the lender a number of different remedies to enforce the debt. The power to appoint a receiver is one of those remedies.

2.2   An understanding of mortgage law in general is necessary for an understanding of receivership for a number of reasons:

(a)   A receiver can only be appointed if there is a mortgage. Thus, it is necessary to know how a valid mortgage is created.

(b)   Mortgages are created[1] by demise or sub-demise (i.e. by lease with a term for redemption) or by charge by deed by way of legal mortgage, which gives the lender the powers and remedies as if the mortgage had been made by demise or sub-demise. What the borrower retains is the equity of redemption and, without additional statutory powers or powers under the mortgage conditions, the borrower cannot – post-mortgage – create interests which bind the lender. That is highly relevant in analysing the receiver's express powers to sell, to lease and to take possession, and when he can use those powers free of interests which bind the borrower, but not the lender.

(c)   It is also necessary to understand the limitations imposed on lenders by equity in order to understand the purpose of receivership (which is necessary to a proper understanding of the relationship between the lender, borrower and receiver). Equity imposed liabilities on a lender in possession. That imposition led to the development of receivership as a way of obtaining payment of the debt without the lender exposing itself to those liabilities. In particular, it led to the receiver's deemed agency as agent of the borrower, not the lender, though the lender appoints the receiver and the borrower cannot control his acts. The analysis of that agency plays a great part in the understanding of receivership.

(d)   The receiver's equitable duties are based on the lender's equitable duties.[2] Thus knowledge of the lender's duties can help inform both why the receiver has equitable duties and what they are.

(e)   It is necessary to understand what rights and powers the lender has, in order to understand what powers the lender can give to the receiver.

---

[1]   Post the Law of Property Act 1925 coming into force.

[2]   Although the duties are not quite the same. See para 6.81.

2.3   For this reason, this chapter sets out a survey of mortgage law. It is necessarily a summary, since mortgage law could itself take up a book. It should be noted, however, that later chapters cross refer to the material in this chapter, in particular when discussing a receiver exercising lenders' powers.

WHAT IS A MORTGAGE?

2.4   If a lender lends money, especially if it is a significant sum, it will likely want some security for its repayment. It will want some piece of property which it can sell, or ask the court to sell, in order to use the price received on that sale to pay off the debt.

2.5   There are two principal types of security which a lender can take in these circumstances: a mortgage or a charge. The essence of both a mortgage and a charge is the appropriation of property to ensure that a debt is repaid or another obligation complied with. A mortgage and a charge each usually consists of a contract under which the lender lends money on terms as to repayment and interest[3] and the grant by the borrower of a charge over the land to secure repayment. Often, the two are in the same instrument.[4]

2.6   A mortgage is a proprietary interest in the mortgaged property, capable of being a legal estate,[5] created by a conveyance of the mortgaged property. The lender with a mortgage has a right to possession.[6]

2.7   A lender with a mere charge[7] did not, historically, have any legal interest in the security. A mere charge in this sense can still be created by a borrower.[8] Since the lender with a mere charge does not have any estate, it has no right to possession and nor can it foreclose. The lender can apply to the court for an order for sale or the appointment of a receiver, and, now, by reason of the extended definition of 'mortgage' in section 205(1)(xvi) of the Law of Property Act 1925, it has these powers out of court if the charge was made by deed.

---

[3]   Or under which a set of obligations on the borrower is set out, for example, an obligation not to dispose of the property by sale or by letting.

[4]   In residential mortgages by high street banks, they are often by deed incorporating standard mortgage conditions and the offer which sets out the interest rate.

[5]   The only legal charges capable of creation are legal mortgages. See Law of Property Act 1925, s 1(2)(c). However, it is not inevitable that a mortgage will be legal. Equitable mortgages arise where an equitable interest is mortgaged, or where a valid legal mortgage is not created because a contract for a legal mortgage is not completed by the grant of a mortgage by deed (such a contract must comply with Law of Property Act (Miscellaneous Provisions) Act 1989, s 2), or because, though a mortgage is granted by a deed, it is not completed by registration as required for it to have legal effect: Land Registration Act 2002, s 27.

[6]   Unless he has postponed exercise of his right under the mortgage conditions.

[7]   All such charges are equitable only: Law of Property Act 1925, s 1(2)(c). The only legal charge is the legal mortgage, the charge by deed by way of legal mortgage.

[8]   Equally, a charging order under the Charging Orders Act 1979 has the same effect as an equitable charge: s 3(4).

2.8   One of the developments of the Law of Property Act 1925 was the introduction of the method of creating mortgages by the grant of the 'charge by way of legal mortgage'.[9] A lender with a charge by deed by way of legal mortgage has all the protection, rights and remedies it would have if it had a legal mortgage by demise or sub-demise.[10] Such a mortgage can create an estate in land[11] and is registrable.[12]

2.9   The question of whether a particular document creates a mortgage or a mere charge is a question of interpretation. A deed creating a mortgage usually says that that is what is being created, using the words 'mortgage' or 'charge by deed by way of legal mortgage'.[13]

2.10   When the lender has a mortgage over the borrower's property, it has considerable power over the property from the grant of a mortgage. The reason is that the lender with a mortgage has a legal estate in the borrower's property, either a lease or an estate which gives it the same protection, powers and remedies as if it had a lease.

2.11   With that estate comes a number of remedies: the power of sale, the right to possession, the power to appoint a receiver, and the power to foreclose.[14] The lender[15] is empowered to take the property and use it by taking possession of and/or selling it to generate the money required for the repayment of the debt of its own motion, provided any conditions precedent to the exercise of its powers have been fulfilled.[16] It thus gives the lender considerable control over the property.

THE HISTORY OF MORTGAGES

2.12   It is important to understand the history of how mortgages came into being in order to understand the reason why the proprietor of a mortgage has a

---

[9]   Law of Property Act 1925, ss 85(1), 86(1) and 87.

[10]   Law of Property Act 1925, s 87.

[11]   Under the extended definition in Law of Property Act 1925, s 1(2) and (4), even though no lease is created.

[12]   Land Registration Act 1925, s 26.

[13]   Law of Property Act 1925, s 87 gives protection, powers and remedies where the charge is 'expressed to be by way of legal mortgage'.

[14]   This is rare in England and Wales and is thus not considered further in any great detail. The other remedies are considered in more detail at para 2.89 *et seq*. The lender will usually also have a contractual right to repayment of the loan with interest.

[15]   The statutory powers of sale, to grant leases and to appoint a receiver are available to the owner of an equitable mortgage (thus made by deed, but not registered on the registered title of the borrower) and under an equitable charge by deed. See below.

[16]   See below.

right to possession and has been given statutory powers, with their statutory effects now set out in the Law of Property Act 1925.[17]

2.13   Prior to the Law of Property Act 1925, mortgages could be created by transferring the title of the borrower's estate, freehold or leasehold, to the lender subject to the borrower's right to have the title re-transferred on redemption on the contractual date set.[18] All that the borrower thus retained was that contractual right of redemption on payment.

2.14   A mortgage was thus typically an even harsher construct for a borrower than it is now, because if the borrower did not repay the loan by the contractual date, the lender retained the property even if its value far exceeded the debt.

2.15   The equity of redemption was an invention of the courts of Chancery to mitigate this unfairness.[19] They intervened to allow redemption later than the contractual date and thus limit the availability to the lender of the windfall of retaining the whole estate for a debt of less than its value.

2.16   At law, the lender had the legal estate in the land,[20] but in equity it had 'a mere charge for the amount due to him'.[21]

2.17   At law, the borrower had no interest in the lender's estate: 'In equity the mortgagor is regarded as the owner of the mortgaged land subject only to the mortgagee's charge, and the mortgagor's equity of redemption is treated as an equitable estate in the land of the same nature as other equitable estates'.[22]

2.18   It was thus said that, until the mortgage was repaid, the borrower had the equity of redemption,[23] the right to call for the reconveyance of the property on payment of the debt, even after the contract date for redemption, with the assistance of the courts.

2.19   Mortgages could also be created by the borrower granting the lender a leasehold interest with a term just shorter than the term held by the borrower. In that case, the borrower had the reversion on the lease and the equitable right to

---

[17]   The statutory effect of the power of sale, for example, is to allow the lender to sell the borrower's estate free of the lender's estate. In any other property context this would be surprising. It is because the statutory scheme is designed to replicate the effect of historical charges that the lender had the borrower's estate subject to the right of redemption – despite the lender with a mortgage granted post the Law of Property Act 1925 coming into force having a more limited estate.

[18]   The right of redemption was thus the right to have the property re-conveyed. Now, it means the right to have the mortgage discharged so that the borrower's estate, which he retains, is no longer subject to the mortgage.

[19]   See *Medforth v Blake* [2000] Ch 86 at 101G.

[20]   *In Re Sir Thomas Spencer Wells* [1933] Ch 29 at 52.

[21]   *In Re Sir Thomas Spencer Wells* [1933] Ch 29 at 52.

[22]   *In Re Sir Thomas Spencer Wells* [1933] Ch 29 at 52.

[23]   *In Re Sir Thomas Spencer Wells* [1933] Ch 29 at 52: the equity of redemption was an equitable estate in the land. The property belonged to the lender.

call for the conveyance of the lease from the lender to him, on repayment of the debt, at which point it would merge with the reversion.

2.20　Mortgages were thus not new and separate forms of legal estate, but rather were the use of existing estates (the borrower's estate by transfer, or a lease) with the addition of the right of redemption. The lender's remedies[24] arise from these estates.

2.21　Thus, the lender had the right to possession 'before the ink is dry on the mortgage'[25] because it had either the borrower's estate or a leasehold estate out of it, and either one would give an immediate right to possession of the estate.

THE LAW OF PROPERTY ACT 1925

2.22　The Law of Property Act 1925 prevented the first method, a mortgage by conveyance of the borrower's estate, from being used.

2.23　Section 85(1) of the Law of Property Act 1925 prevents mortgages of freeholds other than by:

(a)　demise for a term of years certain absolute; or
(b)　a charge by deed expressed to be by way of legal mortgage.

2.24　Section 86(1) of the Law of Property Act 1925 prevents mortgages of leasehold interests except by:

(a)　sub-demise for a term of years absolute of at least one day less than the borrower's term; or
(b)　by a charge by deed expressed to be by way of legal mortgage.

2.25　By section 87(1) of the Law of Property Act 1925, a lender with a charge by deed expressed to be by way of legal mortgage has the powers and remedies as if it had, in the case of a mortgage of a freehold, a term of 3,000 years, and, in the case of a mortgage of a leasehold, a term of one day less than the mortgaged term.[26]

24　Which can seem surprising when divorced from the historical source.

25　*Four Maids v Dudley Marshall (Properties) Ltd* [1957] Ch 317 at 320.

26　Those powers and remedies apply as against third parties: *Grand Junction Co Ltd v Bates* [1954] 2 QB 160 at 168; *Regent Oil Co Ltd v JA Gregory (Hatch End) Ltd* [1966] Ch 402. The lender does not have a lease, however: *Grand Junction Co Ltd v Bates* [1954] 2 QB 160 at 166; *Weg Motors Ltd v Hales* [1962] Ch 49 at 74, though this appears *obiter*. The reason is that under Law of Property Act 1925, s 1(2), a charge by way of legal mortgage is an interest or charge, and not a leasehold estate under s 1(1). However, a charge by way of legal mortgage is a legal estate within the definition in s 1(4).

2.26   Both methods of creating a mortgage give the lender an immediate right to possession.[27]

2.27   The result of sections 85 to 87 of the Law of Property Act 1925 is that although the borrower owns the freehold or the leasehold interest, he does so subject to the mortgage. The borrower thus either has a reversion on the lender's lease only, or it is as if he has a reversion only, because the lender has the powers and remedies as if it had a lease.

2.28   The borrower always remains legal owner of his estate, post the Law of Property Act 1925.

2.29   However, the concept of the equity of redemption remains useful. If the lender's estate is thought of as having effect as if a leasehold estate out of the borrower's estate, then at law, the borrower has only his encumbered estate, as if a reversion on the lender's estate. In equity, the borrower has the whole of his estate unencumbered, and if he pays the debt he can call, even after the contractual date in the mortgage for redemption, for the release of the mortgage, so that its estate will be unencumbered;[28] that is the equity of redemption.

2.30   At law, the lender has the lender's estate, with effect as if it had a leasehold estate. In equity, it has a mere charge.[29]

2.31   The borrower without a power of leasing[30] can grant a lease only out of his equity of redemption.[31] Likewise, if the borrower cannot redeem the mortgage, he can sell only his equity of redemption. The meaning becomes more obvious if one considers the mortgage as if it were a lease.

2.32   Think of the borrower's and the lender's legal estates as a chain, with the borrower's at the top, and the lender's attached below since it comes out of the borrower's estate. The borrower in granting a lease could only grant a lease to sit in the chain between his estate and the lender's. If one follows the analysis as if the lender had a lease, the borrower would be granting a concurrent lease which slots in between the borrower's interest and the lender's, and such a lease would not affect the lender's estate. It would not give the new leaseholder a right to possession against the lender.[32] The lender would still have the bottom

---

[27]   The lender has either a leasehold estate, or the powers and remedies as if it had one. See *Ropaigealach v Barclays Bank Plc* [2000] QB 263 at 271–272, quoted in *Horsham Properties Group Ltd v Clark* [2008] EWHC 2327 (Ch), [2009] 1 WLR 1255 at [16]. Note, though, that the contractual terms of the mortgage can, and usually do, postpone this right.

[28]   *In Re Sir Thomas Spencer Wells* [1933] Ch 29 at 52.

[29]   So that the court in equity would treat him as having a more limited interest than a leasehold.

[30]   Such as that in Law of Property Act 1925, s 99. See *Iron Trades Employers Insurance Association Ltd v Union Land and House Investors Ltd* [1937] Ch 313 at 321–322.

[31]   He can also grant options out of his equity of redemption, or otherwise create any right or estate, against all the world but the lender: *Weg Motors Ltd v Hales* [1962] Ch 49 at 74.

[32]   *Corbett v Plowden* (1884) 25 Ch D 678 at 681: the lease is precarious for the borrower and the leaseholder because 'the paramount title of the [lender] may be asserted against both of them'. Applied in *Dudley and District Benefit Building Society v Emerson* [1949] Ch 707 at 714: a

estate. For that reason, provided that the lender could exercise its right to possession under the terms of the mortgage, the lender could treat the new lessee as a trespasser if the new lessee were occupying the land.[33]

2.33   At common law, the only way that the borrower could grant a lease binding the lender would be if the lender concurred, by being a party to it, or by later recognition of it. Under the Law of Property Act 1925, the borrower whilst in possession has a power of leasing which will bind the lender, unless the mortgage conditions exclude it. This is discussed further below.[34]

2.34   Similarly, the borrower, unable to redeem the mortgage can only sell his equity of redemption. What is meant by this is that the borrower can only sell his reversion on the mortgage (if it is by lease) or his estate subject to the mortgage (if it is a charge).

2.35   This understanding of the nature of a mortgage also explains why a lender cannot take possession against a tenant whose lease binds the lender, but can against a tenant whose lease binds only the borrower.

2.36   If the tenant's lease pre-dates the mortgage, then the mortgage takes effect as if a concurrent lease between the borrower's estate and the tenant's, so that the lender's estate is the reversion on the pre-existing lease. The lender's right to possession is a right to possession of the lender's estate. If the lender is bound by a lease, it is the tenant under that lease who has the better right to possession of the physical land since he has the right to possession of his estate, which is the last in the chain. The lender has only the right to possession of the rents and profits from the tenant.[35]

2.37   When there is no lower estate or interest in the chain, then the lender's right to possession of its estate allows the lender to take physical possession of the land.[36] Thus, if the borrower grants a lease without a power to bind the

---

right of possession is given by the borrower to the leaseholder by the lease, but it is effective only 'until destroyed or defeated' by the lender. It is as if the leaseholder had a right to possession of the reversion on the mortgage. Since the mortgage reserves no rent, the effect is simply that the leaseholder would be entitled to possession once the mortgage was redeemed, and to redeem the mortgage. The leaseholder would be one of the persons interested in the equity of redemption.

[33]   *Iron Trades Employers Insurance Association Ltd v Union Land and House Investors Ltd* [1937] Ch 313 at 318–319; *Parker v Braithwaite* [1952] 2 All ER 837 at 841; *Nijar v Mann* (2000) 32 HLR 223 at 227.

[34]   See para 2.63.

[35]   *Rogers v Humphreys* (1835) 4 Ad & E 299 and *Moss v Gallimore* 1 Doug 279 referred to In Re *Ind, Coope & Co Ltd* [1911] 2 Ch 223 at 231–232; *Rhodes v Allied Dunbar Pension Services Ltd* [1989] 1 WLR 800, extending this analysis to post-Law of Property Act 1925 mortgages. The same analysis applies if the borrower creates a lease, after the date of the mortgage, which binds the lender by reason of Law of Property Act 1925, s 99, or the mortgage covenants, or by some act of the lender.

[36]   Note, though, that often the lender contracts out of that immediate right to possession, and allows the borrower back into possession, pending default. This might make it appear as though the borrower has the right to grant leases in possession, but he does not (absent some statutory

lender, that lease is as if concurrent to the lender's mortgage, and the lender has the right to take possession of the land free of the borrower's tenant (even if the borrower has allowed the tenant into occupation).

2.38   A similar analysis, based on standard ideas of priority, helps explain why the lender can take possession free of the borrower's licensees, and beneficiaries under trusts created by the borrower, provided they do not bind the lender.[37]

2.39   The analysis then helps explain why the receiver with suitable powers can deal with the land free of occupiers whose interests bind the borrower and not the lender.[38]

2.40   The analysis also explains the limits to the remedies for lenders with second mortgages. A borrower can create more than one mortgage out of his estate.[39] If there is a first mortgage, then a subsequent mortgage will take effect as if a concurrent lease between the borrower's estate and the first lender's. The second lender will have an interest in the equity of redemption arising out of the first mortgage. The second lender will not be able to sell free of the first mortgage, since it is an interest out of the second lender's estate.

THE LAND REGISTRATION ACT 2002

2.41   Mortgages over a registered estate must be completed by registration.[40] A registered charge, on registration, takes effect as a charge by deed by way of legal mortgage.[41] Thus mortgages by sub-demise are now rare.

2.42   For registered mortgages of registered land, under the Land Registration Act 2002, it is even clearer than for unregistered land that the borrower retains his estate. The borrower is the registered legal proprietor of his legal estate, though it is subject to the mortgage. The borrower appears, by virtue of his registration, to have more control over his mortgaged property than historically.[42]

---

or contractual power in the mortgage). His right to possession is purely contractual, and he cannot confer any right to possession on a third party which will bind the lender unless and to the extent that the terms of the mortgage so provide.

[37]   See para 2.111, paras 2.112–2.117 and para 8.91 *et seq* (licences) and para 8.111 *et seq* (beneficiaries).

[38]   See Chapter 8 on third parties, Chapter 10 on possession, and Chapter 11 on sale.

[39]   Although many mortgages prohibit it without consent, and limit the borrower's ability to do so by entering a restriction on the borrower's title. However, this does not prevent the creation of an equitable mortgage and its protection by entry of a Form UN1. A subsequent equitable mortgagee will have the usual powers of a mortgagee if the mortgage is created by deed.

[40]   Land Registration Act 2002, s 27(2)(f).

[41]   Land Registration Act 2002, s 51.

[42]   He retains owners' powers, under Land Registration Act 2002, s 23(1), and see discussion of those powers in *The Keepers and Governors of the Possessions, Revenues and Goods of the Free Grammar School of John Lyon v Helman* [2014] EWCA Civ 17, [2014] 1 WLR 2451 at [30].

LEGAL AND EQUITABLE MORTGAGES

2.43   Most mortgages are legal mortgages. A mortgage is legal only if:

(a)   it is created by deed;[43] and

(b)   if the borrower's estate is registered, then the grant of the mortgage must be completed by registration.[44] The effect of completion by registration is that the charge so registered takes effect as a charge by deed by way of legal mortgage within the meaning of the Law of Property Act 1925 even if it would not otherwise have done so.[45]

2.44   A mortgage will be equitable, not legal, if:

(a)   a mortgage created by deed has not been registered;[46]

(b)   if the mortgage was not made by deed, and there is a contract for the grant of a legal mortgage;[47] or

(c)   if it is a mortgage of an equitable estate only.[48]

---

[43]   Law of Property Act 1925, ss 52(1) and 205(1)(ii) (which includes the grant of a mortgage in the definition of conveyance). The grant of a mortgage by deed requires execution by the borrower only, not the lender. Compliance with Law of Property (Miscellaneous Provisions) Act 1989, s 2 is not required: *McLaughlin v Duff* [2008] EWCA Civ 1627, [2010] Ch 1. The grant of a mortgage is a disposition of land, caught by s 52, and not a contract for the disposition. See also *Bank of Scotland Plc v Waugh* [2014] EWHC 2117 (Ch) at [37].

[44]   Land Registration Act 2002, s 27(1) and (2)(f). Where the mortgaged property is unregistered, there may be registration requirements on the mortgage, depending on the form of mortgage created, under the Land Charges Act 1972. This is outside the scope of this book.

[45]   Land Registration Act 2002, s 51. For example, if the signature of the borrower on the charge was forged. It will have such effect unless and until removed by alteration, by rectification or otherwise, of the Register. The statutory powers under Law of Property Act 1925, s 101 will be exercisable to the person registered as proprietor of the charge. That person will also have the right to possession: *Paragon Finance Plc v Pender* [2005] EWCA Civ 760, [2005] 1 WLR 3412 (decided under the Land Registration Act 1925, though it is suggested that the decision under the Land Registration Act 2002 would be the same).

[46]   This most usually occurs in the gap between the grant of the mortgage and registration. Sometimes, by accident, there is a failure to register. In addition, if a second mortgage is granted in breach of a first mortgage which prohibits further charging, and, as is common, the first mortgage-holder has the benefit of a restriction on the borrower's title prohibiting its registration, then the second mortgage will take effect in equity only, though its priority against further dispositions usually will be protected by entry of a Form UN1. The problem with a failure to register and the absence of a Form UN1 is that it makes the mortgage at risk from the borrower selling or granting another interest which, when registered, will likely take priority over the mortgage. See Land Registration Act 2002, s 29.

[47]   See, for example, *Bank of Scotland Plc v Waugh* [2014] EWHC 2117 (Ch), where the borrower's signature had not been witnessed, as required for the borrower to have executed by deed under Law of Property (Miscellaneous Provisions) Act 1989, s 1. Unusually, the lender had also signed the mortgage, hence it took effect as a contract since it complied with Law of Property (Miscellaneous Provisions) Act 1989, s 2, and hence took effect as an equitable mortgage.

[48]   For example, where the borrower has only an interest under a trust of land. This situation most commonly arises where a mortgage was purportedly entered into by deed by the two co-owners of the legal estate, but the signature of one was forged by the other, and/or was entered into by reason of the other's undue influence, and subsequently avoided. In that case, the mortgage will be over the beneficial interest of the other co-owner, if any. An equitable mortgage (or any

2.45   The powers which arise under the different types of equitable mortgage are different.

2.46   If an equitable mortgage of a legal estate has been made by deed, then the lender will have express powers under it, and statutory powers under the Law of Property Act 1925.[49]

2.47   If an equitable mortgage is by contract only, the lender will have any powers given to it by the contract,[50] but it will not have the statutory powers under section 101 of the Law of Property Act 1925, since they require the grant of the mortgage to have been made by deed. Thus even if the lender has by contract a power of sale, the statutory magic in the Law of Property Act 1925 which allows it to sell free of the mortgage and other interests later in priority to the mortgage will not be available.[51]

---

charge) of an equitable interest must be made in writing signed by the borrower or his agent lawfully authorised in writing: Law of Property Act 1925, s 52(1)(a). It need not be by deed.

[49]   Under Law of Property Act 1925, s 101. This includes the power to appoint a receiver: s 101(1)(iii). Moreover, the power of sale will be to sell the mortgaged property, i.e. the legal title, despite the failure to register the mortgage: *Re White Rose Cottage* [1965] Ch 940 (doubting *Re Hodson & Howes' Contract* (1887) 35 Ch D 668, which decided to the contrary). The lender may not have the right of possession since it has no estate, save perhaps if a right to possession expressly provided. A charge by deed by way of legal mortgage appears to require to be registered (and hence a legal mortgage) before the powers in s 87(1) arise because s 87 applies where 'a legal mortgage' has been created by that method. It is likely that the right to possession in an equitable mortgage is enforceable by the lender at least against the borrower because equity looks on as done that which ought to have been done.

[50]   Provided that such a power is capable of being given by contract without a deed. A power to sell the borrower's estate which is not the lender's statutory power of sale is a power operating in equity: Law of Property Act 1925, s 1(7). The Act does not contain any formal requirements as to creation of such powers. However, if the power is not created by deed, then the donee will not be able to perform any acts of the borrower required to be by deed, for example, the execution of a disposition of property which must be by deed by s 52: *Steiglitz v Egginton* (1815) Holt 141; *Berkeley v Hardy* (1826) 5 B&C 355, which assumes this is the case as a long-standing rule of common law; *Powell v London & Provincial Bank* [1893] 2 Ch 555 at 563, though this was about an agent's power to deliver a deed of his principal, and the requirement that the agent's power to do so must be by deed has been abolished by Law of Property (Miscellaneous Provisions) Act 1989, s 1(1)(c); *Windsor Refrigerator Co v Branch Nominees* [1961] Ch 88; *Phoenix Properties Ltd v Wimpole Street Nominees Ltd* [1992] BCLC 737, in which the court determined that an appointment by the lender of a receiver in writing without a deed to a power of sale in the mortgage conditions where the mortgage was made by deed was sufficient for the then requirement that an agent, to have power to deliver a deed on sale, must be appointed by deed. See also Powers of Attorney Act 1971, ss 1 and 7, which give statutory effect to a power of attorney created by deed. The only alternative to creation by deed is execution in the presence of the borrower: Law of Property (Miscellaneous Provisions) Act 1989, s 1(3). It seems to follow from these cases that a power to perform an act which must be performed by deed, for example a power to make a disposition of another's land, must be by deed, even if the act is not to be in the other's name. The purpose of the requirement for a deed for a disposition of land is to make the act more certain. It seems likely that that requirement for certainty should be echoed in the appointment of an agent. However, the reasoning for the rule relied on in the above cases is unclear. Thus the contractual powers may be practically useless without the assistance of the court.

[51]   See para 2.121 *et seq* for the lender's power of sale.

2.48   The assistance of the court will likely be required either under a claim by the lender for specific performance of the contract, by an order requiring the borrower to grant the mortgage by deed,[52] or via a claim, for example, for an order for sale to enforce the equitable mortgage.[53]

2.49   An equitable mortgage over an equitable interest, if made by deed, will give the lender the statutory powers,[54] but only over the equitable interest.[55] Thus his powers may be of limited benefit.[56] An equitable mortgage over an equitable interest where the mortgage has not been made by deed will require the assistance of the court as above.

2.50   A lender with an equitable charge which is not a mortgage,[57] if made by deed,[58] will have the statutory powers, for example, to sell and to appoint a receiver.

2.51   If it is not by deed, the lender will have only the right to ask the court to assist in the enforcement of the debt or obligation by, for example, ordering sale[59] or the appointment of a receiver under Part 69 of the Civil Procedure Rules 1998 (CPR).[60]

2.52   The lender with a mere charge will have no right of possession, however,[61] since the right under a mortgage comes from the mortgage estate.[62]

---

[52]   As happened in *Bank of Scotland Plc (No 2) v Waugh* [2014] EWHC 2835 (Ch).

[53]   See Law of Property Act 1925, s 90(1) for the interest which the court will vest in the lender if it makes such an order. The other remedies of a lender under s 101 are not available. The court has power to appoint a receiver, who will be an officer of the court, to assist with ensuring repayment of the debt, under CPR, Pt 69. That is outside the remit of this book.

[54]   Under Law of Property Act 1925, s 101(1).

[55]   For example, the lender will have the power of sale over the equitable interest, but if sale of the legal estate is sought, where the borrower has charged his beneficial interest in it under a trust, so as to release that part of the proceeds due to the borrower by reason of his beneficial interest, then the lender will have to apply as someone with an interest in property subject to a trust of land, under Trusts of Land and Appointment of Trustees Act 1996, s 14. See paras 8.126–8.127.

[56]   There may be very little income from the mortgaged equitable interest, and hence little benefit in appointing a receiver.

[57]   See paras 2.44 and 2.47–2.49. A lender with an equitable charge is usually in a worse position than a lender with an equitable mortgage over a legal estate because the latter may well be able to require registration, and or execution of a mortgage by deed.

[58]   Under Law of Property Act 1925, s 205(1)(xvi), 'mortgage' in s 101 includes a charge.

[59]   In which case, the lender is vested with an estate by demise or sub-demise, and the effect of the statutory power of sale, under Law of Property Act 1925, s 90. The court has various sources of jurisdiction to order a sale, relevant, for example, to different types of charge, the different types of interest charges, and the different situations, but these are outside the scope of this book.

[60]   SI 1998/3132. This form of receivership is outside the scope of this book. The receiver is an officer of the court.

[61]   Under Law of Property Act 1925, s 90, on an order for sale the court can vest a demise or sub-demise in the lender to allow sale, and that will give the lender a right to possession so that sale can be with vacant possession.

[62]   It is possible that the borrower would give the lender his right to possession of the mortgaged property in the charge.

REDEMPTION

2.53   The mortgage is redeemed when the borrower[63] pays the debt (including any interest and expenses) and hence discharges the mortgage, and the mortgage term ceases.[64] The borrower then holds his estate free of the mortgage.

2.54   The mortgage covenants often set out a contractual date for redemption of the mortgage. That is the borrower's first opportunity to redeem.

2.55   However, equity permits redemption after the contractual date. In principle, the lender is entitled to notice before redemption.[65]

2.56   In order to redeem the mortgage, the borrower must pay the charged sum. He is entitled to know how much is owed. If the lender tells him a figure that is too small, the redemption of the mortgage will often not prevent the lender pursuing him for the difference.[66] If the lender tells him a figure which is greater than what is owed,[67] then the borrower may be able to seek repayment of the difference after redemption.[68]

2.57   If the borrower unconditionally tenders all that is due, and the lender will not allow redemption, then the borrower can issue a claim for redemption.[69]

2.58   On such a claim, the court will usually:

(a)   order an account of the mortgage to determine the amount of the debt if there is a dispute. The account is up to the date of tender since no interest is payable thereafter;

---

[63]   Anyone with an interest in the equity of redemption can redeem, for example, a transferee of the borrower's property, a lender with a mortgage later in priority or a leaseholder save if the lease is short term.

[64]   The mortgage term ceases on repayment automatically, leaving the borrower's estate free of the mortgage: Law of Property Act 1925, ss 5 and 116. If the mortgage is registered over registered land, the lender should apply to the Land Registry for the charge to be removed, using Form RX1. The borrower may ask for the mortgage to be conveyed to a third party instead, provided the lender is not in possession: s 95(1).

[65]   The reason is said to be to allow the lender to find an alternative investment for his money, and that this is what the courts of equity would require to allow redemption by the borrower after the contractual date. Six months' notice is usually found reasonable. Interest can be paid in lieu. The requirement for notice, and the length of any notice required, is subject to the terms of the mortgage.

[66]   Subject to estoppel arguments.

[67]   This is not uncommon when there are costs added to the mortgage. The parties may dispute them; any dispute is resolved through the courts by the taking of an account of the mortgage, which, when it is legal costs which are the issue, is done by a detailed assessment. The borrower may well choose to redeem at the higher figure, if for example he has a sale pending, so as to avoid delays.

[68]   As money had and received, or paid under a mistake, or under a constructive trust. See W Clarke, *Fisher and Lightwood's Law of Mortgage* (LexisNexis, 14th edn, 2014) at 47.37.

[69]   The lender will risk costs, and further interest from the date of tender will not be payable.

(b)   order redemption on payment of the sum so determined, by the borrower to the lender within a time period, usually 6 months after judgment. A failure by the borrower to tender the necessary payment unconditionally within the time limit results in foreclosure and the loss of the right to redeem. The lender becomes entitled to the borrower's estate free of the mortgage and all subsequent mortgages.[70] The time period will only be extended in special circumstances.

2.59   Claims for redemption are thus risky and are rare in practice.

2.60   The court can, in a redemption action or an action for sale of the mortgaged property, order a sale of the mortgaged property by the borrower[71] free of the charge,[72] even if the proceeds will be insufficient to allow redemption, where it is just and equitable to do so in all the circumstances.[73]

2.61   The cases in which the jurisdiction has been exercised have been negative equity cases, where the lender has not wanted to sell, but the borrower cannot pay the current monthly instalment and is in financial hardship.[74]

2.62   The right of redemption is lost if:

(a)   the lender has contracted to sell the property under its power of sale;[75]
(b)   foreclosure has occurred;
(c)   where the mortgaged property is unregistered, by limitation.[76] Possession by the lender of the mortgaged property for 12 years prevents an action to redeem[77] and allows the lender to enlarge its title up to the borrower's estate,[78] unless the lender within that period acknowledges the borrower's title, or his equity of redemption, or receives any sum in

---

[70]   Law of Property Act 1925, ss 88(2) and 89(2).

[71]   Law of Property Act 1925, s 91(1).

[72]   Law of Property Act 1925, 50(1)(b).

[73]   The mortgage will continue, in the sense that the mortgage conditions will continue to bind the borrower and the lender, so that, for example, the lender can sue the borrower for the debt, but the security will be lost, thus the proprietary remedies, such as the lender's right to possession, and to sell, will no longer be capable of exercise. See Chapter 13 for a discussion of receivership in this situation.

[74]   See for example *Palk v Mortgage Services Funding Plc* [1993] 2 WLR 415.

[75]   *Waring v London and Manchester Assurance Company Ltd* [1935] Ch 310; *Property & Bloodstock Ltd v Emerton* [1968] Ch 94; *Horsham Properties Group Ltd v Clark* [2008] EWHC 2327 (Ch), [2009] 1 WLR 1255 at [22]. The reason given in *Waring* was that the statutory powers gave the lender a power to bind the borrower, so that when the lender contracted to sell, that contract bound the borrower and the court would not grant an injunction against completion of the sale unless the contract was entered into in bad faith. The equity of redemption is extinguished on completion.

[76]   Land Registration Act 2002, s 96(2).

[77]   Limitation Act 1980, s 16.

[78]   Law of Property Act 1925, ss 88(3) and 89(3).

respect of principal or interest of the mortgage debt.[79] In that case the 12-year period runs from the acknowledgment or payment.

STATUTORY POWERS OF LEASING AND SURRENDER

Leasing

2.63   The development of mortgage law in the 18th century might be thought of as a history of equity assisting borrowers by treating them as if they were the legal owners of the mortgaged land.[80] The Law of Property Act 1925 supported that development.

2.64   In relation to leasing, the Law of Property Act 1925 intervenes to allow the borrower to grant leases binding on the lender in certain circumstances, unless the mortgage covenants provide otherwise.[81] Under section 99(1), a borrower, while in possession, has power to make a lease[82] of the mortgaged land[83] 'as against every incumbrancer'.[84]

2.65   Moreover, under section 98(1) of the Law of Property Act 1925, the borrower who has granted a lease in his sole name, whilst entitled to possession or receipt of the rents or profits of the land, and provided the lender has not given notice of its intention to take possession or enter into receipt of the rents and profits, may sue for possession or for those rents and profits in his sole name, without joining the lender. Since section 99(1) has an effect as if the lease so granted sits below the lender's estate in the chain, the court would, but for

---

[79]   Limitation Act 1980, s 29(4).

[80]   By treating them as owning the equity of redemption which made them the owner in equity of the lender's estate. See *In Re Sir Thomas Spencer Wells* [1933] Ch 29, referred to at paras 2.16–2.17.

[81]   Law of Property Act 1925, s 99(13).

[82]   A contract to grant a lease under Law of Property Act 1925, s 99 will do: it is enforceable on anyone on whom a lease so granted would be binding: s 99(12). The borrower must within 1 month after making the lease deliver to the lender a counterpart of the lease executed by the lessee: s 99(8) and (11). However, the letting need not be in writing. Reference to a lease 'shall be construed to extend and apply, as far as the circumstances admit, to any letting, and to any agreement, whether in writing or not, for leasing or letting': s 99(17).

[83]   'The mortgaged land' is the borrower's land or estate as it was just prior to the grant of the mortgage. See similarly the meaning of this phrase in Law of Property Act 1925, s 101(1)(i), the statutory power of sale, said in *In Re White Rose Cottage* [1964] Ch 483 (as noted with agreement in *Swift 1st Ltd v Colin* [2011] EWHC 2410 (Ch), [2012] Ch 206) to mean 'the property over which the mortgage deed purported to extend'.

[84]   Thus the borrower can create a lease which sits below the lender's estate in the chain of estates discussed above. A proper understanding of possession is that possession in property law usually means of an estate in land, rather than of physical land. To be able to lease so as to bind the lender, under Law of Property Act 1925, s 99(1), the borrower must be in possession of the mortgaged land. Thus if the borrower had a freehold estate unencumbered by any lease, and charged it to the lender, he would remain in possession of the mortgaged land in the sense that the lender, via his estate, would be entitled to physical possession of the land, but under the mortgage covenants would postpone that right or otherwise not take possession until the borrower was in breach of mortgage.

section 98, require the lender to be a party to the claim since it would have the immediate right to possession or to the rents and profits on an analysis of the estates.[85]

2.66   When the lender is in possession, it is the lender which has the power to make leases[86] 'as against all prior incumbrancers, if any, and as against the mortgagor'.[87] It appears that the lender can grant such leases in the borrower's name, but the statutory power does not entitle it to impose personal liability on the borrower.[88]

2.67   The powers in section 99(1) and (2) of the Law of Property Act 1925 apply only if and so far as a contrary intention is not expressed by the lender and the borrower in the mortgage deed or otherwise in writing, and have effect subject to the terms of the mortgage deed or of any such writing.[89]

2.68   The borrower is not prevented by the common law or by section 99(2) of the Law of Property Act 1925 from leasing his equity of redemption, or indeed his legal estate as encumbered by the charge.[90] The point of section 99(1) is that

---

[85]   The borrower would only have the right to possession of his own estate, the equity of redemption. He can at any time sue for possession of that estate without relying on Law of Property Act 1925, s 98(1): see s 98(2).

[86]   I.e. a lease of the mortgaged land, being the whole of the borrower's estate as it was just prior to the grant of the mortgage. See fn 83.

[87]   Prior chargeholders sit below the lender in the chain of estates. The lender's power, whilst in possession, is thus to create leases which sit at the bottom of the chain, and in addition which bind the borrower in the sense that the borrower would have to recognise such a lease even if he redeemed all the charges. The lender always has power to lease its own estate, whether in possession of the mortgaged land or not, but in principle a lease granted by a lender which did not bind the borrower would end on redemption of the mortgage. The granting of a lease by a lender is an act of taking possession since it shows an intention to control and manage his estate in place of the borrower (*Mexborough Urban District Council v Harrison* [1964] 1 WLR 733 at 736–737; *Berkshire Capital Funding Ltd v Street* (2000) 32 HLR 373 at 377). Where Law of Property Act 1925, s 99(2) is not excluded by the mortgage conditions, it seems that any lease granted by the lender will have the s 99(2) effect.

[88]   Law of Property Act 1925, s 8(1).

[89]   Law of Property Act 1925, s 99(13). The, s 99 powers cannot be excluded in relation to a mortgage of agricultural land: (a) made after 1 March 1948 and before 1 September 1995 (i.e. the period when the Agricultural Holdings Act 1948, and then the Agricultural Holdings Act 1986 governed the creation of tenancies of agricultural land, and before the Agricultural Tenancies Act 1995 came into force); or (b) to which the Agricultural Holdings Act 1986 would apply by reason of Agricultural Tenancies Act 1995, s 4, which permits the creation of new leases governed by the 1986 Act after 1 September 1995 in certain circumstances. Under Landlord and Tenant Act 1954, s 36(4), a new lease granted on a business tenancy renewal is deemed to be one authorised by s 99.

[90]   *Corbett v Plowden* (1884) 25 Ch D 678; *Iron Trades Employers Insurance Association Ltd v Union Land and House Investors Ltd* [1937] Ch 313 at 321 approved in *Dudley and District Benefit Building Society v Emerson* [1949] Ch 707. Such a lease, if the mortgage is thought about as if it were a lease, would be a concurrent lease. It is sometimes described in commentary as taking effect by estoppel. That might have been the case for mortgages created by transfer of the borrower's estate to the lender, prior to the Law of Property Act 1925 coming into force, since then the borrower would have had no estate out of which to grant a tenancy. Mortgages created by sub-demise or charge by deed by way of legal mortgage leave the borrower with a legal estate. Insofar as in the tenancy granted the borrower represents that he

it is only when the borrower is in possession of the mortgaged land that he has the power to grant leases which bind the lender,[91] and once the lender goes into possession,[92] the borrower's powers under section 99(1) cease.

2.69   The borrower's power of leasing under section 99(1) of the Law of Property Act 1925 also ceases, with the section 99 powers of leasing being exercisable by the lender instead, once a receiver of income of the mortgaged property has been appointed by the lender under its statutory power[93] under section 101(1)(iii). It is the lender which can then exercise 'the powers of leasing conferred by this section'.[94]

2.70   The power to lease given by section 99(1) and (2) of the Law of Property Act 1925 is not a power to grant any lease. Section 99(3) limits the type of leases the borrower or lender can grant, when using their section 99 powers, to: (a) agricultural or occupation leases for a term not exceeding 50 years;[95] and (b) building leases[96] for a term not exceeding 999 years.

2.71   Moreover, section 99(5) of the Law of Property Act 1925 requires any such lease to take effect in possession not later than 12 months after its date. Section 99(6) requires the lease to reserve the best rent that can reasonably be obtained in the circumstances of the case, without a fine being taken. Section 99(7) requires the lease to contain a covenant for payment of rent and a right of re-entry on non-payment within a time period to be specified in the lease, but not exceeding 30 days.

---

has an unencumbered estate and/or purports to grant the tenant a tenancy which is not encumbered so that he is to be entitled physically to occupy the land, the borrower is likely estopped from denying that representation.

[91]   So that the leaseholder has a right of possession good against the lender's.

[92]   By reason of the lender's estate.

[93]   Law of Property Act 1925, s 99(19). See the discussion in paras 9.141–9.149 as to the statutory power of leasing and delegation to the receiver. Section 99(19) suggests that it would be preferable if the power in a mortgage deed to appoint a receiver was expressly an extension of the statutory power, so that s 99(19) has effect. Alternatively, any contractual power given to the borrower to grant leases should be expressly limited to the period when he is in possession and whilst there is no receiver appointed.

[94]   The reference to 'the powers' suggests that the powers of leasing are not two different powers, one exercisable by the lender and one by the borrower, from time to time, but one power, with the identity of the party who can exercise it changing.

[95]   If the borrower's estate is leasehold, the s 99 powers do not permit the borrower to grant a lease longer than the term of the leasehold less 1 day, and nor can a s 99 lease be granted save on conditions which could have been granted or imposed by the borrower: Law of Property Act 1925, s 99(15).

[96]   A lease under which the leaseholder or some person directing the grant of the lease, having erected, or agreeing to erect, within not more than 5 years from the date of the lease, buildings, new or additional, or having improved or repaired buildings, or agreeing to improve or repair buildings within that time, or having executed, or agreeing to execute within that time, on the land leased, an improvement for or in connection with building purposes: Law of Property Act 1925, s 99(9). A peppercorn or a nominal or other rent may be payable for the first 5 years or any lesser part of the term: s 99(10).

2.72   Under section 99(14) of the Law of Property Act 1925, the borrower and lender can agree in writing, outside the mortgage deed, to confer on one or other more extensive powers of leasing[97] to take effect as if under section 99(1) or section 99(2),[98] provided that they do not prejudice the rights of other existing lenders unless such a lender joins in or adopts that agreement.

Surrender

2.73   Section 100 of the Law of Property Act 1925 similarly gives the borrower and the lender, when in possession, powers to accept surrenders of leases so as to bind the other.

2.74   Under section 100(1) of the Law of Property Act 1925, the borrower in possession has the power to accept a surrender[99] of a lease[100] of the mortgaged land as against every incumbrancer, provided that the surrender is for the purpose of enabling a lease authorised under section 99 or under an agreement made pursuant to section 99, or by the mortgage deed,[101] to be granted.[102] That is, the borrower in possession can accept a surrender provided it is to grant a lease he can grant under section 99 or an extension of the powers in section 99.

2.75   Thus, if there is a lease binding both borrower and lender, at the bottom of the chain of interests, the borrower in possession can accept a surrender, despite the lender having the reversionary estate on it,[103] so as to grant a new lease which will sit at the bottom of the chain.

2.76   There is an exception. If the surrender is for payment of a premium, then on a surrender to the borrower, the consent of the mortgage holders is needed. If the surrender is to the lender, then the consent of a prior mortgage holder is needed.[104]

---

[97]   Not restricted by the statutory term length limits, or the rent requirement, for example.

[98]   I.e. with the binding effects given by those sections. Presumably, they can thus by agreement, after the grant of a mortgage excluding Law of Property Act 1925, s 99, agree to the borrower having s 99(1) powers and the lender having s 99(2) powers.

[99]   A contract to make or accept a surrender may be enforced by or against every person on whom the surrender, if completed, would be binding: Law of Property Act 1925, s 100(6). Thus a surrender by deed is not needed for s 100 to assist.

[100]   'Lease' extends to any letting, and to an agreement, whether in writing or not, for leasing or letting: Law of Property Act 1925, s 100(9).

[101]   For the surrender to be valid, a lease under Law of Property Act 1925, s 99, or an agreement pursuant to it, or permitted by the mortgage deed, of the whole of the surrendered land to take effect in possession immediately or within 1 month must be granted; the term of the new lease must be not less than the unexpired term under the surrendered lease; and the rent reserved by the new lease must be not less than under the surrendered lease: s 100(5).

[102]   A surrender of part only of the demised land can be accepted, the rent apportioned, and the lease of the remaining demise varied provided the remaining lease would be valid under Law of Property Act 1925, s 99 had it been then granted: s 100(3).

[103]   If the mortgage is by lease. If the mortgage is by charge by deed by way of legal mortgage, the lender has the rights, powers and remedies as if he had the reversionary lease: Law of Property Act 1925, s 87.

[104]   Law of Property Act 1925, s 100(4).

2.77   Likewise, under section 100(2) of the Law of Property Act 1925, the lender while in possession can accept a surrender as against all prior incumbrancers and the borrower, provided it is for the same purpose.

2.78   The borrower's section 100(1) powers to accept surrenders are not exercisable once and while a receiver is appointed by the lender under the lender's statutory power. The power to accept surrenders is the lender's as if it were in possession.

2.79   The section 100 powers apply only if and so far as the contrary intention is not expressed in the mortgage deed or in writing between borrower and lender and have effect subject to the terms of the deed and any such writing.[105] Thus the power to accept surrenders can be excluded.

2.80   As with the section 99 powers, the powers in section 100 can also be extended by an agreement in writing between the borrower and the lender, and any further powers are exercisable as if conferred by the Law of Property Act 1925, hence so as to bind other incumbrancers, provided the agreement does not prejudicially affect any lender under a mortgage subsisting at the date of the agreement (or it joins in or adopts the agreement).[106] Thus, it is possible to confer a power to accept surrenders for purposes other than the grant of a new lease under section 99 powers.

2.81   If the borrower grants a lease, postdating the mortgage and other than under section 99 powers, so that that lease does not bind the lender, the borrower can accept a surrender of that lease. In the pre-Law of Property Act 1925 terminology, the lease was not a lease of the mortgaged land but of the borrower's equity of redemption.[107]

2.82   Likewise, it is hard to see why a lender could not accept a surrender of a lease granted by the lender but not under section 99 powers, thus, which did not affect the borrower's estate. The effect of that surrender could not change the position of the borrower.

2.83   If the borrower's section 100 power to accept surrenders is excluded by the mortgage, but nevertheless he accepted a surrender of a lease which bound the lender, the effect would be a surrender which bound the borrower but not the lender. For example, suppose the borrower had granted a lease prior to the grant of the mortgage, so that the mortgage took subject to that lease. The position would be as if the chain of estates was: borrower's, lender's, lease.

2.84   If the borrower accepted a surrender of the lease without the consent of the lender and without section 100 powers, or without compliance with that section,

---

[105]   Law of Property Act 1925, s 100(7).

[106]   Law of Property Act 1925, s 100(10).

[107]   See the discussion above. Note, though, that if the land is registered land, the lease will be shown as granted out of the borrower's estate, but the registered charge will have priority which can be seen on the register by its earlier date to the date of the lease.

then that surrender would not bind the lender, and the lease would continue unchanged as against the lender.[108] If the borrower granted a new lease in breach of mortgage, then that new lease would take effect as a concurrent lease out of the borrower's estate only.[109]

TRANSFER BY THE BORROWER

2.85   If a mortgage on a registered estate is itself registered, then the borrower will not be able to sell free of it, and if he grants any interests they will not take priority over the charge.[110] Thus the lender's primary protection against the borrower's dispositions is registration.

2.86   However, many lenders prefer if possible to be able to prevent any disposition at all. It is common on the grant of a mortgage for the lender to require the borrower to enter a restriction on the register for the borrower's estate preventing any disposition without the lender's consent.

TRANSFER BY THE LENDER

2.87   A mortgage, as a property interest, can be transferred by the lender to another person. Such a transfer has to be by deed,[111] and, if the mortgage is registered, itself be completed by registration,[112] if it is to take effect at law.

2.88   The effect of a transfer of the mortgage by deed, unless a contrary intention is shown, is to transfer the right to the mortgage money and interest, the benefit of all securities for it, the benefit and right to sue on the covenants, the right to exercise the lender's powers, and the mortgage estate.[113]

---

[108]   *E S Schwab & Co Ltd v McCarthy* (1975) 31 P & CR 196 at 209.

[109]   *Barclays Bank Ltd v Stasek* [1957] Ch 28. The result in that case was that the lender could not take possession against the occupiers because their original lease continued as against the lender, though it did not against the borrower. See also the discussion in *Caroll v Manek and Bank of India* (2000) 79 P & CR 173. The apparent oddity is in line with the position on with surrender of leases more generally. A surrender of an intermediate lease to the reversioner ends the lease between those two parties but does not end underleases out of the intermediate lease, though there are no direct landlord–tenant relationships between the reversioner and the underlessees.

[110]   Land Registration Act 2002, s 29(1) and (2)(a)(i).

[111]   Law of Property Act 1925, s 52.

[112]   Land Registration Act 2002, s 27.

[113]   Law of Property Act 1925, s 114. Although see *Paragon Finance Plc v Pender* [2005] EWCA Civ 760: s 114 does not apply to registered land (though note that the case was about the right to possession and was decided under the Land Registration Act 1925). The registered proprietor of a mortgage is in a like position to that resulting from s 114 by reason of that registration. Presumably, registration under the Land Registration Act 2002 has the same effect as found in *Pender* by reason of s 51, s 52 and s 58, though note that the equivalent provision in Land Registration Act 1925, s 34(1) referred to in *Pender* expressly gave the registered proprietor of a charge the powers conferred by law on the owner of a legal mortgage, and that is not replicated in the 2002 Act. Although a registered proprietor of a charge would have a right to possession,

THE LENDER'S REMEDIES

2.89   An understanding of the remedies open to a lender is necessary for an understanding of receivership for two reasons:

(a)   it provides the context for a consideration of the circumstances in which a receiver might be appointed, by revealing what other options the lender has; and

(b)   it enables an understanding of the powers which can be delegated by the lender to the receiver.

2.90   When considering the lender's remedies, it is important to remember that the mortgage creates both a contract and an interest in land. The lender therefore has both contractual remedies and remedies arising from its proprietary interest. The first section of this chapter examines the main contractual remedy: a claim in debt. Then the principal proprietary remedies are considered in detail.[114]

2.91   Most mortgage lenders are regulated by the Financial Conduct Authority (FCA).[115] These lenders are required to treat their customers fairly, or face enforcement or other action by the regulator. The regulatory requirements curtail the lender's ability to exercise some of its remedies. The key points are noted in the relevant sections below.

A MONEY CLAIM

2.92   The mortgage deed will invariably[116] contain a covenant to repay the principal sum lent, interest at a specified (and often variable) rate and the costs which the lender incurs in protecting or enforcing its security.[117]

---

since it is inherent in the estate, and statutory powers to appoint a receiver, and to sell, for example, because those belong to the mortgagee as defined in Law of Property Act 1925, s 205, it is less obvious that it would have all express powers and rights. Given that omission, rights and powers under the mortgage are often expressly assigned in the transfer deed and the borrower given notice of that assignment so that Law of Property Act 1925, s 136 is complied with. See also paras 9.26–9.27 and 9.34–9.35.

[114]   Guidance about the lesser used proprietary remedies of foreclosure and an order for sale, which are principally used where the mortgage is equitable, is outside the scope of this book, but can be found in specialist works. Foreclosure is discussed briefly above in the context of redemption of the mortgage.

[115]   The FCA website contains a lists of firms which are or have been regulated by the FCA at https://register.fca.org.uk.

[116]   If such a covenant is not present, it is likely to be implied, unless the mortgagor is providing security for a loan to a third party.

[117]   The lender's right to costs is a topic of some complexity. If the mortgage is silent, the lender is entitled to its costs reasonably and properly incurred in enforcing or preserving the security from the mortgaged property on sale, though if there is a shortfall, he will not be able to sue for the costs portion as a debt. The question of whether receiver's expenses can be added to the mortgage debt is a question of interpretation of any express costs provision in the mortgage conditions.

2.93 Once these sums have fallen due on the true construction of the mortgage,[118] the lender can therefore bring a money claim for these sums. However, free-standing money claims are comparatively rare.[119] Most borrowers have no means to repay the loan without selling the security, so it is frequently easier for the lender to obtain possession and sell the security itself.

2.94 Money claims against the borrower are generally only contemplated where:

(a)   the security is defective; or
(b)   the security is inadequate.

2.95 It is generally no bar to a money claim that a possession order has previously been made[120] or that the security has been sold.[121] As a result, in many cases where the security is inadequate, the lender will often seek the shortfall from the borrower(s) many years later when the borrowers have got back on their feet. The limitation period for such claims is 12 years from the date when, as a matter of construction of the mortgage deed, the principal sum fell due or could have been demanded,[122] unless in the meantime there has been a part-payment or written acknowledgment.[123] If the Mortgages and Home Finance: Conduct of Business Sourcebook (MCOB) applies,[124] the lender must notify borrowers within 6 years of the date of sale if it intends to pursue the shortfall.[125]

2.96 A money claim cannot be brought against the borrower if he (or it) is insolvent.[126]

---

[118] Note that in many cases a demand will be required before the cause of action crystallises. Such a demand must be made before the proceedings are issued: *Esso v Alstonbridge* [1975] 1 WLR 1474 at 1483. Demands are considered in more detail at paras 4.39–4.54.

[119] A money claim is often included in a possession claim. They are then sometimes adjourned pending sale, especially if the borrower disputes the figures. If there is a dispute, the court will take an account. If the costs are the cause of the dispute, that will be by detailed assessment.

[120] Even if a money judgment was sought in the possession proceedings and then not proceeded with: *UCB v Chandler* (1999) 79 P & CR 270.

[121] *Rudge v Richens* (1872–73) LR 8 CP 358.

[122] Limitation Act 1980, s 20; *West Bromwich Building Society v Wilkinson* [2005] UKHL 44. Note that if, on the true construction of the mortgage, the only covenant was to repay a shortfall, then the applicable period would be 12 years from the date of sale, under s 8. Note also that a shorter period applies to arrears of interest (6 years under s 20(5)), but the lender will generally apportion the proceeds of sale to pay off the arrears of interest first, so the shortfall amount will be principal.

[123] Limitation Act 1980, s 29.

[124] See www.handbook.fca.org.uk/handbook/MCOB/1/?view=chapter. The MCOB applies to most mortgage lending to an individual where at least 40% of the land is used as, or in connection with, a dwelling. See the discussion in Chapter 3.

[125] MCOB 13.6.4R.

[126] Where the borrower is an individual: Insolvency Act 1986, s 285(3). Where the borrower is a company:

   –   s 130(2) precludes any claim without leave, where a compulsory winding up order has been made;

2.97   A money claim can be brought by the original lender[127] or by an assignee of a registered mortgage who has itself been registered as the proprietor of it.[128] A claim can be brought by an assignee of the debt, even without the mortgage, provided that notice in writing of the assignment has been given to the borrower.[129] If the lender is dissolved, the right vests in the Crown[130] as *bona vacantia*.

2.98   A money claim can also be brought against any guarantor who has covenanted to repay the loan. Such claims are more common than claims against borrowers, because guarantors are more likely to have the means to satisfy the claim. The same principles apply: the lender must ensure that the money is due as a matter of contract, that the guarantor is not insolvent and that the claim is not statute-barred.

THE RIGHT TO PRESERVE THE SECURITY

2.99   The mortgage will generally be construed so as to enable the lender to take any steps necessary to preserve the value of its security, whether against the borrower or a third party. This means that the lender is able to, for example:

(a)   seek injunctive relief if a third party seeks to remove fixtures from the property, even if the third party was entitled to do so as against the borrower;[131] or

(b)   take possession to protect it from vandalism.[132]

2.100   In addition, statute confers further rights on the lender to preserve its security:

(a)   it can insure the security against fire and add the premiums to the mortgage account;[133] and

(b)   if the security is leasehold, it can seek relief from forfeiture.[134]

-    s 112 enables the liquidator to apply to the court for a stay of any claim in a voluntary winding up; and

-    Sch B1, para 43(6) prevents any legal process being taken against the company without permission of the administrator or the court.

In all cases, the court is unlikely to sanction any course of action which allows one creditor to obtain priority over others.

[127]   If the lender was an individual, his personal representatives can claim after his death, and his trustee in bankruptcy can claim if he is bankrupt.

[128]   Law of Property Act 1925, s 114(1)(a) if the transfer was by deed and/or *Paragon Finance Plc v Pender* [2005] EWCA Civ 760, and Land Registration Act 2002, s 58: see fn 113.

[129]   Law of Property Act 1925, s 136.

[130]   Or the Duchy of Cornwall or the Duchy of Lancaster.

[131]   *Ellis v Glover* [1908] 1 KB 388.

[132]   *Western Bank v Schindler* [1977] Ch 1 at 9.

[133]   Law of Property Act 1925, s 101(1)(ii). This power can be excluded or modified by the terms of the mortgage deed.

[134]   Law of Property Act 1925, s 146.

POSSESSION

2.101 Whilst possession might be an end in itself, for example if the occupiers are damaging the property, generally the lender takes possession as a prelude to exercising its power of sale so that it can sell with vacant possession.[135] This is very common.

The lender's right to possession from the borrower

2.102 As set out above, historically, mortgages involved the demise of the security to the lender. It follows that the lender was entitled to possession, just as any other tenant would be.

2.103 This method of creating mortgages was abolished by the Law of Property Act 1925, but the lender has the same rights, including the right to take possession, as if a term had been demised to it.[136]

2.104 It has been said that the lender is entitled to possession 'before the ink is dry on the mortgage'[137] even if the borrower is not in default. However, the following points should be noted:

(a) The lender is only entitled to exercise its right to take possession if it does so in good faith and for the purpose of preserving or enforcing the security.[138]

(b) Most mortgage conditions limit the lender's right to possession, until, typically, the lender's power of sale has arisen, in recognition of the fact that institutional lenders do not want to take possession unless they have to in order to sell with vacant possession[139] and borrowers do not expect that the lender will be able to do so if they are not in default. In each case, the mortgage conditions must be carefully examined in order to establish when the lender's right to possession occurs.

(c) Where the MCOB applies,[140] the lender cannot (without risking enforcement action by the FCA) repossess the property until all other reasonable attempts to resolve an arrears situation have failed.[141]

(d) If the lender brings possession proceedings,[142] the court has a discretion to adjourn the proceedings, postpone the date on which possession is given,

---

[135] Discussed at paras 2.121–2.140. Indeed, where the MCOB applies, the lender is obliged to take steps to market the property for sale as soon as possible after taking possession: MCOB 13.6.1. See Chapter 3 for a discussion of the MCOB.

[136] Law of Property Act 1925, s 87.

[137] *Four Maids v Dudley Marshall (Properties) Ltd* [1957] Ch 317 at 320; see also *Ashe v National Westminster Bank Plc* [2008] EWCA Civ 55, [2008] 1 WLR 710 at [26]–[27].

[138] *Quennell v Maltby* [1979] 1 WLR 318.

[139] See fn 135 in relation to MCOB 13.6.1.

[140] See Chapter 3.

[141] MCOB 13.3.2A.

[142] Which will be necessary if the borrower is in occupation and the mortgagor cannot obtain possession without violence against the person or the property: Criminal Law Act 1977, s 6. If

or suspend the order on terms, if it appears likely that the borrower will be able to pay the sums due[143] within a reasonable period.[144]

The lender's right to possession from third parties

2.105 The lender has no right to possession against any third party occupying the mortgaged property unless and until it is entitled to possession from the borrower, unless the terms of the mortgage provide otherwise. Before this time, the borrower has the right to decide who should be in possession.[145]

2.106 When the lender is entitled to take possession against the third party, it will often have no means of knowing the identity or the status of the person in occupation of the property as against the borrower. Generally,[146] the lender will simply sue the borrower, serve notice addressed to the occupiers at the property[147] and wait and see what rights (if any) the third party asserts.[148]

---

the property is vacant, the lender can physically retake possession without the need for any court proceedings: *Ropaigealach v Barclays Bank Plc* [2000] 1 QB 263. In that case, the court will have no jurisdiction to postpone or suspend possession at the request of the borrower under Administration of Justice Act 1970, s 36. See also Consumer Credit Act 1974 (CCA 1974), s 126 which requires a court order before possession is taken for certain mortgages. See the discussion at paras 3.89–3.99.

[143] In ascertaining the sums due, any acceleration of the date when the principal falls due by reason of the default is to be ignored: Administration of Justice Act 1973, s 8.

[144] Administration of Justice Act 1970, s 36. In the context of receivership, this is discussed at paras 10.142–10.148.

[145] See *Turner v Walsh* [1909] 2 KB 484 at 494: prior to the lender giving notice of an intention to take possession or the income, the borrower's right to possession continues because 'it was in the nature the transaction that the mortgagor could continue in possession. His possession was rightful and not wrong'. See the discussion in Chapter 9, fn 60.

[146] Since a lender's claim for possession is not enforcement of the mortgage, but simply a right to recover land he is entitled to because of his right to possession, the lender may, as an alternative, issue a claim against the occupiers alone: *Esso Petroleum Co Ltd v Alstonbridge Properties Ltd* [1975] 3 All ER 358. That case suggests that a lender should sue the occupiers only, if the only remedy sought is an order for possession. However, if the lender wishes to claim a money judgment, or even if he wishes simply to ensure that the borrower is bound by the court's determination that the right to possession has arisen, he can and should join the borrower. It is, in fact, common to claim possession against the borrower alone, even when the borrower is known not to occupy, because the order obtained will be enforceable at the date of the eviction by the bailiffs against any occupant. Although that may not be correct practice, it rarely leads to argument. Service of notice on the occupants should suffice to ensure that if they have any claim to a right to occupy as against the lender, they assert it.

[147] Pursuant to CPR, r 55.10.

[148] Note that even if the occupier does not assert a right at the time of the possession hearing, a further notice must be served before the order is enforced, and the occupiers will have a further opportunity to assert their rights at this stage: Mortgage Repossessions (Protection of Tenants etc) Act 2010, s 2; Dwelling Houses (Execution of Possession Orders by Mortgagees) Regulations 2010 (SI 2010/1809).

Tenants

2.107 If the occupier asserts that he has a tenancy, the next step is to ascertain whether the tenancy is binding on the lender. The tenancy will be binding in the following circumstances:

(a) If it was granted before the mortgage,[149] and it was registered at the Land Registry[150] or it amounts to an overriding interest under section 29 of, and Schedule 3 to, the Land Registration Act 2002,[151] and the tenant is not estopped from asserting its interest binds the mortgagee.[152]

(b) If the borrower was authorised to grant tenancies by the terms of the mortgage[153] and complied with any conditions stipulated in the mortgage.

(c) If the lender consented to the grant of the tenancy, before or after it was granted, [154] or if the lender has accepted the tenant and treated him as its own, for example, by accepting rent from him in circumstances where it is fair to infer that the lender intended to create a tenancy. For the lender to become bound by the tenancy in this way, it must have acted, with knowledge of the tenancy, in such a way that it may be taken to have

---

[149] If a purchaser does not own the property, buys it with a mortgage, and purports to grant a tenancy before the completion date of the purchase, the tenant does not obtain priority over a lender whose charge is completed on completion of the purchase: *Abbey National v Cann* [1991] 1 AC 56. The same is true for a tenancy granted at completion: *Southern Pacific Mortgages Ltd v Scott (Mortgage Business Plc intervening)* [2014] UKSC 52, [2015] AC 385 (known as the North Eastern Property buyers litigation). But see *Universal Permanent BS v Cooke* [1952] 1 Ch 95 for an example of a case where there was a gap between completion of the purchase and completion of the mortgage, despite the mortgage financing the purchase, and the lender was bound by the tenancy granted in the gap.

[150] See Land Registration Act 2002, s 29. Where there is already a registered lease, the mortgage will be of the reversion, and as if a concurrent lease.

[151] See *Woolwich BS v Dickman* (1996) 28 HLR 661, decided under the Land Registration Act 1925.

[152] Frequently, lenders require occupiers to sign a form postponing any interest they might have to the lender's charge. There is relatively little authority on the effectiveness of this postponement despite it being standard for lenders to seek such a postponement; but see *Abbey National BS v Cann* [1991] AC 56; *Bristol and West BS v Henning* [1985] 1 WLR 778; *Skipton BS v Clayton* (1993) 25 HLR 596 at 602.

However, note that a Rent Act 1977 protected or statutory tenant cannot postpone his priority so as to allow a lender to take possession against him as a trespasser: *Woolwich Building Society v Dickman* [1996] 3 All ER 204. Two reasons were given. First, because under Land Registration Act 1925, s 70(1)(g) then in force, registered land was deemed subject to the rights of a person in actual occupation unless the contrary was expressed on the register. The Land Registration Act 2002 reversed this position. Even so, it is not obvious, were the case to turn on this provision only, why the equivalent provision in the Land Registration Act 2002 would not apply in Rent Act and other cases, save that in other cases, the tenant is likely estopped from denying the priority of the mortgage over the lease. The better explanation for the decision is the second. Rent Act 1977, s 98(1) prevents a possession order being made by the court save in specific circumstances which did not apply and the court cannot by estoppel be given a jurisdiction it does not have. See also *Barclays Bank Plc v Zaroovabli* [1997] Ch 321. It is possible that there are similar issues with assured and assured shorthold tenancies under the Housing Act 1988 since the court has jurisdiction to grant possession only in specific circumstances.

[153] Law of Property Act 1925, s 99 gives the borrower a power to lease in certain circumstances, but this power can be, and generally is (unless the mortgage is a buy to let mortgage), excluded. See the discussion above.

[154] Or indeed granted it, under Law of Property Act 1925, s 99(2), for example.

acquiesced in the tenancy.[155] A mere failure by the lender to evict the tenant is unlikely to be enough, even if for a long time.[156] The question of whether the lender has recognised the tenancy so as to be bound by it is to be determined by looking at the whole picture.[157] The most common form of acquiescence by a lender is acceptance of rent from the tenant knowing of the tenancy. The effect of acceptance of the tenancy by the lender will be to create a new tenancy between the lender and the tenant.[158]

2.108 If the tenancy is not binding on the lender, it can obtain possession from the tenant, once its right to possession as against the borrower has arisen under the terms of the mortgage, without the need to show that any grounds exist under the tenancy for doing so, and regardless of any statutory protection that the tenant would have as against the borrower.[159]

2.109 However, if the tenant has an assured or Rent Act protected tenancy (as against the borrower), the tenant can apply to postpone the date on which he must give up possession for up to 2 months.[160] The court will consider the tenant's circumstances and whether the tenant is in breach of his tenancy when determining whether to grant the application.

2.110 Conversely, if the tenancy is binding on the lender, it can only obtain possession from the tenant in accordance with the terms of the tenancy and any applicable statutory protection.[161]

Licensees

2.111 The lender will be entitled to possession from any licensee regardless of the terms of the licence,[162] unless the lender has estopped itself from seeking possession from him.

---

[155] *Iron Trades Employers Insurance Association Ltd v Union Land and House Investors Ltd* [1937] Ch 313 at 318–319; *Parker v Braithwaite* [1952] 2 All ER 837 at 841; *Stroud BS v Delamont* [1960] 1 WLR 431 at 434: the lender had informed the tenant that the terms of the tenancy which she held as tenant of the lender were the same as those of the borrower, expressly representing that there was such a tenancy. She paid rent by cheque to the lender. The court held that the lender was bound by the tenancy even though it did not appreciate that it could have treated her as a trespasser despite appointing a receiver. See also *Chatsworth Properties Ltd v Effiom* [1971] 1 WLR 144 where the lender appointed a receiver, and the lender's solicitor wrote to the tenant requiring him to pay rent to the receiver, but without mentioning the mortgage or the deemed agency of the receiver. The lender was found to have accepted the tenant and to be bound by the tenancy. A reasonable man would have understood the letter as requiring payment to the receiver as agent of the lender: *Nijar v Mann* (2000) 32 HLR 223 at 226–227.

[156] *Taylor v Ellis* [1960] 1 All ER 549 at 551 cited in *Nijar v Mann* (2000) 32 HLR 223 at 227.

[157] *Nijar v Mann* (2000) 32 HLR 223 at 228.

[158] *Stroud BS v Delamont* [1960] 1 WLR 431 at 434.

[159] *Dudley & District Benefit BS v Emerson* [1949] Ch 707; *Bolton BS v Cobb* [1966] 1 WLR 1.

[160] Mortgage Repossessions (Protection of Tenants etc) Act 2010, s 1.

[161] This is considered in more detail in Chapter 10.

[162] Because a licence takes effect only between the parties to it.

Beneficiaries

2.112 If the borrower holds the property on trust, then just as with tenants, it is necessary to ask whether the lender is bound by the trust, and, if it is, whether and to what extent that will affect its right to possession.

2.113 If the borrower held the legal and beneficial title for himself at the date of the grant of the mortgage and later declares a trust of his estate, then it is unlikely that the trust will affect the mortgage.[163]

2.114 The issue most often arises on mortgages post-dating the borrower's acquisition of the property where the borrower held the property in his sole name.[164] If a beneficiary's interest existed at the date of the mortgage grant and he was in actual occupation of the property at that date, then that interest binds the mortgage unless the lender knew of the interest and ensured the beneficiary postponed his rights to the lender's as a condition of the mortgage being entered into, by deed or otherwise in writing.[165]

2.115 For example, a property may be registered in the sole name of A. A few years after purchase, A mortgages the property. A's partner contributed to the price on the purchase of the property and, on the particular facts, has a beneficial interest in the property in proportion to his contribution. He is living in the property when the mortgage is granted and hence is in actual occupation.[166] His beneficial interest binds the lender if he has not signed a consent agreeing to postpone any interest he has to the lender.

2.116 If the trust has the purpose of permitting the beneficiary to occupy the property, the lender will not be able to exercise its right of possession against the beneficiary if in occupation, because the lender takes subject to the beneficiary's right.

2.117 A similar problem arises when the property is owned by two or more people, but one successfully proves that he entered into the mortgage by the undue influence of the other. In those circumstances, the effect of what purported to be a mortgage of the legal title to the property will be an equitable mortgage binding only the beneficial interest of the person whose consent was not vitiated. The lender's rights and remedies will be effective against that

---

[163] If the mortgage is registered, the trust could have no effect. In any event, a trust is equitable, and priorities in equity are as to time of creation. Thus problems should only arise if the lender agrees to postpone his priority to the trust.

[164] Where there is more than one trustee registered with the title to the property who granted the mortgage, or the trustee was a trust corporation, then the grant of the mortgage will have overreached the beneficial interests under Law of Property Act 1925, s 2(1)(ii) and (2) as long as the provisions in s 27 as to payment of the capital money have been complied with, and the lender will take free of the trust.

[165] See a similar discussion in relation to pre-existing leases at para 2.107.

[166] See Land Registration Act 2002, s 29 and Sch 3, para 2. The partner's beneficial interest would be overriding and hence bind the mortgagee.

person's beneficial interest only, and it will not be able to seek possession of the legal estate against the beneficiary whose interest is not bound.

Trespassers

2.118   The lender is also entitled to possession from trespassers[167] once its right to possession has arisen as against the borrower.

The consequences of taking possession

2.119   If the lender takes any of these steps and succeeds in obtaining and enforcing an order for possession, it will become a mortgagee in possession. That has a number of serious consequences, and is not a step that the lender will take lightly. The following are the most important:

(a)   The lender will be liable to account to the borrower (and anyone else interested in the equity of redemption) not only for all the sums which he has in fact received, but also for any sums which it would have received, but for its wilful default.[168]

(b)   The lender is obliged to take reasonable care of the property.

(c)   The lender may be liable for breaches of restrictive covenants and on landlord leasehold covenants.[169]

(d)   The lender will be treated as the person in possession or occupation for all purposes. The lender might therefore be liable:

  (i)   to pay rates (but not council tax);

  (ii)   under environmental legislation, such as the contaminated land regime; and

  (iii) under the Occupiers Liability Acts.

---

[167]   I.e. occupants with no rights from the borrower, as well as occupants who are trespassers as against the lender despite having rights from the borrower.

[168]   Note that for older leases the lender will not be liable to the landlord of the borrower, if the borrower's estate is leasehold, because there is no privity of estate. The lender's estate is at the end of the chain: landlord-borrower-lender, if the mortgage were considered as a lease. That is save for new leases, granted after 1 January 1996. The landlord may be able to enforce against the lender under Landlord and Tenant (Covenants) Act 1995, ss 3(5) and 15(4).

[169]   Landlord and Tenant (Covenants) Act 1995, s 15(2), for tenancies created after 1 January 1996. For such tenancies, the lender will be able to enforce tenant covenants in a lease binding on the mortgage: s 15(1). The position in relation to old tenancies granted prior to that date is governed by Law of Property Act 1925, ss 141 and 142. If there is a lease out of the mortgaged property binding on the lender, the lender will likely be entitled to enforce tenant covenants, under s 141(2), even if the mortgage is a charge by deed by way of legal mortgage, because it is entitled to the income by reason of s 87. A lender with a mortgage by lease will be liable on the landlord obligations by s 142(1). It is less obvious whether a lender with a charge by deed by way of legal mortgage could be liable for landlord obligations under s 142 since obligations go with the reversionary estate, and the lender in those circumstances do not have it: *Weg Motors Ltd v Hales* [1962] Ch 49 at 74, though this part of the decision appears *obiter*.

(e) If the security is a leasehold estate, the lender taking possession might trigger the landlord's entitlement to forfeit the lease.[170]

2.120 The lender will also, of course, have to find the resources to manage the property if it takes possession.

SALE

The power of sale

2.121 The Law of Property Act 1925 confers a statutory power of sale on the lender where the mortgage is made by deed,[171] 'when the mortgage money has become due'.[172] This enables the lender to sell the borrower's estate in the property itself, not just the lender's interest under the mortgage.

When exercisable

2.122 The statutory power of sale is not exercisable until one of the following statutory conditions has been satisfied:

(a) notice requiring payment of the mortgage money has been served on the borrower, and the borrower has failed to pay within 2 months;
(b) some interest under the mortgage is in arrear and unpaid for 2 months after becoming due; or
(c) the mortgagor is in breach of some other term.[173]

2.123 However, the statutory terms only apply if they are not modified by the mortgage terms. Frequently they are. In each case, the mortgage terms must be considered to ascertain when the lender's power of sale arises and is exercisable.

2.124 Once the power of sale is exercisable, the lender can, if it chooses, exercise it without obtaining possession from the borrower.[174] However, this is rarely done in practice: those lenders who are members of the Council of Mortgage Lenders have agreed not to do so where the security is owner-occupied; and in all other cases, the lender will be mindful that any purchaser may seek an inflated reduction in the purchase price for the trouble of obtaining vacant possession after completion.

---

[170] For example, if there is a covenant against parting with possession.

[171] The mortgage, if made by deed, need not be registered for the right to arise: *Swift 1st Ltd v Colin* [2011] EWHC 2410 (Ch), [2012] Ch 206. Similarly, an assignee of the mortgage is entitled to exercise the power of sale before being registered as proprietor of the charge: *Skelwith (Leisure) Ltd v Armstrong* [2015] EWHC 2830 (Ch), [2016] Ch 345 (contrary to the *obiter* comment to the contrary in *Lever Finance v Needleman's Trustee* [1956] Ch 375 decided under the Land Registration Act 1925).

[172] Law of Property Act 1925, s 101. The meaning of this phrase is considered in detail at paras 4.36–4.60.

[173] Law of Property Act 1925, s 103.

[174] *Horsham Properties Group Ltd v Clark* [2008] EWHC 2327 (Ch), [2009] 1 WLR 1255.

2.125 Normally, the lender will take possession first and then sell with vacant possession.

Extent of the power

2.126 The power of sale is extensive. It is:

> To sell,[175] or to concur with any other person in selling, the mortgaged property, or any part thereof, either subject to prior charges or not,[176] and either together or in lots, by public auction or by private contract, subject to such conditions respecting title, or evidence of title, or other matter, as the mortgagee thinks fit, with power to vary any contract for sale and to buy in at any auction, or to rescind any contract for sale, and to re-sell without being answerable for any loss occasioned thereby.[177]

2.127 The 'mortgaged property' is 'the property over which the mortgage deed purports to extend and operate',[178] i.e. the unencumbered estate the borrower had just prior to the mortgage.[179] The power of sale allows sale of part only of that property.[180]

2.128 The lender can exercise its section 101(1)(i) power by public auction or by private contract and can agree any conditions in the contract. The lender is given further powers incident to the power of sale, by section 101(2),[181] so as to be able to operate as any seller of an estate in land.

---

[175] Sale is a key concept in the Law of Property Act 1925. Presumably, it means a transfer of title for money or monies worth. See for example the definition of 'purchaser' in s 205(1)(xxi) as a purchaser for valuable consideration. Sale is to be distinguished from a conveyance, which, at s 205(1)(ii) includes mortgages, charges, leases, etc. The precise meaning of 'sale' in the Act is not set out. In s 205(1)(xxiv), 'sale' is defined as 'a sale properly so called'.

[176] Since under Law of Property Act 1925, s 104(1) the lender exercising its statutory power of sale conveys the property subject to 'all estates, interests, and rights which have priority to the mortgage', this phrase, 'either subject to prior charges or not', cannot mean that the power is to sell free of prior mortgages without discharging them.

[177] This power to vary or rescind contracts is unlimited and appears to apply to a contract for the sale of the mortgaged property entered into by the borrower. In any event, if the borrower enters into a contract to sell the mortgaged property, whether or not the lender's power of sale has arisen, the existence of that contract does not affect the lender's power of sale, or its other rights. The borrower's contract would have effect as a contract for the sale of the equity of redemption only, if the charge is not redeemed: *Duke v Robson* [1973] 1 WLR 267.

[178] *In Re White Rose Cottage* [1964] Ch 483 at 496 (reversed on appeal in [1965] Ch 940 on other grounds), with this interpretation approved in *Swift 1st Ltd v Colin* [2011] EWHC 2410 (Ch), [2012] Ch 206.

[179] At law, the lender has a proprietary estate by reason of the mortgage. In equity, the lender is treated as having only a charge to secure the lending.

[180] Save that under Law of Property Act 1925, s 101(1A), sale of a part-unit of a commonhold unit is not possible, under Commonhold and Leasehold Reform Act 2002, s 21. This relates to commonhold land, introduced by that Act, a way of owning blocks of flats for the benefit of the owners of the individual flats, which is little used.

[181] (i) A power to impose or reserve or make binding, as far as the law permits, by covenant, condition, or otherwise, on the unsold part of the mortgaged property or any part thereof, or on the purchaser and any property sold, any restriction or reservation with respect to building on or

2.129 Under section 88(1)(b) and section 89(1) of the Law of Property Act 1925, as set out above, the lender may convey the borrower's estate, under its power of sale and with the above effect, in the borrower's name,[182] rather than expressly as the lender under its power of sale.[183]

The lender's duties

2.130 The lender does not owe any general duty of care to the borrower in deciding whether or when to sell. The lender is not under any obligation to improve the property, for example by carrying out works or obtaining planning permission, before selling. However, it must act in good faith and for proper purposes in deciding whether to sell and, if it decides to sell, it must take reasonable care to obtain the best price reasonably obtainable.[184] This is an equitable duty, and the lender will not be found to be in breach unless it has failed to expose the property to the market adequately, bearing in mind the circumstances, and the price obtained falls outside the bracket of values which different valuers could properly place on the property.[185]

---

other user of land, or with respect to mines and minerals, or for the purpose of the more beneficial working thereof, or with respect to any other thing:

(ii) A power to sell the mortgaged property, or any part thereof, or all or any mines and minerals apart from the surface—

(a) With or without a grant or reservation of rights of way, rights of water, easements, rights, and privileges for or connected with building or other purposes in relation to the property remaining in mortgage or any part thereof, or to any property sold: and

(b) With or without an exception or reservation of all or any of the mines and minerals in or under the mortgaged property, and with or without a grant or reservation of powers of working, wayleaves, or rights of way, rights of water and drainage and other powers, easements, rights, and privileges for or connected with mining purposes in relation to the property remaining unsold or any part thereof, or to any property sold: and

(c) With or without covenants by the purchaser to expend money on the land sold.

[182] The wording of Law of Property Act 1925, ss 88 and 89 suggests that it is the conveyance which can be in the borrower's name. There is no express power to contract in the borrower's name.

[183] If the lender has a power of attorney for the borrower, then some care will be needed, on a sale by the lender in the borrower's name, to ensure that that sale takes effect as a sale under the statutory power, or an express power, of sale, with its effects, rather than under the power of attorney where sale will not be free of charges later in priority to the mortgage in question, if the former is intended. See Law of Property Act 1925, s 104(3) which deems a conveyance on sale by a lender to have been made in exercise of the statutory power of sale unless the contrary intention appears. See, for example, *In Re White Rose Cottage* [1965] 1 Ch 940, in which the question of which method of sale had been used was precisely in issue. The sale was said to be under a power of attorney, and there was an express discharge of the selling lender's mortgage. It followed that the sale was not under the statutory or an express power of sale. Presumably, the lender with power to sell in the borrower's name can execute a conveyance in the borrower's name in exercise of that power, and does not require the borrower to so execute. See s 9(1)(d) and (e), under which a conveyance by the lender in the borrower's name or on that person's behalf under the statutory power operates to convey the legal estate in like manner as if the conveyance had been executed by the estate owner.

[184] *Silven Properties Ltd v Royal Bank of Scotland Plc* [2003] EWCA Civ 1409, [2004] 1 WLR 997.

[185] *Michael v Miller* [2004] EWCA Civ 282, [2004] 2 EGLR 151.

2.131 If the duty is breached, the lender must account to those interested in the equity of redemption for the price that it should have received.[186]

2.132 In addition, where the lender is regulated by the FCA, it is obliged to treat the customer fairly. A lender which disregards the borrower's interest entirely will risk facing regulatory action.

Position of the borrower

2.133 A borrower can, in principle, seek to prevent the lender entering into a contract for sale of the mortgaged property or completing that sale, by seeking an injunction, if the power of sale has not arisen, or is being exercised by the lender in bad faith.[187] Prior to entry into the contract, the borrower can also prevent the contract by tendering the total amount due under the mortgage[188] to the lender or by paying it into the court if the lender will not accept it. Once the lender has entered into a contract for sale, the borrower's equity of redemption is suspended[189] and he cannot prevent completion even by tender of the full sum.[190]

2.134 Entry into a contract for sale by the borrower will not prevent the lender from contracting. A sale by the borrower is of his equity of redemption and subject to the registered mortgage,[191] unless and until the borrower obtains the

---

[186] *Silven Properties Ltd v Royal Bank of Scotland Plc* [2003] EWCA Civ 1409, [2004] 1 WLR 997.

[187] See *Waring v London and Manchester Assurance Company Ltd* [1935] Ch 310 and the discussion in *Property & Bloodstock Ltd v Emerton* [1968] Ch 94 at 114. A court might well decide that the borrower could be adequately recompensed in damages, and thus not grant an injunction.

[188] That is the total amount the lender says is due for principal, interest, costs and expenses unless the lender seeks something for which he is obviously not entitled (e.g. expenses which he has no right to recover, or interest at a greater rate than provided for by the mortgage). If the full amount the lender asks for is paid, and it is in excess of what is due, the excess can be recovered by the borrower. Likewise, if the lender seeks less than he is entitled to, he can seek the remainder after redemption.

[189] *Waring v London and Manchester Assurance Company Ltd* [1935] Ch 310; *Property & Bloodstock Ltd v Emerton* [1968] Ch 94; *Horsham Properties Group Ltd v Clark* [2008] EWHC 2327 (Ch), [2009] 1 WLR 1255 at [22]. The reason given in *Waring* was that the statutory powers gave the lender a power to bind the borrower, so that when the lender contracted to sell, that contract bound the borrower and the court would not grant an injunction against completion of the sale unless the contract was entered into in bad faith. The equity of redemption is extinguished on completion.

[190] Unless the power of sale has not arisen, or the lender is not acting properly, i.e. the sale is in bad faith.

[191] See *Duke v Robson* [1973] 1 WLR 267. It is usual for a lender with a registered mortgage to enter a restriction on the register preventing completion of a disposition without the lender's consent. This is how a lender prevents sale of the property by the borrower without redemption of the mortgage. If the mortgage is registered only, without a restriction, then sale by the borrower is possible though it will be subject to the mortgage.

discharge of the mortgage by the lender, which is usually on redemption by payment of the full sums.[192]

Position of the purchaser

2.135 If the lender sells, it is deemed to sell pursuant to the statutory power of sale unless the contrary appears.[193] Under section 101(3) of the Law of Property Act 1925, the power of sale may be varied or extended by the mortgage deed and, if so varied or extended, the power will operate in a like manner and with the incidents, effects and consequences of the power of sale in the Act. Thus, an express power of sale can have the same effect (as set out in this section) on the position of the purchaser as the statutory power.

2.136 A sale pursuant to the statutory power vests the borrower's estate in the property in the purchaser free of the mortgage and of any interests over which the mortgage has priority.[194]

---

[192] Under Law of Property Act 1925, s 91(1), the court has the power to put the sale into the hands of the borrower not the lender, for example, where it will realise greater sums, or permit sale by the borrower at lower than the redemption figure, where the sale will not realise sufficient monies for discharge of the mortgage where it is just and equitable to do so in all the circumstances. The cases in which the jurisdiction has been exercised have been negative equity cases, where the lender has not wanted to sell, but the borrower cannot pay the current monthly instalment (i.e. the monthly sum payable under a standard high street mortgage, consisting of a contribution towards repayment of the principal and/or interest) and is in financial hardship. See, for example, *Palk v Mortgage Services Funding Plc* [1993] 2 WLR 415 CA.

[193] Law of Property Act 1925, s 104(3). Further, in any contract for the sale or exchange of a mortgage term, where the vendor has power to convey the fee simple or, for a mortgage of a leasehold, that lease (i.e. where the power of sale has arisen), the contract is deemed to extend to the fee simple or leasehold reversion: s 42(4)(i).

[194] Law of Property Act 1925, ss 88, 89 and 104(1). The mortgage term merges with the borrower's estate on the conveyance: ss 88 and 89. The subsequent interests are overreached by these provisions and/or under s 2(1)(iii), if the capital money arising is paid to the lender. This is similar to the overreaching that occurs when purchase monies are paid to two trustees or a trust corporation. The purpose of the overreaching provisions has been described in D Cavill, et al, *Ruoff & Roper: Registered Conveyancing* (Sweet & Maxwell, looseleaf) at 15.011.01 as a transfer of the interest from an interest in land to an interest in the proceeds of sale. Thus a transfer by two trustees, under s 2(1)(ii), will turn the interest of a beneficiary in the property into an interest in the money raised by its sale.

The question of which equitable interests are 'capable of being overreached' is not an easy one, and case law has not provided a clear answer. In *Birmingham Midshires Mortgage Services Ltd v Sabherwal* (2000) 80 P & CR 256 in which Walker LJ said at [28] that since an equitable easement or right of entry could not 'shift from the land affected to it to the proceeds of sale', those interests were of the kind not capable of being overreached. But in *Mortgage Express v Lambert* [2016] EWCA Civ 555, the right to avoid an unconscionable bargain was held capable of being overreached by the grant of a mortgage; the suggestion in *Baker v Craggs* [2016] EWHC 3250 (Ch) that the grant of an equitable easement could overreach has been refuted on appeal in [2018] EWCA Civ 1126 as only conveyances of legal estates in land can overreach under s 2(1), and an easement is a legal estate but not a legal estate in land.

However, there can be little doubt that a mortgagee can sell free of interests over which the mortgage has priority, because of the terms of s 104.

2.137 The statutory power of sale does not enable the lender to overreach any interests which have priority over the mortgage[195] and, in particular, does not enable it to clear off prior charges.[196]

2.138 Generally, a purchaser will not want to take the property subject to a charge (or other prior interest) and will seek an undertaking that the prior charge be discharged from the proceeds of sale on completion. If such an undertaking is given by the lender's solicitor, and honoured, the purchaser will take free of prior charges also.

Protection of the purchaser

2.139 The purchaser must ascertain that the power of sale has arisen.[197] However, the statute provides that the purchaser need not enquire as to whether the power of sale was exercisable, or whether the power of sale was improperly or irregularly exercised.[198] His title is not impeachable on this ground,[199] unless the purchaser (or his solicitor) knew of the irregularity or shut his eyes to it. In such a case, the borrower can obtain an order setting the sale aside, if he acts promptly.[200]

Proceeds of sale

2.140 The proceeds must be distributed in accordance with the statutory regime:

(a)   discharge of prior incumbrances (which permits the lender's solicitor to honour an undertaking to do so);
(b)   the costs of sale;
(c)   the monies due under the mortgage; and
(d)   the residue is to be paid to 'the person entitled to the mortgaged property, or authorised to give receipts for the proceeds of the sale thereof'.[201]

---

[195]   Law of Property Act 1925, s 104(1). There is an argument that s 2(1)(iii) allows sale free of certain equitable interests, for example, a beneficial interest in the mortgaged property, which has priority over the mortgage. It is no bar to overreaching for example by trustees that they are bound by the equitable interest. However, the wording of s 104, and the use of the words 'paramount powers' suggests that a lender cannot overreach by sale an interest to which the mortgage is subject, since the lender's powers on sale are not paramount over such interests.

[196]   Although, of course, if the charge is not registered, the purchaser may take free of such interests in any event under Land Registration Act 2002, s 29 and Sch 3.

[197]   I.e. within the meaning of Law of Property Act 1925, s 101(1): *Bailey v Barnes* [1894] 1 Ch 25. If it had not, the lender would sell its mortgage only.

[198]   Law of Property Act 1925, s 104(2). If the power of sale is irregularly exercised, those suffering loss as a result have a personal claim against the lender.

[199]   Ibid.

[200]   *Tse Kwong Lam v Wong Chit Sen* [1983] 1 WLR 1349.

[201]   Law of Property Act 1925, s 105. This regime is considered in more detail at paras 12.84–12.88.

POWER OF ATTORNEY

2.141 Frequently, the mortgage terms will provide that the borrower irrevocably appoints the lender as his attorney, so that the lender can execute documents in the borrower's name. Typically, this will enable the lender to take out insurance policies in the borrower's name, to convey the property in the borrower's name and make claims against third parties relating to the property, including claims for possession of the property, in the borrower's name. The lender is entitled to exercise its right to do these things as attorney of the borrower, even if the borrower does not concur in the taking of such steps.[202] The lender's power of attorney survives the borrower's bankruptcy.[203]

APPOINTMENT OF A RECEIVER

2.142 Unless the mortgage terms provide otherwise, the lender is entitled to appoint a receiver when it is entitled to exercise the power of sale.[204] The preconditions and formalities required for a valid appointment are dealt with in more detail below.[205]

2.143 Almost invariably, the mortgage terms provide that the receiver will have power to collect income from the property[206] and will do so as agent of the borrower.[207] Frequently, the mortgage terms also give the receiver much wider powers, such as the power to let the property and terminate existing leases,[208] the power to take possession[209] and a power to sell the property.[210] In addition, the lender can delegate some of its powers to the receiver.[211]

2.144 The advantages of appointing a receiver for the lender are as follows:

(a) The lender can avoid the liabilities that flow from taking possession itself.[212] Since the receiver is the borrower's agent, the borrower remains in possession even if the receiver is in fact 'running the show' on the ground.

---

[202] In *Garrett v The Licensing Justices of the District of St Marylebone, Middsx* (1884) 12 QBD 620, the lender applied for a premises licence in the borrower's name. The borrower appeared at the hearing, and said he did not want the licence. On appeal, it was held that a licence should nonetheless have been granted.

[203] Cf the receiver's power of attorney. see paras 6.229–6.243.

[204] Law of Property Act 1925, s 109.

[205] Chapter 4.

[206] This is considered in detail in Chapter 9.

[207] The agency relationship is considered in Chapter 6.

[208] See Chapter 9.

[209] See Chapter 10.

[210] See Chapter 11.

[211] This is considered in more detail in Chapter 9.

[212] See paras 6.7–6.8.

(b) The lender will not be liable for any acts carried out by the receiver as agent for the borrower, unless the lender interferes with the conduct of the receivership.[213]

(c) The lender is unlikely to be subject to regulatory sanction if the receiver treats the borrower unfairly, unless the lender directs the receiver to act in that way.

(d) The lender does not itself have to resource the management of the property or supervising agents instructed to do so.

2.145 Of course, the corollary to the freedom from liability from the receiver's acts is that the lender cannot control what the receiver does. A receiver may seek to sell the security (if he has the power to do so), but he will try to manage the property in such a way that it will generate enough income to service the mortgage and clear the arrears so that it can be returned to the borrower if he considers this possible. In practice, the lender may be able to ascertain from a prospective receiver what he is likely to do, but once he is appointed, it will be for the receiver to decide how best to discharge his primary duty to the lender of recovering the sums due under the mortgage.[214] That said, the lender does retain ultimate control, because it can terminate the receivership at any time if it does not like what is being done.[215]

2.146 A further disadvantage of appointing a receiver is that the receiver will, of course, expect to be paid for the work he does.[216] The lender must therefore expect that the receiver will recover sufficient monies to pay the receiver's remuneration and still leave the lender better off than if it had exercised some other right. Often, the receiver will also seek an indemnity from the lender against any liability which he may incur to the borrower or a third party.

2.147 A receiver is typically appointed where some or all of the following circumstances exist:

(a) It is fair to the borrower for a receiver to be appointed.[217]

(b) The mortgage terms confer wide powers on the receiver, and/or provide that the receiver is to be the agent of the borrower even when he exercises lender-delegated powers;

(c) Sufficient money is likely to be realised to cover the receiver's remuneration.

(d) The lender does not wish to sell, for example because there are tenants paying sufficient rent to cover the mortgage instalments and receivers' remuneration.

---

[213] This is considered in more detail at paras 7.44–7.57.

[214] See para 6.88 and paras 7.19–7.24.

[215] Termination is dealt with in Chapter 14.

[216] The receiver's remuneration is considered at paras 12.25–12.45.

[217] Any lender regulated by the FCA must satisfy itself that it is fair to appoint a receiver before doing so.

(e)   The borrower is acting irrationally, or does not appear to be maximising the money that could be made from the property, and the lender believes that with better management, the property need not be sold.

(f)   The property is not suitable for an immediate sale, for example because it is in course of development, or repair works need to be undertaken.

(g)   The borrower has a portfolio of properties, and the receiver will be able to consider how many and which properties need to be sold to clear the arrears, whilst enabling the borrower to retain as many as possible.

(h)   The lender-borrower relationship has broken down, and the lender believes that the borrower may co-operate with a receiver.

2.148   Receivers will rarely be appointed where the property is residential and owner-occupied. Lenders which are members of the Council of Mortgage Lenders have agreed to seek a possession order rather than appoint receivers to sell the property,[218] and such properties will not have existing tenants whose rent can be collected by receivers.

---

[218]   However, it is hard to see how that could give a borrower any right to seek an injunction to prevent the appointment of a receiver.

Chapter 3

Consumer Protection Legislation

3.1   This chapter addresses the impact of consumer protection legislation on mortgage agreements generally and receivership in particular. It covers the following:

(a)   The general[1] regulatory framework of consumer protection legislation under:

    (i)   the Consumer Credit Act 1974 (CCA 1974);
    (ii)   the Financial Services and Markets Act 2000 (FSMA 2000); and
    (iii) the Mortgage Credit Directive 2014/17/EU (MCD).[2]

(b)   The impact of consumer protection legislation on mortgage agreements and the enforcement of those agreements by the appointment of a receiver.

3.2   The CCA 1974 offers wide-ranging protection to individual consumers regulating for example the form of contracts, cancellation rights and the process of enforcement. Where the CCA 1974 applies, the breach of its provisions can render a regulated agreement unenforceable.[3] Application of the CCA 1974 to mortgages is limited. This has always been the case, but recent legislative changes have further reduced the class of mortgages which are regulated agreements and, as a result, the number which are caught by the majority of the regulation in the Act.

---

[1]   Only a general overview of the legislative framework concerning consumer protection is provided. Emphasis is placed on the relevance of the legislation to mortgages relating to land and receivership. For a more in-depth treatment of consumer protection, reference should be made to specialist texts such as R Goode, et al (eds), *Goode: Consumer Credit Law and Practice* (LexisNexis Butterworths, looseleaf), which contains commentary on the position following the passing of the MCD (see fn 2) and its implementation by the MCD Order 2015 (see fn 10); and E Lomnicka and D Bowden (eds), *Encyclopaedia of Consumer Credit Law* (Sweet & Maxwell, looseleaf).

[2]   Directive 2014/17/EU of the European Parliament and of the Council of 4 February 2014 on credit agreements for consumers relating to residential immovable property and amending Directives 2008/48/EC and 2013/36/EU and Regulation (EU) No 1093/2010. Other Acts of Parliament and Statutory Instruments which have now been repealed (such as the Unfair Terms in Consumer Contracts Regulations 1994 and 1999) may be relevant to old agreements.

[3]   See for example CCA 1974, Pt IX, which gives the court a wide power to supervise regulated agreements by limiting or preventing enforcement, and s 86D(3) and (4), which restricts the ability to recover arrears where appropriate notices have not been given.

3.3   Prior to the introduction of the MCD, first legal mortgages did not fall within the general regulatory framework of the CCA 1974. In general, second legal mortgages were more likely to be caught by the CCA 1974.

3.4   However, with the introduction of the MCD, credit agreements which are made with the purpose of acquiring land or to retain property rights in land no longer fall to be regulated by the CCA 1974.

3.5   The exceptions to the above are two areas of regulation by the CCA 1974. First, the unfair relationships provisions[4] which give the court oversight of unfair terms and the exercise by the creditor of its rights, in credit agreements made by individuals. These provisions will apply to certain[5] mortgages made by individuals, however else they are regulated.

3.6   Secondly, section 126 of the CCA 1974, which requires certain types of mortgages to be enforced on an order of the court only,[6] applies to a larger class of mortgages than regulated agreements under the CCA 1974.[7]

3.7   Those agreements which fall outside the remit of the CCA 1974[8] will be regulated under the FSMA 2000,[9] the Mortgage Credit Directive Order 2015 (MCD Order 2015),[10] or not at all.

3.8   The consequences of a breach of the FSMA 2000 are potentially severe. Agreements made by unauthorised persons in the course of carrying out a regulated activity may be rendered unenforceable.[11]

3.9   However, the impact of a breach of the MCOB, which forms part of the FCA[12] Handbook[13] and is the part directed at certain types of residential mortgages,[14] is more limited, at least in the sense that such breaches do not

---

[4]   Consumer Credit Act 1974, ss 140A–140C. See paras 3.100–3.115.

[5]   Any mortgage which is not exempt under RAO 2001, art 60C. Thus, the unfair relationship provisions do not apply to regulated mortgage contracts and regulated home purchase plans.

[6]   See paras 3.89–3.99.

[7]   It applies also to regulated mortgage contracts and to consumer credit agreements which are exempt from being regulated agreements by reason of RAO 2001, art 60D. See fn 163.

[8]   A detailed exposition of this subject is outside the remit of this book.

[9]   As amended by the Financial Services Act 2012.

[10] SI 2015/910. Effective from 21 March 2016.

[11] See also, FSMA 2000, s 26.

[12] The FCA which, with the Prudential Regulation Authority at the Bank of England, replaced the Financial Services Authority in 2013. The FCA is the conduct regulator for financial markets which aims, among other things, to protect consumers. The Prudential Regulation Authority rules are intended to ensure financial institutions have adequate capital and risk controls.

[13] See www.handbook.fca.org.uk/handbook/MCOB/1/?view=chapter. The Handbook also includes the Consumer Credit Sourcebook (CONC) being that part directed towards credit-related regulated activities, see www.handbook.fca.org.uk/handbook/CONC/.

[14] The MCOB, introduced in 2004 by the FSA, applies to firms which carry on 'home finance activity' or 'communicates or approves a financial promotion of qualifying credit, of a home purchase plan, of a home reversion plan or of a regulated sale and rent back agreement': see

prescriptively prevent mortgage enforcement.[15] Furthermore, while the FCA has the power to enforce the provisions of the MCD Order 2015, it is unclear what the precise consequences of a breach would be.

3.10 This chapter addresses the relevant framework before considering the consequences for receivership of a particular regime applying to a mortgage or loan agreement.

OVERVIEW OF REGULATORY FRAMEWORK

3.11 There are two main statutory regimes which provide consumer protection in relation to loan agreements concerning land:

(a) the CCA 1974; and
(b) the FSMA 2000.

3.12 The provisions of the CCA 1974 and the FSMA 2000 have been the subject of several amendments over the years.[16]

3.13 The most recent wave of amendments took place following the MCD[17] and its transposition into UK domestic law by the enactment of the MCD Order 2015. This statutory instrument amended both the CCA 1974 and the FSMA 2000 and has also led to changes to the FCA rules and guidance in relation to residential immovable property. The legislative intention was to provide a single regulatory regime for mortgage contracts under the MCOB from 21 March 2016. The MCD Order 2015 has, by Part 3, also introduced a new, self-contained framework for the regulation of consumer buy-to-let mortgages.

3.14 Before 21 March 2016 and prior to the implementation of the MCD, the CCA 1974 dealt primarily with certain second charge mortgages while the FSMA 2000 covered certain first legal charge residential mortgages. The fundamental change effected by the MCD Order 2015 was the removal of most second and later mortgages from regulation under the CCA 1974 consumer credit regime and the FCA's Consumer Credit Sourcebook (CONC)[18] and their transfer to the mortgages regime under the FSMA 2000 and the FCA's MCOB. Equitable mortgages are now also covered by the FCA. The parallel regime of

---

MCOB 1.2.1 and further for definitions. The mortgages caught are generally agreements regulated under the FSMA 2000.

[15] See paras 3.158–3.170.

[16] Notably, under the Financial Services and Markets Act 2000 (Regulated Activities) Order 2001 SI 2001/544), the Consumer Credit Act 2006, and the Financial Services Act 2012, which amended the FSMA 2000 to replace the Financial Services Authority with two institutions: the FCA, to regulate financial institutions' conduct, and the Prudential Regulation Authority at the Bank of England, which regulates the sufficiency of financial institutions' capital and risk controls.

[17] This was adopted on 4 February 2014 (also known as CARRP).

[18] The CONC is the FCA's specialist sourcebook for credit-related regulated activities.

regulation for consumer buy-to-let mortgages created by the MCD Order 2015 applies to both first and subsequent consumer buy-to-let mortgages.

3.15   The CCA 1974 does continue to have application in relation to some older mortgages. For those land related agreements created before 21 March 2016[19] which still fall to be regulated by the CCA 1974 (typically second charge legal mortgages), the CCA 1974 sets out certain requirements as to the form and content of agreements, as well as provisions as to their withdrawal and termination.[20] The parties to the contract are not permitted to contract out of its provisions,[21] and the breach of certain provisions under the CCA 1974 can render the agreement unenforceable.[22] It is important, therefore, to be clear on those agreements which fall outside the CCA 1974 regime.

3.16   However, even where an agreement falls outside the three regimes set out above, it may still be caught under the unfair credit relationship provisions under sections 140A to 140C of the CCA 1974[23] and section 126 of the CCA 1974, which requires a court order before enforcement.[24] The relevant provisions of the CCA 1974 are considered in the following section.

THE CCA 1974

3.17   The CCA 1974 regime imposes various requirements on various types of credit agreements. Requirements are imposed on consumer credit agreements, which are regulated agreements.[25] For example, Part V of the CCA 1974 regulates entry into the agreement, including requirements as to form[26] and signature,[27] with breach of those requirements rendering the agreement enforceable against the debtor on the order of the court only.[28] It also gives cancellation rights,[29] requires specific information to be given to the debtor prior to enforcement for arrears and default[30] and makes certain types of mortgage

---

[19]   See transitional provisions under MCD Order 2015, Pt 4.

[20]   See paras 3.77–3.85.

[21]   CCA 1974, s 173 provides that 'a term contained in a regulated agreement or linked transaction, or in any other agreement relating to an actual or prospective regulated agreement or linked transaction, is void if, and to the extent that, it is inconsistent with a provision for the protection of the debtor or hirer or his relative or any surety contained in this Act or in any regulation made under this Act'.

[22]   See para 3.84.

[23]   See paras 3.100–3.115.

[24]   See paras 3.89–3.99

[25]   See also the CONC within the MCOB.

[26]   CCA 1974, s 60.

[27]   CCA 1974, s 61.

[28]   CCA 1974, s 65.

[29]   CCA 1974, s 67–73.

[30]   CCA 1974, Pt VII.

enforceable on an order of the court only.[31] These provisions are discussed further below.[32]

3.18 One of the difficulties with the CCA 1974 regime is that it has been subject to numerous amendments since 1974. These amendments have changed membership of the class of credit agreements to which the Act applies. In particular, the types of mortgage which have been caught by the Act thus necessitating compliance with its various requirements, have changed over time. The latest amendments, and the introduction of the MCD, are a further example of this process.

3.19 Care must be taken when determining whether a particular agreement is caught by the CCA 1974 to identify the specific provisions of the CCA 1974 which were in force at the time at which the agreement was made whether or not the agreement was then, and/or later, regulated and whether any applicable requirements under the CCA 1974 were breached at any time.

3.20 When the CCA 1974 was first enacted, it did not apply to agreements that provided credit over £15,000.[33] In May 1998, that limit was increased to £25,000, and this remained the position until 2006.[34] This meant that the CCA 1974 was not relevant to the majority of loan and mortgage agreements concerning residential property. However, the amendments introduced by the Consumer Credit Act 2006 removed this financial limit, so that mortgages relating to land more frequently fell within its remit. [35] Except as set out in exemptions,[36] there is now no general financial limit to what constitutes a regulated credit agreement under the CCA 1974.

3.21 In addition to the financial limits, the historic position was that first legal mortgages for owner-occupiers were usually exempt,[37] and buy-to-let mortgages were usually exempt.[38]

3.22 As discussed in this chapter, the latest statutory changes have excluded more mortgages from much of the CCA 1974 regime. The starting point, however, is to identify the correct description for a mortgage, within the

---

[31] CCA 1974, s 126(1). These are regulated agreements, regulated mortgage contracts, and consumer credit agreements which but for RAO 2001, art 60D would be regulated agreements.

[32] See paras 3.77–3.99.

[33] CCA 1974, s 8(2), prior to its amendment by Consumer Credit (Increase of Monetary Limits) Order 1983 (SI 1983/1878), Sch 1(II), para 1

[34] CCA 1974, s 8(2), prior to its amendment by the Consumer Credit Act 2006.

[35] CCA 1974, s 8(2) has been repealed by Consumer Credit Act 2006, Sch 4, para 1. The financial limit does not apply to agreements made after 6 April 2008 unless the agreement is a 'relevant agreement' for the purposes specified in Consumer Credit Act 2006 (Commencement No 4 and Transitional Provisions) Order 2008 (SI 2008/831), art 3(1) and Sch 2. The financial limit does not apply to 'relevant agreements' made after 1 October 2008. Although note the exemptions under RAO 2001, art 60C discussed at paras 3.14–3.57.

[36] See RAO 2001, arts 60C–60AH.

[37] By, CCA 1974, s 16(6C), which was repealed from 1 April 2014.

[38] By, CCA 1974, s 16C, which was repealed from 1 April 2014.

meaning of the CCA 1974, so that any obligations imposed by the CCA 1974 on the mortgage can be identified. That requires discussion of various definitions used to identify agreements to which provisions in the CCA 1974 apply.

Regulated credit agreements

3.23   The latest version of the CCA 1974 defines 'consumer credit agreement' in section 8(1) and then 'regulated credit agreement' in section 8(3).

3.24   'Credit' is defined in section 9(1) of the CCA 1974 as including 'a cash loan, and any other form of financial accommodation'.[39]

3.25   A 'consumer credit agreement' under section 8(1) of the CCA 1974 is 'an agreement between an individual ("the debtor") and any other person ("the creditor") by which the creditor provides the debtor with credit of any amount'.

3.26   'Individual' includes a partnership of two or three persons provided that not all are bodies corporate, and an unincorporated body of persons which does not consist entirely of bodies corporate and is not a partnership.[40]

3.27   It thus appears by inference that the CCA 1974 does not regulate agreements solely with corporate bodies.[41]

3.28   Most of the obligations imposed on agreements by the CCA 1974 are imposed on 'regulated agreements', i.e. consumer credit agreements which are regulated agreements within the meaning of section 8(3).[42]

3.29   Section 8(3) of the CCA 1974[43] says that:

> A consumer credit agreement is a regulated credit agreement within the meaning of the Act if it (a) is a regulated credit agreement for the purposes of Chapter 14A of Part 2 of the Regulated Activities Order;[44] and (b) if entered into on or after 21st March 2016,[45] is not an agreement of the type described in Article 3(1)(b) of

---

[39]   See, CCA 1974, s 189(1), which defines 'credit' by reference back to s 9(1).

[40]   CCA 1974, s 189(1).

[41]   Note CCA 1974, s 185(5), which includes within 'consumer credit agreement' agreements with joint debtors where one or more is an individual and one or more is not. Note also that the definition of 'consumer credit agreement' does not exclude agreements with an individual for the purposes of his business.

[42]   Or consumer hire agreements which are regulated agreements within the meaning of CCA 1974, s 15(2). See s 189(1) for the definition of 'regulated agreement'. Consumer hire agreements are outside the remit of this book. Oddly, s 8(3) refers to a 'regulated credit agreement' not a 'regulated agreement'. The definition of the latter refers back to s 8(3), so it is presumed they are intended to have the same meaning.

[43]   This came into force on 17 March 2016.

[44]   RAO 2001: CCA 1974, s 189(1).

[45]   For agreements entered into after 21 March 2016, both conditions must be satisfied. This second provision appears to take out of CCA regulation mortgages granted since that date for the purpose of acquiring the property, or re-mortgages of such mortgages. See paras 3.71–3.74.

Directive 2014/17/EU of the European Parliament and of the Council of 4th February 2014 on credit agreements for consumers relating to residential immovable property.

3.30 There are thus two limbs to the relevant definition of 'regulated agreement'. A regulated consumer credit agreement is an agreement that is:

(a) a regulated credit agreement for the purposes of Part II, Chapter XIVA of the Financial Services and Markets Act 2000 (Regulated Activities) Order 2001 (RAO 2001);[46] and

(b) an agreement made after 21 March 2016 which is not of the type described in Article 3(1)(b) of the MCD.

These two limbs are considered in turn in the following sections.

Regulated credit agreements for the purposes of RAO 2001, Part II, Chapter XIVA

3.31 Section 8(3)(a) of the CCA 1974 provides that a consumer credit agreement is a regulated credit agreement if it is a regulated credit agreement for the purposes of Part II, Chapter XIVA of the RAO 2001.[47] The RAO 2001 is a statutory instrument made under the FSMA 2000[48] to specify activities which if carried on by way of a business are regulated under that Act.[49]

3.32 The RAO 2001 defines the terms 'credit agreement' and 'regulated credit agreement' in article 60B(3).[50]

3.33 First, the definition of 'credit agreement'. A credit agreement: (a) in relation to an agreement other than a green deal plan,[51] means an agreement between an individual or relevant recipient of credit (A) and any other person (B)

---

[46] SI 2001/544 as amended by the Financial Services and Markets Act 2000 (Regulated Activities) Order (Amendment) (No 2) Order 2013 (SI 2013/1881).

[47] Under CCA 1974, s 8(3)(b), for agreements entered into on or after 21 March 2016 falling within s 8(3)(a), there is a second condition to be satisfied for regulation under the CCA 1974. Under s 8(3)(b), the agreement must not be of the type described in MCD, Art 3(1)(b), i.e. any purchase mortgage or remortgage it seems: see paras 3.71–3.74.

[48] FSMA 2000, s 22 and Sch 2, para 25.

[49] Including provision of credit under agreements regulated by the CCA 1974.

[50] RAO 2001, Pt, II, Ch XIVA.

[51] 'Green deal plan' has the meaning given by Energy Act 2011, s 1 (see RAO 2001, art 3). In summary, a green deal plan is an energy plan (an arrangement by the owner or occupier of property for a person to make energy efficiency improvements to it) where payment is to be wholly or partly by instalments, the property is eligible, the improvements fall within a description specified in an order made by the Secretary of State, and various other conditions are met. That is, green deal plans are designed as ways of financing particular energy efficiency improvements to property.

under which B provides A with credit of any amount; and (b) in relation to a green deal plan, has the meaning given by article 60LB of the RAO 2001.[52]

3.34   Most mortgages will not be green deal plans; most are likely to be credit agreements. Credit includes a cash loan and any other form of financial accommodation.[53]

3.35   Under article 60B(3) of the RAO 2001, a regulated credit agreement is, in the case of an agreement entered into on or after 1 April 2014, any credit agreement which is not an exempt agreement.[54]

3.36   In the case of an agreement entered into before 1 April 2014, a regulated credit agreement is a credit agreement which:[55]

(a)   was a regulated agreement within the meaning of section 189(1) of the CCA 1974 when the agreement was entered into;[56] or

(b)   became such a regulated agreement after being varied or supplemented by another agreement before 1 April 2014, and would not be an exempt agreement pursuant to article 60C(2) of the RAO 2001[57] on 21 March 2016 if the agreement were entered into on that date.

Exempt agreements relating to land after 1 April 2014

3.37   A credit agreement which is an exempt agreement will not be a regulated credit agreement within the meaning of article 60B of the RAO 2001 and, hence, not a regulated agreement, for the purposes of the CCA 1974.[58] Thus many of the requirements imposed by the CCA 1974, in particular as to form and signature of the agreement and steps before enforcement, will not apply.[59]

3.38   Exempt agreements are defined in Part II, Chapter XIVA of the RAO 2001 at articles 60C to 60H.[60] Those provisions have been amended significantly

---

[52] Under RAO 2001, art 60LB, a green deal plan is to be treated as a credit agreement for the purposes of the RAO 2001 if (and only if): (a) the property in relation to the plan is a domestic property at the time when the plan is commenced; or (b) if sub-paragraph (a) does not apply, the occupier or owner of the property who makes the arrangement for the plan is an individual or relevant recipient of credit.

[53] RAO 2001, art 60L, repeating the definition in CCA 1974, s 9(1).

[54] As to which, see below.

[55] An analysis of past versions of the CCA 1974 is outside the scope of this book. Reference should be made to the statute in its earlier forms, and to any practitioner's text on consumer credit.

[56] To analyse if this is the case, one must identify the CCA 1974 as it was in force when the agreement was entered into.

[57] See the discussion of this article at paras 3.41–3.56.

[58] RAO 2001, art 60B(3).

[59] The requirement under CCA 1974, s 126 requiring a court order before enforcement, and the unfair relationships provisions under ss 140A–140C will apply. See below.

[60] This replaced the provisions of CCA 1974, ss 16–16C, which were repealed by Financial Services and Markets Act 2000 (Regulated Activities) (Amendment) (No 2) Order 2013 (SI 2013/

since the introduction of the MCD and its implementation into domestic law by the MCD Order 2015. The most recent version of articles 60C to 60HA came into effect on 17 March 2016. The exemptions are considered in general terms in the following paragraphs.[61]

3.39   Exempt agreements fall into six categories. Exemptions are based on:

(a)   the nature of the agreement;[62]
(b)   the purchase of land for non-residential purposes;[63]
(c)   the nature of the lender;[64]
(d)   the number of repayments to be made;[65]
(e)   the total charge for credit;[66] and
(f)   the nature of the borrower.[67]

The nature of the agreement

3.40 Article 60C of the RAO 2001 contains numerous categories of agreements which are exempt agreements[68] due to the nature of those agreements. It includes the following categories:

(a)   entering into a regulated mortgage contract;[69]
(b)   entering into a regulated home purchase plan;[70]
(c)   administering regulated mortgage contracts;[71]
(d)   agreements where the lender provides over £25,000 to the borrower, and the borrower enters into the agreement wholly or predominantly for the

---

1881), Pt 5, art 20(5) (1 April 2014: the repeal has effect subject to transitional provisions specified in Pt 8).

[61]   The exemptions are based on various factual matters being true. The court tends to look unfavourably on borrowers' attempts to argue at the stage of enforcement of a mortgage that this and similar provisions did apply when at the time of grant they stated in the documentation that they did not apply. See, for example, *Fortwell Finance Ltd v Halstead* [2018] EWCA Civ 676. See also *Waterside Finance Ltd v Karim* [2012] EWHC 2999 (Ch) under the Consumer Credit Act 1974 as then in force: parties could agree that matters should be treated as fact so that exemptions from regulation applied whatever the true facts. The decision suggests that s 173 was not discussed. See conversely *Wood v Capital Bridging Finance Ltd* [2015] EWCA Civ 451, decided prior to the 2014 amendments, in which a declaration of business purpose did not engage the presumption as to business exemption under s 16B since the borrower told the lender of the true use at the date of the loan she entered into.

[62]   RAO 2001, art 60C. See paras 3.41–3.57.

[63]   RAO 2001, art 60D. See paras 3.58–3.61.

[64]   RAO 2001, art 60E. See para 3.62.

[65]   RAO 2001, art 60F. See paras 3.63–3.65.

[66]   RAO 2001, art 60G. See paras 3.66–3.68.

[67]   RAO 2001, art 60H. See paras 3.69–3.70.

[68]   I.e. exempt from the definition of regulated credit agreement in RAO 2001, art 60B, and hence from CCA regulation under CCA 1974, s 8(3).

[69]   RAO 2001, arts 60C(2)(a) and 61, and para 3.43.

[70]   RAO 2001, art 60C(2)(b). See fn 79 for meaning.

[71]   RAO 2001, art 60C(2)(c).

purposes of a business carried on, or intended to be carried on, by the borrower;[72]

(e)   agreements where the lender provides £25,000 or less to the borrower and the borrower enters into the agreement wholly for the purposes of a business carried on, or intended to be carried on, by the borrower, and the agreement is a green deal plan made in relation to non-domestic property;[73] and

(f)   agreements made in connection with certain trade in goods or services.[74]

REGULATED MORTGAGE CONTRACTS

3.41   The exemption under article 60C(2) of the RAO 2001 will be of the most relevance to a receiver as it relates to entering into a regulated mortgage contract and is hence most likely to exempt a mortgage from CCA regulation.

3.42   A credit agreement is an exempt agreement if, by entering into the agreement as lender, a person is entering into a regulated mortgage contract.[75] A regulated mortgage contract in this context means regulated under the FSMA 2000 rather than under the CCA 1974. The purpose of this exemption is to limit CCA regulation to mortgages not already regulated by the FCA by reference to the MCOB. As set out below, the definition of which mortgages are regulated mortgage contracts has been extended by amendments due to the MCD.

3.43   Chapter XV of the RAO 2001 contains provisions relating to regulated mortgage contracts. Following the amendments made by the MCD Order 2015, article 61(3) of the RAO 2001 defines a regulated mortgage as a contract which, at the time it is entered into, meets the conditions stated below:

(i)   the contract is one under which a person ('the lender') provides credit to an individual[76] or to trustees ('the borrower');

(ii)   the contract provides for the obligation of the borrower to repay to be secured by a mortgage[77] on land in the EEA;

(iii)   at least 40% of that land is used, or is intended to be used:

(aa)   in the case of credit provided to an individual, as or in connection with a dwelling;[78] or

(bb)   in the case of credit provided to a trustee which is not an individual, as or in connection with a dwelling by an individual who is a beneficiary of the trust, or by a related person,

---

[72]   RAO 2001, art 60C(3).

[73]   RAO 2001, art 60C(4).

[74]   RAO 2001, art 60C(8).

[75]   RAO 2001, art 60C(2).

[76]   'Individual' is not defined.

[77]   The definition of mortgage in RAO 2001, art 61(4) includes a charge. It will include equitable mortgages. See paras 2.43–2.52 for the distinction.

[78]   Note that if the contract says that the property is not to be used as a dwelling, it will not fall within this definition even if as a matter of fact it is so used: *Waterside Finance Ltd v Ashraf Karim* [2012] EWHC 2999 (Ch).

but such a contract is not a regulated mortgage contract if it falls within article 61A(1) or (2).

3.44   The reference to article 61A(1) of the RAO 2001 excludes from the definition of regulated mortgage agreement regulated home purchase plans,[79] limited payment second charge bridging loans,[80] second charge business loans,[81] investment property loans,[82] exempt consumer buy-to-let mortgage contracts,[83] exempt equitable mortgage bridging loans[84] and exempt housing authority loans.[85]

---

[79]   An arrangement under which the home purchase provider buys a qualifying interest or share of a qualifying interest in land, it is held on trust for the provider and an individual or trustees, the individual or trustees have an obligation to buy the interest over the course of or at the end of a specified period, and the home purchaser, or a beneficiary of the trust, or a related person is entitled to occupy at least 40% of the land as or in connection with a dwelling over the period: RAO 2001, arts 63F(3) and 61A(6).

[80]   Defined by RAO 2001, art 61A(6) as a loan complying with (i)–(iii) of the definition of a regulated mortgage contract, is a borrower-lender-supplier agreement financing the purchaser of land, is used by the borrower as a temporary financing solution while transitioning to another financial arrangement for the land subject to mortgage, the mortgage ranks in priority behind one or more other mortgages, and the number of payments to be made by the borrower under the contract is not less than four.

[81]   A loan complying with (i)–(iii) of the definition of a regulated mortgage contract, but where the lender provides credit exceeding £25,000, the mortgage ranks in priority behind one or more other mortgages, and the agreement is entered into by the borrower wholly or predominantly for the purposes of a business carried on, or intended to be carried on by the borrower: RAO 2001, art 61A(6). Entry of the borrower into a statement that the agreement is entered into wholly or predominantly for the purposes of a business carried on, or intended to be carried on, by the borrower, that he understands he will not have the benefit of FSMA 2000, and that he is aware that if he is in any doubt he should seek independent legal advice raises a presumption that the borrower did enter into the agreement for business purposes unless the lender or a person acting on its behalf knows or has reasonable cause to suspect that the agreement is not entered into for that purpose: RAO 2001, s 61A(3) and (4).

[82]   Under RAO 2001, art 61A(6), these are loans complying with (i)–(iii) of the definition of a regulated mortgage contract, but where less than 40% of the land is used or intended to be used as or in connection with a dwelling by the borrower or, where the loan is to trustees, by an individual who is a beneficiary of the trust or a related person, and the agreement is entered into by the borrower wholly or predominantly for the purposes of a business carried on, or intended to be carried on, by the borrower. See the end of fn 81 as to the statement of business purposes.

[83]   Under RAO 2001, art 61A(6), such a contract is one which when entered into is a consumer buy-to-let contract within the meaning of MCD Order 2015, art 4 and is of a kind the MCD does not apply to by virtue of MCD, Art 3(2), or is a bridging loan. A consumer buy-to-let mortgage contract is a buy-to-let mortgage contract not entered into by the borrower wholly or predominantly for the purposes of a business carried on, or intended to be carried on, by the borrower. See the end of fn 81 as to the statement of business purposes. See also s 61A(5) as to the presumption as to business purpose where the agreement is a buy-to-let mortgage contract.

[84]   Under RAO 2001, art 61A(6), these are bridging loans, secured by an equitable mortgage on land, and exempt within the meaning of art 60B(3) (regulated credit agreements) by virtue of art 60E(2) which excludes agreements made by, for example, local authorities and housing associations as lenders.

[85]   Under RAO 2001, art 61A(6), these are contracts for credit to be granted by a housing authority, and if entered into on or after 21 March 2016, are contracts of a kind to which the MCD does not apply by virtue of MCD, Art 3(2), is a bridging loan, or is a restricted public loan within the meaning of art 60HA.

3.45   The reference to article 61A(2) of the RAO 2001 excludes from the definition of regulated mortgage contracts limited interest second charge credit union loans,[86] where the borrower receives timely information on the main features, risks and costs of the contract at the pre-contractual stage, and any advertising of the contract is fair, clear and not misleading.

3.46   Regulated mortgage contracts, in simple terms, are owner-occupier residential mortgages.

3.47   The scope of the revised definition is wider than that which existed previously in earlier versions of article 61 of the RAO 2001. The previous definition of regulated mortgage contracts in article 61 referred to the obligation to repay being secured by a 'first legal mortgage' of land in the United Kingdom.[87] It was for this reason that, subject to exemptions, first legal mortgages of land in the United Kingdom did not fall under the CCA 1974 general regulatory provisions[88] while second legal mortgages could. However, the test has since been expanded so that second and subsequent mortgages are now capable of being regulated mortgage contracts, subject to any applicable exemptions.

3.48   In addition, by article 61(4) of the RAO 2001, references to mortgages are defined as including a charge. Thus, equitable charges are also now within the definition of a regulated mortgage contract.[89] Furthermore, the land charged need not be in the United Kingdom, as reference is now made to the European Economic Area.

3.49   Until 20 April 2015, article 61(3)(iii) of the RAO 2001 required that at least 40% of the land be used, or be intended to be used as, or in connection with, a dwelling by the borrower, or a beneficiary or related person. The amendments which took effect from 20 April 2015 do not seem to require, for credit to an individual, that the individual use at least 40% of the land himself, though, oddly, that requirement is retained for beneficiaries of a trust. This amendment to the definition in principle suggests that, subject to the exclusions set out above,[90] buy-to-let mortgages could be regulated mortgage contracts.

3.50   However, the exclusion of investment property loans from the definition of regulated mortgage contracts seems likely to exclude buy-to-let mortgages, so that they will not be regulated under the FSMA 2000. There is a separate

---

[86]   Defined under RAO 2001, art 61A(6) as a contract complying with (i)–(iii) of the definition of a regulated mortgage contract, which is a borrower-lender agreement, the mortgage ranks in priority behind one or more other mortgages, the lender is a credit union and the rate of the total charge for the credit does not exceed 42.6%.

[87]   This was the position until the end of 19 April 2015.

[88]   CCA 1974, s 16, when in force, had exempted mortgages regulated under the FSMA 2000 from CCA regulation; those were FSMA regulated mortgage contracts under the narrower definition in the earlier version of RAO 2001, art 61.

[89]   See para 2.44 *et seq* for a discussion of equitable charges.

[90]   See paras 3.39 and 3.40.

exception to CCA regulation for non-residential mortgages (in the sense of mortgages not for owner-occupation) at article 60D of the RAO 2001.[91] It follows that many buy-to-let mortgages will not be regulated by either the FSMA 2000 or the CCA 1974.

3.51   There is provision for another form of regulation of consumer buy-to-let mortgages under the MCD Order 2015.[92] Notwithstanding this, those buy-to-let agreements which are entered into wholly or predominantly for the purposes of a business carried on by the borrower will likely remain unregulated.[93]

3.52   The definition in article 61(3) of the RAO 2001 of a regulated mortgage contract is subject to the provisions of article 61(5). That sub-article alters the definition of a regulated mortgage contract in relation to contracts made before 21 March 2016. Its purpose is to include within the class of 'regulated mortgage contracts' both regulated mortgage contracts, as that expression was defined when the agreement was entered into, and contracts which would be regulated mortgage contracts had they been granted after that date, but which were, when granted, regulated under the CCA 1974.

3.53   Thus, via article 61(5) of the RAO 2001, a contract entered into before 21 March 2016 will only be a regulated mortgage contract if:

(a)   at the time it was entered into, entering into the contract was an activity of the kind specified by paragraph (1);[94] or
(b)   the contract is a consumer credit back book mortgage contract within the meaning of article 2 of the MCD Order 2015.[95]

---

[91]   Further consideration is given to the MCD and its impact on both buy-to-let mortgages and bridging loans at paras 3.116–3.125.

[92]   See paras 3.116–3.125.

[93]   See also the discussion of exemptions relating to the purchase of land for non-residential purposes at paras 3.58–3.61.

[94]   I.e. entering into the contract was at the time, and under the version of RAO 2001, art 61(2) then in force, entering into a regulated mortgage contract, then owner-occupier first legal mortgages.

[95]   The definition of 'consumer credit back book mortgage contract' is divided into two, depending on the date of entry into the contract. If the contract was entered into before 21 March 2016, then to be a consumer credit back book mortgage contract, immediately before that date it must have been a regulated credit agreement within the meaning of RAO 2001, art 60B(3), not an exempt agreement within the meaning of art 60B(3) by virtue of art 60D (purchase of land for non-residential purposes) if it were entered into immediately before 21 March 2016, and it would be a regulated mortgage contract if it were entered into on or after 21 March 2016. The requirement that it be a regulated credit agreement means that, if the contract was entered into on or after 1 April 2014 (and before 21 March 2016) it must have been a credit agreement which was not an exempt agreement, to be a regulated credit agreement. If it was entered into on or before 1 April 2014, it must have been a credit agreement which was a regulated agreement within the meaning of CCA 1974, s 189(1) when entered into, or became such a regulated agreement after been varied or supplemented by another agreement before 1 April 2014, and would not be an exempt agreement pursuant to art 60C(2) (a regulated mortgage contract, or regulated home purchase plan) on 21 March 2016 if the agreement were entered into on that date. Thus older CCA regulated mortgages are picked up by this extended definition of regulated mortgage contract. For contracts entered into on or after 21 March 2016, the definition in MCD Order 2015, art 2 is that it was entered into in the circumstances set out in

3.54 Where an agreement is a regulated mortgage contract, it will not be a regulated credit agreement for the purposes of Part II, Chapter XIVA of the RAO 2001. It will thus not be a regulated credit agreement within the meaning of section 8(3)(a) of the CCA 1974, nor will it be a regulated agreement within the meaning of section 189(1).

3.55 The general supervisory provisions of the CCA 1974 which – when breached – can render an agreement unenforceable,[96] will not apply to a regulated mortgage contract.[97]

3.56 Instead, regulated mortgage contracts are governed under the FSMA 2000 and the MCOB.

3.57 However, entering into a regulated credit agreement as a lender is a specified kind of activity within the meaning provided in the FSMA 2000[98] and is an activity which is subject to the provisions of the FSMA 2000 and the MCOB.[99]

Purchase of land for non-residential purposes

3.58 Article 60D of the RAO 2001 sets exemptions[100] relating to the purchase of land for non-residential purposes. It provides:

> (1) A credit agreement is an exempt agreement for the purposes of this Chapter if, at the time it is entered into, any sums due under it are secured by a legal or equitable mortgage on land and the condition in paragraph (2) is satisfied.
> (2) The condition is that less than 40% of the land is used, or is intended to be used, as or in connection with a dwelling
>
> > (a) by the borrower or a related person of the borrower, or
> > (b) in the case of credit provided to trustees, by an individual who is a beneficiary of the trust or a related person of a beneficiary.
>
> (3) For the purposes of paragraph (2)—
>
> > (a) the area of any land which comprises a building or other structure containing two or more storeys is to be taken to be the aggregate of the floor areas of each of those stories;

---

art 28 (a credit agreement was entered into before 21 March 2016 and this is a further agreement relating into the same credit required to be entered into before the borrower was entitled to the credit), it would be a regulated credit agreement within the meaning of RAO 2001, art 60B(3) if it had been entered into immediately before 21 March 2016, and is a regulated mortgage contract immediately after it is entered into. This provision picks up some agreements subject to transitional provisions in the statutory scheme.

[96] CCA 1974, Pt V. See paras 3.77–3.85.

[97] Nor will the unfair relationships part of the CCA 1974 apply. See below.

[98] Specified activities are subject to the general prohibition under FSMA 2000, s 19.

[99] See the further discussion at paras 3.151–3.171.

[100] I.e. from the definition of regulated credit agreement in RAO 2001, art 60B(3), and hence from CCA regulation under s 8(3).

    (b)   'related person' in relation to a person ('B') who is the borrower or (in the case of credit provided to trustees) a beneficiary of the trust, means—

        (i)   B's spouse or civil partner,

        (ii)   a person (whether or not of the opposite sex) whose relationship with B has the characteristics of the relationship between husband and wife, or

        (iii)   B's parent, brother, sister, child, grandparent or grandchild.

    (4)   This article does not apply to an agreement of the type described in Article 3(1)(b) of the mortgages directive[101] that is entered into on or after 21st March 2016 and does not meet the conditions in paragraphs (i) to (iii) of article 61(3)(a) (regulated mortgage contracts).

3.59   This exemption is directed towards pre-21 March 2016 agreements relating to investment properties or buy-to-let mortgages, or mortgages of commercial property. It is in some senses the inverse of the definition of a regulated mortgage contract under article 61 of the RAO 2001.[102]

3.60   The result of this exemption is that commercial mortgages to individuals and many buy-to-let mortgages will not be regulated either as regulated mortgage contracts under the FSMA 2000[103] or as regulated credit agreements under the CCA 1974.

3.61   The impact of article 60D(4) of the RAO 2001 is that the exemption under article 60D from the definition of regulated credit agreement does not apply to agreements made on or after 21 March 2016 which fall within Article 3(1)(b) of the MCD (purchase mortgages or re-mortgages)[104] and which do not fulfil (i) to (iii) of article 61(3) of the RAO 2001.[105] Since mortgages granted on or after 21 March 2016 will be excluded from CCA regulation by reason of falling within Article 3(1)(b) of the MCD,[106] this exclusion will not add to CCA 1974 regulated mortgages.

The nature of the lender

3.62   Article 60E of the RAO 2001 sets out exemptions[107] in relation to the nature of the lender. A credit agreement is an exempt agreement in certain cases where the lender is: (a) a local authority;[108] (b) a housing authority;[109] or (c) an

---

[101] See paras 3.71–3.74.

[102] See para 3.43.

[103] Because they are investment property loans under FSMA 2000, s 61A(1). See paras 3.44–3.45 as to exemption from the definition of regulated mortgage contract.

[104] The apparent meaning of that article. See paras 3.71–3.74.

[105] I.e. the extended owner-occupier requirement. See para 3.43.

[106] CCA 1974, s 8(3)(b).

[107] That is from being a regulated credit agreement, and hence from regulation under CCA 1974, s 8(3).

[108] RAO 2001, art 60E(2).

[109] RAO 2001, art 60E(5).

investment firm or credit institution.[110] In addition, article 60E(3) provides that the FCA may specify other categories of lenders.[111]

The number of repayments

3.63   Article 60F of the RAO 2001 sets out exemptions[112] in relating to number of repayments to be made. It is applicable to agreements which finance the purchase of land[113] as well as conditional sale agreements,[114] hire purchase agreements and agreements secured by pledge.

3.64   The agreements in this exemption are those where a lender, for example under an agreement for the purchase of land, with a pre-existing arrangement with the seller, also finances the insurance premium or the life insurance premium.

3.65   Thus, a credit agreement will be exempt in certain cases:

(a)   borrower-lender-supplier agreement[115] for fixed-sum credit[116] with no more than 12 payments to be made within 12 months or fewer of the date of the agreement, and where the credit is secured on land or provided without interest or other charges, and where (paragraph (7)) the agreement is not to finance the purchase of land, not a conditional sale agreement or hire-purchase agreement, nor an agreement secured by pledge;[117]

(b)   borrower-lender-supplier agreement for running account credit[118] where the borrower is to make payments in relation to specified periods which must be, unless the agreement is secured on land, of 3 months or fewer, the number of payments to be made by the borrower in repayment of the whole amount of credit provided in each period is not more than one, the

---

[110] RAO 2001, art 60E(6).

[111] RAO 2001, art 60E(3) provides that the FCA may specify: (a) an authorised person with permission to effect or carry out contracts of insurance; (b) a friendly society; (c) an organisation of employers or organisation of workers; (d) a charity; (e) an improvement company (within the meaning given by Improvement of Land Act 1893, s 7); (f) a body corporate named or specifically referred to in any public general Act; (g) a body corporate named or specifically referred to in, or in an order made under, a relevant housing provision; (h) a building society (within the meaning of the Building Societies Act 1986); and (i) an authorised person with permission to accept deposits.

[112] From the definition of regulated credit agreement, and hence from regulation under CCA 1974, s 8(3).

[113] RAO 2001, art 60F(7)(a).

[114] Where the purchase price is payable by instalments and the property remains vested in the seller even though the buyer has possession: RAO 2001, art 60L(1).

[115] A borrower-lender-supplier agreement is one where the transaction being financed is one with the lender, or where the lender has an arrangement with the supplier. See RAO 2001, art 60L(1) for the precise definition.

[116] Where the facility allows credit in one amount or by instalments but is not running account credit.

[117] RAO 2001, art 60F(2).

[118] Where the borrower is entitled to receive cash, goods or services from time to time. See RAO 2001, art 60L(1).

credit is secured on land or provided without interest or other significant charges, and paragraph (7)[119] does not apply;[120]

(c)　borrower-lender-supplier agreement financing the purchase of land, the number of payments is not more than four, and the credit is secured on land or provided without interest or other charges;[121]

(d)　borrower-lender-supplier agreement for fixed sum credit, where the credit is given to finance a premium under a contract of insurance relating to land or anything on land with the lender a lender under a credit agreement secured by a mortgage, credit to be repaid within the period to which the premium relates, which must be less than 12 months, and with the number of repayments not more than 12, and with either no interest or charges (if not secured on land), or only with interest not exceeding that under the credit agreement (if secured on land);[122] or

(e)　borrower-lender-supplier agreement for fixed sum credit, the lender is the lender under a credit agreement secured by a mortgage, where the credit is to finance a premium under a whole life insurance contract and, as above, either no charges or interest (if not secured on land), or at most at the interest rate under the credit agreement (if secured on land). The total number of payments must be no more than 12.[123]

The total charge for credit

3.66　Article 60G of the RAO 2001 sets out the exemptions based on limits to the total charge for credit.

3.67　It applies to certain borrower-lender agreements where:

(a)　the lender is a credit union[124] and the rate of the total charge for credit does not exceed 42.6%, and either the agreement falls outside the Article 3(1) of the MCD provisions or falls within those provisions, but is not an agreement made with the purpose of acquiring or retaining property rights in land or an existing or projected building, or it is a bridging loan within the meaning of the MCD;[125] or

---

[119] See above.

[120] RAO 2001, art 60F(3).

[121] RAO 2001, art 60F(4).

[122] RAO 2001, art 60F(5).

[123] RAO 2001, art 60F(6).

[124] See RAO 2001, art 60G(2).

[125] Paragraph (2A) applies to an agreement where:

　(a) the agreement is not of a type described in Article 3(1) of the mortgages directive; (b) the agreement is of such a type and—

　　(i) the agreement is of a kind to which the mortgages directive does not apply by virtue of Article 3(2) of that directive,

　　(ii) the agreement is a bridging loan within the meaning of Article 4(23) of the mortgages directive, or

　　(iii) in relation to the agreement—

(b)   it is an agreement of a kind offered to a particular class of individual or relevant recipient of credit and not offered to the public generally, provides that the only charge included in the total charge for credit is interest which may not at any time be more than the sum of 1% and the highest of the base rates published by the banks specified in paragraph (7) on the date 28 days before the date on which the interest is charged;[126] or

(c)   similarly to the above, save that instead of including interest only in the total charge, the agreement does not permit an increase in the rate of any item included in the total charge for credit.[127]

3.68   The second and third exemptions set out above will not apply to credit agreements entered into on or after 21 March 2016 unless the agreement meets the general interest test, the borrower receives timely information on the main features, risks and costs of the agreement at the pre-contractual stage and any advertising of the agreement is fair, clear and not misleading.[128]

The nature of the borrower

3.69   Article 60H of the RAO 2001 sets out exemptions[129] in relation to the nature of the borrower. A credit agreement is exempt under this article where, subject to article 60HA:[130]

(1)   the borrower is an individual,

(2)   the agreement is either—

     (i)   secured on land, or

     (ii)   for credit which exceeds £60,260 and, if entered into on or after 21st March 2016, is for a purpose other than—

          (aa) the renovation of residential property, or

          (bb) to acquire or retain property rights in land or in an existing or projected building,

---

         (aa) the borrower receives timely information on the main features, risks and costs of the agreement at the pre-contractual stage, and

         (bb) any advertising of the agreement is fair, clear and not misleading; or

   (c) the agreement was entered into before 21st March 2016.

[126]   RAO 2001, art 60G(3). Paragraph (5) must not apply to the agreement. Paragraph (5) applies if the total amount to be repaid varies according to a formula in the agreement and has effect by reference to movements in an index, such as RPI, or other factor, or if the agreement is: (a) not secured on land or is not offered by a lender to a borrower as an incident of employment with the lender or an undertaking in the same group; and (b) does not meet the general interest test in paragraph (6), which requires credit more favourable to the borrower than those prevailing in the market.

[127]   RAO 2001, art 60G(4).

[128]   RAO 2001, art 60G(8).

[129]   From falling within the definition of regulated credit agreement within the meaning of RAO 2001, art 60B, and hence from CCA regulation by reason of CCA 1974, s 8(3).

[130]   RAO 2001, art 60HA sets out exemptions which are not permitted under the mortgages directive. Under art 60H(2), where a credit agreement would be an exempt agreement pursuant to art 60H but for para (1)(b)(ii)(bb) or art 60HA, the FCA may treat the agreement as an exempt agreement except for the purpose of the application of the requirements of the MCD.

(3) the agreement includes a declaration made by the borrower which provides that the borrower agrees to forgo the protection and remedies that would be available to the borrower if the agreement were a regulated credit agreement and which complies with rules made by the FCA,

(4) a statement has been made in relation to the income or assets of the borrower which complies with rules made by the FCA,

(5) the connection between the statement and the agreement complies with any rules made by the FCA (including as to the period of time between the making of the statement and the agreement being entered into), and

(6) a copy of the statement was provided to the lender before the agreement was entered into.[131]

3.70 This is similar to the old exemption for high net worth individuals under a previous version of the CCA 1974.

Agreements which are not of the type described in MCD, Article 3(1)(b)

3.71 Section 8(3)(b) of the CCA 1974 provides a second condition, applying to agreements entered into on or after 21 March 2016, which must be fulfilled if a consumer credit agreement falling within section 8(3)(a)[132] is to be a regulated credit agreement. That is, that the agreement is not an agreement of the type described in Article 3(1)(b) of the MCD.

3.72 Article 3(1) of the MCD says:

This Directive shall apply to:

(a) credit agreements which are secured either by a mortgage or by another comparable security commonly used in a Member State on residential immovable property or secured by a right related to residential immovable property; and

(b) credit agreements the purpose of which is to acquire or retain property rights in land or in an existing or projected building.

3.73 The first limb of Article 3 of the MCD relates to the nature of the security; all land mortgages in England and Wales appear apt to fall within Article (3)(1)(a) provided they are on 'residential'[133] property. The second limb is concerned with the purpose of the agreement; this appears apt to pick up any mortgage entered into by the debtor so as to buy land or a re-mortgage of such a first mortgage. It would not include a mortgage to secure borrowing for other purposes, for example, financing a business or works to the property.

3.74 What is excepted from regulation under the CCA 1974, for mortgages granted on or after 21 March 2016, is agreements falling within Article 3(1)(b)

---

[131] RAO 2001, art 60H.

[132] See para 3.29.

[133] This is not defined.

of the MCD, hence any mortgage obtained for the purpose of acquiring or retaining property rights in land.

Effect of the MCD

3.75   The main effects of the implementation of the MCD by the MCD Order 2015 have been twofold. First, as the MCD applies to both first and second charge mortgages, the regulation of second charge mortgages has moved to the FCA's mortgage regime under the FSMA 2000 and the MCOB.[134]

3.76   Secondly, the MCD covers consumer buy-to-let mortgages which previously did not fall to be regulated under UK consumer protection legislation. The MCD Order 2015 contains a parallel regime of regulation for consumer buy-to-let mortgages.[135] The current position is that any agreement made on or after 21 March 2016 which is an Article 3(1)(b) agreement will not be a regulated credit agreement for the purposes of the CCA 1974.

THE EFFECT OF THE CCA 1974 ON THE STEPS REQUIRED TO ENFORCE A MORTGAGE

Effect on regulated credit agreements

3.77   If an agreement is a regulated credit agreement within the meaning of section 8 of the CCA 1974, it will be governed by the requirements and limitations imposed by the CCA 1974, the FCA's CONC and RAO 2001.[136]

CCA 1974 requirements on entry into the agreement

3.78   The requirements under the CCA 1974 include in Part V[137] extensive provisions as to entry into credit or hire agreements and the form, contents and signature of agreements once entered into. Non-compliance renders the agreement unenforceable. The most relevant provisions in the CCA 1974 which apply to regulated agreements which are secured on land and which are currently in force[138] are:[139]

---

[134]   MCD, Art 3(1)(b) agreements are not regulated credit agreements under the CCA 1974, however, but MCOB 14 may apply in respect of some art 3(1)(b) credit agreements.

[135]   MCD Order 2015, art 4(2). See paras 3.116–3.125.

[136]   The CCA 1974's provisions in relation to unfair relationships will apply to credit agreements which are not exempt under RAO 2001, art 60C(2) (regulated mortgage contracts and regulated home purchase contracts). See paras 3.100–3.115. Moreover, s 126 applies to regulated mortgage contracts as well as regulated agreements. See paras 3.89–3.99.

[137]   CCA 1974, s 74 sets out a list of agreements which are excluded from the provisions of Pt V.

[138]   Requirements no longer in force may be relevant to the enforceability of older agreements.

[139]   See also CCA 1974, ss 56 and 67 in relation to antecedent negotiations, ss 57 and 58 (in relation to some land mortgages), which relate to the rights of the debtor to withdraw, and s 59, which renders an agreement to enter a future agreement void.

(a) requirements as to disclosure of information,[140] a failure to comply renders the agreement enforceable on the order of the court;[141]

(b) requirements as to the form and content of agreements;[142]

(c) requirements as to signature of the agreement,[143] breach of which makes the agreement enforceable on the order of the court only;[144]

(d) requirements to supply a copy of the unexecuted agreement to the debtor;[145]

(e) requirements to give notice of cancellation rights;[146] and

(f) requirements as to the form and content of certain securities.[147]

3.79 Not all of these provisions specify any consequence of breach. Breach of the disclosure requirements, and the requirements as to execution do, however, prevent enforcement without the order of the court.[148] Enforcement seems likely to include any of the steps the lender can take under the mortgage, including the appointment of a receiver,[149] since this appears to be the natural meaning of the word.

CCA 1974 requirements during currency of agreement

3.80 Part VI of the CCA 1974 sets out requirements during the currency of a regulated agreement. This section includes steps required prior to enforcement, which are relevant to the appointment of a receiver. The most relevant are:

(a) the requirement on the creditor to give at least 7 days' notice in prescribed[150] form before enforcing a term of the agreement, including demanding earlier payment of any sum, recovering possession of land or treating any right conferred on the debtor by the agreement as terminated,

---

[140] CCA 1974, s 55(1), the Consumer Credit (Disclosure of Information) Regulations 2004 (SI 2004/1481), the Consumer Credit (Disclosure of Information) Regulations 2010 (SI 2010/1013), and the Consumer Credit (Green Deal) Regulations 2012 (SI 2012/2798).

[141] CCA 1974, s 55(2). Enforcement includes the retaking of land.

[142] CCA 1974, s 60 and the Consumer Credit (Agreements) Regulations 1983 (SI 1983/1553) as amended by the Consumer Credit (Agreements) Regulations 2010 (SI 2010/1014) as to form; s 61 (signature)

[143] CCA 1974, s 61.

[144] CCA 1974, s 65(1). Enforcement includes the retaining of land: s 65(2).

[145] CCA 1974, s 61A (under which agreements secured on land are excluded), an, ss 62 and 63 (which apply to excluded agreements under s 61).

[146] CCA 1974, s 64 and see also ss 68–71.

[147] CCA 1974, s 105 in relation to securities other than that provided by a debtor or hirer, i.e. guarantees and indemnities.

[148] As to which, and the consequences of failure, see below.

[149] In *Ropaigealach v Barclays Bank Plc* [1999] 3 WLR 17, a well-known case that a lender need not obtain a possession order before taking possession, the agreement was not regulated. In *Waterside Finance Ltd v Ashraf Karim* [2012] EWHC 2999 (Ch), [2013] 1 P & CR 21, it was conceded for the purposes of that hearing that appointment of a receiver was enforcement for the purposes of CCA 1974, s 126.

[150] The Consumer Credit (Enforcement, Default and Termination Notices) Regulations 1983 (SI 1983/1561).

restricted or deferred, where the agreement specifies a period for the duration of the agreement and the enforcement is prior to that date.[151] This will apply to lender's possession claims;[152]

(b)   requirements to give information as to the debt to the debtor;[153]

(c)   requirements to give notice of variations to the agreement in the prescribed form.[154]

3.81 The sanction for non-compliance is not obvious.[155]

CCA 1974 requirements for enforcement

3.82   Part VII of the CCA 1974 sets out detailed provisions as to default and termination.

3.83   Under sections 86B to 86E of the CCA 1974, creditors and owners are under obligations as to the form, content and timing of notices relating to arrears.

3.84   The consequences of a breach of these provisions is that the creditor or owner shall not be entitled to enforce[156] the agreement during the period of non-compliance, and the debtor or hirer shall have no liability to pay the sums due or interest which would otherwise accrued during the period of non-compliance.[157] The sanction for non-compliance is not obvious.

3.85   By section 87 of the CCA 1974 the service of a default notice[158] is necessary before a creditor can become entitled by reason of any breach by the debtor to, amongst other things, demand earlier payment of any sum or recover

---

[151]   CCA 1974, s 76(1).

[152]   Under CCA 1974, s 189(1), 'creditor' includes 'the person to whom [the lender's] rights and duties under the agreement have passed by assignment or operation of law'. That does not seem apt to include a receiver with the lender's right to possession since it does not seem correct to say that the right has passed.

[153]   On the debtor's request: CCA 1974, s 77; periodic statements: s 77A (both fixed-sum credit agreements) and s 78 (running account credit – that is where the debtor can draw down further sums from time to time such as with an overdraft facility: s 10); as to a change of interest: s 78A. See also s 97, which imposes a duty post the debtor's request to give a statement in the prescribed form as to the amount to discharge the debt, and s 97A as to the duty to give information on a partial repayment, and the duty to give a termination statement under s 103. Under, CCA 1974, s 172, the court can grant relief to a creditor where a mistake has been made in the giving of information.

[154]   CCA 1974, s 82 and see Consumer Credit (Notice of Variation of Agreements) Regulations 1977 (SI 1977/328).

[155]   But see paras 3.93–3.99 in relation to enforcement of other breaches of the Act, which are likely to be relevant to any relief application by the lender if there is a sanction.

[156]   This appears to include the appointment of a receiver. See paras 3.90 and 3.91 on the similar wording in s 126, and fn 165.

[157]   CCA 1974, s 86D(3) and (4). See also s 86E, which prevents liability of default sums if notice is not given.

[158]   The default notice must be served in accordance with CCA 1974, s 88, which sets out the required content as well as its effect. See Consumer Credit Enforcement, Default and Termination Notices) Regulations 1983 (SI 1983/1561), as amended.

possession of any goods or land, to enforce any security.[159] That disentitlement will likely prevent the valid appointment of a receiver,[160] although there is no clear sanction for non-compliance.[161]

CCA 1974, section 177

3.86   Section 177 of the CCA 1974 sets out an important saving provision.

(1)   Nothing in this Act affects the rights of a proprietor of a registered charge (within the meaning of the Land Registration Act 2002), who—

(a)   became the proprietor under a transfer for valuable consideration without notice of any defect in the title arising (apart from this section) by virtue of this Act, or

(b)   derives title from such a proprietor.

3.87   This saving provision is subject to the qualification under section 177(3) of the CCA 1974, which provides that the saving provision does not apply to a proprietor carrying on a consumer credit business, a consumer hire business or a business of debt-collecting or debt administration.

3.88   While this might not be directly applicable to receivers, it may affect the rights and obligations of the lender and thus have an impact on the validity of the receiver's appointment. Nothing in the CCA 1974 affects the operation of section 104 of the Law of Property Act 1925, which concerns the protection of the purchaser where the mortgagee exercises power of sale.[162]

Judicial control of enforcement

3.89   Section 126 of the CCA 1974 contains provisions as to the enforcement of land mortgages. This provides that a land mortgage securing a regulated agreement[163] is enforceable 'so far as is provided in relation to the agreement', on an order of the court only.[164]

3.90   If a lender seeks to enforce a regulated agreement by appointing a receiver under an express power in the mortgage conditions, by section 126 of the CCA 1974 it seems likely that a court order is required.[165]

---

[159]   Note that CCA 1974, s 86 disentitles the creditor under a regulated agreement taking any of these things on the death of the debtor if the agreement is fully secured, and on taking any of these steps without an order of the court, if the agreement is only partly secured.

[160]   See fn 165.

[161]   See fn 155.

[162]   CCA 1974, s 177(2).

[163]   CCA 1974, s 126 also applies to a regulated mortgage contract and a consumer credit agreement which would, but for RAO 2001, art 60D (exempt agreements: exemption relating to the purchase of land for non-residential purposes), be a regulated agreement.

[164]   CCA 1974, s 126.

[165]   In *Ropaigealach v Barclays Bank Plc* [1999] 3 WLR 17, a well-known case that a lender need not obtain a possession order before taking possession of the mortgaged property, the mortgage

3.91   However, it appears from the wording 'so far as is provided in relation to the agreement' that where a lender seeks to enforce by appointing a receiver under its statutory power, the provisions of section 126 of the CCA 1974 do not bite. Since a receiver with only the statutory powers under section 109 of the Law of Property Act 1925 is limited, this is likely to be of little assistance. ·

3.92   It is unclear what sanction there is for non-compliance with section 126 of the CCA 1974, for example by the appointment of a receiver without a court order.[166] In *Waterside Finance Ltd v Karim*,[167] it was accepted that section 126 applied, yet a receiver had been appointed without a court order and sold the mortgaged property at auction. The borrower sought an injunction to restrain registration of the transfer. Norris J refused, in part because the borrower had stood by, knowing of the receivership, the auction and the sale. However, Norris J noted the lack of sanction for a failure to obtain a court order under section 126 and, in particular, that nothing in the CCA 1974 prevented the passing of good title to the purchaser on a sale by the lender or receiver in such circumstances.[168]

3.93   A mortgagee or receiver who enforces a mortgage by taking possession of the mortgaged property and exercising the power of sale can pass good title to the purchaser.[169] Given the terms of section 104 of the Law of Property Act 1925 and section 177(2) of the CCA 1974, once a sale has already taken place, it is difficult to see how its effects could be undone in the absence of statutory sanctions for breach.

3.94   Although in principle, a borrower might be able to obtain an injunction to prevent a sale where the application is made earlier in the process, it is unlikely that the court would prevent enforcement by the lender at all, given that the borrower would have received and used the loan.[170] Indeed, it seems likely that the court would use the hearing of the application for an injunction either as an opportunity to make an order under section 126 of the CCA 1974 or list for a hearing to consider making such an order.

3.95   It also seems likely that the court would apply similar principles as those under section 127 of the CCA 1974 in deciding any application to enforce. Even though that section does not specifically apply to section 126, its emphasis on

---

agreement was not regulated. In *Waterside Finance Ltd v Ashraf Karim* [2012] EWHC 2999 (Ch), it was conceded for the purposes of that hearing that appointment of a receiver was enforcement for the purposes of CCA 1974, s 126.

[166] And indeed for non-compliance of other provisions in the CCA 1974 which are said to prevent or disentitle enforcement, or prevent enforcement without an order of the court.

[167] [2012] EWHC 2999 (Ch), [2013] 1 P & CR 21.

[168] *Waterside Finance Ltd v Karim* [2012] EWHC 2999 (Ch) at [23], quoting a passage in W Clarke, *Fisher and Lightwood's Law of Mortgage* (LexisNexis, 14th edn, 2014) at 20.65 to that effect.

[169] See, Law of Property Act 1925, s 104, and CCA 1974, s 177(2), which provides that nothing in the Act affects the operation of Law of Property Act 1925, s 104.

[170] *Waterside Finance Ltd v Karim* [2012] EWHC 2999 (Ch) at [24].

the question of prejudice caused by the failure to comply with the CCA 1974, and the degree of culpability, is echoed by Norris J's comments.

3.96   Does section 126 of the CCA 1974 require a receiver to obtain a court order whenever he exercises any of his powers, assuming he was validly appointed under a court order? That seems unlikely, since it is the appointment of the receiver with his statutory and express powers which is the enforcement, not his exercise of them. In any event, the court order appointing him, if properly drawn, should expressly permit him to use his powers, so that their exercise would be via that court order. It would be cumbersome and costly to require a new application for each of the receiver's acts.

3.97   Section 126 is not the only limit to enforcement of mortgages regulated under the CCA 1974. Section 127 sets out the court's powers when the creditor applies for an enforcement order because it has not complied with, for example, requirements of disclosure,[171] and where the agreement is not properly executed.[172] In those cases:

> the court shall dismiss the application if, but only if, it considers it just to do so having regard to (i) prejudice caused to any person by the contravention in person, and the degree of culpability for it, and (ii) the powers conferred on the court by subsection (2) and sections 135 and 136.[173]

3.98   Consideration of (i) above is unlikely to lead to prevention of enforcement of a mortgage by the lender at all, since the result would be a considerable windfall to the borrower disproportionate to the breach.

3.99   Much more likely is an order disallowing interest or costs, or giving the debtor more time to repay arrears or to pay in instalments or to remedy any other breach of the mortgage. The court's jurisdiction is:

(a)   Under section 127(2) of the CCA 1974, if it appears to the court just to do so, it may, in making the enforcement order, reduce or discharge the sum payable by the debtor so as to compensate him for prejudice caused by the contravention.

(b)   Under section 129(1) of the CCA 1974,[174] to make a time order allowing time to repay, or payment by instalment at such times as the court, having regard to the means of the debtor, considers reasonable,[175] or the remedy of another breach.

---

[171]   CCA 1974, s 55(2).

[172]   CCA 1974, s 65(1).

[173]   CCA 1974, s 177(1).

[174]   The court has this jurisdiction on an application to enforce where the creditor has breached a requirement, and hence must apply to court for permission, or on an application by the debtor, or on an application under CCA 1974, s 126.

[175]   CCA 1974, s 129(2)(a), and see s 130.

(c)　Under section 135 of the CCA 1974 the court, if it thinks it just to do so, may make a term of the order conditional on the doing of specified acts by any party or suspending the operation of the terms.

(d)　Under section 136 of the CCA 1974, the court may include in the order such provision as it thinks just as for amending the mortgage.

UNFAIR CREDIT RELATIONSHIPS

3.100　The other part of the CCA 1974 regime which may well affect the appointment of a receiver is the unfair relationship provisions in sections 140A to 140C.

3.101　Sections 140A and 140B of the CCA 1974 govern 'unfair relationships'. Section 140A sets out to which agreements a section 140B order may be made by the court. Section 140B sets out the court's powers. Section 140C is an interpretation provision.

3.102　The provisions apply to all new credit agreements[176] made on or after 6 April 2007 and to all existing agreements from 6 April 2008.[177] That is, save that under section 140A(5), no unfair relationship order under section 140B shall be made where the credit agreement is exempt for the purposes of Chapter XIVA or Part II of the RAO 2001 by virtue of article 60C(2) (regulated mortgage contracts and regulated home purchase plans).[178] Credit agreements are defined as any agreement between an individual (the 'debtor') and any other person (the 'creditor') by which the creditor provides the debtor with credit of any amount.[179] It therefore follows that these sections not only apply to regulated agreements, but also to some exempt agreements.[180]

3.103　Where the unfair relationship provisions apply, the court may make an order under section 140B of the CCA 1974. It may make it where it determines that the relationship between the creditor and debtor is unfair to the debtor

---

[176]　CCA 1974, s 140A(1).

[177]　The general equitable jurisdiction of the court was previously supplemented by the Moneylenders Act 1990. That Act was repealed following the enactment of CCA 1974, ss 137–140, which enabled debtors to reopen a credit agreement on the ground that it was an extortionate credit bargain. Sections 137–140 have now been repealed. Additional transitional provisions apply to preserve the court's ability to make orders under the repealed sections in certain circumstances and those provisions may therefore be relevant to agreements made prior to the introduction of CCA 1974, ss 140A and 140B.

[178]　See para 3.43 *et seq* for the definition of a regulated mortgage contract, and fn 79 for the definition of a regulated home purchase plan. This exception from the unfair relationship jurisdiction is an extension of the pre-April 2014 exception for credit agreements exempt under the now repealed CCA 1974, s 16(6C) which was the exemption under which first legal mortgages of residential land fell.

[179]　CCA 1974, s 140C(1).

[180]　Under, CCA 1974, s 140B the court's powers also extend to agreements which are related to a credit agreement.

because of any of the terms of the agreement or related agreement,[181] the way the creditor has exercised or enforced the agreement or related agreement,[182] and any other thing done (or not done) by, or on behalf of, the creditor (either before or after the making of the agreement or any related agreement.[183] The term 'unfair' is not defined. However, it is clear that it is the relationship which must be unfair, and not the agreement.[184]

3.104 In deciding whether to make a determination, the court will have regard to all matters it thinks relevant (including matters relating to the creditor and matters relating to the debtor).[185] For example, where it is the term which is said to be unfair, this will include whether the term is commonplace, whether there are sound commercial reasons for the term and whether it reflects a legitimate and proportionate attempt by the creditor to protect its position.[186] While the court is concerned with unfairness to the debtor, a balance will need to be struck between the interests of both the debtor and the creditor.[187]

3.105 The court has extensive powers to make orders in relation to agreements where there is an unfair credit relationship. The court can order the repayment of money to the debtor or surety, require the creditor and his associates to do anything in connection with the agreement, reduce or discharge any sum payable by the debtor or surety, direct a return of property to a surety, set aside any duty imposed on the debtor or surety, alter the terms of the agreement or related agreement or direct that accounts be taken.[188]

3.106 Sections 140A to 140C of the CCA 1974 can provide debtors with both a defence to a claim and a cause of action. These are also often used by debtors to prolong litigation, arguing that the court's jurisdiction to take into account all matters it thinks relevant under section 140A(2), and the provisions of Practice Direction 7B of the CPR which limit the requirements for the consumer to put in a defence, for example,[189] put the court on enquiry, unlike in most other claims, and that summary judgment is therefore not appropriate against a debtor who raises such a case.[190] Notwithstanding the wide ambit of an unfair relationship case, however, summary judgment is available.[191]

---

[181] CCA 1974, s 140A(1)(a).

[182] CCA 1974, s 140A(1)(b).

[183] CCA 1974, s 140A(1)(c).

[184] See the decision of the Supreme Court in *Plevin v Paragon Personal Finance Ltd* [2014] UKSC 61, which reviewed the unfair relationship provisions and offered guidance as to its operation.

[185] CCA 1974, s 140A(2).

[186] *Deutsche Bank (Suisse) SA v Khan and others* [2013] EWHC 482 (Comm); see also *Maple Leaf Macro Volatility Master Fund v Rouvroy* [2009] EWHC 257 (Comm); *Paragon Mortgages Ltd v McEwan-Peters* [2011] EWHC 2491 (Comm); *Rahman v HSBC Bank Plc* [2012] EWHC 11 (Ch); *Nelmes v NRAM Plc* [2016] EWCA Civ 491 at [101].

[187] *Plevin v Paragon Personal Finance Ltd* [2014] UKSC 61, [2014] 1 WLR 4222 at [10].

[188] CCA 1974, s 140B.

[189] CPR, PD 7B, para 5.3.

[190] See *Bevin v Datum Finance Ltd* [2011] EWHC 3542 (Ch), [2011] GCCR 11400.

[191] *Axton v GE Money Mortgages Ltd* [2015] EWHC 1343 (QB), [2015] GCCR 13105.

3.107 The appointment of a receiver and the exercise of his powers may be vulnerable to an unfair relationship challenge.

3.108 However, the inclusion in the mortgage conditions of the power to appoint a receiver is unlikely to be a successful ground for an unfair relationship.

3.109 In *Graves v Capital Home Loans Ltd*,[192] a borrower brought an unfair relationship case following appointment of a receiver and then the sale of the mortgaged property by the lender under a buy-to-let mortgage. The Court of Appeal held that it could not be said that it was unfair for the creditor to have included a power to appoint a Law of Property Act 1925 receiver (LPA receiver) in the event of the debtor becoming unable to manage his financial affairs. The appointment of a receiver to collect the rents and to manage the property, thereby maintaining the payment of the mortgage, was as much in the interests of the mortgagor as it was in the interests of the mortgagee.[193] In addition, the fact that the power of sale had to become exercisable in order for an LPA receiver to be appointed and that the power to appoint a receiver arose upon breach under the terms of the agreement did not render the inclusion of such powers unfair.[194] The real question was whether there was any unfairness in the way the power was exercised.

3.110 In that case, the court went on to hold that there had been no unfairness in the way the powers had been exercised. It was considered that the borrower's complaint that he lost his property stemmed not from the appointment of the receiver, but from the lender's exercise of its power of sale. Whilst the court did not consider what the position would have been if it was the receiver who had conducted the sale, it seems likely that exercise of the receiver's power of sale in accordance with his duties would not be unfair.

3.111 The appointment of a receiver and the exercise of his powers in the usual way under a mortgage is unlikely to be unfair, especially if the receiver is complying with his duties. Indeed, the existence of the receiver's duties to the borrower is likely to militate against a finding of unfairness. The law already protects the borrower.

---

[192] [2014] EWCA Civ 1297.

[193] [2014] EWCA Civ 1297 at [21] per Patten LJ. This appears part of a pattern of decisions in which challenges to established property law via person protective statutes have failed. See for example human rights decisions in relation to property and mortgage law more generally, for example *Horsham Properties Group Ltd v Clark* [2008] EWHC 2327 (Ch), [2009] 1 WLR 1255; *McDonald v McDonald* [2016] UKSC 28, [2017] AC 273; and the failure of defence under the Equality Act 2010 to a mortgage possession claim in *Green v Southern Pacific Mortgage Ltd* [2018] EWCA Civ 854, [2018] All ER (D) 94 (Apr).

[194] [2014] EWCA Civ 1297 at [21] per Patten LJ; the court applied the earlier decision in *Rahman v HSBC Bank Plc* [2012] EWHC 11 (Ch). In *Rahman*, upon the challenge of the defendant bank's decision to appoint receivers over some of the borrowers' properties, it was held that in a large-scale commercial lending transaction where both parties had equal bargaining power, there were sound commercial reasons for a clause which permitted the bank to enforce its securities and the bank's decision to enforce its securities could not be described as unfair.

3.112 Section 140A of the CCA 1974 requires, for unfairness, something arising out of the terms of the agreement, the way in which the creditor has exercised his rights or any other thing done by or on behalf of the creditor.

3.113 Can this include the way a receiver exercises the powers given to him? The existence of his powers is because of the terms of the agreement, but his exercise of them could not be unfair to the debtor because of any of the terms, if the terms giving him such powers were not unfair. Exercise of the powers by the receiver is not 'the way in which the creditor has exercised' his rights. Nor is anything the receiver does within his deemed agency something done by or on behalf of the creditor. It thus appears that the receiver's exercise of his powers ought not to be capable of amounting to an unfair relationship between the debtor and the creditor.[195]

3.114 What might be unfair is a lender's decision to appoint a receiver where there are few arrears or the continued appointment of the receiver and his strategy to sell the property when the appointment has resulted in all arrears having been paid, if there is plenty of equity in the property and plenty of years left in the term.

3.115 The most interesting challenge to receivership under the unfair relationship provisions would be to the deemed agency. Any such challenge is likely to be hard, given the long history and statutory basis of it.

CONSUMER BUY-TO-LET MORTGAGE REGIME UNDER THE MCD ORDER 2015

3.116 Article 3 of the MCD provided member states with an option as to how to implement its provisions in relation to buy-to-let mortgages. The United Kingdom implemented this aspect of the MCD by creating an appropriate framework to govern consumer buy-to-let mortgages under the MCD Order 2015. This framework operates outside the provisions of the CCA 1974 and the FSMA 2000. Prior to this, consumer buy-to-let mortgages did not fall to be regulated under any consumer protection regime.[196]

3.117 A consumer buy-to-let contract is a buy-to-let mortgage contract which is not entered into by the borrower wholly or predominantly for the purposes of a

---

[195] Unless the receiver is within the definition of the creditor in CCA 1974, s 189(1) as a person to whom the lender's rights have passed by assignment or operation of law. Even if the receiver under the mortgage conditions has lender's powers, this does not seem an apt description of him.

[196] A distinction was previously drawn between agreements made with owner-occupiers and with those intending to let the mortgaged property. Until 31 March 2014, under CCA 1974, s 16C, mortgages where less than 40% of the land was used as, or in connection with, a dwelling by the debtor, or, where the credit is provided to trustees, by a beneficiary, were excluded from CCA regulation.

business carried on or intended to be carried on by the borrower.[197] Part 3 of the MCD Order 2015 provides a self-contained framework for the regulation of consumer buy-to-let mortgages. It does not apply in relation to any agreement entered into before 21 March 2016.[198]

3.118 The MCD Order 2015 sets out conduct standards[199] that apply to firms conducting broking or other lending activities relating to consumer buy-to-let mortgages.

3.119 Under article 4(1) of the MCD Order 2015, a consumer buy-to-let mortgage firm is defined to mean a person carrying on a consumer buy-to-let mortgage business. The same provision defines 'consumer buy-to-let mortgage business' as one or more of the following activities: (a) acting as a creditor; (b) acting as a credit intermediary; or (c) providing advisory services.

3.120 Lenders are likely to be caught. However, the provision does not expressly apply to receivers. It seems unlikely that a receiver would be considered to be acting as a creditor, credit intermediary or proving advisory services, and thus it is unlikely that a receiver will be a consumer buy-to-let mortgage firm for the purposes of the MCD Order 2015.[200]

3.121 Whilst the FSMA 2000 and the RAO 2001 are of no application to consumer buy-to-let contracts, there are some aspects of the FCA Handbook which do apply. The FCA does not have the ability to create rules in relation to consumer buy-to-let mortgages, but there is power to register, supervise and enforce the provisions of the MCD Order 2015.[201] Although article 21 of the MCD Order 2015 provides that the FCA must maintain arrangements for enforcing its provisions, to date, it is unclear what arrangements have been put in place and the precise consequences of a breach. The Financial Ombudsman Service can, however, deal with complaints made against registered consumer buy-to-let firms.

3.122 Schedule 2, paragraph 19 to the MCD Order 2015 sets out the requirements for registered consumer buy-to-let mortgage firms in relation to arrears and possessions:[202]

---

[197] MCD Order 2015, art 4(1). See also the definition of a 'buy-to-let contract' as set out in art 4(1) by reference to the RAO 2001.

[198] MCD Order 2015, art 3A. See above for commentary on whether such an agreement granted earlier than 21 March 2016 would be CCA regulated.

[199] See MCD Order 2015, Sch 2.

[200] See the definitions of a 'consumer buy-to-let mortgage firm' and 'consumer buy-to-let mortgage business' under MCD Order 2015, art 4.

[201] MCD Order 2015, arts 19–21.

[202] Consumer buy-to-let mortgage firms are required by MCD Order 2015, art 18(1)(a) to comply with Sch 2.

(1)   A creditor must exercise reasonable forbearance before initiating possession proceedings.

(2)   Any charges that the creditor imposes on the borrower arising from the borrower's default must be no greater than is necessary to compensate the creditor for costs incurred by the creditor as a result of the default.

(3)   Where the price obtained for the secured property affects the amount owed by the borrower under the contract, the creditor must take all reasonable steps to obtain the best possible price for the secured property.

(4)   Where, after possession proceedings, outstanding debt remains, the creditor must put in place measures to facilitate repayment by the borrower.

3.123 Nothing in the MCD Order 2015 suggests that the above provisions could be directly enforced by a debtor as against a creditor.

3.124 The FCA can direct a consumer buy-to-let mortgage firm to take steps in order to comply with its obligations under Schedule 2 of the MCD Order 2015, and article 13(b) provides that the FCA may revoke the registration of a registered consumer buy-to-let mortgage firm if it contravenes a requirement under Schedule 2 which applies to it.

3.125 The MCD Order 2015 provisions do not appear to place a greater obligation on lenders than would otherwise be the case. In relation to a buy-to-let mortgage, a mortgagee will generally appoint a receiver if the property has the potential to generate income. The receiver will not be a consumer buy-to-let mortgage firm, and therefore the Schedule 2 provisions will not apply to him.[203]

FCA REGULATION

3.126 The FCA is the conduct regulator for financial markets, which aims, among other things, to protect consumers.

3.127 In particular, the FCA has regulatory power over lenders who carry out financing in relation to particular types of home purchase, for example, via the requirement that the firms be authorised to carry on activities and by imposing particular duties on them in dealing with consumers.

The receiver and authorisation

3.128 The first way the FCA regulates is by making certain activities ones which require authorisation.

---

[203]   CCA 1974, s 126 will still apply to the enforcement of a consumer credit agreement which would, but for RAO 2001, art 60D (which deals with the exemption relating to the purchase of land for non-residential purposes, see paras 3.58–3.61), be a regulated agreement. See also paras 3.90–3.91 and fn 165, which discusses the applicability of s 126 to the exercise by a receiver of his powers. Note that the unfair relationship provisions of the CCA 1974 will likely apply to consumer buy-to-let mortgages.

3.129 Section 19 of the FSMA 2000 prevents any person from carrying out a regulated activity in the United Kingdom, or purporting to do so, unless he is an authorised person or an exempt person.[204]

3.130 An authorised person includes someone who has a Part 4A permission to carry on one or more regulated activities and a person who is otherwise authorised by a provision of or made under the FSMA 2000.[205]

3.131 Under section 22 of the FSMA 2000, an activity is a regulated activity if it is an activity of a specified kind, which is carried on by way of business, and relates to an investment of a specified kind, or, in the case of an activity of a kind which is also specified for the purposes of section 22(1)(b), is carried on in relation to property of any kind.

3.132 'Specified' means in an order made by the Treasury. One such order is the RAO 2001.[206]

3.133 An agreement made by a person carrying out a regulated activity in contravention of the prohibition under section 19 of the FSMA 2000 is unenforceable against the other party,[207] unless the court finds that it is just and equitable in the circumstances of the case to allow it to be enforced, or the money and property paid under it to be retained.[208]

3.134 There are exemptions to the requirement for authorisation, relevant to particular specified activities. In particular, there is a general exemption under section 39 of the FSMA 2000 for appointed representatives of authorised persons. That does not seem apt for receivers, since they are not the agents of lenders.

3.135 Thus, if a receiver is not an authorised person, yet carries out a regulated activity, he will fall foul of the general prohibition under section 19 of the FSMA 2000.

3.136 Will a receiver, in carrying out his functions, be engaging in specified activities in breach of the FSMA 2000?

3.137 There are some activities in the RAO 2001 which might, in principle, be activities of a receiver specified for the purposes of FSMA authorisation.

---

[204] A contravention of this is an offence. See FSMA 2000, s 23.

[205] FSMA 2000, s 31(1).

[206] RAO 2001, art 4(1).

[207] FSMA 2000, s 26(1). 'Agreement' means the making or performance of which constitutes, or is part of, the regulated activity in question (s 26(3)), which seems apt to extend as far as a sale of a mortgaged property if sale by a lender or receiver is a specified activity.

[208] FSMA 2000, s 28(3). The court must consider whether the person carrying on the activity without authorisation reasonably believed he was not contravening the s 19 prohibition in making the agreement.

3.138 For example, taking steps to procure the payment of a debt due under a credit agreement[209] is, under article 39F of the RAO 2001, a specified activity. Article 39G also provides that performing the duties of a lender under a credit agreement or taking steps to exercise or enforce rights under such an agreement on behalf of the lender are both capable of being specified activities.

3.139 It seems unlikely that a receiver would, in carrying out his functions, be considered to be carrying out a specified activity given the multiple exceptions which exist under the RAO 2001. By article 39H, steps taken by certain persons, including the lender, in connection to the agreement are excluded from articles 39F and 39G.[210]

3.140 The likely argument that a receiver does not carry out a specified activity of one of these kinds is that the receiver is not taking steps to procure payment of a debt, nor performing duties on behalf of the lender, nor exercising or enforcing rights on behalf of the lender. What the receiver is actually doing is collecting in the income, or the proceeds of sale, and passing them to the lender as he must. He does it on behalf of the borrower, not the lender, or in his own name.[211]

3.141 In relation to CCA 1974 regulated mortgages, article 60B(2) of the RAO 2001 makes it a specified activity to exercise, or have the right to exercise, the lender's rights and duties under a regulated credit agreement. Such specified activities cannot be carried out by unauthorised persons.

3.142 Performing a receivership is not as a matter of generality an exercise of the lender's rights and duties. It might be said that the receiver, with the lender's right of possession, or delegated power of leasing, or the lender's power of sale, is exercising the lender's rights. If the rights are given in the mortgage conditions, it is arguable that the receiver is not to be viewed as exercising the lender's rights, but his own, given by the borrower in the mortgage when the mortgage was created, notwithstanding that they are co-extensive with the lender's rights.[212] If the lender separately delegated its rights, for example the power of leasing, that argument would be more difficult.

3.143 There are exemptions to the requirement of authorisation. In particular, article 60J of the RAO 2001 says:

> A person who is not an authorised person does not carry on an activity of the kind specified by art 60B(2) in relation to a regulated credit agreement if that person exercises or has the right to exercise the lender's rights and duties under the agreement pursuant to an agreement with an authorised person who has permission to carry on an activity of the kind specified by article 60B(2).

---

[209] An agreement between an individual or relevant recipient of credit and any other person who provides him with credit of any amount: RAO 2001, art 60B(3)(a).

[210] See RAO 2001, art 39H(1)(a) and (3). See also art 39J.

[211] However, No decision that the receiver is not carrying out a specified activity is known.

[212] No case law on this is known.

3.144 Since the receiver has his powers under the mortgage and his appointment, both of which are agreements with the lender, and the lender is authorised, this exception appears to apply.[213]

3.145 Article 61 of the RAO 2001 provides that administering a regulated mortgage contract is also a specified kind of activity where:

(a)   the contract was entered into by way of business on or after 31st October 2004; or

(b)   the contract:

   (i)   was entered into by way of business before 31st October 2004, and
   (ii) was a regulated credit agreement immediately before 21st March 2016.

3.146 Article 61(3) of the RAO 2001 defines 'administering' to include notifying the borrower of changes in interest rates or payments due under the contract, or of other matters of which the contract requires him to be notified; and taking any necessary steps for the purposes of collecting or recovering payments due under the contract from the borrower.

3.147 Strangely, however, it goes on to state that a person is not to be treated as administering a regulated mortgage contract merely because he has, or exercises, a right to take action for the purposes of enforcing the contract (or to require that such action is or is not taken). There is an obvious tension which this provision causes as it is not clear how a person can take steps to enforce a loan contract secured by a mortgage without taking steps to procure payment.[214] In any event, litigation by a receiver under his powers is unlikely to be the specified activity of administering a mortgage contract.

3.148 In any event, article 63 of the RAO 2001 provides that a person who is not an authorised person does not carry on an activity of the kind specified by article 61(2) in relation to a regulated mortgage contract where he administers the contract pursuant to an agreement with an authorised person who has permission to carry on an activity of that kind.

3.149 Presumably, the agreement made between a lender and a receiver when the receiver accepts his appointment will fall into this category, as with article 60J of the RAO 2001. If the lender is an authorised person, a receiver administering a mortgage agreement on his behalf will not be carrying on an activity of a specified kind.

3.150 It thus seems likely that receivers do not need FCA authorisation, but this does not appear to have been tested.

---

[213] Although no decision to this effect is known.

[214] This exception was applied to a lender in *Fortwell Finance Ltd v Halstead* [2018] EWCA Civ 676: entry into a consent order compromising the lender's possession claim could not be administering a regulated mortgage contract since taking legal proceedings was exempted, and was in any event not a necessary step for collecting or recovering payments.

The FCA Handbook

3.151 Much of the FCA regulation is set out in the FCA Handbook, which sets out standards to be expected of the financial services industry.

3.152 The FCA Handbook contains specific sections setting out the standards expected of lenders dealing with consumers relevant to the particular regulatory regimes, i.e. the consumer credit regime and the regulated mortgage contract regime.

3.153 The part of the FCA Handbook directed at regulated mortgage contracts is the MCOB, which sets out similar standards and similar requirements on lenders when there are arrears. The latter is the basis of the CPR Pre-Action Protocol for Possession Claims based on Mortgage or Home Purchase Plan[215] Arrears in Respect of Residential Property[216] (the Protocol).

3.154 The part of the FCA Handbook directed to lender dealings with consumers with consumer credit agreements is the CONC. It sets out standards of lending in this context, including for enforcement. For example, CONC 7.3 sets out standards of treatment of customers in arrears, including a requirement on the lender to forbear from enforcement.

To whom do the MCOB and the CONC apply?

3.155 The first question relevant to receivership is to which firms the CONC and the MCOB apply.

3.156 The MCOB applies to firms including those which carry on home finance activities.[217]

3.157 The CONC applies[218] to any firm carrying on credit-related regulated activities and connected activities.[219]

---

[215] Defined in para 1.1 of the Protocol as a method of purchasing property by way of sale and lease without payment of interest.

[216] The Protocol applies to first charge residential mortgages and home purchase plans regulated by the FCA, second charge mortgages regulated under the CCA 1974 and unregulated residential mortgages, but not buy-to-let mortgages. Its provisions, which are intended to encourage discussion between the lender and borrower on steps to repay arrears without, or prior to, a possession claim being issued. It includes a requirement that the lender consider postponing a claim where the borrower has complained to the Financial Ombudsman Service.

[217] The MCOB, introduced in 2004, applies to firms which carries on 'home finance activity' or 'communicates or approves a financial promotion of qualifying credit, of a home purchase plan, of a home reversion plan or of a regulated sale and rent back agreement': see MCOB 1.2.1 and further for definitions. A home finance providing activity includes entering into a regulated mortgage contract and administering it.

[218] CONC 1.2.1.

[219] Save where rules specify otherwise. 'Credit related regulated activity' includes entering into a regulated credit agreement as lender (RAO 2001, art 60B(1)), exercising or having the right to exercise, the lender's rights and duties under a regulated credit agreement (RAO 2001,

3.158 Under MCOB 1.2.1 and CONC 1.2.1, a firm is an authorised person[220] (as defined in section 31 of the FSMA 2000 to include those with permission to carry out regulated activities). Authorised mortgage lenders, administrators, arrangers and advisers will therefore need to comply with the provisions of the MCOB.

Enforcement of MCOB provisions

3.159 The MCOB, like much of the FCA regulation, is a scheme enforceable by the FCA against lenders. For example, the FCA can impose penalties against the lender or its staff for breach of the MCOB, such as fines, suspension of FCA authorisation to trade or an order prohibiting certain functions. The FCA can also order the lender to pay compensation to the borrower.[221]

3.160 In addition, imposition of penalties by the FCA against the lender, or a history of mortgage enforcement in the face of complaints by borrowers, may have reputational consequences, and hence many high street lenders will agree to adjourn possession proceedings or other enforcement whilst complaints are resolved.

3.161 The obligations in the MCOB will likely not apply to a receiver[222] who owes a duty primarily to the mortgagee who appoints him.[223] A receiver must act in good faith,[224] and as such, it is likely that in complying with this obligation (e.g. the receiver must obtain the best price reasonably obtainable at the time of the sale), the provisions of MCOB 13 will be fulfilled in any event. The mortgagee's obligations under the MCOB, however, will remain, notwithstanding the appointment of the receiver.

3.162 The obligations imposed by the provisions of the FSMA 2000 and the MCOB do not add much to the general obligations which a mortgagee is under when taking possession of a property and taking steps to arrange a sale of the property. They include procedures which are to be followed in relation to customers in arrears.[225] For example, steps are not to be taken to repossess the property unless all other reasonable attempts to resolve the position have

---

art 60B(2)), debt collecting (art 39F(1) and (2)), debt administration (art 39G(1) and (2)) carried on by way of a business.

[220] But not a professional firm unless it is an authorised professional firm.

[221] See the FSMA 2000 for the FCA's powers.

[222] MCOB 13 imposes obligations on 'a firm', defined by reference to authorised persons as defined in, FSMA 2000, s 31. See para 3.157.

[223] See para 6.66 and paras 7.19–7.24.

[224] See Chapter 6 for a discussion of the duties of a receiver, and in particular para 6.89 as to his duty of good faith.

[225] MCOB 13.3.

failed,[226] and where steps are taken to market the property for sale, the best price is to be obtained.[227]

3.163 The consequences of a breach of the MCOB are therefore much less severe than a breach of the CCA 1974 provisions. Such a breach does not render the security unenforceable. A breach may result in a complaint to the Financial Ombudsman Service, disciplinary procedures and possibly the payment of compensation.

3.164 However, a breach of the MCOB gives borrowers few direct rights against a lender for breach of that regulatory regime, assuming that the matter complained of does not itself give the borrower a cause of action recognised by the court.[228] It is not uncommon for borrowers to complain in court about regulatory issues and find that they have no recourse there.

3.165 First, though the principles behind the Protocol are informed by the MCOB,[229] breach of the Protocol will not usually prevent a possession order being made. Breach of it may lead to an adjournment on the first hearing of a lender's mortgage possession[230] to force the lender to comply, or other sanctions,[231] but it does not defeat the lender's right to possession arising.[232] It thus does not prevent the making of a possession order.[233] Breach of the Protocol may be relevant to the reasonableness of costs under the CPR and, likely, under the mortgage.[234]

---

[226] MCOB 13.3.2A(6).

[227] MCOB 13.6.

[228] Thus, for example, if the complaint was that the borrower had not agreed to the mortgage and had not executed the mortgage deed, and that it was entered into via a fraud perpetuated by or with the assistance of a lender employee, then the borrower would have a court-based remedy.

[229] The Protocol repeats provisions in MCOB 13.

[230] The Protocol applies to possession claims by lenders brought on the basis of arrears. It is unlikely to apply to claims for possession brought by receivers.

[231] Practice Direction – Pre-Action Conduct and Protocols, para 15(b).

[232] *Thakker v Northern Rock (Asset Management) Plc* [2014] EWHC 2107 (QB) applying *National Westminster Bank Plc v Skelton* [1993] 1 WLR 72 to mortgages regulated by the MCOB. The reason given in *Thakker* was that FSMA 2000, s 151(2) (now s 138E(2)) states that 'no such contravention [of rules set out in a code made under regulatory powers granted to the FCA] makes any transaction void or unenforceable'.

[233] Sanctions include provisions on costs and interest. Breach of the Protocol could be said to be relevant to the court's jurisdiction to adjourn, stay or suspend the possession order under the Administration of Justice Act 1970, s 36 (its extension under the Administration of Justice Act 1973, s 8) in the sense that the Protocol is intended to encourage exploration of whether the borrower can repay the arrears, since the court's jurisdiction under those Acts arises only where the borrower is likely to be able within a reasonable period to pay the arrears, whether or not the Protocol has been complied with, compliance with it is likely only to be relevant to whether the court gives the borrower who can show such a likelihood the benefit of any doubt.

[234] Practice Direction – Pre-Action Conduct and Protocols, para 16 specifically includes costs consequences, though the specified sanctions are payment of the other side's costs, not expressly deprivation of, in particular, a contractual entitlement to costs. Paragraph 16 also permits the court to reduce interest or lower the rate.

3.166 This is even though a damages counterclaim for an unliquidated sum for breach of the MCOB[235] is brought as a defence by equitable set-off,[236] because the lender has an immediate right to possession which is merely postponed by the mortgage conditions, for example, until there is a failure to pay a monthly instalment.[237]

3.167 The court's only power to adjourn or to suspend a possession order made on a claim by a lender is under section 36 of the Administration of Justice Act 1970 (with its extension under section 8 of the Administration of Justice Act 1973) in relation to dwelling-houses. Since an order made under the Acts must be for a specified period,[238] it is rare that a counterclaim for an unliquidated sum, which otherwise would not prevent a possession order being made, is sufficient for it to be likely that within a reasonable period, the arrears will be paid off. Thus, such a counterclaim rarely assists the borrower, unless it is already very close to resolution in his favour.

3.168 The lender's statutory right to appoint a receiver arises when the mortgage money has become due,[239] and is exercisable when the lender has become entitled to exercise the power of sale.[240] An express right under the mortgage conditions is often linked – as the right to possession is linked – to a failure to pay a monthly instalment or another breach of mortgage. A claim by the borrower for damages for breach of the MCOB is unlikely to be sufficient to prevent the mortgage money becoming due, unless it exceeds the total owed. It is more likely that breach of the MCOB will prevent the right being exercisable on the ground of arrears, because of the possibility of an equitable set-off preventing the existence of arrears.

---

[235] The question of whether such a damages claim is available was left undecided in *Thakker v Northern Rock (Asset Management) Plc* [2014] EWHC 2107 (QB). The issue has now been resolved by rules made by the FCA under FSMA 2000, s 138D, which lists which of the rules in the FCA Handbook allows a private claim for damages for breach. In particular, in relation to the MCOB, the majority of rules are enforceable privately.

[236] *Mobil Oil v Rawlinson* (1981) 43 P & CR 221; *National Westminster Bank Plc v Skelton* [1993] 1 WLR 72 (where the lender was entitled to possession after demand for the whole debt); *Thakker v Northern Rock (Asset Management) Plc* [2014] EWHC 2107 (QB), though it has been left undecided whether a cross-claim for a liquidated sum extinguishing the mortgage debt (not the arrears only) would suffice. See *Woodeson v Credit Suisse (UK) Ltd* [2018] EWCA Civ 1103, [2018] All ER (D) 95 (May) at [51] *et seq*.

[237] Where the lender's right of possession is postponed until there has been non-payment of a monthly instalment, it will be a question of interpretation of the mortgage conditions whether an equitable set-off could bar that right, assuming that breach of the MCOB does allow a damages claim and that such a breach is sufficiently closely connected to the mortgage for an equitable set-off to arise in the sense set out in *British Anzani (Felixstowe) Ltd v International Marine Management (UK) Ltd* [1980] QB 637. In general, it is not equitable to allow set-off. See *Woodeson v Credit Suisse (UK) Ltd* [2018] EWCA Civ 1103 at [51] *et seq*.

[238] *Royal Trust Co of Canada v Markham* [1975] 1 WLR 1416.

[239] Law of Property Act 1925, s 101(1)(iii).

[240] See Law of Property Act 1925, ss 109(1) and 103, and paras 4.61–4.62.

3.169 Secondly, a borrower can complain to the Financial Ombudsman Service[241] about MCOB breaches and other matters, both of which would give him a cause of action recognised in civil litigation, and otherwise. The Ombudsman will determine the complaint by reference to what is fair and reasonable in the circumstances of the case.[242] The Ombudsman has powers to make compensatory awards[243] and to direct the financial institution complained about to take such steps as the Ombudsman considers just and appropriate.[244]

3.170 However, a borrower's complaint to the Financial Ombudsman Service will not prevent the lender's claim in court, for example for possession, from succeeding, though the lender will often, for reputational reasons, agree to adjourn whilst the complaint is being resolved.[245] A complaint to the Ombudsman will not prevent the right to appoint a receiver from arising; nor will it prevent it from being exercisable, unless the mortgage conditions expressly prevent this.

3.171 Once an award is made by the Financial Ombudsman Service, it becomes *res judicata* as to the facts and will prevent a borrower raising the complaint in court by action, assuming he has a cause of action arising out of the same facts, if he has accepted the award.[246] Hence, even if the complaint is of something actionable in the court, resolution of a complaint by the Ombudsman may lead to its loss as a defence to the lender's claim or enforcement action.

Enforcement of CONC provisions

3.172 Breach of the CONC is unlikely to allow a borrower to be able to obtain an injunction to prevent the appointment of a receiver, for similar reasons to those set out in relation to the MCOB.[247] Although breach of the CONC can give the borrower a claim for damages under section 138D of the FSMA 2000,[248] it is unlikely this could prevent a valid appointment of a receiver unless the damages exceeded the money owed.

---

[241] FSMA 2000, Pt XVI.

[242] FSMA 2000, s 228(2).

[243] FSMA 2000, s 229(2)(a), though the FCA can limit the maximum the Financial Ombudsman Service can award.

[244] FSMA 2000, s 229(2)(b). The Financial Ombudsman Service's powers are not co-extensive with a court's. The current maximum is £150,000 including interest and costs.

[245] As it is required to consider doing in the Protocol.

[246] FSMA 2000, s 228(5) and *Clark v In Focus Asset Management & Tax Solutions Ltd* [2014] EWCA Civ 118, [2014] 1 WLR 2502.

[247] Unless the breach is also a breach of the CCA 1974 and hence there are enforcement issues under that Act.

[248] See CONC, Sch 5.

Chapter 4

Appointment

4.1   This chapter addresses:

(a)   the preconditions to a valid appointment of a receiver;
(b)   who can be appointed as receiver;
(c)   the formalities; and
(d)   the consequences of acting under an invalid/defective appointment.

4.2   However, there are two preliminary points which need to be appreciated. The lender owes no duty of care to the borrower in deciding whether to appoint a receiver.[1] Provided that any preconditions have been met, an appropriate person is appointed as receiver and the formalities are complied with, the borrower cannot complain that a receiver has been appointed.

4.3   The only possible exception to this principle if the lender has acted in bad faith.[2]

4.4   The second point is that for some mortgages regulated under the CCA 1974, there are limits on enforcement if there has been non-compliance with various formal requirements. Moreover, for such mortgages and others, including those regulated under the FSMA 2000, a court order is needed for the appointment of a receiver, under section 126 of the CCA 1974.[3] These aspects are discussed in Chapter 3.

PRECONDITIONS TO APPOINTMENT

4.5   The appointment of a receiver will only be valid if any applicable preconditions have been met. Some preconditions apply in every case. Others apply if the terms of the mortgage so provide.

4.6   The preconditions are:

---

[1]   *In Re Potters Oils* [1986] 1 WLR 201 at 206; *Shamji and Others v Johnson Matthey Bankers Ltd* (1986) 2 BCC 98910; *Medforth v Blake* [2000] Ch 86; *JL Homes Ltd v Mortgage Express and Diakiw and Heap* [2013] EWHC 3928 (Ch), [2013] All ER (D) 115 (Dec).

[2]   *Shamji and Others v Johnson Matthey Bankers Ltd* (1986) 2 BCC 98910.

[3]   See *Waterside Finance Ltd v Karim* [2012] EWHC 2999 (Ch), [2013] 1 P & CR 21, where the lack of consequence for non-compliance with CCA 1974, s 126 was discussed.

(a)   there is a valid mortgage under which the power arises;
(b)   the person appointing has power to make the appointment;
(c)   there is no bar to the appointment because of the status of the borrower;
(d)   other conditions precedent to exercise of the power have been met.

These divide into:

(a)   express pre-conditions;
(b)   statutory pre-conditions.

4.7   Each of the above is considered in turn.

Valid mortgage

4.8   A receiver cannot be appointed unless there is valid mortgage at the time the appointment is made.[4]

4.9   The lender's statutory power[5] to appoint a receiver only arises where the mortgage has been made by deed.[6] The deed must be properly executed by the borrower.[7] A receiver cannot validly be appointed if there is some defect in the execution of the deed, unless:

(a)   a separate power to appoint a receiver is created by the mortgage agreement;[8] or
(b)   the lender can rely on rights of subrogation to an earlier valid legal charge by deed.[9]

4.10   It follows that in the situation where one of two co-owners forges the other's signature, although an equitable mortgage over the forger's share arises,

---

[4]   See Chapter 2 for a discussion of the nature of mortgage. A receiver cannot be appointed under a mortgage which is void *ab initio* (e.g. in the event of a forgery of the borrower's signature). However, a receiver can be validly appointed under a mortgage which is voidable (e.g. for fraudulent misrepresentation), if the appointment occurs before the mortgage is set aside. If it is subsequently set aside, that will terminate the receiver's authority. See para 13.31. *Day v Tiuta* [2014] EWCA Civ 1246, [2015] 1 P & CR DG10 should not be read as suggesting the contrary.

[5]   See para 5.6 for an explanation of the different sources of a receiver's powers.

[6]   Law of Property Act 1925, s 101(1): 'A mortgagee, *where the mortgage is made by deed*, shall, by virtue of this Act, have the following powers....' (emphasis added).

[7]   Borrowers who are individuals must have complied with the requirements of Law of Property (Miscellaneous Provisions) Act 1989, s 1 (as amended from time to time). Borrowers who are companies must have complied with the requirements in Companies Act 2006, ss 44 and 46 (or, for mortgages executed prior to 1 October 2009, those in Companies Act 1985, ss 36A and 36AA(1)).

[8]   For an example, see *Byblos Bank v Al-Khudhairy* (1986) 2 BCC 99549.

[9]   *Day v Tiuta* [2014] EWCA Civ 1246, [2015] 1 P & CR DG10, where the Court of Appeal held that an appointment which was made under a particular charge could operate as a valid appointment as at that date under a right of subrogation to an earlier, valid, charge, *even if* the particular charge was subsequently set aside. It follows that an appointment which purports to be made under an invalid charge can be a valid appointment under an earlier, valid charge if there is a right of subrogation to that charge.

the lender will have no statutory power to appoint a receiver over the legal title.[10]

4.11   If the mortgage is over registered land, it will not operate at law until it is registered at the Land Registry.[11] Although a failure to register the mortgage might, in practice, impact the receiver's ability to sell the property, the failure to register a valid charge will not, *per se*, preclude a lender from making a valid appointment as receiver.[12] However, the failure to register should always be considered a warning that there might be an underlying problem with the charge.[13]

4.12   Conversely, where the mortgage is registered, the lender has the power to appoint a receiver, even if there is some defect in the validity of the execution of the legal charge,[14] unless and until the register is rectified.[15] The receiver is entitled to rely on the register. Even if the register is subsequently rectified, no claim will lie against the receiver in respect of acts done before the rectification.[16]

Company borrower

4.13   If the mortgagor is a company, the charge should also be registered at Companies House.[17] An unregistered charge is void against a liquidator, administrator and creditors of the company.[18] However, it is not void against the company, so unless and until the company goes into liquidation or administration, the failure to register would not preclude the lender from appointing a receiver.[19]

---

[10]   Unless it has rights of subrogation. As for the equitable mortgage, since this is made by deed, the lender will have the statutory powers over the forger's equitable interest. The lender could also rely on any express contractual power to appoint a receiver, or such a power under the equitable mortgage. However, the powers that the receiver would have would be limited to those provided for in the contract, and in relation to the forger's equitable interest.

[11]   Land Registration Act 2002, s 27.

[12]   *Swift 1st Ltd v Colin* [2011] EWHC 2410 (Ch), [2012] Ch 206.

[13]   The lack of registration of the mortgage also exposes it to the risk of loss of priority if other interests are registered since these will very likely take priority over it: Land Registration Act 2002, s 29.

[14]   Or the charge is *ultra vires*: see para 4.14.

[15]   *Bank of Scotland v Waugh* [2014] EWHC 2117 (Ch), [2015] 1 P & CR D6 especially at [65]–[67]. The reason is the effect of Land Registration Act 2002, s 51. The point does not appear to have been run in *Day v Tiuta* [2014] EWCA Civ 1246, though it would appear to have been open to the lender and receivers, [2015] 1 P & CR DG10.

[16]   Rectification is not retrospective: Land Registration Act 2002, Sch 4, para 8, but see *MacLeod v Gold Harp Properties Ltd* [2014] EWCA Civ 1084, [2015] 1 WLR 1249 as to the ability to change priorities for the future.

[17]   Companies Act 2006, s 859A.

[18]   Companies Act 2006, s 859H.

[19]   This was assumed to be the law in *Burston Finance Ltd v Speirway* [1974] 1 WLR 1648 at 1657E.

4.14   In addition, where the mortgagor is a company, the mortgage will not be valid if the company had no capacity to borrow or charge its assets (i.e. if the mortgage was *ultra vires*).[20]

4.15   A distinction must be drawn between acts which are truly *ultra vires* and acts which the company can do, but the directors had no authority to do.[21] It is only the former situation which results in an invalid mortgage. The company's powers do not have to be spelled out in the memorandum. The company has power to do any act which is reasonably incidental to the attainment or pursuit of any of its objects, unless expressly prohibited.[22]

Person entitled to exercise the power

4.16   A receiver can only be appointed by the person entitled for the time being to the charge.[23]

4.17   Where the property and charge are registered, the person named as proprietor of the charge is usually the person entitled to appoint the receiver.[24] This may not be the person named as lender on the mortgage, for example, if there has been an assignment of the mortgage as part of a securitisation or otherwise.

4.18   There are also situations where persons who might appear to have authority to act on behalf of the named proprietor of the charge cannot appoint a receiver, and, conversely, other situations where someone who is not the registered proprietor of the charge can appoint a receiver. In particular, it appears that an assignee of a charge may be able to appoint a receiver before the assignment has been registered.[25]

---

[20]   For an example of a case where a mortgage was void because it was *ultra vires*, see *Rosemary Simmons Memorial Housing v United Dominions Trust* [1986] 1 WLR 1440.

[21]   *Rolled Steel v British Steel Corp* [1986] Ch 246, where the Court of Appeal held that the mortgage was not *ultra vires*.

[22]   *Rolled Steel v British Steel Corp* [1986] Ch 246 at 287.

[23]   A mortgagee in possession is not precluded from appointing a receiver: *Refuge Assurance v Pearlberg* [1938] Ch 687.

[24]   Under Land Registration Act 2002, s 58(1), the person registered as proprietor of a legal estate will be deemed to have it vested in him. 'Legal estate' includes a mortgage: Law of Property Act 1925, s 132(1) and s 1(2)(c) and (4). Thus by Land Registration Act 2002, s 51, as set out above, the person so registered will have the power to appoint a receiver.

[25]   This conclusion appears consistent with Law of Property Act 1925, s 114(2). In *Skelwith (Leisure) Ltd v Armstrong* [2015] EWHC 2830 (Ch), [2016] Ch 345, the court held that an assignee of a mortgage was entitled to exercise the power of sale before being registered as proprietor of the charge. A mortgagee is entitled to appoint a receiver when he is entitled to exercise the power of sale: Law of Property Act 1925, s 109(1). Accordingly, the same result ought to follow. However, in *Skelwith*, the judge commented that he was not suggesting that cases decided under the Land Registration Act 1925 would have been decided any differently under the provisions of the Land Registration Act 2002. In one of the cases the judge specifically had in mind, *Lever Finance v Needleman's Trustee* [1956] Ch 375, the court held until an assignee is registered as proprietor of the charge at the Land Registry, it cannot appoint a receiver. As can be seen from (*inter alia*) paras 10, 13–15 and 17 of the explanatory note at

Lender insolvency

Corporate lender

4.19   The directors and secretary of a corporate lender lose their power to execute documents on its behalf when:

(a)   an administrator is appointed;[26]
(b)   a winding up order is made;[27] or
(c)   a liquidator is appointed in a voluntary winding up, except to the extent that the directors and secretary are sanctioned by the liquidator (in a members' voluntary winding up) or the liquidation committee (in a creditor's voluntary winding up).[28]

4.20   Thereafter, documents can only be executed on behalf of the lender by the administrator[29] or liquidator.[30] A Companies House search should reveal the status of the lender.

4.21   In addition, liquidators and administrators can apply for an entry recording their appointment to be made in the register.[31] However, an appointment made by the directors will be invalid even if no such entry is made.

Individual lender

4.22   Similarly, when an individual lender becomes bankrupt, the charge vests in the trustee in bankruptcy on the appointment taking effect.[32] The better view is that the lender no longer has the power to appoint a receiver, even if it is registered as proprietor of the charge and there is nothing on the register about the bankruptcy.[33] Registration at the Land Registry is not required,[34] although it

---

the end of the Act, the Land Registration Act 2002 was intended to strengthen the sanctity of the register. However, the decision in *Skelwith* means that the register is not conclusive as to who is entitled to appoint the receiver, or sell the property. The position is therefore not altogether free from doubt. It is prudent to ensure that the assignee is registered before a receiver is appointed. See also Chapter 2, fn 113.

[26]   Insolvency Act 1986, Sch B1, para 64, and Sch 1.

[27]   *Re Mawcon* [1969] 1 WLR 78.

[28]   Insolvency Act 1986, ss 91(2) and 103.

[29]   Insolvency Act 1986, Sch B1, para 64, and Sch 1.

[30]   Insolvency Act 1986, Sch 4, para 7.

[31]   Land Registration Rules 2003 (SI 2003/1417), r 184, Land Registry Practice Guide 35, para 3.3 shows the type of entries typically made on liquidation; Land Registry Practice Guide 36, para 2.4 relates to administration.

[32]   Insolvency Act 1986, s 306; Land Registration Act 2002, s 27(5)(a).

[33]   The bankrupt lender will probably retain his 'owner's powers' set out in Land Registration Act 2002, s 23 in that situation: *The Keepers and Governors of the Possessions, Revenues and Goods of the Free Grammar School of John Lyon v Helman* [2014] EWCA Civ 17, [2014] 1 WLR 2451 at [30]. However, the power to appoint a receiver is not within 'owner's powers'. There is an argument that an analogy should be drawn, but not one that is considered to have strong prospects.

[34]   Land Registration Act 2002, s 27(5)(a).

is advisable.[35] Unlike a purchaser, a receiver cannot take advantage of section 86 of the Land Registration Act 2002 because no disposition is made to the receiver. The appointment will[36] be invalid.

Joint lender

4.23   Individuals may lend jointly. Co-lenders must hold the legal charge as joint tenants at law.[37] A receiver can only properly be appointed by both co-lenders.[38]

4.24   If one of two co-lenders becomes bankrupt, the two co-lenders remain the legal owners of the charge.[39] An appointment by the co-owners will be valid.[40] A purported appointment by the trustee in bankruptcy, with or without the other co-lender, would not be valid.

Lender's death

4.25   The personal representatives of a deceased lender can appoint a receiver, even if they are not registered as proprietors of the charge.[41] However, it is best practice for the personal representatives to register themselves as proprietors of the charge before seeking to appoint a receiver.[42] If this is not done, the receiver will need to check the grant of probate or letters of administration to verify that the person purporting to appoint is, indeed, the personal representative of the lender.

4.26   If one of two co-lenders dies, the survivor (and only the survivor) is entitled to appoint a receiver,[43] unless and until the mortgage is assigned by the survivor. The personal representatives of the deceased co-lender have no ability to appoint a receiver.[44]

---

[35]   Land Registry Practice Guide 34 provides details of the forms to use and the procedure. Note that the statement in para 4.7 of this Practice Guide that a receiver is not exercising the chargee's power of sale may, in some circumstances, be wrong. See para 11.87 *et seq*.

[36]   Subject to the argument set out in fn 33.

[37]   Law of Property Act 1925, ss 34(2) and 36(3). They may hold the charge on trust, but it is the two as trustees who will have the power to appoint the receiver, not the beneficiaries under the trust.

[38]   One of two co-lenders can only appoint a receiver under the statutory power on behalf of himself and his co-lender if he has a power to attorney authorising him to do so.

[39]   Only the bankrupt's beneficial interest under the trust of the charge if any will vest in the trustee in bankruptcy.

[40]   Land Registry Practice Guide 34, para 5.1.

[41]   Land Registration Act 2002, s 27(5)(a).

[42]   Land Registry Practice Guide 6 provides details of the form to use and the procedure.

[43]   If the Land Registry entries still show the deceased as a registered proprietor of the charge, the receiver will need to see evidence of the death.

[44]   This is the effect of the right of survivorship where there is a joint tenancy of an estate.

Borrower status: insolvency, dissolution and death

Insolvency

Company insolvency

4.27   If a company borrower is in administration,[45] a receiver cannot be appointed without the consent of the administrator or the permission of the court.[46]

4.28   However, liquidation of the borrower[47] does not prevent a receiver being appointed.[48]

4.29   Entry by a company into a company voluntary arrangement (CVA)[49] will also not prevent appointment of a receiver by a secured lender. If, however, the company has obtained a moratorium prior to entry into a CVA,[50] then a receiver cannot be appointed during its continuation without the leave of the court and subject to such terms as the court may impose.[51]

---

[45]   Under Insolvency Act 1986, Pt II and Sch B1. An interim moratorium operates from the date an application for an administration order is made, but does not prevent a receiver appointed previously from acting: *SS Agri Power Ltd v Dorins* [2017] EWHC 3563 (Ch).

[46]   Insolvency Act 1986, Sch B1, para 43(2); *Sinai Securities Ltd v Hooper* [2003] EWHC 910 (Ch). It is unlikely that consent or permission will be given if to do so would impede the achievement of the statutory purpose of the administration. Where the statutory purpose of the administration would be impeded by granting leave, the court will balance the proprietary rights of the secured creditor in this asset against the interests of the unsecured creditors: *Re Atlantic Computer Systems Plc* [1990] BCC 859 at 880. Administration should not be used to prejudice a secured creditor, or override its decisions, at least where there will be no surplus for the unsecured creditors; *Promontoria (Chestnut) Ltd v Craig* [2017] EWHC 2405 (Ch) especially at [60] and [63]. However, if the aim of the administration is to rescue the company as a going concern, and possession of the property is necessary for the continuation of the company's business, then permission is unlikely to be given: *Innovate Logistics v Sunberry Properties* [2008] EWCA Civ 1321. However, if the purpose is to realise more for the creditors than in a winding up, and the receiver is in a better position to maximise the value of the property, permission is more likely to be given: *Sinai Securities Ltd v Hooper* (above).

Guidance on the procedure and the evidence required for making such a claim can be found in M Watson-Gandy, *Corporate Insolvency Practice: Litigation, Procedure and Precedents* (Wildy, Simmonds and Hill, 2nd edn, 2017) at Chapter 15. See also para 4.106. The receiver's status is considered at para 6.183.

[47]   Under Insolvency Act 1986, Pt IV.

[48]   *In Re Northern Garage Ltd* [1946] Ch 188. See para 6.167 *et seq* for a discussion of the receiver's status if appointed whilst the borrower is in liquidation.

[49]   Under Insolvency Act 1986, Pt 1.

[50]   Insolvency Act 1986, s 1A and Sch A1.

[51]   Since that would be a step to enforce security over the company's property within the meaning of Insolvency Act 1986, Sch A1, para 12(1)(g). It is likely that the court will apply similar principles to those in relation to administration, set out in fn 46, when considering any application for permission.

Personal insolvency

4.30   Bankruptcy[52] of an individual borrower is also no bar to a receiver being appointed.[53] However, if the lender has proved for the full debt without disclosing the security, it must surrender the security unless the court, on application by the lender, grants relief on the grounds that the omission was inadvertent or the result of an honest mistake.[54] If the security is surrendered, the lender will not be entitled to appoint a receiver.

4.31   If the insolvency is the ground for appointing the receiver, leave from the court is required.[55] In addition, the receiver will require the court's permission to take possession from an officer of the court.[56]

4.32   Entry by the borrower into an individual voluntary arrangement (IVA)[57] does not prevent the lender from appointing a receiver. However, if an interim order is granted, a receiver cannot be appointed without leave of the court.[58]

Dissolution and death

4.33   The dissolution[59] of a company borrower will not prevent the lender from appointing a receiver. On such a dissolution, the mortgaged property will go to the Crown *bona vacantia*.[60] The Crown could disclaim the property,[61] but this would not prevent the lender from appointing a receiver.[62]

4.34   Similarly, the death of an individual borrower does not prevent a receiver being appointed.[63]

---

[52]   Under Insolvency Act 1986, Pt VIII, Ch 1.

[53]   However, the receiver should take care to verify that there is no basis to set the charge aside as a preference/transaction at an undervalue: see para 13.31.

[54]   Insolvency (England and Wales) Rules 2016 (SI 2016/1024) (Insolvency Rules 2016), r 14.16. If the lender does specify the security, but puts no value on it and proves for the entire debt, the security is not surrendered and the lender can rely on his charge until paid in full: *Evans v Finance – U Ltd* [2013] EWCA Civ 869, [2013] BPIR 1001.

[55]   See para 4.63.

[56]   *Re Henry Pound Son & Hutchins* (1889) LR 42 Ch D 402. This is considered in more detail at para 4.106.

[57]   Insolvency Act 1986, Pt VIII.

[58]   Insolvency Act 1986, s 252: no execution or other legal process can be taken without leave. This wording appeared in s 11(3)(d). In *Sinai Securities Ltd v Hooper* [2003] EWHC 910 (Ch), the applicants sought leave under this provision and others, and it does not appear to have been suggested that appointing a receiver would not breach it.

[59]   This is discussed in further detail at para 6.106 *et seq*.

[60]   Companies Act 2006, s 1012.

[61]   Companies Act 2006, s 1013.

[62]   *In Re Fivestar Properties Ltd* [2015] EWHC 2782 (Ch), [2016] 1 WLR 1104 at [25]. See para 4.54 for service of a demand on a dissolved company. However, note that the receiver cannot be the agent of a dissolved entity.

[63]   *Re Hale, Lilley v Foad* [1899] 2 Ch 107. The receiver appears to be the agent of the personal representatives in this situation. See the discussion at para 6.198 *et seq*.

Express terms

4.35   The mortgage terms may disapply some or all of the statutory preconditions for appointment[64] and/or may add additional preconditions. Indeed, a wholly separate contractual right to appoint a receiver which bears little resemblance to the statutory power may exist. It is therefore essential to check the mortgage terms to identify, in the particular case, whether the power is statutory or contractual and what preconditions apply. It is also important to enquire as to whether there has been any enforceable side agreement at the time of the mortgage or subsequently which restricts the exercise of the right to appoint a receiver.[65]

The first statutory condition: 'when the mortgage money has become due'

4.36   The statutory power arises 'when the mortgage money has become due'.[66] The terms of the mortgage must be checked in each case to ascertain what the parties have agreed about when the mortgage money will become due.

Immediately

4.37   Some mortgage conditions stipulate that for the purposes of section 101 of the Law of Property Act 1925, the mortgage money is due on the date that the mortgage deed is executed. In such cases, a receiver can be appointed immediately, without the need to show any default by the borrower.

Default

4.38   Other mortgage conditions say that the mortgage money is due on default or after some specific default.[67] In these cases, whether the receiver has been validly appointed turns on whether the identified default has in fact occurred.

Demand

4.39   Many mortgages provide that the mortgage money is due 'on demand' or that the lender has the right to demand repayment in certain circumstances, for example, if one monthly repayment is missed.

---

[64]   Considered at paras 4.36–4.63.

[65]   This was suggested, but rejected, in *SS Agri Power Ltd v Dorins* [2017] EWHC 3563 (Ch).

[66]   Law of Property Act 1925, s 101(1)(iii).

[67]   See para 4.39 *et seq* for the position where the lender is entitled to demand the sums due in the event of a default. It is important to consider, on the true construction of the terms of the mortgage, whether the sums are due on default or on demand in the event of default, in each particular case.

4.40   Sometimes the mortgage conditions are unclear as to whether a demand is required, due to inconsistencies between the clauses. If there is any suggestion that a demand is required, a demand should be made.

Content of a demand

4.41   The demand must comply with any requirements in the charge. The demand must make it clear that it is an immediate demand for payment and not a letter before action or a notification of the balance.

4.42   The demand must also make it clear that it is a demand for payment of the full amount owing, not just for the arrears to be cleared. It is good practice for the amount of the debt to be stated. However, a failure to state the amount of the debt will not invalidate a demand.[68] Furthermore, a mistake in the amount demanded will also not invalidate the demand.[69]

Service of the demand

4.43   The demand must be served on the borrower.

4.44   It is important to identify whether the mortgage terms impose any mandatory requirements as to service. If they do, these must be followed.

4.45   Unless the mortgage conditions require some other method of service to be used, the safest course is to employ a process server to serve the demand personally. If possible, the process server should obtain the borrower's signature[70] acknowledging receipt of the demand.

4.46   Sometimes the mortgage conditions expressly provide for service of demands and notices under the mortgage to be deemed to have occurred in certain circumstances. In such cases, provided the requirements of the clause are strictly complied with, service will be deemed to have occurred at a particular time. This means that the borrower will be treated as if he had received the demand at the stated time, even if he proves that he did not receive it then or at all.

4.47   If such a provision does not exist, a lender which does not wish to effect personal service may seek to rely on section 196 of the Law of Property Act 1925, which provides that notices left at or sent to the last known place of abode or business by registered post or recorded delivery[71] are deemed served.

---

[68]   *Bank of Baroda v Panessar* [1987] 1 Ch 335. However, it may mean that more time needs to be given to the borrower to comply before a receiver can be appointed: para 4.58.

[69]   *Bank of Baroda v Panessar* [1987] 1 Ch 335 at 347A–B; *Arab Banking Corp v Saad Trading and Financial Services* [2010] EWHC 509 (Comm) at [34].

[70]   Or, where the borrower is a company, the signature of an officer of the company.

[71]   By reason of Recorded Delivery Service Act 1962, s 1(1).

4.48 However, this provision applies in terms to 'any notice' required to be served. It does not expressly say that 'demands' are covered, and it would be possible to argue that a notice and a demand have different meanings: notices tend to give information, whereas demands tend to require the recipient to take action of some sort. It is considered on balance that a distinction should not be drawn between a 'notice' and a 'demand', for the following reasons:

(a) The draftsman of the Law of Property Act 1925 referred to a 'notice requiring payment' in section 103. It does not seem that there was an intention to distinguish between notices and demands.

(b) Other notices require action to be taken. An example is a notice under section 146 of the Law of Property Act 1925.

(c) There is no principled reason why Parliament would have intended to facilitate the service of notices but not demands. In particular, there is no obvious reason why Parliament should have intended that the lender should be obliged to take more onerous steps to serve a demand to make the mortgage money due than those required when serving the 'notice requiring payment', which permits the lender to exercise a power of sale and/or appoint a receiver.[72]

4.49 It is therefore considered that a lender could rely on section 196 of the Law of Property Act 1925 when serving a demand.

4.50 If a demand is to be equated with a 'notice', two other statutory provisions will assist the lender to serve a demand if the borrower should die.

4.51 The first such situation arises if the lender has no reason to believe that the borrower is dead. Section 17 of the Law of Property (Miscellaneous Provisions) Act 1994 provides that a 'notice' which would have been effective but for the borrower's death will be effective notwithstanding his death.

4.52 Where the lender is aware that the borrower has died, the first port of call should be the register of personal representatives at the Principal Registry of the Family Division. If a grant of probate has been taken out, or letters of administration granted by the court, the lender will be able to identify the personal representative and serve the demand on him.

4.53 Where there is no personal representative, the lender can (if a 'demand' is to be equated with a 'notice', and unless this provision is excluded by the mortgage terms) address its demand to 'the Personal Representatives of [*Insert Name of Borrower*]' and leave it or send it by post to the borrower's last known place of residence of business in the United Kingdom, with a copy to the Public Trustee.[73]

4.54 Unfortunately, there is no equivalent provision where the borrower is a company which has been dissolved. It will often be possible to argue that, on the

---

72 Law of Property Act 1925, ss 103 and 109.

73 Law of Property (Miscellaneous Provisions) Act 1994, s 18.

true construction of the mortgage, a demand is not necessary in this situation.[74] However, it is considered prudent to serve a demand on the Crown's Bona Vacantia Division.[75]

Time for payment

4.55   A receiver cannot be appointed until sufficient time for the borrower to make the payment has elapsed after service (or deemed service) of the demand.

4.56   The time allowed will be short. The starting point is that a person who is obliged to pay money on demand must have it ready at all times. The borrower is not entitled to time to raise finance to pay the money back. He is simply entitled to the time to undertake the administrative arrangements necessary to convey the money to the lender.[76]

4.57   If the demand is made outside banking hours, a receiver cannot be appointed until the banks have re-opened and the borrower has had a chance to pay the sums due.[77]

4.58   The period allowed for payment will also be extended if the borrower raises a legitimate question about the validity of the demand or the amount owing. The lender must answer the borrower's legitimate questions and then allow the borrower time to make the payment.

4.59   However, if the borrower makes clear to the lender that he cannot or will not pay, the lender can appoint a receiver immediately.[78] So, too, if the borrower cannot in fact pay, and the lender is aware of this from their prior dealings.[79]

4.60   A borrower who can pay should contact the lender promptly after receiving the demand[80] and explain the steps that he is taking to make the payment and how long these are likely to take.

---

[74]   Because the debt 'dies' with the company, there is no one liable to pay on demand. The parties cannot have intended a demand to be served when there was no one liable to pay. The requirement to serve a demand is spent. See by analogy the reasoning of Neuberger J in *Crest Nicholson v McAllister* [2002] EWHC 2443 (Ch) (reversed on other grounds).

[75]   It is sensible to make clear, when the demand is served, that the lender recognises that the Crown has no liability to pay the debt, and the demand is being issued solely as a precursor to appointing a receiver.

[76]   *Bank of Baroda v Panessar* [1987] 1 Ch 335 at 347E *et seq*. Earlier authorities are summarised there. In several cases, a gap of about an hour has been held to be sufficient, but these were cases where, in fact, the debtor did not have the ability to pay. Each case turns on its own facts. The question is how long, in fact, would it take to effect the payment assuming the sums were available?

[77]   *Shepherd & Cooper v TSB Bank Plc (No 2)* [1996] BCC 965 at 969D, but see para 4.59.

[78]   *Sheppard & Cooper v TSB Bank Plc (No 2)* [1996] BCC 965.

[79]   *Sullivan v Samuel Montagu & Co Ltd* [1999] BPIR 316. There is a suggestion in this case that the onus is on the borrower to show that he could, in fact, have paid if given a proper amount of time, before he can make any complaint about the short time period given. This suggestion is not thought by the authors to be correct, because the onus is on the lender (or receiver) to prove that the appointment was valid.

[80]   The authors suggest: within minutes rather than hours.

The second statutory condition: 'entitled to exercise the power of sale'

4.61   A receiver cannot be appointed under the statutory power until the lender is entitled to exercise the power of sale.[81]

4.62   Unless the mortgage terms provide otherwise, the power of sale cannot be exercised unless:

(a)   notice requiring payment of the mortgage money has been served and default has been made in payment of the mortgage money, or part thereof, for 3 months after service;

(b)   some interest under the mortgage is in arrears and unpaid for 2 months after becoming due; or

(c)   there has been a breach of the mortgage conditions, other than a condition requiring the payment of money.[82]

Bankruptcy and liquidation

4.63   However, where the mortgage conditions provide that the power of sale and/or right to appoint a receiver become exercisable if the borrower is adjudged bankrupt, or enters into compulsory or voluntary liquidation, the lender is *not* entitled to appoint a receiver on this ground alone, without leave of the court.[83]

4.64   The application for leave should be made:

(a)   in a voluntary liquidation, by claim form under Part 8 of the CPR[84] issued in the Chancery Division of the High Court or, if the amount owing does not exceed £350,000, in a county court;[85]

(b)   in the case of a bankruptcy or compulsory liquidation, by application in the existing proceedings.[86]

---

[81]   Law of Property Act 1925, s 109(1).

[82]   Law of Property Act 1925, s 103.

[83]   Law of Property Act 1925, ss 110 and 205(1)(i).

[84]   Law of Property Act 1925, s 203(2) provides that every application to the court under that Act shall be made by summons at chambers subject to any rules of court to the contrary. CPR, r 7.2 requires all proceedings (other than insolvency proceedings and other types listed in CPR, r 2.1) to be commenced by the issue of a claim form. In a creditors' voluntary liquidation, the company is insolvent, but the application is not 'insolvency proceedings' within the definition in the Practice Direction – Insolvency Proceedings [2014] BCC 502.

[85]   County Courts Act 1984, s 23(c).

[86]   Where there are existing insolvency proceedings, it seems sensible for the application to be made within those proceedings, even though the Insolvency Rules 2016 do not expressly apply to applications made under the Law of Property Act 1925. Insolvency Rules 2016, r 10.122 *et seq* provide a procedure for a mortgagee to seek an order for sale by application in bankruptcy proceedings. It cannot have been intended that a separate claim should also be issued under Law of Property Act, s 110. If an application under s 110 can be made by application in the existing proceedings under the Insolvency Rules 2016 when the mortgagee wants to sell, there is no reason why the application cannot also be made that way when the mortgagee wants permission

4.65   In a bankruptcy or compulsory liquidation, the application should also seek permission to take possession from the trustee in bankruptcy/the liquidator, where taking possession from them is likely to be necessary.[87]

THE IDENTITY OF THE RECEIVER

4.66   The lender can, subject to the points discussed below, appoint 'such person as he thinks fit' to be receiver.[88]

Not limited to an insolvency practitioner

4.67   Unless there is anything in the mortgage to the contrary, anyone can be appointed a receiver. No formal qualification is required.

Lender's duty not to appoint incompetent

4.68   The lender owes a duty to take reasonable care not to appoint an incompetent person as receiver.[89] The lender also owes a duty not to appoint a person who it knows intends to exercise his powers for an improper purpose.[90]

4.69   In practice, most lenders therefore appoint receivers who have obtained voluntary accreditation as a Registered Property Receiver, under a scheme regulated by the Joint Regulation Committee of the Royal Institution of Chartered Surveyors, the Insolvency Practitioners Association and the various professional bodies representing Chartered Accountants.[91] However, this is not the only way the lender can discharge the duty of care.

Person connected with lender

4.70 A person connected with the lender can be appointed as receiver. Indeed, it seems that the lender can appoint itself as receiver.[92]

Number of receivers

4.71   Unless the terms of the mortgage make it clear that the power is to appoint a single receiver, two (or more) receivers can be appointed.[93] There are

---

to appoint a receiver. There is no prescribed form for applications under the Insolvency Rules 2016, although content is prescribed in r 1.35. Any application made in the existing proceedings should contain that content.

[87]   This is dealt with in more detail at para 4.106.

[88]   Law of Property Act 1925, s 109(1).

[89]   *Shamji and Others v Johnson Matthey Bankers Ltd* (1986) 2 BCC 98910 at 98915.

[90]   *Downsview Nominees Ltd v First City Corp Ltd* [1993] 1 AC 295 at 317.

[91]   Further information about this scheme can be found at www.nara.org.uk/how-to-join/member-categories.

[92]   *Mace Builders (Glasgow) Ltd v Lunn* [1987] Ch 191.

[93]   Because the singular includes the plural in both: Law of Property Act 1925, s 109 (Interpretation Act 1978, s 6(c) and Sch 2, para 2), and any contractual power to appoint a receiver (Law of

legal advantages to having more than one receiver,[94] and this is the general practice.

4.72 Where two (or more) receivers can be appointed, they must be appointed jointly, so must act together in exercising any of their powers, unless:

(a) on the true construction of the mortgage deed, it authorises multiple receivers to act severally as well as jointly;[95] or

(b) a term can be implied into the mortgage deed authorising multiple receivers to act severally as well as jointly.[96]

4.73 The appointment should make it clear whether multiple receivers are being appointed to act jointly and severally, or simply jointly. If it is not made clear, then the appointment will probably be construed as permitting the receivers to act jointly and severally if such an appointment could validly have been made.

4.74 If the appointment purports to authorise multiple receivers to act jointly and severally when the lender only had power to appoint jointly, the appointment will be valid as a joint appointment, and acts done jointly[97] will be valid.[98]

4.75 Where receivers are appointed jointly,[99] certain steps should be taken by the receivers so that problems arising from the joint appointment are minimised. Day-to-day practicalities can be achieved by each authorising the other to receive monies due to them and to enter into certain types of contract on behalf

---

Property Act 1925, s 6(c)). The equivalent legislation in Northern Ireland was considered in *Doherty v Perrett* [2015] NICA 52.

[94] In particular in order for a sale by receivers to overreach trust interests: see para 11.71.

[95] In some cases, there is little room for a doubt, for example a clause which states: 'Any act required or authorised to be carried out by the receivers may be done by one of more of the receivers holding office' (as in *TBAC Investments v Valmar Works Ltd* [2015] EWHC 1213 (Ch), [2015] P & CR DG15). In other cases, there may be more room for doubt. In *Gwembe Valley Development Co Ltd (in receivership) v Koshy and Others* [2000] BCC 1127 at 1141A–C, Rimer J was persuaded, on slender indication in the mortgage deed, that the mortgage deed should be construed as permitting the appointment of receivers to act severally as well as jointly. The decision was appealed, successfully, on a different point: [2000] WL 33116499, Court of Appeal, 14 December 2000.

[96] A term can only be implied where the agreement would be commercially or practically incoherent without it: *Marks and Spencer Plc v BNP Paribas* [2015] UKSC 72, [2016] AC 742 especially at [21]. It is perfectly possible (though inconvenient) for multiple receivers to be required to act jointly: see para 4.75. It is therefore unlikely that a term permitting several receivers to be appointed will be implied. See, too, *Gwembe Valley Development Co Ltd (in receivership) v Koshy and Others* [2000] BCC 1127 at 1142E–H.

[97] By both receivers together, or by one under a validly delegated authority to act on behalf of both: see para 4.75.

[98] There is Australian authority to this effect: *Kerry Lowe Management Pty v Isherwood* (1989) 15 ACLC 615 at 618; *Melsom v Velcrete Pty Ltd* (1996) 14 ACLC 778.

[99] Or if there is any doubt as to whether an appointment which purports to convey power to act severally is valid.

of both receivers. Each receiver could, if so desired, execute a power of attorney in favour of the other authorising him/her to execute deeds on his/her behalf. Doing so when the appointment is made is perhaps prudent, in case one receiver comes under a disability, or is unexpectedly absent, which might delay or prevent a disposal of the property.

Company borrower

4.76 There are some limitations as to the identity of the receiver which apply where the borrower is a company.

Body corporate

4.77   A body corporate[100] cannot be appointed as a receiver where the borrower is a company.[101] Any attempt to do so will result in the appointment being invalid[102] and the body corporate being liable for a fine.[103]

Bankrupts

4.78 A person commits an offence if he acts as receiver of the property of a company whilst bankrupt.[104] Such an appointment would, probably, be valid, but it is unlikely to occur in practice for a receiver will not want to risk 'imprisonment, a fine or both'.[105]

Disqualification order

4.79   If the court has made a disqualification order[106] under the Company Directors Disqualification Act 1986 against a person, that person cannot act as receiver of a company's property, without leave of the court, while the disqualification order remains in force.[107]

---

[100] Body corporate includes a body incorporated outside Great Britain, but does not include a corporation sole or a partnership that, whether or not a legal person, is not regarded as a body corporate under the law by which it is governed: Insolvency Act 1986, s 436.

[101] Insolvency Act 1986, s 30.

[102] *Portman Building Society v Gallwey* [1955] 1 WLR 96.

[103] Insolvency Act 1986, s 30.

[104] Insolvency Act 1986, s 31. A debenture includes any security of a company, whether or not constituting a charge on the assets of the company: Insolvency Act 1986, s 436(2); Companies Act 2006, s 738.

[105] Insolvency Act 1986, s 31(2). The maximum punishment is 2 years' imprisonment and a fine on indictment, or 6 months and a fine if dealt with summarily: Insolvency Act 1986, Sch 10. Nor would a lender likely wish to use a bankrupt receiver if it knew of the bankruptcy.

[106] Or accepted an undertaking.

[107] Company Directors Disqualification Act 1986, ss 1 and 22; Companies Act 2006, s 1170A. Although the court has a wide discretion, the authors suggest that obtaining leave to appoint such as person as receiver will be unlikely, unless there is a good reason why another person, who is not subject to such an order could not be appointed instead. CPR Practice Direction:

FORMALITIES FOR APPOINTMENT OF A RECEIVER

4.80   The appointment will not be valid unless the formalities set out in the mortgage deed and/or section 109 of the Law of Property Act 1925 are strictly complied with.[108]

4.81   The starting point is to ascertain whether the lender wishes to rely on the statutory power[109] to appoint a receiver. If it does, then it must make the appointment 'by writing under his own hand'.[110]

4.82   If there are additional requirements in the mortgage deed, the lender must also comply with those.[111] It is only if the lender is relying on a purely contractual power to appoint that it can ignore the statutory requirement.

By writing under his hand

4.83   The appointment must be in writing, but, absent anything in the mortgage requiring a deed, no deed is required.[112] If a deed or a document purporting to be a deed but which is not a valid deed is used, this will not invalidate the appointment.[113]

4.84   The appointment must be made by the lender 'under his hand'. The meaning of this is not clear. In particular, it is unclear whether the lender can delegate the act of appointing a receiver[114] to an agent.

Directors Disqualification Proceedings, Pt Four provides guidance on the procedure for making the application.

[108]   There is Northern Irish authority for this proposition: *Farrell v Brien* [2016] NICh 9.

[109]   Under Law of Property Act 1925, s 109.

[110]   Law of Property Act 1925, s 109(1).

[111]   The terms of the mortgage deed must be checked, to see what additional requirements, if any, there are in any given case.

[112]   *Phoenix Properties v Wimpole Street Nominees Ltd* [1992] BCLC 737. If the mortgage deed does not appoint the receivers as attorneys for the borrower (or there was a defect in executing the mortgage deed: as to which see para 4.9), and the lender wishes to delegate to the receiver the lender's power of sale (or other powers which require the receiver to execute deeds), the appointment is better made by deed to ensure that the receiver has power to execute: *Steiglitz v Egginton* (1815) Holt 141; *Berkeley v Hardy* (1826) 5 B&C 355; *Powell v London & Provincial Bank* [1893] 2 Ch 555; *Windsor Refrigerator Co v Branch Nominees* [1961] Ch 88; *Phoenix Properties Ltd v Wimpole Street Nominees Ltd* [1992] BCLC 737. See para 2.121. An unsuccessful attempt to delegate such powers to a receiver in an appointment under hand will not invalidate the appointment. A subsequent deed can be executed before those powers are exercised: *Byblos Bank v Al-Khudhairy* (1986) 2 BCC 99549.

[113]   *Windsor Refrigerator Co Ltd v Branch Nominees Ltd* [1961] 1 Ch 375. However, note that the mere fact that a valid deed (or a document purporting to be a deed) has been executed does not necessarily mean that the bank has validly appointed the receiver 'by writing under its hand': *McCleary v McPhillips* [2015] IEHC 591, where the bank had authorised different people to execute deeds and documents under hand.

[114]   Whether the lender can delegate the decision to appoint and the decision who to appoint may be a separate question to the question of whether appointment can be under an agent's hand.

4.85   In the absence of authority on point, the authors suggest that the position is as follows:

(a)   An agent (who does not have a power of attorney) acting in his own name cannot make a valid appointment.[115]

(b)   An agent acting under a validly executed power of attorney entitling him to make appointments in the name of the lender would be able to make a valid appointment.[116]

(c)   An agent who does not have a power of attorney probably cannot make a valid appointment, even if he has authority to, and does, act in the name of the lender.[117]

4.86   However, given the uncertainties, it is prudent for the appointment to be made by the lender itself.

4.87   How should the lender make the appointment?

Unlike a trustee's powers, the powers given to the lender are the lender's powers, inherent by statute in the lender's estate and affecting that estate, to be exercised on the lender's behalf, with only limited duties to the borrower in equity, so it is hard to see why they should not be delegable. The borrower has not given the lender a power to be exercised using its personal trust and confidence, unlike, for example, a trustee power.

[115]   There are authorities to this effect in other contexts: *Wilson v Wallani* (1880) 5 Ex D 155; *Hilmi & Associates v 20 Pembridge Villas Freehold* [2010] EWCA Civ 314, [2010] 1 WLR 2750; but cf *R v the Justices of Kent* (1872–3) LR 8 QB 305; *Re Whitley Partners Ltd* (1886) 32 Ch D 337; *R v Assessment Committee of Saint Mary Abbotts, Kensington* [1891] 1 QB 378; *Bevan v Webb* [1901] 2 Ch 59; *Diptford Parish Lands* [1934] Ch 151 for cases in which statutory requirements are valid if performed by an agent. It seems likely that the requirement for an appointment in writing under hand is directed, like many requirements for writing in property law, at certainty of appointment, not as a limit on delegation.

[116]   Certainly, this appears to be the position where the lender is a company, by virtue of Companies Act 2006, s 47(2), and it appears to have been assumed, in relation to a corporate lender, in Northern Ireland in *Smith & Hughes v Black* [2016] NICh 16 (approved in [2017] NICA 56, which contains (at [13]) some support for the contention that a simple delegation without a power of attorney would not suffice). The position is less clear where the lender is an individual, but the authors consider it likely that Parliament would have intended individual lenders to be able to delegate the making of appointments to an attorney, given the obvious practical advantages that this would bring. But cf *St Ermins Property Co v Tingay* [2002] EWHC 1673 (Ch), [2003] L&TR 70 in another context, where the judge said that the particular wording of the statute precluded signing on behalf of an individual by an agent including an agent with a power of attorney.

[117]   *Technocrats International Inc v Fredic Ltd* [2004] EWHC 692 (QB): a legal assignment required to be 'by writing under the hand of the assignor' (Law of Property Act 1925, s 136) must be signed by the assignor himself. The words 'do not admit of the possibility of someone other than the assignor signing in the assignor's name' ([53]) since other provisions of the Law of Property Act 1925 permitted signature by an agent expressly. This also appears to be the view taken in *Smith & Hughes v Black* [2017] NICh 56, and to be good practice in any event. It seems to the authors to make sense as a matter of policy that the lender ought either to execute himself in accordance with the appropriate formalities requiring signed writing, or should be required to have gone through a formal process to appoint an agent before the agent can make appointments on its behalf. That appears to the authors to be a logical place to draw the line.

4.88   An individual lender should sign the notice of appointment personally.[118]

4.89   A company should:

(a)   affix its common seal;
(b)   state that it is executed by the company and ensure that it is signed by two authorised signatories (directors and/or the company secretary); or
(c)   state that it is executed by the company and obtain the signature of one director in the presence of a witness who attests the signature.[119]

4.90   A building society, registered under the Co-operative and Community Benefit Societies Act 2014,[120] should execute the notice of appointment as follows:

(a)   if it has a common seal, it can affix it; or
(b)   by recording on the face of the notice that it is executed by the registered society and having two authorised signatories sign it. Each of the members of the society's committee and the society's secretary is an authorised signatory.[121]

Form of appointment

4.91   No form of notice is mandated by the statute. However, it is wise to state the following:

(a)   the names of the lender, borrower and proposed receiver(s);
(b)   the address of the property and the title number;
(c)   the date of the legal charge, the parties to it and a summary of relevant terms;
(d)   that it is an appointment as receivers pursuant to the statutory and/or any contractual power in the mortgage, and (if this is the case) that the receiver is deemed to be the agent of the borrower;[122]
(e)   what powers the receiver is to have and what the receiver is to do;
(f)   the default or other event giving rise to the appointment;[123]
(g)   the date on which the notice of appointment is being given;

---

[118]   A document which is not signed is not a document 'under hand': *Watersons' Trustees v St Giles' Boys' Club* (1943) SC 369. A telex is not a document under hand, because it is typed and sent by a machine, so it cannot be assumed that the person whose name it bears accepts any responsibility for it: *Re a company* [1985] BCLC 37 at 43. For the same reason, it is likely that an appointment made by email would not be valid: see *Cowthorpe Road 1–1A Freehold Ltd v Wahedally* [2017] L&TR 4 at [53].

[119]   Companies Act 2006, s 44.

[120]   Which includes those registered under the Industrial and Provident Societies Act 1965.

[121]   Co-operative and Community Benefit Societies Act 2014, s 53.

[122]   Preferably reciting the statutory and/or contractual words deeming agency.

[123]   The lender should endeavour to list all grounds. But, the lender will not be precluded from relying on a ground which is not stated: *JL Homes Ltd v Mortgage Express and Diakiw and Heap* [2013] EWHC 3928 (Ch). This is the case even if the ground stated did not justify the appointment: *Byblos Bank v Al-Khudhairy* (1986) 2 BCC 99549 at 99560.

(h)   any powers which the lender is delegating to the receiver;[124]

(i)   what remuneration the lender is offering.

4.92   It is also wise to insert a place where the receiver can sign to indicate acceptance of the appointment and the date and time on which this occurs.

Service of the appointment

4.93   The statute does not in terms require that the appointment should be drawn to the receiver's attention for it to be effective. However, the law is clear. An appointment is of no effect unless and until it has been served on the receiver[125] and the receiver has accepted the appointment.[126] It follows that a document appointing a receiver can be prepared long before it is needed.[127]

4.94   Service must be by a person with authority to appoint and in circumstances from which it can properly be inferred that he was intending to effect an appointment.[128]

FORMALITIES IMMEDIATELY FOLLOWING THE APPOINTMENT

Acceptance

4.95   As discussed above, the appointment must be accepted. An acceptance is generally not required to be in any particular form, but if the mortgage contains requirements, these must be followed.

4.96   An appointment can be accepted by conduct,[129] by the receiver starting to carry out the receivership. If, therefore, a receiver wishes to carry out some investigations before deciding whether to accept the appointment, he should make clear that he is reserving his position as to whether to accept the appointment. Equally, to avoid any doubt, the receiver should also expressly and in writing accept the appointment as and when he decides to do so. The simplest way for this to occur is for him to counter-sign a copy of the lender's appointment document and return it to the lender.[130]

4.97   Where multiple receivers are appointed, each should accept. However, if one has been appointed as agent of the other, after receipt of the instrument of

---

[124]   This is considered at paras 5.6 and 9.172, and in relation to the lender's power of sale at para 11.90 *et seq.*

[125]   *Windsor Refrigerator Co v Branch Nominees* [1961] 1 Ch 375.

[126]   *RA Cripps & Son Ltd v Wickenden* [1973] 1 WLR 944.

[127]   *Windsor Refrigerator Co v Branch Nominees* [1961] 1 Ch 375.

[128]   *RA Cripps & Son Ltd v Wickenden* [1973] 1 WLR 944.

[129]   *RA Cripps & Son Ltd v Wickenden* [1973] 1 WLR 944 at 954.

[130]   The acceptance must be communicated, on ordinary contractual principles.

appointment, an acceptance by the authorised agent on behalf of himself and the other receiver will be valid.

Company borrower

4.98   Where the borrower is a company, the acceptance must contain certain information[131] and be made before close of business on the business day following the day on which the instrument of appointment is received by him or on his behalf.[132] However, if this occurs, the appointment is deemed to have occurred at the time when the receiver receives the instrument of appointment.[133] It is therefore wise to record the date and time on which the instrument of appointment is delivered to the prospective receiver. There is no similar rule in the case of an individual borrower.

Notifying the borrower/his tenant

4.99   There is no statutory obligation to notify the borrower or the occupiers of the property of the appointment. However, it is clearly wise to do so.[134] The borrower remains able to give tenants a valid receipt for rent, even though they are aware of the receivership, unless and until the receiver has given the tenants notice to pay their rent to him.[135]

Notification to third parties

4.100   If the property is leasehold, the receiver should contact the landlord. He should also obtain a copy of the lease to check for any outstanding breaches.

4.101   He should also contact utility suppliers and HM Revenue and Customs (HMRC). He will also need to set up a bank account for the receivership.

4.102   If the receiver has power to do so, he can apply to the Land Registry to change the borrower's address for service to the address of his office.[136] No fee is payable for this, and it is wise to ensure that Land Registry correspondence is, in fact, sent to the receiver. Although it is possible to change the service address, the Land Registry will not note the receiver's appointment in the register.[137]

---

[131] Insolvency Rules 2016, r 4.1(4)

[132] Insolvency Act 1986, s 33(1)(a). The acceptance need not be in writing, but it must be confirmed in writing within 5 business days: Insolvency Rules 2016, r 4.1(3). Prescribed information must be included: r 4.1(4).

[133] Insolvency Act 1986, s 33(1)(b).

[134] Particularly in the case of a company borrower because of the need to ensure that all letters state that a receiver has been appointed. This is considered at para 4.103.

[135] *Vacuum Oil Co v Ellis* [1914] 1 KB 693

[136] Land Registry Practice Guide 36A, para 8(2) contains guidance on the form and evidence required to make the application.

[137] Land Registry Practice Guide 36A, para 8(1).

Company borrower

4.103 All invoices, orders and business letters issued by or on behalf of the company or the receiver, and the company's website, should bear a statement that a receiver has been appointed.[138] If this is not done, the receiver will be liable to a fine.[139] There is no grace period in the statute. This ought therefore to be a priority on accepting an appointment.[140] It is helpful if this statement indicates the date on which the receiver was appointed.

4.104 Notice of appointment must be filed at Companies House, within 7 days.[141] Information which must be included is prescribed,[142] and it is simplest to use Form RM01, which can be downloaded from the Companies House website. If the requirements are not complied with, the lender is guilty of an offence and liable to a fine.[143]

Domestic property in Wales

4.105 The Housing (Wales) Act 2014 requires a landlord of domestic premises to be registered. It is arguable that a receiver comes within the definition of landlord.[144] Receivers should therefore seek to register themselves within 28 days of appointment, if the property is residential and is let or if they intend to let it. If they do not, they risk committing a criminal offence.[145]

Insolvency

4.106 If the borrower is bankrupt,[146] in administration[147] or in compulsory liquidation,[148] the receiver will require the court's permission to take

---

[138] Insolvency Act 1986, s 39(1), as amended by the Companies (Trading Disclosures) (Insolvency) Regulations 2008 (SI 2008/1897).

[139] Insolvency Act 1986, s 39(2).

[140] It is unclear how the receiver can avoid breaching this rule, bearing in mind that the appointment is backdated so that it takes effect before he has accepted it.

[141] Companies Act 2006, s 859K. It is arguable that the requirement does not apply where the receiver is appointed under statutory powers.

[142] Companies Act 2006, s 859K(2)(b). The requirements vary depending on whether the charge was created before or after 6 April 2013.

[143] Companies Act 2006, s 859K(7).

[144] Housing (Wales) Act 2014, s 2 defines the landlord as anyone entitled to possession, but for the tenancy.

[145] Housing (Wales) Act 2014, s 4. It should be noted that there is also a requirement for an agent to be licensed. Receivers appointed over domestic property in Wales should either themselves obtain a licence or appoint licensed agents to collect the rent, etc.

[146] Trustees in bankruptcy are officers of the court: *Re Carnac, ex parte Simmons* (1885) 16 QBD 308.

[147] All administrators are officers of the court: Insolvency Act 1986, Sch B1, para 5. However, since permission to appoint a receiver will always be necessary, a separate application for permission to take possession of the property will not be needed. It is good practice for that application to seek permission to take possession from the administrator in terms.

[148] But not if the borrower is in voluntary liquidation, since the liquidator is not an officer of the court: *Re TH Knitwear (Wholesale) Ltd* [1988] 1 Ch 275 at 288.

possession.[149] Permission will be granted as a matter of course, provided the receiver is a fit and proper person.[150]

4.107 The application should be made in the winding up/bankruptcy.[151] An application by a properly appointed receiver is probably adequate,[152] but the safe course is for the lender also to be joined as a party.

CONSEQUENCES OF ACTING UNDER AN INVALID OR DEFECTIVE APPOINTMENT

4.108 A purported appointment is invalid if the appointor had no power to appoint a receiver or if a pre-condition had not been met. A purported appointment will be defective if the appointor had an exercisable power to appoint a receiver, but did not comply with the formalities in making the appointment, or purported to appoint someone who was not legally able to act as receiver.

4.109 Either way, the receiver has no right to take possession of the property. He commits a clear trespass.[153] However, a receiver who acts in good faith under an invalid or defective appointment will not be liable for procuring a breach of contract.[154] Moreover, an invalid appointment will not amount to a repudiation of the mortgage.[155]

The borrower's perspective

4.110 If the borrower wishes to challenge the appointment of the receiver, there are a number of steps which he should consider. He must take these steps promptly. If he does not, there is a risk that he will be estopped from challenging the appointment,[156] or the receiver will acquire ostensible authority to act on behalf of the borrower.[157]

---

[149] *Re Henry Pound Son & Hutchins* (1889) LR 42 Ch D 402.

[150] *In Re Potters Oils* [1986] 1 WLR 201 at 206.

[151] In the existing proceedings, in accordance with Insolvency Rules 2016, r 1.35.

[152] *Re Henry Pound Son & Hutchins* (1889) LR 42 Ch D 402 at 423.

[153] And can be liable to the borrower for such: *Ford & Carter v Midland Bank* (1979) 129 NLJ 543.

[154] *OBG and Others v Allan and Others* [2007] UKHL 21, [2008] 1 AC 1. If the receiver does not carry out any acts which are otherwise unlawful, he will also not be liable for the tort of causing loss by unlawful means. The House of Lords also dismissed a suggestion that receivers could be liable in conversion in respect of causes of action, as opposed to chattels.

[155] *Byblos Bank v Al-Khudhairy* (1986) 2 BCC 99549 at 99552 (first instance). The Court of Appeal did not deal with the point: above at 99565.

[156] In *Bank of Baroda v Panessar* [1987] 1 Ch 335, the judge indicated (*obiter* at 351–353) that he would have found an estoppel arose from the director's dealings with the receiver over a period of 8 months in which (*inter alia*) his right to sell the property was recognised, and (although this is not spelt out in terms) the receiver's reliance by not seeking a re-appointment.

[157] See para 4.130.

Possession proceedings

4.111 If the receiver has taken physical possession of the property,[158] the borrower should issue trespassers possession proceedings pursuant to Part 55 of the CPR.[159] Under this procedure, a hearing is generally listed about a week after issue. The proceedings must be served no less than 2 clear days (in the case of non-residential property) and 5 clear days (in the case of residential property) before the hearing.[160] These time periods exclude weekends and bank holidays.[161]

4.112 The first hearing is typically a short 15-minute hearing. If the receiver asserts that his appointment is valid, a longer hearing is likely to be necessary. The court will fix this by reference to the urgency of recovering possession in the particular case.

4.113 Possession will not be ordered if, before the hearing, the lender has remedied the defect in the appointment.[162] However, the borrower should be able to recover its costs down to the date when he has been notified that the defect has been remedied.[163] In circumstances where the defect or invalidity is capable of being cured and there is no urgent need to recover possession, it is wise to give the receiver the opportunity to cure the defect before the proceedings are issued.

Injunction and declaration

4.114 Where the receiver has not taken physical possession, the borrower can issue proceedings seeking a declaration that the appointment is invalid or defective and an injunction preventing the receiver from acting.[164] It is wise for the borrower to notify the receiver beforehand that it intends to take this step and give the receiver the opportunity to correct the defect or irregularity before proceedings are commenced, if there is no urgency.

4.115 In cases of urgency, the borrower will need to seek an interim injunction. The borrower will have to give a cross-undertaking in damages. Whether the borrower will be able to pay any compensation which it is ordered to pay at trial will be an important consideration for the court in determining whether to grant interim relief.

---

[158] As opposed to taking steps to collect rents from existing third party occupiers.

[159] There are prescribed forms of claim form and particulars of claim. All of the borrower's evidence must be served with the claim.

[160] CPR, rr 55.5(2) and 2.8(1).

[161] CPR, r 2.8(4). Note also that if the proceedings are served by posting them or delivering them through the door of the property, service will only be deemed to have occurred on the second business day afterwards: r 6.14. Personal service will often be necessary in order to effect service in time.

[162] Or, ensured that all pre-conditions have been met and re-appointed the receiver.

[163] But, if the receiver asserts that the original appointment was valid and has obtained a re-appointment which cures the alleged defect/invalidity without prejudice to that contention, this will not follow.

[164] For an example, see *RA Cripps & Sons v Wickenden* [1973] 1 WLR 944.

Damages

4.116 In either sort of proceedings, the borrower can also claim damages, against the receivers, for losses which it has suffered due to the receiver's trespass during the period when he acted under a defective or invalid appointment. If the receiver disposes of assets belonging to the borrower, the borrower can claim in conversion.

The receiver's perspective

Remuneration

4.117 The receiver will have no statutory entitlement to any remuneration. If the contract with the lender so provides, he may be able to claim remuneration from the lender. Or he may be able to claim from the borrower, on a '*quantum meruit*' basis for the value to the borrower of any work done by him.[165]

Claims against the receiver

4.118 The receiver will be personally liable to the borrower for trespass (and conversion if he has disposed of the borrower's assets).

4.119 The receiver will also be liable for breach of warranty of authority to any third parties who dealt with the receiver believing him to be the borrower's agent, if the borrower is able to avoid the contract.

4.120 The receiver must have appropriate indemnity insurance against such claims.[166]

Indemnity

4.121 In some cases, the receiver will also be able to obtain an express indemnity from the lender.

4.122 Where no express indemnity is given or sought, will any warranties by the lender as to its entitlement to appoint be implied? It is considered unlikely that the lender will be taken to have warranted anything which the receiver could himself check. So, for example, if the lender is not registered as proprietor of the charge, or has not complied with a formal requirement in the charge as to the way in which the appointment should be carried out, then it is unlikely that the receiver will be able to rely on any implied warranty. However, where the invalidity or defect arises from something which the receiver could not himself easily check, it is thought more likely that a warranty by the lender about these matters might be implied, if there is nothing in the other terms or the circumstances to negate such an implication.

---

[165] See *Monks v Poynice Pty* (1987) 8 NSWLR 662.

[166] And other claims. See para 14.85 *et seq.*

Company borrower

4.123 Even where no express indemnity has been taken, the court has a statutory power to order the lender to indemnify the receiver against liabilities which arise solely as a result of the invalidity of the appointment.[167]

The lender's perspective

4.124 An invalid or defective appointment does not render the receiver the lender's agent. Accordingly, the lender is not liable to the borrowers or any third parties for the acts of the receiver merely because the appointment was invalid or defective.[168]

4.125 However, if there is some other basis for suggesting that the receiver is the agent of the lender,[169] the lender may well be liable for acts of the receiver within the ordinary course of his employment.[170] In particular, if the receiver sells the property as agent of the lender, the lender will be liable to the borrower for any loss which it suffers as a result.[171]

4.126 In addition, as discussed above, a lender may well have to indemnify the receiver in this situation against claims made by the borrower and/or third parties against him, and/or the lender may be liable for breach of an implied warranty that the lender was entitled to appoint a receiver.

Third parties

4.127 A person paying money, including rent, to a receiver is not concerned with any defect in the appointment.[172] The receiver's receipt will operate to discharge the third party from liability to the borrower.

4.128 If the receiver sells the property pursuant to the lender's statutory powers, a third party buying property from the receiver in good faith and without notice of any defect in the appointment is protected and acquires good title provided there was no defect in the delegation of the power of sale.[173] A

---

[167] Insolvency Act 1986, s 34. It is considered that defective appointments would also fall within this section. Guidance about the form of application and the evidence in support can be found in M Watson-Gandy, *Corporate Insolvency Practice: Litigation, Procedure and Precedents* (Wildy, Simmonds and Hill, 2nd edn, 2017) at Chapter 19.

[168] *Bank of Baroda v Panessar* [1987] 1 Ch 335 at 354.

[169] See para 7.70.

[170] Under ordinary vicarious liability principles. This is outside the scope of this book.

[171] Law of Property Act 1925, s 104(2).

[172] Law of Property Act 1925, s 109(4). It is likely that this protects against an invalid appointment of a receiver under the lender's statutory power where the lender was not then entitled to exercise the power of sale because it had not complied with, s 103, but not if the invalidity was because the power of sale had no arisen within the meaning of s 101(1). See the discussion in relation to the protection of purchasers under s 104(2) on the lender's exercise of its power of sale at para 2.139.

[173] Law of Property Act 1925, s 104(2).

third party who is concerned as to the delegation should seek a conveyance by the lender itself, in order to ensure that it gets the protection of section 104 of the Law of Property Act 1925.

4.129 However, if the receiver sells the property as attorney for the borrower and does not rely on the lender's statutory powers,[174] and the buyer is registered as proprietor at the Land Registry, the position is more complicated:

(a) If the buyer moves in, the borrower can only get the property back if he can meet the stringent tests in Schedule 4, paragraph 3 to the Land Registration Act 2002.[175] Otherwise, the buyer will keep the property.

(b) If the buyer is not in possession, the borrower will obtain an order for alteration of the register so as to restore the property to him, unless there are 'exceptional circumstances which justify not making the alteration'.[176] The buyer will be left, at best, with a claim to an indemnity from the Land Registry.[177]

4.130 If the receiver purports to grant a tenancy[178] or enter into any other sort of contract with a third party on behalf of the borrower, the borrower will not be bound by it, unless the third party can establish that the receiver had ostensible authority to act on behalf of the borrower. Ostensible authority only arises if the borrower did something to hold the receiver out as being authorised to act on its behalf.[179] If the borrower is not bound by the contract, the third party's recourse is against the receiver for breach of warranty of authority.

---

[174] And the appointment was invalid or defective.

[175] The borrower must show that:

(a) The purchaser has by fraud or lack of proper care contributed to the mistake being made, or

(b) It would for some other reason be unjust for the alteration not to be made.

The mere fact that the borrower will otherwise be deprived of this property is unlikely to be sufficient to satisfy the second test. If the borrower cannot meet these tests, at best, he will get an indemnity from the Land Registry under Land Registration Act 2002, Sch 8 (although if the 'receiver' has sold the property for market value and accounted to the lender for the proceeds, the borrower may struggle to establish that it has suffered any loss). Note also para 5 deprives a claimant of an indemnity if the situation has been caused by his own lack of proper care. Conceivably, failing to take any steps to challenge the receiver's appointment or halt the sale might deprive the borrower of the indemnity.

[176] Land Registration Act 2002, Sch 4, para 3(3). Guidance about this test is given in *Paton v Todd* [2012] EWHC 1248 (Ch), [2012] 2 EGLR 19.

[177] Land Registration Act 2002, Sch 8.

[178] Other than a tenancy which is completed by registration. If the tenancy is registered, the position is as set out in para 4.129.

[179] However, knowing that someone is purporting to act as the company's agent and failing to take any steps to stop that person from continuing to hold himself out as authorised to do so is enough: *Freeman & Lockyer v Buckhurst Park Properties (Mangal) Ltd* [1962] 2 QB 480. It might be different if a person purported to act as an LPA receiver in respect of a property when there was no legal charge over that property.

Chapter 5

Key Themes

5.1   The chapters which follow discuss receivers' powers, for example to collect income, to lease, to take possession of the mortgaged property and to sell it.

5.2   Exercise of those powers will bring the receiver into contact with three categories of people:

(a)   the borrower and anyone else interested in the equity of redemption;
(b)   the lender; and
(c)   third parties, for example any landlord, leaseholders, beneficiaries where the property is held by the borrower on trust and trespassers, as well as other people who have legal relationships with the borrower, such as employees and suppliers.

5.3   For each category, the receiver's ability to affect the person in that category and their respective rights and liabilities will depend on the receiver's powers, and their source, which are analysed in the chapters which follow.

5.4   Although the receiver's relationship with the lender rarely gives rise to difficulties in practice, difficulties can arise from aspects of the receiver's relationship with third parties and with the borrower. The receiver is, of course, appointed by the lender, but he is the deemed agent of the borrower both if he has only the statutory powers[1] and if the mortgage conditions give him express powers expressly exercisable by him as deemed agent of the borrower.

5.5   A key question is how that deemed agency works, which is considered in para 5.7 *et seq*. First, however, the chapter sets out a summary of the different sources of powers that a receiver can have.

5.6   The source of a receiver's powers is discussed in Chapter 9. In summary, a receiver can have powers of three types:

(a)   The basic receivership power conferred by the Law of Property Act 1925: the power to collect income.
(b)   Additional powers under the mortgage deed. Such powers divide into:

(i)   borrower's powers which the receiver will exercise as the borrower's agent, but with a limited equitable duty primarily focused on

---

[1]   Law of Property Act 1925, s 109. See Chapter 9.

repayment of the debt, rather than usual agency duties to act in the borrower's interest. Examples of such powers are the power to carry on a borrower's business, for example, or the power to sell as the borrower could, or a power of attorney for particular acts; and

(ii) lender's powers which it is agreed the receiver will exercise as the borrower's deemed agent, for example the right to possession or the lender's power of sale.

(c) Additional powers conferred by the lender on appointment which the receiver is not given by the mortgage deed. These divide into two:

(i) first, lender's statutory powers which are delegable under the Law of Property Act 1925, for example, leasing.[2] These the receiver exercises as deemed agent of the borrower;

(ii) secondly, rights of the lender which are not so delegable, but which the lender delegates nonetheless. Unless the mortgage terms provide for any powers delegated by the lender to be exercised as the borrower's agent, the receiver will act on his own account as donee of the power, or, if it is appropriate to infer that the parties intended that he should act as the lender's agent, in that capacity.[3]

THE DEEMED AGENCY

5.7   That the receiver is the deemed agent of the borrower is central to receivership. Deemed agency gives rise to four issues:

(a) What is the extent of the deemed agency?
(b) How does the deemed agency affect the relationship between the borrower and the lender?
(c) How does the deemed agency affect the relationship between the borrower and the receiver and between the lender and the receiver?
(d) How does the deemed agency affect the relationship between the borrower and third parties and between the lender and third parties?

5.8   As explained in more detail in the following chapters, it is the thesis of this book that the answer to those questions is:

(a) The deemed agency extends not only to the statutory powers of a receiver under section 109 of the Law of Property Act 1925, but also to all those powers which it is agreed in the mortgage conditions the receiver can

---

[2]   See Chapter 9.

[3]   This is a question of construction of the appointment, or other document by which the powers are delegated. If the lender has given the receiver a power to act in the lender's name, the receiver will be able to act as the lender's agent rather than as a pure donee of a power, if he so chooses. However, in other cases, it is unlikely that a power to act as the lender's agent will be inferred, particularly where the power is a power to take possession. The receiver is appointed precisely because the lender wishes to avoid going into possession himself.

exercise as the deemed agent of the borrower. It can therefore result in powers which have been delegated by the lender being exercised as the deemed agent of the borrower.[4] However, precisely what this means is determined by the answers to the following questions.

(b) The borrower cannot hold the lender liable for acts performed by the receiver within the scope of the deemed agency. As between the lender and the borrower, the borrower cannot deny that the receiver is his agent. The lender will not be liable to the borrower for the 'receiver's' acts, unless the lender interferes in the 'receiver's' decisions.[5] So, for example, if the receiver takes possession exercising a lender-delegated right, the borrower is not entitled to treat the lender as a lender in possession.

(c) The deemed agency gives rise to complications when considering whether there is a contract on which the receiver could sue, for example for remuneration. The mortgage conditions are a contract between the lender and the borrower under which a named class, receivers, to be peopled by the lender, has rights.[6] The authors' view is that there is usually, in addition, a contract between the lender and the receiver in the appointment, even though the result of the appointment is that the receiver is deemed to act as the borrower's agent. The receiver's primary duty is owed to the lender, but the receiver also owes equitable duties to the borrower. Notwithstanding the deemed agency, the receiver does not owe the borrower the same duties that an ordinary agent would.

(d) The deemed agency enables the receiver to act (assuming an appropriate delegation of powers) on the borrower's behalf where the borrower has power to do the act in question or the lender has power to do the act on behalf of the borrower.[7] This means that the receiver can affect the borrower's relationships with third parties, for example, by causing it to breach contractual obligations, or to enter into fresh contracts.[8]

5.9 What is far less clear is whether the deemed agency enables the receiver to exercise on behalf of the borrower powers which the borrower did not have and which the lender could not have exercised on the borrower's behalf, so as to affect the borrower's relationship with third parties. This is considered in detail below.

---

[4] For example, the lender's power of sale, the lender's power of leasing and accepting surrenders, and the lender's power to take possession.

[5] See paras 7.49–7.57, where this is considered in more detail.

[6] On which the receiver should be able to sue under the Contracts (Rights of Third Parties) Act 1999 if the conditions so provide, for example, were there a term making the borrower liable to the receiver for the receiver's remuneration.

[7] The obvious example of this is the lender's power to sell in the name of the borrower.

[8] Where the receiver enters into a fresh contract, he can do so either in the borrower's name or his own name. If he acts in his own name, whether the receiver was acting on his own account (as donee of the power) or as agent for an undisclosed principal (the borrower) must be ascertained by reference to what the receiver (and the other party to the contract) are to be taken to have intended. See paras 8.201–8.206.

5.10   To explain the issues in more detail requires a brief consideration of the nature of powers and agency. A power to deal with property 'is a power of disposition given to a person over property not his own'.[9]

5.11   Powers are what principals give to their agents, but someone given a power need not be an agent at all. They may be a trustee, for example. They may be given a right or power over someone else's property exercisable in their own name and on their own behalf.[10] They may be an agent in name, but have been given simply the right to affect the property of another without having to take that person's interests into account, for example under an irrevocable power of attorney which gives the attorney rights whilst limiting usual agency obligations.

5.12   A typical agency relationship has three aspects:

(a)   the agent is given powers to affect the principal's property;
(b)   the agent has duties to the principal;
(c)   the principal has liabilities to third parties as a result of the agent's actions.

5.13   It is not, however, necessary, that because someone is described as an agent, that they have all three. For example, an attorney with an irrevocable power will have powers and will make the principal liable, but may have limited duties, just as a receiver does not have the usual agency duties.

5.14   It is also possible for a principal to give his agent the power to make him liable to third parties in relation to a property even though he does not own the property himself. For example, a principal may appoint an agent with the power to lease Property A. If he does not own Property A, but the agent lets it nonetheless, then the principal will be liable to the tenant. It is said that there is a tenancy by estoppel between them.

5.15   Thus, the description of a receiver as an agent of the borrower does not automatically mean that the receiver must always exercise his powers in the borrower's name. It does not mean that he owes duties of loyalty to the borrower.[11] It does not mean he can only exercise powers which the borrower could exercise.

5.16   Thus, the thesis of this book is that mortgage conditions can be agreed between lender and borrower which allow the lender to appoint a receiver with powers the borrower does not have, for example, to collect income in the

---

[9]   *Freme v Clement* (1881) 18 Ch D 499 at 504.

[10]   For example, a right of re-entry under a lease given to someone who does not have the reversion. Mortgage receivership gives another example: the receiver's appointment survives the death of dissolution of the borrower (see para 6.10 *et seq*, and paras 13.19–13.27) though his agency does not (see para 6.170 *et seq*, for example). The receiver retains his powers, despite the borrower, said to be the source of them, no longer existing to exercise them.

[11]   His duties are equitable and are not duties of loyalty. See paras 6.83–6.85.

lender's name;[12] to take possession, as the lender could, free of leases the borrower enters into in breach of mortgage and which do not bind the lender; or, in the authors' view, to exercise a lender's express power of sale.[13]

5.17   Moreover, those conditions can make the receiver the deemed agent of the borrower although he is exercising a power the borrower would not have.[14]

5.18   The most difficult issue is what is the effect of the deemed agency as between the various parties to the mortgage and third parties when the receiver is exercising a power the borrower does not have.

5.19   As set out above,[15] if the lender has the power to do the act in the borrower's name and on his behalf,[16] no difficulty arises: the third party acquires title (if appropriate) and the borrower (and not the lender) is bound in contract.

5.20   Conversely, where the lender does not have that power, it might be said that the receiver's acts in the borrower's name can be no more effective than if the borrower had himself purported to do the act in question. Thus, if the borrower did not have title, the receiver cannot confer title.[17]

5.21   However, if the borrower purported to grant a lease when he did not have title, he would be bound as a matter of contract or deed; he would be estopped from denying he had title. So, too, if the receiver purported to grant a lease in

---

[12]   The wording of Law of Property Act 1925, s 109(3) is that the receiver can demand and recover income 'in the name either of the mortgagor or the mortgagee'. Similarly, the lender can delegate the lender's statutory powers of leasing and accepting surrenders to the receiver as deemed agent of the borrower, so as to bind both borrower and lender to the receiver.

[13]   See Chapter 11.

[14]   Under Law of Property Act 1925, s 109(2), the receiver is the deemed agent of the borrower despite the extent of his powers to collect income in the lender's name, and similarly when he exercises the lender's statutory power of leasing, which, by s 99(19) the borrower does not have.

[15]   See para 5.8(d).

[16]   This power could derive from statute (e.g. the lender's power to lease in the name of the borrower: see para 9.146) or the terms of the mortgage. Questions of construction can arise when seeking to determine whether the lender has the power to do a particular act in the borrower's name. Note that some lender's powers to act in the borrower's name allow the lender to do more than the borrower could.

[17]   '*Nemo dat quod non habet*' is a fundamental principle of property law. The principle of ostensible authority does not assist in this situation: that only applies where the borrower does have the power to do the act in question and there is an issue as to whether the borrower has delegated authority to the receiver. The only argument that the receiver's act in the borrower's name could be effective to pass title is if the receiver had the lender's power to pass title, was entitled to act in the borrower's name, and his act in the borrower's name in the circumstances did pass title under his power, for example, because of an express recitation in the deed that he was passing title by reason of his power. The act binding the borrower and the receiver's act under his power would result in the borrower being bound and title passing. This seems consistent with an understanding of receivership as focussed on powers not agency, shown by the survival of the powers on insolvency of the borrower, for example. See *Sowman v David Samuel Trust Ltd* [1978] 1 WLR 22 at 30C; *Swift 1st Ltd v Colin* [2011] EWHC 2410 (Ch), [2012] Ch 206 at [15]. This argument has not been tested in case law.

the borrower's name when the borrower did not have title, the borrower would still be bound as a matter of contract or deed.[18]

5.22   In addition, as between the borrower, the receiver and the lender, the borrower cannot be heard to complain that the receiver did not act on his behalf, if he purported to confer the power to so act so on the receiver.

5.23   This analysis provides the starting point to understanding the issues which arise when the receiver is seeking to take possession from the borrower's tenants,[19] in circumstances where the borrower has no right to obtain possession from them:[20]

(a)   The borrower could not complain that the receiver had brought proceedings in its name (because he has agreed that the receiver could, in this respect, act as his deemed agent).

(b)   However, the third party might well succeed in objecting that the borrower has no cause of action if the proceedings are brought in the borrower's name.[21]

(c)   The proceedings should be brought in the receiver's name.[22]

(d)   The proceedings will succeed because the lender has, in fact, delegated its power to take possession to the receiver. The deemed agency is causally irrelevant to the reason why the proceedings would succeed.

(e)   The tenants will retain a cause of action against the borrower on the lease. This is not because the receiver has acted on the borrower's behalf; it is because a stranger to the borrower/landlord-tenant relationship has interrupted the tenant's possession, resulting in a breach of the covenant for quiet enjoyment.[23]

(f)   The borrower will not be able to complain to the lender that the receiver did this, because, as between the borrower and the lender, the receiver is deemed to be the agent of the borrower.

(g)   The borrower cannot complain against the receiver either because he is doing what the mortgage conditions allow.

---

[18]   The receiver's power to lease is considered in detail in paras 9.141–9.156. Note that once a receiver is appointed, the borrower may not retain a power of leasing at all: Law of Property Act 1925, s 99(19). However, the lender may have a power to grant leases in the borrower's name under s 8(1) and/or under the mortgage terms.

[19]   Relying on the lender's right to do so, and assuming that the mortgage conditions permit the receiver to exercise this power as the borrower's deemed agent.

[20]   Where the receiver is relying on the borrower's cause of action, different principles apply. See paras 10.51–10.57 in general, and the more detailed analysis in specific situations which follows.

[21]   Unless the mortgage conditions provide, on their true construction, that the lender can bring such proceedings in the name of the borrower, which would be rare, or it can be argued successfully that the express agreement by the borrower in the mortgage conditions that the receiver can act as his deemed agent simply means that the receiver can exercise any of the powers conferred by the mortgage in the borrower's name, as to which, see *Edenwest Ltd v CMS Cameron McKenna (A Firm)* [2012] EWHC 1258 (Ch), [2013] BCC 152 at [66].

[22]   See paras 10.151–10.156, where this is discussed in more detail, but see Chapter 10, fn 149.

[23]   See paras 8.6–8.9, where the receiver's ability to end a borrower's contract, and the third party's remaining rights against the borrower are discussed more generally.

(h) If, as we suggest, such proceedings were brought in the receiver's name, the lender would not be in possession as a result, and would not incur any liabilities to the borrower (as mortgagee in possession) or to third parties. It would not incur liabilities to third parties because the receiver is not acting as its agent in that the lender would not be the receiver's principal in exercising the powers.

5.24   The following is thought the likely analysis of how a receiver's exercise of other lender's powers typically delegated to receivers will affect a third party:

(a) A lender's express power of sale which permits the lender to sell in the name of the borrower[24] and to delegate that power: if the receiver exercises the power in the borrower's name,[25] it will be the borrower who is the party to the contract and any deed of transfer, and the purchaser's claim will lie against the borrower, not the lender.[26] Nonetheless, the purchaser will take free of interests which bound the borrower, if the lender was not bound by those interests.[27] Accordingly, there is a real difference between a sale under the lender's power of sale but in the name of the borrower and a sale under the borrower's power of sale.[28]

(b) The lender's power of leasing under section 99(2) of the Law of Property Act 1925: the power is to grant certain leases of the mortgaged land, binding both borrower and landlord. It appears that the lender could grant a lease in the borrower's name,[29] and that in any event the borrower would be bound by this lease in the sense that he could not complain of the tenant's possession.[30] The borrower would also be bound by the lease covenants, if that power is exercised by a receiver, absent something in the mortgage conditions excluding that liability, because the receiver acts as his deemed agent in exercising this power.[31]

(c) The lender's power of accepting surrenders under section 100(2) of the Law of Property Act 1925: the power is to accept surrenders of leases of the mortgaged land.[32] The borrower has no power to accept surrenders so

---

[24]   Which would usually be the case by reason of Law of Property Act 1925, ss 88 and 89.

[25]   Although the delegation might permit exercise in the lender's name the receiver would usually contract in the name of the borrower to limit lender liabilities.

[26]   Unless the lender delegated his power of sale to the receiver to act as the lender's agent, the lender would not be the receiver's principal, and the third party could not sue him.

[27]   See para 11.87.

[28]   A sale under the borrower's power of sale would not be free of interests binding the borrower See para 11.63.

[29]   Law of Property Act 1925, s 8(1), which presumably applies because, s 99 is a repeat of a pre-existing provision in, for example, the Conveyancing Act 1881, but see the commentary on s 99(19) in JT Farrand, *Wolstenholme and Cherry's Conveyancing Statutes* (Oyez Publishing Ltd, 13th edn, 1972), which suggests this follows from s 7(4); unless the sub-section applies by reference to some earlier statute which the commentary does not identify, this suggestion is not understood.

[30]   Law of Property Act 1925, s 99(2).

[31]   Law of Property Act 1925, s 109(2).

[32]   Law of Property Act 1925, s 100(2), by reference to s 100(1).

as to bind the lender after the receiver is appointed.[33] The lender would have power under section 100(2) to accept surrenders so as to bind the borrower as well as itself, but there is nothing in the statute to suggest that this power is a power to act in the borrower's name. Certainly, if the receiver with the delegated power accepted a surrender in his own name, it would bind both lender and borrower. However, it is less obvious whether the receiver exercising the lender's power to accept surrenders can do so in the borrower's name simply because the mortgage terms permit him to act as the borrower's deemed agent.

(d)   The power to insure: the borrower is not precluded from insuring by reason of the appointment of the receiver. Accordingly, if the lender instructs the receiver to insure, and the receiver is entitled (on the mortgage terms) to do so as deemed agent of the borrower, the insurance can (and should) be in the borrower's name. The third party insurer would have a claim, for example, for the cost, against the borrower.

POWERS IN THE MORTGAGE DEED

Examples of powers

5.25   Frequently, the mortgage deed will convey wider powers on the receiver than the statutory powers. For example:

(a)   'Any receiver appointed by the bank shall have ... powers ... to sell, lease, surrender or accept surrenders of leases, charge or otherwise deal with and dispose of the [mortgaged property] without restriction'[34] as deemed agent of the borrower.

(b)   Powers including a power of sale, and a power 'to exercise all powers which the [lender] has by statute or under this mortgage' as deemed agent of the borrower.[35]

(c)   Powers to '(a) take possession of collect and get in any property hereby charged ... (b) to carry on manage or concur in carrying on and managing the business of the farmer and ... to raise or borrow any money that may be required upon the security of the whole or any part of the property hereby charged (c) to sell or concur in selling all or any of the property

---

[33]   Law of Property Act 1925, s 100(13). The effect of the borrower accepting a surrender is that the surrender would take effect as between him and the leaseholder, but the lender could still sue the leaseholder on the lease. See para 2.78.

[34]   The mortgage conditions referred to in the first instance decision in *Silven Properties Ltd v Royal Bank of Scotland Plc* [2002] EWHC 1976 (Ch) at [26]. The receivers sold under the power. Their duties are not agency duties, but the same equitable duty to those interested in the equity of redemption as owed by the lender: at [22] and [27](2). The receiver will have any incidental powers necessary to the performance of his express powers: *M Wheeler & Co Ltd v Warren* [1928] Ch 840; *McDonald v McDonald* [2014] EWCA Civ 1049. See references to these cases in Chapter 9, and see para 10.62 for more detail on these cases.

[35]   The mortgage conditions in *Horsham Properties Group Ltd v Clark* [2008] EWHC 2327 (Ch), [2009] 1 WLR 1255 at [20]. The receivers contracted to sell the mortgaged property under their power of sale, as deemed agent of the borrower, and then executed the transfer as agents of the lender: [4] and [5].

hereby charged ... (g) to do any such other acts and things as may be considered to be incidental or conducive to any of the matters or powers aforesaid and which he or they lawfully may or can do as agent for the farmer' with the receivers 'deemed to be the agent of the famer and the farmer shall be solely responsible for his or their acts or defaults and for his or their remuneration'.[36]

(d) The same powers as the lender, but as agent of the borrower.[37]

(e) A power 'to exercise all powers conferred by the Law of Property Act 1925 in the same way as if the receiver had been duly appointed thereunder ... in particular to sell or concur in selling any of the property hereby charged by the [borrower] in such manner and generally on such terms and conditions as he shall think fit and to carry any such transactions into effect in the name of and on behalf of the [borrower]'.[38]

Construction of powers

5.26   As set out above, the express powers given to receivers in the mortgage conditions may extend beyond the powers of the borrower, though the deemed agency is still expressed to apply.

5.27   Care is needed in construing the powers given by the mortgage conditions, to determine whether the receiver's powers emanate from the borrower or the lender. This is a question of ascertaining what the parties to the mortgage are to be taken to have intended from the language used, bearing in mind the context.

5.28   In general, the argument that a lender has the power to appoint a receiver only once the borrower is in default and has that power for the purpose of recovering its loan is likely to militate in favour of construing the mortgage as conferring wide powers on the receiver.

5.29   That said, if, on the true construction of the mortgage, the powers emanate from the borrower, then the receiver in exercising them cannot do what the borrower could not do.[39]

---

[36]   The mortgage conditions in *Medforth v Blake* [2000] Ch 86, recorded at 90. In that case, the Court of Appeal found that the receivers had an equitable duty to those interested in the equity of redemption in carrying on the farming business. They did not have the usual duties of agency. Note that where, as here, a receiver is given powers over a business as well as real property, some care may be needed as to over which assets the powers extend since he may not use assets not charged: *SS Agri Power Ltd v Dorins* [2017] EWHC 3563 (Ch) at [55] contrasting *Britannia Building Society v Crammer* [1997] BPIR 596, in which the charge was of the real property, not the business, only.

[37]   The mortgage conditions in *McDonald v McDonald* [2014] EWCA Civ 1049 at [8]. This is an example of the receiver having lender's powers as agent of the borrower.

[38]   *Phoenix Properties Ltd v Wimpole Street Nominees Ltd* [1992] BCLC 737 at [741]d. This was not sufficient for the receiver to have a power of sale since the lender's statutory power of sale was not delegable under the Law of Property Act 1925.

[39]   The powers in para 5.25(c) at (g) seem to be an example of borrower's powers.

5.30   Similarly, if the receiver's powers emanate from the lender, then the receiver can do only what the lender could do.

5.31   Any right of possession given to the receiver should likewise be construed carefully. When a mortgage is granted by a borrower to a lender, the lender has the right to possession of the mortgaged property 'before the ink is dry on the mortgage',[40] unless this is varied by the terms of the mortgage. The lender usually postpones that right until a breach of mortgage by a borrower.[41] Once there has been a breach, then the lender has the right to possession[42] of 'the mortgaged property' or 'the property charged'. Thus the expression 'the power to take possession of the property charged' or of 'the mortgaged property', within the receiver's powers likely gives the receiver a power to take possession, or a right of possession, as the lender could, i.e. free of any interests which do not bind the lender. Indeed, the receiver can likely take possession against the borrower.[43]

5.32   Receivers are often given a power of attorney by the mortgage conditions, for example, in the form: the borrower 'hereby irrevocably appoints the ... receiver ... to be its attorney for it and in its name and on its behalf ...', including 'to sign seal and deliver and otherwise perfect any such legal or other mortgage, charge, security or assignment ... which may be required or may be deemed proper by the receiver ...'.[44]

5.33   That power is not usually said to be a power to act under a deemed agency. The power is a real agency, save that insofar as it is expressed to be irrevocable, it is unlikely that the receiver has the usual duties of an agent. Indeed, since it is a device to assist the realisation of the asset to pay back the loan, it is likely that the receiver has the equitable duties discussed in Chapter 6 below only, not the duties associated with real agency.

ADDITIONAL POWERS CONFERRED BY THE LENDER

5.34   The lender may give a receiver further powers – lender's powers – not given to the receiver in the mortgage conditions. Such powers can only be conferred by the lender at the time of appointment or subsequently.

5.35   There are two types of lender-conferred powers.

---

[40] *Four Maids v Dudley Marshall (Properties) Ltd* [1957] Ch 317 at 320.

[41] For example, in the GMAC conditions in *Horsham Properties Group Ltd v Clark* [2008] EWHC 2327 (Ch), [2009] 1 WLR 1255, once there was a breach of mortgage including a failure to pay a monthly instalment, the lender had the right 'to require the borrower to leave the property so that the [lender] may take possession of the property': at [19].

[42] Although the borrower need not join the lender to a claim for possession until the lender has given notice of his intention to take possession: Law of Property Act 1925, s 98(1) and see para 2.65.

[43] See para 10.175 *et seq*.

[44] *Phoenix Properties Ltd v Wimpole Street Nominees Ltd* [1992] BCLC 737 at 741f. Sale was under the power of attorney.

Delegable statutory powers

5.36   The lender's statutory powers of leasing[45] and accepting surrenders[46] in the Law of Property Act 1925 are expressed in that Act as being delegable to the receiver by writing.[47]

5.37   Likewise, the lender can direct the receiver in writing to insure the property.

5.38   If the lender delegates those powers, then the receiver exercises them as deemed agent of the borrower.[48] However, the effect of that deemed agency is not straightforward.[49]

Other powers of the lender

5.39   The lender can delegate other powers to the receiver, for example, the power to take possession, even though the receiver is not given any such powers in the mortgage conditions.

5.40   Where the right conferred is a proprietary right which the lender has by virtue of its estate, such as the right to take possession, no difficulty arises.[50]

5.41   However, the analysis is a little more complicated where the lender is seeking to sub-delegate a power which it has been given by the borrower, either expressly in the mortgage conditions or under statute. The lender's power of sale is such a power. The extent to which the lender is able to delegate its power of sale is considered in detail in Chapter 11.[51]

5.42   Where delegation is possible, delegation of such powers can be in any form sufficient to allow exercise of the power by the receiver. A power of attorney compliant with section 1 of the Powers of Attorney Act 1971 might be appropriate, though not necessary. The delegation should be by deed if the receiver is to execute deeds in the borrower's or the lender's name.[52]

---

[45]   See Law of Property Act 1925, s 99(19).

[46]   Law of Property Act 1925, s 100(13).

[47]   See the discussion at paras 9.144 and 9.157.

[48]   Law of Property Act 1925, s 109(2), (3) and (7).

[49]   See para 5.24(c).

[50]   Because the lender is not attempting to sub-delegate a power which has been delegated to him. His right to possession is a proprietary right arising from his estate. Conversely, the lender's power to sell the borrower's estate is not a proprietary right out of his estate, but a power delegated to the lender.

[51]   See paras 11.90–11.102.

[52]   The common law rule is that if an agent is to be given a power to execute deeds in someone else's name, then he must be appointed by deed: *Berkeley v Hardy* (1826) 5 B&C 355; *Powell v London & Provincial Bank* [1893] 2 Ch 555 at 563; *Windsor Refrigerator Co v Branch Nominees* [1961] Ch 88; *Phoenix Properties Ltd v Wimpole Street Nominees Ltd* [1992] BCLC 737. See Chapter 2, fn 50. It seems likely to follow that a deed is required for the delegation of a

5.43   The receiver will not exercise any such powers as the deemed agent of the borrower, because there is neither express agreement by the borrower to deemed agency, nor is it imposed by statute.

5.44   Whether the receiver is a mere donee of a power to act on his own behalf, or whether the lender has conferred upon the receiver the ability to act as the lender's agent, is a question of construction of the document by which the delegation was made. In some cases, the receiver will have a choice whether to act as the lender's agent or on his own account.

5.45   If he acts as the lender's agent, the lender will be liable to third parties for the receiver's acts. The lender will also be liable to the borrower if there is a breach of the lender's duties.

5.46   When the 'receiver' acts as the lender's agent, he will usually act in the lender's name.[53]

5.47   When he acts on his own account, he will usually act in his own name. If the receiver acts on his own account, he will likely be liable to the borrower for any breach of his equitable duties.[54]

---

power to do an act which must be done by deed even if the act is not to be done in another's name. The requirement for a deed is to make the act more certain.

[53]   It would be wrong for the receiver to act in the borrower's name since he would have no deemed agency from the borrower, and no right to make the borrower liable on the transaction. He could act in his own name, with the lender as undisclosed principal, but would be unlikely to wish to do so. The position is different if the delegated power were the lender's power of sale, since the power includes to sell in the borrower's name: Law of Property Act 1925, ss 88 and 89.

[54]   These are discussed in Chapter 6.

Chapter 6

The Receiver's Relationship with the Borrower

INTRODUCTION

6.1   This chapter analyses the nature of the relationship between the receiver and the borrower. Typically, the relationship is described as one of 'deemed agency'.

6.2   The question that arises is how like to agency this deemed agency is. Although it is a real agency,[1] the usual law of agency 'cannot be applied mechanically to the somewhat complex position of a receivership' and is 'primarily a device to protect the mortgagee'.[2]

6.3   The extent to which this device is like real agency sheds light on questions such as:

(a)   When can the receiver prevent the borrower from dealing with the property?
(b)   When can the receiver deal with the property in a way in which the borrower could not?
(c)   What are the receiver's obligations to third parties?
(d)   What are the receiver's obligations to the borrower and lender?[3]

6.4   This chapter thus discusses the nature of the receiver's deemed agency, comparing it with agency in general, and setting out when it does and does not coincide, the former, in particular, including a discussion of the receiver's duties, which are quite unlike those of an agent. The chapter then discusses the receiver's position once the deemed agency ends, for example, on insolvency.

6.5   The analysis in this chapter explains the theory behind much of the particular consequences in the later chapters on the receiver's role in particular circumstances: sale, possession and relationship with third parties, for example.

---

[1]   *Silven Properties Ltd v Royal Bank of Scotland Plc* [2003] EWCA Civ 1409, [2004] 1 WLR 997; *Rhodes v Allied Dunbar Pension Services Ltd* [1989] 1 WLR 800 at 807H (good faith).

[2]   *Gomba Holdings UK Ltd v Minories Finance Ltd* [1988] 1 WLR 1231, CA.

[3]   The relationship between the lender and the receiver is described in more detail in Chapter 7.

HISTORICAL ORIGINS OF THE AGENCY

6.6   A number of cases[4] dealing with the effect of the deemed agency explain how the practice grew out of appointing receivers as deemed agents. These references to the history are used to justify non-agency analyses of the receiver's relationship with the borrower.

6.7   A lender in possession of the property is prevented by equity from securing any advantage beyond securing repayment. The lender in possession is held liable to account for rent and profits it would have received but for its wilful default.[5] The duty on the lender when in possession to account to the borrower and those interested in the equity of redemption is strict[6] and particularly onerous[7] in the sense that that account imposes on the lender the burden of showing the steps taken are within the duty.

6.8   It was in order to avoid this potential liability and the risk it imposes as to full recovery of the principal and interest under the loan that mortgage receivership as a remedy of the lender was introduced.[8] First, lenders started the practice of obtaining agreement from the borrower in the mortgage conditions that the borrower would appoint a receiver, its agent, to receive the rents and profits and use them to pay down the mortgage debt. Then the mortgage conditions allowed the lender, not the borrower, to appoint the receiver, but with the receiver still being the borrower's agent. The purpose of the agency was to put the liability for any default of the receiver on the borrower, not the lender.

6.9   That latter practice of appointment of a receiver as deemed agent of the borrower was then enacted, the statutory version now in force being section 109 of the Law of Property Act 1925.[9]

---

4   *Gaskell v Gosling* [1896] 1 QB 669 at 691–692; (underlying decision reversed in [1897] AC 575; the receiver post the borrower's winding up did not become the lender's agent); *Medforth v Blake* [2000] Ch 86 at 93–94.

5   *White v City of London Brewery Company* (1889) 42 Ch D 237, for example. See *Medforth v Blake* [2000] Ch 86 at 93H. An account on the footing of wilful default is an equitable remedy. It requires the lender to set out its account of monies received into the mortgage account and monies spent, but the monies taken as received will include anything it should have received but for 'its wilful default', i.e. where lack of receipt is due to breach of the applicable duty, whether or not that breach was intentional. The lender will have to make good any such loss found under the account. The taking of an account on the basis of wilful default allows the court to undertake an extensive enquiry into its administration, and is hence something lenders would wish to avoid.

6   *Yorkshire Bank v Hall* [1999] 1 WLR 1713 at 1728.

7   *Medforth v Blake* [2000] Ch 86.

8   Receivership is a device designed to insulate the lender from liability for the receiver's acts: *Edenwest Ltd v CMS Cameron McKenna (A Firm)* [2012] EWHC 1258 (Ch) at [61]–[62].

9   Note that a receiver will only be a deemed agent of the borrower if Law of Property Act 1925, s 109 applies, or the mortgage terms otherwise provide: see paras 6.13–6.22.

6.10   It is for that reason that in many cases it has been suggested that the law of agency is not a good guide for understanding the receiver's role and relationship to the borrower, the lender and third parties.[10]

6.11   What a review of the case law suggests, however, is that across the cases the analysis of the deemed agency as different from real agency has not been consistent. In some cases, for example, the ratings cases discussed below, the deemed agency of the receiver has been analysed as if a true agency. In others, for example, the cases on the continuation of the receiver's powers after the insolvency of a company borrower, or the cases on the receiver's duties, the law of agency has been used little as a guide. This leaves an apparent discrepancy of principle and an uncertainty as to the correct approach in relation to currently unanswered questions, for example, the question of whether a receiver can take possession against his own borrower.*

6.12   In this chapter and in this book, a theory of the receivership is suggested which attempts a consistent answer.

WHEN THE DEEMED AGENCY ARISES

6.13   A receiver does not always act as the deemed agent of the borrower. Whether he does or does not depends on the power under which he is appointed and what provision that power makes for his agency.

6.14   A receiver appointed under, and in accordance with, section 109 of the Law of Property Act 1925 will be the deemed agent of the borrower, by reason of section 109(2): 'the mortgagor shall be solely responsible for the receiver's acts or defaults unless the mortgage deed otherwise provides'.

6.15   However, his agency will only be deemed insofar as he is exercising the powers permitted by section 109 of the Law of Property Act 1925.[11]

6.16   If his appointment alone were to give him any further powers, then his exercise of those further powers would not be as deemed agent of the borrower.[12]

6.17   A receiver appointed under an express right to do so in the mortgage conditions, and with powers provided for in the mortgage conditions, is the deemed agent of the borrower only if the mortgage conditions so provide.

---

[10]   See, for example, *Gomba Holdings UK Ltd v Minories Finance Ltd* [1988] 1 WLR 1231 at 1233E; *Silven Properties Ltd v Royal Bank of Scotland Plc* [2003] EWCA Civ 1409, [2004] 1 WLR 997 at [28]; *Edenwest Ltd v CMS Cameron McKenna (A Firm)* [2012] EWHC 1258 (Ch) at [62]–[64].

[11]   Including demanding and recovery of income, and exercising any of the powers delegated to him by the lender pursuant to the Law of Property Act 1925.

[12]   Whether he is, in those circumstances, the lender's agent or a mere donee of a power is considered in Chapter 7.

• But see now Menon v Pask [2019] EWHC 2611 (Ch)

Jo

6.18   Even if the appointment is silent as to agency, if the mortgage conditions make the receiver the deemed agent of the borrower, unless the appointment provides otherwise, that provision will prevail.

6.19   Mortgage conditions do, usually, now provide that the receiver will be the deemed agent of the borrower, and it will be rare now for the receiver to be the lender's agent save through the lender's intermeddling.[13]

6.20   However, in the early years of the 20th century, mortgage conditions that were silent as to agency were more common.

6.21   If the mortgage conditions state that they are an extension of section 109 of the Law of Property Act 1925, then the receiver will be a deemed agent of the borrower, due to the incorporation by reference to that provision.[14]

6.22   Conversely, where the mortgage conditions fail to incorporate section 109 and fail to provide on their true construction that the receiver is to be the agent of the borrower, the receiver will not be the agent of the borrower.[15]

THE NATURE OF THE DEEMED AGENCY

6.23   A receiver's deemed agency is a 'real agency', albeit with peculiar incidents.[16] In this section, the extent to which the deemed agency has the incidents of 'real agency'[17] is considered.

6.24   First, the usual incidents of 'real agency' are sketched.

6.25   Secondly, the extent to which the receiver is to be treated as if a real agent is discussed, with emphasis on those cases in which treatment of the

---

[13]   If the receiver acts on the lender's instructions or direction, then to the extent of those instructions or direction, he will be the agent of the lender, though he may remain the agent of the borrower in relation to other matters on which he has not been so directed: *Bicester Properties Ltd v West Bromwich Commercial Ltd*, 10 October 2012, unreported, ChD, at para 15 per Master Bowles. See Chapter 7 for further discussion of when the receiver will be the agent of the lender.

[14]   *Cully v Parsons* [1923] 2 Ch 512, where deemed agency under the relevant provision of the Conveyancing and Law of Property Act 1881, a precursor of the Law of Property Act 1925, was incorporated by reference in the mortgage conditions.

[15]   *Re Vimbos Ltd* [1900] 1 Ch 470, in which the mortgage conditions were silent as to agency, and did not refer to the Conveyancing and Law of Property Act 1881; *Robinson Printing Company Ltd v Chic Ltd* [1905] 2 Ch 123. In *Deyes v Wood* [1911] 1 KB 806, the mortgage conditions did refer to the Conveyancing and Law of Property Act 1881, but not to the specific provision in that Act which deemed the receiver agent of the borrower. Although the judge thought it was likely that the intention was to incorporate that provision, it was not incorporated, and the receiver was agent of the lender. Given the ubiquity of deemed agency in receivership, and the current case law on interpretation, it is unclear that the same result would be reached today.

[16]   *Gaskell v Gosling* [1896] 1 QB 669 per Rigby LJ; approved by the House of Lords at [1897] AC 575.

[17]   *Silven Properties Ltd v Royal Bank of Scotland Plc* [2003] EWCA Civ 1409, [2004] 1 WLR 997.

receiver as an agent of the borrower has been relied on. These are principally ratings and tax cases; the agency of the receiver has been used by the courts to avoid the receiver's personal liability arising.

6.26   Thirdly, the non-agency aspects of receivership are considered by reference to cases in which the analysis of the receiver's role has not coincided with agency: the duties on the receiver, the limit in the receiver's obligation to provide the borrower with documents and the receiver's ability to control the actions of the borrower.

Real agency

6.27   The central point in agency law is that the principal gives the agent the power,[18] or authority, to change the legal relationship between the principal and third parties, and so that the principal has liability to those third parties for the acts of the agent.

6.28   In 'real agency', in addition, the agent will usually have fiduciary duties, and a duty of due diligence, imposed by equity if not express, to the principal.[19] This aspect is not adopted in receivership.[20]

Powers of the agent

6.29   Save in contexts which expressly prohibit actions by someone other than the principal,[21] an agent with appropriate authority can enter into contracts for the principal and he can perform a contract on his principal's behalf. He can receive property or money on his behalf and give good receipt for it, for example. He may be able to make critical decisions for his principal; for example, a director of a company is an agent of that company. He may be able to waive rights of his principal, for example, the right to forfeit a lease for

---

[18]   A power is simply the power given to a person to affect property (including rights) of another who directs the mode in which the power is to be exercised: *Freme v Clement* (1881) 18 Ch D 499 at 504. It is not just agents who can exercise a power over the rights of another, in the sense that someone exercising a power given to him by another need not have the usual agency duties. The notion of powers, and their delegability, is relevant for example in trust law and in relation to wills. There is no universal principle that someone with a power must exercise it in the name of the person who gave it to them, unless the required mode so requires. See, for example, Powers of Attorney Act 1971, s 7(1).

[19]   See PG Watts (ed), *Bowstead & Reynolds on Agency* (*Bowstead & Reynolds*) (Sweet & Maxwell, 21st edn, 2017) at Article 1 for the formulation of agency expressed in these two paragraphs, as quoted in for example *UBS AG v Kommunale* [2017] EWCA Civ 1567 at [83]; *London Borough of Haringey v Ahmed* [2017] EWCA Civ 1861 at [27].

[20]   See paras 6.88–6.94.

[21]   For example, the right to initiate a claim for a lease extension of a residential flat, prior to December 2014, under the Leasehold Reform, Housing and Urban Development Act 1993. Prior to amendment, the statute required signature of the s 42 notice by the tenant personally. It is also possible for a contract between a principal and a third party to require performance by the principal himself, not an agent, or by reference to a principal, so that the third party need not accept performance by an agent even if appointed under a power of attorney. Some powers cannot be delegated, for example, some trustee powers. See the discussion at para 8.129 *et seq*.

breach, even though his principal is unaware of the breach or does not instruct him to do so.

6.30   The extent of the authority of an agent is dependent on the contract or other agreement, for example a power of attorney, under which he acts as the agent. In principle, his power to act is limited by the power given to him by the principal or consented to by the principal. That is save for two situations. The first is when the agent has apparent authority beyond his principal's agreement, i.e. the principal has put him into the position of seeming to third parties to have sufficient authority, or represented to the third party that he has sufficient authority. In that case, the principal is bound by the agent's actions though the agent did not have the power to take them. The second is when the principal afterwards ratifies his agent's actions though his agent's actions were beyond that authority.

The principal and third parties

6.31   As between the principal and third parties, the principal has the benefit of any valid contract[22] made on his behalf by his agent provided that contract was within the scope of his actual authority.

6.32   The principal is bound by any act of the agent within his actual or apparent authority. Thus, the principal can be sued by the third party on a contract made by his agent within his actual or apparent authority.

6.33   The principal will, in addition, be vicariously liable for his agent's torts, provided those torts occurred within the scope of the agent's actual or apparent authority.[23] The principal will be liable to repay money paid by a third party to the agent by mistake, if the money has been passed to him.[24]

The agent and third parties

6.34   An agent will not be liable to a third party on a contract he entered into provided he disclosed to the third party that he was making the contract for his principal, even though he did not name that principal. Likewise, he cannot sue in his own name on such a contract. If the agent does not disclose that he is contracting for his principal, then he can sue or be sued on that contract in his own name, though the third party may prefer to sue the principal once he knows of him.

---

[22]   Various contracts must comply with formal requirements to be valid, for example contracts for dispositions in land, which must be in writing signed by or on behalf of each party, under Law of Property (Miscellaneous Provisions) Act 1989, s 2.

[23]   The precise extent of vicarious liability is itself a matter of considerable legal commentary and case law, and for the precise principles, see any practitioner's text on agency.

[24]   Assuming none of the defences available on such a claim are available, for example, assumption of risk by the third party, or change of position by the principal.

6.35   An agent will be liable in contract for breach of warranty of authority if he indicates he has the authority of his principal to contract and does not.

6.36   An agent will be liable to a third party for his own torts, notwithstanding that his principal is vicariously liable for torts provided the agent's actions were authorised, but it is common for the third party to sue the principal, in particular where this is likely to be the better option for enforcement once judgment is entered.

The agent's duties

6.37   Central to the usual relationship between the principal and his agent (at least in relation to contractual, not gratuitous, agents) are a series of duties commonly imposed on agents:

(a)   A duty to carry out instructions from his principal and not to exceed authority.
(b)   A duty to exercise care and skill and, where the agent has a discretion, to exercise it in his principal's interests.
(c)   A duty to keep the principal informed and to act with necessary speed and diligence.
(d)   Equitable fiduciary duties and duties of loyalty. The relationship between a principal and his agent is a relationship of trust and confidence. The agent should not, for example, place himself in a position of conflict, for example, by acting for the benefit of a third person.

6.38   In return, a principal usually has duties to his agent: to pay him (if it is not a gratuitous agency) and to indemnify him against expenses and liabilities incurred by him,[25] provided he is acting within his authority.

Termination of agency

6.39   Lastly, it is usually the case that the principal can terminate his agent's authority.

6.40   There are, however, exceptions where the agency is irrevocable. At common law, an irrevocable agency can arise, by agreement and for so long as the agent's proprietary interest exists, where 'the authority is given to secure an interest of the agent, being a proprietary interest ... owed him personally'.[26]

6.41   Section 4(1) of the Powers of Attorney Act 1971 reflects this.[27] It makes irrevocable[28] a power of attorney, granted by deed, and so long as the

---

[25]   *Thacker v Hardy* (1878) 4 QBD 685, though if there is a written contract of agency, the existence of such an indemnity will depend on the interpretation of that contract.
[26]   *Bailey v Angove's Pty Ltd* [2016] UKSC 47, [2016] 1 WLR 3179.
[27]   Although it appears it does not replace the common law irrevocable agency. See *Bowstead & Reynolds* at 10-008.
[28]   See paras 6.229–6.243 for a discussion of powers of attorney under mortgages.

attorney (the donee) has a proprietary interest or the performance of an obligation owed to him remains undischarged:

> Where it is expressed to be irrevocable and is given to secure—
>
> (a)   a proprietary interest of the donee of the power; or
> (b)   the performance of an obligation owed to the donee.[29]

6.42   The effect is that the power cannot be revoked by the principal, without the consent of the donee, not even by 'the death, incapacity or bankruptcy of the donor, or, if the donor is a body corporate, by its winding up or dissolution'.[30]

Introduction to the receiver's agency

6.43   This survey of the key concepts in agency helps identify which of the incidents of 'real agency' the receiver has and those which he does not. In summary:

(a)   in relation to third parties, where the deemed agency applies, the receiver is to be treated as a real agent of the borrower in the sense that his acts bind the borrower, and the borrower is liable for his acts to the extent that he would be for his true agent;[31]
(b)   the deemed agency is effective to prevent the lender from being liable for the receiver's acts, unless it interferes with the conduct of the receivership;[32] but
(c)   there are significant differences between the position of a receiver and that of a real agent in other respects. In particular, the receiver does not have an agent's duties to the borrower, he cannot be directed by the borrower, and the receivership cannot be ended by the borrower, or his death or dissolution;[33]
(d)   the starting point for remuneration of receivers is not a duty on the borrower, but recovery of it from receipts from the mortgaged property.[34]

6.44   These similarities and differences between a receiver and a real agent are explained in more detail in the following sections.

---

[29]   Powers of Attorney Act 1971, s 4(1).
[30]   Powers of Attorney Act 1971, s 4(1).
[31]   This is considered further in Chapter 8.
[32]   This is considered further at paras 7.49–7.57.
[33]   Although the agency may be: see para 6.161 and the discussion which follows it.
[34]   Law of Property Act 1925, s 109(6). See Chapters 7 and 12.

Principles of real agency which apply to the receiver

The receiver can give good receipts

6.45   The receiver can receive monies on behalf of the borrower and give a good receipt.[35]

The borrower is liable to third parties for the receiver's acts

6.46   The purpose of the deemed agency in section 109[36] of the Law of Property Act 1925 or in the mortgage conditions is to make the borrower, not the lender, liable for the receiver's acts.[37] A receiver with the deemed agency will be entitled to bind the borrower by entering into contracts within his powers in the borrower's name.[38]

---

[35]   This is express in the statutory receivership under Law of Property Act 1925, s 109 and otherwise a result of the deemed agency. The borrower could have given good receipt for the money, and has given the receiver a deemed agency by express agreement in the mortgage conditions. See *Edenwest Ltd v CMS Cameron McKenna (A Firm)* [2012] EWHC 1258 (Ch) at [66].

[36]   The wording of Law of Property Act 1925, s 109(2) is that the receiver 'shall be the deemed to be the agent of the mortgagor; and the mortgagor shall be solely responsible for the receiver's acts or defaults unless the mortgage deed otherwise provides'.

[37]   An express agency between a principal and his agent will affect a third party entering into a contract with the agent, by creating contractual relations between him and the principal: see the description of the effect of authority in *Freeman & Lockyer v Buckhurst Park Properties (Mangal) Ltd* [1964] 2 QB 480 at 502: 'To this agreement [the agency agreement] the [third party] is a stranger; he may be totally ignorant of the existence of any authority on the part of the agent. Nevertheless, if the agent does enter into a contract pursuant to the "actual authority", it does create contractual rights and liabilities between the principal and the [third party]'. It is suggested that the statutory deemed agency in Law of Property Act 1925, s 109(2) and any express deemed agency in the mortgage conditions works in the same way.

[38]   See *Cully v Parsons* [1923] 2 Ch 512 at 518. See also *Cox v Hickman* (1860) 11 ER 431, in which creditors benefitting from a trust they controlled which operated the debtor's business in the debtor's name were not themselves liable for new contracts made. The deed creating the trust created an agency. The debtor remained the person interested in the profits, though he had agreed that they would only be applied to the benefit of the creditors. This is relied on in the decision in *Gaskell v Gosling* [1897] AC 575 in the context of receivership. Similarly, *Mollwo, March & Co v Court of Wards* (1872) LR 4PC 419 referred to by Rigby LJ in his dissenting judgment in *Gosling v Gaskell* [1896] 1 QB 669 at 690, in which a creditor had total control of the debtor's business but the agreement by the debtor that acts would be in his name amounted to an agency notwithstanding the reality of where that control lay. The agreement as to agency binds the purported principal and makes him liable to third parties. See also *Edenwest Ltd v CMS Cameron McKenna (A Firm)* [2012] EWHC 1258 (Ch) at [66]: 'ordinarily, if a receiver wishes to bind the company to a contract with a third party he will contract in the name of the [borrower], as he is entitled to do as its agent and attorney, so that the [borrower] itself becomes a party and he does not'. Note that a receiver may wish to contract in his own name, as in that case. As set out at para 5.20, there are issues as to whether the receiver can act in the borrower's name if the borrower did not have the power the receiver is exercising, for example, whether a receiver with the lender's delegated power of leasing can lease in the borrower's name. In any event, a lease granted by the receiver with such a power in his own name will bind the borrower as landlord because that is the effect of the power. Since the receiver's acts are the borrower's, provided he was appointed prior to an application for an administration order over a company, his subsequent steps are not continuation of legal process contrary to Insolvency Act 1986, s 43(6), both because of the agency, and because his steps are not 'legal' process: *SS Agri Power Ltd v Dorrins* [2017] EWHC 3563 (Ch) at [11]–[15].

6.47   In addition, the receiver is generally treated no differently from a real agent for the purpose of determining whether the borrower is liable for his torts.[39]

The receiver's actions and limitation

6.48   The deemed agency of the receiver can affect limitation on a claim by the lender or a third party against the borrower because payment by the receiver is an act of the borrower and hence an acknowledgment within the meaning of section 29(5) of the Limitation Act 1980.[40] Presumably, any acknowledgement of the lender's title by the receiver would have the effect of extending time both for a money claim and a claim to recover the land.[41]

The lender is not liable

6.49   The deemed agency of the receiver is also real in the sense that it prevents the lender from being liable for the receiver's acts.[42] The lender is not liable for the acts of the receiver when the receiver acts as deemed agent of the borrower, unless it interferes.[43]

6.50   In particular, the deemed agency prevents the lender going into possession of the mortgaged property. Appointment of a receiver with power to collect rents does not end the lender's permission to the borrower to retain possession and to retain the income of the mortgaged property, because the appointment of the receiver does not put the lender in possession.

6.51   Therefore, the lender is not liable for rates, or under other statutes where liability turns on occupation, either. Nor is it under any of the duties of a lender in possession.[44]

---

[39]   See paras 8.214–8.217.

[40]   Limitation Act 1980, s 29(5); *In Re Hale* [1899] 2 Ch 107 under the then Statute of Limitations. Cf *Portman Building Society v Gallwey* [1955] 1 WLR 96, where payments by a person purporting to act as receiver, but who was not validly appointed, had no effect on the limitation period. The case suggests that a payment by a validly appointed receiver acting beyond his authority would suffice, contrary to the suggesting in *In Re Hale*. There is some uncertainty as to whether the receiver must be acting within the scope of his authority, or simply be validly appointed, in order for his acts to be effective. The authors suggest that the receiver must have actual or ostensible authority before any payment or acknowledgment by him could re-start time.

[41]   Assuming that the borrower is in possession and the receiver acts as the borrower's agent. Limitation Act 1980, s 29(2) only applies where the acknowledgement is made by the person in possession of the land. Section 29(3) also only applies to payments made by the person in possession of the land. No case discusses whether a receiver in possession as against the borrower would be in possession *qua* borrower for the purpose of this subsection because of the deemed agency.

[42]   This is discussed in detail in Chapter 7. *Cully v Parsons* [1923] 2 Ch 512 at 518. See, however, Chapters 5, 7 and 9 in relation to the lender's delegated power of leasing. The lender will be bound by a lease granted by the receiver under such a power because that is the statutory effect of the power.

[43]   See paras 7.49–7.57.

[44]   See para 6.7.

6.52   Similarly, the right to receive rents from sub-tenants is not assigned to the lender as a result of the appointment of a receiver because the receiver is the borrower's agent. In *Rhodes v Allied Dunbar Pension Services Ltd*,[45] a landlord was entitled to demand payment of rent directly from sub-tenants[46] when his lessee's leasehold property was subject to a receivership and the rent under that lease was unpaid. The receiver failed in his argument that the right to the sub-tenants' rent had been assigned to the lender by the crystallisation of floating charge, so the leaseholder no longer had a right to the rents, and the notices were ineffective.

Limits on the receiver's personal liability

6.53   A receiver who is the deemed agent of the borrower can choose whether to enter into contracts in the borrower's name, as deemed agent, or in his own name, which may be more appropriate in some circumstances.[47] If the receiver contracts in the borrower's name, then the borrower, not the receiver, will be liable on the contract, because of the agency. This has been extended, *qua* real agency, to other more complicated situations.

6.54   For example, a receiver who causes the borrower to breach a pre-existing contract is not liable for the tort of procuring or causing a breach of contract, because, as a result of the agency, his acts were acts of the borrower.[48]

6.55   In general, the receiver has no personal liability to pay rates,[49] even where the receiver has a right of possession in the mortgage covenants[50] and

---

[45]   [1989] 1 WLR 800.

[46]   Under Law of Distress Amendment Act 1908, s 6.

[47]   See *Edenwest Ltd v CMS Cameron McKenna (A Firm)* [2012] EWHC 1258 (Ch) at [66]. In that case the receiver had entered into his own contract with solicitors for advice as to the receivership, which was appropriate so that they did not owe a conflicting duty of care to the borrower.

[48]   *Welsh Development Agency v Export Finance Co* [1992] BCC 270 at 287–288 and 295G relying on *Said v Butt* [1920] 3 KB 497 (but note that Dillon LJ doubted the reasoning and left open this rule being reversed by a higher court: at 288C–290A). The principle does not apply if the receiver did not act *bona fide* and within the scope of his authority: *Lathia v Dronsfield Bros* [1987] BCLC 321. See the commentary at para 8.9.

[49]   See for example *In Re Marriage, Neave & Co* [1896] 2 Ch 663, where there was no liability where the receiver entered the property to manage the business, but had no right to possession; and *Ratford v Northavon DC* [1987] 1 QB 357: receivers were appointed with powers to take possession of the charged property and to carry on and manage a company's business as deemed agents of the company. Slade LJ started from the proposition that 'a receiver appointed out of court ... in properly carrying out his functions, will ordinarily be under no personal liability' (at 371E). He would be acting as the deemed agent for the company, unless he was acting as agent for the debenture holder. An agent occupying property as part of his agency would not normally be liable for rates. See also *Rees v Boston BC* [2001] EWCA Civ 1934: a receiver simply carrying on the management of the company's business would not be in occupation for rating purposes. Note, however, that the effect of receivership of tax liability depends on the statute imposing that liability and the particular facts. See, for example, *Farnborough Airport Properties Company v HMRC* [2017] UKUT 394 (TCC) on group relief in corporation tax when a member of the group is subject to the appointment of receivers.

[50]   *Brown v City of London Corp* [1996] 1 WLR 1070 at 1082E. However, in that case, Arden J indicates (*obiter*) that a receiver who exercised his right of possession would become liable for rates, though this was a case in which that had not happened.

even if the borrower has become insolvent.[51] The lack of liability on the receiver for rates has been cited as an example of the reality of the agency.[52]

6.56   In principle, a receiver can be liable for rates if he is in independent possession to that of the borrower,[53] having dispossessed the borrower so that he occupied it as principal.[54]

6.57   However, even when the receiver takes possession, that may not amount to a change in occupier for rating purposes.[55] Whether or not it does depends on the quality of the possession. What has to be shown, for a change in rateable occupation to make the receiver liable, is that the quality of occupation was not that of a mere agent.

6.58   There is no modern case in which a receiver in possession has been held liable for rates. Such liability is, in the authors' view, only likely if possession has been taken from the borrower rather than a third party and the mortgage terms do not provide for the receiver to possess as the deemed agent of the borrower.[56]

6.59   Likewise, a receiver is not liable for capital gains tax (CGT) or income tax on the realisation of the borrower's property, by reason of his agency.[57]

---

[51]   *Rees v Boston BC* [2001] EWCA Civ 1934, [2002] 1 WLR 1304: the insolvency of the borrower does not end the receivership though it does terminate the deemed agency: see para 6.161 and the analysis which follows it.

[52]   *Silven Properties Ltd v Royal Bank of Scotland Plc* [2003] EWCA Civ 1409, [2004] 1 WLR 997 at [26].

[53]   *Ratford v Northavon DC* [1987] 1 QB 357 at 373C.

[54]   *Richards v Overseers of Kidderminster* [1896] 2 Ch 212, in which a receiver who had a right to possession and had taken possession was liable for rates. The ability of the receiver to take possession was said by North J to defeat the deemed agency even though the receiver's power to take possession was expressly as deemed agent. The decision might well be doubted now, since North J describes the receiver's occupation as being on behalf of the lender, which is not how more recent case law puts it. More recent case law rarely sees the receiver's acts as acts of the lender unless the lender has intermeddled. See also *Brown v City of London Corp* [1996] 1 WLR 1070, in which Arden J suggests this, *obiter*.

[55]   *Rees v Boston BC* [2001] EWCA Civ 1934, [2002] 1 WLR 1304 at [64]: 'there can be no change of rateable occupation by reason of acts done by a receiver within the scope of this authority since even if such acts amount to rateable occupation of the premises, the rateable occupation is that of the company and not of the receiver'.

[56]   Where the mortgage terms do provide for the possession to be as deemed agent of the borrower, the fact that possession has been taken from the borrower would not, in the authors' view, render the receiver liable. It is not impossible for a principal to give his agent power to do something instead of him, for example, under an irrevocable power of attorney, so that the agent could prevent the principal taking the step himself. It would not follow that the agent's agency was not real, though the effect was the dispossession of the principal. To the outside world, the effect of the deemed agency can be that the possession of the receiver is the possession of the borrower, just as the sale by the receiver can be the sale of the borrower though he would resist entry into the contract.

[57]   In *Re Piacentini* [2003] EWHC 113 (Admin), [2003] QB 1497, the court concluded that a court-appointed receiver was not liable for taxes such as CGT, on the basis that his liability was, by statute, the same as if he had been appointed out of court, and as a receiver appointed out of court is ordinarily the agent of borrower or lender, that receiver is not liable for tax (see especially [15]). Tax is discussed in more detail at paras 12.16–12.20.

6.60   It is likely that a receiver is not personally liable on other statutes imposing obligations on the borrower, for similar reasons, though each case will hinge on the wording of the particular statute.

Limits on receiver's powers

6.61   There are cases where the deemed agency of the receiver, treated just like 'real' agency, has led to an apparent limit in the receiver's powers. However, a number of decisions in later cases, even in lower courts, have endeavoured to confine them to their own specific facts in some way so as to treat receivers as having much wider powers.[58]

6.62   For example, in *Cretanor Maritime Co Ltd v Irish Marine Management Ltd*,[59] the Court of Appeal held that a receiver could not apply to discharge a freezing injunction over the charged property made against the borrower on the application of an unsecured creditor, although the secured lender could have, because the receiver was the deemed agent of the borrower.[60]

6.63   This does not mean that a receiver can never obtain the discharge of a freezing injunction. If the borrower could obtain the discharge, for example, by arguing that the appointment of the receivers negated the risk of dissipation of his assets, then the receiver can equally do so.[61]

Principles of real agency which do not apply to receivers

The receiver's duties to the borrower

6.64   A key difference between receivership and real agency is that a receiver does not have the duties of an agent to his principal. Although he does have duties,[62] they are quite unlike the duty of an agent to his principal.

---

[58]   See paras 6.148–6.155 and fn 61.

[59]   [1978] 1 WLR 966.

[60]   The suggestion that the receiver was able to get in the assets subject to prior contractual rights in *Cretanor Maritime Co Ltd v Irish Marine Management Ltd* [1978] 1 WLR 966 at 975 appears to be *per incuriam*: see the discussion at paras 8.6–8.9.

[61]   See, for example, *Capital Cameras Ltd v Harold Lines* [1991] 1 WLR 54, where the receiver's application to discharge a freezing injunction did succeed. The injunction was justified only while there was a real risk of dissipation of assets, and since the receivers were reputable insolvency practitioners, there was no longer such a risk once they had been appointed. Harman J in the High Court agreed with Buckley LJ's analysis, but disputed that *Cretanor Maritime Co Ltd v Irish Marine Management Ltd* [1978] 1 WLR 966 had laid down any general principle. It turned on its own facts. He can receive money and property and give good receipt for it. See paras 6.148–6.155 for further discussion of the receiver's powers contrary to the agency.

[62]   The equitable duties discussed below apply whether or not the receivership is statutory or express: *Yorkshire Bank Plc v Hall* [1999] 1 WLR 1713, quoted in *Medforth v Blake* [2000] Ch 86 at 98F.

To whom does the receiver owe duties?

6.65   The first difference between the duty of the receiver and the duty of a 'real agent' is the person to whom the duty is owed. Most agents owe duties to their principal and no one else.[63] The receiver does not owe duties to the borrower alone.

6.66   A receiver's principal duty is to the lender, to collect in the income to pay down the debt.[64]

6.67   The receiver also owes duties to anyone interested in the equity of redemption.[65] The receiver's duties are owed to the class of people so interested; he does not have a separate duty to each of the individuals in it. If the receiver breaches his duty, then he must account[66] not to the borrower as an individual, but to 'the persons interested in the equity of redemption for what he would have held as receiver but for his default'.[67]

6.68   Thus, the receiver does not owe duties of loyalty to the borrower, as a real agent would. The relationship is not one of trust and confidence. The receiver does not have a fiduciary duty to the borrower to avoid conflicts of interest. Nor is it his duty to carry out instructions from the borrower, to use reasonable care and skill or to exercise any discretion in the borrower's best interests.

---

[63]   Although it is not impossible to think of situations in which more complicated duties arise, where, for example, two principals have agreed that an agent should work for both of them, though they have potentially conflicting interests.

[64]   This is a separate and primary duty: see *Re B Johnson & Co (Builders) Ltd* [1955] Ch 634 at 661–662. The duty owed to the lender is considered at paras 7.19–7.24. Although the lender has no duty to any prior lender in deciding whether to appoint a receiver, the receiver must use the income he collects first to pay off any charged loans which have priority to the charge under which he has been appointed. Clearly, a prior chargeholder has an interest in the receivership of a subsequent mortgagee being carried out in good faith, and it has a property interest, though not in the equity of redemption. The case law on, for example, guarantors by analogy, suggests that this is enough for the imposition of an equitable duty. Although the authors do not know of any authority on the issue, it thus seems likely that the receiver (and, indeed, the subsequent lender) owes a like duty to any prior mortgagee.

[65]   See *Silven Properties Ltd v Royal Bank of Scotland Plc* [2003] EWCA Civ 1409, [2004] 1 WLR 997 at [27] for a clear exposition of the principles of the receiver's duty. *Silven* gives a good account more generally of the lender's and the receiver's respective duties. *Ahmad v Bank of Scotland* [2016] EWCA Civ 602 at [38] also sets out a helpful summary, adopted in *Centenary Homes Ltd v Gershinson*, 19 September 2017, unreported, QBD, at [29]. See also *Davey v Money* [2018] EWHC 766 (Ch). Although this is a case on administration, at [254] is a useful paragraph in which the difference between the duties in administration and receivership, in which the receiver is freer than an administrator, is summarised, and the discussion of the administrator's decisions could be taken as some illustration of the perhaps more limited duties of a receiver.

[66]   In the sense of the remedy of taking an account, i.e. setting out what he should have received in income, as well as in the sense of paying any difference between the sums received and the sums he should have received to the persons interested in the equity of redemption.

[67]   *Silven Properties Ltd v Royal Bank of Scotland Plc* [2003] EWCA Civ 1409, [2004] 1 WLR 997 at [27]. See also *Parker-Tweedale v Dunbar Bank Plc* [1991] Ch 12 as to like duties on the lender.

The class of people with an interest in the equity of redemption

6.69   Someone has an interest in the equity of redemption if they are interested in the mortgaged property, so that they are interested in its return free of the charge.[68]

6.70   The persons interested in the equity of redemption clearly include the borrower,[69] but only so long as his estate remains vested in him, because once he has lost that he has no interest in the equity of redemption.

6.71   Thus the original borrower, if an individual, is no longer in the class if he is made bankrupt, as his estate would vest immediately in the Official Receiver and then in the trustee in bankruptcy once appointed.[70] It is the trustee who would be in the class of people to whom the receiver would owe a duty. This is even though the borrower remains liable personally on the debt secured by the mortgage until he is discharged from the bankruptcy.[71] The reason is that the borrower retains no estate in the mortgaged property[72] and hence has no interest in the equity of redemption. Whether or not the mortgage is redeemed, the property will not be returned to the borrower but to the proprietor of it, the trustee in bankruptcy or his successor.[73]

6.72   The class of people interested in the equity of redemption includes any subsequent mortgagees.[74]

6.73   Other chargeholders, for example, those of equitable charges of the various kinds, are also interested in the equity of redemption on the first charge.

6.74   The class also includes the owner A of properties charged to B, whose charge is charged to C, when C appoints receivers over B's charges and sells A's properties under B's power of sale.[75] The receivers appointed by C have a duty to A since A has an interest in the equity of redemption.[76]

---

[68]   The nature of the equity of redemption is discussed at paras 2.15–2.18 and 2.29.

[69]   But not the beneficiary under a trust of the mortgaged property: *Parker-Tweedale v Dunbar Bank Plc* [1991] Ch 12 at 19D in relation to the lender's duty. Not does it include a tenant at will since he has no interest in the proceeds of sale of the mortgaged property: *Jarrett v Barclays Bank Ltd* [1947] Ch 187.

[70]   Insolvency Act 1986, ss 291A and 306.

[71]   *Purewal v Countrywide Residential Lettings Ltd* [2015] EWCA Civ 1122, [2016] 4 WLR 31.

[72]   Although it may revert to him under Insolvency Act 1986, in which case he would return to the class of people interested in the equity of redemption.

[73]   *Purewal v Countrywide Residential Lettings Ltd* [2015] EWCA Civ 1122, [2016] 4 WLR 31 at [18].

[74]   Their interests are interests in the equity of redemption. If one were to think of mortgages as leases, subsequent mortgages would be granted by the borrower as if concurrent leases between the borrower's interest and the first lender's lease. They would fall to be redeemed with any surplus income after payment of the first lender. See *Downsview Nominees Ltd v First City Corp Ltd* [1993] AC 295; *Midland Bank Ltd v Joliman Finance Ltd* [1967] 203 EG 1039.

[75]   *Raja v Austin Gray (a firm)* [2002] EWCA Civ 1965, [2003] BPIR 725.

[76]   *Raja v Austin Gray (a firm)* [2002] EWCA Civ 1965, [2003] BPIR 725 at [28]. It is not clear from the reasoning that Clarke LJ had distinguished between the equity of redemption in A's

6.75   The receiver's duty is also owed to the guarantor of a mortgage because 'the guarantor is liable only to the same extent as the [borrower]. The more the overdraft is reduced, the better for the guarantor'.[77] Although that is true, this justification for the imposition of a duty does not sit well with *Purewal v Countrywide Residential Lettings Ltd*,[78] because a bankrupt is equally interested in the amount of realisations that the receiver is able to make, and yet no duty is owed to the bankrupt. Moreover, the guarantor does not have an interest in the equity of redemption in the sense discussed in *Purewal*.

6.76   The better explanation for the receiver's duty to the guarantor is that the guarantor who makes payment under the guarantee would acquire the security for the debt under the doctrine of subrogation under section 5 of the Mercantile Law Amendment Act 1856.[79]

6.77   In *Knight v Lawrence*,[80] Browne-Wilkinson V-C decided that the receiver's duty in managing property A was owed to Mrs Knight, a joint borrower and co-owner of property B charged under the same charge as the charge of A, even though she had no proprietary interest in it and hence was not interested in the equity of redemption in A. The reason was that the receiver's management could reduce the debt.[81] Thus, his duty in managing one property was owed to all the borrowers.

6.78   The explanation is similar to that in *Standard Chartered Bank v Walker*[82] and is unsatisfactory since it imposes a duty on the receiver managing a property to someone without an interest in its equity of redemption.

---

    properties versus the equity of redemption in B's charge. If one thinks of the charges as a chain of leases, with A having the reversion on a lease to B, and B having granted a sub-lease to C, then A is in a similar position to someone with a second charge. The receivers appointed by C would have a duty to A in those circumstances.

[77]   *Standard Chartered Bank Ltd v Walker* [1982] 1 WLR 1410 especially at 1415H. This case was about whether the defendant guarantor should have been given leave to defend, i.e. whether his defence that the receiver owed him a duty had reasonable prospects of success. It is cited as authority for the proposition that a guarantor is owed duties by the receiver, but it is not decide more than that the argument he did had reasonable prospects. The decision in *Walker* was considered positively in the QBD in *American Express International Banking Corp v Hurley* [1985] 3 All ER 564 despite it being argued that its decision showed no more than the existence of the duty was arguable. See also *China and Southsea Bank Ltd v Tan* [1990] 1 AC 536 at 544: equity intervenes to protect a surety; *Barclays Bank Plc v Kingston* [2006] EWHC 533 (QB): a creditor owes a duty to a guarantor, if he sells the security for the debt, to do so at a proper price.

[78]   [2015] EWCA Civ 1122, [2016] 4 WLR 31.

[79]   *Burgess v Auger* [1998] 2 BCLC 478, though in that case the guarantor had made no payment and the claim against him was statute barred.

[80]   [1991] BCC 411.

[81]   *Knight v Lawrence* [1991] BCC 411 at 417E. But see *Jarrett v Barclays Bank Ltd* [1947] Ch 187, in which someone jointly liable for the mortgage debt without a proprietary interest in it was found without standing to complain of sale by a lender at an undervalue.

[82]   [1982] 1 WLR 1410.

6.79   In *Knight v Lawrence*,[83] however, the receiver was the deemed agent of both borrowers, and his receivership was over all of the properties, so that the joint borrower, Mrs Knight, had an interest in the equity of redemption of some of the properties under receivership. The issue was whether the receiver should have operated the rent review provisions in a lease to which one of the properties was subject. He owed his duty to do so to all the borrowers regardless of whether or not they had interests in the property subject to that lease. The explanation might be that he had a duty to Mrs Knight in managing property B because she had an interest in the equity of redemption of property B, and that that duty encompassed management of property A since the receiver's decisions about property B were contingent on his decisions about property B, and vice versa.

6.80   The receiver does not owe a duty to the directors or other officers, nor to the members, of a company borrower unless any of those persons have an interest in the equity of redemption.[84] Nor does he owe duties to the unsecured creditors of the borrower.[85]

When the duties arise

6.81   Although the receiver's duties are similar to the lender's, the receiver's duties are different from the lender's in that they arise immediately on his appointment. A lender has no duty to exercise his power to sell, to take possession or to appoint a receiver. 'He is entitled to remain totally passive',[86] and need not consider anybody but its own interests in deciding whether to act.[87]

6.82   Conversely, the receiver, once appointed, 'has no right to remain passive if that course would be damaging to the interests of the mortgagor or mortgagee'.[88] Thus, a receiver has no general duty to exercise a power of sale,

---

[83]   [1991] BCC 411.

[84]   *Burgess v Auger* [1998] 2 BCLC 478 (but see *Barclays Bank Plc v Kingston* [2006] EWHC 533 (QB), which distinguished its decision that no duty was owed by a receiver to a guarantor because in *Burgess* the guarantor shareholder had not paid any of the debt and the lender's claim against him was statute barred). See also *Yorkshire Bank Plc v Hall* [1999] 1 WLR 1713: a secure lender has no duty to shareholders. It likely follows that a receiver has no such duty.

[85]   *Lathia v Dronsfield Bros Ltd* [1987] BCLC 321 at 324, approved in *International Leisure Ltd v First National Trustee Ltd* [2012] EWHC 1971 (Ch), [2013] Ch 346 at [32]; *Alpstream AG v AK Airfinance Sarl* [2015] EWCA Civ 1318 (in relation to the lender's duties).

[86]   *Silven Properties Ltd v Royal Bank of Scotland Plc* [2003] EWCA Civ 1409, [2004] 1 WLR 997 at [13].

[87]   However, once the lender has taken possession it assumes a duty to take reasonable care of the mortgaged property: *Downsview Nominees Ltd v First City Corp Ltd* [1993] AC 295 at 315a, which requires him to take active steps to protect and exploit the security, maximising the return, but without taking undue risks: *Palk v Mortgage Services Funding Plc* [1993] Ch 330 at 338a, both quoted in *Silven Properties Ltd v Royal Bank of Scotland Plc* [2003] EWCA Civ 1409, [2004] 1 WLR 997 at [13].

[88]   *Silven Properties Ltd v Royal Bank of Scotland Plc* [2003] EWCA Civ 1409, [2004] 1 WLR 997 at [23]. This is reminiscent of a real agent's duty of due diligence, though it is more likely it comes from the lender's duties when in possession referred to in fn 87.

unless his failure to do so would result in loss, but if he has the power of sale, he should consider whether to exercise it.

The nature of the duty owed to the borrower

6.83   The receiver's duty is one imposed by equity only, as the lender's duty is.[89]

6.84   Although the content of the duty has been said to be little different to a common law duty of care,[90] cases in which the receiver's duty has been described as in negligence, or based on the neighbour principle,[91] have been since said to be wrong in so describing it.[92]

6.85   The duty has also been described as fiduciary,[93] but since the receiver's first duty is to the lender to get in the property to pay down the debt, and his secondary duty is owed to a class of people, rather than a single person, it is not at all similar to the fiduciary duty of an agent to his principal. It is not the receiver's duty to carry out instructions from the borrower. Nor is it his duty to use reasonable care and skill, nor to exercise any discretion in the borrower's best interests.

6.86   Moreover, it is not, unlike most agency relationships, imposed by a contract between principal and agent. The receiver's duty is not an implied term of the mortgage conditions.[94]

6.87   It is unlikely that it would be possible to exclude the duty by express words in the mortgage covenants.[95]

What is the duty?

6.88   The receiver's primary duty in exercising his powers is a duty owed to the lender 'to try and bring about a situation in which the secured debt is

---

[89]   *Medforth v Blake* [2000] Ch 86 at 101H.

[90]   *Medforth v Blake* [2000] Ch 86 at 102D.

[91]   Lord Denning in *Standard Chartered Bank Ltd v Walker* [1982] 1 WLR 1410, for example, bases his analysis on the neighbour principle. See also *American Express International Banking Corp v Hurley* [1985] 3 All ER 564 in which the duty was said to be negligence.

[92]   *Parker-Tweedale v Dunbar Bank Plc* [1991] Ch 12 at 18C–H, in relation to the lender's duty. See also *Downsview Nominees Ltd v First City Corp Ltd* [1993] AC 295, in which a prior lender and its receiver's duty to a subsequent lender was said not to be in tort and not to be a duty to use reasonable care, but rather, an equitable duty to exercise their powers in good faith for the purpose of obtaining repayment.

[93]   For example, in argument in *Downsview Nominees Ltd v First City Corp Ltd* [1993] AC 295; in the decision it was described as imposed by equity.

[94]   There is no contract between the receiver and the borrower, let alone between the receiver and others interested in the equity of redemption. In any event, a lender's like duties are not contractual: *Raja v Lloyds TSB Bank Plc* [2001] EWCA Civ 210, where this point is made in relation to the lender's duties.

[95]   *Bishop v Bonham* [1988] 1 WLR 742.

repaid'.[96] The receiver 'is not managing the mortgagor's property for the benefit of the mortgagor, but the security, the property of the mortgagee, for the benefit of the mortgagee'.[97] It is not his role to benefit the borrower.

6.89 Subject to that primary duty to bring about repayment of the interest and the debt, the receiver's duty to those interested in the equity of redemption includes a duty of good faith,[98] so that were the receiver to act fraudulently or with *mala fide*, he would be in breach.[99] Bad faith does not require dishonesty.[100] The receiver's duty, like the lender's, is to exercise his powers in good faith for the purpose of obtaining repayment.[101]

6.90 The origin of both lender's and receiver's duties is the same, in equity.[102] Thus case law on the lender's duties can thus be indicative of likely receiver's duties.[103] Like the lender, the receiver is not allowed to act so as unfairly to prejudice the borrower.

6.91 However, the duty on the receiver goes further than the lender's since the lender, unless in possession, is under no duty to take active steps in relation to the property.[104] The receiver has a duty to manage the property with

---

[96] *Silven Properties Ltd v Royal Bank of Scotland Plc* [2003] EWCA Civ 1409, [2004] 1 WLR 997 at [27]; *Medforth v Blake* [2000] Ch 86. See paras 7.19–7.24. A borrower alleging a receiver's breach of duty to him must identify a duty to him not in conflict with the receiver's duty to the lender. He cannot rely on evidence of an alternative decision of benefit to the borrower to that made by the receiver as defining the duty he relies on and evidence of the breach: *Centenary Homes Ltd v Gershinson*, 19 September 2017, unreported, QBD, at [35]–[36].

[97] *Silven Properties Ltd v Royal Bank of Scotland Plc* [2003] EWCA Civ 1409, [2004] 1 WLR 997 at [27]; and see *B Johnson & Co (Builders) Ltd* [1955] Ch 634 at 661 and 646; *Downsview Nominees Ltd v First City Corp Ltd* [1993] AC 295 at 313B (a New Zealand case of the PC); *Medforth v Blake* [2000] Ch 86 at 95H–96A.

[98] *Medforth v Blake* [2000] Ch 86, where it was common ground that there was a duty of good faith. The lender is under a similar duty: see at 100H, quoting *Kennedy v De Trafford* [1897] AC 180.

[99] *Mogridge v Clapp* [1892] 3 Ch 382 at 391: good faith, or *bona fide*, is an absence of bad faith.

[100] *Horn v Commercial Acceptances Ltd* [2011] EWHC 1757 (Ch) at [76].

[101] *Downsview Nominees Ltd v First City Corp Ltd* [1993] AC 295 at 296. Purity of purpose is not necessary: *Meretz Investments NV v ACP Ltd* [2006] EWHC 74 (Ch) (overturned on a different point on appeal in [2007] EWCA Civ 1303, [2008] Ch 244). The receiver's duties on sale are considered at paras 11.174–11.178.

[102] *Medforth v Blake* [2000] Ch 86 at 101H.

[103] See a useful summary of the lender's duties to the borrower in *Saltri III Ltd v MD Mezzanine Sa Sicar* [2012] EWHC 3025 (Comm) at [127] and [128]. A receiver in possession of the mortgaged property will likely have similar duties to the lender's to take reasonable care of it, including a duty to carry out reasonable repairs. Note, however, that a statutory receiver of income only cannot recover the cost of repairs from the income unless the lender agreed to the works: Law of Property Act 1925, s 109(8)(iii). See paras 12.57–12.58.

[104] *Silven Properties Ltd v Royal Bank of Scotland Plc* [2003] EWCA Civ 1409, [2004] 1 WLR 997 at [13]. Nor is the lender under a duty to enforce. His rights of enforcement are the result of the borrower's bargain with him on entering into the mortgage, and the lender can choose whether and when to enforce by consulting his own interests: at [14]. The receiver in contrast has a duty to pay down the mortgage.

due diligence.[105] Moreover, he must use the income he receives in the way required by section 109 of the Law of Property Act 1925, or any express variation to it in the mortgage conditions.[106]

6.92   A receiver's duties remain limited; a receiver is not required to protect the borrower's interests. For example, the receiver owes no duty to the borrower not to place it in breach of pre-existing contracts.[107] The principal focus is repayment of the debt, and more extensive duties could conflict with that focus. Just like a lender, a receiver is thus not required to spend money in the attempt to repay the debt.

6.93   For the same reason, as his primary duty, the receiver is not required to follow instructions from the borrower.

6.94   The extent of the duty of care on the receiver in equity depends on all of the circumstances of the case. The question to be asked is 'What standard of conduct in all the circumstances does the law require of the receiver managing the mortgaged properties?'.[108]

Examples of the receiver's duties

6.95   The following are examples of the receiver's duties to those interested in the equity of redemption in various specific contexts which have arisen in case law:[109]

(a)   A receiver need not carry on the business of the borrower,[110] but if he does, he must take reasonable steps to try to do so profitably.[111]

(b)   A receiver of mortgaged property which is let has a duty to read the lease and to trigger an upwards only rent review if otherwise the value of the property would be adversely affected.[112]

(c)   A receiver can only sell to a company in which he is interested if he takes reasonable precautions to obtain the best price reasonably obtainable at the time of sale.[113]

---

[105]   *Silven Properties Ltd v Royal Bank of Scotland Plc* [2003] EWCA Civ 1409, [2004] 1 WLR 997 at [23]. It might be said that the receiver has a general duty to consider whether and how to use his powers. In the context of sale, see para 11.175 and Chapter 11, fn 199.

[106]   This is discussed in detail in Chapter 12.

[107]   See paras 8.7–8.9.

[108]   *Medforth v Blake* [2000] Ch 86 at 99G.

[109]   See also Chapter 11 on sale, where the receiver's duties on sale are discussed at paras 11.174–11.178.

[110]   Assuming the mortgage conditions and appointment give him that power.

[111]   *Medforth v Blake* [2000] Ch 86, a case about a pig farm.

[112]   *Knight v Lawrence* [1991] BCC 411. That claim was made against the receivers, successfully, in negligence, but is said in *Medforth v Blake* [2000] Ch 86 at 99G that it should have been a claim for breach of the duty in equity.

[113]   *Medforth v Blake* [2000] Ch 86 at 99D, *obiter*, applying to receivers the decision as to similar sales by a lender, in *Tse Kwong Lam v Wong Chit Sen* [1983] 1 WLR 1349.

(d) A receiver may be in breach of his duties if he fails to take specialist advice, for example on valuation, where he is not a specialist in the property to be sold and it has special features,[114] or if he did not advertise the property in specialist press.[115]

(e) A receiver would be liable (to the borrower) for a misstatement in auction particulars.[116]

(f) A receiver is under no common law duty[117] to notify the borrower that he intends to take possession of the mortgaged property against occupiers, even if these are tenants or licensees of the borrower.[118]

(g) A receiver may be liable to the borrower for the negligence of his agent, even though his own duty to the borrower is the lesser obligation of good faith.[119]

Remedies for breach of duty

RELEVANCE OF THE LENDER'S CLAIM

6.96   The receiver owes duties not only to the borrower and those interested in the equity of redemption, but also to the lender. The receiver's duty to the lender is the primary duty.[120] The duties are similar. It follows that if the receiver has breached its duty to the borrower, then it is likely he has breached his duty to the lender. Although it appears both claims can be made concurrently,[121] the lender's claim for breach of duty is primary, and the

---

[114] *American Express International Banking Corp v Hurley* [1985] 3 All ER 564.

[115] *American Express International Banking Corp v Hurley* [1985] 3 All ER 564, where the property for sale was specialist machinery.

[116] *Medforth v Blake* [2000] Ch 86 at 99F, *obiter*, applying to receivers the decision as to similar sales by a lender, in *Tomlin v Luce* (1889) 43 ChD 191.

[117] It is possible he will have an express obligation to do so in the mortgage conditions.

[118] *JL Homes Ltd v Mortgage Express and Diakiw and Heap* [2013] EWHC 3928 (Ch).

[119] In *Cuckmere Brick Co Ltd v Mutual Finance Ltd* [1971] 1 Ch 949, the court considered whether a lender has liability to the borrower for negligence of its agent (rather than just the agent's wilful default which would amount to a breach of good faith). Cross LJ at 973E said, *obiter*, it would, based on earlier case law likely decided before the law of negligence was developed in relation to third party claims, but the point was not decided since it had been conceded. Sir Richard Scott V-C suggested that the same reasoning would likely apply to receivership in *Medforth v Blake* [2000] Ch 86 at 99F. In *Raja v Austin Gray (A Firm)* [2002] EWCA Civ 1965, [2003] BPIR 725 at [34]–[35], it was decided that a receiver could not avoid liability to the borrower for the negligent act of his agent on a sale; the reasoning was a passage in G Lightman and G Moss (eds), *Lightman & Moss on The Law of Receivers and Administrators of Companies* (Sweet & Maxwell, 3rd edn, 2000). Nothing about the statutory scheme of receivership in Law of Property Act 1925 suggests that a receiver is not entitled to employ agents in the performance of his duties, and his ability to do so has been assumed in cases, and is likely an incident of those powers, especially for example in litigation which would usually require employment of solicitors. It is unlikely that an express receivership would be interpreted as preventing the receiver from acting through agents save possibly in executing deeds for example in the name of the borrower.

[120] *International Leisure Ltd v First National Trustee Ltd* [2012] EWHC 1971 (Ch), [2013] Ch 346 at [28], for example. See Chapter 7 and paras 7.19–7.24.

[121] *International Leisure Ltd v First National Trustee Ltd* [2012] EWHC 1971 (Ch), [2013] Ch 346 at [36] *et seq*. That was an appeal of a decision to strike out the lender's claim because the

lender has the primary entitlement to that portion of the damages representing its loss.[122]

EQUITABLE PRINCIPLES

6.97   *Knight v Lawrence*[123] is one of the few cases to discuss remedy for breach of the receiver's duties to the borrower and those with an interest in the equity of redemption. The receiver was found to have breached that duty by failing to exercise a rent review.

6.98   However, the court's analysis of the receiver's duty was as if it was a duty of care in negligence, though there is little discussion of whether this is the correct analysis. For example, the court talks of the neighbourhood principle,[124] which it has been suggested is not the correct understanding of the receiver's duty,[125] and the possibility of contributory negligence by the borrower is discussed[126] and, on the facts, rejected.

6.99   As set out above, later case law has identified the duty as one in equity and not negligence.[127] Thus the principles to be applied are equitable and not tortious.

6.100   Since there is little case law, the principles set out below are those common to equity, in part by reference to a claim for breach of fiduciary duty, since that duty is owed by agents to their principals, though taking into account the differences between the deemed agency of a receiver and real agency.

6.101   The most common equitable remedies in principle available for a breach by the receiver of his duty to the persons in the class are an account,[128] equitable compensation for any loss caused to those persons by reason of a breach of the duty and injunctive relief to prevent acts in breach of duty.

---

borrower had also claimed. What is not discussed is whether the borrower's claim for the whole of the damages should be struck out if: (a) no lender's claim has been brought; or (b) when there is a concurrent lender's claim, though at [51] it is stated that the borrower's claim will only be for any sums exceeding the lender's damages. Presumably, if the borrower succeeds on a claim for the whole of the damages, the lender's charge will attach to it. Many mortgages would make this express.

[122]   *International Leisure Ltd v First National Trustee Ltd* [2012] EWHC 1971 (Ch), [2013] Ch 346 at [52] and in the headnote. See also *Meretz Investments NV v ACP Ltd* [2006] EWHC 74 (Ch) at [292], which suggests that the measure of damages in a claim for breach of duty by a second mortgagee against the first is limited by the extent of the second mortgagee's security.

[123]   [1991] BCC 411.

[124]   [1991] BCC 411 at 417.

[125]   See *Parker-Tweedale v Dunbar Bank Plc* [1991] Ch 12 at 18C–H; *Medforth v Blake* [2000] Ch 86.

[126]   [1991] BCC 411 at 418.

[127]   See fn 92.

[128]   In the sense of the remedy of taking an account, i.e. setting out what he should have received in income, as well as in the sense of paying any difference between the sums received and the sums the receiver should have received to the persons interested in the equity of redemption.

6.102 Unlike damages remedies in contractual or tortious claims, all of the remedies available to a borrower or anyone else interested in the equity of redemption based on breach of duty by a receiver are equitable, and hence the court has a discretion in equity whether to award the remedy even if the breach is made out, and perhaps more flexibility in fashioning a remedy to the circumstances of the case.

6.103 The claim of a breach of duty by the receiver is made not for the benefit of the borrower alone. The duty is owed to everyone with an interest in the equity of redemption. Any remedy is awarded for the benefit of the class. This may affect the award of a remedy.

6.104 That the claim is for the benefit of the whole class of those interested in the equity of redemption might also affect the willingness of the court to award a remedy in a claim by the borrower without reassurance that the borrower would himself account for that benefit to the others in the class or the joinder of the others into the action. For example, a court might well be unwilling to order payment of equitable compensation direct to a borrower when a guarantor also stood to have lost from a breach of duty by the receiver selling at an undervalue where the sale price was not sufficient to pay off the debt.[129]

AN ACCOUNT

6.105 The first remedy mentioned in para 6.101, an account, is a remedy which allows the borrower, with the assistance of the court, to determine what income or purchase monies the receiver has received and on what he has spent that money. This is likely to assist him in identifying from the information provided as to what has been done, whether any steps have been in breach of duty.

6.106 Anyone in the class of people interested in the equity of redemption is entitled to such an account[130] unless the account has been settled, for example, by the borrower settling with the lender the amount owed under the mortgage after the receiver's appointment has ended.

6.107 The process of the account is a little like a detailed assessment of costs in that the receiver will submit verified accounts and documents in support, and the borrower can then raise objections to particular items. The court will then determine if those objections are made out, applying, where appropriate, the terms of section 109 of the Law of Property Act 1925 and/or the covenants

---

[129] Likewise, the court might be concerned that compensation/damages should be directed to the lender, to the extent of the shortfall, not the borrower. See *International Leisure Ltd v First National Trustee Ltd* [2012] EWHC 1971 (Ch), [2013] Ch 346, discussed at para 6.96 and fn 121.

[130] An account is often sought when the mortgage is redeemed, if there is a dispute about the redemption figure. See Chapter 2.

in the mortgage which determine what (e.g. of a receiver's expenses) can be added to the account and what cannot.

EQUITABLE COMPENSATION

6.108 More generally, if the receiver is in breach of duty and that breach has caused a reduction in the value of the equity of redemption, then the receiver could be ordered to pay equitable compensation, as part of the account, so as to make up the difference. The test for causation is likely 'but for': but for the breach of duty, the diminution in value would not have occurred. It is likely that the burden of proof that diminution has been caused is on the person claiming it.

6.109 Quantum, in assessing compensation for a breach of the receiver's duty, is likely[131] to be measured by the difference between the value of the equity of redemption had the duty not been breached as against its value given the breach.[132] This accords with the principles for breach by a lender of its equitable duties and the general principles for the quantification of damages in contractual and tortious cases.

6.110 Thus, where the breach is having failed to advertise prior to selling the mortgaged property, the difference would be between the sale price which could have been achieved had there been an advertisement, compared to the price achieved.

6.111 This approach to quantum seems to have been the one followed in *Knight v Lawrence*,[133] although the discussion there was centred on the specific facts of the case, rather than the principles which might be applied.

6.112 The receiver will usually only be required to pay equitable compensation if the breach has resulted in a loss. Not every wrong changes the position of the class of people with an interest in the equity of redemption. For example, a failure to advertise planning permission already obtained

---

[131] Equitable compensation is, however, more flexible than damages in tort and contract. It may seek to remedy a breach even if there would be no compensation were a contractual or tortious analysis of damages used. Reparative compensation (to compensate actual loss to a fund or a person) and substitutive compensation (the equivalent of a lost asset which may not be the same for example if there is no causation of loss; this includes a requirement on a fiduciary to disgorge his profits, for example to account for property he acquired via his principal's property even though the principal did not wish to acquire it: *Boardman v Phipps* [1967] 2 AC 46) are both available. See J McGhee (ed), *Snell's Equity* (Sweet & Maxwell, 33rd edn, 2017), for example, for a discussion.

[132] See, for example, *Downsview Nominees Ltd v First City Corp Ltd* [1993] AC 295, the damages due to the second mortgagee from the first and its receiver for wrongly displacing its receiver were the difference between what would have been recovered by the second lender had the original receivership proceeded undisturbed, and the amount actually recovered. See *Meretz Investments NV v ACP Ltd* [2006] EWHC 74 (Ch) at [305]. Evidence of loss should be given: see *Investec Bank (Channel Islands) Ltd v Kamyab*, 28 January 2014, unreported, QBD, for an example of the loss of a case where there was a failure to do so.

[133] [1991] BCC 411.

might be a breach of the receiver's duties without loss, if the evidence was that in the circumstances there was little chance that on sale a greater price would have been obtained.

6.113 The reason for the use of 'usually' in the paragraph above is that it is unclear whether a receiver could be ordered to pay out any profits he had personally made from the charged property whether or not there was a loss in the value of the equity of redemption.

6.114 The court could certainly order the receiver to pay equitable compensation or to pay into the mortgage account[134] any profits he has made himself in breach of duty, for example, by purchasing the charged property at an undervalue and then selling it on at profit, if the transaction in question could not be undone. The reason for this is that the taking of a profit would have caused a loss.

6.115 However, it is not obvious that the remedy of an account of profits would be available against a receiver if there was no loss, i.e. that a receiver could be required by the court to pay out any profits he had made which had not caused loss to the equity of redemption.

6.116 An account of profits is available against an agent since he has fiduciary duties, including duties of loyalty to his principal, and should not make personal profits out of his principal's property without his consent.

6.117 A receiver does not owe a duty of loyalty to the borrower, or those with an interest in the equity of redemption, so it is doubtful whether the disgorgement of profits would be required. If the receiver bought the property, paying market value for it, but then later sold it for profit, it is not obvious he should be made to account for that sum.

INJUNCTIVE RELIEF

6.118 Injunctive relief can, in principle, be sought by the borrower, and anyone else with an interest in the equity of redemption, to prevent a transaction such as a sale by the receiver in breach of duty,[135] for example, on a sale in a particular forum – such as a private sale rather than a sale by auction, or a sale without advertising planning permission already acquired – were a case for a breach made out.

---

[134] If the mortgage has not been discharged.

[135] See *Watts v Midland Bank* (1986) 2 BCC 98961 in which Peter Gibson J suggested, by reference to *Newhart Developments Ltd v Co-operative Commercial Bank Ltd* [1978] 1 QB 814, that proper exercise by a receiver of a power of sale cannot be interfered with by the borrower, but that it is common sense that the borrower can seek to restrain an improper act even during his appointment, just as a liquidator of a company borrower could so sue: at 98967. However, there is one way in which the borrower can interfere with a proper exercise of power by the receiver: he could apply under Law of Property Act 1925, s 91: see *National Westminster Bank Plc v Hunter* [2011] EWHC 3170 (Ch), and Chapters 2 and 11.

6.119 The test for the court in exercising its equitable discretions on both an interim application of this kind, and also finally at trial, are common to litigation more generally.[136]

6.120 For the court to grant an injunction at trial, the borrower must have a cause of action, i.e. he must show that the receiver is in breach of duty.[137]

6.121 Likewise, at the interim injunction stage, it must be satisfied that there is a serious issue to be tried that there is such a breach. Then the court must consider the balance of convenience.[138] If the borrower cannot give an adequate cross-undertaking, and there is insufficient equity in the property, it is likely to be difficult for such a claim to succeed, although the remedy would no doubt be available on suitable facts.[139]

RESCISSION

6.122 The position of the borrower and the others in the class of persons with an interest in the equity of redemption if the receiver has already contracted to sell the property in breach of duty is more difficult.[140] Equity has a remedy of rescission exercisable by the court.[141] However, it is not obvious whether a borrower has standing to call for it.

6.123 Rescission is available to a principal whose agent has sold property in breach of fiduciary duty, for example, by selling to himself or an associate at an undervalue. Yet that is not obviously available to a borrower on a receiver's sale because the borrower does not have the power to control the

---

[136] See Chapter 14 for a more general discussion on litigation. See Chapter 8 (receiver's relationship with third parties) and Chapter 11 (sale) for a discussion of injunctions against receivers in the context of sale.

[137] *Watts v Midland Bank* (1986) 2 BCC 98961, and see fn 135.

[138] As for the other parts of the test, for example, where the receiver intends to sell, the question of whether damages would be an adequate remedy for the borrower will depend in the commercial context on whether its sale would devastate the business, and in the residential whether the borrower will be homeless; the borrower if impecunious may well not be able to give an undertaking in damages; the balance of convenience may well rest, as it did in *J&N Cowden LLP v Ulster Bank Ltd* [2014] NIQB 138, on whether the loan is being repaid and/or the equity in the property thus whether there is likely to be a shortfall on repayment of the loan if the sale is delayed.

[139] In *Watts v Midland Bank* (1986) 2 BCC 98961, an interim injunction sought by borrower to prevent completion of a sale under a contract made by the receiver on the basis, they said, that the contract had been made in breach of duty, was both because the case on breach was weak, but also that damages would be an adequate remedy. *J&N Cowden LLP v Ulster Bank Ltd* [2014] NIQB 138, where there was an interim injunction application by the borrower and the guarantor against the lender and the receiver from dealing with the mortgaged property on the basis that there was a serious issue as to the meaning of the breach provisions in the mortgage conditions, and hence whether the receiver could properly be appointed. This was a case not on breach of receiver's duty, but on the validity of the appointment.

[140] See the discussion in Chapter 8 and at para 11.41.

[141] Unlike the common law rescission available in contract, for example, which is an election by one party to the contract allowed in various circumstances.

receiver's acts. A validly appointed receiver with a power of sale can sell in the borrower's name whatever the borrower's wishes, and the borrower, under suitably worded mortgage covenants, will have given all his powers to sell away.[142]

6.124 The answer may well be that the court would have the power to rescind a sale entered into by the receiver in breach of duty, in particular if it was entered into fraudulently or *mala fide*, so as to give the receiver a profit, for example, by selling knowingly at an undervalue to himself or an associate so as to generate a profit. The court might well do so in order to protect the equity of redemption.

6.125 If rescission were possible as a matter of principle, then the court would apply usual principles in determining whether rescission was available, for example, whether the borrower had affirmed the contract for sale prior to the application, and whether the parties (including any third party buyer in a sale, for example) can be restored to their positions before the contract. A court might well conclude that the more appropriate remedy would be an award of equitable compensation against the receiver.

Defences to a claim for breach of duty

6.126 The first defence that may be available is that the receiver has already accounted for damages on a claim by the lender for breach of his duty to the lender, and that that extinguishes or reduces the borrower's claim.[143]

6.127 In principle, the usual equitable defences may be available to the receiver: delay, waiver and, to the extent discussed below, contributory fault.

6.128 In *Knight v Lawrence*,[144] the court considered and dismissed on the facts a defence by the receiver of contributory negligence by the claimant. However, the court did not consider the question of principle as to whether contributory negligence is an available defence in a claim based on breach of a receiver's duties. Since the duty is equitable, not tortious, it is not obvious that contributory negligence is an available defence in the way it would be available in a negligence claim.

6.129 Contributory fault would not be available in a claim by a principal against his agent for breach of fiduciary duty where that breach was based on

---

[142] The court will not interfere with a proper exercise of the receiver's discretion (see below and paras 8.19–8.34 and paras 11.43–11.53 for the position where a third party seeks specific performance of the borrower's contract), save in exercise of its discretion under Law of Property Act 1925, s 91, though that would likely be rare: see Chapters 2 and 11 for a discussion of this provision.

[143] I.e. by reducing the shortfall in the debt. The borrower could not receive for a second time damages for the sums for which he had obtained credit due to sums paid to the lender being applied to reduce his account.

[144] [1991] BCC 411.

conscious disloyalty by the agent, for example, in diverting a principal's property to himself.

6.130 The duty on the receiver is not a fiduciary one, however, and to the various extents discussed below and in the rest of this book, the appointment supplants the borrower's rights to deal with the mortgaged property,[145] for example, to let it or to collect income from it. Any action by the borrower, or anyone else interested in the equity of redemption, which interferes with the exercise by the receiver of his powers could well reduce the value of the equity of redemption itself, regardless of any breach of duty by the receiver.

6.131 It seems likely that contributory fault would not be an available defence for a receiver whose breach of duty was a fraudulent action, or action with *mala fide*, or was such as to give himself a profit, for example, by selling the property to himself at an undervalue.

6.132 Conversely, it is likely that equity would recognise contributory fault where the breach of duty by the receiver was not of those kinds and was more akin to a failure to use reasonable skill and care, for example, a failure to advertise, and where the borrower or other person with an interest in the equity of redemption had impeded the receiver.[146]

6.133 The availability of a defence of failure to mitigate loss may also depend on the particular circumstances in which the claim against the receiver arose. If the receiver is in breach of duty and the result is, for example, sale of the property at a lower value than it would have obtained if it had been properly advertised, then the purpose of the equitable compensation is to restore the value of the equity of redemption to what it should have been but for the breach.

6.134 In that case, a defence of failure to mitigate loss may well be available and appropriate, though it is hard to imagine what mitigation a borrower could have taken given that the appointment of the receiver has put the property and its management out of his hands.

6.135 If, however, the receiver's actions have resulted in a loss of the mortgaged property which should not have occurred, then the equitable compensation might be analysed as substitutive compensation, i.e. intended to represent a like benefit to the one lost.[147] In similar contexts, for example,

---

[145] See paras 6.148–6.155 on the receiver's power to control the borrower, Chapter 9 on collection of income and leasing, and Chapter 10 on possession.

[146] Although it might be that the better analysis was simply a lack of causation of all of the loss in those cases.

[147] A possible example is if the receiver wrongly sold the mortgaged property after receiving enough income to clear the debt, so that the property should have been returned unsold to the borrower, then the compensation would be intended to represent the property lost, not a diminution in the value of the equity of redemption. The receiver's wrong would perhaps not be a breach of the duties discussed above, however, but a failure to return the property once the debt had been repaid. See, similarly, the commentary in *Rottenberg v Monjack* [1992] BCC 688

misuse of trust property, commentary has suggested that the analysis is not of loss caused to the claimant beneficiary, but of restoration of something like to the property lost, and remoteness of damage and mitigation of loss are not relevant concepts.[148]

LIMITATION PERIOD

6.136 A claim for breach of the duty owed to the borrower is not a claim for breach of the mortgage deed for the purposes of limitation and hence is not a claim on a speciality.[149]

6.137 Although the duty is equitable, the tortious limitation period of 6 years under section 2 of the Limitation Act 1980 has been applied by analogy.[150]

6.138 This application of limitation is similar to that in claims of breach of fiduciary duty for example by an agent. A claim for breach of fiduciary duty is treated as analogous to a claim for breach of trust, for the purposes of limitation, with a 6-year limitation period by analogy with the time period for such a breach at sections 21 and 23 of the Limitation Act 1980, or by analogy with a breach of contract or tort, where there is sufficient similarity in the claims, under section 36.[151]

Entitlement to documents

6.139 In 'real agency', documents that the agent creates or that come into his custody by reason of his agency must usually be passed to his principal, if the principal demands them, because they are the principal's. Similarly, a principal can require his agent to give him information about the conduct of his agency, including his accounts. The same is not true of receivership.

6.140 A receiver is under an equitable duty to account to the borrower.[152] Moreover, a receiver appointed under a fixed charge, where the borrower is a company, is caught by section 38 of the Insolvency Act 1986 and must provide accounts half-yearly to Companies House.[153]

---

at 690H *et seq*, which suggested that a receiver would be trespassing on the mortgaged property if he remained there after receiving enough income to repay the debt.

[148] Reference should be made to commentary on equitable remedies.

[149] *Raja v Lloyds TSB Bank Plc* [2001] EWCA Civ 210 in particular at [25] and [27], doubting the apparent suggestion in *Bishop v Bonham* [1988] 1 WLR 742 that the duty was an implied term.

[150] *Raja v Lloyds TSB Bank Plc* [2001] EWCA Civ 210 at [32].

[151] *Cia de Seguros Imperio v Heath (REBX) Ltd and others* [2000] EWCA Civ 219, [2001] 1 WLR 112.

[152] *Jefferys v Dickson* (1866) LR 1 Ch App 183, where the right to such an account was said to stem from the deemed agency

[153] *Smiths Ltd v Middleton (No 1)* [1979] 3 All ER 842.

6.141 However, a borrower does not have an 'unrestricted right of access to receivership documents'[154] or information.

6.142 There is no 'general obligation' on the receiver to provide information to the borrower.[155] The receiver's primary duty is to manage the property to pay off the debt. He cannot have a duty to provide the borrower with documents or information insofar as that would impede that duty: 'if the receiver considers that disclosure of information would be contrary to the interests of the [lender] in realising the security, I think he must be entitled to withhold it ...',[156] though his decision must be taken in good faith.

6.143 Documents created or obtained by the receiver in pursuit of his receivership are not necessarily the property of the borrower, despite the deemed agency.[157] Documents which are the records of the company belong to the company, though they were created by the receivers. In *Gomba Holdings UK Ltd v Minories Finance Ltd*,[158] the receivers had been appointed as receivers and managers of the company under a floating charge, rather than as receivers under a fixed charge. Documents created by them as managers, such as the ordinary correspondence of the company sent and received by the receivers, were the property of the company.[159] Documents created or received as part of the conduct of the receivership were not the property of the company, whether these were created to advise or inform the lender, or for the purpose of the performance of the receivership more generally.[160] Such documents belonged to the receivers. They were not 'brought into being for the purpose of the companies' business or affairs'.[161]

The receiver's power to restrain the acts of the borrower

6.144 There is no doubt that a receiver can seek the court's assistance, by injunction, to restrain the acts of the borrower if they interfere with the receiver performing his duties. In *Bayly v Went*,[162] the receiver obtained an injunction to prevent the borrower from distraining for rent payable by an under-tenant, on that basis, even though the receiver was the deemed agent of the borrower. Kay J said that 'even if the receiver had been guilty of default in

---

[154] *Silven Properties Ltd v Royal Bank of Scotland Plc* [2003] EWCA Civ 1409, [2004] 1 WLR 997 at [28], though this refers to the then like provision at Companies Act 1985, s 498.

[155] *Gomba Holdings UK Ltd v Homan* [1986] 1 WLR 1301 at 1307G.

[156] *Gomba Holdings UK Ltd v Homan* [1986] 1 WLR 1301 at 1307E.

[157] *Gomba Holdings UK Ltd v Minories Finance Ltd* [1988] 1 WLR 1231.

[158] [1988] 1 WLR 1231.

[159] *Gomba Holdings UK Ltd v Minories Finance Ltd* [1988] 1 WLR 1231 at 1234E. It is not obvious that such documents would belong to the borrower if created by a fixed charge receiver. See similarly *Global Gaming Ventures (Group) Ltd v Global Gaming Ventures (Holdings) Ltd* [2018] EWCA Civ 68, where it appears the receivers' documents ordered to be disclosed on the appeal of an interim application were documents of the company not the receivership.

[160] [1988] 1 WLR 1231 at 1234F.

[161] [1988] 1 WLR 1231 at 1234E.

[162] (1884) 51 LT 764.

neglecting to collect the rent, the mortgagors could not have interfered in this way, that is, by distraining for the rent', which suggests a recognition that the borrower has given the receiver via the mortgage conditions such extensive powers that the receiver usurps the borrower.[163]

6.145 In 1912, it was said that the appointment of a receiver and manager of a company 'entirely supersedes the company in the conduct of its business ...'.[164] This is a position quite contrary to 'real agency' where the principal is not prevented from acting himself even though he has instructed his agent to do so.

6.146 Although this was said of a receiver and manager, with more extensive powers to manage the company's business than a fixed charge receiver usually has, it seems a clear statement of principle of the extent to which a borrower has agreed, for the consideration of provision of the loan, to give away his power and control if he is in breach of the mortgage terms.

6.147 Nevertheless, the case law since the early 20th century has been slower to recognise the extent of the powers of the receiver to control the borrower's actions.

6.148 What is less clear is the extent to which the appointment of a receiver prevents the borrower from exercising powers which have been delegated to the receiver, but whose exercise in the particular way proposed by the borrower would not impede the receivers from carrying out their functions.[165]

---

[163] See also *Woolston v Ross* [1900] 1 Ch 788: so long as the receivership is in force, the borrower cannot distrain even if the receiver refuses to. 'It is a fallacy to suggest that the mortgagor, as principal, can exercise the statutory power vested in his agent, the receiver'. The cause of action on which a receiver's claim for an injunction to restrict such an act is not discussed in either case, and the majority of the later cases relate to claims brought by the borrower, rather than a positive claim by a receiver against a borrower. The receiver in possession or occupation of the land, including by having the right to receive the rents, might have standing to sue in nuisance or trespass (including as to the rents) if the borrower's interference were of that kind, especially if the receiver could be said to have taken possession against the borrower. See *Jennings v Quinn* [2017] NICh 21, in which Morgan LCJ granted an interim injunction to receivers requiring the borrower to trespassing onto the mortgaged property with a claim based in trespass. There was 'no serious to be tried concerning the entitlement of the plaintiff to possession of the subject lands' (at [19]), though the point was not properly argued by the borrower. Now, it might also be said that he can sue on the mortgage conditions by reason of the Contracts (Rights of Third Parties) Act 1999 since the mortgage conditions presumably impliedly impose an obligation on the borrower not to interfere with the receivership. The alternative explanation would be that the borrower has a duty to the receiver in equity to allow him to carry on his work; there is no case law to that effect, though in *Newhart Developments Ltd v Co-operative Commercial Bank Ltd* [1978] 1 QB 814 at 819, Shaw LJ said that the borrower could not do something 'which would interfere with the proper discharge of the receiver's function in gathering in the assets of the company, so far as they were available, in order to put him the position to discharge the claims of his appointer', which suggests the possibility of such a duty.

[164] *Moss Steamship Company Ltd v Whinney* [1912] AC 254 at 263.

[165] See, for example, *Freevale Ltd v Metrostore (Holdings) Ltd* [1984] 1 Ch 199, in which the fact of appointment of receivers did not prevent a buyer succeeding in a claim for specific

6.149 In *Newhart Developments Ltd v Co-operative Commercial Bank Ltd*,[166] the Court of Appeal decided that the appointment of a receiver did not prevent the company borrower, via its directors, issuing a claim against the lender for breach of contract in withdrawing financial support for a development. The receivership was said not to divest the directors of their powers, so that the claim could be made if it did not interfere with the receiver's function in gathering in the assets to repay the loan, since such an action should not be allowed.[167] In this case, the claim would have been a difficult one for the receivers to bring (since the appointing lender was the defendant), and the company was not prejudiced by the claim because the directors had agreed to indemnify it in respect of costs.

6.150 The decision in *Newhart Developments Ltd v Co-operative Commercial Bank Ltd*[168] has been doubted or distinguished in subsequent first instance cases where these features were not present.

6.151 In *Gomba Holdings v Homan*,[169] the apparent generality of the decision of the Court of Appeal in *Newhart Developments Ltd v Co-operative Commercial Bank Ltd*[170] was doubted by Hoffmann J. *Newhart*, he said, was peculiar because the claim the company, acting by its directors, issued was against the lender itself, which was a claim the receiver, with a duty to the lender, would not consider issuing. In general, however, once receivers were

---

performance of a contract for sale of the borrower's estate made by the borrower before that appointment because it was said that the appointment did not destroy the buyer's equitable interest. The borrower's ability to perform the contract and transfer the property free of the charge given the lender's interest does not appear to have been considered. Nor were the questions of whether the receivers' acts in accordance with their duties would be impeded, or whether it could be said that the buyer could seek an order directly against them. This case is discussed in further detail at paras 8.14–8.17 on the receiver's relationship with third parties, and at paras 11.45–11.46, which discusses the case in the context of sale. See also *Telemetrix Plc v Modern Engineers of Bristol (Holdings) Plc* (1985) 1 BCC 99417, in which receivers joined as third parties to a claim for specific performance for contracts for the assignment of the mortgaged property were found properly to have been joined, and hence liable for costs. The case followed *Freevale*. As with *Freevale*, the issues of whether the receivers' acts in accordance with their duties, and how the buyer could have a cause of action against the receivers, were not discussed. The receivers conceded that they would agree to the assignment.

[166] [1978] 1 QB 814.

[167] [1978] 1 QB 814 at 819B and see 821B: 'what, of course, the directors cannot do, and to this extent their powers are inhibited, is to dispose of the assets within the debenture charge without the assent or concurrence of the receiver', a statement approved in *In Re Emmadart Ltd* [1979] 1 Ch 540 at 544B. See also *Lawson v Hosemaster Co Ltd* [1966] 1 WLR 1300, which assumes the directors cannot act after the appointment of the receiver: at 1315. It seems unlikely that even where wide powers have been delegated to a receiver, that delegation would be of the power to sue the lender for breach of the mortgage. See also *Watts v Midland Bank Plc* (1986) 2 BCC 98961: a borrower (in that case a company) can sue its receiver during the appointment in respect of the improper discharge of his duties even without indemnifying the lender as to costs which might otherwise deplete the asset (at 98966).

[168] [1978] 1 QB 814.

[169] [1986] 1 WLR 1301.

[170] [1978] 1 QB 814.

appointed, the directors did not have a continuing duty or ability to exploit the company assets:[171]

> I cannot accept that the Court of Appeal contemplated some kind of diarchy over all the company's assets. This would be contrary to principle and wholly impractical. In my judgment the board has during the currency of the receivership no powers over assets in the possession or control of the receiver.[172]

6.152 In *Tudor Grange Holdings Ltd v Citibank NA*,[173] the directors had issued a claim in the company's name against the lender without the receiver's consent and without indemnifying the company in costs. On the bank's strike out application, the court decided that the directors did not have the power to issue the claim, without the directors providing an indemnity, since the cause of action was subject to the rights of the receiver. Sir Nicolas Browne-Wilkinson distinguished *Newhart Developments Ltd v Co-operative Commercial Bank Ltd*[174] because the indemnity given in that case prevented the company being prejudiced by the proceedings.

6.153 However, Sir Nicolas Browne-Wilkinson doubted that *Newhart Developments Ltd v Co-operative Commercial Bank Ltd*[175] had been correctly decided, though he did not need to decide that point, and in any event recognised he was bound by that decision:

> The decision seems to ignore the difficulty which arises if two widely differing sets of people, the directors and the receivers, who may have widely differing views and interests, both have power to bring proceedings on the same causes of action.[176]

6.154 The two different lines of cases have not been reconciled by a case in the Court of Appeal or Supreme Court.[177] It is the position of this book that the 1912 position and the position of the judges doubting *Newhart Developments Ltd v Co-operative Commercial Bank Ltd*[178] is right.[179]

---

[171] In that case, such a duty was being asserted as the basis for a claim that the receiver was obliged to provide the directors with information about the company.

[172] [1986] 1 WLR 1301 at 1307D. This decision was followed, and *Newhart* doubted, by the Outer House in *Independent Pension Trustee Ltd v L A W Construction Co Ltd* 1997 SLT 1105.

[173] [1992] Ch 53.

[174] [1978] 1 QB 814.

[175] [1978] 1 QB 814.

[176] [1992] Ch 53 at 63C.

[177] See, however, the attempt to do so referred to, but not adopted since there was no need to do so, *Enigma Technique Ltd v the Royal Bank of Scotland* [2003] EWHC 3340 (Ch) at [20], a costs decision against a director who brought proceedings in the company's name when receivers had been appointed.

[178] [1978] 1 QB 814.

[179] Subject, of course, to the particular receivership provisions in the mortgage.

6.155 If the receiver is appointed to have particular powers of the borrower, then the borrower can no longer exercise them[180] and can be restrained by the receiver from doing so.[181] The borrower has given the receiver his powers, just as if he had executed an irrevocable power of attorney, and cannot interfere with the receiver's exercise of them by insisting on exercising them himself.

The borrower's inability to control the receiver

6.156 In 'real agency', the principal can control his agent by giving instructions to him, or by terminating his appointment.

6.157 The position in receivership is quite different. The receiver has 'an uncontrolled discretion'[182] subject to his duties. The borrower can only prevent the receiver's exercise of his powers if the powers are being exercised in breach of the receiver's powers or duties,[183] or the receiver's appointment is invalid,[184] or the receiver has sufficient money in his hands to repay the debt.[185] Thus, the receiver cannot be restrained even from repudiating a contract made by the borrower before his appointment, save if that would be in breach of duty.[186] The fact that this will open the borrower to a claim by the third party is of no avail.

---

[180] The case law is not clear, but it seems to be the case that a contract made by a borrower after the appointment of a receiver, and within the scope of the receiver's powers, is void. See, for example, the quotations at paras 6.151 and 6.153. Nevertheless, if the other contracting party has no knowledge of the receivership, it may be that the contract takes effect between borrower and that other party by estoppel so that the borrower could still be sued on it. The point was not argued in *National Westminster Bank Plc v Hunter* [2011] EWHC 3170 (Ch), in which it was assumed that the borrower's contract was not void. In *Bower Terrace Student Accommodation Ltd v Space Student Living Ltd* [2012] EWHC 2206 (Ch), the question of whether the contracts were effective between the borrower and the other party was not decided (at [45]). The contracts were not binding on the receiver because the other party knew they were in breach of the mortgage. Since the receiver need not perform a contract entered into by a borrower pre his appointment (*Airlines Airspares Ltd v Handley Page Ltd* [1970] Ch 193; *Lathia v Dronsfield* [1987] BCLC 321; and see paras 8.6–8.9), it is hard to see why a receiver would have to perform a contract made by the borrower after the appointment. Thus the distinction between the contract being void and voidable may not be great. If entry into the contract would be within the receiver's duty, then he could ratify it or enter into it afresh.

[181] The borrower has not assigned his powers and rights to the receiver. The powers remain to be exercised in his name, but he has given the receiver free rein to exercise them. See *Moss Steamship Company Ltd v Whinney* [1912] AC 254 at 263: 'this appointment of a receiver and manager over the assets and business of a company does not dissolve or annihilate the company, any more than the taking possession by the mortgagee of the fee of land let to tenants annihilates the mortgagor'.

[182] *Rottenberg v Monjack* [1992] BCC 688 at 693H.

[183] So that, for example, the borrower can claim an injunction to restrain sale of a property to allow for payment to himself of more in remuneration than he is entitled to where the receiver already has sufficient funds to redeem the charge given the right level of remuneration: *Rottenberg v Monjack* [1992] BCC 688. *Watts v Midland Bank Plc* (1986) 2 BCC 98961.

[184] For example, *J&N Cowden LLP v Ulster Bank Ltd* [2014] NIQB 138.

[185] And hence the receivership is at an end: *Rottenberg v Monjack* [1992] BCC 688.

[186] *Airlines Airspares Ltd v Handley Page Ltd* [1970] 1 Ch 193. See further Chapter 8.

6.158 Moreover, the borrower cannot himself terminate the receivership.

6.159 To these extents, the receiver's deemed agency is more akin to an irrevocable power of attorney, though receivership is not described as such in the case law,[187] and the analogy with an irrevocable power of attorney is not exact. The deemed agency appears to be a particular creation of mortgage law.

LOSS OF DEEMED AGENCY

6.160 In 'real agency', if the principal dies or becomes bankrupt, or if a company is dissolved, then the agency ends so that the agent no longer has any powers to deal with the principal's property.[188]

6.161 In contrast, the insolvency, death or dissolution of the borrower will not end a receiver's appointment, nor his powers to deal with the mortgaged property, though the deemed agency may end in certain circumstances.

6.162 Most of the case law in this area relates to liquidation in company insolvency, and hence the effects set out below on deemed agency in receivership of other forms of company insolvency, and for personal insolvency and death, are less well supported by case law.

Company insolvency

6.163 The Insolvency Act 1986[189] contains a number of statutory schemes for the management of an insolvent company[190] out of insolvency or towards the repayment of debts (in whole or in part) and its dissolution:

(a) CVAs:[191] the company, administrator (for a company in administration), or liquidator (for a company being wound up) proposes to its creditors a scheme for satisfaction of its debts or arrangement of its affairs with an insolvency practitioner supervising or acting as trustee. If the creditors at the creditors' meeting agree to the proposal, all of the creditors of debts

---

[187] Although in Land Registry Practice Guide 36A, the receiver with usual powers is said to have a power of attorney by his appointment even if no separate power is granted.

[188] This is not true of irrevocable powers of attorney at common law which survive death (though the case law in support of this proposition is said in *Bowstead & Reynolds* to be weak), personal insolvency, and company liquidation and dissolution. Irrevocable powers of attorney under the Powers of Attorney Act 1971 survive death, incapacity or bankruptcy, winding up or dissolution: s 4(1)(ii). The reason, as set out in *Bowstead & Reynolds*, is that the power is a property interest. This is the same reasoning as in the case law on the survival of receivership on liquidation. See *Bowstead & Reynolds* at 10-006–7.

[189] See any practitioner's text on insolvency for more detail. See Chapter 4 for a discussion of the effect of insolvency on the lender's power to appoint a receiver.

[190] 'Company' here refers to a company registered under the Companies Act 2006 or otherwise caught by the Insolvency Act 1986 provisions. Companies incorporated outside the Companies Act 2006 and not caught by the Insolvency Act 1986 are beyond the remit of this book.

[191] Insolvency Act 1986, Pt I.

caught by the arrangement are bound by it and can thus expect payment of those debts at the rate specified in the arrangement provided it continues in effect. The company continues to exist, and its property remains vested in it, and can enter new contracts and incur new debts.

(b) Administration:[192] an insolvency practitioner[193] is appointed[194] as administrator of the company with the objective of rescuing the company as a going concern, achieving a better result for the creditors than likely if the company were wound up, or realising property in order to make a distribution to one or more secured or preferential creditors.[195] The company continues to exist, and its property remains vested in it, unless and until it is wound up and dissolved by the administrator, but is run by the administrator, rather than the directors, until the purpose of administration is achieved by repayment of debts, or sale for that purpose, or the company is dissolved. There is a moratorium on legal process without the consent of the administrator or the permission of the court against a company whilst in administration,[196] including against enforcement of security over company property.[197] The purpose is to limit the creation of further obligations on the company without control by the administrator or the court.[198]

(c) Appointment of a receiver, manager, administrative receiver and/or, by court order, the official receiver:[199] such a person is appointed under a debenture or charge, or, in the case of the official receiver, on an application to the court by creditors. The Insolvency Act 1986 governs, for example, who can act, their obligations and remuneration. The company continues to exist, and its property remains vested in it. It is run by the receiver or manager, to the extent of the powers given to them, and with the purpose of repaying the debt, for example, under the debenture or charge. Once the debt is repaid, the appointment will end, and the company will continue under the direction of the directors alone.

(d) Winding up (also known as liquidation):[200] an insolvency practitioner (the liquidator) is appointed, either by reason of the company's resolution for a voluntary winding up;[201] or a creditors' decision at a meeting of the creditors that there be a creditors' voluntary winding up;[202] or on a winding up by

---

[192] Insolvency Act 1986, Pt II and Sch B1.

[193] Insolvency Act 1986, Sch B1, para 6.

[194] By the court, the holder of a debenture, or the company.

[195] Insolvency Act 1986, Sch B1, para 3.

[196] Insolvency Act 1986, Sch B1, para 43.

[197] Insolvency Act 1986, Sch B1, para 43(2). This applies to the appointment of a receiver by a lender *Sinai Securities Ltd v Hooper* [2003] EWHC 910 (Ch). See Chapter 4.

[198] The receiver's powers are limited statutorily by the administration. Under Insolvency Act 1986, Sch B1, para 41(2), the receiver must vacate his office if the administrator requires. He cannot exercise any management powers or enforce the security without the administrator or the court's consent, under para 43(2). See Chapter 4 for further discussion of the effect of the administration on the receiver's powers.

[199] Insolvency Act 1986, Pt III.

[200] Insolvency Act 1986, Pt IV. Part V deals with winding up companies not registered under the Companies Act 2006 in the United Kingdom.

[201] Insolvency Act 1986, Pt IV, Chs II, III, V, VII and VIII, and s 84.

[202] Insolvency Act 1986, Pt IV, Chs II, IV, V, VII and VIII.

the court, for the reason that the company cannot pay its debts.[203] The effect of winding up is that the company is run not by the directors, but by the liquidator with the purpose of securing the assets of the company, realising and distributing them to the creditors, thus repaying its debts in whole or in part, and then dissolving the company.[204] Prior to dissolution, the company's property remains vested in it.[205] Once the company's assets have been got in and distributed to the creditors, the company will be dissolved and cease to exist.

6.164 In each case, the effect of the insolvency on the deemed agency of the receivership needs to be considered.[206] Liquidation is considered first since there is a clear answer in case law for that situation.

Liquidation

6.165 The making of a winding up order does not end the receivership.[207]

6.166 The explanation for the continuation of the receivership in *Gaskell v Gosling*[208] is that the position of the borrower is not improved by its liquidation; after the winding up order, it cannot revoke the receivership, or the lender's power to appoint a receiver, when it could not have done so before. The property was not the company's at all; the company borrower had only the equity of redemption.[209]

6.167 *Gaskell v Gosling* is a late 19th-century case. Post the Law of Property Act 1925, the same point applies, though the borrower retains a legal title after charging the property.[210] The company dissolution on insolvency does not prevent the receiver from exercising the powers given him because 'the rights

---

[203] Insolvency Act 1986, Pt IV, Chs VI, VII and VIII. The company's inability to pay its debts is one ground for a court order: s 122(1)(f). It is not the only ground, but is the most common.

[204] Insolvency Act 1986, Pt IV, Ch IX.

[205] Save on a successful application for vesting in the liquidator: Insolvency Act 1986, s 145.

[206] The effect of company insolvency on the lender's power to appoint a receiver is discussed in Chapter 4.

[207] *Gaskell v Gosling* [1896] 1 QB 668 (decision on liability of lender for receiver's acts reversed in [1897] AC 575); *Thomas v Todd* [1926] 2 KB 511 at 516 (voluntary liquidation), *Gough's Garages Ltd v Pugsley* [1930] 1 KB 615 at 626; *Sowman v David Samuel Trust Ltd (In Liquidation)* [1978] 1 WLR 22; *Barrows v Chief Land Registrar* (1977) *The Times*, 20 October 1977. See Chapter 4 for a further discussion of the effect of insolvency on the power to appoint a receiver. A receiver with a right to possession of company assets and powers to do acts incidental or conducive to that power has the power to present a winding up petition since winding up protects the assets: *In Re Emmadart Ltd* [1979] 2 WLR 868.

[208] [1896] 1 QB 669 at 699 per Rigby LJ. See also *Gough's Garages Ltd v Pugsley* 1930] 1 KB 615, where a similar explanation is given.

[209] This was before the reforms in mortgages brought about by the Law of Property Act 1925.

[210] See para 2.22 *et seq.*

and powers given by [the mortgage] are themselves property, but not the property of the company'.[211]

6.168 That is why the receiver can continue to deal with the secured property and be indemnified out of it in doing so. His powers come from the mortgage and are not ended by the liquidation.[212]

6.169 Even if the security is disclaimed by the liquidator under section 178(2) of the Insolvency Act 1986, the rights of the lender, including the right to appoint a receiver, would not be affected, save 'so far as necessary for the purpose of releasing the company from any liability'.[213] Quite what this means in different contexts has yet to be worked out in the case law.

6.170 The making of a winding up order is, however, said in the case law[214] to end the deemed agency.[215]

6.171 The reasoning from the case law is based on the purpose of the liquidation.[216] Although the company continues to exist[217] until its dissolution at the end of the winding up, it is run by the liquidator and not the directors, and the liquidator's powers are to get in the assets and distribute them. His

---

[211] *Sowman v David Samuel Trust Ltd (In Liquidation)* [1978] 1 WLR 22 at 30C.

[212] For the same reason, a receiver can be appointed by the lender even though a winding up order has already been made: *In Re Northern Garage Ltd* [1946] Ch 188 at 191. The receiver's deemed agency is not of the essence of his role. See para 4.28.

[213] Insolvency Act 1986, s 178(4)(b); *Scmlla Properties Ltd v Gesso Properties (BVI) Ltd* [1995] BCC 793, where the lender exercised its power of sale of a freehold property after a disclaimer. The effect would be to prevent liability being imposed on the company from any continuation of the lease, hence, for example, sale of the lease in the company's name might well not be possible.

[214] *Gaskell v Gosling* [1897] AC 575 suggests that this is the effect, see at the end of 591 per Lord Herschell. The receiver's acts post the winding up order did not bind the borrower. They could not be the principals. But see the earlier comments of Rigby LJ: [1896] QB 669 at 700. The proposition has been agreed in a number of cases thereafter: *Thomas v Todd* [1926] 2 KB 511 at 516 (relying on the decision in *Gaskell v Gosling*); *Gough's Garages Ltd v Pugsley* [1930] 1 KB 615 at 626; *Sowman v David Samuel Trust Ltd (In Liquidation)* [1978] 1 WLR 22 at 30 (likewise); *Yorkshire Bank Plc v Mashford*, 3 April 1987, unreported, CA.

[215] Note that in the case of an administrative receiver, as defined in Insolvency Act 1986, s 29(2) (a receiver or manager of the whole (or substantially the whole) of a company's property appointed by or on behalf of the holders of any debentures of the company secured by a charge which, as created, was a floating charge, or by such a charge and one or more other securities, or a person who would be such a receiver or manager but for the appointment of some other person as the receiver of part the company's property), the deemed agency under s 44(1) ends on liquidation: s 44(1)(a). This was the situation in *Rees v Boston BC* [2001] EWCA Civ 1934.

[216] Although purpose alone, not directly reflected by statutory restrictions, is unlikely to be sufficient for the termination of the deemed agency.

[217] The statement in *Gaskell v Gosling* [1896] 1 QB 668 that the company 'from the date of the [liquidator's appointment] the company ceased to exist as a company, and ceased to exist as a going concern' was said by Lord Watson in the House of Lords at [1897] AC 575 to be 'approximately correct' (at 587), though the company continues to exist until dissolution. See, however, Lord Herschell at 593: the company 'had not ceased to exist; it could still hold and also acquire property'.

ability to carry on the business of the company is limited.[218] Although this is not set out expressly in the case law, presumably the reasoning for the termination of the deemed agency is that entry by the company into any new liabilities would be beyond its powers,[219] limited as they are by the insolvency, and thus the receiver cannot bind the company personally by any deemed agency because to do so would be outside those powers.[220]

6.172 The meaning of this is, however, more limited than it seems.

6.173 The termination of the deemed agency:

> does not in the least affect [the receiver's] powers to hold and dispose of the company's property comprised in the [mortgage], including his power to use its name for that purpose, for such powers are given by the disposition of the company's property which it made (in equity) by the [mortgage] itself.[221]

6.174 After liquidation, the receiver can sell the property under the power of sale given to him, in the name of the borrower,[222] and he can issue and continue a lease extension claim under the Landlord and Tenant Act 1954,[223] even though both of those acts would impose liabilities on the borrower and would seem to be acts of agency. It seems likely, by the same reasoning, that the receiver can grant a lease of the mortgaged property, if that power is

---

[218] *Gaskell v Gosling* [1897] AC 575 at 588 and 591. Under the Insolvency Act 1986, the relevant provisions are s 87 (voluntary winding up), which requires the company to cease to carry on its business, except so far as may be required for its beneficial winding up, but preserves its corporate state and powers; in a winding up by court order, the liquidator's functions are to secure that the assets are got in, realised, and distributed to the company's creditors: s 143(1). The liquidator's powers in a winding up are in Sch 4, including at para 5 the power to carry on the business of the company so far as may be necessary for its beneficial winding up. It is not clear from any of these provisions that the company is in truth incapable of having a receiver as its agent so as to justify the termination of the deemed agency. If personal liability were imposed on the company, the liquidator could disclaim it, under s 178. The lender's interest would be protected (s 178(4)), and it could seek a vesting order under s 181. It is less clear whether the receiver with, for example a power of sale, could do so, since it is unclear whether that power would be sufficient for the receiver have an interest in the disclaimed property under s 181(2)(a), or a liability under s 181(2)(b). In any event, it is unlikely that the receiver would wish to have the property directly vested in him, the result of a court order under s 181.

[219] Even a liquidator has limited powers to create new liabilities.

[220] For example, in a winding up by the court, any disposition of the company's property is void unless the court orders otherwise under Insolvency Act 1986, s 127(1). This reasoning, however, depends on the effect of a company's creation of a new liability being void, rather than voidable.

[221] *Sowman v David Samuel Trust Ltd (In Liquidation)* [1978] 1 WLR 22 at 30A, but this is subject to Insolvency Act 1986, s 127(1), which makes a disposition of company property made after the commencement of the winding up void unless the court orders otherwise.

[222] *Sowman v David Samuel Trust Ltd (In Liquidation)* [1978] 1 WLR 22 at 30A. The power to do so in the borrower's name is likely under the irrevocable power of attorney usually given in the mortgage covenants: at 30F, but see Insolvency Act 1986, s 127(1).

[223] *Gough's Garages Ltd v Pugsley* [1930] 1 KB 615 under a precursor to that Act. Just like that precursor, the Landlord and Tenant Act 1954 and s 67 specifically provides that the receiver once appointed can serve notices and claim a lease extension.

delegated to him,[224] even though that too would impose liabilities on the borrower.

6.175 It has been said that termination of the deemed agency is in the sense that the receiver cannot impose new liabilities on the borrower which would be provable in the litigation against the unsecured assets.[225] Provided it is within his receivership powers, he can trade with the mortgaged property and seek an indemnity from it for costs and liabilities incurred in so doing.[226]

6.176 Thus, it appears, in relation to sale, lease extensions and leasing, that the receiver can transfer, extend or create a property interest in the borrower's name, but any third party (the buyer, landlord or tenant) could not sue the borrower directly on the transfer or lease whilst the winding up order remained in force. It would seem advisable for any contract or disposition entered into by the receiver in the borrower's name after a liquidation to make clear that the borrower is insolvent and hence the limits on its personal liability.

6.177 The receiver of a company in liquidation does not inevitably become the agent of the lender on termination of his deemed agency for the borrower.[227] The receiver may no longer be an agent at all, i.e. he could act in his own right.[228]

6.178 If the receiver purports to act in the name of the borrower, so as to make debts provable in the liquidation out of unsecured property, when he does not have authority to do so, he may be liable to third parties for a breach of his warranty of authority.[229]

CVA

6.179 A CVA does not affect the existence of the mortgage and does not apply to a secured debt under a mortgage. It will not end the receivership for the reasons set out in relation to liquidation. It seems unlikely that it would end the lender's power to appoint a receiver.[230]

---

[224] Although see the discussion of this in Chapters 5 and 9.

[225] See the dissenting judgment of Rigby LJ in *Gaskell v Gosling* [1896] QB 669 at 700 (approved in [1897] AC 575), and *Sowman v David Samuel Trust Ltd (In Liquidation)* [1978] 1 WLR 22 at 30A.

[226] *Gosling v Gaskell* [1897] AC 575, provided the mortgage deed gave him such an indemnity.

[227] *Gaskell v Gosling* [1897] AC 575. This is unless the lender interferes so as to make the receiver its agent: see *American Express International Banking Corp v Hurley* (1986) 2 BCC 98993, and paras 7.49–7.57.

[228] *American Express International Banking Corp v Hurley* (1986) 2 BCC 98993, for example. See also the suggestion in *Gaskell v Gosling* [1897] AC 575 at 592 that there could be no principal. It is not necessary that there be a principal for the receiver's acts.

[229] *Gaskell v Gosling* [1897] AC 575 at 592. See para 8.206.

[230] Once any pre-CVA moratorium obtained by the directors of the borrower under Insolvency Act 1986, s 1A and Sch A1 has ended. During the moratorium, the lender will need permission from the court to appoint a receiver, under Sch A1, para 12(1)(g). See the discussion at para 4.29.

6.180 A CVA, once passed, leaves management of the company with the directors, though an insolvency practitioner oversees the arrangement. There is no moratorium on the company continuing to trade. Thus, the reasoning given in the case law for the termination of the deemed agency on liquidation does not appear to apply to a CVA. The deemed agency of the receiver is therefore likely to continue, so that the receiver can impose new liabilities on the company.

Administration

6.181 Administration does not affect the existence of a mortgage.[231] However, specific statutory provisions affect both the power to appoint a receiver[232] and, very likely, the receivership.

6.182 An administration order does not end receivership.[233]

6.183 There is no authority on whether an administration order ends the deemed agency. The administrator's powers are not as limited as they are in liquidation; the administrator is expected to run the company and the business. Thus the apparent basis for the loss of deemed agency in liquidation does not appear to apply in administration.

6.184 The purpose of administration, to rescue the company as a going concern, or ensure a better return for the creditors than on a liquidation, or realisation of company property so as to make a distribution, is protected by Schedule B1, paragraph 64 of the Insolvency Act 1986. The company is prohibited from exercising management powers[234] without the consent of the administrator.[235] This suggests that the receiver can continue to be the deemed agent of the borrower, but the exercise of any of his powers must be with the administrator's consent,[236] which may be an effective bar to the receivership being of any practical benefit.[237]

---

[231] Although see para 13.24 for the court's power to permit the administrator to deal with the mortgaged property free of the mortgage.

[232] See para 4.27.

[233] *In Re Fivestar* [2015] EWHC 2782 (Ch), [2016] 1 WLR 1104 at [4] states this to be the case but gives no reasoning. It is likely that the reasons set out above when considering liquidation also apply here. See also *Promontoria (Chestnut) Ltd v Craig* [2017] EWHC 2405 (Ch) on the exercise of the administrator's power to require the receiver to vacate office, also discussed in Chapter 13.

[234] A power which could be exercised so as to interfere with the exercise of the administrator's powers: Insolvency Act 1986, Sch B1, para 64(2)(a); even when the power was conferred by an instrument: para 64(2)(b).

[235] Insolvency Act 1986, Sch B1, para 64(1).

[236] Assuming they are management powers within the meaning of Insolvency Act 1986, Sch B1, para 64(2)(b).

[237] See also the discussion at para 13.24.

Receivership and management

6.185 The effect of a second receivership or the appointment of a manager will depend on the priority of the mortgages/debentures. This is discussed in Chapter 2.

Company dissolution

6.186 Company dissolution[238] can occur either simply, if a company is struck off the company register, for example, for failure to file company accounts,[239] or as a result of winding up under the Insolvency Act 1986.

6.187 If the charged property is still owned by the company when it is dissolved, the property is not destroyed; it goes *bona vacantia* to the Crown under section 1012(1) of the Companies Act 2006. It vests in the Crown subject to the mortgage and hence subject to the right to appoint a receiver and the receiver's powers. Even if the Crown disclaims the charged property, under section 1013, that does not affect the lender's rights[240] or the receiver's rights.

6.188 Just as with liquidation of the company, the receiver would retain any powers he had to collect income, to sell the mortgaged property, or to lease it, because those powers are, by reason of the lender's mortgage, not dependent on the existence of the company.

6.189 On dissolution of the company, it ceases to exist and hence the company can no longer be the principal for any agency. Thus a receiver's deemed agency with the company as principal ends on the dissolution of a company borrower in the sense that there is no company to be liable for the receiver's acts.[241] Sale or leasing in the borrower's name would be inappropriate, though a receiver with appropriate powers would remain able to sell or lease the mortgaged property.

6.190 It does not follow that there is no principal for deemed agency.[242] The mortgaged property has vested in the Crown *bona vacantia*. In principle, the statutory deemed agency under section 109(2) of the Law of Property Act 1925 has as principal 'the mortgagor', where 'the mortgagor' 'includes any person from time to time deriving title under the original mortgagor or entitled

---

[238] See Companies Act 2006, Pt 31 and Insolvency Act 1986, Pt IV, Ch IX.

[239] Although in that case it is likely it could be restored.

[240] Companies Act 2006, s 1015(2). The lender could apply to have the property vested in it. It is unclear whether the receiver would have standing to do so: see fn 218 in relation to insolvency. In any event, the receiver would unlikely wish to have the property vested in him.

[241] Unless the company were restored to the register to make it liable.

[242] There is no authority on this point.

to redeem a mortgage according to his estate interest or right in the mortgaged property' under section 205(1)(xvi). That appears apt to include the Crown.[243]

6.191 Similarly, it seems likely that a suitably worded express deemed agency in the mortgage conditions would be apt to include the Crown.[244]

6.192 Likewise, if the receiver has the lender's power of sale, then he has the power to sell in the name of the 'estate owner in whom [the mortgaged property] is vested'.[245] It thus appears that the sale could be in the name of the Crown, in whom the estate has vested *bona vacantia*.

6.193 However, the Crown would no doubt disclaim the mortgaged property if it were being exposed to any potential liability by the receiver's acts. Once the Crown has disclaimed, the receiver could only act either as the lender's agent or in his own right.

Individual insolvency and death

6.194 For borrower individuals, the question is whether receivership, and the deemed agency, survives individual insolvency and/or death.

6.195 There is even less case law on these issues than for company insolvency. What case law there is[246] relates to the effect of death on the receivership and the deemed agency, and hence this issue is considered first.

6.196 The position for both individual insolvency and death must follow the reasoning in the company liquidation cases. Neither bankruptcy nor the death of the borrower could end the right to appoint a receiver or the receivership, because the receivership emanates from the charge, an estate owned by the lender and not the borrower, so the change in ownership of the borrower's property on bankruptcy[247] or death[248] cannot affect the receivership.[249]

6.197 The thesis of this book is that, as with company insolvency and dissolution, the deemed agency will be ended on the individual's insolvency insofar as that is necessary to avoid conflict with the statutory provisions for the particular insolvency scheme under the Insolvency Act 1986, or the powers of the executors or administrators of the borrower's estate.

---

[243] Similarly, under Law of Property Act 1925, s 109(3), the receiver with statutory powers could collect income in the name of the Crown.

[244] See paras 9.36–9.41 for a discussion of the possible ways in which an express deemed agency might be said to affect a successor in title.

[245] Law of Property Act 1925, ss 88(1) and 89(1).

[246] *In Re Hale* [1899] 2 Ch 107. See the discussion below.

[247] It vests in the official receiver, and then the trustee in bankruptcy once appointed.

[248] It vests in the executors of there is a will, or the administrators once appointed if not.

[249] See paras 4.30–4.34.

Death

6.198 There is a suggestion in *In Re Hale*[250] that the deemed agency can survive the death of the borrower because 'mortgagor' in the mortgage covenants includes the executor as the successor in title.[251]

6.199 A standard analysis of the effect of a transfer of the borrower's title on the mortgage is that the new owner will take subject to the mortgage and hence to the lender's right to take possession, which is inherent in the mortgage.[252] The lender's right to sell if the mortgage payments are not maintained is a statutory right under section 101(1)(i) of the Law of Property Act 1925[253] and is hence similarly incident to the lender's estate so that it remains enforceable against a borrower's successor in title. Similarly, the lender's statutory right to appoint a receiver under section 101(1)(iii)[254] is a right which remains enforceable against the borrower's successor in title. This is consistent with the explanations for the continuation of the right to appoint a receiver and the receivership on a liquidation set out above.[255]

6.200 Conversely, the obligation to pay the debt does not in general fall on the successor in title, since that is a personal obligation only. The covenant to pay is not an incident of the lender's estate.[256]

6.201 The question which remains is whether the deemed agency in receivership applies to the borrower's successor in title.

6.202 Statutory receivership, under section 109(2) of the Law of Property Act 1925, is imposed on 'the mortgagor'. Since 'mortgagor' 'includes any person from time to time deriving title under the original mortgagor or entitled to redeem a mortgage according to his estate interest or right in the mortgaged property' under section 205(1)(xvi), the answer is that the statutory deemed agency does apply to successors in title of the borrower.[257]

---

[250]   [1899] 2 Ch 107.

[251]   There is little reasoning in *In Re Hale* [1899] 2 Ch 107 as to why the deemed agency continues beyond that the executors fell within the definition of 'the mortgagor'. See the first instance decision at 113: 'the executrix of the testator Hale occupied the same position as between herself and the mortgagee under the agreement – that is to say, the position of mortgagor and mortgagee within the meaning of the phrase as used in the document' and as to payment by the receiver was 'clearly a payment made on behalf of the mortgagor and by the agent of the mortgagor ...'. The Court of Appeal gives no reasoning on this point.

[252]   Even if it is postponed until a breach, by the mortgage covenants.

[253]   The statutory provisions expressly include the statutory rights of possession and sale as modified by the mortgage deed: Law of Property Act 1925, s 101(4).

[254]   The statutory right to appoint a receiver similarly expressly includes modifications of it in the mortgage covenants.

[255]   See para 6.165 *et seq*.

[256]   Although the rights to possession and sale are contingent on the debt not having been paid. The covenant to pay will bind the estate of a deceased borrower since the estate is subject to the deceased's obligations unless they are purely personal so as to end with death.

[257]   See also discussion on successors in title at paras 9.24–9.41. Similarly, the receiver with statutory powers to collect income will be able to do so in the successor in title's name.

6.203 In a suitably worded mortgage, the deemed agency of a receiver with extended powers would also apply to a successor in title of the borrower, as per the decision in *In Re Hale*.[258] The power to appoint a receiver with a deemed agency is part of the property interest of the lender conferred by the mortgage. It is a covenant 'touching and concerning the land' and thus binds successors of the borrower.[259]

6.204 However, the receiver cannot make the successor personally liable if statute prevents that kind of successor from being so liable. As set out above, that appears to be the explanation for the termination of deemed agency in the liquidation cases; the company in liquidation cannot make itself personally liable on new contracts, and hence the receiver cannot.

6.205 In the case of individual death, since the executors and/or the administrators of the deceased's estate are not limited in their powers to deal with the deceased's estate, on this analysis, the receiver can make the executors/administrators as such[260] personally liable via the deemed agency.

6.206 The receiver with suitable power to sell the mortgaged property in the name of the estate owner[261] will remain able to sell the property, though he will do so in the name of the executors or the administrators of the borrower's estate, since those persons will be the estate owner.

Individual insolvency

6.207 The Insolvency Act 1986 contains a number of schemes for administration of an insolvent individual's estate:[262]

(a) IVA:[263] the individual proposes to his creditors a scheme for satisfaction of his debts or an arrangement of his affairs with an insolvency practitioner supervising or acting as trustee. If the creditors at the creditors' meeting agree to the proposal, all of the creditors of debts caught by the arrangement are bound by it and can thus expect payment of those debts at the rate specified in the arrangement provided it continues in effect. The debtor's property remains vested in him, and he can enter new contracts and incur new debts.

---

[258] Where the executors were found to be 'the mortgagor' within the meaning of that phrase in the agreement: [1899] 2 Ch 107 at 118 (the first instance decision under appeal; the Court of Appeal does not discuss the point).

[259] See the discussion at paras 9.24–9.41.

[260] I.e. to the extent of the estate. See *Re Hale* [1899] 2 Ch 107 at 113 as to the difference as regards the executor versus the borrower's liability. See also *Fairholme and Palliser v Kennedy* (1890) 24 LR Ir 498, which suggests that the receiver can act in the name of the borrower's personal representatives if he gives an indemnity.

[261] As per the lender's power of sale in Law of Property Act 1925, ss 88(1) and 89(1).

[262] The second group of parts of the Insolvency Act 1986, starting at Pt VIII. See paras 4.30–4.32 for a discussion of the effect of insolvency on the lender's power to appoint a receiver.

[263] Insolvency Act 1986, Pt VIII.

(b)   Bankruptcy:[264] a bankruptcy order is made on the presentation of a petition by a creditor, temporary administrator, insolvency practitioner, supervisor of or someone bound by an IVA, or where a criminal bankruptcy order has been made,[265] on the basis of the insolvency of the debtor.[266] An insolvency practitioner[267] (the trustee in bankruptcy) is appointed to administer the bankrupt's estate so as 'to get in, realise and distribute the bankrupt's estate'.[268] The bankrupt's estate, including the mortgaged property,[269] vests in the trustee in bankruptcy on his appointment.[270]

IVA

6.208 For the same reasons as those in company liquidation, entry by a borrower into an IVA does not terminate a receivership or the receiver's powers.

6.209 During an IVA, the mortgaged property will remain vested in the borrower, and the borrower's powers in dealing with it are not limited. It thus seems likely that the receiver can continue as deemed agent of the borrower during an IVA.

Bankruptcy

6.210 It follows from the reasoning in the case law relating to company liquidation that the making of a bankruptcy order does not terminate the receivership.[271]

6.211 Between the bankruptcy petition and the making of the bankruptcy order, the estate remains vested in the borrower. Since the borrower cannot in this period deal with his own property, there is an argument, similar to that in company liquidation, that the receiver's deemed agency is suspended at least insofar as it would impose personal liability on the bankrupt borrower.

6.212 From the point of view of mortgage law, the receiver will retain any power he has to sell in the name of the estate owner of the mortgaged property; in this period, it is the borrower. However, since the borrower cannot make any disposition of property in this period without the order

---

[264] Insolvency Act 1986, Pt VIII, Ch I.

[265] Insolvency Act 1986, s 264(1).

[266] See Insolvency Act 1986, ss 267 and 268.

[267] Insolvency Act 1986, s 292(2).

[268] Insolvency Act 1986, s 305(2).

[269] See the definition of 'bankrupt's estate' at Insolvency Act 1986, s 283. The bankrupt's home will cease to form part of the estate after 3 years, and revest in the bankrupt, save in specific circumstances: see s 283A.

[270] Insolvency Act 1986, s 306(1). The official receiver is the first trustee in bankruptcy, but the bankrupt's estate does not vest in him.

[271] See para 4.30 for a discussion of the effect of bankruptcy on the lender's power to appoint a receiver.

consent of the court or its subsequent ratification,[272] a sale (or, indeed, the grant of a lease) in the borrower's name would not be possible without the permission of the court.[273]

6.213 Once the bankrupt's estate vests in the trustee in bankruptcy,[274] the trustee becomes the 'mortgagor' within the meaning of section 205 of the Law of Property Act 1925. The receiver with statutory powers under section 109 is the deemed agent of the trustee, save insofar as the Insolvency Act 1986 prevents it, and likewise, for the same reasons as with individual death, it is likely that the receiver who in the mortgage conditions is the express deemed agent of 'the mortgagor' where that term includes successors in title, is the deemed agent of the trustee in bankruptcy save insofar as the Insolvency Act 1986 prevents it.[275]

6.214 The trustee in bankruptcy's powers include carrying on any business of the bankrupt so far as may be necessary for winding it up beneficially,[276] and the power to deal with any property in the bankrupt's estate as the bankrupt might have dealt with it.[277]

6.215 It seems likely that a court would find that the deemed agency is terminated by the bankruptcy at least insofar as necessary to prevent personal liabilities being imposed on the trustee in bankruptcy. The purpose of bankruptcy, the trustee's function and his powers, are similar to the purpose of liquidation, the function of the liquidator and the powers of the company, in a company liquidation.

6.216 However, it is not obvious that the Insolvency Act 1986 does prevent the trustee from having personal liability.[278] Personal liability would not be

---

[272] Insolvency Act 1986, s 284. Such a disposition is void.

[273] It is arguable that the receiver could sell in his own name, if he has the lender's power of sale, but the effect of such a sale as against Insolvency Act 1986, s 284 is not the subject of authority. The lender could sell in its own name since this is permitted under s 285(4), so presumably the receiver with sufficient delegation could also do so. See also *Sowman v David Samuel Trust Ltd* [1978] 1 WLR 22 at 30C: sale by the receiver is not a disposition of the borrower's property because the receiver's powers are themselves property given away by the borrower at the date of the mortgage.

[274] Or the Official Receiver on the bankruptcy order: Insolvency Act 1986, ss 291A and 306.

[275] Certainly it is the trustee in bankruptcy who can complain of a lender, or presumably, a receiver's sale of the mortgaged property at an undervalue: *Jarrett v Barclays Bank Ltd* [1947] Ch 187 at 193. It is unclear why he cannot be the deemed agent.

[276] Insolvency Act 1986, Sch 5, para 1.

[277] Insolvency Act 1986, Sch 5, para 13.

[278] See fn 218 for a similar argument in relation to liquidation. The case of *In Re Simms* [1934] Ch 1 does not assist the analysis. In that case, the bankrupt, S, had before the bankruptcy order assigned his business to a company who had charged it. The lender appointed a receiver. S was then made bankrupt and the assignment found by the court to be void. The trustee elected to treat the receiver as a trespasser and sought an account of the business from him. The argument was whether the trustee could seek profits the receiver made from chattels as well as their value. The court decided he could not. He could choose to treat the receiver as trespasser and have the value of the chattels, or as his agent and call for the profits, but not both. The case is not about

contrary to his liabilities under section 304 since that 'section is without prejudice to any liability arising apart from this section'. If personal liability were imposed on the trustee, it is likely that he would disclaim the mortgaged property as onerous under section 315.[279]

6.217 Whether bankruptcy terminates the deemed agency, or the receiver thereafter acts as deemed agent of the trustee in bankruptcy, the bankruptcy will not prevent sale[280] by a receiver with suitable powers, nor leasing.[281]

6.218 It seems that the disposition should be made in the name of the trustee in bankruptcy.[282] However, it appears that the receiver does retain a power to act in the name of the borrower where this is necessary.[283]

6.219 It does not follow that the receiver can do everything he could have done before the bankruptcy. For example he cannot serve a valid notice to acquire the freehold of a leasehold house under the Leasehold Reform Act 1967,[284] because that requires the borrower to be the leaseholder for 2 years, and the effect of the bankruptcy is that the leasehold estate vests in the trustee.

6.220 If the deemed agency is terminated by bankruptcy, then the receiver does not necessarily become the agent of the lender, for the same reasons as in liquidation: he could act in his own right.[285]

---

whether a trustee in bankruptcy can treat the receiver of the bankrupt as a trespasser. *In Re Goldburg (No 2), ex parte Page* [1912] 1 KB 606, cited in that case, has similar facts.

[279] The lender's interest would not be affected: Insolvency Act 1986, s 315(3), and the lender could apply to court for an order vesting the disclaimed property in it: s 320. It is less clear that the receiver would have standing to do so, absent an appropriate delegation of the lender's power to him. See fn 218 in relation to liquidation. The receiver would, in any event, not likely wish to have the property vested in him.

[280] See para 6.174, and *Sowman v David Samuel Trust Ltd* [1978] 1 WLR 22.

[281] Nor an application for a lease extension under the Landlord and Tenant Act 1954. See *Gough's Garages Ltd v Pugsley* [1930] 1 KB 615.

[282] Since the trustee is the estate owner within the meaning of Law of Property Act 1925, ss 88(1) and 89(1) or assuming an express power of sale in 'the mortgagor's name' where mortgagor includes successors in title.

[283] In *The Keepers and Governors of the Possessions, Revenues and Goods of the Free Grammar School of John Lyon v Helman* [2014] EWCA Civ 17, [2014] 1 WLR 2451, notice to acquire the freehold under the Leasehold Reform Act 1967 was served by the receiver in the borrower's name after his bankruptcy. That notice failed because the property was vested in the trustee in bankruptcy. The question of whether the receiver could be the deemed agent of the trustee in bankruptcy was not addressed, but nor was it said that service of notice in the name of the original borrower was wrong.

[284] *The Keepers and Governors of the Possessions, Revenues and Goods of the Free Grammar School of John Lyon v Helman* [2014] EWCA Civ 17, [2014] 1 WLR 2451. Presumably, the same point would apply in relation to a lease extension under the Leasehold Reform, Housing and Urban Development Act 1993.

[285] See para 6.177.

SUMMARY OF THE DEEMED AGENCY

6.221 The key to understanding the receiver's deemed agency is to focus not on the usual idea of agency, i.e. the principal getting someone else to act in his name but on his instructions, but on two key elements.[286] First, powers: the borrower gives the receiver powers to act in his name. Secondly, liability: the borrower agrees that he will be liable for the receiver's acts.

6.222 The powers which a receiver can be given and which on standard mortgages usually are given, include the borrower's powers to deal with his property: to lease it, to collect rent, to end leases by serving notices and accepting surrenders and to sell the borrower's property. This is the first of the two key elements to the deemed agency. The borrower, by the mortgage covenants, gives the lender the power to appoint a receiver with the borrower's powers to lease and sell in the borrower's name. When the receiver is appointed by the lender, he is appointed with those powers.

6.223 The mortgage covenants usually go further. They usually allow the lender to appoint a receiver who can also exercise the lender's powers: to lease, to end leases by serving notices and accepting surrenders and, sometimes, to sell. It is usual for the receiver's deemed agency to extend to these powers, too, so that the receiver, though he is exercising the lender's powers, is exercising them as the borrower's deemed agent.

6.224 The effect is where the second of the two key elements in the deemed agency comes in. The borrower has promised the lender in the covenants to be liable for the receiver's acts even when the receiver is exercising the lender's powers. That is the extent of the deemed agency.[287] It means that the borrower cannot complain to the lender about their exercise. The borrower cannot make the lender account to him for leasing or sale of the property. Thus the lender avoids the onerous burden imposed by the courts of equity of accounting to the borrower for management of the property once the lender is in possession.

6.225 The above distinguishes between the borrower's powers to lease and sell his property and the lender's powers to lease and sell. The difference between the borrower's powers and the lender's powers are considered further in later chapters in this book.[288] The key is that in mortgage law, the borrower

---

[286] See also the summary at para 5.11.

[287] It is not inconsistent with agency for a principal to be liable for the agent's acts even though the agent, for example on the principal's instructions, contracts to sell something the principal does not have. Thus this idea of deemed agency extending to exercise of lender's powers is not inimical to ideas of agency. See the reasoning in *Cox v Hickman* (1860) 11 ER 431, quoted in *Gaskell v Gosling* [1896] 1 QB 669 at 579–583: 'the company is still the person solely interested in the profits, save only that it has mortgaged them to its creditors. It receives the benefit of the profits as they accrue, though it has precluded itself from applying them to any other purpose than the discharge of the dents'. The suggestion appears to be that the agreed fiction of the agency is to be recognised, not the reality of the debtor's lack of control.

[288] See Chapter 8 on the receiver's relationship with third parties, Chapter 10 on possession, and Chapter 11 on sale.

and the lender deal with different property. The borrower encumbers his freehold or leasehold property with the charge. From the charge come powers, rights and remedies as if it were a lease just shorter than the borrower's estate.

6.226 Thus, the borrower can only deal with his property, the charged estate. The powers emanating from the borrower which a receiver can exercise[289] relate to that encumbered estate.

6.227 The lender has greater powers. The lender's estate is, for example, free of any underleases the borrower has entered into in breach of the mortgage, or after the appointment of the receiver. Moreover, the lender can sell the property free of the charge. The powers emanating from the lender which a receiver can exercise[290] are thus more extensive. Nevertheless, the receiver exercises those more extensive powers as the borrower's deemed agent, subject only to his equitable duties to those with an interest in the equity of redemption.

6.228 This understanding of the role of deemed agency in receivership by separating ideas related to powers and ideas relating to liabilities accords with the case law about termination of the deemed agency discussed above: where the company borrower goes into liquidation, the deemed agency may end, but the powers of the receiver continue.[291] Powers can continue without the agency because the powers do not come from agency. As Vaisey J said in *In Re Northern Garage Ltd*,[292] having discussed the conceptual difficulty of the idea that the receivership can exist without the agency:

> It seems to me that if a receiver can continue to be receiver after the loss of the prescribed agency, he could equally well become receiver without ever obtaining such agency. I suppose that the receiver's contemplated position as agent of the mortgagor must be regarded as not of the essence of his position and status as receiver.

POWER OF ATTORNEY

6.229 The deemed agency discussed above is not the only possible agency relationship between the borrower and a receiver. Many mortgage conditions include the grant by the borrower to the lender, and often separately to any receiver appointed, of a power of attorney to take steps to deal with the property, including for example the sale of the charged property, in the borrower's name.

6.230 The first question which arises is whether this gives rise to a separate power, or whether it merely enhances the deemed agency, which entitles the

---

[289] If they are given to him.

[290] If they are given to him.

[291] See para 6.165 *et seq.*

[292] [1946] Ch 188 at 192.

receiver to act in the borrower's name. It is thought that the better view is that it gives rise to a separate power, although it is unclear why this is necessary, since the receiver's express right to exercise its powers in the borrower's name is itself a power of attorney.[293]

6.231 The usual interpretation of such a power of attorney is that it permits the receiver to do anything the borrower could do in his name. If the receivers carry out a transaction under the power of attorney, rather than the deemed agency of their receivership, that transaction can only deal with something owned by the borrower.

6.232 Thus, if the receiver brings a possession claim against occupiers of the charged property relying on his power of attorney only, on that interpretation, he can only succeed if the borrower could have succeeded. If for example the occupiers occupy under an assured shorthold tenancy from the borrower, the receiver, acting under the power of attorney, can only succeed if the right to serve a notice under section 21 or section 8 of the Housing Act 1988 has arisen, and he has validly served such a notice. This is even though the lender could have brought a possession claim against the occupiers as trespassers because the tenancy granted by the borrower for some reason does not bind the lender.[294]

6.233 Similarly, if the receiver sells the charged property under such a power of attorney, he can only sell the borrower's interest, which is subject to the mortgage and any beneficial interests which bind the borrower but not the lender. He cannot sell free of the mortgage, as the lender can, unless the price is enough to discharge the mortgage. He cannot sell free of the beneficial interests, though they do not bind the lender, because he cannot, by using a power of attorney granted by the borrower, use the lender's powers of overreaching.[295]

6.234 Such a power of attorney complies with the requirement in section 1(1) of the Powers of Attorney Act 1971 that an instrument creating a power of attorney must be executed as a deed by the donor because the mortgage, which incorporates the mortgage conditions, has been granted by the borrower by deed.[296] It is not necessary for the mortgage conditions to name the specific receivers later appointed by name.[297]

---

[293] See Land Registry Practice Guide 36A which makes this point. Although the express powers do not comply with the formality requirements in Powers of Attorney Act 1971, s 10, powers of attorney existed at common law before that Act was passed, so that those formalities are not necessary to the creation of a power of attorney. See *Bowstead & Reynolds* at 10-008.

[294] See Chapter 10 on possession.

[295] See Chapter 11 on sale.

[296] *Phoenix Properties Ltd v Wimpole Street Nominees Ltd* [1992] BCLC 737 at 742c. See also *Byblos Bank S A L v Al-Khudhairy* (1986) 2 BCC 99549 at 99564, col 2. Even if the mortgage was not by deed, the receiver would have powers though he might be unable to execute a conveyance of land: at 99565, col 1.

[297] *Phoenix Properties Ltd v Wimpole Street Nominees Ltd* [1992] BCLC 737 at 742f.

6.235 If the power of attorney is: (a) expressed to be irrevocable and (b) given to secure a proprietary interest in the donee of the power, or the performance of an obligation owed to the donee, then it is irrevocable, so that it cannot be ended at the choice of the borrower and will survive the death or insolvency of the borrower.[298] The power of attorney continues, and cannot be revoked by the borrower for so long as the interest or obligation remains undischarged.[299]

6.236 Under section 4(2) of the Powers of Attorney Act 1971, 'a power of attorney given to secure a proprietary interest may be given to the person entitled to the interest and persons deriving title under him to that interest'.

6.237 Clearly, an irrevocable power of attorney can be granted to the lender to secure the charge, since the charge is its proprietary interest, and the borrower has an obligation to pay the lender which the power of attorney secures.

6.238 It is less obvious that an irrevocable power of attorney can be granted to the receiver who has no proprietary interest and no title to the charge. This issue was not considered in *Phoenix Properties Ltd v Wimpole Street Nominees Ltd*.[300] The problem is mentioned in *Sowman and Others v David Samuel Trust Ltd*,[301] though it is not resolved because it was unnecessary to determine it for the purpose of the case. In that case, the receivership powers were sufficient for the receiver to have power to sell the charged property in the company's name despite the liquidation of the company.

6.239 The answer may be that the Powers of Attorney Act 1971 did not replace the common law before it, under which irrevocable powers could be granted to secure a proprietary interest of someone other than the donee of the power.[302] Furthermore, since the receiver's powers are part of the lender's power to appoint a receiver, and the lender's power cannot be revoked, it would be anomalous if the receiver's powers could themselves be revoked:[303] indeed, the lender would be able to simply re-appoint the receiver with all the powers.

6.240 Just as in *Sowman*, it is hard to see when the question of the irrevocability of the receiver's power of attorney would become an issue in litigation. Most mortgage covenants give the receiver sufficient powers as receiver to undertake most necessary transactions in the borrower's name, so the

---

[298] Powers of Attorney Act 1971, s 4. This is the enactment of a common law rule: see *Sowman and Others v David Samuel Trust Ltd* [1978] 1 WLR 22 at 30F.

[299] Powers of Attorney Act 1971, s 4(1).

[300] [1992] BCLC 737. See at 742f, where it is said that the receiver's appointment was irrevocable without any discussion.

[301] [1978] 1 WLR 22 at 30–31.

[302] See *Bowstead & Reynolds* at 10-008.

[303] *Sowman v David Samuel Trust Ltd* [1978] 1 WLR 22 at 31B: 'The receiver's power is given to him only for the protection of the debenture of the [lender], and why should it be revoked in circumstances that do not affect a power given to [the lender] direct?'.

problem is likely to arise only if the receiver's powers as receiver are limited to those in the Law of Property Act 1925, his only power to sell is under the power of attorney and the borrower has become insolvent or died, or claims to have revoked the power before sale.

6.241 If the receiver has been given a power of attorney in the conditions, it is likely the lender will have been given a like power, and that will be irrevocable. If there is any doubt about the receiver's powers, the lender could for example execute the transfer in the borrower's name or appoint the receiver as its attorney for the purpose of execution.[304]

6.242 The question of whether the receiver's appointment with a power of attorney is irrevocable has a potential relevance beyond the ability to revoke. Outside receivership, an agent under a non-irrevocable power of attorney would have the duties to his principal a real agent. An agent with an irrevocable power of attorney likely does not, because it is clear from the irrevocability that his appointment is not for the borrower's benefit, but for the purpose of securing the proprietary interest or the principal's obligation. The conflict of interest inherent in the agency has been expressly agreed by the principal in the appointment.

6.243 Whatever the status of the power of attorney, and assuming that the receiver has been appointed as receiver as well as with a power of attorney, it is likely that the receiver's duties would be no more than as receiver, notwithstanding the power of attorney. The existence of the receivership already creates a conflict of interest between the receiver and the borrower, which suggests that the usual agent's duties would not be imposed. The power of attorney has been created by the borrower to assist the receiver to get in the debt. It has not been created to assist the borrower.

---

[304] See Chapter 11.

Chapter 7

The Receiver and the Lender

7.1   Statute and/or the terms of the mortgage give the lender the ability to appoint a receiver to act as if he were the borrower's agent, but for the lender's benefit. A key question is how to analyse this.

7.2   The correct view, in the authors' opinion, is that a contract arises between the lender and the receiver at the time of the appointment under which the receiver agrees to act in return for remuneration.[1] The reason is a simple offer, acceptance and consideration analysis.

7.3   It follows that the terms of the contract and contractual rules and principles frequently provide the answers to questions about the relationship between the lender and the receiver.

7.4   It is, however, important to note that the contract operates against the background of the mortgage which regulates the dealings between the lender and the borrower, and that the power to appoint the receiver derives from the mortgage and the Law of Property Act 1925. The contract is unusual in that the receiver's primary duty to the lender under it is equitable,[2] and he also owes equitable duties to the borrower.[3]

7.5   In addition, the borrower is almost invariably solely responsible for the receiver's acts or defaults by reason of a deemed agency.[4] The way in which this impacts the interpretation of the contract between the receiver and the lender, and the relationship between the lender and the borrower, is considered below.

BEFORE THE APPOINTMENT

7.6   Typically, there will be contact between the proposed receiver and the lender before any appointment is made. At this time, the lender will provide information to the receiver about the property, which the receiver may take into account in deciding whether to accept the appointment or in fixing the terms of his remuneration.

---

[1]   Although not necessarily from the lender. See para 7.30 *et seq*.

[2]   *Silven Properties Ltd v Royal Bank of Scotland Plc* [2003] EWCA Civ 1409, [2004] 1 WLR 997 at [27] item (3).

[3]   See para 6.83 *et seq*.

[4]   See para 6.46 *et seq*.

7.7   If the lender misrepresents the position, and the receiver relies on the misrepresentation in accepting the proposed terms, the receiver will[5] be entitled:

(a)   to rescind the contract that arises on the appointment (i.e. terminate the receivership), or seek damages from the lender in lieu of rescission;[6] and

(b)   to seek damages for any loss he suffers,[7] unless the lender can prove that he had reasonable grounds to believe, and did believe, that the representation was true.[8]

7.8   However, in practice, such situations are readily resolved, for example, by allowing the receiver to resign if the job was not as he was led to believe.

AFTER THE APPOINTMENT

7.9   The terms of the contract arising on appointment are a matter of construction of the document of appointment and the terms in which any acceptance is made, bearing in mind the context.[9] Specialist works on the construction of contracts should be consulted if there is any doubt about the terms of the contract between the lender and the receiver in any given case.

7.10   The contractual terms will generally include the matters considered in the following paragraphs.

The receiver's powers

7.11   The receiver will usually be given in the appointment all the powers that the mortgage provided that a receiver would have. It is important for the receiver to check what those powers are, in any particular case.[10]

7.12   In many cases, the powers will include a power to sell the property as attorney for the borrower.

7.13   The lender may also delegate to the receiver, in the appointment, additional powers.

7.14   The receiver has power to exercise any powers which may have been delegated to him by the lender pursuant to the Law of Property Act 1925.[11]

---

[5]   Unless such liability has been excluded by the terms of the contract, which is unusual.

[6]   This is available for innocent as well as negligent misrepresentation, provided rescission is still available.

[7]   Measured as against the position had the misrepresentation not been made by the lender. Damages for negligent misrepresentation are not referable to losses by comparison to the situation if the misrepresentation were true, but if it had not been made.

[8]   Misrepresentation Act 1967, s 2. In that case, the misrepresentation would not be a negligent misrepresentation, and if rescission were no longer possible, the receiver would have no remedy.

[9]   This, of course, will include the terms of the mortgage.

[10]   See para 5.6 and Chapter 9 for discussions of the types of powers a receiver might have.

[11]   Law of Property Act 1925, s 109(3).

7.15   The only powers which can be delegated to the receiver pursuant to the Law of Property Act 1925 are:[12]

(a)   the power of leasing and accepting surrenders;[13] and
(b)   the power to insure.[14]

7.16   If these powers are delegated to the receiver, he will be acting *qua* receiver in carrying out these tasks and, under section 109(2) of the Law of Property Act 1925, as deemed agent of the borrower.

7.17   However, if the lender purports to appoint the receiver as the borrower's agent to do acts which are not in section 109 of the Law of Property Act 1925, nor do the mortgage terms provide for them to be exercised by the receiver as the borrower's deemed agent, then the 'receiver' will not be acting *qua* receiver in carrying out these functions.[15] The receiver will usually be a simple agent of the lender if he exercises such lender's powers.

7.18   One example is when the lender, by the appointment or subsequently, delegates the lender's power to take possession to the receiver, so that the receiver can obtain possession free of interests which do not bind the lender in preparation to sell with vacant possession.

The receiver's primary duty

7.19   Notwithstanding that the receiver is deemed to be the agent of the borrower, the receiver's primary duty is owed to the lender. It is a duty to seek to recover the sums due under the mortgage.[16] In performing that duty, the receiver must act in good faith and exercise reasonable care and skill. This duty arises in equity even if it is not expressed in the appointment, because it is of the essence of being a receiver.[17] The receiver is only entitled to exercise the powers he is given for the purpose of obtaining repayment of the debt.[18]

---

[12]   *Phoenix Properties v Wimpole Street Nominees* [19992] BCLC 737 at 743f. See the discussion of this case at para 11.97 *et seq*.

[13]   Law of Property Act 1925, ss 99(19) and 100(13).

[14]   Law of Property Act 1925, s 109(7).

[15]   *Phoenix Properties v Wimpole Street Nominees* [1992] BCLC 737 at 743f. It is common to insert in the mortgage conditions a clause which provides that the receiver shall act as the borrower's agent at all times (i.e. even when exercising a lender delegated power).

[16]   *Silven Properties Ltd v Royal Bank of Scotland Plc* [2003] EWCA Civ 1409, [2004] 1 WLR 997 at [27]–[29]. See also *B Johnson & Co (Builders) Ltd* [1955] Ch 634; *Ahmad v Bank of Scotland* [2016] EWCA Civ 602.

[17]   *Re B Johnson & Co (Builders) Ltd* [1955] Ch 634 at 645: 'it is the whole purpose of his appointment'; see also *International Leisure Ltd v First National Trustee Ltd* [2012] EWHC 1971 (Ch), [2013] Ch 346 at [20] and [28], in relation to administrative receivership. That the duties arise in equity even if they do not arise contractually is the counterpart of the equitable duties arising between lender and borrower, and receiver and borrower.

[18]   *Downsview Nominees Ltd v First City Corp Ltd* [1993] AC 295 at 312 and 314.

7.20   The lender can sue the receiver for breach of the duty even though the loss suffered by the lender is the same as the loss suffered by the borrower, since the receiver's primary duty is to the lender not the borrower.[19] There is little case law on the remedies available for breach of the receiver's duties to the lender. Unless there is a different contractual duty, it is likely that similar principles as apply to a breach of the receiver's duties to the borrower would apply here.[20]

7.21   Where the receiver has a power of sale (whether as attorney of the borrower or as agent for the lender), the receiver is not obliged to sell the asset immediately in order to avoid a breach of his primary duty. However, he is obliged to consider whether to do so would be the best way for the lender to recover the monies due under the mortgage.[21] If he concludes that a sale of the asset is the best way to protect the lender's interest, he should proceed with it, even if sale will be detrimental to the borrower.[22]

7.22   However, the receiver's duties to the borrower[23] do temper the primary duty in some respects. So, for example, the receiver cannot simply sell the security for just enough to repay the mortgage debt. He must take reasonable care to obtain a proper price.[24]

7.23   Similarly, if the receiver is unable to sell, or decides not to sell immediately, he is under a duty to manage the property with due diligence.

7.24   The receiver must also act in accordance with the statutory and contractual framework. It follows that, for example, the receiver cannot prioritise paying the lender the sums due under the mortgage if the applicable statutory or contractual regime which governs the use of monies he receives requires him to pay other items, such as payment of rent and rates, ahead of the mortgage monies.[25]

The extent of the receiver's duty to liaise with the lender

7.25   The receiver owes a fiduciary duty to the lender to keep the lender fully informed about the receivership.[26]

---

[19] *International Leisure Ltd v First National Trustee Ltd* [2012] EWHC 1971 (Ch), [2013] Ch 346 at [36] discussing reflective loss. It was assumed that the borrower could then only claim for any sums above the lender's loss: at [52]. The lender would have the primary entitlement to the damages for the breach of duties by the receiver.

[20] See para 6.97 *et seq*.

[21] *Downsview Nominees Ltd v First City Corp Ltd* [1993] AC 295 at 313.

[22] *Re B Johnson & Co (Builders) Ltd* [1955] Ch 634 especially at 661–663.

[23] Considered at para 6.64 *et seq*.

[24] *Downsview Nominees Ltd v First City Corp Ltd* [1993] 1 AC 295 at 315.

[25] See Chapter 12.

[26] *Gomba Holdings v Minories Finance* [1988] 1 WLR 1231 at 1233; *Re Magadi Soda* (1925) 94 LJ Ch 217.

7.26 However, the receiver does not generally[27] owe the lender any duty either to seek the lender's directions in relation to the progress of the receivership or to consult with the lender before taking any particular step.

7.27 A duty to do one or both might arise if the contract expressly so provided,[28] or if it was appropriate in all the circumstances to make that implication.[29]

The lender's duty to remunerate the receiver

7.28 Remuneration is considered in detail below.[30] The starting point, as set out there, is recovery of remuneration out of receipts.

7.29 This section considers whether the receiver can sue for unpaid remuneration. This issue is, of course, most likely to arise if the receipts are insufficient to pay the receiver.

7.30 Whether the lender is liable as a matter of contract to pay remuneration to the receiver (so that he will be paid even if receipts are insufficient to allow him to take his remuneration from them) turns on the true interpretation of the terms of the appointment.

7.31 The terms of the mortgage are plainly going to be relevant in construing the terms of the appointment:

(a) Where (unusually) the terms of the mortgage provide that the receiver is to be the lender's agent, the lender will generally be liable to pay the receiver's remuneration,[31] unless it appears that the parties intended that the receiver should be limited to remuneration from the receipts.

---

[27] The position may be otherwise when the receiver is exercising a lender delegated power as the lender's agent.

[28] If a duty to seek directions were written into the contract, and were complied with, the lender would be liable for the receiver's acts: see paras 7.49–7.50.

[29] It is highly unlikely that a duty to follow the lender's directions will be implied, other than in relation to lender delegated powers, because the consequence of the receiver complying would be to render the lender liable for the receiver's acts. It is also more likely that an obligation to consult will be implied where the power which the receiver is considering exercising is a lender delegated power which the receiver is to exercise as the lender's agent, not the borrower's deemed agent.

[30] See para 12.25 *et seq.*

[31] *Deyes v Wood* [1911] 1 KB 806. More commonly, now, the receiver acts as the borrower's agent in exercising powers conferred by the mortgage conditions. However, the lender can delegate additional powers to the receiver in the appointment, and where the mortgage does not provide for the deemed agency to cover the exercise of these powers, the lender will be liable for the remuneration of the receiver in respect of these powers even if he is not liable for the rest of it, at the least, on a *quantum meruit* basis. If there is any doubt about whether the lender is liable to pay all the remuneration, the receiver should keep separate time sheets for mortgage powers and lender-delegated powers outside the mortgage, so that he can prove the time spent on the lender delegated powers in case he should need to enforce the lender's obligation to pay his remuneration in respect of these powers.

(b)   Where the receiver is the borrower's deemed agent, it is easy to see that the starting point in construing the appointment might be that the borrower should be liable for the remuneration and not the lender,[32] but if there were wording in the mortgage conditions indicating that it was not intended that the receiver could sue the borrower, that would preclude any claim by the receiver against the borrower.[33]

(c)   In circumstances where the borrower is not liable, there would be a reasonable prospect of persuading the court to imply a term into the appointment that the lender is obliged to pay the remuneration. On the other hand, the court might, depending on the circumstances, take the view that it was intended that the receiver should not be able to recover remuneration beyond the receipts – i.e. that the receiver took the chance that he would not recover his remuneration in full, or indeed any remuneration.

7.32   Given the uncertainties, it is plainly wise for the receiver to ensure either that there is an express contractual obligation on the lender in the appointment to pay the remuneration even if receipts are insufficient, or that he has investigated the likelihood of receipts being insufficient, before he accepts the appointment.

The lender's duty to indemnify the receiver

7.33   One specific part of the receiver's remuneration package calls for further comment. Frequently, the receiver will want an obligation on the lender to indemnify the receiver for any loss and damage which he may suffer as a result of the appointment.

7.34   The scope of any indemnity is a question of construction. Generally, an obligation to indemnify will not extend to losses caused by:

(a)   acts beyond the receiver's powers;
(b)   negligent acts or defaults by the receiver;
(c)   acts which the receiver knows are otherwise tortious;[34]

unless these acts were done at the direction of the lender.[35]

7.35   Whether an obligation to indemnify can be implied will turn on the facts of each case. Where the receiver is acting as the deemed agent of the borrower, it is unlikely that any obligation on the lender to indemnify will be implied into the appointment if the terms of the mortgage do not, on their true construction, permit an indemnity to be given.[36]

---

[32]   With the receiver able to sue the borrower by reason of the Contracts (Rights of Third Parties) Act 1999. See para 5.8.

[33]   Contracts (Rights of Third Parties) Act 1999, s 1(2).

[34]   *W Cory & Son v Lambton and Hetton Collieries* (1916) 86 LJKB 401.

[35]   *Re B Johnson & Co (Builders)* [1955] 1 Ch 634 at 647–648.

[36]   Because the costs could not be recharged to the mortgage account.

7.36   However, where the receiver acts as the lender's agent, an obligation by the lender will be implied.[37]

7.37   However, a lender may also be obliged to indemnify a receiver (in full or in part) under the Civil Liability (Contribution) Act 1978 if the lender is liable to the borrower or third party for the same damage.[38] The size of the contribution is 'such as may be found by the Court to be just and equitable having regard to the extent of that person's responsibility for the damage in question',[39] so if the receiver exercised no discretion at all and simply relied on the lender's directions, it is at the very least possible that the lender may be obliged to provide the receiver with a complete indemnity under this provision.

The receiver's duty to indemnify the lender

7.38   Unless the terms of the contract preclude this, the receiver will be liable to indemnify the lender against any liability it may incur as a result of the receiver's acts if:

(a)   the receiver is negligent; and
(b)   the receiver was not simply acting in accordance with directions from the lender.[40]

7.39   Similarly, the lender could also rely on the Civil Liability (Contribution) Act 1978 if both the receiver and the lender were liable to the borrower or a third party for the same damage.[41]

IMPACT OF INVALID OR DEFECTIVE APPOINTMENT

7.40   If the appointment is invalid or defective, the purported receiver has no statutory or other powers deriving from the mortgage[42] and is not to be treated, as against the borrower, as a receiver at all. However, as between the lender and the purported receiver, a contract will nonetheless come into existence.[43]

7.41   A term will readily be implied into that contract which relieves the receiver of any obligation to carry out the primary duty of the receiver if he does not have power to perform it because his appointment is invalid or

---

[37]   *Bank of Baroda v Panessar* [1987] 1 Ch 335 at 354.

[38]   See para 7.44 *et seq* for the circumstances in which a lender will be liable for the receiver's acts.

[39]   Civil Liability (Contribution) Act 1978, s 2(1).

[40]   *American Express International Banking Corp v Hurley* (1986) 2 BCC 98993. See para 7.44 *et seq* for the circumstances in which a lender will be liable for the receiver's acts and omissions.

[41]   See para 7.37.

[42]   However, if the appointment validly delegates powers to act on behalf of the lender, the receiver will have those powers.

[43]   See paras 7.69–7.70 for the impact of an invalid appointment on the lender's liability for the receiver's acts.

defective. The lender will not be able to complain that the receiver has not fulfilled that duty in the circumstances.

7.42   However, to the extent that the lender has an obligation to remunerate the receiver, that remains effective. Furthermore, it is suggested that the court will readily imply into that contract:

(a)   a warranty of authority by the lender (upon which the receiver can sue for any losses he suffers as a result of relying on that authority to appoint); and/or

(b)   a covenant by the lender to indemnify the receiver against any liabilities which he suffers as a result of acting on the purported appointment;[44]

if the invalidity or defect stems from something which the receiver could not easily check.

Company borrower

7.43   In addition, where the borrower is a company, the court can order a lender to indemnify the supposed receiver for any losses arising solely by reason of the invalidity of the appointment.[45] This is a statutory power and exists even where the terms of the mortgage preclude any implication.

THE LENDER'S LIABILITY FOR THE RECEIVER'S ACTS AND DEFAULTS

7.44   Both the borrower and third parties may wish to claim that the lender is liable for the receiver's acts.

7.45   When considering any such claim, the starting point is to ascertain the capacity in which the receiver was acting when he committed the relevant act or default.[46]

As lender's agent

7.46   If the receiver is acting as the lender's agent, the lender will, in accordance with the general rules about a principal's liability for the acts of his agent, be liable for any wrongful acts or defaults of the receiver when acting in this capacity.[47] In brief, this means that the lender will be liable on contracts

---

[44]   See para 4.108 *et seq*, especially para 4.122, for a discussion of the consequences of acting on an invalid appointment.

[45]   Insolvency Act 1986, s 34.

[46]   See Chapter 5.

[47]   *In Re Vimbos* [1900] 1 Ch 470 at 473; *Robinson Printing Company Ltd v Chic Ltd* [1905] 2 Ch 123; *Deyes v Wood* [1911] 1 KB 806; *In Re Goldburg (No 2), ex parte Page* [1912] 1 KB 606.

made by the receiver as agent of the lender and will be liable for his torts if it authorised the action in question.[48]

As borrower's agent

The general rule

7.47   Generally, the mortgage terms will provide for the receiver to act as the borrower's agent.[49] In these circumstances, the general rule is that the lender is not liable for any acts or defaults of the receiver it appointed.

7.48   That general rule applies even if the receiver acted outside his powers,[50] unless, on the facts, it is proper to infer that the receiver acted as agent for the lender rather than on his own account.[51]

The exception

7.49   If the lender interferes with the conduct of the receivership, the lender can be liable for the receiver's acts and defaults.[52]

7.50   It is a question of fact whether the lender's acts amount to interference, but the following guidance can be given:

(a)   If the lender is merely the passive recipient of information given to it by the receiver, interference is unlikely to be found. There is therefore no difficulty with the receiver keeping the lender informed as to the progress of the receivership and his plans.[53] The fact that the lender has the opportunity to, and does not, object to the receiver's proposed course of action does not result in the lender becoming liable for it.[54]

(b)   However, if the lender tells the receiver what to do (whether or not he is invited to), interference is likely to be found.[55]

---

[48]   See paras 6.32–6.33.

[49]   For examples, see para 5.25.

[50]   *Gosling v Gaskell* [1897] 1 AC 575 at 595. In *Gosling*, the defendant was, on the facts, found to be estopped from disputing the scope of the receiver's powers. It is, therefore, arguable that the case should be distinguished in a case where this feature was not present. However, the reasoning does not appear to turn on this fact.

[51]   See paras 7.69–7.70.

[52]   *Standard Chartered Bank v Walker* [1982] 1 WLR 1410.

[53]   In *Gosling v Gaskell* [1897] AC 575 at 582 per Lord Halsbury: 'The fact of the [lender] keeping a check upon the mode in which the produce of the trade carried on was dealt with ... appears to me to reflect no light whatever on the relation of the [lender] to outside creditors'. Indeed, the receiver has a duty to keep the lender informed: see para 7.25.

[54]   *National Bank of Greece v Pinios* [1990] 1 AC 637 especially at 648–649.

[55]   In *Standard Chartered Bank v Walker* [1982] 1 WLR 1410, the allegation was that the lender had instructed the receiver to sell the borrower's stock as quickly as possible, and had given directions as to how the sale was to be publicised. This was said to give rise to a triable issue.

7.51   The difficult cases are those where the receiver 'consults' the lender, and the lender expresses a preference for a particular course of action.[56]

7.52   Here, the receiver's discretion is not 'taken away',[57] for the receiver is, on the face of things, entitled to disregard the lender's views. However, in practice it may be that a suggestion or request from the lender has the same effect as a statement which is in terms a direction, because the receiver will wish to keep his appointing lender happy, in the hope of securing further appointments in the future.

7.53   Where, as a matter of fact, the receiver did consider matters for himself, the lender will not be liable, but where the receiver simply did as the lender asked without exercising any independent thought, the lender is likely to be liable.[58]

7.54   Lenders would therefore be well advised to make it clear that receivers are to be free to form their own judgment about the best way forward when making requests or suggestions (which should be framed as such), and receivers should record their reasons for reaching their decision in a contemporaneous note, at least in cases where it is clear that the borrower dissents from the proposed course of action.

7.55   If there is 'interference', the lender does not automatically become liable for all acts and defaults of the receiver, even those unrelated to the interference. The lender is liable only for the acts or defaults of the receiver which have some causal connection with the interference.[59]

7.56   The lender will not be liable to the borrower for any acts which it directed the receiver to perform if the borrower also agreed that the receiver should so act. The borrower will be estopped from complaining about these acts.

7.57   However, where the claim is brought by a third party, it will be a question of fact whether the lender's direction was the sole cause of the receiver acting as he did, or whether the receiver considered the matter himself.

---

[56]   Note that there is generally no duty to consult: see para 7.26.

[57]   See *Standard Chartered Bank v Walker* [1982] 1 WLR 1410 at 1417B.

[58]   *Bicester Properties Ltd v West Bromwich Commercial Ltd*, 10 October 2012, unreported, Master Bowles, at [15] and [17].

[59]   *Bicester Properties Ltd v West Bromwich Commercial Ltd*, 10 October 2012, unreported, Master Bowles, at [15]. In *Standard Chartered Bank v Walker* [1982] 1 WLR 1410, the test was put in this way (at 1416A): '... the bank is not responsible for what the receiver does except insofar as it gives him directions or interferes with his conduct of the realisation ...'; and (at 1419A): '... one is left with the question, was the conduct of the auction the consequence of instructions from the Bank'.

When the receiver exercises a lender-delegated power as deemed agent of the borrower[60]

7.58   The borrower will not be able to claim against the lender unless there is interference by the lender in the receiver's exercise of the power, because, by agreeing that the receiver would act as his (the borrower's) agent, the borrower has agreed that he and not the lender would have liability for the receiver's acts.[61]

7.59   However, the position is more complicated where it is a third party who seeks to claim. The third party is not, of course, bound by the mortgage, so the question in a third party claim is who the true principal of the receiver was.

7.60   When the lender gives the receiver a lender's delegated power, it is not necessary for the lender to give the receiver the power to make the lender liable for the receiver's acts as his principal. A power to sell property owned by A can be given by A to someone, B, who does not own that property without B being A's agent in dealing with the property. A will be bound by the sale of the property by B in the sense that A cannot protest when the buyer, C, says he now owns it. It does not follow that B must act in A's name in selling the property (and if he does not then A will not be liable on the contract). B need only show that he has the power of sale. Nor must A be principal for all of B's acts in selling the property (e.g. if B were to commit a tort as part of the process of selling).

7.61   Thus, a distinction must be made between the potential liability of a lender as principal[62] and its liability, because the power given to the receiver is a power to affect the lender's mortgage and hence relationship with third parties.

7.62   Unless the lender agrees that the receiver is to act as its agent, it will not be the principal for the receiver's actions. If the receiver contracts in the borrower's name, or his own name as the deemed agent of the borrower, then it is the borrower who will be liable as principal to third parties for any breach of contract.[63]

7.63   The lender may, however, be affected by the receiver's acts.

7.64   The clearest example is on delegation of the lender's power of sale to the receiver. Since the power is exercisable in the name of the borrower,[64] and assuming exercise by the receiver in the borrower's name, it will be the borrower who is the party to the deed of transfer, and any third party claim will

---

[60]   See para 7.46 for the position where the receiver acts as the lender's agent

[61]   See para 5.22.

[62]   Which would make the lender liable on all contracts entered into by the receiver, and vicariously liable for the receiver's torts carried out within the agency.

[63]   See Chapters 5, 6 and 8 for discussions of why and whether the borrower would be liable to the third party under the deemed agency.

[64]   Law of Property Act 1925, ss 88(1) and 89(1).

lie against the borrower, not the lender. However, the effect of the transfer would be sale free of the mortgage,[65] and hence the lender could not seek to enforce mortgagee remedies against the third party buyer.

7.65   If the power is the lender's power of leasing under section 99(2) of the Law of Property Act 1925, then the power is to grant leases of the mortgaged land, binding both borrower and landlord. The lease can be granted in the borrower's name.[66] The borrower is liable as landlord under the lease, since that is the effect of exercise of the power.[67] In any event, the lender would be bound by a lease so granted and, therefore, could not, for example, take possession against the tenant as a trespasser.

7.66   Likewise, if the power is the lender's power of accepting surrenders under section 100(2) of the Law of Property Act 1925, the power is to accept surrenders of leases of the mortgaged land.[68] The effect of the surrender would be to bind both borrower and lender in the sense that neither could contend against the third party that the lease continued.[69]

7.67   If the power is the lender's statutory power to insure,[70] then if the lender instructs the receiver to insure as deemed agent of the borrower, that insurance will be in the borrower's name, and the third party insurer would have a claim, for example, for the cost, against the borrower, not the lender. There could be no claim by a third party against the lender, since the exercise of the power does not affect the lender's interest.

The receiver acting on his own account

7.68   This section is concerned with situations in which the receiver does not act as agent for either the lender or the borrower and considers the extent to which the lender can be liable for his acts in those situations.[71]

7.69   The receiver will rarely willingly act on his own account. There are, however, two particular situations in which this can occur:

---

[65]   This possibility is discussed at para 11.87 *et seq*.

[66]   See para 9.141 *et seq*.

[67]   However, if the lender takes possession, the lender could be liable. For leases granted after 1 January 1996, a tenant can claim on landlord covenants against a lender in possession entitled to the rents and profits: Landlord and Tenant (Covenants) Act 1995, s 15(2) by reference to s 15(1)(b). For a lease granted before that date, the lender in possession is likely to be liable under Law of Property Act 1925, s 142(1). The deemed agency may give the lender a right to an indemnity from the borrower for any liabilities and/or allow the lender to add such costs to the mortgage debt.

[68]   Law of Property Act 1925, s 100(2) by reference to s 100(1).

[69]   See para 9.157 *et seq* for a discussion of whether the receiver could accept surrenders in the name of the borrower.

[70]   Law of Property Act 1925, s 101(1)(ii).

[71]   This is not the same question as whether the receiver has liability to third parties on any contracts he enters into. The receiver can have such liability even if he is acting within the scope of the deemed agency. This is considered at para 8.201 *et seq*.

(a)   if the appointment was invalid or defective; or

(b)   the borrower becomes insolvent, is dissolved, or dies, and the receiver's deemed agency ceases.[72]

7.70   In both cases, the receiver will likely act on his own account unless it is possible to infer either from the terms of the appointment, interpreted against the background,[73] or from the lender's subsequent acts,[74] that the lender agreed to become the receiver's principal in these circumstances.[75]

7.71   Where the receiver does act on his own account, the lender will not be liable for his acts or defaults unless interference[76] is shown. The general rule set out above[77] applies.

---

[72]   See para 6.160 *et seq* for a discussion of when the deemed agency ends.

[73]   There is no suggestion in the authorities that such a term is readily to be implied. No such term was implied in *Gosling v Gaskell* [1897] AC 575 (insolvency) or *Bank of Baroda v Panessar* [1987] 1 Ch 335 (invalid appointment). However, it is considered that a term might now be implied where:

   (a)   the defect or invalidity in the appointment was not a matter which the receiver could have verified easily: cf para 4.122; or

   (b)   the borrower was insolvent at the time of the appointment.

[74]   The lender's subsequent acts were sufficient to persuade the court to infer that the lender had agreed to become the receiver's principal in *Amercian Express v Hurley* (1986) 2 BCC 98993 at 98997. The basis for this finding appears to be that there was 'constant communication between the bank and the receiver and the latter sought the former's approval to such actions as he proposed to take'. However, it is clear that mere knowledge that the receiver is continuing to act is not enough: *Gosling v Gaskell* [1897] AC 575 at 592–593. Presumably, what is required is some active encouragement to continue acting as receiver.

[75]   If the lender did agree to become the principal, the lender will be liable for the receiver's acts: see para 7.46.

[76]   In the sense described at para 7.50 *et seq*.

[77]   See para 7.47. Where the appointment was invalid/defective: *Bank of Baroda v Panessar* [1987] 1 Ch 335 at 354. In *Panessar*, the defendant was, on the facts, found to be estopped from disputing the validity of the appointment. It is, therefore, arguable that it should be distinguished in a case where this feature was not present. However, the reasoning does not appear to turn on this fact. In a case on insolvency, *Yorkshire Bank Plc v Mashford & Others*, 3 April 1987, unreported, CA, the defendant does not appear to have advanced an argument that, on the construction of the mortgage, or by virtue of the lender's acts, the receivers had become the agent of the lender.

Chapter 8

The Receiver and Third Parties

INTRODUCTION

8.1   This chapter is concerned with the receiver's relationship with the various third parties with whom he may deal during the receivership.

8.2   The first part of the chapter deals with how the receiver is to deal with third parties with whom the borrower had some sort of pre-existing relationship before the receivership began: third parties with whom the borrower has a contract; occupiers (leaseholders, licensees, beneficiaries under a trust, trespassers or other occupiers); landlords; and neighbours.

8.3   Later in the chapter, the question of the receiver's liability on new relationships formed by the borrower is considered, as well as the receiver's ability to form new relationships himself.

8.4   Lastly, the chapter discusses the receiver's liability in tort for acts committed whilst acting as receiver and the extent to which he might have statutory liabilities.

THE BORROWER'S PRE-EXISTING CONTRACTS

8.5   In this section, the situation envisaged is that prior to the appointment of the receiver, the borrower entered into a contract with a third party, for example, a contract for the sale of the mortgaged property, or an employment contract, or a contract for a utility. First, some general principles about the effect of the receivership on those contracts are discussed. Next, principles particular to certain types of contract are considered.

General principles

8.6   Contracts which the borrower entered into prior to the appointment of the receiver do not terminate automatically on that appointment.[1] Should it be within his powers to do so,[2] the receiver can adopt and enforce them.[3]

---

[1]   However, if there is an express term in the contract bringing it to an end if a receiver is appointed, that will be effective. Some hire purchase contracts, in particular, contain such a clause, giving the third party the right to repossess the goods.

[2]   See Chapter 9 for a discussion of receivers' powers.

[3]   Furthermore, he can ratify a previous agent's acts, and adopt the contract, even when that agent was acting with apparent not actual authority: *Lawson v Hosemaster Co Ltd* [1966] 1 WLR 1300.

8.7   However, a receiver is not generally obliged to perform the borrower's obligations under any contract which the borrower has entered into before his appointment.[4] Indeed, he can actively frustrate the contract if to do so is in the best interests of the lender,[5] even though the borrower could not,[6] and regardless of the impact on the borrower's commercial interests.[7] The reason is that the receiver's principal duty is to the lender and to get in the assets in order to repay the debt.[8]

8.8   If a receiver fails to perform the borrower's contract, or frustrates or repudiates it, and does so within his powers whilst acting as the borrower's deemed agent, then his act will be the borrower's. Thus the borrower's relationship with the third party will be affected.

8.9   In general, if the borrower's contractual obligations are not performed:

(a)   The borrower will be in breach of contract and will be liable to pay damages to the contracting party.

(b)   If the receiver is acting properly[9] and within his powers, the borrower will have no cause of action against the receiver despite these losses. Nor will the borrower likely be able to prevent the receiver by injunction from failing to perform the contract.[10]

(c)   If the receiver has not been validly appointed, or is acting outside his powers, or is in breach of duty in failing to perform the contract[11] then the borrower will have a cause of action against the receiver.

---

[4]   *Airlines Airspares Ltd v Handley Page Ltd* [1970] Ch 193; *Lathia v Dronsfield* [1987] BCLC 321. In principle, any party to a contract can seek to repudiate or frustrate it. The cases suggest that the court will permit the receiver to frustrate or repudiate, and prevent the other party insisting on performance, where that would not seriously affect the assets of the borrower or its future prospects, i.e. presumably, where the receiver is acting in accordance with his duties in deciding not to perform the contract. The question will be whether the other party can insist on performance, with the assistance for example of a court order for specific performance or an injunction. See paras 8.10–8.18.

[5]   *Airlines Airspares Ltd v Handley Page Ltd* [1970] Ch 193.

[6]   *Airlines Airspares Ltd v Handley Page Ltd* [1970] Ch 193.

[7]   *Lathia v Dronsfield* [1987] BCLC 321 at 326.

[8]   See para 6.66. If the receiver could not do so, 'almost any unsecured creditor would be able to improve his position and prevent the receiver from carrying out, or at any rate carrying out as sensibly and equitably as possible, the purpose for which he was appointed': *Airlines Airspares Ltd v Handley Page Ltd* [1970] Ch 193 at 198. See also *Edwin Hill & Partners v First National Finance Corp* [1989] 1 WLR 225 as to a lender's insistence on a borrower breach of a post-mortgage contract. The lender was not liable for the tort of procuring a breach since it was justified by the lender's superior right. Moreover, the lender could obtain the same result via its remedies.

[9]   See Chapter 6 for the receiver's duty to the borrower (paras 6.64–6.95), and remedies on breach (paras 6.96–6.138).

[10]   See para 6.157.

[11]   That might be so if the borrower had entered into a *bona fide* contract for sale at a price which would redeem the mortgage, for example.

(d)   In particular, the receiver owes a duty to the borrower to use monies coming into his hands in accordance with the agreed distribution scheme,[12] so in some circumstances the receiver will owe a duty to the borrower (but not to the contracting party) to comply with the contract. If he breaches that duty, the borrower can sue the receiver.

(e)   The third party has no cause of action against the receiver,[13] provided the receiver acts *bona fide* and within the scope of his authority.[14] If, however, he exceeds his authority[15] or acts *mala fide* in preventing the borrower from performing its contractual obligations, the receiver may be liable to the third party for procuring a breach of contract.

Specifically enforceable contracts

8.10   Is the position different if the third party seeks an order for specific performance of the contract against the borrower, or the receiver?

8.11   All contracts are in principle capable of the equitable remedy of specific performance, but there is a threshold for the court to make the order, whether damages are an adequate remedy. If damages are not adequate, the court may order specific performance of the contract provided it is equitable to do so in the circumstances.

8.12   It is more common for an order for specific performance to be granted where the contract is for the sale of land or an agreement for a lease than for other contracts because land is more often treated as unique, so that damages are not an adequate remedy.[16] A contract to supply specific goods is also more likely to be capable of specific performance.[17]

8.13   Where the third party to the contract makes a claim against the borrower for its specific enforcement after a receiver has been appointed, how will the court approach the application?

8.14   The appointment of the receiver does not, without more, prevent an order for specific performance of the borrower's contract being made against the

---

[12]   See Chapter 12.

[13]   *Welsh Development Agency v Export Finance Co* [1992] BCC 270 at 287–288 and 295 (but note that Dillon LJ left open this rule being reversed by a higher court).

[14]   *Lathia v Dronsfield* [1987] BCLC 321. Alleging that there is a lack of *bona fide* is the same as alleging fraud or improper motive: *Lathia* at 326. See para 6.89.

[15]   Note that a receiver is unlikely to have authority to sell goods which are subject of a retention of title clause. If he does this, the receiver may be liable to the party entitled to the goods in conversion.

[16]   However, this is not a universal proposition. If the land has been purchased to provide an income, for example it is a reversion on a lease, or is not for personal use, but simply an investment, then damages are more likely to be adequate than if, say, a residential property is bought for occupation by the buyer, or a commercial property bought to set up a shop or a factory.

[17]   *Land Rover Group Ltd v UPF (UK) Ltd* [2002] EWHC 3183 (QB), [2003] 2 BCLC 222.

borrower.[18] The reason is that the appointment of the receiver does not end the buyer's equitable interest[19] in the property. The mere fact that a receiver has been appointed does not destroy that interest.[20] The appointment itself does not have the legal effect of raising a defence to the claim.[21]

8.15   Nor does the possibility of the receiver having direct liability to ensure the performance of the contract, for example, by executing a transfer where the contract is for sale of the mortgaged property, provide a successful argument against an order for specific performance, without more.[22]

8.16   It does not follow from those propositions, however, that the court will usually order specific performance in these cases. Specific performance is an equitable remedy, and there are a number of reasons why specific performance might be refused.[23] The court will not likely order specific performance against a borrower after receivers have been appointed in the following situations:

(a)   Where the borrower cannot in practice comply.[24] It should be noted that the fact of receivership does not mean that the borrower cannot comply. If the

---

[18]   *Freevale Ltd v Metrostore (Holdings) Ltd* [1984] 1 Ch 199 at 211A. In *Freevale*, the litigation was between the borrower and the purchaser on a borrower's contract to sell the mortgaged property. The only defence suggested was the appointment of the receiver, not, for example, that the receiver could get a better price. The parties agreed that the contract would have been specifically enforceable had there been no appointment. The receiver does not seem to have been a party to the litigation. The decision in *American Airspaces Ltd v Handley Page Ltd* [1970] Ch 193 was distinguished because specific performance would not have been ordered of that contract even if a receiver had not been appointed. See also *Land Rover Group Ltd v UPF (UK) Ltd* [2002] EWHC 3183 (QB), [2003] 2 BCLC 222, which followed *Freevale*. Note the suggestion in *Astor Chemical Ltd v Synthetic Technology Ltd* [1990] BCC 97 that in *Freevale* the pre-existing contract bound the lender, though that does not appear in *Freevale* itself.

[19]   The interest of the purchaser on a contract for sale of land. The buyer is described as having an equitable interest in the property from the date of the contract, under something akin to a trust, though that equitable interest remains the right to call for specific performance of the contract if the buyer is ready, willing and able to perform his side of it. The same arguments apply where the contract does not relate to land, since the other contracting party has an equity in the sense that he can ask the court in its equitable discretion to make an order for specific enforcement.

[20]   *Freevale Ltd v Metrostore (Holdings) Ltd* [1984] 1 Ch 199 at 210E.

[21]   *Freevale Ltd v Metrostore (Holdings) Ltd* [1984] 1 Ch 199 at 211A.

[22]   *Freevale Ltd v Metrostore (Holdings) Ltd* [1984] 1 Ch 199 at 206. The receiver should not incur personal liability because the subject matter of the contract will remain the property of the borrower. The reference to personal liability in *Freevale* was because of discussion of a Scottish case where, under different law, there could have been personal liability. There was no discussion in *Freevale* of how the receiver could be made to execute the transfer so as to have personal liability.

[23]   The equitable interest of the buyer which is not destroyed by the appointment of a receiver is the right to call for specific performance, which right is subject to the equitable bars and subject to the court's equitable jurisdiction.

[24]   *Freevale Ltd v Metrostore (Holdings) Ltd* [1984] 1 Ch 199 at 206. This is a general bar to specific performance. For an example of such a circumstance, if the contract is for sale of the mortgaged property free of encumbrances, and the lender has the benefit of a restriction on the title and the sale price will not redeem the mortgage, the court is unlikely to order specific performance (at least without some abatement of the purchase price) since the borrower cannot deliver the property free of encumbrances.

borrower does not comply with the order for specific performance, at least in the case of an order to transfer real property, the court can execute the transfer in his place.[25] Moreover, a corporate borrower can comply with the order through the receiver.[26] In principle, for any kind of borrower, the receiver could be joined to the proceedings[27] and an order for specific performance sought directly against the receiver. It is unclear, however, with what jurisdiction the court could make an order for specific performance directly against the receiver.[28]

(b) Where enforcing the contract would cause hardship to the borrower, for example, if the borrower has contracted to sell at a significant undervalue.[29]

(c) Where enforcing the contract is impossible or futile.[30] This seems likely if the mortgage cannot be redeemed, and hence either the transfer to the borrower's purchaser would be subject to the mortgage, which a purchaser usually would not accept,[31] or could not be registered because there is a

---

[25] Senior Courts Act 1981, s 39.

[26] *Freevale Ltd v Metrostore (Holdings) Ltd* [1984] 1 Ch 199 at 206.

[27] Under CPR, Pt 19.

[28] The difficulty is determining what cause of action the buyer would have against the receiver. The purchaser would only have a cause of action against the receiver if, by reason of the equitable interest arising from his contract, he was interested in the equity of redemption. Since, however, that equitable interest is trust-like, though an odd sort of trust, and beneficiaries are not so interested (see Chapter 6, fn 69), it seems unlikely that the borrower's purchaser would have a cause of action. Even if he did, it would only be in limited circumstances, for example, where the price was sufficient to redeem the mortgage, that the receiver's duty would be to transfer the property to the buyer under the buyer's contract. In principle, it might be possible to argue that the receiver would be in breach of duty to the borrower in refusing to execute the transfer, thus putting the borrower in breach of the order for specific performance, but see *Gomba Holdings UK Ltd v Homan* [1986] 1 WLR 1301: the receiver has an unrestricted power of sale. Unless the receiver is in breach of duty to the borrower, the borrower cannot control him, and it is unclear how a court could. A court does not have unrestricted jurisdiction over all persons where there is no cause of action. The case law does not explain the basis for an order against the receiver directly even when it appears to suggest it is possible, for example, in *Freevale Ltd v Metrostore (Holdings) Ltd* [1984] 1 Ch 199.

[29] If the borrower's contract was at a price sufficient to redeem the mortgage debt, then it is hard to see how a receiver would not be in breach of duty if he refused to allow its completion. If the contract is below the sum required, then assuming the lender can prevent registration, or the buyer will take subject to the mortgage because it is registered, and that is in breach of the contract, then it seems likely arguable the borrower would suffer sufficient hardship to prevent completion. Indeed, it is unclear why the buyer would want to complete.

[30] Where the lender could achieve the same result as the receiver's refusal to act by exercising its other remedies, for example, a sale under its power, it is hard to see why specific performance would be ordered. See *Edwin Hill & Partners v First National Finance Corp* [1989] 1 WLR 225. A decision to the contrary would give the buyer preference over the lender's secured rights. What is key seems to be whether the receiver's resistance would be in breach of duty. See the reference to whether the receiver's refusal to perform the contract would adversely affect the company assets in *Airlines Airspares Ltd v Handley Page Ltd* [1970] Ch 193 and *Astor Chemical Ltd v Synthetic Technology Ltd* [1990] BCC 97.

[31] And would usually be a breach of the contract for sale. Note that the lender could appoint a receiver to sell the buyer's registered estate if the buyer took subject to the mortgage, which suggests a futility in the sale.

restriction on the title preventing registration without the consent of the lender.[32]

(d) Where enforcing the contract would result in the receiver coming under some personal liability.[33]

(e) Where the contracting party had actual knowledge[34] that the borrower was in breach of the terms of its charge in entering into the contract.[35]

8.17   Furthermore, whilst unlikely to be determinative, the intervention of a third party interest will be a relevant factor in determining whether specific performance ought to be granted.

8.18   If an order for specific performance were made against the receiver,[36] the receiver will be obliged to take any steps within his authority to cause the borrower to perform this obligation and to refrain from doing anything which would cause the borrower to breach this obligation.

Contracts for sale of the mortgaged property

8.19   It is not uncommon for the borrower to have entered into a contract for the sale of the mortgaged property before the receiver is appointed,[37] sometimes at below market value perhaps as an attempt to defeat the receivership and/or the lender's other routes of enforcement.

8.20   In addition, if the receiver is appointed over a site in the course of development, the receiver may find that the borrower has already contracted to sell some or all of the units to third parties.[38]

8.21   The receiver's role in relation to that contract will depend on his powers. If he has no power to deal with the mortgaged property (in particular, if he has no power of sale), then it is likely that any dispute over performance of the contract will be between the borrower and the lender, without involving him.

---

[32] In principle, it is impossible for the borrower to complete the purchase once a receiver with a borrower's power of sale has been appointed because it is the receiver and not the borrower who has the power of sale.

[33] For the reasons set out above, it is unclear how this could be so, though it is considered in *Freevale Ltd v Metrostore (Holdings) Ltd* distinguishing a Scottish case, where the receiver's liability was discussed since the receiver in that jurisdiction would incur liability.

[34] The question of what amounts to actual knowledge has not been explored.

[35] *Bower Terrace Student Accommodation Ltd v Space Student Living Ltd* [2012] EWHC 2206 (Ch).

[36] The jurisdiction for such an order is unclear. See fn 28.

[37] Borrowers also enter such contracts after the receiver is appointed. The effect of a contract made after appointment is considered at paras 8.197–8.200. See also paras 11.37–11.53 for a discussion of the possible battle between a borrower's and a receiver's contracts for sale

[38] The receiver's power to make contracts for sale himself after appointment is considered at para 8.24.

8.22   The receiver with suitable powers must consider whether to adopt the contract.

8.23   If the receiver wishes to adopt the contract the borrower has made, the question may arise as to whether the receiver can enforce it. This depends on the scope of his powers, [39] but it seems likely that if he has a power of sale he will have incidental powers in relation to pre-existing contracts. If he has the power to enforce the contract, it is likely that a notice to complete served on his authority will be valid.[40]

8.24   If the receiver does not want to adopt the contract, he may wish to enter into another contract to sell the same property. The existence of the borrower's contract does not preclude the receiver with suitable powers from entering into a further contract to sell the property.[41] The existence of such a contract will be relevant to the exercise of the court's discretion on any claim for specific enforcement of the borrower's prior contract.

8.25   If the borrower's purchaser becomes aware that the receiver does not intend to honour the contract, he may seek an injunction to prevent him from entering into an inconsistent contract or completing it.[42]

8.26   How an application to restrain entry into a contract would be treated in circumstances where the receiver is acting in accordance with his powers and in good faith so as, for example, to obtain better terms, is unclear. However, the authors suggest that if there is evidence that significantly better terms are likely to be available, an injunction will likely not be granted (because the purchaser would not be able to obtain an order for specific performance, on borrower hardship grounds).

8.27   If the application is made after a further contract has been entered into, to restrain completion of it, then the subsequent purchaser's interest must also be taken into account. In effect, the court must decide which contract to enforce.[43] It is more likely that an injunction to benefit the borrower's buyer will be refused in these circumstances.

8.28   Conversely, if the receiver contemplating entering into a contract, or completing it, is not acting properly, and is in breach of duty, an injunction is far more likely to be granted.

---

[39]   But, for an example or a receiver with sufficient powers to adopt such a contract, see *Mills v Birchall and Gilbertson* [2008] EWCA Civ 385, [2008] 1 WLR 1829.

[40]   *TBAC Investments v Valmar Works* [2015] EWHC 1213 (Ch), [2015] P & CR DG15.

[41]   *National Westminster Bank Plc v Hunter* [2011] EWHC 3170 (Ch) at [42].

[42]   *National Westminster Bank Plc v Hunter* [2011] EWHC 3170 (Ch) at [60]. *Ash & Newman v Creative Devices* Research [1991] BCLC 403. The safest course for the potential purchaser is to sue the borrower for specific performance and join the receiver in as a necessary party; and then seek an injunction preventing either the borrower or the receiver from making any further contracts pending determination of the specific performance claim.

[43]   *National Westminster Bank Plc v Hunter* [2011] EWHC 3170 (Ch) at [42].

8.29 If the receiver's power of sale is the lender's, then the borrower's pre-existing contract will not affect the buyer under the receiver's contract.[44]

8.30 However, if the receiver's power of sale is only the borrower's, then the equitable interest of the buyer under it which arises on exchange of contracts[45] will be later in priority than the buyer under the borrower's pre-existing contract.

8.31 If the receiver's contract completes and his purchaser is registered with title, then:

(a) If the borrower's purchaser has registered a notice in the charges register at Land Registry to protect his contract, or if he is in actual occupation of the property,[46] the receiver's subsequent buyer will be bound by the borrower's purchaser's equitable interest. The borrower's purchaser will be able to sue the receiver's purchaser for an order requiring him to sell the property to him on the terms of the first contract. That claim could only be defeated by the usual equitable defences.[47] In reality, a subsequent buyer is unlikely to contract if the first contract is registered, at least without an indemnity for the value of the property.

(b) If the borrower's purchaser did not register a notice to protect the contract[48] and is not in actual occupation, the receiver's purchaser will take free of the borrower's purchaser's claim.[49]

8.32 Entry by the receiver into a second contract on the borrower's behalf will inevitably result in a situation where the borrower is in breach of one contract or

---

[44] Assuming it post-dates the mortgage, or was unregistered at the date of the mortgage, so the lender took free of it. The lender's sale will overreach it.

[45] From exchange of contracts, a purchaser has an entitlement to specific performance of that contract, in equity, and hence is said to have an equitable interest in the property; he is the owner in equity. The seller holds the property on trust for the buyer, though it is an odd trust because the seller is entitled to the property until the purchase price is paid, and it is not inevitable that the court would order specific performance, for example if equitable bars such as delay, or the intervention of a third party, operate. See, for example, C Harpum, S Bridge and M Dixon, *Megarry & Wade: The Law of Real Property* (Sweet & Maxwell, 8th edn, 2012) (*Megarry & Wade*) at Ch 15.

[46] Land Registration Act 2002, s 29 and Sch 3, para 2.

[47] Delay for example. It is unclear, as a matter of general property law, whether purchase by the receiver's buyer without knowledge of the prior contract could be enough, even though he is bound by the borrower's buyer's interest. The intervention of a third party interest can be an equitable defence to a claim for specific performance. It is unclear, as a matter of general property law, whether purchase by the receiver's buyer without knowledge of the prior contract could be enough, even though he is bound by the borrower's buyer's interest.

[48] It is not standard practice for contracts to be registered, although solicitors who do not do so may commit a negligent breach of duty. If the first buyer's contract is not registered and he loses out against a second buyer, it is likely the first buyer's solicitor will have to compensate him for any shortfall between the damages he can recover from the borrower and his actual losses (subject to the usual rules on remoteness, etc).

[49] Land Registration Act 2002, s 29.

the other[50] and liable to pay damages to the disappointed purchaser. However, the receiver will not be liable to the other contracting party, or the borrower, absent *mala fide*, if he acts within the scope of his authority.[51]

8.33   Given the potential difficulties outlined above, a receiver with only the borrower's power of sale and good reason to believe that he will be able to obtain a better price than under the borrower's contract, may wish to try and rescind that contract.

8.34   However, he could only do so if:

(a)   the borrower has grounds for setting aside the contract, for example because the purchaser fails to comply with a notice to complete;[52] and

(b)   he has power to do so under the terms of the mortgage and his appointment. Where the receiver has power to 'take possession and get in the property hereby charged', a receiver does have power to sue in the name of the borrower when the borrower is entitled to rescind the contract.[53]

Other circumstances where the receiver may be bound

8.35   It has been suggested[54] that there is a further exceptional situation when a receiver will be bound by a prior contract (i.e. even if it is not capable of specific performance). If the contract pre-dated the charge, and the lender had actual knowledge of the contract and its terms at the time the charge was accepted, the receiver might be obliged to perform the contract. However, the analytical basis for this suggestion is not understood.[55]

---

50   Where the receiver's purchaser takes subject to the borrower's purchaser, he will likely have a claim for breach of contract against the borrower unless the existence of the first contract was disclosed, since it would be a latent defect in title. Failure by the receiver to disclose the existence of the first contract might be a breach of his duty to the borrower. The problem is most likely to arise when the receiver does not know of the borrower's contract until after he has entered his own.

51   See paras 6.88–6.94 as to the receiver's duty to act *bona fides*.

52   Whether the receiver has power to serve a notice to complete is a question of construction of his powers. If he does not, he will have to persuade the borrower to do so. However, a receiver who has the power to enforce the contract is likely to have the power to serve a notice to complete: *TBAC Investments v Valmar Works* [2015] EWHC 1213 (Ch), [2015] P & CR DG15.

53   *M Wheeler & Co Ltd v Warren* [1928] Ch 840. Lord Hanworth MR suggested that the action was an action for getting in the property charged because the receivers had claimed specific performance in the alternative. The other two judges did not comment on this. Query whether receivers with these powers have power to sue for rescission alone.

54   *Land Rover Group Ltd v UPF (UK) Ltd* [2002] EWHC 3183 (QB), [2003] 2 BCLC 222.

55   In *Welsh Development Agency v Export Finance* [1992] BCC 270 at 274, the contract pre-existed the charge, and the lender knew of the contract (but not its terms). The third party did not suggest that this *per se* rendered the receiver bound by the contract; it did argue that this was part of the factual matrix which might bear on the construction of the charge. However, the Court of Appeal held that the wording of the charge was clear that all of the company's assets were charged, despite the terms of the prior contract.

Employees

8.36   If the receiver has, and exercises, the power to manage the borrower's business, the question of the receiver's liability to its employees is likely to arise.

8.37   The appointment of a receiver does not of itself determine any employment contracts or contracts of service.[56]

8.38   Where section 37 of the Insolvency Act 1986 applies,[57] the receiver is personally liable on any contracts of employment he adopts. The receiver has a period of 14 days to consider matters, before he will be taken to have adopted any contract of employment. However, if the receiver knows that a person is an employee of the borrower[58] and does not give him notice within that 14-day period,[59] it is likely that the receiver will be taken to have adopted the contract.[60] The receiver should confirm the potential exposure and seek an appropriate indemnity from the appointing lender if the receivership assets will not be adequate.[61] If there is any doubt about the entitlement to an indemnity from the assets, he should seek the authority of both the lender and the borrower to pay the wages from income received.

OCCUPIERS

8.39   Often, third parties are in occupation of the property when the receiver is appointed. The receiver will need to understand the basis of their occupation, and what – if any – rights they have, in order to determine whether he can collect income from them,[62] take possession from them[63] or sell free of those interests.[64]

8.40   Some will occupy under contracts such as leases or licences;[65] others will occupy by reason of other rights, for example under a trust; or they will occupy under no right, in which case they are trespassers.

---

[56]   *In Re Mack Trucks (Britain) Ltd* [1967] 1 WLR 780.

[57]   See para 8.201.

[58]   *Re Antal International Ltd* [2003] EWHC 1339 (Ch), [2003] 2 BCLC 406.

[59]   Specialist advice should be sought as to the entitlement to terminate any contract of employment before any attempt to do so is made.

[60]   *Powdrill v Watson* [1995] 2 AC 394. This is the case even if the receiver writes to the employee stating that he will continue as an employee of the company and the company will remain liable for his wages.

[61]   The receiver is entitled to an indemnity out of the assets: Insolvency Act 1986, s 37.

[62]   See Chapter 9.

[63]   See Chapter 10.

[64]   See Chapter 11.

[65]   In which case the general principles above will be relevant.

8.41   The following sections consider the different kinds of occupiers a receiver may come across.

8.42   One of the themes of this book is that the receiver may be given powers of two types: the powers of the borrower, under which he can only do what the borrower could do; and the powers of the lender, which are often more extensive than the borrower's powers.

8.43   In particular, in relation to occupiers of the mortgaged property, the lender's mortgage may have priority over occupiers' rights, so that the lender can sell free of those rights or take possession against those occupiers as trespassers even though the borrower has given them rights to occupy.

8.44   This occurs, for example, if the borrower has given the occupier a lease in breach of mortgage, or the occupier has postponed his interest to the lender's. These situations are explored in more detail in Chapters 10 and 11.

8.45   Thus, the receiver, presented with an occupier put into occupation by the borrower, will need to understand, first, which of his powers to deal with that occupier are co-extensive with the borrower's powers and which with the lender's, and, secondly, what right – if any – the occupier has to occupy the property and whether that right binds the borrower, or the lender, or both.

8.46   Thus, for each type of occupier, whose occupation pre-exists the appointment of the receiver, the analysis below considers whether the borrower is bound, whether the lender is bound and the consequences for the receiver, for example how he can and must treat the occupier.

8.47   Thereafter, issues which arise for the receiver in relation to that occupier are discussed, insofar as they are not dealt with specifically elsewhere.[66]

The difference between a lease and a licence

8.48   If someone occupies under a contract granted by the borrower, he may do so under a licence, or under a lease or tenancy.[67]

8.49   There are a number of distinctions between licences and leases/tenancies,[68] and it can be difficult at times to determine whether a contract giving a right to occupy is a lease/tenancy or a licence.

8.50   The essential difference, however, is that under a lease or tenancy, the occupier is given an interest in land, the right to exclusive possession of identified property for a determinate term (from one date to another) or for a

---

[66]   In Chapter 9 (receiver's powers, which deals with collection of income, and powers of leasing), Chapter 10 (possession), and Chapter 11 (sale).

[67]   The two terms can be used interchangeably for the present purposes.

[68]   For more detailed commentary, see any practitioner's text on landlord and tenant law.

rolling period (e.g. weekly, monthly or yearly), in return for paying a rent. He can control its use to the exclusion of all others.

8.51   A licence, conversely, is a mere personal privilege whether it is contractual, or merely gratuitous. Although it may give a right to exclusive occupation, it is more often characterised by an inability in the licensee to exclude the property owner who granted him the licence.

Tenants

8.52   The first thing that the receiver will wish to do is establish the terms on which any tenants are occupying.

8.53   The terms are to be found in the written document if the tenancy is in writing. However, where the tenancy is oral, it can be more difficult to identify what the terms are. Key pieces of information are how long the tenants have been there, what they pay, how often they pay and what they are using the property for.[69] Whether the tenants have, in fact, been paying will also be highly material to the receiver.

8.54   Should the receiver choose to do so, he can enforce the terms of the tenancy, insofar as he has power (under the statute and/or mortgage terms and his appointment). A receiver with statutory powers to collect income has the power to do so in the names both of the borrower and the lender.[70]

8.55   In many cases, the receiver will not want to terminate the tenancy. A receiver will often be appointed when the borrower has let the property, so as to ensure that the net rents are paid to the lender.[71]

8.56   However, the receiver should not take any steps to enforce the terms until he has considered: (a) whether he is obliged to recognise the lease and (b) if not, whether it is advantageous for him to do so.

8.57   If the receiver accepts payments from the occupier, he may lose any right he may have[72] to treat him as a trespasser. The receiver must be particularly careful not to do any acts which could be construed as an acceptance of the tenant on behalf of the lender, since then the lender, too, would not be able to treat the tenant as a trespasser.

---

[69]   Since some conclusions about the nature of the tenancy may be possible from this information, for example, whether it is a periodic tenancy or a fixed term tenancy. See any practitioner's text on landlord and tenant law.

[70]   Law of Property Act 1925, s 109(3). See paras 9.52–9.59.

[71]   See paras 9.47–9.133 for the receivers' powers to collect income and Chapter 12 for the receivers' duties to distribute income.

[72]   See paras 8.60–8.76.

8.58   If the receiver simply accepts rent from the tenant in his capacity as deemed agent of the borrower, this is unlikely to be an action on which acceptance by the lender of the tenancy can be found.[73]

8.59   However, if the receiver acts as the lender's agent, the receiver's acts can amount to recognition of the tenancy by the lender,[74] even if the receiver and the lender so acted in ignorance of the deemed agency principle, which would have enabled the receiver to act as the borrower's agent.[75] Care should, therefore, be taken before any rent is accepted in any case where there is a possibility that the receiver will wish to rely on a lender power to evict the tenant.

Is the receiver bound by the lease?

8.60   The question of whether the receiver will be required to treat the leaseholder as such, rather than as a trespasser, will depend on whether his powers are borrower powers, or lender powers, and in the case of the latter, whether the lease binds the lender.

8.61   It is a question of construction of the mortgage (and the appointment) whether the receiver has only borrower's powers, or lender's powers, or both.

Receiver with borrower's powers

8.62   A tenancy, once granted,[76] gives the tenant an estate in land. That part of the borrower's obligation has been performed. A landlord's refusal to perform landlord obligations, even if expressed as a permanent refusal, does not end that estate.[77] If the receiver with the borrower's right of possession[78] sought to bring it to an end simply by retaking possession, hence other than by one of the recognised means of bringing a lease to an end under the common law,[79] a court on the occupier's claim would order possession to be returned to him because he has the estate in the land and the receiver would not have the better

---

[73]   *Lever Finance Ltd v Needleman's Trustee* [1956] 1 Ch 375 at 381–382, cited in *Nijar v Mann* (2000) 32 HLR 223 at 228; *Barclays Bank Ltd v Kiley* [1961] 1 WLR 1050.

[74]   *Lever Finance Ltd v Needleman's Trustee* [1956] 1 Ch 375: in that case the right to appoint a receiver had not arisen so that the receiver in collecting rent was acting as agent of the bank.

[75]   As happened in *Nijar v Mann* (2000) 32 HLR 223: see at 232.

[76]   Contrast a contract for a tenancy which, although it operates in equity, requires the estate to be granted before it operates at law.

[77]   And the tenant can usually obtain an order for specific performance of the obligations. It is far from obvious, as a matter of landlord and tenant law, that the tenant could accept, so as to end the tenancy, even a refusal by the landlord to act which amounted to so fundamental a refusal as to be a repudiation of the lease. The better analysis would be that such actions by the parties would amount to a surrender by operation of law.

[78]   See paras 10.22–10.27 for a discussion of the situation when the receiver has the lender's right of possession.

[79]   See the Appendix for the methods of bringing a lease to an end and for statutory restrictions on ending leases of particular kinds. If the occupier accepted the receiver's act, there would likely be a surrender by operation of law.

right to possession. Thus a receiver with borrower's powers[80] cannot end the lease by his refusal to perform the landlord obligations. He can only terminate the tenancy if the borrower could. The extent to which he is entitled to enforce the covenants and obliged to perform the obligations is considered below.[81]

8.63   A receiver who, on the true interpretation of the mortgage conditions, is given the borrower's right to possession (but only the borrower's right) will be entitled to take possession from a lessee only if the borrower could have taken possession, for example, if the lease has ended or could be ended validly by the borrower.[82]

8.64   In these circumstances, the receiver would have to take the same steps to terminate the tenancy as the borrower would have to take before any possession proceedings could be taken.

8.65   There are various types of tenancy at common law. The different types of tenancy can be terminated in different ways. There are also a number of different statutory regimes which prevent the termination of tenancies or require specific steps to be taken. Information about these topics can be found in the Appendix.

8.66   If a receiver has power to sell only the borrower's estate,[83] he will not be able to sell it free from any lease that binds the borrower.[84]

Receiver with lender's powers

8.67   A receiver with lender's powers must determine whether any tenancy binds the lender, to determine whether he can deal with the property free of that tenancy.

8.68   The lender will be bound by some tenancies created by the borrower, but not all of them.[85]

8.69   If the lender is bound by the tenancy, the lender is not bound to perform the landlord covenants, but it cannot take possession, or sell,[86] free of it unless the tenancy can be ended.

---

[80]   See paras 10.22–10.27 for a discussion of the position when the receiver has the lender's right of possession.

[81]   See paras 8.77–8.90.

[82]   Discussed in further detail at para 10.51 *et seq* and in the Appendix.

[83]   I.e. his estate subject to the mortgage.

[84]   Discussed further at para 11.11 *et seq*.

[85]   See paras 2.63–2.72 and paras 9.141–9.156 for discussions. Acts by the lender itself might mean that the lender has recognised the tenancy, so that it becomes bound by it. The receiver would therefore be well advised to warn the lender not to have any contact with the tenant.

[86]   Law of Property Act 1925, ss 88(1), 89(1) and 104(1). See para 11.87 *et seq*.

8.70   Where the lender is not bound by the tenancy, the lender could take possession from the tenant, even if, as between the borrower and the tenant the fixed term has not expired and/or the tenant is entitled to statutory protection.[87] The lender can also sell free of it.[88]

8.71   The lender's right to take possession can be delegated to the receiver,[89] so the receiver can obtain possession from the tenant relying on the lender's right.[90] A receiver given the lender's right of possession can take possession free of a lease which binds the borrower only and not the lender. He can maintain a claim in trespass against the occupier, just as the lender could,[91] though he cannot take possession from a leaseholder whose lease binds the lender unless that lease can be ended.

8.72   Likewise, a receiver, were he given the lender's power of sale,[92] could sell free of any lease which does not bind the lender.[93]

8.73   A receiver who is given the lender's right of possession and who takes possession will be able to collect income which the lender could collect, even if the borrower had granted an intermediate lease between his estate and the leasehold interest.[94]

8.74   A receiver with lender's powers must determine whether any tenancy binds the lender, to determine whether he can deal with the property free of that tenancy.

8.75   If the lender is not bound by the tenancy, the receiver must determine nonetheless, in light of his duties,[95] whether to recognise the tenancy or treat the occupant as a trespasser.

8.76   In many cases, this will depend on the scope of the receivers' powers to re-let, the state of the market and the rent payable. However, in some cases a consideration of the liabilities under the lease (and any other rights granted beyond receipt of a rent) will be of greater importance.

---

[87]   *Dudley & District Benefit BS v Emerson* [1949] Ch 707; *Bolton BS v Cobb* [1966] 1 WLR 1. See for example paras 2.32, 2.68 and 2.108, and para 10.162 *et seq.*

[88]   Law of Property Act 1925, ss 88(1), 89(1) and s 104(1). See paras 2.136–2.137 and para 11.87.

[89]   The common assumption that a receiver has only the powers of the borrower, and can deal only with the borrower's estate, is an error. Presumably, this misconception derives from the fact that the receiver is usually the deemed agent of the borrower. That may not, however, be the extent of the powers given to a receiver, on a true interpretation of the mortgage conditions: see paras 5.25–5.33.

[90]   See the discussion at paras 10.22–10.27.

[91]   See the discussion at para 10.23.

[92]   The lender's power of sale when it arises extends to the whole of the borrower's estate but unencumbered. See the discussion at paras 2.135–2.138, and para 11.106.

[93]   See the discussion at para 11.126 for example.

[94]   See the discussion in Chapter 9, fn 49.

[95]   See para 6.64 *et seq.*

The receiver and the borrower as landlord

8.77   In what follows, knowledge of the basics of landlord and tenant law is assumed, and the specific issues relating to receivers are covered.

Landlord rights

8.78   If the tenancy is not determined by the receiver, it is important to appreciate the extent to which the receiver has landlord rights and must comply with landlord obligations, as the tenancy continues.

8.79   A receiver will have an implied power to do any act necessary to enable the receiver to carry out the functions for which he was appointed and/or to exercise any power given to him expressly.[96]

8.80   As already seen, a receiver with statutory powers has the power to demand and recover rent. A court is likely to construe this as implying any powers necessary to enable him to obtain the rent.[97]

8.81   Where the receiver also has power to grant leases, that will similarly give the receiver the power ancillary powers such as the power to terminate existing tenancies.[98] However, it is considered that the power does not include giving consent to an underletting because it is not necessary for the receiver to have this power in order to be able to grant leases.

8.82   If a receiver has additional powers delegated by the mortgage deed, for example, a power to sell the property (whether as delegate of the lender or attorney for the borrower), he is likely to have incidental powers to do anything which he needs to do in order to effect the sale.[99] This might include resolving any disputes with the tenants.

8.83   In some cases, the receiver will be given extremely wide powers. If the mortgage appoints the receiver the borrower's attorney:

> to do all ... things as the... receiver shall in [his] absolute discretion think fit for the full exercise of any of the powers confirmed by this clause to which may be deemed expedient by ...the receiver or in connection with any sale lease or disposition realisation or getting in by the receivers ...

the receiver will have power to serve a counter-notice opposing an application under the right to manage legislation, on the basis that the management of the block might affect the sale price.[100] It therefore seems that a receiver appointed

---

[96] *McDonald v McDonald* [2014] EWCA Civ 1049, [2015] Ch 357 at [65]. The Supreme Court decision ([2016] UKSC 28) does not address this point. See also *In Re Emmadart Ltd* [1979] 1 Ch 540 (discussed at paras 10.61–10.62); *M Wheeler & Co Ltd v Warren* [1928] Ch 840.

[97] This is considered in more detail in Chapter 9, fn 123.

[98] Termination of tenancies is dealt with at para 10.103 *et seq* and in the Appendix.

[99] See for example para 10.25.

[100] *Alleyn Court RTM Co v Mich'al Abou-Hamdan* [2012] UKUT 74.

under a mortgage with wide terms such as these would have the power to deal with any applications by tenants for consent to make alterations or change the use of the property.

Landlord obligations

8.84 The receiver does not step into the borrower's obligations under the lease[101] unless there is something in the mortgage deed which, on its true construction, provides that he does.

8.85 The position in relation to the borrower's obligations to insure, repair, maintain and provide services may, however, be different. If the service charge contributions are held on trust,[102] the receiver cannot use any monies he receives by way of service charges to pay down the mortgage debt.[103] If he spends service charges, he must spend them on the provision of services, works and insurance for which the tenants have paid.[104]

8.86 If there is no trust, the receiver must apply the income in accordance with the applicable statutory or contractual regime.[105]

8.87 Regardless of whether there is a trust, if the receiver does not inherit a reserve fund, he is not obliged to make up any shortfall in the sums received from the service charges in order to carry out all the works which the borrower is obliged to do under the lease.

8.88 The receiver must also consider to what extent he is bound by statutory obligations imposed on landlords. Generally, if the statute imposes an obligation on the borrower (or the lender), the receiver will not be obliged to perform that obligation (unless there is something in the terms of the mortgage deed that requires him to do so). However, the receiver cannot be in a better position than the person from whom he derives his power, so if the statute precludes the

---

[101] The tenant could obtain an order for specific performance against the borrower for performance of landlord obligations. The court would not require the receiver to perform the landlord obligations under it. The receiver can choose to cause the borrower to breach the lease, though the borrower may be liable to the tenant: see para 8.7. Where the lease is a new lease within the meaning of the Landlord and Tenant (Covenants) Act 1995, it is considered that the receiver is not 'the holder for the time being of the interest of the landlord', and is not therefore caught by s 15(2). Chapter 7, fn 67 and Chapter 9, fn 118. For old leases, the position is the same: Law of Property Act 1925, s 142.

[102] A statutory trust is imposed where tenants of two or more dwellings have to pay service charges: Landlord and Tenant Act 1987, s 42. In addition, a trust will exist if, on the true construction of the lease, this was intended. In *Frobisher (Second Investments) Ltd v Kiloran Trust Co* [1980] 1 WLR 425, the court declined to imply any trust. See Chapter 9.

[103] It is considered that the trust trumps the statutory or any contractual regime for distributing the income received, because the service charge money is not money 'received by him', and in addition the receiver if he used the monies to pay the mortgage could become a constructive trustee of them. See also para 9.95(c).

[104] There is no obligation on the receiver to undertake the landlord obligations paid for by service charges he has collected.

[105] See Chapter 12.

borrower (or the lender) from exercising a power until its terms have been complied with, the receiver will also be precluded from doing so.

8.89 For example, the Landlord and Tenant Act 1987[106] precludes a landlord from selling the property (or making any other relevant disposal[107]) without giving the tenants a right of first refusal. A mortgagee exercising its power of sale is under the same duty.[108] A receiver must therefore comply with this requirement, whenever he sells the property, whether he sells with the borrower's or the lender's power of sale.

8.90 Further, some statutes make express provision for the tenant to be entitled to treat the receiver as its landlord for certain, defined purposes. Good examples can be found in the enfranchisement legislation: a tenant who is seeking to enfranchise can serve notice on the receiver instead of on the landlord.[109]

Licensees

8.91 Licences are simple contracts between the borrower and the occupier under which the borrower agrees that the occupier can occupy the land, but which do not fulfil the requirements for being a lease.[110] They can be very informal, for example, if a simple permission is given orally, or they can be conferred by a written contract, under which consideration is payable.

8.92 Many informal licences are terminable immediately by the grantor, or on reasonable notice. Such licences rarely cause difficulties, though it is important: (a) to check that the receiver's powers are sufficiently wide to allow him to terminate the licence as the borrower's agent; and (b) to follow any contractual requirements for termination precisely. The receiver should usually serve any notices in the borrower's name.

8.93 There are certain statutory requirements which apply when a licence of a dwelling is to be terminated. Any notice to terminate must comply with

---

[106] This applies to premises if they contain two or more flats held by qualifying tenants and the number of flats held by such tenants exceeds 50% of the total number of flats in the buildings; and any non-residential parts of the building occupy less than 50% of the internal floor area, disregarding any common parts. Assured and assured shorthold tenants are not qualifying tenants (although their landlord, if holding a leasehold estate, could be).

[107] Landlord and Tenant Act 1987, s 4 defines relevant disposals.

[108] Landlord and Tenant Act 1987, s 4(1A).

[109] Leasehold Reform Act 1967, Sch 3, para 9(1); Leasehold Reform, Housing and Urban Development Act 1993, Sch 2, para 2(4). If the tenant does not serve notice on the receiver, the recipient of the notice must serve a copy on the receiver. The appointment of a receiver has other consequences for a tenant who seeks to enfranchise: the lender can elect to conduct the proceedings on behalf of the borrower (Leasehold Reform Act 1967, s 25(5); Leasehold Reform, Housing and Urban Development Act 1993, Sch 8, para 2(3)), and the lender can require the price to be paid into Court (Leasehold Reform Act 1967, s 13(3)(b); Leasehold Reform, Housing and Urban Development Act 1993, Sch 8, para 4(3)).

[110] Discussed at paras 8.48–8.51.

section 5(1A) of the Protection from Eviction Act 1977, unless the licence falls into one of the statutory exceptions under the Act. The exceptions are limited and can be found in section 5(1B), and the definition of 'excluded licence' can be found at section 3A.

8.94   For example, licences are excluded where accommodation is shared by the occupier with the licensor or a member of his family occupying the premises as his only or principal home both at the date of the licence and the date when it comes to an end; where the licence was granted as a temporary expedient to persons entering as a trespasser, or the licence gives a right to occupy for a holiday only, or is granted otherwise than for money or money's worth. The Protection from Eviction Act 1977 itself should be consulted for precise detail of the exclusions. The notice must be in writing, give not less than 4 weeks' notice and contain certain prescribed information.[111]

8.95   If a receiver decides not to terminate a licence which the borrower could terminate and instead accepts money for use of the property, a question may arise as to whether the receiver has created a tenancy. This is considered below.

8.96   Licences are mere personal privileges and do not create any interest in land. Accordingly, they could not bind the lender, unless the lender joined in the granting of the licence so that it is bound as a matter of contract. If the receiver can rely on the lender's right of possession, the receiver will be able to obtain possession from the licensee as a trespasser even if the borrower could not under the terms of the licence.[112]

8.97   Where the receiver cannot or does not rely on the lender's right to possession, it is considered that the receiver may not simply be able to take possession, if the borrower could not, because of the terms of the licence. Even though licences do not create interests in land, a licence could, at least in some circumstances, be capable of being protected by an order for specific performance of the obligation in it to give the occupier possession, or allow him to occupy, or an injunction to prevent breach by the borrower of those obligations.[113]

Telecoms operators

8.98   Sometimes, receivers discover electronic communications apparatus, such as mobile phone masts, on the roof (or in a field). They will want to know

---

[111]   Set out in Notices to Quit etc. (Prescribed Information) Regulations 1988 (SI 1988/2201), Sch 1.

[112]   The authors' view is that the receiver is bound by the licence in these circumstances (assuming it would be capable of specific performance) unless and until he exercises the lender's right to go into possession. However, in *Bower Terrace Student Accommodation Ltd v Space Student Living Ltd* [2012] EWHC 2206 (Ch), the court required the occupiers to give up possession to the receivers (who had sought injunctions in proceedings commenced in the borrower's name) without requiring the receivers to sue for possession.

[113]   See the discussion above on specific performance. Key will be whether damages, in the claim by the occupier against the borrower, would be an adequate remedy, and the reason why the receiver seeks to end the licence.

if they can collect any income due from the operators and they may wish to know to what extent it is possible to get rid of such apparatus, particularly if they are contemplating a sale.

8.99   Operators have for many years had specific rights and protections, under various statutes. On 28 December 2017, a new Electronic Communications Code (New Code) conferring such rights and protections came into force.[114] The New Code applies to existing agreements, subject to transitional provisions.[115] It is necessary to consider the New Code and the transitional provisions in order to answer the receiver's questions. A summary of the relevant provisions is set out below, but reference should be made to specialist texts for a more detailed explanation.[116]

8.100   The first step is to ascertain who is actually in occupation of the site and on what basis. In general, it will be possible to find an agreement with an operator ('the main operator').[117] The receiver will be able to step into the borrower's shoes and collect the monies due from the main operator under the contract, in the borrower's name.

8.101   Whether the receiver can obtain the removal of the apparatus is more complicated. As ever, the receiver can only succeed by relying on either the borrower's right or the lender's right and only if that right has been delegated to him.

8.102   A person with an interest in land[118] has the right to require the removal of electronic communications apparatus on, under or over the land if (and only if) one of a list of statutory conditions is met.[119] The person with the interest in

---

[114]   The New Code can be found in Digital Economy Act 2017, Sch 1.

[115]   Digital Economy Act 2017, Sch 2.

[116]   See Falcon Chambers, *The Electronic Communications Code and Property Law: Practice and Procedure* (Routledge, 2018).

[117]   Operators have power to obtain rights over land by court order, in the absence of agreement. This procedure has been rarely exercised to date. The juristic nature of the operator's right when created by court order has not been considered. It seems likely that it is a *sui generis* right which can bind successors as set out in the New Code (or, under the previous code set out in Telecommunications Act 1984, Sch 2, if the order provided that it should), even if the order does not confer exclusive possession of any particular part of the site on the operator. It is thought that the better view is that this right is an interest in land, *sed quere*?

[118]   Thus the receiver could act on behalf of either the borrower or the lender, assuming appropriate delegation of powers. However, note that the receiver cannot serve a notice in his own name under this provision. This is a change from the position under the old code, where the equivalent, s allowed any person for the time being entitled to require the removal to trigger the process: Telecommunications Act 1984, Sch 2, para 21.

However, note that there is a separate scheme, in Digital Economy Act 2017, Sch 1, para 41, which enables persons who are not 'landowners' within the definition, to require removal of the apparatus. There is no guidance as to who might fall within the definition of a 'third party', but it seems unlikely that this extends to the agents of 'landowners'. Agents can exercise landowners' rights in their name. It would be contrary to principle for a separate and different scheme to apply to agents.

[119]   Digital Economy Act 2017, Sch 1, para 37.

land is referred to as a 'landowner', but the definition is sufficiently wide to include a lender. The final three statutory conditions cover obsolescence (of the equipment or the right) in one form or another and are unlikely to be of assistance to the receiver often. The remaining two statutory conditions are:

(a) The landowner has never since the coming into force of this code been bound by a code right entitling an operator to keep the apparatus on, under or over the land.

(b) A code right entitling an operator to keep the apparatus on, under or over the land has come to an end or has ceased to bind the landowner.

8.103 The landowner does not meet the first or second conditions if:

(a) the land is occupied by a person who:

    (i) conferred a code right (which is in force) entitling an operator to keep the apparatus on, under or over the land, or

    (ii) is otherwise bound by such a right, and

(b) that code right was not conferred in breach of a covenant enforceable by the landowner.

8.104 As a result, the receiver will have the right to remove the equipment if:

(a) the operator was from the outset a pure trespasser, who was never given a right to occupy by anyone;

(b) the code right was conferred by a tenant of the borrower in breach of a covenant in the lease (under the borrower's delegated power);

(c) the code right was conferred by the borrower in breach of a covenant in the mortgage (under the lender's delegated power); or

(d) the person who conferred the code right is no longer in occupation, and the code right did not bind the borrower or lender as the case may be, or has been lawfully terminated.

8.105 To establish if the code right has been lawfully terminated requires a consideration of the nature of the agreement, what contractual right to terminate existed and any statutory restrictions and procedures applicable. Under the New Code, an agreement will either be a lease capable of protection under Part II of the Landlord and Tenant Act 1954 (where the purpose of the lease is not to grant code rights) or a Code Agreement which must be terminated in accordance with Part 5 of the New Code. As regards leases in existence at 28 December 2017, if the lease is protected by the Landlord and Tenant Act 1954 at that date,[120] it will continue to be so protected, and the New Code provisions about termination will not apply to it, even if the primary purpose of the agreement was to grant code style rights to the operator.[121]

---

[120] I.e. it is not 'contracted out' of the protection of the Landlord and Tenant Act 1954.

[121] Digital Economy Act 2017, Sch 2, para 6.

8.106 If a right to require removal exists, there is a mandatory statutory procedure. This requires the service of a notice on the operator requiring him to remove the apparatus and restore the land within a reasonable time. If no agreement can be reached, the landowner can apply to court for an order requiring the operator to remove the apparatus. A detailed explanation as to the content of the notice and the way in which the application will be dealt with are outside the scope of this book.

8.107 The key point to appreciate is that the operator can take steps to secure a right against the landowner to keep the apparatus on the land. The operator can seek rights against the lender or the borrower under Part 4 of the New Code. A right will be given if:

(a) the prejudice caused by the order is capable of being adequately compensated by money; and
(b) the public benefit likely to result from the making of the order (i.e. the public interest in access to a choice of high quality electronic communications services) outweighs the prejudice,

provided that the person against whom the order is sought is not intending to redevelop the land, and the order would prevent that.[122]

8.108 If a fresh right is granted, the receiver will not be able to remove the apparatus. If no fresh right is granted, the receiver will obtain an order entitling him to remove the apparatus.

Site sharers

8.109 Frequently, the main operator has entered into arrangements with other operators entitling them to share the site. The borrower has no right to collect income from these site sharers, so the receiver cannot collect income from them.

8.110 It is important to appreciate that there are two different kinds of site sharers: those who simply use the main operator's equipment, and those who the main operator permits to install their own equipment. If the site sharer is simply using the main operator's equipment, it is likely that there is no need to serve notice on the site sharer under paragraph 40 of the New Code.[123]

8.111 However, if the main operator has permitted the site sharer to install their own equipment on the site, the receiver will need to consider what steps he can and should take to get rid of the site sharer's apparatus. It is thought that an order under paragraph 44 of the New Code against the main operator will not require the main operator to remove apparatus belonging to and used solely by

---

[122] Digital Economy Act 2017, Sch 1, para 21.

[123] Digital Economy Act 2017, Sch 1, para 40 requires a notice to be given 'to the operator whose apparatus it is'. This odd wording is, presumably, supposed to connote ownership of the apparatus as opposed to encompassing every operator who is, in fact, using the apparatus.

third parties: paragraph 44 refers to 'the electronic communications apparatus', but this must refer back to the apparatus referred to in the paragraph 40 notice.

8.112 It therefore seems that in order to remove apparatus belonging to someone other than the main operator, the receiver must consider whether he has any right to require its removal under paragraph 37 of the New Code, and, if he does, operate the procedure separately in respect of each site sharer.

Occupiers with a beneficial interest

8.113 A borrower may well hold the mortgaged property on trust. A trust arises wherever the legal ownership (i.e. what appears on the title register) differs from the beneficial (i.e. true) ownership of the property. A trust is also imposed whenever the legal title is owned by more than one person, even if they own both the legal title and the beneficial interest in the property jointly.

8.114 There are a number of different kinds of trust:

(a) Express trusts, where a trust has been declared by deed. In these cases, the Land Registry title for the property will usually have a Form A or other trust restriction on the proprietorship register.[124]
(b) Resulting trusts. These typically arise in a non-domestic context where the purchase money for the property has been provided by someone other than the registered proprietor, in circumstances where there was no intention that the money be a gift.
(c) Constructive trusts. There are a variety of circumstances where a constructive trust can arise. A common example of a circumstance where a constructive trust is imposed is where an unmarried partner claims to have contributed to the purchase of a house in the name of the other on the promise that it would be co-owned; or where one partner claims that even though the property was in joint names, he or she is entitled to more than half of the net proceeds, because of some agreement or understanding that this would be so.

8.115 The existence of a trust has no bearing on the validity of that mortgage.

8.116 However, the existence of a trust which pre-dates the grant of the mortgage can affect the lender's remedies. If a beneficiary in actual occupation of the property did not postpone his interest to the mortgage,[125] the lender's

---

[124] A Form A restriction says 'No disposition by a sole proprietor of the registered estate (except a trust corporation) under which capital money arises is to be registered unless authorized by an order of the court'. If there is an express trust of any complexity, it is likely there will be a restriction requiring compliance with provisions of the trust deed on a disposition for value.

[125] His beneficial interest will take priority over the mortgage on its registration by reason of Land Registration Act 2002, s 29 and Sch 3, para 2, unless the mortgage was granted by more than one trustee or a trust corporation so that any beneficial interest is overreached under Law of Property Act 1925, s 2. See Chapter 2, fn 194.

ability to enforce the mortgage remedies against the beneficiary would be limited.

8.117 Moreover, the validity of a mortgage granted by more than one legal co-owner is at risk if one of those borrowers suggests that the mortgage should be set aside because, for example, it was executed under undue influence.

8.118 In this situation, the receiver must proceed with great care. If the legal charge is set aside, the receivership will terminate at that point.[126] However, unless and until the mortgage is set aside, the receiver is entitled (and, indeed, obliged because of his primary duty to pay down the debt) to proceed with the receivership.

8.119 Unless there is a risk that the mortgage will be set aside, the receiver is only likely to be concerned about trust interests if he is seeking to obtain possession or sell the mortgaged property. Of course, a receiver must check that he has power to do these things before becoming embroiled in any consideration of the trust. If he has, the receiver will want to know to what extent the existence of the trust interest can preclude him from getting possession, and, if he sells, whether he is obliged to pay any part of the proceeds over to the beneficial owner.

8.120 In order to answer those questions, it is necessary to consider:

(a) the borrower's obligations *qua* trustee;
(b) whether the receiver can ignore the borrower's obligations *qua* trustee if he is relying on the borrower's powers;
(c) if he can ignore them if he relies on the lender's powers.

The borrower's obligations qua *trustee*

8.121 The precise nature of the borrower's obligations may depend on the terms of the trust. However, the following general points can be made.

8.122 First, trustees must operate the trust and, in particular, distribute income and capital to those entitled to it, under the terms of the trust.

8.123 Secondly, beneficiaries can have rights to occupy the land. A right to occupy arises where:

(a) the beneficiary has an interest in possession (as opposed to in reversion);
(b) the terms of the express trust provide that the beneficiary has the right to occupy; or

---

[126] Save insofar as the mortgage continues to bind the other co-owner's beneficial interest, in which case the receivership will continue in relation to that interest, but the receiver's ability to deal with the legal title will be limited so that the receivership's effectiveness will be limited.

(c)   the purposes of the trust include making the land available for his occupation or the land must be held so as to be available for his occupation;[127]

(d)   the property is not unavailable or unsuitable for occupation by him.[128]

8.124   Where two or more beneficiaries are entitled under section 12 of the Trusts of Land and Appointment of Trustees Act 1996 to occupy, the position is regulated by section 13. In particular, under section 13(3), 'the trustees may from time to time impose reasonable conditions on any beneficiary in relation to his occupation of land by reason of his entitlement under section 12', including the requirement on the beneficiary to pay outgoings and expenses in respect of the land, or assume any other obligation in relation to the land or any activity which is or is proposed to be conducted there.[129] The conditions may include a requirement on the occupying beneficiary to pay an excluded beneficiary compensation.[130]

8.125   In exercising the powers conferred to impose conditions, or to exclude a beneficiary with a right to occupy where there is more than one such beneficiary, the trustees must take into account the intentions of the person who created the trust, the purposes for which the land is held, and the circumstances and wishes of each of the beneficiaries entitled to occupy.[131] That is in addition to the trustees' more general obligation under section 6(5) of the Trusts of Land and Appointment of Trustees Act 1996, to have regard to the rights of the beneficiaries in exercising their powers.

8.126   Under section 14 of the Trusts of Land and Appointment of Trustees Act 1996, any person who is a trustee of land or has an interest in property subject to a trust may apply to the court for an order relating to the exercise by the trustees of any of their functions, and declaring the nature and extent of a person's interest in the property subject to the trust. Via this method, a trustee or a beneficiary could seek an order determining which of two beneficiaries should be permitted to occupy the property, and whether and what compensation should be paid by the one in occupation to the other, for example.

8.127   On such an application, the court must have regard to: (a) the intentions of the person who created the trust; (b) the purposes for which the property is held; (c) the welfare of any minor who occupies or might reasonably be expected to occupy any land subject to the trust as his home; and (d) the interests of any secured creditor of any beneficiary.[132] In addition, on applications relating to occupation of the property under section 13 of the Trusts

---

[127]   Trusts of Land and Appointment of Trustees Act 1996, s 12. In trusts arising under co-ownership of houses intended to be occupied by the owners, the court will likely infer such a right, though such an inference is far less likely if the property is mortgaged under a buy-to-let mortgage, or was bought as an investment property.

[128]   Trusts of Land and Appointment of Trustees Act 1996, s 12(2).

[129]   Trusts of Land and Appointment of Trustees Act 1996, s 13(5).

[130]   Trusts of Land and Appointment of Trustees Act 1996, s 13(6).

[131]   Trusts of Land and Appointment of Trustees Act 1996, s 13(4).

[132]   Trusts of Land and Appointment of Trustees Act 1996, s 15(1).

of Land and Appointment of Trustees Act 1996, the court must have regard to the circumstances and wishes of each beneficiary entitled to occupy the land under section 12.[133]

8.128 If a beneficiary is already in occupation, the court's approval is required before the beneficiary's right to occupy is terminated.[134]

The effect of trust on the scope of the receiver's powers

8.129 The first issue is whether the receiver, in fact, has all the powers which it appears, on the face of the mortgage, the borrower has delegated to him.[135] The receivers' powers where these issues are most relevant are regulation of occupation by beneficiaries, which is considered in Chapters 9 and 10, in relation to income from occupying beneficiaries in Chapter 9,[136] and in relation to sale in Chapter 11.[137] The issues also arise on sale under a borrower's power of attorney, which is discussed in Chapter 11.[138]

8.130 Insofar as the borrower acts in relation to the property, he is doing so as a trustee. This adds a potential complexity because there is statutory regulation of the delegation of trustee powers which may interfere with the delegation of powers to the receiver in the mortgage deed insofar as the powers that are so delegated are trustee powers.

8.131 The issue arises whenever the borrower holds the property on trust, because there is a question of whether and to what extent the entry of the borrower into a mortgage deed which gives the lender power to appoint a receiver is an act by the trustees delegating their powers. Moreover, insofar as the receiver is not exercising lender's powers, he may well have those powers only insofar as the borrower can delegate trust powers.

8.132 This section now considers a trustee's powers to delegate his trustee functions.

Trustee Act 2000

8.133 Prior to the coming into force of the Trustee Act 2000, although trustees, acting together, could instruct agents to exercise their management functions in relation to the trust, they could not delegate functions in relation to the exercise of which they had a fiduciary duty: those which required them to take decisions

---

[133] Trusts of Land and Appointment of Trustees Act 1996, s 15(2). That includes a beneficiary entitled to occupy but excluded by the trustees.

[134] Trusts of Land and Appointment of Trustees Act 1996, s 13(7).

[135] Note that the discussion in this section of Chapter 8 does not have any bearing on the receiver's statutory powers, or lender delegated powers, since these are simply a result of the mortgage. See Chapter 5 for the different sources of the receiver's powers.

[136] See paras 9.86–9.90.

[137] See paras 11.16–11.23.

[138] See para 11.85.

about the assets of the trust, for example, investment, sale or distribution. The Trustee Act 2000 changed this so as to give trustees more freedom to appoint agents, though surrounded by more safeguards.

8.134 The principal power of trustees[139] to employ agents is in either the trust deed, if there is one, or in Part IV of the Trustee Act 2000.[140] That Act limits which of the trustees' functions are delegable and imposes limits on the way in which delegable functions are delegated.

8.135 Section 11(1) of the Trustee Act 2000 permits the trustees, acting all together, to delegate their delegable functions.[141] The delegable functions are[142] all functions of a trustee, i.e. everything the trustees are permitted to do and must do under the trust deed, common law and statute,[143] except for: (a) any function relating to whether or in what way any assets of the trust should be distributed;[144] (b) any power to decide whether any fees or other payment due to be made out of the trust funds should be made out of income or capital; (c) any power to appoint a person to be a trustee of the trust; or (d) any power conferred by any other enactment or the trust instrument which permits the trustees to delegate any of their functions or to appoint a person to act as nominee or custodian.

8.136 None of these are likely to be powers which a mortgage deed usually seeks to give to a receiver, or indeed a lender. Accordingly, an ordinary delegation of powers by a trustee to the receiver is likely to be effective.

8.137 However, there are four ways in which Part IV of the Trustee Act 2000 could affect the exercise of receivership powers:

(a) Under section 13(1), a person authorised by trustees to exercise a trustee function under section 11(1), is subject to any specific duties or restrictions attached to that function. The example given by the Act is the duties imposed on trustees by Part II[145] when exercising their power of investment, and hence this is unlikely to apply to receivers.

(b) The terms of the agency may not include a term: (i) permitting the agent to appoint a substitute; (ii) restricting the liability of the agent or his

---

[139] This power is common to all trusts, not just those of land.

[140] The Trustee Act 2000 is subject to any powers otherwise conferred on trustees, and subject to any restriction or exclusion imposed by the trust deed or any enactment: s 26.

[141] The trustees cannot authorise two or more persons to exercise the same function unless they are to exercise the function jointly: Trustee Act 2000, s 12(2). That is unlikely to be an issue for receivers who, if appointed, are appointed jointly.

[142] For a trust other than a charitable trust.

[143] Trustees' functions include powers to sell trust property, invest income, distribute income and assets, manage trust property, but also obligations to consult beneficiaries for example, where the trust is a trust of land.

[144] This would include a decision as to how the proceeds of sale are to be paid out to the beneficiaries, if this were not fixed by the trust.

[145] To consider a standard investment criteria set out in Trustee Act 2000, s 4, and obtain and consider proper advice.

substitute to the trustees or any beneficiary; or (iii) permitting the agent to act in circumstances capable of giving rise to a conflict of interest, unless it is reasonably necessary for them to do so. Although a receiver by nature has a conflict of interest between his duties to the lender and the duties he owes the borrower if appointed as his agent, it is considered that it is reasonably necessary for the trustees to agree this, since it is not possible to obtain mortgage finance in the general market without agreeing such a term.

(c)   There are specific restrictions under section 15(1) when the functions that the trustees authorise their agent to exercise are 'asset management functions': the investment of assets subject to the trust, the acquisition of property which is to be subject to the trust, and managing property which is subject to the trust and disposing of, or creating or disposing of, an interest in such property.[146] This picks up a receiver's powers to sell in the name of the borrower[147] and more general management functions insofar as the receiver has them. For those powers, section 15(1) requires the authorisation of the agent to be in writing, which will be fulfilled by the mortgage deed and the lender's appointment of the receiver.[148] However, section 15(2) also requires the trustees before authorising their agent to prepare a statement giving guidance as to how the functions should be exercised ('a policy statement'),[149] and the agreement under which the agent is to act must include a term that he will secure compliance with the policy statement, or any revised or replacement version. This appears unlikely to be consistent with appointment of a receiver, though it should be noted that a failure by the trustees to act within the limits of the statutory powers does not invalidate the authorisation of the agent.[150]

(d)   Lastly, a trustee is not liable for any act or default of the agent unless the trustee has failed to comply with duties imposed by the Trustee Act 2000[151] in entering into arrangements or reviewing the appointment of the agent or review of the policy document under section 22.[152] This section is directed towards liability of the trustee to beneficiaries, since the duty of care is to the beneficiaries, and hence does not appear to be inimical to the borrower's liability to third parties for the receiver's acts imposed by the deemed agency.

Delegation by individual trustees

8.138   There are two further methods by which an individual trustee can give someone else his trustee functions. Neither assists the lender or the receiver:

---

[146]   Trustee Act 2000, s 15(5).

[147]   I.e. not a delegation of the lender's power of sale.

[148]   *Phoenix Properties Ltd v Wimpole Street Nominees Ltd* [1992] BCLC 737.

[149]   To be in or evidenced in writing: Trustee Act 2000, s 15(4), and formulated with a view to ensuring that the functions will be exercised in the best interests of the trust: s 15(3).

[150]   Trustee Act 2000, s 24.

[151]   Trustee Act 2000, Sch 1, para 3.

[152]   Trustee Act 2000, s 23(1).

(a) The first is under section 25 of the Trustee Act 1925, which allows an individual trustee by power of attorney[153] to delegate execution or exercise of all or any of the trusts, powers and discretions vested in him alone or jointly for a period up to 12 months from a specified date or the date of grant.[154] This is unlikely to be the form of any power of attorney granted in the mortgage conditions.

(b) The second is under section 9(1) of the Trusts of Land and Appointment of Trustees Act 1996, which permits the trustees of land by power of attorney to delegate any trustee functions to beneficiaries of full age and beneficially entitled to an interest in possession. This does not assist the receivers since they are not beneficiaries.

Powers of attorney

8.139 The grant of powers of attorney is governed by the common law and by the Powers of Attorney Act 1971.[155] The donee of a power of attorney has 'authority to do on behalf of the donor anything which he can lawfully do by attorney'.[156] However, this does not apply 'to functions which the donor has as a trustee',[157] unless at the time when the power of attorney is relied on, the donor has a beneficial interest in the land.[158] Typically, the donor will have a beneficial interest, but receivers must check that this is the case before relying on a power of attorney conferred by a trustee. Any purchaser will, if well advised, require the receiver to provide an 'appropriate statement', being a statement signed by the receiver within three months of the sale that the donor of the power has a beneficial interest, or had one at the time.[159] If the statement is false, the receiver will be liable as if the statement were contained in a statutory declaration.[160] If the receiver is not willing to provide the statement, he will not be able to rely on a power of attorney created by a borrower who is a trustee.

The effect of trust on the exercise of the receiver's powers

8.140 There is little authority on the questions considered here. Although not free from doubt, it is considered that the better view is that if the receiver simply

---

[153] In a specific form of words set out in Trustee Act 1925, s 25(6), which specifically refers to s 25(5), the provision which delegates the trusts, powers and discretions.

[154] It is said in commentary that the power in Trustee Act 1925, s 25 cannot be used to provide a series of powers of attorney taking effect for consecutive 12 months, but this has not been tested and is not obvious from the statute.

[155] It does not appear that the Powers of Attorney Act 1971 superseded the previous common law position: see *Bowstead & Reynolds* at 10-008.

[156] Powers of Attorney Act 1971, s 10(1).

[157] Powers of Attorney Act 1971, s 10(2).

[158] Trustee Delegation Act 1999, s 1.

[159] Trustee Delegation Act 1999, s 2.

[160] Trustee Delegation Act 1999, s 2(4). Under Perjury Act 1911, s 5, if any person knowingly and wilfully makes a false statement in a statutory declaration, he is guilty of an offence for which he could be imprisoned.

steps into the borrower's shoes, he will have not be able to avoid the borrower's obligations *qua* trustee, just as he cannot ignore leases and other proprietary interests created by the borrower. This is the case whether the trust was created before or after the mortgage.

8.141 However, there are two situations in which it is likely that the receiver could ignore the terms of the trust (without relying on the lender's powers):

(a) If the trust pre-existed the mortgage, and all the beneficiaries executed the mortgage (e.g. where husband and wife hold on trust for themselves).

(b) If the trust was created after the mortgage, the trustee acted in breach of the mortgage in creating the trust, and the beneficiary was aware of the mortgage at the time it was created and that the trustee had acted in breach of the mortgage.[161]

8.142 Assuming that the receiver is bound by the borrower's obligations under the trust, how will this affect him? Unless he can rely on the lender's powers, he cannot take possession from a beneficiary with rights of occupation.

8.143 However, if the beneficiary has no right to occupy, the receiver could exercise the borrower's right to seek possession from that beneficiary (subject to the points made above in relation to the delegation of the borrower's functions to the receiver). It is therefore necessary to understand when the beneficiary has rights to occupy.

8.144 Assuming a suitable delegation of the borrower-trustee's functions, the receiver could make an application under the Trusts of Land and Appointment of Trustees Act 1996 in the borrower's name,[162] if the borrower itself could make one.

Exercising the lender's powers

8.145 In order to establish whether the receiver can ignore the trust by relying on the lender's rights, it is necessary to consider the following questions:

---

[161] See Chapter 12 for the discussion of whether the receiver has to pay the beneficiary out of the proceeds of sale, if he sells under the borrower's power.

[162] It is unlikely that a receiver could be said himself to have an interest in property, and hence that he could make an application under Trusts of Land and Appointment of Trustees Act 1996, s 14 in his own name. It is arguable that a receiver who has a right to possession has an interest, though 'interest' more naturally means something akin to an estate rather than a right only. See *Stevens v Hutchinson* [1953] Ch 299 as to the meaning of a similar phrase in Law of Property Act 1925, s 30 then in force. A receiver appointed by the court by way of equitable execution over a beneficiary's interest in a trust for sale of land, where the receiver had a power to collect income, did not give the receiver rights *in rem* and hence he personally was not a person interested in the property. 'Person interested' required some proprietary right. However, note that this case has been criticised in *Levermore v Levermore* [1979] 1 WLR 1277.

(a)   Could the lender obtain possession from the beneficiary?
(b)   Would the lender be obliged to account to the beneficiary if it sold the property?
(c)   In what circumstances can the receiver exercise the lender's rights?

Trusts not binding the lender

8.146 If the trust is not binding on the lender, the lender is entitled to possession from the beneficiary (if it is entitled to possession under the terms of the mortgage) and can disregard the terms of the trust when distributing the proceeds of sale.

8.147 Trusts arising after the mortgage is granted do not bind the lender.

8.148 The lender is also not bound by pre-existing trusts where:

(a)   The beneficiary executed the mortgage (and cannot set it aside, for example, as having been executed under undue influence).
(b)   The overreaching mechanism is triggered. Where there is more than one trustee registered with the title to the property who granted the mortgage, or the trustee was a trust corporation, then the grant of the mortgage will have overreached the beneficial interests under section 2(1)(ii) and (2) of the Law of Property Act 1925, as long as the provisions in section 27 as to payment of the capital money have been complied with.[163]
(c)   The beneficiary does not have an overriding interest.[164] Typically, a beneficiary will only have an overriding interest if he is in actual occupation of the property at the time the mortgage is taken out.
(d)   The beneficiary agreed to postpone its rights to those of the lender, and that postponement cannot be attacked as having been executed under undue influence.

Trusts binding on the lender

8.149 The lender is likely to be bound where, for example, the property is registered in the sole name of A, and, a few years after purchase, A mortgages the property, but A's partner contributed to the price on the purchase of the property and, on the particular facts, has a beneficial interest in the property at a percentage reflecting his contribution. He is living in the property when the mortgage is granted and hence is in actual occupation. He is not asked to sign any postponement form. His beneficial interest binds the lender.

---

[163]   See the discussion in Chapter 2, fn 194.
[164]   See Land Registration Act 2002, s 29 and Sch 3, para 2. The partner's beneficial interest would be overriding and hence bind the mortgagee.

The effect of a binding trust on the lender's remedies

8.150 The lender retains his legal charge (unless and until it is set aside). This means that the lender retains his remedies and, in particular, that the lender retains the ability to sell. However:

(a) The lender can only sell subject to the beneficiaries' interest.[165] If none of the beneficiaries are bound by the mortgage, it is unlikely any sale will be possible. The lender's sale will have no purpose since it will not raise any funds for repayment of the mortgage.[166]

(b) The lender will not be entitled to possession against a beneficiary entitled under the terms of the trust to occupy the property[167] whose interest ranks ahead of the mortgage, because the beneficiary has a prior and better right to possession than the lender. This means that the lender cannot sell with vacant possession (if the beneficiary is in occupation).

8.151 In practice, the lender will not generally be able to exercise his remedies against the property.

The receiver with lender's powers

8.152 If the trust does not bind the lender, the receiver can exercise the lender's powers if delegated to him.

8.153 If the trust does bind the lender, the receiver will be in no better position than the lender as regards the ability to sell or obtain possession.

8.154 The question as to whether the receiver has power to collect income, and, if he does, to whom it should be distributed, is one which has not received much attention. On balance, it is considered that the better view is that the receiver does have power to collect income and is obliged to distribute it in accordance with the statutory regime (or any alternative scheme mandated by the mortgage), provided that the trustees had power to create the mortgage.[168]

---

[165] Law of Property Act 1925, s 104(1), though in registered conveyancing the question of whether the purchaser takes free of the trust is dependent on the provisions of Land Registration Act 2002, s 29 and Sch 3. If the trust is a bare trust, so that the beneficiaries together have all of the beneficial interest, they will be able to require the transfer of the legal title to them (on the principle in *Saunders v Vautier* (1841) Cr & Ph 240), and hence will be able to call for this prior to the lender's sale, which would defeat it, or from the purchaser.

[166] It seems likely that the lender will have to account to the beneficiaries whose interests bind him for the sale proceeds first, before using them to pay the mortgage, on the basis that they are incumbrances. See Chapter 12, fn 95.

[167] See paras 2.116–2.117.

[168] The trustees of a trust of land have all the powers of an absolute owner, save where a contrary intention is expressed in any disposition creating the trust: Trusts of Land and Appointment of Trustees Act 1996, ss 6 and 8.

8.155 If they had power to do it, then the legal charge is valid, and the power to appoint a receiver to collect the income follows, just as the lender's statutory power to sell the property exists regardless of the trust (albeit subject to the beneficiary's interest by reason of section 104 of the Law of Property Act 1925), absent anything in the mortgage conditions indicating that the receiver should distribute otherwise than in accordance with the ordinary regime, i.e. what the receiver should do.

Home rights holders

8.156 The Family Law Act 1996 makes provision for spouses and civil partners of home owners to obtain 'home rights' over property if it has at some time been, or has been intended to be, a matrimonial or civil partnership home.

8.157 Home rights arise, under section 30 of the Family Law Act 1996, where A has a beneficial interest, interest or contract, or statutory right, under which he is entitled to occupy a dwelling-house, and his spouse or civil partner, B, has no such entitlement. In addition, where B has an equitable interest but no legal estate, he will be entitled to home rights.[169]

8.158 B's home rights are:

(a) if in occupation, a right not to be evicted or excluded without leave of the court under section 33 of the Family Law Act 1996;
(b) if not in occupation, a right with the leave of the court to enter and occupy.

8.159 Section 33 of the Family Law Act 1996 gives the court jurisdiction to regulate the occupation of the dwelling-house, where there are home rights, including to restrict or terminate those rights.[170]

8.160 B's home rights also allow him to pay the mortgage. A payment by B is as good as if by A,[171] and the lender may treat it as a payment by A.[172]

8.161 Home rights prevent the home owner from evicting the spouse or civil partner without a court order under the Family Law Act 1996. The rights last only so long as the marriage or civil partnership lasts, save where extended by a court order.[173]

8.162 Since the borrower is affected by home rights regardless of whether they are protected by notice, a receiver may well face an argument that since the receiver is the deemed agent of the borrower, the spouse or civil partner cannot be evicted by the receiver in exercise of a borrower-delegated power, save by

---

[169] Family Law Act 1996, s 30(9).
[170] Family Law Act 1996, s 33(3)(e).
[171] Family Law Act 1996, s 30(3).
[172] Family Law Act 1996, s 30(5).
[173] Family Law Act 1996, s 33(8)(a).

the court exercising its jurisdiction under section 33 of the Family Law Act 1996.[174]

8.163 Can the receiver get round this by relying on the lender's right of possession?

8.164 If the mortgage has priority over the home rights, the lender will not be bound by the rights. If the receiver can rely on a lender delegated right to possession, then he will be able to obtain possession against the spouse or civil partner asserting the home rights.

8.165 However, if the home rights are registered[175] prior to the grant of a mortgage, or its registration, then the home rights will rank in priority to the mortgage, and the lender will be unable to pursue its remedies against the spouse or civil partner[176] without an application to the court under the Family Law Act 1996 for an order either terminating the home rights, or in any event allowing vacant possession so that the receiver can carry out his receivership.[177]

8.166 A question which is unanswered at present is whether the outcome of the application would be different if the lender made the application, as against an application made by the receiver in the borrower's name. The court is mandated to take all the circumstances into account[178] and hence can take into account the lender's rights, and indeed the receivership, provided evidence about the arrears and the lender's position is before the court. An application by the lender may be preferable, however, since on an application by the receiver in the borrower's

---

[174] The application should be made in the borrower's name, assuming that the receiver has sufficient powers delegated by the borrower to allow him to do this. The receiver himself if unlikely to have standing to make an application in his own name as he has no title.

[175] Family Law Act 1996, s 31. The charge is registrable by registering a notice on the title. Home rights are not an overriding interest under Sch 3: s 31(10).

[176] The home rights last only so long as A's rights last, save where the rights are a charge on A's estate or interest: Family Law Act 1996, s 30(8)(b). Thus a mortgagee with a right of possession will be able to evict B, but not if B's home rights have been registered as a charge with priority over the mortgage.

[177] Under Family Law Act 1996, s 33 and via s 34(1)(b), which applies s 33 to 'any person deriving title under the other spouse and affected by the charge'. The receiver may be able to apply in the lender's name if appropriate powers to do so are delegated by the lender. It is unclear whether the receiver could apply in his own name, without such delegation, and rather than in the borrower's name. It seems inapt to suggest that the receiver has title, even if he has a right to possession, hence he does not appear to fall within s 34(1)(b) on his own account.

[178] Family Law Act 1996, s 33. Section 33 also provides a list of specific factors which the court should consider: including:

(a) the housing needs and housing resources of each of the parties and of any relevant child;

(b) the financial resources of each of the parties;

(c) the likely effect of any order, or of any decision by the court not to exercise its powers under subsection (3), on the health, safety or well-being of the parties and of any relevant child; and

(d) the conduct of the parties in relation to each other and otherwise.

name, the court might conclude that the receiver could not argue a case contrary to that of the borrower.[179]

Trespassers

8.167 This is the final category of occupier which the receiver might meet. Trespass to land is the entry onto and/or occupation of land without the consent of the person or persons entitled to possession of that land. The word thus encompasses both the entry onto land and the occupation of it by someone who has never had consent from the person or persons entitled to possession, and someone who fails to leave the land after the termination of any right to occupy that they had, for example, a licence or a lease, even after the owner of the land tells them to leave.[180]

8.168 Trespass, in particular of the first kind, may well be a problem in receivership. Property which is left empty for any period of time, which may well occur if the owner is having financial difficulties, is vulnerable to trespass.

8.169 If the occupier is a trespasser against the borrower, then the receiver can treat him as a trespasser. The receiver will be able to obtain possession from him.

8.170 If the occupier is not a trespasser against the borrower, he will have either a lease or a licence. Where the receiver has the lender's right to possession, an occupier occupying with the consent of the borrower is a trespasser against the receiver, because he is a trespasser against the lender. Thus, the receiver can evict him.

8.171 Both scenarios are considered in more detail in Chapter 10. The collection by the receiver of mesne profits from the trespasser is considered in Chapter 9.[181]

LANDLORDS

8.172 Where the security is a leasehold estate, the receiver will have to consider to what extent he is obliged to perform the tenant covenants in the lease and to what extent he is entitled to enforce the landlord's obligations.

---

[179] Although the case law on the nature of receivership would perhaps suggest otherwise.

[180] Although note that the definition in CPR, Pt 55 is different and hence the procedure to be used where the occupier entered as a trespasser versus that to be used where he remained in occupation after a tenancy, licence, or other right has ended, is different. See paras 10.228–10.231.

[181] At paras 9.91–9.94.

Tenant obligations

8.173 The receiver has power to discharge the rents and other outgoings (which would include the sums due under the lease) from the income received by him.[182] The receiver's duty to make these payments is owed only to the lender and borrower. The landlord cannot claim the rent from the receiver, even if the receiver has had sufficient income to discharge the rents.[183]

8.174 Generally, the receiver will not owe any duty to anyone to make up any shortfall, or to comply with other tenant covenants in the lease.

8.175 However, where the landlord is entitled to forfeit the lease[184] because the rents have not been paid or the other covenants have not been complied with, the lender will usually wish to ensure that forfeiture is prevented, since that will involve the loss of the security.

8.176 The landlord must generally serve a notice under section 146 of the Law of Property Act 1925 before forfeiting on a ground other than rent arrears.[185]

---

[182] See below.

[183] In this situation, the landlord would sue the borrower, who would apply to join the receiver as third party suing him for breach of duty to the borrower to apply receipts per the statutory regime.

[184] Forfeiture is the retaking of possession by the landlord, by reason of breach for which the landlord is entitled by the lease to forfeit. The landlord forfeits by physical re-entry (known as peaceable re-entry) or by the issue and service of a possession claim. Peaceable re-entry is rarely used with residential leases since there is a risk of a criminal penalty under Protection from Eviction Act 1977, s 2 where the premises are let as a dwelling and any person is lawfully residing in the property. A brief discussion of forfeiture can be found at para 10.105 *et seq* and para A.12 *et seq*. See also any practitioner's text on landlord and tenant law for further detail on this complicated subject.

[185] However, by Law of Property Act 1925, s 146(9), a s 146 notice is not required if the ground is 'the taking in execution of the lessee's interest' in:

(a) agricultural or pastoral land;

(b) mines or minerals;

(c) a house used or intended to be used as a public-house or beershop;

(d) a house let as a dwelling-house with the use of any furniture, books, works of art, or other chattels not being in the nature of fixtures; or

(e) any property with respect to which the personal qualifications of the tenant are of importance for the preservation of the value or character of the property, or on the ground of neighbourhood to the lessor, or to any person holding under him.

It is considered that there is a real risk that the 'taking in execution of the lessee's interest' would be interpreted so as to include the appointment of a receiver. There is no definition of 'execution' in the Law of Property Act 1925. In *Blackman v Fysh* [1892] 3 Ch 209, where there was a proviso that operated if 'the estates hereby given ... shall be taken in execution by any process of law for the benefit of any creditors', it was held that the appointment of a receiver by the court did fall within that proviso. In addition, execution against land is defined in a different context as being completed by seizure, by the appointment of a receiver or by the making of a charging order: Insolvency Act 1986, s 346(5). But cf *Norburn v Norburn* [1894] 1 QB 448 on the meaning of 'execution' in the then Rules of the Supreme Court (RSC) and *In Re Potts, ex parte Taylor* [1893] 1 QB 648 at 650 on the meaning of 'execution' in Bankruptcy Act 1883, s 45. If s 146 does not apply, then the lender, the borrower, and hence the receiver, could not seek relief under the section.

The landlord must serve the notice on 'the lessee'. The landlord's notice will be valid if served on the borrower. There is no obligation on the landlord to serve notice on the receiver or the lender.[186]

8.177 Some leases entitle the landlord to forfeit if a receiver is appointed.[187]

8.178 If the receiver becomes aware of forfeiture or a threat of forfeiture, he may wish to seek additional funds from the lender to meet the costs of complying with the lease covenants. If any breaches can be remedied before peaceable re-entry or proceedings, costs can usually be limited.

8.179 If, however, this does not occur and forfeiture proceedings are issued, a question may arise as to the receiver's right to seek relief from forfeiture.[188]

8.180 A lender has a right to seek relief from forfeiture itself, but it may be more convenient for the receiver to seek relief in the name of the borrower, than for the lender to act, for example, so that, if the forfeiture is by proceedings, the lender will not need to be joined as a separate party. Thus, the lender may prefer to advance the money to the receiver to pay on the borrower's behalf than to seek relief from forfeiture itself.

8.181 First, the receiver's right to seek relief on behalf of the borrower needs to be considered. The terms of the mortgage deed and the deed of appointment need to be scrutinised carefully in order to ascertain whether the receiver has an express power to litigate on the borrower's behalf or whether it is a necessary incident to any of the powers the receiver has.

8.182 If the receiver does not have power to act on the borrower's behalf in claiming relief, the lender will have to make its own claim for relief[189] or delegate its power to do so to the receiver as the lender's agent.

---

[186] *Smith v Spaul* [2002] EWCA Civ 1830, [2003] QB 983.

[187] A Law of Property Act 1925, s 146 notice must be served even though the appointment of a receiver is outside the tenant's control: *Halliard Property Co Ltd v Jack Segal* [1978] 1 WLR 377; *Ivory Gate Ltd v Spetale* (1999) 77 P & CR 141, but see fn 185.

[188] The right to relief is explained at paras A.28–A.32. The court has powers to grant relief from forfeiture on terms usually directed at remedy of the breach, principally under County Courts Act 1984, s 138 (forfeiture for rent arrears alone), Law of Property Act 1925, s 146 (discretionary relief forfeiture including for another breach of lease than rent arrears). The effect of relief, if the terms are performed within the time period specified, is that the lease continues as if not forfeited.

[189] Where forfeiture is for rent arrears alone, the lender can seek relief from forfeiture either in the name of the borrower, in which case the lease will continue with the borrower as lessee since 'lessee' in County Courts Act 1984, s 138 includes person deriving title under the lessee (s 140), which includes the lender; or in its own name under s 138(9C) or Law of Property Act 1925, s 146(4), in which case the lender will become lessee, though the lease so vested will remain subject to the mortgage conditions so that on sale the proceeds after payment of the mortgage must be passed to the borrower. Where forfeiture is for breach of other terms, a similar dichotomy applies under s 146(2) (since lessee includes someone deriving title under the lessee:

8.183 In the period between the service of the forfeiture claim and a decision as to whether relief is to be granted, the receiver can and should continue to manage the property and collect rents from any sub-tenants.[190] He is entitled to use those monies to discharge current outgoings. A question may arise as to whether he should pay to the landlord the mesne profits the borrower is liable to pay instead of rent during this period. Unless and until a judgment is obtained, the borrower has no obligation to pay the mesne profits, so it is considered that the right course is for the receiver to withhold such payments from the landlord.

8.184 If relief is given on terms requiring the 'arrears' to be paid, it is likely to be in both the lender's and borrower's interest for the sums collected by the receiver during this period to be paid to the landlord in satisfaction of the condition imposed. However, it is wise to obtain both the lender's and the borrower's agreement to this course, because it is arguable that such a payment would not fall within the 'outgoings' which the receiver can properly pay.

8.185 If a forfeiture order is made, the receiver must vacate. If he does not, he becomes a trespasser. If there is a balance in the receiver's hands which has arisen during the 'twilight' period, then the question arises whether the receivers have to pay the balance to the landlord. Typically, the landlord will seek an order for mesne profits against the borrower. If it does this, then it will be issue estopped from claiming that the receivers should deliver up the balance.[191]

8.186 If the rent is not paid, and the premises are commercial premises, the landlord may seek to recover the unpaid rent under the commercial rent arrears recovery procedure (known as CRAR) in section 72 of, and Schedule 12 to, the Tribunals, Courts and Enforcement Act 2007 (2007 Act). This involves the landlord taking the tenant's goods. As such, it is of no concern to the receiver, save that:

(a) if CRAR occurs because the receiver has breached his duty to the borrower to pay the rent out of receipts, he will be liable to the borrower for any loss arising; and

(b) he must take care not to pay rent which the landlord has already recovered by CRAR.

8.187 If the receiver seeks to assign the lease, the receiver must consider the terms of the lease and ensure that if landlord's consent is needed, it is obtained. It is considered that if the receiver has power to sell the lease, the receiver will also have an implied ancillary power to seek landlord's consent. If the lease provides that the landlord is entitled to withhold consent unless an authorised

---

s 146(5)(b)), and s 146(4). A lender will often prefer relief to be as per borrower so that it does not incur direct liability to the landlord.

[190] *Official Custodian for Charities v Mackey (No 2)* [1985] 1 WLR 1308.

[191] *Official Custodian for Charities v Mackey (No 2)* [1985] 1 WLR 1308.

guarantee agreement (AGA) is provided, the landlord may seek to argue that it is not obliged to give consent unless the receiver provides the AGA personally. However, such an argument is unlikely to succeed.[192]

Tenant rights

8.188 As with landlord's rights, the terms of the charge and the appointment will determine the extent to which the receiver is able to exercise rights which the borrower has. If the only power delegated to the receiver is the power to collect income, he will have no rights *qua* tenant.

8.189 A power to 'take possession of, collect and get in the property charged ... and for that purpose to take any proceedings in the name of the [borrower] or otherwise as may seem expedient' might entitle the receiver to claim a new lease under the Landlord and Tenant Act 1954[193] or to exercise a contractual option to renew.

8.190 If the receiver has power to 'do all other things he might consider desirable or necessary for realising the security', he probably has an implied

---

[192] In *Legends Surf Shops Plc v Sun Life Assurance Society Plc* [2005] EWHC 1438 (Ch), [2006] BCC 204, a landlord sought to require administrative receivers to give an AGA. The Court held that it was the tenant who was obliged to provide the AGA, even though it was in administrative receivership, but left open (albeit subject to negative comments) whether the landlord could argue that the obligation to give an AGA 'in such form as the Landlord reasonably requires' might entitle it to insist on an AGA from the administrative receiver. Where the lease annexes a copy of the AGA, and provides that the AGA shall be in the form annexed, such an argument could not be run.

[193] In *Gough's Garages Ltd v Pugsley* [1930] 1 KB 615, the Court of Appeal upheld a receiver's claim for a new lease. This was decided under the Landlord and Tenant Act 1927, but it is not thought that this would provide any basis for differentiating the case. However, it might be possible to distinguish the case on the basis that 'the property charged' was, there, all the assets of the company. Where a fixed charge is over the leasehold interest only, there is an argument that the property charged does not include the right to seek a new lease. This argument proceeds on the premise that the right to seek the new lease is a separate property right, rather than an incident of the existing lease.

A similar argument arises, outside the receivership context, when the freehold is sold after the claim for a new lease has been made. Is that claim an overriding interest which binds the purchaser simply because the lease is a binding overriding interest? If the claim is an incident of the existing lease, then it is; but if the claim is a separate property right, it would not be an overriding interest (even if the person claiming is in actual occupation since he would be in actual occupation of the continuation of the lease, not of the claim), and a pending land action would have to be protected by notice prior to the transfer of the freehold in order for the claim to be protected. Despite long controversy on the latter question, it has not yet been determined.

It is considered that the better view is that the right to claim a new tenancy is an incident of the existing tenancy, so that if the existing tenancy is charged, and the receiver is given power in the terms set out above, a claim by a receiver in the borrower's name for a new tenancy would be good.

ancillary power to give notice to enfranchise,[194] at least where his purpose in doing so is to render the property more valuable and/or more marketable.[195]

8.191　It is considered that such a power would also entitle the receiver to:

(a)　settle a rent review;
(b)　seek the landlord's consent to make alterations, and then to make those alterations; and
(c)　seek the landlord's consent to change the use of the property;[196]

where this is being done in order to improve the marketability of the asset.

NEIGHBOURS

8.192　Receivers[197] can find themselves in dispute with the neighbours, or with other third parties claiming to have real property rights over the mortgaged property, or with third parties owning property over which the receivers need to exercise a real property right in order, for example, to access the property. There might be a boundary dispute with a neighbour, for example, or there might be no formal right of way giving access to the security.[198] Or a third party might assert that it has a right of way (or some other right[199]) over the security.

8.193　In such a situation, the receiver should ascertain whether his powers are sufficiently wide to give him the power to deal with resolving or litigating the dispute. If they are, he should seek an indemnity from the lender for any costs he will incur or may be ordered to pay in that resolution or litigation and then refer the dispute to solicitors.

---

[194]　For long residential leases, under the Leasehold Reform Act 1967 (houses) or the Leasehold Reform, Housing and Urban Development Act 1993 (flats).

[195]　The benefit of an enfranchisement notice can be assigned on sale of the lease. In *The Keepers and Governors of the Possessions, Revenues and Goods of the Free Grammar School of John Lyon v Helman* [2014] EWCA Civ 17, [2014] 1 WLR 2451, it was conceded that but for the borrower's bankruptcy, a notice to enfranchise given by the receivers would have been valid, despite an express provision in the mortgage requiring the borrower to give any notice which the lender deemed expedient (which might have militated against the receivers having implied power to give notices on the borrower's behalf).

[196]　The related question of whether the receiver has power to apply for planning permission to permit development and/or a change of use will turn on construction of the receiver's express powers, and whether the power to so apply is incidental to any of those express powers and necessary to their performance.

[197]　Primarily, these problems affect receivers with a power of sale, but a receiver with a power to take possession or to grant new leases can also be affected by some of these issues.

[198]　Sometimes, this arises where it is alleged that there is a ransom strip owned by a third party, over which there is the only access to the landlocked mortgaged property.

[199]　Rights to light are particularly important if the security is development land. Or there may be third parties claiming to have acquired part of the land by adverse possession, or by virtue of some sort of proprietary estoppel.

8.194 In some cases, the right course will be to revert to the solicitor who acted for the borrower when the security was purchased so as to obtain information from the conveyancing file. However, that solicitor may have a conflict of interest. In some cases, the borrower and/or the lender may have a cause of action against the conveyancing solicitor if the security is subject to some incumbrance they were not advised about at the time of the purchase.

8.195 In general, the receiver will not be entitled to prosecute that claim and recover any resulting damages from the solicitor, but if the mortgage expressly grants such a power (or if there is a charge over all the borrower's assets so as to include the borrower's claim), then the receiver with appropriate powers will have the power to bring the claim.

8.196 Litigation is dealt with in more detail in Chapter 14.

NEW RELATIONSHIPS

Contracts entered into by the borrower

8.197 It is not unusual for a borrower to enter into contracts with third parties after the appointment of a receiver, even though the contracts are within the scope of the receiver's powers.[200]

8.198 The case law set out in Chapter 6[201] suggests that the borrower is not entitled to enter into new contracts within the powers of the receiver once the receiver has been appointed. The receiver can prevent the borrower from entering into such contracts by injunction. However, it is likely that the contract would not be void between the borrower and the third party.[202]

8.199 Certainly, the receiver cannot be required to perform a contract made by the borrower after his appointment, for the same reasons as set out above in relation to borrower contracts entered into before the appointment of the receiver.

8.200 If entry into the contract were of such benefit to repayment of the mortgage debt that it would be a breach of duty by the receiver not to adopt it or enter into afresh, then no doubt he could be required to do so by the borrower suing in breach of duty.

---

[200] See, for example, *National Westminster Bank Plc v Hunter* [2011] EWHC 3170 (Ch), in which the borrower entered into a contract for sale of the mortgaged property after the appointment of the receiver, and it appears possibly after the receiver had himself contracted with a third party for sale of the borrower's property.

[201] See paras 6.144–6.155.

[202] Presumably by estoppel. See *National Westminster Bank Plc v Hunter* [2011] EWHC 3170 (Ch), in which it was assumed that the borrower's contract was not void; *Bower Terrace Student Accommodation Ltd v Space Student Living Ltd* [2012] EWHC 2206 (Ch) at [45], though the judge made no decision on the point. However, the point was not considered in detail in either of these cases.

Contracts entered into by the receiver

The receiver's position

8.201 Section 37(1) of the Insolvency Act 1986 provides:

> A receiver or manager appointed under powers contained in an instrument (other than an administrative receiver) is, to the same extent as if he had been appointed by order of the court—
>
> (a) personally liable on any contract entered into by him in the performance of his functions (except in so far as the contract otherwise provides) ... and
> (b) entitled in respect of that liability to indemnity out of the assets.

8.202 It therefore seems clear, at least in the case of a company borrower, that the receiver is personally liable on the contracts he makes, unless 'the contract otherwise provides'. Plainly, it is wise for the receiver to exclude his liability expressly. In other cases, there may be an argument about whether, on the true construction of the contract, the liability has been excluded.

8.203 There is an argument that this provision applies to all receiverships and not just those where the borrower is a company. Unlike most of the provisions in the Insolvency Act 1986 which relate to receivers, there is nothing in this provision which expressly limits its application to the case where the borrower is a company.[203]

8.204 Where this provision does not apply, it is a question of fact, in each case, whether the receiver is to be taken to have made the contract on his own behalf, or on behalf of the borrower, or the lender. This is the case even where the mortgage terms provide that the receiver is to act as the borrower's agent: it does not follow that all contracts which the receiver makes within the scope of his power are, in fact, made on behalf of the borrower.[204] However, the starting point will be that the receiver will be taken to have intended to contract on behalf of the borrower in respect of acts within the scope of the deemed agency and not on his own behalf.

8.205 The receiver will be taken to have contracted on his own behalf if:

(a) he has expressly agreed to undertake personal liability;
(b) he did not disclose that he was acting as the borrower's agent when making the contract;
(c) on the true construction of the contract, it was intended by the other party and the receiver that he would be personally liable;
(d) he is estopped from denying that he has personal liability;

---

[203] However, there is reference in Insolvency Act 1986, s 37(4) to 'the company', so it is not straightforward to argue that s 37 applies to all receiverships. The section was not referred to in *Dammerman v Lanyon Bowdler LLP* [2017] EWCA Civ 269.

[204] *Edenwest Ltd v CMS Cameron McKenna (A Firm)* [2012] EWHC 1258 (Ch); *Dammerman v Lanyon Bowdler LLP* [2017] EWCA Civ 269.

(e)   possibly, if the contract is made by deed (but not a deed poll) and the borrower is not a party; or

(f)   the contract was entered into after the borrower has become insolvent.[205]

8.206 If the receiver purports to enter into a contract on the borrower's behalf but acts outside his powers in doing so, so that the borrower would not be bound, the receivers would be liable (for breach of warranty of authority) for any losses the third party suffered.

The borrower's position

8.207 If the receiver acts within the scope of his powers and contracts on behalf of the borrower, the borrower will be liable on the contract.

8.208 The borrower will not have a claim against the receiver for any losses it suffers as a result of being bound by a disadvantageous contract, absent an implied contract, or the use of unlawful means by the purported receiver and an intention to cause the borrower loss.[206]

8.209 Even if there were some defect in the receiver's appointment, or if the receiver acts beyond his powers in making the contract, the borrower will generally not be in any different position than if the receiver was properly authorised to act on its behalf. The borrower will often be bound by any contracts the receiver makes because the third party will be able to rely on the doctrine of ostensible authority.[207]

Employment

8.210 If the receiver enters new contracts of employment, he generally does so as agent of the borrower, for the purposes of considering continuity of employment.[208] However, the receiver will be personally liable on the contract, at least where the borrower is a company.[209]

---

[205] *Thomas v Todd* [1926] 2 KB 511. The receiver's agency likely ends on insolvency: see para 6.170 and the discussion that follows. Any contracts he makes after this time, he must make as principal.

[206] *OBG and Others v Allan and Others* [2007] UKHL 21, [2008] 1 AC 1 especially at [93] and [218].

[207] *OBG and Others v Allan and Others* [2007] UKHL 21, [2008] 1 AC 1 at [92], but note that ostensible authority only exists where the principal (i.e. the borrower) has held the person out as its agent. Knowledge that a person is holding himself out as your agent and failing to take any steps to prevent him from continuing to do so will suffice: *Freeman & Lockyer v Buckhurst Park Properties (Mangal) Ltd* [1964] 2 QB 480.

[208] *In Re Mack Trucks (Britain) Ltd* [1967] 1 WLR 780.

[209] Insolvency Act 1986, s 37.

Power to grant new leases

8.211 A receiver who only has the statutory power to collect income does not automatically have the power to grant new leases.

8.212 The lender will usually have a statutory power of leasing[210] and a statutory power of accepting surrenders[211] which arise when the receiver is appointed.[212] These are delegable to the receiver.[213] The statutory powers may be extended or varied by the mortgage conditions, or by an agreement between the borrower and the lender. Alternatively, the receiver may be given different express powers of leasing and accepting surrenders in the mortgage conditions.

8.213 The receiver's power of leasing and accepting surrenders is discussed in detail in Chapter 9,[214] with reference to Chapter 2, where the borrower's and the lender's statutory powers are set out.

THE RECEIVER'S LIABILITY IN TORT

8.214 Generally, the fact that a receiver is the agent of the borrower has little relevance in the law of tort. The starting point in establishing whether the receiver is liable in tort is whether he committed a tort.[215] If he trespasses on a third party's land or causes a nuisance, for example, by obstructing a third party's exercise of a right of way over the property, he is likely to be liable to the third party, even if he has carried out these actions in his capacity of receiver.[216]

8.215 The following anomaly should be noted:[217] a receiver is not liable for inducing a breach of contract if he induces the borrower to breach its contracts with third parties. The fact that the receiver is the agent of the borrower precludes him from being treated as independent of the borrower for the purpose of such a claim.

---

[210] Under Law of Property Act 1925, s 99(2), unless the mortgage conditions provide otherwise.

[211] Law of Property Act 1925, s 100(2).

[212] Law of Property Act 1925, ss 99(19) and 100(14).

[213] Law of Property Act 1925, s 109(3).

[214] At paras 9.141–9.163.

[215] Where there is a statutory duty, the starting point is to establish upon whom the duty is placed. If the duty is the borrower's, then it is the borrower (and not the receiver) who is in breach of statutory duty if the duty is not complied with. The receiver is not 'the occupier', so it is thought that the receiver will not be liable to third parties under statutes such as the Occupiers' Liability Acts 1957 or 1984. For a general discussion on who is an occupier for the purpose of these statutes, see *Wheat v Lacon* [1966] AC 552. For the same reason, a receiver is not likely to be liable for adopting pre-existing nuisances on the premises. However, if he creates a nuisance, he will be liable.

[216] *Welsh Development Agency v Expert Finance Co Ltd* [1992] BCC 270 at 288; *In Re Goldburg (No 2), ex parte Page* [1912] 1 KB 606.

[217] This is discussed at para 8.9 and fn 13.

8.216 Since the receiver is not an employee of either the lender or the borrower, the starting point will be that neither of them is liable for any torts committed by the receiver. If the receiver commits a tort, liability will only attach to someone else if that person directed, or authorised, him to commit the tort.[218]

8.217 If the receiver is fraudulent, different principles are likely to apply: a principal is liable for the fraud of his agent if he clothed him with actual or ostensible authority to perform transactions of the kind in question.[219] It is unclear precisely how that principal might be applied in the case of a receiver and in particular whether the borrower would be liable for the receiver's frauds given that it is the lender, and not the borrower, who appoints him.[220]

STATUTORY LIABILITIES

8.218 This section is not concerned with whether a third party can bring an action for breach of statutory duty against the receiver, but whether a receiver is guilty of a criminal offence or liable to action by a public body, such as a local authority, if the statute is not complied with.

8.219 The starting point is the answer to the question on whom the duty is placed by the statute. If the receiver is a person on whom the duty is placed, then the receiver will be liable if that duty is breached.

8.220 For example, the contaminated land regime imposes liability on persons who cause or knowingly permit substances which contaminate land to be in, on or under that land[221] (as well as on owners or occupiers if the person responsible cannot be found).[222] It is envisaged in the Environmental Protection Act 1990 that a receiver might be liable as a person who caused or knowingly permitted the substances to be in, on or under the land, for there is an express provision that the receiver should not be personally liable for the remediation costs unless the substances were there as a result of an unreasonable act or omission of his.[223] There is no such limitation on the receiver's personal liability in respect of substances which pollute controlled waters: if the receiver caused or knowingly

---

[218] This is from the general analysis of when vicarious liability arises. See any practitioner's text on agency, though note the unusual cases on vicarious liability where there is neither employment nor direction/authorisation by the principal, or a contractor's act is a non-delegable duty of the potential principal.

[219] *Lloyd v Grace, Smith & Co* [1912] AC 716.

[220] No doubt the receiver would be liable to the borrower for breach of duty were there any such fraud.

[221] Environmental Protection Act 1990, s 78F(2).

[222] Environmental Protection Act 1990, s 78F(4). See below in relation to occupiers.

[223] Environmental Protection Act 1990, s 78X(3) and (4)(f)(ii).

permitted the matter to be in the controlled water or to be at a place from which it was likely to enter the controlled water,[224] he will be liable.

8.221 If a planning enforcement notice is served, whilst the receiver will not be liable for the cost of the works or for failure to carry out works,[225] the receiver is at risk of committing a criminal offence[226] if he carries on any activity which is required by the notice to cease.

8.222 Many statutes impose obligations on owners and occupiers of property. Typically, the receiver will not be obliged to comply with these requirements, for the receiver is merely the borrower's agent, and the borrower remains in occupation.[227]

8.223 However, the following should be noted:

(a) If the receiver remains in possession after his agency for the borrower has ceased (e.g. on insolvency), he may be liable as the occupier.[228]
(b) If the receiver has acted beyond his powers in taking possession, his occupation is unlikely to be construed as agent for the borrower.
(c) If the receiver has taken possession in his own right (i.e. he has brought possession proceedings against the borrower, or in reliance on the lender's right when the borrower did not have power to obtain possession) and he has not taken any steps to put the borrower back into possession, he may be liable as occupier.

---

[224] Water Resources Act 1991, s 161.

[225] This liability falls on the owner: Town and Country Planning Act 1990, ss 178(1)(b) and 179(1).

[226] As a person with control of the land, under the Town and Country Planning Act 1990, s 179(4).

[227] *Ratford v Northavon DC* [1986] 3 WLR 771.

[228] But cf *Rees v Boston Borough Council* [2001] EWCA Civ 1934, [2002] 1 WLR 1304.

Chapter 9

The Receiver's Powers

INTRODUCTION

9.1   This chapter is about the powers that may be given to a receiver and their sources.

9.2   As this chapter explains, a receiver appointed solely under section 101(1)(iii) of the Law of Property Act 1925 will have the powers specified in section 109 and nothing more. Such a receiver can be called an LPA receiver.

9.3   This chapter sketches the statutory provisions governing LPA receivership and gives, where relevant, references for more detailed discussion.

9.4   It then considers the LPA receiver's powers under section 109(3) of the Law of Property Act 1925. The powers to collect income and the lender's statutorily delegable powers of leasing and surrender are discussed in some detail.

9.5   The terms of the mortgage often give the lender either an express right to appoint a receiver, who could be called a fixed charge receiver, or could vary or extend the powers that a receiver appointed under the Law of Property Act 1925 might have.

9.6   Thus, in contrast, additional powers commonly given to fixed-charge receivers are set out briefly.

9.7   Lastly, the chapter sets out the consequences of a receiver acting beyond his powers.

9.8   Collection of income is a statutory power given to every LPA receiver by section 109(3) of the Law of Property Act 1925, whether or not any such power is included in the mortgage conditions, and whether or not the LPA receiver's powers are extended. It is also commonly given to fixed charge receivers. It is central to the role of a receiver, at least as it was originally used.[1]

9.9   Even if there is no power to appoint a receiver with greater powers than those under the Law of Property Act 1925, the appointment of a receiver with a

---

[1]   It is common now for a receiver's role to be directed towards sale of the mortgaged property.

power to collect income is useful to a lender.[2] The lender can ensure that an income source from the mortgaged property available to the borrower is made available for the repayment of the interest on the loan and the loan itself, without incurring the obligations to account to the borrower or liability as landlord to any tenants which would be imposed if it went into possession itself.

LPA AND FIXED CHARGE RECEIVERS

9.10   In the introduction to this chapter, a distinction in name was made between an LPA receiver, i.e. a receiver appointed under section 109 of the Law of Property Act 1925 with precisely the powers given by section 109, and a fixed charge receiver, who is appointed under an express power to do so in the mortgage conditions and perhaps with different or additional powers.

Are all receivers LPA receivers?

9.11   If, on the true construction of the mortgage, it grants a separate express power to appoint a receiver in certain circumstances, the receiver will, once appointed, be a fixed charge receiver, not an LPA receiver.[3]

9.12   However, in many cases, the mortgage conditions will, on their true construction, purport to vary or extend the statutory conditions so as to give an LPA receiver additional powers.[4] The receiver's status in those circumstances is more difficult to analyse.

9.13   Under section 101(3) of the Law of Property Act 1925:

> The provisions of this Act relating to the foregoing powers, comprised either in this section, or in any other section regulating the exercise of those powers, may be varied or extended by the mortgage deed, and as so varied or extended, shall as far as may be, operate in the like manner and with all the like incidents, effects, and consequences, as if such variations or extensions were contained in this Act.

9.14   Despite the impression given by this section on first reading, it appears that it does not make every express power to appoint a receiver simply a variation or extension of the statutory power. In *Phoenix Properties Ltd v*

---

[2]   Especially if the lender delegates its power of leasing to the receiver so that the receiver can ensure there are occupants to generate income.

[3]   An express power to appoint a receiver expressly exercisable 'at any time after the date of' the mortgage deed is not to be read as a variation of the statutory power to appoint a receiver, and hence does not include Law of Property Act 1925, s 109(1), and with it the requirement (via the need for the statutory power of sale to have arisen) for the mortgage money to be due: *Silven Properties Ltd v Royal Bank of Scotland Plc* [2002] EWHC 1976 (Ch) at [105]–[106]: appealed on other grounds in *Silven Properties Ltd v Royal Bank of Scotland Plc* [2003] EWCA Civ 1409, [2004] 1 WLR 997.

[4]   I.e. beyond those of an LPA receiver. These are discussed at paras 9.172–9.175.

Wimpole St Nominees Ltd,[5] a power of sale[6] given to the receiver in the mortgage conditions was held not to be a variation or extension within the meaning of section 101(3) of the Law of Property Act 1925.[7]

9.15 It is unclear what the variations and extensions envisaged by section 101(3) of the Law of Property Act 1925 are in the case of receivership.[8]

9.16 Nevertheless, the result is that it is possible for a receiver to be an LPA receiver in respect of the statutory powers and a fixed charge receiver in relation to the additional powers, at the same time. If the legal charge purports to extend the statutory powers by conferring additional non-delegable powers to the receiver, then it is likely that on the true construction of the charge, the statutory preconditions and other terms will also apply to the fixed charge receivership. However, a receiver who has both LPA powers and fixed charge powers should

---

[5] [1992] BCLC 737.

[6] To sell or concur in selling any of the property hereby charged: see *Phoenix Properties Ltd v Wimpole St Nominees Ltd* [1992] BCLC 737 at 741d. The case did not discuss whether that was to be interpreted as a lender's power of sale, or a borrower's power of sale, though the wording at 743h suggests that it was interpreted, as is likely right, as a borrower's power of sale. See Chapter 11, fn 120 and para 11.97 for a discussion.

[7] The reasoning of Mummery J (*obiter*) in *Phoenix Properties Ltd v Wimpole St Nominees Ltd* [1992] BCLC 737 was that the lender's statutory power of sale is not expressed in the Law of Property Act 1925 to be delegable to receivers, and thus the power of sale in the mortgage conditions was not to be regarded as a statutory provision varied or extended by the mortgage deed: at 743d. But for this authority, it might have been possible to argue that s 101 gives a wide power to vary what the receiver's powers should be at the time the mortgage is made, and that the reference in s 109(3) to powers delegated to the receiver by the mortgage pursuant to the Act is intended to refer to delegations which occur outside the mortgage terms. However, unless and until *Phoenix* is overruled, that argument would face real difficulties, even though the comments about the scope of s 101 were *obiter*. This book, therefore, adopts the analysis that the LPA powers are limited to those set out in this chapter, and other powers can only be conferred on the receiver by right of some separate but parallel receivership created by the terms of the fixed charge.

[8] The only statutorily delegable lender's powers are leasing, the power to accept surrenders and insurance: see below. Thus *Phoenix Properties Ltd v Wimpole St Nominees Ltd* 1992] BCLC 737 suggests that no other lender's powers could be given to an LPA receiver within the meaning of Law of Property Act 1925, s 101(3). Since few borrower powers are referred to in the Act (leasing and surrender being the only obvious examples) are not expressed to be delegable, the reasoning in *Phoenix* would suggest that these cannot be given to the receiver. This appears to make s 101(3) of extremely limited effect. Section 101(3) is a provision common to the four powers in s 101(1): sale, insure, appoint receivers, cut and sell timber. The distinctions made in the two cases referred to do not seem to have been made into the most commonly litigated of those, sale. Moreover, Law of Property Act 1925, Pt III (and the statutes which proceeded it, such as the Conveyancing Act 1881), which includes the provisions on mortgages, appears to have been designed in various of its sections to ensure that what was previously common under express mortgages was on a statutory footing which enabled mortgages other than by transfer of the borrower's property to the lender, or by actual sub-demise, would work within the context of property law. There thus seems to be room to challenge the apparent effect of the above two decisions, if an appropriate case came before the Court of Appeal.

take care to consider the source of the particular power he seeks to exercise in order to ensure that the exercise of the power is valid in the circumstances.[9]

What distinctions are there?

9.17 An LPA receiver is regulated by the Law of Property Act 1925. The lender's right to appoint him, its right to remove him, the form of appointment or removal, the deemed agency of the receiver, the receiver's remuneration and the obligations and powers with which a receiver can be appointed by the lender are all regulated by the Act.

9.18 A fixed charge receiver is regulated by the mortgage conditions. The lender only has a right to appoint him, or remove him, if the conditions allow it, and in the circumstances provided by the conditions. The conditions govern the form of appointment and removal. A fixed charge receiver will only be the deemed agent of the borrower if the conditions so provide. The powers and obligations of the receiver are those given to him in the conditions and then in his appointment.

9.19 When the mortgage conditions expressly include the statutory power to appoint a receiver, but appear to modify those terms, for example as to requirements for an appointment or give the receiver additional powers, then it will be a matter of construction to what extent if at all there has been a variation or extension under section 101(3) of the Law of Property Act 1925, so that section 109 continues to apply, or whether the receivership in whole or in part is better considered as express.

9.20 For the most part, the distinction will not be critical since the question will be simply interpretation of the mortgage conditions.

9.21 Many of the differences between the two types of receivership are dealt with elsewhere in this book. For example, the requirements for appointment of a receiver,[10] including the specific requirements for appointment of an LPA receiver, are discussed elsewhere.[11] Similarly, the application by the receiver of the money received by him,[12] the process for termination of a receivership[13] and remuneration of a receiver, are all discussed elsewhere.[14]

9.22 Law common to both types of receivership is also discussed elsewhere. Any LPA receiver is the deemed agent of the borrower.[15] It is relatively rare for

---

[9] Note that there is a third potential source of powers for a receiver, namely those delegated by the lender. This is discussed at para 5.34 *et seq*.

[10] Both the requirement under Law of Property Act 1925, s 109(1) that the power of sale under the Act has arisen, and the requirements as to the form of appointment.

[11] See Chapter 4.

[12] See Chapter 12.

[13] See Chapter 13.

[14] See Chapter 7.

[15] Law of Property Act 1925, s 109(2).

the conditions of a mortgage which provides expressly for the appointment of a receiver not to deem him the agent of the borrower. The operation of that deemed agency and the duties imposed by equity on the receiver are the same whether the source of the deemed agency is section 109(2) of the Law of Property Act 1925 or the mortgage conditions. This aspect of receivership is dealt with elsewhere in this book.[16]

9.23   Similarly, the receiver's relationship with the lender, for example that intermeddling with the receivership would make the receiver the agent of the lender rather than of the borrower, is similar whatever the source of the receivership.[17] An LPA receiver's relationship with third parties is similar to that of a fixed charge receiver, save that an LPA receiver usually has fewer powers and hence can create fewer contractual relationships with third parties than a fixed charge receiver.[18]

The power to appoint a receiver, and successors in title

9.24   One issue where the distinction between LPA receivers and fixed charge receivers does make a possible difference is the effect of changes in the proprietor of the mortgaged property, and in the proprietor of the mortgage, on the power to appoint a receiver.

The LPA receiver

Change in proprietor of the mortgage

9.25   A transferor of the mortgage, where the transfer is by deed and 'unless a contrary intention is therein expressed' will have the right to exercise all powers of the lender.[19]

9.26   This does not extend to changes of proprietor of the charge by automatic vesting, for example, on the death of bankruptcy of a personal lender. However, section 101(1) of the Law of Property Act 1925 gives the power to appoint a receiver to the 'mortgagee'. Under section 205(1)(xvi),[20] 'mortgagee includes and person from time to time deriving title under the original mortgagee'. Thus, if the lender transfers his mortgage, and certainly once the transfer has been

---

[16]   See Chapter 6.

[17]   See Chapter 7.

[18]   See Chapter 8 for a discussion of the relationship between receivers and third parties.

[19]   Law of Property Act 1925, s 114(1)(b). What is said is that a deed executed by the lender purporting to transfer his mortgage will transfer the right to exercise all the powers of the lender. The powers are not simply the statutory powers, but include the express powers. Section 114 is a general section transferring rights and powers under a mortgage on its transfer. It applies where only the benefit of the mortgage is transferred. Section 114 appears to be limited to charges over unregistered land: *Paragon Finance Plc v Pender* [2005] EWCA Civ 760, [2005] 1 WLR 3412. See Chapter 2, fn 113.

[20]   'Unless the context otherwise requires': see Law of Property Act 1925, s 205(1). The context does not otherwise require.

registered at the Land Registry, the new proprietor of the mortgage will have the power to appoint an LPA receiver.[21]

9.27   If the mortgage is registered, and a transferee is registered as the proprietor of it, then the transferee will have the estate vested in it[22] and hence will have the statutory powers because it will be deemed to be the proprietor of a charge by deed by way of legal mortgage.[23]

Change in proprietor of the mortgaged property

9.28   The power in section 101(1)(iii) of the Law of Property Act 1925 is to appoint a receiver over the income of the mortgaged property. That is not a concept dependent on who the mortgagor is. However, under section 109(2), the receiver so appointed 'shall be deemed to be the agent of the mortgagor', and under section 109(3), the receiver can demand and recover income 'in the name ... of the mortgagor' and 'the mortgagor shall be solely responsible for the receiver's acts or defaults unless the mortgage deed otherwise provides'.

9.29   Under section 205(1)(xvi) of the Law of Property Act 1925, '"mortgagor" includes any person from time to time deriving title under the original mortgagor or entitled to redeem a mortgage according to his estate interest or right in the mortgaged property'.

9.30   If the borrower sells the mortgaged property and it is not redeemed so remains subject to the charge,[24] then at least on registration of the purchaser as proprietor of the mortgaged property,[25] 'mortgagor' will refer to the purchaser, and the receiver will be the purchaser's deemed agent.

9.31   Thus the power to appoint a receiver survives changes in the proprietor of the mortgage and of the mortgaged property by statute.

---

[21]   As well as the other statutory powers under Law of Property Act 1925, s 101(1). See Chapter 4 for further discussion, including the situation where there has been no registration.

[22]   Land Registration Act 2002, s 58(1).

[23]   Land Registration Act 2002, s 51(10).

[24]   Where the mortgaged property and the mortgage are registered, the priority of the mortgage is protected on sale, so the purchaser when registered takes subject to it. A transfer of the borrower's title is rare where there is a mortgage since usually the lender requires at grant that a restriction is entered on the title to prevent registration of a transfer without its consent. Thus this scenario is most likely to arise on vesting of the mortgaged property in the successor in title automatically, for example on the borrower's death or bankruptcy. See Chapter 6 for a discussion.

[25]   It is unlikely that the definition of mortgagor extends to the beneficiary under a trust of the mortgaged property, since 'title' is not usually used to refer to equitable interests under a trust, but legal title. Nor does a beneficiary have the right to redeem, though he may be able to call on his trustee to do so. Otherwise, those interested in the equity of redemption may well be entitled to redeem.

The fixed charge receiver

Transfer of the mortgage

9.32   As above, if the transfer of the mortgage is by deed, then the transferee will have the power to appoint a receiver.

9.33   This, however, does not assist if the transfer is automatic, for example, on the death or bankruptcy of an individual lender.

9.34   If it is right that an express power to appoint a receiver need not be a variation or extension of the statutory power, despite section 101(3) of the Law of Property Act 1925, then the effect of changes in the proprietor of the mortgage and of the mortgaged property are a little more difficult to analyse, though it is usually assumed that the power continues on those changes.[26]

9.35   The mortgage conditions will give 'the mortgagee' a power to appoint a receiver. Usually, a power given by one person is exercisable by anyone in the class of people described in the power.[27] It follows that if the definition of 'mortgagee' in the mortgage conditions includes successors in title to the original lender, then on a transfer of the mortgage, the new proprietor of it, at least once registered, will be able to exercise the power to appoint a receiver.[28]

Transfer of the mortgaged property

9.36   What if the borrower sells the mortgaged property? Insofar as the express power to appoint the receiver gives the receiver powers over the mortgaged property, then the receiver once appointed will be able to exercise those powers. Thus, for example, if he has the power to collect income, he will be able to do so. If he has the power of letting, he will be able to let. If he has the power to sell the property,[29] he will be able to sell the property, notwithstanding that it is registered in the purchaser's name, because the purchaser will have taken subject to the mortgage and thus subject to the power to appoint a receiver with such a power to sell.

---

[26]   There is no case law commentary on this issue, hence what is set out is the analysis of the authors only.

[27]   See, for example, *In Re Crunden and Meux's Contract* [1909] 1 Ch 690 at 695; *In Re Rumney and Smith* [1897] 2 Ch 351 at 356.

[28]   This could also be analysed as if the mortgage were a lease: (a) for a mortgage entered into before 1 January 1996, under the rule in *Spencer's Case* (1583) 5 Co Rep 16a, on the basis that the mortgagee's powers are the benefit of leasehold covenants since the power to appoint a receiver touches and concerns the land. See *Megarry & Wade* at para 20-043 for an explanation; (b) for a mortgage entered into on or after 1 January 1996, under the Landlord and Tenant (Covenants) Act 1995, in both cases provided that on a true interpretation the power is not intended to be personal.

[29]   Either the property as the borrower could sell it, subject to the mortgage and any other interests which bind the equity of redemption, or as the lender could sell it, free of the mortgage and those interests, depending on the power of sale the receiver has been given.

9.37   Two questions arise:

(a)   Will a receiver be able to exercise a power which is, on its proper interpretation, a power strictly limited to a requirement that it be done in the 'mortgagor's' name?[30]

(b)   Will an express deemed agency make the receiver the deemed agent of the purchaser?

9.38   If the definition of 'mortgagor' in the mortgage conditions is, on a proper interpretation, limited to the original borrower, then any power the receiver has may be of no benefit. For example, a power to sell the original borrower's estate would be of no benefit once that borrower had transferred the estate to a purchaser.

9.39   In a mortgage with the limited meaning of the original borrower for 'mortgagor', after transfer of the borrower's estate to the purchaser the receiver retains any powers, then the receiver when exercising them will remain the deemed agent of the borrower so that the original borrower could be sued by third parties on any contracts entered into by the receiver.

9.40   If, as will be more common, the definition of 'the mortgagor' includes successors in title on its true interpretation, it does not necessarily follow that the receiver could exercise any powers strictly to act in 'the mortgagor's name', and/or as deemed agent of 'the mortgagor', and so as to make the purchaser liable to third parties.

9.41   An analysis which suggests that the receiver could so act as against the purchaser is a leasehold analysis, thinking of the mortgage as if it were a lease out of the borrower's estate.[31] If the mortgage were a lease, then the receiver's powers appear likely to bind the purchaser.[32]

---

[30]   It may be possible to interpret the power as a power to sell which would continue to be exercisable as a power to convey the estate from whomsoever owns it to someone else, with the reference to the mortgagor's name simply an emphasis on the deemed agency of the mortgagor, so that the mortgagor can be made liable on the transaction. In that case, the power would continue, but it may be that the purchaser could not be made liable on the transaction, and the receiver would have to proceed in his own name. It may, however, be that the power is strictly limited to a power to sell the estate vested in the mortgagor only. If the reference to the mortgagor is incapable of referring to a successor in title, then the power ends with the transfer to the purchaser.

[31]   Where the mortgage is by demise or sub-demise, then it is indeed a lease, and such an analysis is obviously appropriate. If it is by charge by deed by way of legal mortgage, then the mortgagee has 'the same protection, powers and remedies' as if there was a lease: Law of Property Act 1925, s 87(1). The mortgagee, if he had a lease, would be able to enforce leasehold covenants against a successor in title to the mortgage, provided the rules for the covenant passing on transfer of the borrower's estate were complied with.

[32]   Note that a mortgagor is the lease out of the borrower's estate, so the borrower is the landlord, and the lender the tenant. If the mortgage were granted before 1 January 1996, then the obligations on the mortgagor would pass on transfer of the mortgagor's estate under Law of Property Act 1925, s 142 – as obligations under landlord covenants. If the mortgage were

Power of attorney

9.42   The same analysis as suggested for fixed charge receivership suggests that if mortgage conditions give the receiver a power of attorney from 'the mortgagor', and that expression is apt to include successors in title: (a) a receiver appointed by a successor mortgagee will have a power of attorney from the borrower; and (b) a receiver appointed by the original lender or a successor will have a power of attorney from the purchaser, on a sale of the borrower's estate subject to the charge.

THE STATUTORY REGIME

9.43   The statutory power of a lender to appoint a receiver is given by section 101(1)(iii) of the Law of Property Act 1925.

9.44   The statutory power is given to a lender 'where the mortgage is made by deed', and is a power 'to the like extent as if [it] had been in terms conferred by the mortgage deed, but not further'.[33]

9.45   The power given to the lender by section 101(1)(iii) of the Law of Property Act 1925 is 'a power, when the mortgage money has become due, to appoint a receiver of the income of the mortgaged property, or any part thereof …'. That power is qualified by section 109(1): where the lender has the power to appoint a receiver under section 101(1)(iii), he 'shall not appoint a receiver until he has become entitled to exercise the power of sale conferred by [the Act]'. The question of when the mortgage money has become due, and when the power of sale has arisen, and hence when a receiver can be appointed under the statute, is considered in Chapter 4. Appointment must be in under the hand of the lender.[34]

9.46   Section 109 of the Law of Property Act 1925 then sets out various provisions about the operation of the receivership:

(a)   An LPA receiver is deemed to be the agent of the borrower, under section 109(2). Deemed agency is discussed in Chapter 6.
(b)   The LPA receiver's power to demand and recover income, and its operation, is set out in section 109(3) and (4). The power is discussed in detail at para 9.47 *et seq*.
(c)   Section 109(3) allows the receiver 'to exercise any powers which may have been delegated to him by the mortgagee pursuant to this Act'. The

---

granted on or after 1 January 1996, then the obligations would pass under the Landlord and Tenant (Covenants) Act 1995.

[33]   Law of Property Act 1925, s 101(1), which governs all the powers given in that section. The effect of these requirements, and the question of whether the lender must be registered as the proprietor of the mortgage to exercise the statutory power to appoint a receiver is discussed in detail at para 4.11 and paras 4.16–4.18 *et seq*.

[34]   Also considered at paras 4.83–4.90.

delegable powers are the lender's powers of leasing and accepting surrenders. The delegable powers are discussed at para 9.137 *et seq.*

(d) Section 109(5) permits the lender to remove an LPA receiver and appoint a new one. Termination of receivership is the subject of Chapter 13.

(e) Remuneration of LPA receivers is dealt with in section 109(6) and discussed in Chapter 7.

(f) Section 109(7) permits the receiver to insure the mortgaged property if so directed in writing by the lender. Insurance is discussed at para 9.164 and in Chapter 12.

(g) Section 109(8) sets out the order in which the LPA receiver is to apply the money he receives. Use of the money is the subject of Chapter 12.

COLLECTION OF INCOME

9.47   The collection of income is usually under the statutory power, since that will be available whatever the express powers under the mortgage conditions. Since the power under section 109(3) of the Law of Property Act 1925 is wide, in relation to income collection, though express powers to collect income may be given they are unlikely to give much greater power to a fixed charge receiver than an LPA receiver has.

9.48   Section 109(3) of the Law of Property Act 1925 is as follows:

> The receiver shall have power to demand and recover all the income of which he is appointed receiver, by action or under section 72(1) of the Tribunals, Courts and Enforcement Act 2007 (commercial rent arrears recovery), or otherwise, in the name either of the mortgagor or the mortgagee, to the full extent of the estate or interest which the mortgagor could dispose of, and to give effectual receipts accordingly for the same, and to exercise any powers which may have been delegated to him by the mortgagee pursuant to this Act.

9.49   The primary power which section 109(3) of the Law of Property Act 1925 gives an LPA receiver is the power to demand and recover income. That is a limited power.[35]

9.50   Receivership is perhaps most commonly understood as a tool to allow the lender to run commercial property or a borrower's reversionary estate. For example, LPA receivership is apt where the mortgaged property is subject to leases whose rents are not being collected by the borrower, for example, in the residential context, where the mortgage is buy-to-let. An LPA receiver, once appointed, can manage the reversionary estate by collecting those rents and using them to pay down the mortgage.

---

[35]   See *Marshall v Cottingham* [1982] 1 Ch 82 at 89D: 'By itself, the Act gives the receiver no power of sale, and all that s 109(3) authorized the receiver to receive is the "income of which is appointed receiver"... the receiver is not made a receiver of the capital or corpus'.

9.51   The statutory power to appoint a receiver is not in any way limited by the effectiveness of the power to collect income, so it is unlikely that an appointment would be invalidated by the lack of income available for collection.[36] The receivership might, however, be pointless if there were no income for collection and the receiver did not have adequate powers to enable income to be produced. Section 109(3) allows the lender to delegate to the receiver powers of leasing and accepting surrenders.[37] In addition, mortgage conditions often give the receiver additional express, non-statutory powers in a fixed-charge receivership.[38]

Legal Framework under Law of Property Act 1925, section 109(3)

In the name of the mortgagor or the mortgagee

9.52   The LPA receiver, in exercising his power to demand and recover income, is entitled to do so in the name of the borrower or of the lender.[39] For example, if the mortgaged property was let by the borrower prior to his appointment, then the receiver would likely collect the rent under that letting in the borrower's name and would likely use the borrower's name in any necessary litigation.[40]

9.53   If the property were let by the lender, exercising its power of leasing by reason of the appointment of the receiver under section 99(19) of the Law of Property Act 1925, for example, so that the lease bound the lender and the

---

[36]   It was argued at first instance in *Silven Properties Ltd v Royal Bank of Scotland Plc* [2002] EWHC 1976 (Ch) that since the mortgaged property was unlet, so did not produce an income to be collected, the lender could not validly appoint an LPA receiver. The point was not decided because the mortgage conditions contained an express power to appoint a receiver with greater powers. The issue was not part of the appeal in *Silven Properties Ltd v Royal Bank of Scotland Plc* [2003] EWCA Civ 1409, [2004] 1 WLR 997.

[37]   Discussed at para 9.137 *et seq*.

[38]   See para 9.172 *et seq* for a summary of common such powers.

[39]   Presumably, this allows the receiver both flexibility to collect all the income, but also so that he can give good receipt in either name, to avoid disputes with any third party. It is not usually the case that the receiver could recover income in his own name. See, for example, *Re Sacker* (1888) 22 QBD 179. In that case, the receiver was appointed under a charge over goods, and the proceeds of their sale in the hands of a defendant, and an order was made for payment of that sum to the receiver. The receiver was nonetheless not the creditor because he could recover only as the court appointed receiver and hence the cause of action was not vested in him. It may be the case that a receiver who contracts in his own name, by reason of Insolvency Act 1986, s 37 or because, post the insolvency of the company borrower he is not the agent of either the borrower or the lender, is principal and creditor in relation to any contract made by him under which he is to be paid money (just as, as observed in *Re Sacker*, a receiver who holds a bill of exchange is a creditor). See Chapter 14 for further discussion of the correct party in litigation by receivers.

[40]   See Chapter 14 on litigation.

borrower, the LPA receiver would likely be able to collect the rent in the name of the borrower.[41]

9.54   However, even if the receiver collected rent in the name of the lender, he would do so as deemed agent of the borrower under section 109(2) of the Law of Property Act 1925 in the sense that the borrower, and not the lender, would be responsible for his acts or defaults.[42]

9.55   Suppose the borrower granted a lease prior to the appointment of the LPA receiver, but with a power of leasing so that that lease bound the lender. If one thinks of the mortgage as if it were a lease,[43] then that first lease would lie at the bottom of the chain of interests: borrower's estate, lender's estate and then lease.

9.56   If the borrower granted a second lease of the same property after the appointment of the LPA receiver, that lease would not bind the lender[44] and would be concurrent to the lender's interest as if the chain were: borrower's estate, second leasehold estate, mortgage and first leasehold estate. The borrower would no longer have the right to collect the income under the first lease, because that right would have passed to the second leaseholder. The receiver, acting in the name of the borrower, could only collect income from the second leaseholder, unless he is able to bring the second lease to an end either in accordance with its terms or because they need not honour it.[45]

---

[41] The reason is that the lender's power of leasing under Law of Property Act 1925, s 99(2) is a power to lease 'the mortgaged land', by reference to s 99(1), and binds the borrower. 'The mortgaged land' is the borrower's estate. *In Re White Rose Cottage* [1964] Ch 483 (reversed in part in *In Re White Rose Cottage* [1965] Ch 940, but quoted in *Swift 1st Ltd v Colin* [2011] EWHC 2410 (Ch), [2012] Ch 206 at [15]) at 496: the meaning of 'the mortgaged property' in s 101(1) is 'the property over which the mortgage deed purports to extend'. The borrower will be the landlord. Thus the borrower, via the receiver, would be entitled to collect the rents. The lender is also bound by the lease. However, the lender will not be able to enforce the covenants until in possession, which he is unlikely to be whilst the receiver is appointed (Landlord and Tenant (Covenants) Act 1995, s 15(1)(b) for leases granted on or after 1 January 1996, which gives the lender the right when in possession; for leases pre-dating 1996, the lender will be able to collect rents as reversioner on the lease he has granted: Law of Property Act 1925, ss 85–87 and 141(1), but since the lender is not in possession and will not have given notice to the borrower of any intention to receive the rents and profits, the borrower will be able to recover the rents without joining the lender).

[42] See Chapters 5 and 6 for further discussion of the deemed agency.

[43] As per Law of Property Act 1925, s 85(1), where the borrower's estate is a freehold, and s 86(1), where the borrower's estate is a leasehold, and Law of Property Act 1925, s 87(1), though note that a charge by deed by way of legal mortgage only gives the powers and remedies of a lease. It is not itself a lease. See para 2.25.

[44] Law of Property Act 1925, s 99(19).

[45] In *Bower Terrace Student Accommodation Ltd v Space Student Living Ltd* [2012] EWHC 2206 (Ch), receivers succeeded in establishing that due to the circumstances in which the alleged concurrent lease was granted, the receivers were not obliged to honour it. In the circumstances, they were entitled to ignore the alleged concurrent lease, and obtain income directly from the occupiers. See para 8.16(e).

9.57   Case law suggests that the receiver could, indeed, collect the rents due to the borrower only under the second lease, and not the rents under the first lease, despite his ability to collect rents in the lender's name as well.[46] That follows from *Rhodes v Allied Dunbar Pension Services Ltd*,[47] which decided, in the case of a floating charge under which the lender's right to possession was postponed, that the appointment of a receiver did not mean that the lender became entitled to the rent under an underlease.[48]

9.58   Thus the lender would not be entitled to the rent from the first lease, and hence the receiver could not collect it in the lender's name, even though the breach of mortgage which entitled the lender to appoint a receiver would entitle the lender to possession.[49]

9.59   In any event, the receiver could not collect the income under the second lease as agent of the lender, without the lender accepting the second tenancy as binding on him.[50]

---

[46]   But see discussion in the footnotes below.

[47]   [1989] 1 WLR 800.

[48]   This appears consistent *Turner v Walsh* [1909] 2 KB 484, which says at 494 that prior to the lender giving notice of an intention to take possession or the income, the borrower's right to possession continues because:

> it was in the nature the transaction that the mortgagor could continue in possession. His possession was rightful and not wrong. He was entitled to the rents and profits as long as he remained in possession: mesne profits accrued due and received prior to action or demand could not be recovered from him by the mortgagee (a quote from *Heath v Pugh* (1881) 6 QBD 345 at 359).

[49]   Before the grant of the second lease, the borrower was treated as having an estate encumbered directly by the first lease, notwithstanding the mortgage. After grant of the second lease, the borrower has only the reversion on that second lease, and no direct relationship with the first leaseholder whose landlord is the second leaseholder. If the lender was in possession, the lender would be the immediate landlord on the first lease because the second lease would not bind it, and hence would sit above it in the chain of interests. The receiver has the power to demand and recover income 'to the full extent of the estate and interest which the mortgagor could dispose of', which appears to mean the whole of the borrower's estate prior to granting the mortgage. See for example *In Re White Rose Cottage* [1964] Ch 483 (reversed in part in *In Re White Rose Cottage* [1965] Ch 940, but quoted in *Swift 1st Ltd v Colin* [2011] EWHC 2410 (Ch), [2012] Ch 206 at [15]) at 496: the meaning of 'the mortgaged property' in Law of Property Act 1925, s 101(1) is 'the property over which the mortgage deed purports to extend'. If that is right, then the receiver ought to be able to recover rent the lender could have recovered, as well as the rent the borrower could have recovered, thus the rent under both the first and second leases, though perhaps that is pushing the leasehold analogy too far. This situation, in a fixed charge receivership, arose in *Bower Terrace Student Accommodation Ltd v Space Student Living Ltd* [2012] EWHC 2006 (Ch) on an application by the receivers for an interim injunction against occupiers who said that they occupied under a lease granted by the borrower after the receiver's appointment. The judge decided that since the occupiers were very closely involved with the borrowers, and the directors of the occupying company knew that the alleged lease would be in breach of the mortgage, the purported lease could have given no estate in land. The possible issues sketched in this footnote were not canvassed.

[50]   See para 2.107(c).

To the full extent of the estate or interest

9.60   The wording of section 109(3) of the Law of Property Act 1925 is: 'to the full extent of the estate or interest which the mortgagor could dispose of'. The receiver will be able to collect income under tenancies granted prior to the grant of the mortgage as well as those granted thereafter.[51]

The receiver's duties in collecting income

9.61   The receiver's duty in collecting income is a particular application of a receiver duty more generally, which is discussed in Chapter 6. The duty is owed to the lender and to everyone with an interest in the equity of redemption. The receiver's duty is 'to try and bring about a situation in which the secured debt is repaid'.[52] The receiver cannot remain passive once appointed.[53]

What is income?

9.62   No definitive definition of income is given in the Law of Property Act 1925 save that income includes rents and profits.[54] The categories set out below are items which would fall within rents and profits, save where discussed.

Rent

9.63   The most common category of income which a receiver will collect is rent from any leases of the property.[55] The level of that rent under a tenancy or lease entered into by the borrower with the occupant, or the lender under its powers of leasing for example under section 99(19) of the Law of Property Act 1925, will be determined by that tenancy.

9.64   The dates on which rent falls due, the requirement, if any[56] for a prior demand and the availability of interest for late payment will all be set out in the lease. It is useful to note whether payment of rent is required in the lease to be 'without set off or deduction whatsoever' since that, or similar wording,

---

[51]   *In Re White Rose Cottage* [1964] Ch 483 (reversed in part in *In Re White Rose Cottage* [1965] Ch 940, but quoted in *Swift 1st Ltd v Colin* [2011] EWHC 2410 (Ch), [2012] Ch 206 at [15]) at 496: the meaning of 'the mortgaged property' in 1925 Act, s 101(1) is 'the property over which the mortgage deed purports to extend', i.e. what the borrower had available to dispose of at the date the mortgage was granted.

[52]   *Silven Properties Ltd v Royal Bank of Scotland Plc* [2003] EWCA Civ 1409, [2004] 1 WLR 997 at [27]; *Medforth v Blake* [2000] Ch 86.

[53]   *Silven Properties Ltd v Royal Bank of Scotland Plc* [2003] EWCA Civ 1409, [2004] 1 WLR 997.

[54]   Law of Property Act 1925, s 205(1)(xix).

[55]   See the discussion at paras 9.55–9.59 as to under which leases the receiver can collect income, and para 9.141 *et seq* and para 8.42 *et seq* as to leasing more generally.

[56]   It is unusual for there to be any requirement.

prevents payment by the tenant from being reduced by any counterclaim he may have, for example for breach of landlord's repairing obligations.[57]

9.65   Where the mortgaged property is leasehold and is forfeited by the landlord, the receiver will be able to retain rent from sub-lessees and other occupants between service of the landlord's claim for possession on the grounds of forfeiture[58] and until the court grants the possession.[59]

Arrears

9.66   In general, the receiver will be entitled to collect arrears of rent and other income which fell due before he was appointed as receiver, indeed before any breach of mortgage, unless, on their true construction, the mortgage conditions provide otherwise.[60]

---

[57]   See *Gilbert-Ash (Northern) v Modern Engineering (Bristol)* [1974] AC 689; *Connaught Restaurants v Indoor Leisure* [1994] 1 WLR 501; *Electricity Supply Nominees Ltd v IAF Group Ltd* [1993] 2 EGLR 95; *Star Rider v Inntrepreneur Pub Co* [1998] 1 EGLR 53; *Esso Petroleum v Milton* [1997] 1 WLR 938. It seems right that any such set-off would be good as against the receiver collecting the rent in the name of the borrower or the lender. No counterclaim could be brought against the receiver personally on a borrower's or lender's lease. He could only have such a liability had he granted the lease himself, for example post-insolvency of the borrower.

[58]   When a lease is forfeited by proceedings rather than peaceable re-entry, the forfeiture is effected by issue and service of the proceedings. Although the landlord, having elected to forfeit, cannot treat the lease as continuing after service of proceedings, the lessee is entitled to treat the lease as continuing until the court makes a possession order. There is thus a 'twilight' period between service of proceedings and the court order which recognises the forfeiture, during which the lessee will be liable for mesne profits to the landlord if the landlord's claim is successful.

[59]   *Official Custodian for Charities v Mackey (No 2)* [1985] 1 WLR 1308, in which the landlord unsuccessfully sought an injunction against the receivers to prevent them collecting the income and managing the property prior to the court determining that the lease had been lawfully forfeited (and hence the mortgage also ended). In *Mackey*, the court said that the landlord had no claim against the receivers for monies had and received or in equity. However, the borrowers will be liable to mesne profits during that period. If the receiver were in possession of the mortgaged property, he could have a liability for mesne profits, but only if the landlord had not obtained an order against the borrower. If the landlord obtained a possession order and an order for mesne profits for the period against the borrower he would disqualify himself by issue estoppel from recovering against the receiver because the receiver shared privity of interest with the borrower. It is possible that a claim against the receiver in trespass could be made with, or in preference to, the claim based on forfeiture against the borrower.

[60]   It used to be the case that the borrower retained possession, and the rents, by tacit agreement from the lender who had the immediate right to possession and hence to those rents. See *Moss v Gallimore* (1779) 1 Douglas 279 at 283, for example, and *Turner v Walsh* [1909] 2 KB 484 at 494. The borrower receives the rent by 'tacit agreement' with the lender which the lender can end (*Gallimore* at 283) in order to make any pre-existing arrears recoverable by the lender. Standard modern mortgages are expressed as if the lender's right to possession is exercisable only on breach. Such a mortgage with standard wording might be construed as giving the borrower the right to possession and/or to the rents until a breach Since, usually, the receiver cannot be appointed, until there is a breach of mortgage, it seems to follow that the receiver under a mortgage with such covenants may be unable to collect rent arrears which accrued before a breach has occurred of the mortgage covenants. In many cases, however, the correct interpretation will be that although the parties intended the lender's

Rent for dwellings

9.67   There are statutory requirements for the collection of rent from tenants of dwellings.

9.68   Where the mortgaged property 'consists of or includes a dwelling'[61] and Part II of the Landlord and Tenant Act 1954 does not apply,[62] the landlord must by notice give the tenant an address in England and Wales at which notices (including notices in proceedings) may be served on the landlord by the tenant.[63]

9.69   A failure to do so means that any rent[64] is 'treated for all purposes as not being due from the tenant to the landlord at any time before the landlord does comply'.[65]

9.70   Similarly, any written demand for rent or other sums due under a tenancy must contain the name and address of the landlord, and, if that address is not in England and Wales, an address in England and Wales at which notices (including notices in proceedings) may be served on the landlord by the tenant.[66] If there is a failure to comply:

> any part of the amount demanded which consists of a service charge or an administration charge ... shall be treated for all purposes as not being due from the tenant to the landlord at any time before that information is furnished by the landlord by notice given to the tenant.

9.71   Case law on this provision affirms that omission of the required information from a demand simply postpones the tenant's liability for service charges and administration charges, so that once the omission to provide an address has been remedied, they become due from the tenant.[67] No interest is payable for the period prior to remedy. The same is true under section 48(2) of the Landlord and Tenant Act 1987. The failure to give an address for the service of notices simply suspends the tenant's liability. It does not extinguish it.

9.72   Can a receiver give these notices? A receiver with power to collect income will have the power to do all things which are necessarily ancillary to

---

right to take physical possession to be postponed, they did not intend to take away the receiver's right to collect arrears.

[61]   Under Landlord and Tenant Act 1987, s 60(1), 'dwelling' means a building or part of a building occupied or intended to be occupied as a separate dwelling, together with any yard, garden, outhouses and appurtenances belonging to it or usually enjoyed with it.

[62]   Landlord and Tenant Act 1987, s 46(1).

[63]   Landlord and Tenant Act 1987, s 48(1).

[64]   And service charges and administration charges: Landlord and Tenant Act 1987, s 48(2).

[65]   Landlord and Tenant Act 1987, s 48(2). The exception in s 48(3) where a receiver or manager has been appointed by virtue of an order of any court or tribunal does not apply to LPA and fixed charge receivers.

[66]   Landlord and Tenant Act 1987, s 47(1).

[67]   *Tedla v Cameret Court Residents Association Ltd* [2015] UKUT 221 (LC), [2015] EGLR 50.

the collection of the income and thus to serve these notices.[68] Such notices should be served in the borrower's name, not the receiver's. It is 'the landlord' who must give notice, but service of notice in the receiver's name will suffice.[69]

9.73   For the requirement section 47(1)(a) of the Landlord and Tenant Act 1987 to give the landlord's name and address, provision of the address of a landlord's agent is not sufficient. The purpose of the statutory provision is to identify the landlord,[70] with section 47(1)(b) a separate requirement to give an address for notices a separate requirement. It seems likely that the section 48(1) address need not be the landlord's.

9.74   It may well be that there is a pre-existing address notification which satisfies section 48(1) of the Landlord and Tenant Act 1987. For example, the unqualified inclusion of the current landlord's address on the lease is sufficient.[71] Even if there is such an address, the receiver may wish to serve a further notice to update the address to his own, so that notices will be served on him.

9.75   A separate statutory requirement regulates payment of ground rent under long leases[72] of dwellings.[73] Under section 166(1) of the Commonhold and Leasehold Reform Act 2002, a tenant of such a lease is not liable to make a payment of rent unless the landlord has given him notice relating to the payment, and the date on which is liable to make the payment is specified in the notice. The notice may be sent by post,[74] and if it is, it must be addressed to the tenant at the dwelling, unless he has notified the landlord in writing of a

---

[68]   See *M Wheeler & Co Ltd v Warren* [1928] Ch 840 and *McDonald v McDonald* [2014] EWCA Civ 1049, [2015] Ch 357, discussed in more detail at para 10.60 *et seq*, by analogy.

[69]   The definition of 'landlord' is immediate landlord: Landlord and Tenant Act 1987, s 60(1). This does not obviously include the receiver with Law of Property Act 1925, s 109(3) power to collect income. Since the receiver is the borrower's deemed agent under s 109(2), and there is nothing in the Landlord and Tenant Act 1987 to prevent service of notice by the landlord's agent, the apparent limit to this definition does not seem likely to prevent the receiver serving the notice.

[70]   *Beitov Properties Ltd v Martin* [2012] UKUT 133 (LC), [2012] 3 EGLR 21. This has not been tested where there is a mortgage receiver who may not know the address.

[71]   *Rogan v Woodfield Building Services Ltd* (1995) 27 HLR 78.

[72]   The principal category of long lease, in Commonhold and Leasehold Reform Act 2002, s 76(2), is a lease for a term of years certain exceeding 21 years. There are other types of long lease but they are rarely seen, save where they already fall within the 21-year category. Various types of tenancy, those to which Landlord and Tenant Act 1954, Pt 2, agricultural holdings under the Agricultural Holdings Act 1986, and farm business tenancies within the meaning of the Agricultural Tenancies Act 1995 are excluded by Commonhold and Leasehold Reform Act 2002, s 166(8).

[73]   'Dwelling' means the same as under Commonhold and Leasehold Reform Act 2002: s 166(9). The meaning of 'dwelling' in Landlord and Tenant Act 1985, s 38(1) is a building or part of a building occupied or intended to be occupied as a separate dwelling, together with any yard, garden, outhouses and appurtenances belonging to it or usually enjoyed with it.

[74]   Commonhold and Leasehold Reform Act 2002, s 166(5)(b).

different address in England and Wales at which he wishes notices under section 166 to be served.[75]

9.76   The notice must specify: (a) the amount of the payment; (b) the date on which the tenant is liable to make it;[76] and (c) if different, the date on which he would have been liable to make it in accordance to the lease. It must also contain prescribed information[77] and be in prescribed form.[78] That prescribed form and its prescribed information can be found in Landlord and Tenant (Notice of Rent) (England) Regulations 2004[79] and Landlord and Tenant (Notice of Rent) (Wales) Regulations 2005,[80] respectively.

Rent review

9.77   Leases of in particular commercial property often contain rent reviews.[81] If the tenancy or lease has a rent review clause which is operable during the appointment of the receiver, it is likely that the receiver, whether LPA or fixed charge, has power to serve any required landlord notice to operate the rent review in the name of the borrower.[82] A failure to trigger a rent review is likely to be a breach of the receiver's duty to those with an interest in the equity of redemption.[83]

---

[75]   Commonhold and Leasehold Reform Act 2002, s 166(6).

[76]   That date must not be either less than 30 days or more than 60 days after the day on which the notice is given, nor before the date on which the tenant would have been liable in accordance with the lease: Commonhold and Leasehold Reform Act 2002, s 166(3). Any provisions in the lease for late payment, for example interest, have effect in relation to the date in the notice not that in the lease: s 166(4).

[77]   Commonhold and Leasehold Reform Act 2002, s 166(2).

[78]   Commonhold and Leasehold Reform Act 2002, s 166(5)(a).

[79]   SI 2004/3096. This includes a requirement for the landlord's address, as well as the name of the person to whom payment is to be made and the address for payment. It seems likely that the landlord's address cannot be the address of an agent, as in *Beitov Properties Ltd v Martin* [2012] UKUT 133 (LC) in relation to Landlord and Tenant Act 1987, s 47(1)(a).

[80]   SI 2005/1355.

[81]   Reference should be made to any practitioner's text on rent review for the detail of how such clauses work.

[82]   See *Knight v Lawrence* [1991] BCC 411, in which the fixed charge receiver appointed with power to collect the rents and income had power to serve a rent review notice because he was given an express power to 'do all such other acts and things as may be considered incidental or conducive to any of the matters aforesaid which the receiver lawfully may or can do as agent for the borrowers', and his failure to do so was a breach of duty. See also *M Wheeler & Co Ltd v Warren* [1928] Ch 840: a fixed charge receiver has incidental powers necessary to perform his express powers. Although there is no similar case for LPA receivers, it is likely an LPA receiver has an incidental power to serve a rent review notice.

[83]   See Chapter 6 for a discussion of the receiver's duties, in which *Knight v Lawrence* [1991] BCC 411 is discussed in greater detail both as to the persons with an interest in the equity of redemption (paras 6.77–6.79), and as to defences in a claim against a receiver for breach of duty (para 6.128).

Statutory rent review under housing law

9.78 Various of the Housing Acts provide a mechanism for statutory rent review.[84] For example, rent under an assured statutory periodic or other periodic tenancy under the Housing Act 1988 is liable to increase.

9.79 The statutory process for securing an increase in rent is[85] service by 'the landlord' on the tenant of a notice in prescribed form proposing a new rent. That proposed rent takes effect unless,[86] within a specified time period, the tenant applies to the 'appropriate tribunal'[87] or the landlord and tenant agree a rent. If the tenant makes an application, then the tribunal will determine the rent being the rent at which 'the dwelling-house might reasonably be expected to be let in the open market by a willing landlord under an assured tenancy' on various statutory assumptions[88] and disregards.[89] The borrower, as landlord, could serve such a notice. By analogy with *Knight v Lawrence*,[90] it seems likely that a receiver of income could serve such a notice in the borrower's name.

9.80 Similarly, it seems likely that a receiver of income could serve, in the borrower landlord's name, a notice of increase up to the registered income for a Rent Act protected tenancy[91] and apply for the registration of a rent.[92]

Business tenancies

9.81 Conversely, a receiver appointed as deemed agent of the borrower is not likely to be able to apply under section 24A of the Landlord and Tenant Act 1954, as agent for the borrower, for an interim rent during a lease extension claim under Part II. Such an application must be made by 'the landlord'. Once a receiver is appointed and in receipt of the rents and profits, 'the landlord' means the lender, under section 67, not the borrower. Thus a receiver is likely only to be able to pursue such an application as an agent of the lender and with its authority.

---

[84] See paras A.43–A.79 for sketches of the operation of the Housing Acts in the context of possession claims by receivers. Further details of the statutory rent review provisions under various Acts can be found in any practitioner's text on those subjects.

[85] Housing Act 1988, s 13(2). The statute should be read for the precise requirements of the process and the periods when it can be operated.

[86] Housing Act 1988, s 13(4).

[87] The First-tier Tribunal, or the Upper Tribunal in relation to a dwelling-house in England, or the rent assessment committee, where the dwelling-house is in Wales: Housing Act 1988, s 45(1).

[88] Housing Act 1988, s 14(1).

[89] Housing Act 1988, s 14(2).

[90] [1991] BCC 411.

[91] See Rent Act 1977, s 45(2)(b).

[92] See Rent Act 1977, s 67.

VAT

9.82   Where the borrower has elected to waive the exemption from value added tax (VAT) for tenancies and interests in land and thus charged VAT on rent, the receiver must collect that VAT with the rent and must pay it to HMRC.[93]

Licence fees

9.83   Occupation of the mortgaged premises may be under a licence between the borrower[94] and the occupier. A licence may be written and set out a clear licence fee, but it may also be oral and far less formal.[95]

9.84   Where the licence is contractual, the receiver will be able to collect the income payable under it as the borrower's agent.

9.85   A licence may be gratuitous, in which case a receiver with sufficient power may well wish to terminate it so as to be able to let or licence the property for a fee or so as to obtain vacant possession for a sale. An LPA receiver without further powers beyond collection of income will not be able to do this and may have to involve the lender.[96]

Trust income

9.86   It is possible that an occupier, in particular of residential property, will be a beneficiary under a trust of the borrower's estate.[97]

9.87   If the property is held on express trust, that trust may require the occupant to pay during his occupation. A receiver of the income can recover such a sum provided it is properly understood as income from the property.[98]

9.88   The Trusts of Land and Appointment of Trustees Act 1996 makes provision for the payment of compensation in certain circumstances where the occupant as beneficiary of the trust is entitled to 'an interest in possession'[99] in

---

[93]   *Sargent v Customs and Excise Commissioners* [1994] 1 WLR 235 in relation to the position with VAT in the 1990s. See paras 12.17–12.20 for further discussion about the receiver's liability for VAT.

[94]   Or, conceivably the lender, but this will be rare when a receiver is appointed. If the licence is granted by the receiver, this will usually be as the borrower's deemed agent, not as the lender's.

[95]   See paras 8.48–8.51 for a discussion of the difference between a lease and a licence.

[96]   See paras 10.92–10.101 for a discussion of terminating licences, for receivers with suitable powers.

[97]   See paras 8.113–8.114 for a brief sketch of how such a trust may arise.

[98]   A payment for occupation is likely to be income. A payment under the trust unrelated to income, for example in an extensive trust of which the mortgaged property is just one asset, may well not be.

[99]   Trusts of Land and Appointment of Trustees Act 1996, s 12(1). An interest in possession is in contrast to an interest in reversion for example an interest reversionary on the end of someone's life interest. A freehold reversion is an interest in possession because it is an interest in the rents and profits from the land which is regarded as a possessory interest. However, such an interest

the mortgaged property, and the 'purposes of the trust include making the land available for that beneficiary',[100] or 'the land is held by the trustees so as to be so available'.[101] In that case, if two or more beneficiaries are entitled to occupy under section 12(1), the trustees 'may exclude or restrict the entitlement of any one or more (but not all) of them'.[102] The trustees may 'impose reasonable conditions on any beneficiary in relation to his occupation',[103] which conditions may include the payment of compensation to the excluded beneficiary.[104]

9.89   If the borrower is also a beneficiary entitled to occupy under the trust but excluded in favour of the occupier, and if by the time of the appointment of the receiver, the borrower trustee has required the beneficiary occupant to pay him compensation, or the court has so ordered, it is likely that the receiver can collect that compensation[105] on the basis that it is income from the mortgaged property, provided that the mortgage, and the receivership, binds the borrower's beneficial interest, which is likely.[106]

9.90   The LPA receiver of income is unlikely, however, to be able to be able to make a decision as to payment of such compensation because the power to collect income does not give him power to take trustee decisions.[107] Moreover, it

---

would not be held for the purpose of making the land available for occupation by the beneficiary since occupation denotes physical occupation. See also para 8.123.

[100]   Trusts of Land and Appointment of Trustees Act 1996, s 12(1)(a): as named beneficiary, or as one of a class of beneficiaries occupation by whom is one of the purposes of the trust.

[101]   Trusts of Land and Appointment of Trustees Act 1996, s 12(1)(b).

[102]   Trusts of Land and Appointment of Trustees Act 1996, s 13(1).

[103]   Trusts of Land and Appointment of Trustees Act 1996, s 13(3).

[104]   Trusts of Land and Appointment of Trustees Act 1996, s 13(6)(a).

[105]   Whether the receiver has power to litigate in order to secure an order for payment of compensation already required by the trustee or the court is a question of construction of his powers. It is thought that an LPA receiver would have such power, as necessarily incident to the power to collect the income from the property. Where, however, the borrower is the beneficiary who has remained in possession, and another beneficiary is claiming compensation, or a beneficiary is disputing the level of compensation set by a trustee, it is unlikely that an LPA receiver will have power to defend or participate in the claim (because his powers are insufficiently wide). Even a fixed charge receiver whose powers under the mortgage appear sufficiently wide to permit him to defend such a claim might not be able to do so, because there are issues around the ability of the trustees to delegate. Those issues are discussed in more detail at paras 8.124–8.144.

[106]   See also paras 8.116–8.118.

[107]   It seems more likely than not that a fixed charge receiver could be given such a power: see para 8.144. It is unlikely that such a power is a function relating to whether or in what way any asset of the trust should be distributed, under Trustee Act 2000, s 11(2), which is a non-delegable function under s 11. It is likely that an attempt to give the receiver agency to decide on the payment of compensation would fall foul of s 15, since the function would relate to 'managing property which is subject to the trust', which is an 'asset management function' within the meaning of s 15(5)(c), so that the trustees would need to have prepared a policy statement giving guidance as to how the functions should be exercised, and it is unlikely that the receiver's agreement to act would comply with that policy statement as required by s 15(2). Since the failure to comply with this provision does not invalidate the authorisation the, s 15 requirements are unlikely to prevent such a power being given to the receiver: s 24(a). The requirement for a policy document does not appear to have been intended by the Law Commission in its report which led to the Trustee Act 2000 to have an 'effective mechanism'

is unlikely that an LPA receiver has 'an interest in property' to allow him to make an application for an order requiring payment of compensation by a beneficiary under section 14 of the Trusts of Land and Appointment of Trustees Act 1996.[108]

Damages for use and occupation from trespassers

9.91   If the occupiers of the mortgaged property are trespassers as against the borrower, then the receiver of income will be able in the borrower's name to recover mesne profits, i.e. damages for occupation, from the occupiers.[109] The measure of such damages for occupation is often taken to be the market rent for the property.

9.92   If mesne profits are to be collected, it should be made clear to the occupiers that they are collected as such and not as rent or a licence fee for permitted occupation. Otherwise there is a risk that the occupiers will later argue that there is a formal relationship, a tenancy or a licence, between them and the borrower by reason of the receiver's acceptance of money for occupation.[110]

9.93   If the occupiers are trespassers as against the borrower, their eviction may well be a better course of action than collection of mesne profits, especially if they are not occupiers with means. A receiver of income only, without additional powers, will not be able to evict the occupiers, and the lender may have to take possession proceedings in its own name.

9.94   If the borrower has granted a tenancy or licence to the borrower in breach of mortgage, then it will not bind the lender, and the lender can treat the occupiers as trespassers against it. A fixed charge receiver with sufficiently wide powers to take possession as the lender could may thus be entitled to mesne profits against the occupiers notwithstanding the tenancy or licence from the borrower. This may produce a level of income higher than an artificially low or absent rent or licence fee set by the borrower.[111]

---

for enforcement. See Law Commission and Scottish Law Commission, *Trustee's Powers and Duties*, Law Com No 260, Scot Law Com No 172 (12 May 1999) at Pt IV, para 4.20.

[108] It is possible that a receiver who has a right to possession has an interest, though 'interest' more naturally means something akin to an estate rather than a right only. See *Stevens v Hutchinson* [1953] Ch 299 as to the meaning of a similar phrase in Law of Property Act 1925, s 30 then in force. A receiver appointed by the court by way of equitable execution over a beneficiary's interest in a trust for sale of land, where the receiver had a power to collect income, did not give the receiver rights in rem and hence he personally was not a person interested in the property. 'Person interested' required some proprietary right. This case has been criticised in *Levermore v Levermore* [1979] 1 WLR 1277. It is, in addition, possible to understand the receiver with a right to possession over land held under a trust of land as having a proprietary right.

[109] A receiver with a right to possession will be able to evict them as well.

[110] Provided the receiver is acting as the deemed agent of the borrower, not the lender, there is no risk that the acceptance of payment by the receiver could result in a tenancy or licence between the lender and the occupiers.

[111] See paras 10.22–10.27 for a discussion. There is a suggestion in *Kitchen's Trustee v Madders* [1950] Ch 134 at 146 that mesne profits could not be available because the occupant would not

Other sources of income

9.95   There may be other sources of income which a receiver is entitled to collect:

(a)   The mortgage conditions may entitle a fixed charge receiver to operate the borrower's business, for example, where the mortgage is over that business as well as the property.[112] In that case, and subject to the circumstances,[113] the receiver, acting within his duties[114] is not obliged to carry on the business; he may instead close it down, provided he has the power to do so, but he if does choose to carry on the business he must do so with reasonable competence.[115]

(b)   The mortgaged property may be agricultural, or contain game which the property owner is entitled to hunt.[116] The income from the mortgaged property may thus include the crops or the fish or game.[117]

(c)   Where the mortgaged property is a block of flats or commercial units, the leases may contain provisions which allow the landlord to collect service

---

be occupying unlawfully whilst the borrower retained the right to possession and prior to the lender giving the notice required by Law of Property Act 1925, s 98(1). See also *Turner v Walsh* [1909] 2 KB 484 at 494 that prior to the lender giving notice of an intention to take possession or the income, the borrower's right to possession continues though this is not a result of s 98 or its precursor, Judicature Act 1873, s 5, but because:

it was in the nature the transaction that the mortgagor could continue in possession. His possession was rightful and not wrong. He was entitled to the rents and profits as long as he remained in possession: mesne profits accrued due and received prior to action or demand could not be recovered from him by the mortgagee' (a quote from *Heath v Pugh* (1881) 6 QBD 345 at 359).

The need for notice by the lender is because the borrower's tenant 'shall not be prejudiced for any act done by him, as holding under the grantor, till he has had notice of the deed' (*Moss v Gallimore* (1779) 1 Douglas 279 at 282). The need for the lender to give a tenant notice prior to an entitlement to claim possession is not one much now suggested, and would be subject to the mortgage conditions. In any event, a receiver with a right to take possession of the lender's estate can give any required notice after which mesne profits will be payable by the borrower's tenant in any event, even were it correct that the receiver could not do so before. See Chapter 10, fn 11 and para 10.62.

112   See for example *Medforth v Blake* [2000] Ch 86. A detailed exposition of the steps to run a business and collect income from it is outside the ambit of this book.

113   If the business were the only asset, it might well be that the receiver would have to sell it or carry it on, otherwise he would not be performing his obligation to pay down the debt. In addition, if the business is in perishable goods and they were the only asset, then the receiver though he need not carry on the business would likely be in breach of duty if he let the goods simply perish without taking simple steps to avoid that outcome at least insofar as he had the power and the income to do so.

114   As to which, see Chapter 6.

115   *Medforth v Blake* [2000] Ch 86 at 93C. The business was a pig farm. There is some discussion of the extent of the receiver's duty in running the pig farm, once he has decided to do so, and in light of the perishable nature of pigs.

116   I.e. where that right is not another's by reason of a *profit à prendre*, or is itself a *profit à prendre*.

117   An exposition of the steps to recover that income is outside the ambit of this book.

charges. Although these are income,[118] their use is usually to reimburse the landlord's cost of repairs of common parts to the building,[119] and hence issues may arise as to the upkeep of the building and the landlord's liability for disrepair, if funds collected in this way are used to pay down the mortgage debt.[120] It is likely that a receiver with power to collect service charges will have the power to take the necessary preliminary steps, under the lease, for example to prepare service charge accounts.

(d)   Damages for breach of lease by a tenant, for example where the tenant has the repairing obligations, are income.[121]

(e)   If the mortgaged property is a rentcharge, charges under that rentcharge are income.[122]

Steps to collect income

9.96   The steps to collect income are likely to be similar whether the receiver is an LPA receiver or a fixed charge receiver, save that the specific powers to collect income for an LPA receiver come from section 109 of the Law of

---

[118] Or, if they are not income properly so called, then, at least for leases granted before 1 January 1996 when the Landlord and Tenant (Covenants) Act 1995 came into force, a receiver entitled to the income is entitled to enforce the covenants under the lease by reason of Law of Property Act 1925, s 141(2): see *Turner v Walsh* [1909] 2 KB 484 at 494, and hence to collect them in any event. For new leases granted after 1 January 1996, the receiver will have no such right to sue on covenants in the lease unrelated to income, unless expressly given, since Landlord and Tenant (Covenants) Act 1995, s 15 does not extend the right to sue to anyone entitled to the income who is not the immediate reversioner.

[119] If the mortgaged property is a block containing leases of two or more dwellings which require a tenant contribution to service charges, those service charges once collected are subject to a statutory trust under Landlord and Tenant Act 1987, s 42, and are held by the payee under the lease, i.e. the landlord or named management company, on trust to defray costs incurred in connection with the matters for which the charges were payable, and otherwise for the contributing tenants for the time being: s 42(3). It seems likely that service charges thus cannot thus be used to pay down the mortgage debt. Although the receiver is not the payee under the lease, it is likely that were he to use the funds other than to pay for services he would be fixed with a constructive trust or knowing receipt. Residential service charges are subject to considerable statutory regulation under Landlord and Tenant Act 1985, ss 18–40. Outside that regulation, a lease may expressly impose a trust on service charges, though this is unusual.

[120] An LPA receiver will be able to use his receipts to pay down the cost of necessary or proper repairs provided he has been directed by the lender in writing to undertake those repairs: Law of Property Act 1925, s 109(8)(iii), and see *White v Metcalf* [1903] 2 Ch 567 for a case under its precursor, the Conveyancing and Law of Property Act 1881, in which the receiver had no such written direction, so that the cost of repairs could not be added to the mortgage.

[121] The law relating to landlord's claims for damages for disrepair is complicated, and any practitioner's text on this subject and/or advisers should be consulted.

[122] See Law of Property Act 1925, s 101(1)(iii), which mentions receivers appointed over rentcharges specifically. See also the Rentcharges Act 1977 and any practitioner's text on the subject. The Rentcharges Act 1977 abolished the creation of new rent charges which provide for pure income, rather than, for example, the payment of a service charge by freeholders for the maintenance of common land on a freehold estate.

Property Act 1925, whereas for the fixed charge receiver they come from the mortgage conditions.[123]

9.97   Thus an LPA receiver may face more difficulties in collecting the income without the assistance of more extensive powers in the mortgage conditions.

The occupier's obligation to pay the receiver

9.98   The receiver is given power to collect the income, by section 109(3) of the Law of Property Act 1925, or by the mortgage conditions. By section 109(3), or by the mortgage conditions, the receiver can give 'effectual receipts'.[124]

9.99   The effect of the receiver's power to collect the income under section 109(3) of the Law of Property Act 1925, or under the mortgage conditions, is not an assignment of the right to the income by the borrower to the receiver. The power is in substitution for the borrower in the sense that the borrower can no longer collect the rent.[125] This does not mean, however, that the receiver does not act as the borrower's deemed agent.[126]

9.100   An occupier, notified of the receiver's power, who refuses to pay the receiver and continues to pay the borrower, is liable to be sued successfully by the receiver.[127]

9.101   The occupier, by reason of section 109(4) of the Law of Property Act 1925, need not 'inquire whether any case has happened to authorise the receiver to act'.

9.102   The like phrase in section 104(2)(a) of the Law of Property Act 1925, which protects the purchaser on a sale of the mortgaged property under the power of sale conferred by the Act, does not mean that the purchaser need not check that the requirements of section 101(1), that the mortgage was made by deed and the mortgage money has become due, have been satisfied, since these requirements are necessary for the power of sale to arise; if it has not, the lender

---

[123]   And include necessary incidental powers: *M Wheeler & Co Ltd v Warren* [1928] Ch 840. There is no like case for LPA receivers, though it seems likely that LPA receivers have incidental powers necessary for the exercise of their powers under Law of Property Act 1925, s 109(3) insofar as that does not provide them.

[124]   The wording of Law of Property Act 1925, s 109(3).

[125]   It is the receiver who is so entitled not the borrower. See *Woolston v Ross* [1900] 1 Ch 788, in which the borrower distrained for rent after the receiver was appointed, but since the receiver had a statutory power of distress under the Conveyancing Act 1881, a precursor to the Law of Property Act 1925, the borrower did not, and could not, distrain even though the receiver chose not to: 'The statute says that the receiver may distrain in the name either of the mortgagor or of the mortgagee, but it does not say that the mortgagor may himself distrain without any authority from the receiver'.

[126]   *Rhodes v Allied Dunbar Pension Services Ltd* [1989] 1 WLR 800 at 807G.

[127]   See *Moss v Gallimore* (1779) 1 Douglas 279 at 282 in relation to the tenant's obligation to pay the lender once he had notice of him: 'In the case of execution it is uniformly held, that if you act after notice, you do it at your peril'.

cannot sell the mortgaged estate, but only its mortgage. Section 104(2) is protecting the purchaser from having to enquire whether the power of sale once it has arisen is exercisable, i.e. whether any necessary notice has been made, for example, under section 103.

9.103 Thus, similarly, the occupant who pays the receiver is not protected by section 109(4) of the Law of Property Act 1925 if he pays the receiver when no mortgage by deed exists, or when the mortgage money is not due. If he pays, and the borrower shows that there is no mortgage by deed or the mortgage money is not due, then he will have to pay the borrower the same sum.[128]

9.104 The occupant is protected if the power to appoint a receiver had arisen, but could not be properly exercised because section 109(1) of the Law of Property Act 1925 did not apply; the power of sale under the Act could not yet be exercised.[129]

Identifying the basis of occupation

9.105 The first step for any receiver, once appointed, will be to determine who is in occupation of the property and on what basis they occupy so as to find out the chain of leases and licences and the borrower's position in that chain.

9.106 Legal leases for a term of years absolute for more than 7 years from the date of grant are registrable under section 4 of the Land Registration Act 2002. The Land Registry titles for the mortgaged property are a good place to start.

9.107 Shorter term, and equitable, leases usually cannot be discovered by consulting the Land Registry since they are not registrable. Enquiries will have to be made of the borrower and/or the occupants as to the terms of occupation.

9.108 It is not unusual for a borrower to be reluctant to divulge that information if he is hostile to the receivership. Many mortgage conditions entitle the lender at least to require any such documents or information to be produced by the borrower. Thus the lender may assist in ensuring that information is provided.

9.109 With suitably-worded mortgage conditions, it may be possible for a receiver to obtain the assistance of the court in requiring the borrower to produce any written tenancy agreements or licences, or to provide information about occupation.

9.110 A receiver is entitled to obtain an injunction to prohibit the borrower from interfering with the carrying out of the receiver's duties.[130] It does not

---

[128] He may be able to recover the monies paid to the receiver in an unjust enrichment claim.

[129] That is not to say that an occupant would be protected if the person saying they were a receiver was a stranger to the lender. In that case, the receiver would simply not be any such person and would have no powers. Law of Property Act 1925, s 109(4) would not apply.

[130] *Bayly v Went* (1884) 51 LT 764, a case under the predecessor to Law of Property Act 1925, s 109, in which the borrower distrained for rent, and the receiver obtained an injunction

follow that the borrower has a positive duty to assist the receiver unless the mortgage conditions impose such obligations. A claim by a receiver for an injunction requiring the borrower to produce the relevant documents and information, though it is highly likely to find sympathy from the court, does not have a clear cause of action on which the receiver may base his claim, if the mortgage conditions do not expressly assist.

9.111 The receiver, once appointed, will usually inspect the property to identify occupiers and write to them either by name, or addressed 'to the occupiers', to introduce himself and ascertain the basis on which they occupy.

9.112 Occupiers, even once notified by the receiver of his entitlement to collect the income, can be reluctant to deal with the receiver especially if they have any loyalty to the borrower.

9.113 The LPA receiver is empowered by section 109(3) of the Law of Property Act 1925 to recover income by action, which includes court claims. A fixed charge receiver with power to recover income will have the power to issue in the borrower's name, and prosecute, a claim against an occupant for a money judgment for the income either by an express power to that effect in the mortgage conditions, or because that power is incidental to the power to recover the income.[131]

9.114 A receiver may thus be able to make applications under the CPR to assist in making and prosecuting that claim. Once the receiver has notified the occupant that the income is to be paid to him as receiver and asked without success for a copy of the tenancy or licence,[132] he could make an application for pre-action disclosure of any written tenancy or licence, under rule 31.16 of the CPR, on the basis that the occupant is likely to be a defendant to a subsequent claim for a money judgment for the income, and the receiver (or borrower) a claimant, any written tenancy or licence is within the class of documents to which the standard disclosure obligation on the occupant would extend during proceedings, and the disclosure is desirable to dispose fairly of the proceedings, or assist resolution without proceedings, or save costs, for example, the costs of pleading a claim in the alternatives of tenancy, licence, or damages for trespass if the borrower will not produce any relevant written document.[133]

---

prohibiting him from doing so. The reasoning was not set out in any detail, but the basis for such a prohibitory injunction must be that the apparent rights of the borrower are, so far as the receiver has been given powers, to be exercised only by the receiver; see the discussion of the receiver's powers in this regard at para 6.144.

[131] *M Wheeler & Co Ltd v Warren* [1928] Ch 840.

[132] These two steps are likely to assist in relation to costs arguments on the application.

[133] Each case will need individual analysis to determine if the prospects of success on such an application are worth the cost and the costs risk. It is, of course, possible that the occupier will say he has been permitted to occupy the property by the borrower rent free, or is entitled to do so because he is beneficially entitled to the borrower's estate. An LPA receiver without further powers faced with an occupant who has such a right to occupy for no rent may well thus have no income to collect in this situation. See paras 9.85 and 9.86–9.90 for further discussion.

9.115 The problem is more difficult if there is no written tenancy agreement or licence either because any tenancy or licence between the borrower and the occupant is oral, or because the occupant is trespassing. The court's powers to order disclosure relate to documents, not to information. In that case, a receiver faced with an occupier who will not explain the basis of his occupation and will not pay rent, and a borrower who will not assist in explaining the basis of occupation, may need simply to sue for a money judgment for rent, licence fee, or mesne profits, in the alternatives that occupation is by tenancy, licence, or is a trespass, and resist any costs application by the occupier relating to whichever cause of action fails by relying on pre-action correspondence asking for the relevant information.

Litigation

9.116 Section 109(3) of the Law of Property Act 1925 specifically gives an LPA receiver the power to recover income by action, i.e. by litigation. A fixed charge receiver with power to collect income will either have an express power to litigate or will likely have an implied power.[134]

Claims

9.117 A claim for recovery of income will simply be a money claim. Such a claim would usually be made under Part 7 of the CPR. If the claim is for a specified sum of money only[135] and that sum is less than £100,000 and in sterling,[136] then the claim may be started using Money Claim Online, an online portal for issuing claims and for the more straightforward steps in litigation, for example, obtaining judgment in default of a defence.[137] If the claim is contested, it will be sent to a county court hearing centre for case management and trial.[138]

Enforcement

9.118 Once a money judgment has been obtained, if it is not paid by the debtor, it can be enforced by one of a number of procedures. Those which are most likely to result in payment of the debt are third party debt orders,[139] attachment

---

[134] *M Wheeler & Co Ltd v Warren* [1928] Ch 840, though in that case the express terms gave the receiver the powers an LPA receiver had under Law of Property Act 1925, s 109, which include the right to take action.

[135] As a claim for rent or licence fee will be, and a claim for mesne profits will likely be if the sum is specified.

[136] The additional relevant requirements are that the claim is against a single defendant, or is for a single amount against each of two defendants, the defendant is not the Crown and is not a person known to be a child or a protected party (someone lacking mental capacity in relation to the litigation: see CPR, Pt 21), and both parties have addresses for service in England and Wales. See PD 7E, para 4.

[137] See CPR, PD 7E.

[138] See Chapter 14 on litigation more generally.

[139] An order that a third party who owes the debtor money pays it direct to the judgment creditor. It can be used to obtain money from the debtor's bank account directly.

of earnings orders[140] and enforcement by taking control of goods.[141] For larger sums of money, where the debtor owns property, a charging order over the property can be obtained, and a claim then made for an order for sale.[142] If information about the debtor's assets is needed, an order to obtain information from the debtor can be made.[143]

CRAR

9.119 With effect from 6 April 2014,[144] section 109(3) of the Law of Property Act 1925 specifically gives an LPA receiver the power to recover income under section 72(1) of the 2007 Act. The Act created a procedure known as CRAR. Exercise of CRAR allows a landlord to recover rent arrears from a tenant of commercial premises by an enforcement agent collecting and selling the tenant's goods. There is no like power to recovering arrears relating to residential premises.

9.120 This section first outlines how CRAR works[145] and then discusses how it applies to receivers, in particular whether it applies to fixed charge receivers.

KEY FEATURES OF CRAR

9.121 The process by which CRAR is exercised is set out in:

(a) Part 3 of the 2007 Act;
(b) Schedule 12 to the 2007 Act;[146]
(c) Part 84 of the CPR, which governs the procedure on applications to court in relation to the exercise of CRAR for example to shorten the notice period;
(d) Part 85 of the CPR, which regulates the procedure on applications relating to for example ownership of the controlled goods, or that they are exempt goods.[147]

---

[140] Under CPR, Pt 89.

[141] Under CPR, Pt 84.

[142] CPR, Pt 73.

[143] CPR, Pt 71.

[144] Prior to that, the like power given to a receiver by Law of Property Act 1925, s 109(3) was the power to distrain, a common law right given to landlords to seize goods in order to secure payment for rent arrears, which was abolished, for both commercial and residential rent arrears, by 2007 Act, s 71. For distress in the context of receivership, see *Bayly v Went* (1884) 51 LT 764; *Woolston v Ross* [1900] 1 Ch 788.

[145] This is a summary only. For more detail, reference should be made to the 2007 Act and to any practitioner's text on CRAR.

[146] 2007 Act, Sch 12 also regulates the control of goods as part of enforcement of court orders by writ or warrant conferring a power to use the procedure in Sch 12. Schedules 13 and 14 amend various Acts which regulated distress, and the Taking Control of Goods Regulations 2013 (SI 2013/1894) (2013 Regulations), and the Taking Control of Goods (Fees) Regulations 2014 (SI 2014/1).

[147] See, for example, 2007 Act, Sch 12, para 60 which makes provisions for applications to the court by a person claiming that goods taken control of are his not the tenant's. Such applications are governed by CPR, Pt 85.

9.122 The following are key features of CRAR:

(a) CRAR is a process of taking control[148] of goods[149] so that they may be sold to recover rent arrears.[150]

(b) It is not the landlord[151] who takes control of the goods and sells them, but an enforcement agent.[152] Only the enforcement officer may take control of goods and sell them under CRAR.[153] The enforcement power[154] is conferred on a specific enforcement agent, and another enforcement agent can only act if authorised by the enforcement agent with the enforcement power.[155]

(c) Section 72(1) of the 2007 Act gives a landlord under a lease of commercial premises[156] power to use the procedure in Schedule 12 (taking control of goods)[157] to recover from the tenant[158] rent payable under the lease. The goods in question must be the goods of the tenant who is liable for the rent arrears.[159] The goods must be on the demised premises,[160] or on a highway.[161]

(d) 'The landlord' is defined at section 73(1) of the 2007 Act as the person for the time being entitled to the immediate reversion in the property comprised in the lease.

---

[148] Securing them on the premises, or removing them and securing them elsewhere, or entering into a controlled goods agreement with the debtor: 2007 Act, Sch 12, para 13. See 2013 Regulations, regs 14 and 15 for the definition of a controlled goods agreement and its form and content.

[149] Property of any description other than land: 2007 Act, Sch 12, para 3(1).

[150] 2007 Act, Sch 12, para 1(1).

[151] Or the receiver, in the context of this chapter.

[152] An enforcement agent is: (a) someone acting under a certificate under 2007 Act, s 64 which is issued by a judge of the county court; or (b) someone exempt for example a constable, officer of Revenue and Customs (now HMRC), court officer or staff acting in the course of his duty as such; or (c) someone acting in the presence and under the direction of a person in (a) or (b): s 63(2)–(4). Only the enforcement officer may take control of goods and sell them under CRAR: Sch 12, para 2(2). The enforcement power is conferred on a specific agent authorised by the landlord: Sch 12, para 2(3) and (4).

[153] 2007 Act, Sch 12, para 2(2).

[154] Defined in 2007 Act, Sch 12, para 1(2) as the power to use the procedure to recover a particular sum.

[155] 2007 Act, Sch 12, para 2(4).

[156] 2007 Act, s 72(1). 'Commercial premises' is defined in s 75 by exception. A lease A is of commercial premises if none of the demised premises is let under lease A as a dwelling, let under an inferior lease B as a dwelling, or is occupied as a dwelling, where 'let as a dwelling' means on terms permitting that use, and the use under B is not a breach of a superior lease, and the occupation as a dwelling is not a breach of lease A. It cannot thus usually be used for mixed-use dwellings.

[157] I.e. exercise CRAR: 2007 Act, s 72(2).

[158] Defined as 'the tenant for the time being under the lease': 2007 Act, s 87. The process cannot be used against the Crown: s 89(1).

[159] 2007 Act, Sch 12, para 10. For the goods to be the tenant's, the tenant must have an interest in them: Sch 12, para 3(2)(a). Goods which are trust property in which either the tenant or a co-owner has an interest not vested in possession are excluded: Sch 12, para 3(2)(b).

[160] 2007 Act, Sch 12, para 14(4).

[161] 2007 Act, Sch 12, para 9.

(e)   Lease means a lease in law or in equity,[162] including a tenancy at will but not a tenancy on sufferance.[163] The lease must be evidenced in writing. CRAR cannot be used for a purely oral tenancy not so evidenced.

(f)   That rent must be rent properly so called, though the landlord may recover interest under the lease and any VAT chargeable.[164] CRAR does not extend to sums in respect of rates, or council tax, or service charges, even if reserved as rent in the lease.

(g)   CRAR ceases to be exercisable once the lease ends,[165] that is when the tenant ceases to be entitled to possession both under the lease and under any continuation under statute or rule of law.[166]

(h)   Section 79(3) of the 2007 Act makes an exception for this termination of the power. CRAR remains exercisable after the end of the lease in relation to rent arrears due and payable before its end if the lease did not end by forfeiture, not more than 6 months have passed since its end, the rent was due from the person who was the tenant at the end of the lease, that person remains in possession of any part of the demised premises, any new lease under which that person remains is a lease of commercial premises, and the person who was the landlord at the end of the lease remains entitled to the leasehold reversion.[167]

WHAT EXERCISE OF CRAR INVOLVES

9.123   The following is a brief summary of what exercise of CRAR involves:

(a)   The process starts by the landlord authorising an enforcement agent to exercise CRAR on his behalf.[168] This must be done in writing and be signed by the landlord. It must provide prescribed information as to the identity of the landlord and his contact details, the name and contact details of the person authorised to act on his behalf[169] and the commercial premises, as well as the rent owed.[170]

---

[162]   Leases of a term of years absolute of more than 3 years must be created by deed to be legal. Leases of more than 7 years must, in addition, be registered to have legal effect. An equitable lease is one which required, but lacks, creation by deed, or, though made by deed, required and lacks registration.

[163]   2007 Act, s 74(1). See para A.4 for a brief discussion of these terms.

[164]   2007 Act, s 76(2).

[165]   2007 Act, s 79(1).

[166]   2007 Act, s 79(7). Statutory continuations include under Landlord and Tenant Act 1954, Pt II for business tenancies. It is less clear what is covered by continuations by rule of law, since continuations on holding over seem to be dealt with by s 79(3) and (4).

[167]   2007 Act, s 79(3) and (4). This covers tenancies at will or on sufferance, or periodic tenancies, which can arise when the tenant holds over after the end of a term which is not otherwise extended. That such leases are often oral only, and are not usually evidence in writing, but arise because the landlord continues to accept rent for example, is covered by s 79(5) which disapplies the requirement for writing in s 74(2).

[168]   2007 Act, Sch 12, para 2(3).

[169]   I.e. the enforcement agent.

[170]   2007 Act, s 73(8), and 2013 Regulations, reg 51.

(b)   The next step is the service of written[171] notice of enforcement[172] served by the enforcement agent or the enforcement agent's office[173] on the tenant. It must be given not less than 7 clear days before the enforcement officer takes control of the tenant's goods.[174] The notice period, form of notice and contents and method of service are set out regulations 6, 7 and 8, respectively, of the 2013 Regulations. In particular, the notice sets out the debt, interest and costs, and the date and time by which payment must be made to prevent control of goods being taken and sold.

(c)   For CRAR to be exercisable, the rent must: (i) have become due and payable before notice of enforcement is given; and (ii) be certain, or be capable of being calculated with certainty.[175] The amount of rent which is recoverable by CRAR is reduced by what are called 'permitted deductions',[176] i.e. any deduction, recoupment or set-off the tenant would be entitled to claim in law or equity if the landlord claimed the rent.[177]

(d)   For CRAR to be exercisable, the 'net unpaid rent' must be greater than a minimum amount both immediately before the time when notice of enforcement is given and the first time that goods are taken control of after that notice.[178] The 'net unpaid rent' is the rent less interest and VAT and less any permitted deductions.[179] The minimum amount is set by Regulations. It is currently 'an amount equal to 7 days' rent'.[180]

(e)   Special provisions apply if the lease is an agricultural holding within the meaning of the Agricultural Holdings Act 1986. CRAR is not exercisable to recover rent that became due more than a year before the notice of enforcement is given.[181]

(f)   On an application by the tenant, the court[182] has a power to set aside the notice, or prevent further steps being taken before further order.[183]

---

[171] 2007 Act, Sch 12, para 7.

[172] 2007 Act, Sch 12, para 7(1).

[173] 2013 Regulations, reg 8(2).

[174] 2013 Regulations, reg 6(1), though the court may specify a shorter period of notice if satisfied that without it doing so it is likely the goods will be moved away from the demised premises or otherwise disposed of to avoid CRAR: reg 6.

[175] 2007 Act, s 77(1).

[176] 2007 Act, s 77(2).

[177] 2007 Act, s 77(7). For example, an equitable set-off of damages for the landlord's breach of leasehold covenant.

[178] 2007 Act, s 77(3).

[179] 2007 Act, s 77(5). Since it is often hard to know if there is a set-off, it may not be clear if the minimum threshold has been reached.

[180] 2013 Regulations, reg 52. If the rent is reserved annually, the daily rent likely should be calculated from the annual figure, not the monthly or quarterly figure at which rate rent is paid.

[181] 2007 Act, s 80(2) and see that section for further detail as to, for example, the permitted deductions under such leases.

[182] County or High Court: 2007 Act, s 78(3).

[183] 2007 Act, s 78(1).

(g)   The effect of the notice is to bind the property in all goods of the tenant, save for exempt goods,[184] from the time the notice is given.[185] This means that if the goods are sold they are sold subject to the power of enforcement, save as set out in Schedule 12, paragraph 61 of the 2007 Act.[186] The goods remain bound until sold, or if money, when it is used to pay the arrears, or if the amount outstanding is paid, the instrument under which the power is exercisable ceases to have effect, or the power ceases to be exercisable for any other reason.[187]

(h)   After notice has been given, the enforcement agent has 12 months from the date of the notice of enforcement within which to take control of the goods.[188]

(i)   Once the enforcement agent has control of goods,[189] he must take an inventory of them as soon as reasonably practicable and provide it to the tenant.[190] The enforcement agent, within 7 days[191] of removing the goods, must make or obtain a valuation which he must give to the debtor.[192]

(j)   The enforcement agent will then sell the goods[193] on notice to the debtor and any co-owner of the goods as to the date, time and location of the

---

[184]   Including items necessary for use personally by the tenant in his employment, business, trade, profession, study or education up to an aggregate value of £1,500, and such clothing, bedding, furniture and household equipment, items and provisions as are reasonably required to satisfy the basic domestic needs of the debtor and every other member of his household. The full list is in 2013 Regulations, reg 4. The second category, domestic goods, are less likely to be found on commercial premises.

[185]   2007 Act, Sch 12, para 4(4).

[186]   This deals with assignments of bound goods and to whom money from sale is to be paid. If the assignee bought in good faith, for valuable consideration, without notice that the goods were controlled, then he is paid from the proceeds of sale first as if a co-owner. If the assignee does not satisfy those conditions, he is paid from the surplus after the arrears are paid. See 2007 Act, Sch 12, para 61.

[187]   2007 Act, Sch 12, para 6.

[188]   2007 Act, Sch 12, para 8, and 2013 Regulations, reg 9(1). The period for enforcement is affected by any agreements to pay the arrears by instalments, breach of which starts the 12-month period running afresh: reg 9(2). The enforcement agent or the landlord can apply to court to extend the period if he has reasonable grounds for not taking control of goods during the 12 months: reg 9(3) and (4), and CPR, Pt 84.

[189]   There are numerous provisions in 2013 Regulations, Sch 12 governing the aggregate value of the goods of which the enforcement agent can take control, the power of entry onto the premises and its exercise, when there can be a re-entry, the method of controlling the goods, the requirement of notice after taking control, etc. For further details, the 2007 Act and and the 2013 Regulations should be consulted.

[190]   2007 Act, Sch 12, para 34 and 2013 Regulations, reg 34 as to form and content, etc. Schedule 12, para 35 imposes a requirement to take reasonable care of the goods, and to comply with 2013 Regulations, reg 34 as to storage.

[191]   2013 Regulations, reg 37(1).

[192]   2007 Act, Sch 12, para 36(1) and 2013 Regulations, reg 35.

[193]   Specific provisions apply to sales of securities: 2007 Act, Sch 12, paras 47–49 and 55–57 and 2013 Regulations, Pt 4.

sale.[194] The enforcement agent has a duty to obtain the best price that can reasonably be obtained.[195] He cannot sell before the expiry of the minimum period, 7 days from removing controlled goods for sale, without the consent of the landlord and the tenant,[196] unless delay would make the goods unsaleable or substantively reduce or extinguish their value due to their nature and any characteristic.[197] The sale must be by public auction unless the court orders otherwise.[198]

(k)   After sale, the enforcement agent must as soon as possible give to the tenant an itemised list of goods sold or disposed of, the sums received and their application and disbursements such as costs.[199]

(l)   The proceeds of sale are used to the pay the arrears outstanding plus costs, with any surplus to be paid to the tenant.[200]

RECOVERY FROM SUB-TENANTS

9.124   Since a landlord has no privity of estate with his tenant's sub-tenants, he cannot usually collect rent directly from the sub-tenants even if his tenant is in arrears. However, section 80 of the 2007 Act allows recovery direct from sub-tenants.

9.125   When CRAR is exercisable against a tenant for rent arrears, the landlord may serve notice on any sub-tenant.[201] The notice requires the sub-tenant to pay his rent, payable under his tenancy, direct to the landlord up to a notified amount, i.e. the amount the landlord has the right to recover from the tenant under CRAR.[202] The effect of that notice is to transfer to the landlord the right to recover, receiver and give a discharge for any rent payable by the sub-tenant

---

[194]   2007 Act, Sch 12, para 40 and 2013 Regulations, regs 39 and 40. The notice must be given within the permitted period of 12 months from the date on which he takes control of the goods, unless this is extended by agreement: para 40(6) and (7) and reg 37. A new notice may be served if the date, time, or location must be re-arranged in certain circumstances: Sch 12, para 40(3) and 2013 Regulations, reg 39(3).

[195]   2007 Act, Sch 12, para 37(1).

[196]   2007 Act, Sch 12, para 39(1) and 2013 Regulations, reg 37(1).

[197]   2013 Regulations, reg 37(2).

[198]   2007 Act, Sch 12, para 41 and 2013 Regulations, regs 4–43.

[199]   Taking Control of Goods (Fees) Regulations 2014, reg 14.

[200]   2007 Act, Schedule 12, para 50. This makes provision for payment of a share in the surplus to any co-owner of the goods first. See also Taking Control of Goods (Fees) Regulations 2014, reg 13 for application of proceeds of sale when the proceeds are less than the outstanding arrears.

[201]   2007 Act, s 80(1). The sub-tenant need not be a direct sub-tenant of the tenant, but may be further down the chain of tenants and may be a sub-tenant may be a tenant of part only of the premises: s 80(8).

[202]   2007 Act, s 81(3).

under the sub-lease until the notified amount (i.e. the arrears) has been paid[203] or the notice is replaced[204] or withdrawn.[205]

9.126 The form of the notice, its required contents, provisions as to service and what must be done to withdraw it are contained in Regulations.[206] In particular, it must be in writing, signed by the landlord.[207] The notice takes effect 14 days after service on the sub-tenant.[208] Any payment received by the landlord not due under the notice to the sub-tenant is treated as payment of rent by the immediate tenant.[209]

CRAR AND RECEIVERS

9.127 It is the landlord within the meaning of section 73 who is entitled to exercise CRAR. That section does not expressly permit LPA receivers[210] or fixed charge receivers to exercise CRAR.

9.128 That an LPA receiver can do so is clear from section 109(3) of the Law of Property Act 1925, which gives him power to recover the income using CRAR to be done 'in the name either of the mortgagor or the mortgagee'. However, it is not clear whether the LPA receiver has the power as if he were landlord so that if 'the landlord' is given power to do something in the 2007 Act, the LPA receiver can do it in his own name, or only as the landlord borrower's deemed agent.

9.129 Presumably, the LPA receiver should exercise CRAR in the name of the borrower.[211]

---

[203] By the sub-tenant or otherwise, for example by control of goods of the tenant or by the tenant for example.

[204] By the landlord serving another notice on the sub-tenant for a notified amount covering the same rent or part of it (2007 Act, s 83(1)), or the landlord serves notice on another sub0tenant for a notified amount covering the same rent or part of that rent and in relation to any of the premises comprised in the first sub-tenant's sub-lease, the second sub-tenant is an inferior or superior sub-tenant (s 83(2)). The landlord cannot thus require rent to be paid by a sub-tenant who is not receiving rent from his sub-tenant because that second sub-tenant is also paying the landlord. But note that a landlord cannot recover the sub-tenant's rent payable to him because of service of a notice by service of notice on his sub-tenant: s 84(2).

[205] 2007 Act, s 80(4). The landlord must withdraw the notice if it is replaced, or the notified amount is paid other than wholly by the sub-tenant (s 83(3)). A notice must be withdrawn in writing served on the sub-tenant: 2013 Regulations, reg 55.

[206] 2013 Regulations, reg 54.

[207] 2013 Regulations, reg 54.

[208] 2013 Regulations, reg 53(1).

[209] 2007 Act, s 84(3).

[210] And nor does 2007 Act, Sch 13, para 22, which amended, Law of Property Act 1925, s 109(3), make it express.

[211] This is consistent with the position of a court appointed receiver, who invokes CRAR 'in the name of the landlord': 2007 Act, s 73(7). It is possible that Law of Property Act 1925, s 109(3) allows the receiver to act in his own name, hence as if 'landlord' under the 2007 Act, if one

9.130 However, there are a number of steps in the 2007 Act which require the landlord to serve notice or authorise someone to act by a written and signed notice, which make no express provision for that act to be taken by an agent other than an enforcement agent, thus make no express provision for an act by a receiver as the deemed agent of the borrower:

(a) Under section 73(8) of the 2007 Act, 'any authorisation of a person to exercise CRAR on another's behalf must be in writing and must comply with any prescribed requirements'. The prescribed requirements in regulation 51 of the Taking Control of Goods Regulations 2013 (2013 Regulations) only permit a landlord to authorise an enforcement agent, and that authorisation must 'be in writing, [and] be signed by the landlord ...'.[212] It must give the name and contact details of the landlord and of the person authorised to act on behalf of the landlord.

(b) The notice which the landlord may serve on a sub-tenant to obtain rent directly from him 'must be in writing, [and] be signed by the landlord ...'.[213] The notice must include the landlord's name and contact details.[214]

9.131 Section 73(8) of the 2007 Act and regulation 51 of the 2013 Regulations do not make it clear whether a landlord can appoint an agent to serve the relevant notices.[215] Given the terms of section 109(3) of the Law of Property Act 1925, it must be the case that a receiver can exercise CRAR in the name of the borrower, whatever may be the position of other agents. The 2007 Act cannot have specifically included in section 109(3) powers for the receiver which under the 2007 Act the receiver would not be allowed to exercise.

---

reads the reference in s 109(3) to acting in the name of the borrower or the landlord as empowering the receiver, not preventing him from exercising powers in his own name.

[212] 2007 Act, s 73(8) and 2013 Regulations, reg 51 are odd in that the landlord himself can never exercise the power, save by appointing an enforcement agent. Thus, these provisions seem to be directed at the necessary appointment of an enforcement agent, and not giving someone else the power to do so, despite their wording.

[213] 2013 Regulations, reg 54.

[214] 2013 Regulations, reg 54(1).

[215] There is a presumption that a statute requiring an act or signature by a specific person permits that person to act or sign via an agent. That presumption can be overturned by the wording of the statute as a whole. The wording of the 2007 Act appears to exclude the landlord acting by an agent. Section 73(8) is about the landlord authorising someone else 'to exercise CRAR' on his behalf, which one would expect to refer to authorisation of agents. However, the authorisation referred to 2013 Regulations, reg 51 is authorisation only of an enforcement agent to exercise CRAR on the landlord's behalf. Section 73 otherwise talks of the landlord exercising CRAR without express reference. Exercise of CRAR by a landlord is by appointment of an enforcement agent to take all the steps in Sch 12. Since the only place the 2007 Act talks of authorisation of someone else to act is about authorisation of the enforcement agent, it appears the landlord may not authorise an agent other than an enforcement agent to take any steps at all, for example, to serve notice. If that is right, then the reference to the landlord's signature in regs 51 and 54 must be to the specific landlord's signature, not his agent.

9.132 Once a receiver of income with the power to recover income under CRAR has been appointed, the borrower will not be able to do so.[216]

9.133 Under section 73(5) of the 2007 Act, a lender who has given notice of his intention to take possession of the mortgaged property or enter into receipt of the rents and profits is the person entitled to exercise CRAR.[217] However, the lender cannot exercise CRAR in relation to a lease that does not bind him.[218] Thus, the appointment of an LPA receiver is a route to allow exercise of CRAR when the lender could not.

DELEGATED POWERS

9.134 Receivership is used not only when the borrower's property already produces an income, but also it is commonly used as a way to ensure the borrower's property is fully let, or – even when there is nothing to produce income – as a precursor to sale.

9.135 Even an LPA receiver appointed under a mortgage the conditions of which give no additional powers to receivers need not be limited to the collection of income. The end part of section 109(3) of the Law of Property Act 1925 gives the receiver the power 'to exercise any powers which may have been delegated to him by the mortgagee pursuant to this Act'.

9.136 The powers of the lender under the Law of Property Act 1925[219] which the Act says expressly are capable of delegation to the receiver are:

(a) the limited power of leasing exercisable by the lender after the receiver has been appointed;[220]
(b) the limited power to accept surrenders of leases exercisable by the lender after the receiver has been appointed.[221]

---

[216] *Woolston v Ross* [1900] 1 Ch 788 in relation to distress. CRAR is a power given to 'the landlord' in the 2007 Act. The definition of 'landlord' in s 73(1) means the person for the time being entitled to the immediate reversion, unless the immediate reversion, as here, is mortgaged, in which case it is the lender if he has given notice of his intention to take possession or enter into receipt of the rents and profits, but is otherwise the borrower: s 73(5). Nothing in that definition, as against the previous common law right of a landlord to distrain, suggests that *Woolston* does not extend to CRAR as it did to distress.

[217] This echoes Law of Property Act 1925, s 98(1).

[218] See the discussion at para 2.17 as to when leases bind lenders.

[219] In contrast to powers of the lender under express covenants in the mortgage.

[220] Law of Property Act 1925, s 99(19), which expressly permits delegation in writing to the receiver; see below for further discussion of when this power arises. It appears that the lender must appoint the receiver first before the lender's power to lease arises under s 99(19), and thus it must delegate the power to the receiver post-appointment. This supports the argument that a lack of letting does not prevent a valid appointment of an LPA receiver. See paras 9.141–9.145.

[221] Law of Property Act 1925, s 100(13), which expressly permits delegation in writing to the receiver; see below for further discussion of when this power arises.

Are other statutory powers of the lender delegable?

9.137 The Law of Property Act 1925 gives the lender a number of other powers:

(a) the power to sell the mortgaged property;[222]
(b) the power to insure the mortgaged property;[223]
(c) the power whilst in possession to cut and sell timber.[224]

9.138 These powers are not delegable to an LPA receiver. The phrase 'any powers which may have been delegated to him ... pursuant to this Act' means lender's powers that the Law of Property Act 1925 expressly allows to be delegated. 'Pursuant to this Act' qualifies 'delegated' and not 'powers'.[225]

9.139 Thus, if the receiver is to have a power of sale, it must come from the mortgage conditions, and the receiver's appointment, and the receiver will be a fixed charge receiver in this respect.[226]

9.140 Although the lender's power to insure is not delegable, an LPA receiver does have power to insure in certain circumstances. This is considered below.[227]

Leasing

9.141 As set out in Chapter 2,[228] the Law of Property Act 1925 gives the borrower and the lender separate powers of leasing when in possession.

9.142 When the lender is in possession, it is the lender who has the power to make leases.[229]

9.143 The borrower's power of leasing under section 99(1) of the Law of Property Act 1925 also ceases, with the section 99 powers of leasing being

---

[222] Law of Property Act 1925, ss 101(1)(i), 103 and 104; see paras 9.141–9.145 for further discussion of when the power arises, and paras 11.90–11.102 on delegatability of the power of sale to a fixed charge receiver.

[223] Law of Property Act 1925, s 101(1)(ii), but see also s 109(7). Since the receiver can be directed by the lender to insure under s 109(7), it is clear that the receiver can have the power to insure, and hence that power need not fall within s 109(3). It seems inapt to describe this as delegation of the lender's power to insure.

[224] Law of Property Act 1925, s 101(1)(iv).

[225] *Phoenix Properties Ltd v Wimpole Street Nominees Ltd* [1992] BCLC 737. An express receivership power to sell in the mortgage conditions is not a variation or extension by the mortgage deed of the lender's powers in Law of Property Act 1925, s 101 because the Act does not allow delegation of the statutory power of sale to the receiver. See fns 6–8, and Chapter 11, fn 120 and paras 11.97–to 11.98 for further discussion of this case. Indeed, it is questionable whether these powers are delegable at all: see paras 11.90–11.102.

[226] See Chapter 11

[227] See paras 9.164–9.171.

[228] See paras 2.63–2.72.

[229] So far as the contrary intention is not expressed in the mortgage or otherwise in writing by the borrower and lender: Law of Property Act 1925, s 99(1) and (2).

exercisable by the lender instead, once a receiver of income of the mortgaged property has been appointed by the lender under its statutory power[230] under section 101(1)(iii). It is the lender who can then exercise 'the powers of leasing conferred by this section', 'so long as the receiver acts'.

9.144 Under section 99(19) of the Law of Property Act 1925, once a receiver has been appointed under the Act, the section 99 powers of leasing, then exercisable by the lender, can be delegated to the receiver in writing.[231]

9.145 Section 99(19) of the Law of Property Act 1925 refers to 'the powers of leasing conferred by this section'.[232] The powers in section 99(1) and (2) are the same power exercisable by different people. The power of leasing in question is a power to grant a lease of the mortgaged property which binds the lender, and prior incumbrancers and the borrower.

In whose name?

9.146 In whose name could the receiver grant such a lease? If the receiver grants a lease in his own name it will bind both the borrower and the lender, because of the power.[233] It is likely that the receiver can grant the lease in the borrower's name because he is the deemed agent of the borrower.[234] The receiver's exercise of his power would have the effect of the grant of a lease,

---

[230] Law of Property Act 1925, s 99(19). This suggests that it would be preferable if the power in a mortgage deed to appoint a receiver was expressly an extension of the statutory power, so that s 99(19) had effect, if the borrower's s 99(1) powers are not to be excluded or limited.

[231] See also discussion of the receiver's powers of leasing at paras 8.211–8.123.

[232] Although the reference in Law of Property Act 1925, s 99(1) to 'in like manner as if such mortgagee were in possession of the land' might suggest that the power is the s 99(2) power only, i.e. the lender's power.

[233] A power can be given to a person, who can thus act to affect a proprietary interest, even though he has no such interest, without that person truly being an agent of the person who donated the power, and hence without that act being seen as an act of that person. See for example *Swift 1st Ltd v Colin* [2011] EWHC 2410 (Ch), [2012] Ch 206 at [15]: 'a power, including the power of sale, is by its nature an authority to exercise rights over property in which the donee of the power does not necessarily have any proprietary interest, and which therefore enables the donee of the power to dispose of property which that done does not own'. This is, after all, how a lender can grant a lease which binds the borrower, though he is not the borrower's agent, or sell the borrower's estate in the borrower's name.

[234] *Edenwest Ltd v CMS Cameron McKenna (A Firm)* [2012] EWHC 1258 (Ch), [2013] BCC 152 suggests that the effect of the deemed agency is precisely to allow the receiver to act in the borrower's name. See at [66]: 'if a receiver wishes to bind the [borrower] to a contract with a third party he will contract in the name of the [borrower], as he is entitled to do as its agent and attorney, so that the [borrower] becomes a party and he does not'. However, that case was about the receiver instructing solicitors, and did not consider the situation with leasing, where the power the receiver has is not one which the borrower would have. See also the commentary in JT Farrand, *Wolstenholme and Cherry's Conveyancing Statutes, Vol 1* (Oyez Publishing Ltd, 13th edn, 1972). The commentary to Law of Property Act 1925, s 99(19) suggests that the receiver should usually exercise a delegated power of leasing in the name of the lender, though he can do so in the name of the borrower via s 7(4). Unless s 7(3) is referring to pre-existing statute, for example, the Conveyancing Act 1881, allowing conveyance and leasing of the borrower's estate by the lender, it is unclear why it is said that s 7(4) has that effect.

binding both borrower and lender, because the receiver had the power to do so, and the borrower has agreed, via the deemed agency, to the grant in his name.[235] There appears to be no case law on the issue.[236] No doubt, any buyer would wish to see that the receiver had the power to lease and to have it recited in any lease that he was exercising that power, especially if the lease was granted in the borrower's name.

9.147 The receiver cannot lease as agent of the lender, unless the lender expressly permits this. The statutory delegation is to the receiver as deemed agent of the borrower, not of the lender. It would be of little benefit to the lender for the receiver only to be able to exercise the power in the lender's name since then the lender would be in possession[237] and would have the liabilities imposed by equity.[238]

What is the power?

9.148 A receiver's power to lease, if the lender's delegated statutory power of leasing, is to grant leases compliant with the requirements of section 99 of the Law of Property Act 1925:[239]

(a) Term: the receiver cannot grant a lease which is for the same or a longer term than the borrower's estate.[240] Further, he cannot grant a lease other than:

    (i) agricultural or occupation leases for any term not exceeding 21 years, or, in the case of a mortgage made after the commencement of this Act, 50 years; and

    (ii) building leases for any term not exceeding 99 years, or, in the case of a mortgage made after the commencement of this Act, 999 years.[241]

---

[235] The situation is arguably similar to the lender exercising his power to sale in the borrower's name (under Law of Property Act 1925, ss 88(1) and 89(1)). The lender can sell the borrower's estate, unencumbered by the mortgage, in the borrower's name, though the borrower could not do so. No doubt, the buyer would wish to see that the lender does have such a power.

[236] The receiver might also rely on Law of Property Act 1925, s 8(1), as the lender could, to grant the lease in the borrower's name, though that would not make the borrower directly liable on the landlord covenants since, s 8(1) does not authorise the imposition of personal liability.

[237] *Mexborough Urban District Council v Harrison* [1984] 1 WLR 733 at 736–737. *Berkshire Capital Funding Ltd v Street* (2000) 32 HLR 373 at 377.

[238] See Chapter 2, fn 87. It is harder to argue that the lease must be granted by the receiver in the lender's name in the sense of making the lender the receiver's principal, because the receiver's principal is the borrower. The lender will, however, have potential liabilities to third parties on the lease granted because the lease binds him.

[239] See also paras 2.63–2.72 for a discussion. See Law of Property Act 1925, s 152 for the effect of a lease, purportedly granted in pursuance of s 99, but which is invalid for example because of non-compliance with these conditions.

[240] Law of Property Act 1925, s 99(15).

[241] Law of Property Act 1925, s 99(3). If a building lease is granted, there are additional requirements as to terms set out in s 99(9) and (10).

(b)   The lease must take effect in possession not later than 12 months after its date.[242]

(c)   The lease must reserve the best rent that can reasonably be obtained, regard being had to the circumstances of the case, but without any fine being taken.[243]

(d)   The lease must contain a covenant by the lessee for payment of the rent, and a condition of re-entry on the rent not being paid within a time therein specified not exceeding 30 days.[244]

(e)   Probably, the lease is required to be in writing. Statute requires a counterpart to be executed by the lessee and delivered to the lessor.[245]

(f)   Leases on other terms can only be granted if the borrower and lender have so agreed.[246]

9.149   The receiver will have the power to 'execute and do all assurances and things necessary or proper in that behalf' as per section 99(4) of the Law of Property Act 1925, and a counterpart is to be executed by the lessee as required by section 99(8).

Registering the lease

9.150   Land Registry Guide 36A, in particular at section 4, sets out guidance on execution of leases by receivers under the delegated power. The issues which are discussed, in particular where there is a Form A trust restriction,[247] are similar to those discussed in relation to sale, in Chapter 11.[248]

Effect of grant

9.151   Once the lease has been granted, the borrower will be liable on the landlord covenants, because the receiver is deemed to act as the borrower's deemed agent.[249]

---

[242] Law of Property Act 1925, s 99(5).

[243] Law of Property Act 1925, s 99(6).

[244] Law of Property Act 1925, s 99(7).

[245] Law of Property Act 1925, s 99(8).

[246] If there is an extension of the lender's powers, then the lender can delegate the extended powers to the receiver, either expressly in the mortgage conditions and the appointment, or simply in the appointment, because the Law of Property Act 1925, s 99 powers referred to in s 99(19) are the lender's powers of leasing as extended by the mortgage conditions or expressly in writing.

[247] If the receiver is exercising the lender's statutory powers, which arise from the mortgage, the trust issues ought not to arise. Trust issues arise when it is a borrower's power which is being exercised, and the borrower is bound by a trust, because of the problems of delegation of a trustee's powers. A lease granted under lender's powers ought to overreach beneficial interests under a trust which does not bind the lender: Law of Property Act 1925, s 2(1)(iii).

[248] See, for example, paras 11.68–11.73, 11.142 and 11.159.

[249] Under Law of Property Act 1925, s 109(2), because the delegation falls within s 109(3). I.e. unless the deemed agency has ended due, for example, to liquidation. In that case, the receiver could not impose liability on the borrower. See para 6.170. In the case of liquidation, Law of

9.152 The lender will also have potential landlord liabilities to the leaseholder if he is in possession. For leases granted after 1 January 1996, a tenant can claim on landlord covenants against a lender in possession who is entitled to the rents and profits.[250] For a lease granted before that date, the lender in possession is also likely to be liable[251] under section 142(1) of the Law of Property Act 1925.

9.153 However, provided that the lease is not granted in the lender's name, the lender will not go into possession simply because of the grant, so those liabilities will arise only at some later date when it does go into possession.[252]

9.154 The receiver will not be liable on the landlord covenants in the lease.[253]

Power in the mortgage conditions

9.155 The lender's power of leasing, in particular as to the type of lease, may be extended by the mortgage conditions or by agreement in writing between borrower and lender.[254] If there is such an extension, provided that on its proper interpretation, it is an extension of the statutory powers,[255] then the lender can delegate the extended powers to the receiver, either expressly in the mortgage conditions and the appointment, or simply in the appointment, because the powers under section 99 of the Law of Property Act 1925 referred to in section 99(19)

Property Act 1925, s 8(1) would not assist since that section prevents the imposition of personal liability.

[250] Landlord and Tenant (Covenants) Act 1995, s 15(2) by reference to s 15(1)(b).

[251] Under Law of Property Act 1925, s 142(1). When the lender is in possession, then it is likely that the lender is entitled to the reversionary estate on the lease. That seems to follow if one treats the mortgage as if it were a lease. However, s 87(1) gives the lender with a charge by deed by way of legal mortgage the rights and powers as if it had a lease. The mortgage is not a lease, and the lender is not expressly given the obligations.

[252] If the lender granted a lease, it would go into possession: *Mexborough Urban District Council v Harrison* [1984] 1 WLR 733 at 736–737; *Berkshire Capital Funding Ltd v Street* (2000) 32 HLR 373 at 377. The purpose of the statutory delegation to the receiver, who will act as deemed agent of the borrower under Law of Property Act 1925, s 109(2), is to avoid the lender going into possession, and thus incurring the liabilities of a lender in possession, as to which, see para 6.7.

[253] Any lease granted by the receiver in his own name should make clear that he does so as receiver, as deemed agent for the borrower, and in exercise of his power of leasing, and so that he has no liability on the lease granted. This is necessary to avoid him being a landlord under a tenancy by estoppel. For an example of wording intended to avoid direct liability, in a sale by a receiver of a borrower company's assets, see *Edenwest Ltd v CMS Cameron McKenna (A Firm)* [2012] EWHC 1258 (Ch), [2013] BCC 152 at [40]: '[the receiver will incur] no personal liability under, or by virtue of, this agreement, nor in relation to any related matter or claim howsoever, whenever, and wherever arising, and whether such claim be formulated in contract or tort or both or by reference to any other remedy or right, and in whatever jurisdiction or forum'. This would, of course, need considerable variation for use in a lease.

[254] Law of Property Act 1925, s 99(14); provided that such powers do not prejudicially affect the rights of any lender interested under any mortgage subsisting at the date of the agreement, unless that lender joins in or adopts the agreement.

[255] See the discussion at para 9.14 about extensions of statutory powers.

are the lender's powers of leasing as extended by the mortgage conditions or expressly in writing.[256]

9.156 The mortgage conditions might give the receiver a power of leasing which does not affect the lender's estate, for example, a power of leasing of the equity of redemption only, so as to avoid any possible liability of the lender either to the borrower or the tenant under a lease so granted.[257] The power would be to lease only the borrower's estate reversionary on the mortgage, so that any tenancy granted does not bind the lender.

Surrender

9.157 The lender can, similarly, by writing, delegate his powers under section 100 of the Law of Property Act 1925 to accept surrenders[258] to the receiver, once appointed, by section 100(13).[259]

9.158 As above, it is clear that a receiver with this power can enter into surrenders in his own name which bind both borrower and lender.

9.159 The receiver can accept surrenders in the borrower's name because that is the effect of the deemed agency under section 109(2) of the Law of Property Act 1925.[260] The surrender operates to bind both the borrower and the lender, because that is what the receiver has the power to do. It can be done in the borrower's name, because that is the effect of the deemed agency.[261]

9.160 The receiver cannot accept surrenders in the lender's name unless the lender gives him power to do so. The receiver is the deemed agent of the borrower. He is not the agent of the lender.

---

[256] Law of Property Act 1925, s 99(14): any further or other powers so reserved or conferred shall be exercisable, as far as may be, as if they were conferred by this Act, and with all the like incidents, effects, and consequences. That must include statutory delegation to the receiver under s 109(3).

[257] In that case, it is clear that the receiver can exercise the power in the borrower's name.

[258] Provided he has them. Under Law of Property Act 1925, s 100(7), the lender has the powers only if and as far as the contrary intention is not in the mortgage deed, or otherwise expressed by the borrower and lender in writing, and any power is subject to the mortgage deed and any such writing.

[259] See paras 2.73–2.84 for a discussion of the lender's powers of accepting surrender.

[260] The commentary on Law of Property Act 1925, Law of Property Act 1925, s 100(13) in JT Farrand, *Wolstenholme and Cherry's Conveyancing Statutes* (Oyez Publishing Ltd, 13th edn, 1972) suggests that the receiver can act in the name of the borrower by reason of s 7(4). The reasoning is unclear. If he can do so it is because the Conveyancing Act 1881 includes a lender's power to accept surrenders, and 'disposing of' in s 7(4) includes accepting surrenders.

[261] *Edenwest Ltd v CMS Cameron McKenna (A Firm)* [2012] EWHC 1258 (Ch), [2013] BCC 152 at [66]. See Chapter 5, fn 21 and Chapter 6, fn 38, but see para 5.24(c).

9.161 The statutory power to accept surrenders is to accept surrenders compliant with the provisions of section 100 of the Law of Property Act 1925:[262]

(a)   The power is to accept surrenders[263] of leases for the purpose of enabling the grant of a lease[264] compliant with section 99 or under an agreement made pursuant to section 99, or by the mortgage deed.[265]

(b)   Save that a surrender, other than to enable the grant of a section 99 compliant lease, can be made for payment of a premium, provided any prior mortgage holder consents.[266]

9.162 The lender's power of accepting surrenders may be extended by the mortgage conditions, or by agreement in writing between the borrower and the lender.[267] Any such extended powers are delegable to the receiver.[268]

9.163 The mortgage conditions might give the receiver more limited powers to accept surrenders for example of leases granted by the borrower which do not affect the lender.[269] Such powers could, without doubt, be exercised in the borrower's name.

POWER TO INSURE

9.164 The LPA receiver's power to insure is limited. It arises only where the following conditions are met:

---

[262] See also paras 2.73–2.84.

[263] A contract to make or accept a surrender may be enforced by or against every person on whom the surrender, if completed, would be binding: s 100(6). Thus a surrender by deed is not needed for s 100 to assist.

[264] 'Lease' extends to any letting, and to an agreement, whether in writing or not, for leasing or letting: s 100(9).

[265] Law of Property Act 1925, s 100(2) referring back to, s 100(1). For the surrender to be valid, a lease under s 99, or an agreement pursuant to it, or permitted by the mortgage deed, of the whole of the surrendered land to take effect in possession immediately or within 1 month must be granted; the term of the new lease must be not less than the unexpired term under the surrendered lease; and the rent reserved by the new lease is not less than under the surrendered lease: s 100(5). A surrender of part only of the demised land can be accepted, the rent apportioned and the lease of the remaining demise varied provided the remaining lease would be valid under s 99 had it been then granted: s 100(3).

[266] Law of Property Act 1925, s 100(4).

[267] Law of Property Act 1925, s 100(10); provided that such powers do not prejudicially affect the rights of any lender interested under any mortgage subsisting at the date of the agreement, unless that lender joins in or adopts the agreement.

[268] Law of Property Act 1925, s 100(10): any further or other powers so reserved or reserved shall be exercisable, as far as may be, as if they were conferred by this Act, and with all the like incidents, effects, and consequences. That must include statutory delegation to the receiver under s 109(3).

[269] Although since these would be granted by the borrower in breach of mortgage, such a power might be surprising.

(a)   the lender has directed the LPA receiver to insure, in writing;
(b)   the receiver is able to effect the insurance out of the money received by him;[270]
(c)   the insurance extends only to damage by fire; and
(d)   the insurance extends only as far as the lender had a power to insure.[271]

9.165   Where these conditions are met, the LPA receiver has not only a power to insure, but also an obligation. His power is to insure to the extent to which the lender might have insured.[272]

The lender's power to insure

9.166   Section 101(1)(ii) of the Law of Property Act 1925 gives the lender:[273]

> A power, at any time after the date of the mortgage deed, to insure and keep insured against loss or damage by fire any building, or any effects or property of an insurable nature, whether affixed to the freehold or not, being or forming part of the property which or an estate or interest wherein is mortgaged, and the premiums paid for any such insurance shall be a charge on the mortgaged property or estate or interest, in addition to the mortgage money, and with the same priority, and with interest at the same rate, as the mortgage money.

9.167   The lender's power can be varied by the mortgage deed,[274] and only applies 'as far as a contrary intention is not expressed in the mortgage deed'.[275]

9.168   Section 108 of the Law of Property Act 1925 sets out specific requirements on insurance effected by the lender under the power in section 101(1)(ii):

(a)   The amount of insurance is not to exceed the amount specified in the mortgage deed, or, if none is specified, two-thirds of the amount which would be required to restore the property on total destruction.[276]
(b)   The lender shall not effect insurance under the power, if there is a declaration in the mortgage deed that no insurance is needed, where the borrower insures in accordance with the mortgage deed, or where the mortgage deed contains no stipulation as to insurance and the borrower insures, to the amount authorised in section 108(1), with the lender's consent.[277]

---

[270]   Bearing in mind the statutory regime for use of funds received by him; see Chapter 12.

[271]   Law of Property Act 1925, s 109(7)

[272]   Law of Property Act 1925, s 109(7).

[273]   See paras 12.46–12.56 for a further discussion of insurance.

[274]   Law of Property Act 1925, s 101(3). See the discussion at paras 9.12–9.15.

[275]   Law of Property Act 1925, s 101(4).

[276]   Law of Property Act 1925, s 108(1).

[277]   Law of Property Act 1925, s 108(2) and (3).

(c)   Money received on insurance shall be used by the borrower, if the lender requires, in making good loss or damage in respect of which the money is received.[278]

(d)   The lender may require any money received on insurance effected under the Act or on an insurance required of the borrower under the mortgage deed, to be applied towards discharge of the mortgage money.[279]

Exercise of the LPA receiver's power

9.169 If all of the conditions are met, then, since the receiver is the deemed agent of the borrower, under section 109(2) of the Law of Property Act 1925, the insurance can be taken out in the borrower's name.[280]

9.170 Insurance money received by the receiver is to be applied in accordance with section 108 of the Law of Property Act 1925.[281]

Fixed charge receiver's power to insure

9.171 Fixed charge mortgages often expressly permit or require a receiver to insure, in other circumstances. The receiver's powers and obligations will depend on the precise wording.

COMMON POWERS OF A FIXED CHARGE RECEIVER

9.172 A fixed charge receiver is commonly given more extensive powers than an LPA receiver by the mortgage terms. Common additional powers of a fixed charge receiver are:

(a)   a power to lease and to surrender leases, more extensive than the delegable power under sections 99 and 100 of the Law of Property Act 1925;[282]

(b)   a right to take possession;[283]

(c)   a power of sale;[284]

(d)   a power of attorney.[285]

---

[278] That suggests that money from insurance payouts is income to be collected under Law of Property Act 1925, s 109(3). 'Income' in that section is not further defined. The question is whether the receiver has been appointed as receiver over the income in question, under the mortgage conditions.

[279] Law of Property Act 1925, s 108(4).

[280] The reference to 'the extent' in Law of Property Act 1925, s 109(7) is to the extent of the losses to be covered, by reference to ss 101(1)(iii) and 108.

[281] Law of Property Act 1925, s 109(8), which excludes insurance money from the statutory order of application of monies received. This also suggests that insurance payouts are income.

[282] This is covered in the sections on leasing and surrenders above: see paras 9.141–9.163.

[283] See Chapter 10.

[284] See Chapter 11.

[285] See para 6.229–6.243 for the power of attorney in general, and paras 11.79–11.86 for its use in sale by a receiver.

9.173 The fixed charge receiver's power to take possession and sell are considered in detail in the following chapters.[286]

9.174 It is, of course, common for the fixed charge receiver expressly to be made the deemed agent of the borrower, in the mortgage conditions, when exercising these powers.[287]

9.175 The fixed charge receiver is thus usually given powers much closer to those of the lender. Since the purpose of receivership is to give the lender a route to use its powers without the liabilities that fall on it as mortgagee in possession, it is not surprising that the express powers of a fixed charge receiver are extensive and mirror the lender's powers.

THE RECEIVER ACTING BEYOND HIS POWERS

9.176 As already seen, for a receiver to have any particular power:

(a) the power must be one granted by section 109 of the Law of Property Act 1925; or
(b) the borrower must have agreed to delegate that power to the receiver in the mortgage terms, and the receiver must have been given the power in the appointment; or
(c) the power must have been delegated by the lender.

9.177 In general, receivers take careful note of the mortgage terms and the terms of their appointment and will ensure that they do not act beyond the powers.

9.178 However, on occasion, mistakes are made. This section provides a brief summary of the consequences of a receiver acting beyond his powers.[288]

Ratification

9.179 As with other agents, if a receiver acts beyond his powers, his acts can also be ratified if four conditions are met:

(a) the receiver was purporting to act on behalf of the lender or the borrower (and not on his own account) when he carried out the act in question. The reason is that only the person on whose behalf the receiver was purportedly

---

[286] Possession is considered in Chapter 10. Sale is considered in Chapter 11.

[287] See Chapter 6 for a discussion.

[288] For the position where the receiver has not been validly appointed at all, see para 4.108. For the position where the receiver continues to act after the receivership has been terminated, see Chapter 13.

acting could ratify his act. If the receiver was, properly understood, acting on his own account, then neither borrower nor lender could ratify his act;[289]

(b)   the person in whose name the receiver carried out the act has the power to do whatever the receiver did;

(c)   third parties would not be prejudiced by the ratification;[290] and

(d)   the third party did not know that the receiver lacked authority at the time the contract was made.

9.180   For example, if the receiver without a power of leasing purported to grant a lease so as to bind both borrower and lender, the lender could ratify the grant because the lender, not the borrower, would have the power of leasing under section 99(19) of the Law of Property Act 1925, even if the lease was granted in the borrower's name or the receiver's.

9.181   Conversely, the borrower could not ratify the grant of the lease, even if in his own name, because he would not have power to grant a lease to bind the lender.

9.182   Where the receiver has purported to do something as agent of the borrower,[291] which the lender could not have authorised, the lender will not be able to ratify the receiver's acts. The borrower could do so, but borrowers are not often co-operative.

9.183   In general, there are there are no formalities involved in ratifying action taken by the receiver. The question is simply whether it is right to infer, from the acts (or even omissions) of the person with the ability to ratify, that he intended[292] to adopt the receiver's act.

9.184   However, where the act which is to be ratified had to be carried out by deed (e.g. the execution of a Form TR1), the ratification must be by deed.[293] In some cases, it will be prudent for the conveyance to be re-executed.

9.185   In most other cases, it will be prudent for a written document to be prepared evidencing that ratification of the receiver's act has occurred.

9.186   Ratification does not necessarily exonerate the receiver from liability to the lender or borrower for having exceeded his authority in the first place. The ratification may occur in order to ensure that a transfer completes or is not open

---

[289]   See *Edenwest Ltd v CMS Cameron McKenna (A Firm)* [2012] EWHC 1258 (Ch), [2013] BCC 152 at [85]. For the borrower to ratify, he must initially have been intended to be a party to the act or to be bound by it. If the receiver is purportedly exercising a power which binds the borrower, it is likely the borrower can ratify, providing he had the power to do the act, even if the receiver was acting in his own name. Likewise the lender.

[290]   *Lawson (Inspector of Taxes) v Hosemaster Co Ltd* [1966] 1 WLR 1300.

[291]   For example, if the mortgage, and hence the receivership powers, were over part only of the property, and the receiver collected income attributable to the wrong part. Otherwise, issues will most commonly arise where the receiver is given powers to run the borrower's business.

[292]   An objective intention.

[293]   *Kidderminster Corp v Hardwick* (1873–4) LR 9 Ex 13.

to challenge, for example, so as to mitigate possible loss, or avoid the expense of a purchaser's challenge to the validity of a sale, especially where that would require repayment of money used to redeem the mortgage and/or rectification of the Register.

9.187 The question of whether the ratification of the receiver's act is intended to absolve him from liability to the borrower or the lender as well is determined by ascertaining from the acts and omissions of the person ratifying whether they intended[294] to exonerate the receiver as well as ratify the transaction for the benefit of the third party to it.

Consequences of an act outside the receiver's powers

9.188 This section assumes that the receiver has acted outside his powers and his act has not been ratified. It discusses the consequences.

The receiver purporting to contract on behalf of the borrower

9.189 If a receiver purports to contract in the borrower's name when he had no actual authority to do so, the question of whether the borrower will be bound by the contract, and whether the third party to it will be able to enforce it, turns on whether the receiver had ostensible authority to make contracts of that type.[295]

9.190 The receiver will have ostensible (or apparent) authority[296] where the borrower has made representations (by words or conduct) to the third party about the scope of the receiver's authority on which the third party has relied.[297]

9.191 The real agency cases on ostensible authority tend to involve situations where the principal has put the agent into a position which would usually (but not in this case) give the agent a particular power, for example, where agency has been terminated, but the third party already dealing with the agent has not been notified, or where the agent is acting as a sales agent who would normally have power to sell all of the principal's products, but in fact has a limited power.

9.192 A difficult question, which has not been addressed in the authorities to the best of the authors' knowledge, is whether an acknowledgment by the borrower to third parties that the receiver has been appointed imports any representation that the receiver has the 'usual' powers of a fixed charge receiver, and if so, what the 'usual' powers are to be taken to be.

9.193 It is likely that much will depend on the context. For example, if the contract was for cleaning the common parts of a block of flats, an acknowledgment by the borrower that the receiver was a fixed charge receiver

---

[294] This is an objective intention.

[295] *OBG v Allen* [2007] UKHL 21, [2008] 1 AC 1 especially at [92].

[296] A real agency concept. See the brief discussion at para 6.30.

[297] See H Beale (ed), *Chitty on Contracts* (Sweet & Maxwell, 32nd edn, 2017) at 31-056.

might be sufficient to give him ostensible authority to make such a contract, because it would not be reasonable to expect the supplier to verify the terms of the mortgage and the appointment rather than rely on the usual authority of a receiver to enter contracts of this type.

9.194 However, if the receiver purported to sell the freehold or leasehold estate, it is unlikely that a purchaser would be able to rely on 'usual authority' to enforce the contract if, in fact, the receiver did not have power to make it. After all, a purchaser ought to retain solicitors to verify the scope of the receiver's power.

9.195 If the borrower is not bound by the contract, the receiver will be liable to the third party for breach of warranty of authority. The lender will not be bound unless, in all the circumstances, it is proper to infer that the receiver acted as the lender's agent in entering the contract, rather than on his own account.[298]

9.196 If the borrower is bound by the contract, the receiver will be liable to the borrower for any loss caused, under ordinary agency principles and/or for breach of a receiver's duties.[299]

9.197 If the borrower is aware that the receiver is about to contract (or complete a sale) beyond his powers, the borrower can seek an injunction to prevent him from doing so. An injunction will readily be granted in such circumstances.

The receiver purporting to contract on behalf of the lender

9.198 Similar principles apply where the receiver purports to act as agent for the lender, but has no authority to do the particular act in question. For example, where a receiver contracts with a third party purportedly as agent for the lender, the lender will be bound by the contract, and the third party will be able to enforce it if the receiver had ostensible authority to do that act on behalf of the lender.

9.199 However, the lender will have a cause of action against the receiver if he did not direct the receiver to act in that way, because the receiver, in so acting, will be in breach of the contract under which the lender made him his agent.

---

[298] *Gosling v Gaskell* [1897] 1 AC 575 at 595; paras 7.46 and 7.71.
[299] *Fray v Voules* (1859) 1 E & E 839.

Chapter 10

Possession

INTRODUCTION

10.1   This chapter considers issues which arise when a receiver seeks to take possession of the charged property.

10.2   When available, a receiver's power, in the mortgage conditions, to take possession is powerful for the lender. If a receiver takes possession as the deemed agent of the borrower, the lender avoids the duty, which it owes to the borrower if it goes into possession, to be reasonably diligent in realising the estate.[1] Moreover, the receiver, as deemed agent of the borrower, can manage the land without imposing liabilities on the lender.

10.3   Thus, the appointment of receivers can be used as a route for sale of the charged property with vacant possession with more limited risk to the lender. This is a method often used for example in relation to charged commercial properties or residential buy-to-let properties.

10.4   A number of issues do, however, arise:

(a)   Is the receiver given the right or power to take possession of the charged property under the express conditions in the mortgage?
(b)   Has the right so given been included in the appointment by the lender?[2]
(c)   In the particular circumstances of the situation, is the right to possession exercisable against the occupier of the mortgaged property?
(d)   In the particular circumstances of the situation, is taking possession the appropriate action in performance of the receiver's duties?

10.5   These issues are considered in this chapter. However, as regards question (c), the issues considered here are those peculiar to receivership and, in particular, those which arise out of the deemed agency of the receiver: whether a receiver can take possession from a tenant when the borrower does not wish it; whether a receiver can take possession from an occupier if the borrower could not; and whether a receiver can take possession from the borrower. The answers

---

[1]   See para 2.119 *et seq* for a discussion of the consequences of the lender in taking possession of the mortgaged property.

[2]   A lender might give a receiver a power to take possession even if that is no part of a receiver's powers granted in the mortgage deed, but the effect would be that the receiver would act as the lender's agent, not the borrower's. In exercising that right, the lender would be put into possession and would be liable as such.

lie in determining, by interpreting the mortgage conditions, what right of possession the receiver has been given. Has he been given simply the right the borrower has, so that, just as if he were the borrower's agent and the borrower were asking him to obtain possession, he is simply doing what the borrower could, in the borrower's name? Or does the receiver have a more extensive right, which is to take possession as the lender could, against occupiers whose rights bind the borrower, but not the lender, and even the borrower himself?

10.6   Much depends on the precise wording of the mortgage conditions. However, it is the thesis of this book that often those conditions will give the receiver a right of possession coterminous with the lender's right. In that way, the purpose of receivership, which is to give a person appointed by the receiver control of the property to generate money from it to repay the debt, without putting the lender into possession itself, is fulfilled.

10.7   Receivers also face issues common to any situation when possession is claimed, for example, issues of procedure under the CPR. These are considered briefly below.[3] Commentary on termination of landlord and tenant relationships is set out in the Appendix, to assist when the occupier against whom possession is sought is a tenant, as he commonly will be.[4]

10.8   It should be noted that the receiver, whatever his powers, will not be able to obtain possession from the lender, nor resist the lender taking possession from him should it wish to do so. After all, the lender could simply terminate the receivership[5] and any right to possession the receiver has.

The meaning of possession

10.9   The meaning of 'possession', legally, is complicated,[6] since in different contexts it can mean the physical occupation of property, or the more technical legal meaning the right to occupy and control an estate in the land to the exclusion of others.

10.10   It is that latter meaning, the right to control the estate, which is what possession means in this chapter, though the effect of the receiver taking possession will often be to put him into physical occupation as well.

10.11   It is also helpful to the understanding of the analysis in this chapter to understand that possession in the technical sense is possession of an estate: freehold or leasehold. Where the borrower has a freehold estate unencumbered by any lease out of it, then possession of the estate will allow occupation of the physical land; similarly, where the borrower's leasehold estate is not encumbered by a sub-lease.

---

[3]   For more detail, reference should be made to any practitioner's text on civil procedure.

[4]   Although the Appendix is inevitably a summary only of landlord and tenant law. Recourse should be had to any specialist practitioner's text for a detailed exposition.

[5]   See Chapter 13 for a discussion of termination of receivership.

[6]   See M Wannacott, *Possession of Land* (Cambridge, 2006) at Ch 1.

10.12 However, it is possible to be in possession of a freehold or leasehold reversion on a leasehold estate. Possession of a reversion is control of the rents and profits.[7] Thus, the owner of a reversion retains an estate in possession.

THE RECEIVER'S POWER TO TAKE POSSESSION

10.13 The sources of the receiver's powers are: (a) section 109 of the Law of Property Act 1925; and/or (b) the mortgage conditions; and, in each case, (c) the appointment by the lender which determines which of the powers which are, in principle, available have been given to the specific receiver who has been appointed.

10.14 The statutory power given to a receiver appointed under section 109 of the Law of Property Act 1925 is to demand and recover income.[8] That is not a power which alone could permit or require the receiver to take possession for his use.[9]

10.15 Thus, situations in which the receiver might seek to take possession of the charged property are situations which arise when receivers are appointed on express terms in the mortgage conditions rather than only under the Law of Property Act 1925.

10.16 The question of whether the mortgage conditions give a receiver the power or right to possession of the mortgaged property, and the extent of that right, is specific to each particular set of mortgage conditions.

The lender's right versus the borrower's right

10.17 A borrower has a right to possession, by reason of his freehold or leasehold estate, either of the land or the rents and profits from it if it is let or sub-let. The borrower whose estate is a reversion on sub-tenancies is entitled to the receipts and can take possession from his tenants, subject to the terms of the tenancy and any applicable statutory regime,[10] until the lender takes possession

---

[7]   *Megarry & Wade* at 6-017. See also Ch 4 of the same work.

[8]   The additional powers delegable to the receiver under Law of Property Act 1925, s 109(3) are the lender's statutory powers to let and surrender. See paras 2.63–2.94 and paras 9.141–9.163 for discussions.

[9]   An agent with authority to collect rent and other income does not necessarily have authority to serve any notice required to end a tenancy, nor take possession of it in his principal's name.

[10]   By reason of his estate. In *Kitchen's Trustee v Madders* [1950] Ch 134 at 146, a case relating to a tenancy granted by the borrower in breach of mortgage, it was said that the lender could not recover mesne profits from the tenant prior to giving a notice of intention to take possession so that the tenant had no defence against the borrower for rent arrears based on an alleged liability in mesne profits to the lender. The argument was by reference to Law of Property Act 1925, s 98(1), and that section does not give the borrower a right to possession.

(by requiring the rents and profits to be paid to him), or, possibly, until the lender serves notice that he intends to take possession.[11]

10.18 The lender also has a right of possession,[12] because that is the effect of the mortgage. Either the lender has a leasehold estate out of the borrower's estate,[13] which gives it a right to possession as would any other leasehold estate, or it has a charge by deed by way of legal mortgage, and hence 'the same protection, powers and remedies (including the right to take proceedings to obtain possession from the occupiers in receipt of rents and profits, or any of them)' as if it had a lease.[14]

10.19 The lender's right of possession is thus not of the same estate as the borrower's. As a result, where the mortgage has priority over rights of occupation created by the borrower, the lender will be able to take possession against those occupiers as trespassers.

10.20 For example, when a mortgage prohibits the grant of a lease by the borrower, and the borrower grants such a lease, that lease does not bind the lender,[15] and the leaseholder is a trespasser against him. The lender need not serve any notices which the borrower would have to serve to terminate the tenancy. He can simply sue for possession.

10.21 Thus, the lender's ability to obtain possession may be more powerful than the borrower's.

---

[11] Law of Property Act 1925, s 98 certainly prevents a borrower from suing for possession in his own name only once such a notice has been given. Section 98(1), however, does not give a borrower a right to possession: see *Turner v Walsh* [1909] 2 KB 484 at 494. It gives a borrower with an entitlement to possession or to the rents and profits for the time being an entitlement to sue for them in his own name only. This is a statutory scheme to prevent the need for the lender to be joined to proceedings when the borrower wishes to sue for possession or rents against a tenant whose tenancy, under s 99(1), binds them both as if a sub-demise of the mortgage, or against a trespasser given that it would be the lender who would be treated as having the immediate right to possession against him by reason of its estate. That this is the case is clear from s 98(2) which makes s 98(1) without prejudice to the power of the borrower to take proceedings in his own name only in right of any legal estate vested in him. A borrower can always take possession against a tenant whose tenancy he has granted in breach of mortgage since that is a tenancy which takes effect as concurrent to the mortgage with landlord the borrower only. The requirement of the lender to give notice to the borrower's tenant before suing him for rent is to protect prejudice to the tenant. See *Moss v Gallimore* (1779) 1 Douglas 279 at 282. This suggestion of a need for notice as a legal precursor to a right on a lender to claim possession against the borrower's tenant is not one much argued now. In any event, a receiver with the lender's power to take possession of the lender's estate could give any notice necessary, since the lender could treat the tenant as a trespasser: *Thunder v Belcher* (1803) 102 ER 669; *Bolton Building Society v Cobb* [1966] 1 WLR 1.

[12] Albeit that the mortgage conditions frequently postpone the receiver's right to possession.

[13] Law of Property Act 1925, ss 85 and 86. See paras 2.22–2.26.

[14] Law of Property Act 1925, s 87. Note that the lender with such a charge does not have a lease, but rights as if it had a lease.

[15] *Berkshire Capital Funding Ltd v Street* [1999] 32 HLR 373 (CA). See paras 2.31–2.32 for an explanation.

The receiver with the lender's right to possession

10.22 The purpose of mortgage receivership is to take control of the mortgaged property from the borrower and put it into the control of the receiver, appointed by the lender, with primary duty to pay down the mortgage debt, whilst avoiding the additional liabilities on a lender which come when it is in possession itself.

10.23 A receiver with the lender's right of possession would be able to pursue this end with greater ease than if he had only the borrower's right of possession. He would be able to evict the borrower's occupiers as trespassers if their rights did not bind the lender, because he would have a right to possession of, or out of, the lender's estate.

10.24 If the receiver is given the lender's right to possession,[16] and, provided the lender's right to possession has arisen as at the date of appointment of the receiver, then the receiver will have that right to possession of the property. Since the lender's rights to exercise its remedies usually all arise together once there is any breach of mortgage condition, it is highly likely that the lender's right to possession, and hence the receiver's, will have arisen by the date of the receiver's appointment.

10.25 The deemed agency of the receiver does not prevent the receiver having the lender's right of possession. The deemed agency is not what limits the receiver's powers. The receiver has the powers he is given in the mortgage conditions[17] and can exercise the lender's power, though the lender has not chosen to do so.

10.26 Just as the borrower gave the lender a right to possession when granting the mortgage, he can agree to that right being exercisable by the receiver. The effect of the deemed agency is to avoid lender liability and reduce receiver liability. The borrower cannot complain to the lender about the receiver's acts in taking possession, and nor can third parties complain to the lender or the receiver, save in limited circumstances.[18]

10.27 That is the considerable extent of the fiction of the deemed agency. It is a fiction allowing the receiver to use the lender's powers, which the borrower does not have, but without the lender being put into possession, so that the borrower cannot hold the lender in breach of his duties as mortgagee in possession.

---

[16] Either under the terms of the mortgage conditions, or on appointment or subsequently.

[17] See Chapter 6 for a discussion of the nature of the deemed agency, in particular para 6.228 which discusses the receivership as a right not limited by the agency, which can be lost, and for example *Sowman v David Samuel Trust Ltd (In Liquidation)* [1978] 1 WLR 22 at 30C.

[18] See Chapters 5 and 8.

Interpreting the mortgage conditions

10.28 It is thus crucial, when considering the receiver's right of possession, to determine whether the right given to him is the borrower's right to possession of his estate, or the lender's.[19]

10.29 There is little case law about the taking of possession by receivers, and hence few forms of conditions which have passed any sort of judicial testing.

10.30 It was conceded in *McDonald v McDonald*[20] that the mortgage condition permitting the appointment of a receiver, as agent of the borrower, with the same powers as the lender[21] gave the receiver the right to claim possession and that the mortgage conditions gave the receiver the power to sue and issue proceedings. There was no analysis of 'whose right' the receiver had, since the receiver had not sought to do anything which the borrower could not have done.[22]

10.31 Conversely, many mortgages give the receiver 'all the powers which the borrower has'. Although that would include the borrower's power to take possession against occupants, it would not give the receiver the lender's right of possession.

10.32 Often, the mortgage conditions will first give the lender a right to possession of 'the mortgaged property' or 'the property' if the borrower breaches the mortgage conditions, and then gives a right to appoint a receiver with a right to possession of 'the mortgaged property', or 'the property'. It seems likely that the reference to 'the mortgaged property', or 'the property', is the same for the lender and the receiver, and it is certainly arguable that, as a result, these conditions give the receiver the lender's right to possession.

10.33 Where the mortgage conditions simply confer a right to possession without stating whose right this is, it is again certainly arguable that this is the lender's right, since the lender is deemed to have an estate in possession, subject (generally) to the agreement that the borrower can remain in possession until breach. Allowing the receiver the lender's powers of possession is consistent with the purpose of receivership: to give the lender an effective remedy which avoids the liabilities of a mortgagee in possession.

---

[19] The usual principles on interpretation of contracts apply. See, for example, K Lewison, *The Interpretation of Contracts* (Sweet & Maxwell, 6th edn, 2017). In principle, a receiver could be given both, though that would be unusual. Were the receiver to have more than one right to possession, he must consider carefully which right he is purporting to exercise.

[20] [2014] EWCA Civ 1049, [2015] Ch 357.

[21] [2014] EWCA Civ 1049, [2015] Ch 357 at [8]. This seems a perfect example of the kind of use of deemed agency over powers more extensive than the borrower has.

[22] The issue for the court was whether the receiver with these powers had the power to serve the relevant notice to terminate the tenancy. See [2014] EWCA Civ 1049, [2015] Ch 357 at [9].

10.34 Most mortgage conditions will make the receiver the deemed agent of the borrower in exercising receivership powers, including the lender's right to possession.[23]

The appointment

10.35 Where the mortgage conditions are in one of the general forms discussed above, a receiver appointed with all of the powers available to the receiver in the mortgage conditions will have a power to take possession. Thus, for such a general form, it is simply necessary to check that there is nothing in the terms of the appointment which limits the receiver's powers and then to establish whose power the receiver has.

10.36 However, where the mortgage conditions are more limited, the receiver's powers might be extended in the terms of the appointment by the delegation of additional powers by the lender. Where the lender gives the receiver a lender's power to take possession where such a power is not a receivership power in the mortgage conditions, then the receiver exercising it will not be the deemed agent of the borrower, because the deemed agency in the mortgage conditions will apply only to powers in the mortgage conditions. The receiver's exercise of the lender's power will likely be as the lender's agent[24] and will put the lender into possession, which will defeat the purpose of receivership.[25]

PARTICULAR CLASSES OF OCCUPIER

10.37 Put simply, a receiver seeking possession of the charged property wants to remove the occupier of that property from it and secure it for his own use in the performance of the receivership, whether that is, for example, re-letting it to a better tenant, or selling it with vacant possession.

10.38 The first of those aims, removal from occupation, is about the change in physical occupation. The second, however, is about establishing the right to occupy and control an estate in the land to the exclusion of others. The receivers will want to establish that whoever was in occupation and has been removed, cannot, legally, return.

10.39 A receiver will only be able to obtain possession through the court if the receiver's right to possession is better than the occupier's, and a receiver will only be able to avoid a successful action in court against him for taking possession of the charged property unlawfully insofar as the party taking that action does not have a better right to possession than he has.

---

[23] See Chapters 5 and 6.

[24] Unless expressly given to the receiver as a power to be exercised on his own behalf.

[25] See paras 6.7–6.8.

10.40 Thus, it is necessary to consider, in answer to question (c) in the list in the Introduction to this chapter,[26] various categories of occupier of the charged property and the rights of an appointed receiver to take possession against each.

10.41 There are five categories of occupier against whom a receiver might seek to take possession:

(a) Occupiers whom the receiver has himself let into possession.
(b) Occupiers against whom the borrower could have sought possession: for example, trespassers and licensees or leaseholders/tenants whose licence or lease/tenancy could be terminated by the borrower.
(c) Occupiers against whom the borrower could not have sought possession, but against whom the lender could have sought possession.
(d) The borrower.
(e) Occupiers against whom the lender could not have sought possession since they have rights which bind the lender and which the lender cannot terminate.

10.42 In each of the above categories, it is by considering the deemed agency of the receiver, as against the wider powers he has been given by the mortgage conditions and his appointment, that it can be determined whether he can take possession against the occupant in question.

10.43 The possibility of possession by a receiver against each category of occupant listed above is discussed below.

Occupiers let into possession by the receiver

10.44 These are the most straightforward claims. If the receiver has allowed someone into possession after his appointment, then the receiver will be entitled to sue for possession once the occupier's contractual rights and any applicable statutory protection have come to an end, whether or not he had the power to grant the right.[27]

10.45 If the receiver granted the right in the name of the borrower, he should serve notices and sue in the name of the borrower.[28]

10.46 If the receiver granted the right in his own name, he can, however, serve notices and sue for possession in his own name.

10.47 This is straightforward if he granted a licence: he can simply terminate it and then seek possession.[29] Note that it is necessary for the receiver to take court

---

[26] See para 10.4.

[27] See paras 9.141–9.156 for the receivers' power of leasing.

[28] See para 10.51 *et seq* for a discussion of claims made by the receiver on the borrower's behalf. This is unless the borrower is insolvent, in which case the receiver may need to act in his own name. See para 6.165 *et seq* on liquidation, for example.

[29] Although he may have to comply with Protection from Eviction Act 1977, s 5 as to the form of notice. See paras 10.60–10.62.

proceedings, as opposed to re-entering physically, if the premises were let or licensed as a dwelling (other than an excluded lease or licence) and the occupier continues to reside there.[30] In other cases, it will generally be wise to take proceedings for the reasons set out above.

10.48 Things seem more complicated if the receiver granted a lease in his own name. If he has done so under a power of leasing given to him under the mortgage conditions or delegated to him by the lender,[31] the lease granted will be an estate in land. Given suitable mortgage conditions and a suitable appointment, the receiver has a right to possession post his appointment. It is arguable that this is then sufficient for him to terminate any lease he has created, subject to the terms of the contract and any statutory protection.

10.49 In any event, if someone who does not own land purports to grant a lease of it to another, then there is between those two people a tenancy by estoppel.[32] That means that the grantor cannot deny to the tenant that he owned the land, nor can the tenant deny to the grantor that the grantor owned the land and could grant the lease.

10.50 In a possession claim between the two, the court will treat the tenancy as having any statutory protection it would have had had the grantor owned the land and apply the common law rules and/or the statutory rules as to termination. Reference should be made to the Appendix for more detail about these rules. The standard possession procedure, described below,[33] should be followed.

Occupiers against whom the borrower has a right of possession

Introduction

10.51 Since the borrower could take possession against the occupant, the receiver with the borrower's right to take possession[34] is, in taking possession,

---

[30] Protection from Eviction Act 1977, s 3. This refers in terms to 'the owner' enforcing a right of possession, but the prospects of arguing that the receiver is not within the scope of that definition, on the true construction of the statute, appear extremely low, given the purposes of the statute.

[31] See paras 9.141–9.156.

[32] See *Bruton v London & Quadrant Housing Trust* [1999] 3 WLR 150 at 415 per Lord Hoffmann as to the nature of a tenancy by estoppel.

[33] See para 10.218 *et seq*.

[34] If the receiver has only the lender's right to possession, there is nothing to stop him treating the occupier as having a right binding the lender, and hence serving notices. Since he is entitled to act as the deemed agent of the borrower, and the borrower could so act, he can serve notices and take possession in the borrower's name, and hence put the borrower into possession. In so doing, he will not put the lender into possession, nor bind the lender with the occupier's rights, because he does not act as the lender's agent.

doing no more than the borrower can. In that sense, he is simply stepping into the borrower's shoes.[35]

10.52 There is little conceptual difficulty with the receiver, as deemed agent of the borrower, taking possession in the borrower's name, when the borrower can take possession. An agent can do whatever his principal has power to do, provided that he acts within the powers that his principal has given to him.

10.53 If the borrower could take possession against the occupants, the receiver, in doing so, is doing no more than his deemed principal, the borrower, has power to do, provided he follows the steps necessary to the taking of possession which apply in each case.[36]

10.54 If the receiver takes possession as the deemed agent of the borrower, then it is the borrower who will be in possession, not the receiver.

10.55 A little more difficulty arises if the receiver, although he has the borrower's right of possession, were to seek to exercise it in his own name and not as the borrower's agent, so as to avoid making the borrower directly liable for example for litigation costs if his ability to do so is limited because of the borrower's insolvency, or company borrower dissolution.[37]

10.56 In that case, the receiver will have to rely not on the agency but on the right to possession which he has because of the mortgage conditions and his appointment.[38] That right of possession will be a better right of possession than the occupier's provided that any right to occupy given by the borrower has been terminated.[39] It is that termination step that can be difficult, since both at common law and often in statute, the person who can terminate, for example, a lease is the landlord, and it is not always the case that someone without the landlord's estate, but a right of possession coterminous with it, can take a step the landlord could.

10.57 Thus, the analysis below discusses not only the ability of a receiver with a right of possession coterminous with the borrower's to terminate rights of occupation as the borrower's agent, but to take such steps in his own name relying on his right of possession.

---

[35] And hence has the right to take possession against occupiers if the borrower could. See *The Ocean Accident and Guarantee Corp Ltd v the Ilford Gas Company* [1905] 2 KB 493 at 499, in which second mortgagees with an express right of possession had a claim against a trespasser: 'they have the right to stand in the shoes of the mortgagor, and the wrong-doer cannot dispute their title'. Whatever the nature of the receiver's right to possession, the borrower cannot resist it, and nor can any occupier who could not resist the borrower's right.

[36] Further details of which are set out below.

[37] See para 6.160 *et seq* for a discussion of the deemed agency in these circumstances.

[38] For the reasons discussed at para 6.160 *et seq*, the receiver's powers will survive the termination of the deemed agency on the borrower's insolvency. The receiver may have to act in his own name.

[39] *The Ocean Accident and Guarantee Corp Ltd v the Ilford Gas Company* [1905] 2 KB 493 at 499, and fn 35.

10.58 If the receiver takes possession in his own name, it is he, not the borrower, who will be in possession.

Acting against the borrower's wishes

10.59 What if the borrower does not wish relevant notices to be served, or possession to be taken? Unlike a simple agency relationship, the borrower cannot remove the receiver's agency nor instruct him to stop his actions.[40] The situation is similar to the situation of an attorney given wide powers by his principal in a power of attorney,[41] who acts under those powers, which he is entitled to do, without further reference to his principal and without the requirement for specific instruction.

Source of the receiver's powers to take preliminary steps

10.60 In general, the receiver can take the necessary steps to terminate any right of the occupier to occupy and then take possession of the charged property. Even if he does not have the power to terminate the occupier's rights expressly, this is implied from his right of possession.

10.61 In *McDonald v McDonald*,[42] Miss McDonald, who was occupying the charged property under an assured shorthold tenancy granted by her parents, the borrower argued that the receiver, despite being given the power to take possession, could not serve on her a valid notice under section 21 of the Housing Act 1988. She argued that the agency of the receivers could extend only to the enforcement of the terms of the loan, not to the landlord and tenant relationship. This argument did not succeed.

10.62 The wording of the decision of Arden LJ suggests that the powers of the receiver are wide:

> The mortgage conditions have to be interpreted purposively: the clear purpose of the mortgage conditions was to enable the receivers to proceed to realise the charged property in an orderly and efficient way. The powers conferred on the receivers must therefore include power to do anything which is necessarily incidental to the exercise of the specified powers.[43]

---

[40] See paras 6.156–6.159.

[41] It is not suggested here that the mortgagee is acting under the power of attorney which is commonly also given to him in the mortgage conditions.

[42] [2014] EWCA Civ 1049. Appealed to the Supreme Court on other issues.

[43] [2014] EWCA Civ 1049 at [65]. See also *M Wheeler & Co Ltd v Warren* [1928] Ch 840: a receiver once appointed has an implied power to sue in the name of the borrower for the purpose of getting in the charged property. Such a conclusion that incidental powers are implied is consistent with case law on agency. An agent with express authority has incidental powers to do what is necessary: *Pole v Leask* (1860) 54 ER 481; *SMC Electronics Ltd v Akhter Computers Ltd* [2001] 1 BCLC 433, CA; *Nayyar v Denton Wilde Sapte* [2009] EWHC 3218 (QB).

Service of notices

10.63 Despite the generality of the decision in *McDonald v McDonald*,[44] an issue arises as to why a receiver can serve common law notices to terminate tenancies, acts usually required of landlords, and similarly how it is that a receiver can serve statutory notices under, for example under section 21 or section 8 of the Housing Act 1988, under Part II of the Landlord and Tenant Act 1954, or under the Protection from Eviction Act 1977,[45] though he is not the landlord.

By reason of the deemed agency

10.64 The first and simplest reason is agency. At common law, a landlord can act through his agent. A notice to quit served by an agent in his landlord's name is service of a notice to quit by the landlord. Provided the agent has been given authority to serve a notice to quit, he can do so.[46] A receiver, it appears, is no different.[47] Thus, the receiver can serve common law notices to terminate tenancies in the name of the borrower.

10.65 The position for statutory notices is more complicated since not every statutory act to be performed by a person can be performed by his agent; whether an agent can act depends on what the statute says.

10.66 In *McDonald v McDonald*,[48] the possession claim required service of a notice under section 21 of the Housing Act 1988. The receivers' powers 'necessarily incidental to the exercise of the specified powers'[49] included service of a section 21 notice, a step necessary as a precursor to bringing possession proceedings against Miss McDonald, though there was no express provision in the mortgage conditions to that effect.

10.67 The definition of 'landlord', at section 45(1) of the Housing Act 1988, includes:

> any person from time to time deriving title under the original landlord and also includes, in relation to a dwelling-house, any person other than a tenant who is, or but for the existence of an assured tenancy would be, entitled to possession of the dwelling-house.

---

[44] [2014] EWCA Civ 1049.

[45] See the Appendix for summaries of these provisions.

[46] Indeed, agency to receive rents and let was sufficient for an agent to determine a tenancy: *Manvers v Mizem* (1837) 174 ER 212.

[47] A receiver appointed by the Court of Chancery with authority to let lands has authority to serve a notice to quit: *Marsack v Read* (1810) 104 ER 23, but see *Poole v Warren* (1838) 112 ER 959, in which it appears a receiver appointed with powers including to serve a notice to quit could have served notice requiring possession at risk of liability for double rent, but in that case he had been appointed not by the landlord but by beneficiaries of the landlord's interest.

[48] [2014] EWCA Civ 1049.

[49] See above.

10.68 It was argued in *McDonald v McDonald*[50] at Court of Appeal level that under section 21 of the Housing Act 1988, it was 'the landlord' (i.e. the borrower) who had to serve a section 21 notice, and the extended definition of 'the landlord' did not include a receiver because the receiver did not derive title from the landlord. Arden LJ answered this point in short order. The purpose and powers of the receiver under the mortgage conditions were enough. She did not deal expressly with the point on interpretation of 'landlord' in the Act.[51]

10.69 This issue, however, of how it is that service of a notice under section 21 of the Housing Act 1988 by a receiver is compliant with the requirement for service by the landlord within the meaning of Act does require consideration.

10.70 Not every statutory scheme requiring a landlord to give notice permits the notice to be given by an agent.[52] It is possible in principle for a statutory scheme to prevent a receiver from serving a statutory notice as agent of the borrower though he has been given the power to so by the mortgage conditions and his appointment. Thus, the common law position set out above may not be enough.

10.71 For each statutory scheme, it is necessary to determine whether a receiver can take the statutory step as agent of the borrower.[53]

10.72 In the majority of cases this will provide the answer. Indeed, it is far more usual in the interpretation of statutes to find that agents can be used, since otherwise most legislation would be impractical. In general, thus, there is no reason why the receiver cannot serve any necessary notices in the borrower's name simply by reason of the deemed agency, if he has the power to take possession as deemed agent of the borrower.

Where the deemed agency argument is unavailable

10.73 The deemed agency argument discussed above might be unavailable for two different reasons: first, the deemed agency may be unavailable for example because of insolvency, and, secondly, the particular statute under which the notice must be served might not permit an agent to serve it so that the receiver cannot rely on the deemed agency, or a power to act in the borrower's name, to serve notice.

---

[50] [2014] EWCA Civ 1049, in which the receivers served the s 21 notice in their own name though their issued the possession claim in the name of the borrower: at [9].

[51] The parties in *McDonald v McDonald* [2014] EWCA Civ 1049 appear to have agreed that the receiver had a right to possession (at [8]). Thus one analysis would be that since he was entitled to possession, he would fall within Housing Act 1988, s 45.

[52] For example, in an example outside possession, prior to amendment in December 2014, signature of a s 13 or a s 42 notice under the Leasehold Reform, Housing and Urban Development Act 1993 had to be by each tenant giving the notice. An agent's signature was not sufficient for the notice to be valid. There is, however, nothing in the Housing Act 1988 to suggest that an agent for the landlord cannot serve notice on a tenant. That is another way in which the receiver in *McDonald v McDonald* [2014] EWCA Civ 1049 could have been said to have been able to serve notice.

[53] If he cannot, then the receiver will have to fulfil the statutory definition himself. The same applies if the deemed agency cannot be relied on.

10.74 As to the first of these, it is not in every case where the deemed agency is said to have ended that the receiver loses all right to act in the borrower's name.[54] If the receiver can still act in the borrower's name, then the receiver will still be able to serve notices in the borrower's name, which will satisfy a statute which permits service by an agent.

10.75 However, if the deemed agency has ended, and the receiver has to act in his own name,[55] then the question arises whether he can take any necessary steps preliminary to taking possession. It seems odd that he would not be able to, since his powers are intended to allow him to step into the shoes of the borrower, and the loss of the deemed agency is not intended to prevent that.[56] However, his ability to do so is not obvious and is little addressed in case law.

10.76 Although the receiver can serve a common law notice to quit as deemed agent of the borrower, his right of possession alone may not be sufficient to allow him to serve notice in his own name. The receiver's right to possession, assuming it has been given to him, suggests he is put in at least the same position as the borrower. He should be able to end the lease.

10.77 Case law suggests that only the person legally entitled to the reversion on the lease can serve a valid notice to quit.[57] The question is whether the receiver's right of possession is such an entitlement. Although the receiver has no right to have the estate vested in him at the Land Registry,[58] since a right to possession is a right to control the borrower's estate, either the land, or, if let, the rents and profits, it could be said he has such an entitlement.[59] It thus seems possible that a receiver can serve a notice in his own name.

10.78 Were a statute to prohibit service of notice by an agent,[60] or if the receiver could not rely on a right to serve a notice in the borrower's name,[61]

---

[54] Even where it is said that the deemed agency ends due to liquidation, for example, the right to act in the borrower's name appears to continue at least prior to dissolution, and provided no liability is imposed on the borrower. See para 6.174.

[55] This will be rare. Even where it is said that the deemed agency ends due to liquidation, for example, the right to act in the borrower's name appears to continue at least prior to dissolution, and provided no liability is imposed on the borrower. See paras 6.174–6.177.

[56] See Chapter 6, in particular the discussion of the effect of liquidation at para 6.165 *et seq*, and the summary at paras 6.221–6.228.

[57] *Schalit v Nadler* [1933] 2 KB 79; *Stait v Fenner* [1912] 2 Ch 504.

[58] And one would not say the estate was his.

[59] The difficulty arises because historically ownership of estates was by possession of them, and possession was central to ownership. Modern understanding puts more weight on the paper title, and now the ownership as recorded in the Land Register. Thus a right to possession of an estate and ownership of the estate do not seem quite the same. Nevertheless, ownership under English and Welsh law is not detached from the right to recover possession. It thus seems likely that someone with a right to possession does have a title. See *Megarry & Wade* at 4-012.

[60] Or were service by the receiver in his own name necessary by reason of the striking of a company from the register, for example.

[61] But see Chapter 6 on insolvency at para 6.165 *et seq* and, in particular, para 6.174.

consideration would be needed[62] of whether the receiver would qualify himself to serve notice in his own name.[63]

10.79 It is often hard to determine such a question. For example, the notice which must be given under section 166 of the Commonhold and Leasehold Reform Act 2002 must be given by 'the landlord'. Under section 112(3), 'landlord' is construed by reference to 'lease'. The definition of 'lease' at section 112(2) sheds no light on whether a receiver could be included in the definition of landlord and hence whether he can serve notices other than as agent of the borrower.

10.80 In some statutes, for example in section 45(1) of the Housing Act 1988 referred to above, the definition of who can take possession includes someone with an entitlement to possession. A receiver with a power to take possession, or a right of possession, will be entitled to possession and hence will fulfil the definition.

10.81 In section 45(1) of the Housing Act 1988, the person who can take possession includes persons by reference to whether they 'derive title' under the original landlord.[64] The phrase, 'deriving title' and similar phrases are common in definitions of landlord in statutes, and usually no further definitions are given of who falls within the phrase. It is a phrase whose precise meaning seems to lie, and is perhaps lost, in older law.

10.82 Certainly, someone with a legal estate in land carved out of the original landlord's estate, such as a sub-tenant, or indeed the lender, would fall within the definition. However, a receiver has only a right to possession of the property, or a power to take possession of the borrower's estate, and the title remains vested in the borrower at the Land Registry.

10.83 Nevertheless, the reasoning set out above in relation to notices to quit[65] suggests that the receiver could fall within the definition of someone deriving title from the borrower, though the argument is far from straightforward.

10.84 In the sections below, commentary is given on the receiver taking possession with the borrower's right of possession, against different categories of occupier. Where statutory steps are referred to and the question of whether the receiver can take those steps in his own name is discussed briefly.

---

[62] Common statutes in relation to different categories of occupier are discussed below.

[63] If he did not, he could not serve the notice and could not rely on the borrower's right to possession. He would therefore have to consider whether he could rely on the lender's right. If he had this right, and the lender were bound by the interest, the question which would arise is whether the lender could serve the notice. In general, the lender would fall within the definition of 'the landlord', because he has the same rights, remedies and powers as if he had a lease out of the borrower's estate: Law of Property Act 1925, s 87. That is, at least once the lender gave notice of his intention to take possession or enter into the receipt of the rights and profits: s 98(1).

[64] See for example Housing Act 1988, s 45 (above).

[65] See paras 10.76–10.77.

Title to the proceedings

10.85 If a possession claim is brought by a receiver exercising his receivership power as deemed agent of the borrower against an occupier who the borrower could have sued for possession, the claimant in the title to the claim should be described as:

> [the Borrower] (acting by [the Receivers] as fixed charge receivers)

10.86 The reason is that the borrower has a cause of action against the occupier, and hence it is appropriate for the claim to be in the borrower's name.[66]

10.87 If the receiver can no longer exercise his right of possession in the borrower's name,[67] the claimant should be the receiver himself.

The different types of occupier

Trespassers

10.88 If the occupier is a trespasser[68] against the borrower, then it is straightforward, for the reasons set out above, that in those circumstances, since the borrower could retake possession against trespassers, the receiver could do so likewise.

10.89 The usual route to eviction of a trespasser is to seek a possession order requiring the trespassers to leave,[69] rather than seeking possession without assistance from the court, especially where it is suggested that the trespassers are using the land for residential purposes,[70] whether the use before trespass was commercial or residential.

10.90 If, however, there is a threat that separate charged property, currently unoccupied, will be occupied by trespassers, for example, where trespassers on one piece of property threaten to occupy another on their eviction, then the correct route is to seek an injunction to prohibit that further trespass.[71]

---

[66] See the discussion of litigation in Chapter 14.

[67] For example if the company borrower were in liquidation. See for example para 6.170, but note paras 6.173–6.174. The receiver may be able to use the borrower's name notwithstanding the liquidation. But see fn 149. If the argument from *Re Sartoris* [1892] 1 Ch 11 discussed there were right, and the receiver could not claim in his own name because he had no estate in land even if he has a right to possession, then he could not issue a possession claim against occupiers in his own name, though he could it seems obtain an injunction requiring them to leave.

[68] See para 8.167 for a discussion of when there is trespass.

[69] For an outline of the procedure under CPR, Pt 55, see para 10.228 *et seq*.

[70] See the discussion on reasons for litigation at para 10.199 *et seq*.

[71] *Secretary of State for the Environment, Food and Rural Affairs v Meier* [2009] UKSC 11, [2009] 1 WLR 2780, which says that a possession order is not available in relation to land which trespassers are threatening to occupy, but have not yet occupied.

10.91 From 1 September 2012,[72] a person in a residential[73] building as a trespasser having entered as a trespasser,[74] who knows or ought to have known that he is a trespasser, and who is living in the building or intending to live there for any period, commits an offence. It is unclear whether that provision has been of any assistance in obtaining eviction via the police in these circumstances.

Licensees

10.92 The nature of a licence is discussed in Chapter 8.[75] A licence is a mere contract or promise under which a right to occupy or possess land is given. It creates no estate in land, unlike a lease.

10.93 The first question for the receiver is whether he can simply seek to terminate the licence by taking possession, notwithstanding that the licence on its terms could not be ended in that way. A receiver, like the borrower, could seek to end the licence in this way, and if the occupier accepted this repudiatory breach, the licence would end. Similarly, a receiver might seek an injunction requiring the occupier to leave the property on the basis that he is not obliged to perform the borrower's contract. [76]

10.94 If, however, the court would grant an injunction for the benefit of the occupier, recognising the continuation of the licence and requiring the occupier be let back in, then such an approach would fail. The circumstances in which the court would likely do so are discussed in Chapter 8.[77]

10.95 If the licence could not be terminated save in accordance with the licence terms, the receiver's next step should be to consider the terms of the licence in order to establish if the borrower has the right to terminate it.[78]

10.96 If he does, the receiver can give notice on the borrower's behalf as his deemed agent.[79]

---

[72] The date of commencement of Legal Aid, Sentencing and Punishment of Offenders Act 2012, s 144.

[73] A building is 'residential' if it designed or adapted, before the time of entry, for use as a place to live: Legal Aid, Sentencing and Punishment of Offenders Act 2012, s 144(3).

[74] Someone holding over after the end of a lease or licence does not commit an offence under this section: Legal Aid, Sentencing and Punishment of Offenders Act 2012, s 144(2).

[75] At para 8.91.

[76] This was done in *Bower Terrace Student Accommodation Ltd v Space Student Living Ltd* [2012] EWHC 2206 (Ch), though note the particular circumstances in that case.

[77] At para 8.97.

[78] See the discussion at para 8.91 *et seq*.

[79] If the deemed agency has ended by reason of the borrower's death or insolvency, it is likely that the licence will itself have ended, because a licence is a mere personal privilege, so terminates on the death or dissolution of either party. The receiver would have to decide whether to continue it, with himself as licensor, or evict the occupier.

10.97 If the licence is of a dwelling, then for a notice to terminate it to be valid, it must comply with section 5(1A) of the Protection from Eviction Act 1977.[80] The section refers to notices to terminate licences given by 'a licensor'. 'Licensor' is not further defined. It is highly likely that the receiver, as deemed agent of the borrower, can give such a notice in the borrower's name, or on his own account, as above. Even if he is not given an express power to do so, such a power is incidental to his power to enter into possession.[81]

10.98 Once the licence is determined, how can the receiver recover possession? It is unlawful for an owner of premises licensed as a dwelling, where that licence is not exempt, to enforce a right of possession against an occupier at the termination of the licence save via the court.[82]

10.99 The 'owner' means 'the person who, as against the occupier, is entitled to possession' of the premises.[83] That is apt to cover a claim by a receiver, either because his claim is in the name of the borrower, who is thus the owner, where, for example, it was the borrower who granted the licence, or where the receiver has a better right to possession than the licensor by reason of his right of possession.

10.100 Thus, if the licence is of residential property, it is likely that court proceedings for possession will be required.

10.101 Since the licence has ended, and the occupier is holding over without consent, he is a trespasser, and the special procedure for possession claims against trespassers can be used.[84] However, an interim possession order (IPO) cannot be sought, since those are only available where the property was entered without consent.[85]

Tenancies

10.102 The receiver must start by identifying what the contractual terms of the tenancy are, and what, if any, statutory protection applies, in order to determine if the tenancy has already terminated, and if not, whether the tenancy could now be terminated by the borrower. Detailed information about this is set out in the Appendix.

---

[80] See paras 8.93–8.94.

[81] *McDonald v McDonald* [2014] EWCA Civ 1049 at [65] per Arden LJ.

[82] Protection from Eviction Act 1977, s 3(1) and (2B).

[83] Protection from Eviction Act 1977, s 8(3).

[84] Note the definition of 'a possession claim against trespassers' in CPR, r 55.1(b) includes a claim where the claimant alleges that the land is occupied only by a person who remained on the land without consent (but does not include a claim against a former tenant).

[85] CPR, r 55.21(2) prevents an IPO being made against a person who entered with the consent of the person who, at the time the consent was given, had an immediate right to possession. See para 10.240 *et seq*.

10.103   The common thread is that if the borrower granted the lease and can terminate it, then the receiver can terminate it in the borrower's name and take possession proceedings, if the mortgage conditions and his appointment give him sufficient powers. [86]

10.104   Specific issues do, however, arise.

FORFEITURE AND THE RECEIVER

10.105   Most tenancies contain a forfeiture clause, which entitles the landlord to bring the contractual term of the tenancy to an end in certain circumstances. The Appendix sets out basic information about the process. In the following sections, receiver-specific issues are addressed.

CAN A RECEIVER FORFEIT IN HIS OWN NAME?

10.106   It is the landlord who can forfeit a lease, i.e. the person legally entitled to the reversion on the lease.[87] Can a receiver forfeit in his own name?

10.107   First, there is the possible argument that the receiver, by having a right to possession, has sufficient interest in the reversion to be said to be legally entitled to it.[88] This is not an easy case to make.

10.108   A secondary analysis depends on the date of grant of the lease. If it pre-dates 1 January 1996,[89] then it is highly likely that a receiver, who is entitled to the income from the land leased, can forfeit. This is the effect of section 141(1) and (2) of the Law of Property Act 1925. The person entitled to the income can recover, receive, enforce or take advantage of the rent and every covenant or provision in the lease.[90]

10.109   If the lease was granted on or after 1 January 1996, then section 141 of the Law of Property Act 1925 does not apply. The relevant Act is the Landlord and Tenant (Covenants) Act 1995. A landlord's right of re-entry goes with the reversion[91] and is hence exercisable by the person legally entitled to the reversion.

10.110   Section 15 of the Landlord and Tenant (Covenants) Act 1995 extends the class of people who can enforce the right of re-entry where any tenant

---

[86]   See the discussion at paras 10.13–10.36 and 10.60–10.84.

[87]   See para A.12.

[88]   See paras 10.76–10.83.

[89]   The date of entry into force of the Landlord and Tenant (Covenants) Act 1995, which changed the law.

[90]   See *Scribes West Ltd v Relsa Anstalt and Others (No 3)* [2004] EWCA Civ 1744, [2005] 1 WLR 1847, in which someone to whom the right to the income from a lease had been assigned was entitled to forfeit for non-payment of rent. A receiver would thus be able to serve a break notice in his own name, since it is a provision in the lease.

[91]   Landlord and Tenant (Covenants) Act 1995, s 4.

covenant or right of re-entry is enforceable by the reversioner to 'any person (other than the reversioner) who, as the holder of the immediate reversion in those premises, is for the time being entitled to the rents and profits under the tenancy' or 'any lender in possession of the reversion in those premises who is so entitled'. 'The reversioner' means 'the holder for the time being of the interest in the landlord under the tenancy'.[92]

10.111   Section 15(1)(a) of the Landlord and Tenant (Covenants) Act 1995 is not like section 141(2) of the Law of Property Act 1925, because under section 15(1)(a) someone entitled to the rents and profits must also be 'the holder of the immediate reversion' to be entitled by that section to enforce.[93] It does not appear that a receiver, even with a right to possession, could be said to be 'the holder for the time being of the interest of the landlord'.[94] Thus, it seems unlikely that a receiver can forfeit a lease in his own name, if the lease was granted after 1 January 1996.

LONG RESIDENTIAL LEASES

10.112   There are specific statutory requirements regulating forfeiture of long residential leases.[95] For each, the receiver's ability to participate in his own name under the statute is not clear from the statute:

(a)   Section 81 of the Housing Act 1996, which requires a determination that service charges are payable, does not specify who the parties to the proceedings resulting in the determination must be. Clearly, the tenant must be a party, to be bound. It is perfectly possible for the receiver to be a party, not the landlord, as a matter of principle. In any event, there is nothing to prevent the receiver with suitable powers from initiating an application for a determination as agent for the borrower.

(b)   Section 168 of the Commonhold and Leasehold Reform Act 2002, which requires a determination of breach of lease for breaches other than non-payment of service charges or rent, likewise does not specify the parties to a determination.

(c)   In section 166 of the Commonhold and Leasehold Reform Act 2002, which requires notices of rent, it is 'the landlord' who must give the tenant the section 166 notice. Under section 112(3), 'landlord' is construed by reference to 'lease'. The definition of 'lease' at section 112(2) sheds no light on whether a receiver could be included in the definition of landlord and hence whether he can serve notices other than as agent of the borrower. In any event, there is nothing to prevent the receiver with suitable powers from serving notice as agent of the borrower.

---

[92]   Landlord and Tenant (Covenants) Act 1995, s 15(6).

[93]   The reference in Landlord and Tenant (Covenants) Act 1995, s 15(1)(a) to the immediate reversion is odd, given that only the immediate reversioner would be expected to be entitled to forfeit a lease.

[94]   Note that if the receiver were included within that definition then he would be liable on the landlord covenants: Landlord and Tenant (Covenants) Act 1995, s 15(2).

[95]   See paras A.22–A.27.

NOTICES UNDER LAW OF PROPERTY ACT 1925, SECTION 146

10.113　A landlord must serve the tenant with a notice under section 146 of the Law of Property Act 1925[96] before forfeiting a lease, save if the breach is arrears of rent alone.

10.114　The requirement in section 146(1) of the Law of Property Act 1925 is service of notice by 'the lessor', where lessor is defined at section 146(5)(c) as including 'an original or derivative under-lessor, and the persons deriving title under a lessor'.[97] Unless it can be said that a receiver with a right of possession has a title derived from the lessor,[98] it seems that a receiver cannot serve a section 146 notice in his own name in relation to a lease granted by the borrower.

WAIVER OF THE RIGHT TO FORFEIT

10.115　A landlord may lose the right to forfeit for a particular breach of lease if, knowing the facts upon which the right has arisen, he acts unequivocally so as to recognise the continued existence of the lease.[99]

10.116　Various issues as to waiver arise in the context of receivership. First, a receiver may post-appointment discover a breach of lease by the tenant that occurred prior to his appointment and will not know if it has been waived. If the breach is a once and for all breach, then waiver by the borrower will be fatal to any potential attempt to forfeit the receiver might be considering.

10.117　If the breach occurs after the appointment of the receiver, it may be that the borrower will, nevertheless, waive the right to forfeit by some act of his own.[100] If the management of the property, in particular, the collection of rent and any service charges, has been moved across to the receiver successfully, the risk of waiver by the borrower may be low.

10.118　However, in the period just after the appointment of a receiver and before he has management of the property in his control, issues may arise. It is also possible, with a non-acquiescent borrower, that the borrower will deliberately interfere with management after the appointment of the receiver. In that case, if there are particular difficulties, it may be worth considering applying for an injunction to prevent particular interference by the borrower.[101]

---

[96]　See para A.21.

[97]　Law of Property Act 1925, s 146(5) also refers to 'a person making such grant as aforesaid', i.e. 'a grant at a fee farm rent, or securing a rent by condition' under s 146(5)(a). These further inclusions do not assist a receiver.

[98]　See paras 10.76–10.83 for a discussion of this.

[99]　See paras A.16–A.20 for examples.

[100]　In principle, it might be possible to argue that the borrower does not have power to waive after the receiver has been appointed, because that power is vested in the receiver, and only the receiver: see paras 6.144–6.155. No such argument has been tested as far as the authors are aware.

[101]　See *Bayly v Went* (1884) 51 LT 764, and commentary at para 6.144.

10.119 In general, an agent's knowledge of a breach is only imputed knowledge of the landlord if the agent has a duty to report matters to the landlord.[102] Although a receiver owes a duty to the borrower and others interested in the equity of redemption to take account of their interests, it is far from obvious that in general this extends to an obligation to inform the borrower of a breach of covenant by his tenant, rather than an obligation to consider whether to forfeit for that breach.

10.120 However, knowledge of a breach by an agent with full authority to manage property on behalf of a landlord can be imputed knowledge by the landlord. Moreover, an act by that agent, for example, acceptance of rent, will waive the right to forfeit.[103]

10.121 It is highly likely that a receiver who has full powers to manage the property under his appointment will thus fall into this second category. His knowledge of a breach will be imputed to the landlord, so the landlord can waive the right to forfeit. Moreover, an act by a receiver is highly likely to be capable of being an act of waiver. Thus, the receiver must be careful if the right to forfeit may have arisen.

BUSINESS TENANCIES

10.122 Part II of the Landlord and Tenant Act 1954 continues business leases, and allows landlords to seek to terminate them, subject to the lessee's right to seek a new lease, by service of a section 25 notice.

10.123 Under section 67 of the Landlord and Tenant Act 1954:

> Anything authorised or required by the provisions of this Act, ... to be done at any time by, to or with the landlord, or a landlord of a specified description, shall, if at that time the interest of the landlord in question is subject to a mortgage and the mortgagee is in possession or a receiver appointed by the mortgagee or by the court is in receipt of the rents and profits, be deemed to be authorised or required to be done by, to or with the mortgagee instead of that landlord.

10.124 Once a receiver is appointed, the lender is 'virtually substituted for the landlord'.[104] The borrower has no power to obtain possession from a business tenant, so the receiver cannot exercise that power. Further, the receiver is not the person to give or receive notices, despite his appointment, save insofar as he does so not as the deemed agent of the borrower, but as the agent of the lender.[105]

---

[102] *Metropolitan Properties Co Ltd v Cordery* (1980) 39 P & CR 10.

[103] *Central Estates (Belgravia) Ltd v Woolgar (No 2)* [1972] 1 WLR 1048.

[104] *Meah v Mouskas* [1964] 2 QB 23 CA.

[105] The receiver's right to exercise the lender's right of possession is considered at paras 10.22–10.27.

ASSURED TENANTS

10.125   Under the Housing Act 1988, termination of an assured tenancy requires service of a section 8 notice.[106] It is 'the landlord' who must serve the section 8 notice. 'Landlord' is defined in section 45(1), and its applicability to receivers is discussed above.[107]

10.126   The ability of a receiver to serve a notice under section 21 of the Housing Act 1988 to terminate an assured shorthold tenancy is discussed above.[108]

10.127   As set out in the Appendix,[109] there are a number of circumstances in which service of a notice under section 21 of the Housing Act 1988 is invalid.

10.128   The first is if the landlord does not comply with the rules in relation to paying the tenant's deposit into a tenancy deposit scheme, a notice under section 21 of the Housing Act 1988 cannot be served. A receiver may well have great difficulty in getting information about deposits from the borrower and in getting the evidence required to show compliance. Thus a receiver may well find himself considering payment of a sum at the level of the deposit to the tenant in order to ensure he can serve a section 21 notice.[110] The prudent receiver will obtain at minimum the lender's agreement to this course and an indemnity from the lender for this amount.

10.129   Another question which might arise is whether the borrower could seek an order against the receiver for repayment of the deposit (plus a penal sum).[111] The statute provides that the application is to be made against the landlord, but the landlord includes any person acting on his behalf in relation to the tenancy.[112] It is unclear from the wording whether that extended definition only includes whoever was acting for the landlord when the failure to deal with the deposit correctly occurred, or whether, as appears to be the case on first reading, it includes whoever is currently acting for the landlord. Although it appears unlikely that a receiver would have this liability if he were not appointed at the time the tenancy was granted, it cannot be ruled out.

10.130   A second limit on the validity of a notice under section 21 of the Housing Act 1988 is the scheme in section 33 of the Deregulation Act 2015, which is intended to prevent retaliatory evictions. Section 33 is subject to

---

[106]   See para A.48 *et seq.*

[107]   See paras 10.76–10.83.

[108]   See paras 10.66–10.68. Although the s 21 notice under the Housing Act 1988 in *MacDonald v MacDonald* [2014] EWCA Civ 1049 pre-dated the introduction of s 21A and s 21B and a prescribed form of notice. Nothing seems to turn on that.

[109]   At para A.62 *et seq.*

[110]   Tenants sometimes refuse to accept repayment. It seems likely, however, that a court would not permit the effect of Housing Act 2004, s 215(2A) being prevented in this way.

[111]   Of up to three times the deposit: Housing Act 2004, s 214.

[112]   Housing Act 2004, s 212(9)(a).

limitations in section 34 which limit its application where the house is subject to a mortgage granted before the beginning of the tenancy, the lender is entitled to exercise a power of sale and, at the time of service of the section 21 notice, the mortgagee requires possession for sale with vacant possession.[113] Moreover, 'mortgagee' includes a receiver appointed by the lender under the terms of the charge of the Law of Property Act 1925. Thus, a receiver should not be troubled by section 33, provided that he requires possession for sale.

BENEFICIARIES

10.131   A borrower may well hold the mortgaged property on trust.[114]

10.132   Not every beneficial interest gives a beneficiary an interest in possession,[115] and not every beneficiary with an interest in possession has a right to occupy the trust property. For a beneficiary with an interest in possession to have a right to occupy, so that the borrower could not exclude him from the property, it must be the case that 'the purposes of the trust include making the land available for his occupation', or 'the land is held by the trustees so as to be so available' under section 12(1) of the Trusts of Land and Appointment of Trustees Act 1996. Under section 12(2), a right to occupy is not conferred on the beneficiary by section 12(2) if is 'either unavailable or unsuitable for occupation by him'.

10.133   In express trusts, it is often clear whether section 12(1) of the Trusts of Land and Appointment of Trustees Act 1996 gives a beneficiary a right to occupy or not. In trusts arising under co-ownership of houses intended to be occupied by the owners, the court will likely infer such a right, though such an inference is far less likely if the property is mortgaged under a buy-to-let mortgage or was bought as an investment property.

10.134   If the beneficiary has no right to occupy under section 12 of the Trusts of Land and Appointment of Trustees Act 1996, then it is possible for the trustees to evict a beneficiary who is occupying. On that basis, it seems likely that a receiver could also evict a beneficiary, provided he has power to do what the trustees could do. However, since making a claim for possession is a trust function, it is likely that the receiver could face difficulty in showing that he the trust power to do so has been properly delegated to him to allow him to take this step.[116]

---

[113]   Deregulation Act 2015, s 34(7).

[114]   See para 8.114 for a discussion of how this might arise.

[115]   That phrase should be understood as in contrast to an interest in reversion. It is possible to have a reversionary interest in a trust, reversionary on the end of someone else's life interest, for example.

[116]   See the discussion on delegation of trustee powers at para 8.129 *et seq*.

Occupiers against whom the lender has a right to possession

10.135 The next category of occupiers is those against whom the lender has a right to possession, but the borrower does not. A receiver with only the borrower's right of possession will not be able to take possession from any such occupier.

10.136 A receiver with a right of possession co-extensive with the lender's right will have more power. Thus it is assumed for the rest of this section that the receiver has the lender's right of possession under the mortgage conditions.[117]

Disadvantages of relying on the lender's right

10.137 Suppose the mortgage has priority over a lease granted by the borrower. The lender can take possession against the tenant as a trespasser. If the receiver has the lender's right of possession, the receiver, too, can obtain possession against the tenant as trespasser.

10.138 However, the lease is not ended by the receiver[118] taking possession in this way. The reason that possession could be taken is that the lender has a right of possession as if it has a lease out of the borrower's estate. The lease granted by the borrower to the occupier takes effect as if concurrent to the lender's estate. The exercise of the lender's right to possession is not a termination of the lease; it is merely a recognition of the better right to possession of the lender.

10.139 Thus, use of the lender's right of possession by the receiver can be a useful way to obtain vacant possession, but not of terminating interests which bind the borrower and not the lender. If the receiver has only the borrower's power of sale, he will not be able to sell free of those interests, for example, the lease assumed above, despite having obtained vacant possession. He will need the lender to exercise its right of sale to ensure a transfer free of such interests.

10.140 There are certain specific statutory requirements which bite when the lender is bringing a possession claim. If the receiver is exercising the lender's right of possession, even though not as the lender's agent, there are arguments as to whether those statutory regimes apply. If they do, then reliance on the lender's right brings with it the disadvantage of statutory regulation of possession which the receivership appears otherwise to avoid.

10.141 It follows that if the borrower has a right of possession against the occupant it may be better to rely on that, than to rely on the lender's right.

---

[117] And that he is entitled to exercise that power as the deemed agent of the borrower, and not as agent of the lender.

[118] Or the lender.

The Administration of Justice Acts

10.142   In a mortgage possession claim, where a mortgagee claims possession of a mortgaged property which consists of or includes a dwelling-house, the court has powers to adjourn proceedings, stay, suspend execution of the possession order, or postpone the date for possession, if:

> It appears to the court that in the event of its exercising the power the mortgagor is likely to be able within a reasonable period to pay any sums due under the mortgage or to remedy a default consisting of a breach of any other obligation arising under or by virtue of the mortgage.[119]

10.143   It would be a benefit to lenders if the appointment of a receiver to take possession were a method of avoiding this provision.

10.144   This is particularly relevant where the receiver is seeking to take possession against the borrower,[120] though section 36 of the Administration of Justice Act 1970 applies if the lender's claim is for 'possession of the mortgaged property' and so the court's powers are available on a lender's claim for possession against the borrower's tenants, and it is likely that the borrower can apply to be joined as a party, so as to be able to make section 36 arguments, under rule 40.9 or rule 19.2 of the CPR, on such a claim.

10.145   The meaning of 'mortgagee' in section 36 of the Administration of Justice Act 1970 'includes any person deriving title under the original ... mortgagee'. The question of whether the section 36 powers are available to the court on a claim for possession brought by a receiver thus depends on whether it can be said that the receiver has title derived under the lender.

10.146   The arguments that the receiver with the lender's right of possession does derive title from the lender are like those set out above in relation to the receiver's right to serve notices in his own name when he has the borrower's right of possession.[121] The argument that he does is that 'title' simply means entitled, and in any event in property law, the meaning of 'title' is based in possession so that someone with a right of possession must be said to have title in the way it is used in most property law statutes even though he is not registered as the owner of the estate at the Land Registry.

10.147   The contrary argument is that the reference to 'title' denotes a requirement for some proprietary right, which the receiver does not have. His right to possession does not derive from a proprietary right he has, but from a power granted by the person with the proprietary right.

---

[119]   Administration of Justice Act 1970, s 36. See also Administration of Justice Act 1973, s 8 which limits the sums the court treats as due to the arrears only, not the principal sum, where the borrower is entitled or permitted to defer payment of the whole or part of the principal sum.

[120]   See the discussion at paras 10.175–10.191.

[121]   See paras 10.76–10.83.

10.148   Conversely, a receiver with the borrower's right of possession does not derive title from the lender, though his appointment is under the mortgage, because his right of possession is the borrower's only.[122]

The Housing Act 1980

10.149   There are some similar consequences in the statutory framework surrounding residential possession claims resulting from this approach. Section 89(1) of the Housing Act 1980, which limits the court's powers to postpone the date on which possession is given up,[123] does not apply where 'the order is made in an action by a lender for possession'.[124]

10.150   If a claim for possession by a receiver were to fall within section 36 of the Administration of Justice Act 1970, then it could be an action by a mortgagee under section 89(2)(a) of the Housing Act 1980. 'Mortgagee' is not further defined in section 89, so it is unclear whether this is a possible interpretation.

In whose name should the receiver act?

10.151   The other issue which arises when the receiver is exercising the lender's right to possession is in whose name the receiver should act.

10.152   The receiver is not the lender's agent. First, he has been appointed as the borrower's deemed agent.[125] Secondly, even if the lender has given him a right of possession, it has not given him the power to act in its name.[126] The lender is not put into possession of the mortgaged property by the receiver's acts.

10.153   It follows that the receiver cannot act in the lender's name in serving any notices and in issuing proceedings.

10.154   If the borrower had a right of possession against the occupier whom the lender seeks to evict, then there is no reason why the receiver cannot serve notices and issue proceedings in the borrower's name. That is what the borrower agreed to when he agreed to the deemed agency.[127]

---

[122]   That suggests a subtle argument, if the receiver has the lender's right to possession but serves notices as the borrower must to end occupiers' rights, that despite him apparently exercising the borrower's right of possession, he is exercising the lender's and is hence within the Administration of Justice Act 1970. It is likely, however, that the court would look at the reality of whose power is being exercised in determining whether the section applies.

[123]   See summary of Housing Act 1980, s 89 at para 10.223.

[124]   Housing Act 1980, s 89(2)(a).

[125]   *Cully v Parsons* [1923] 2 Ch 512 at 518.

[126]   Someone can give someone else a power without making him his agent.

[127]   See *Edenwest Ltd v CMS Cameron McKenna (A Firm)* [2012] EWHC 1258 (Ch) at [66].

10.155 There is something odd, however, about the receiver acting in the borrower's name exercising a right of possession against an occupier when the borrower could not. The better view is that the receiver should act in his own name if evicting occupiers that the borrower could not.[128] Likewise, the receiver should issue proceedings in his own name; proceedings issued in the borrower's name will face difficulties because the borrower has no cause of action.[129]

10.156 If the receiver obtains possession in his own name, then it is he who will be in possession, not the borrower.[130]

Occupiers whose rights have been created by the borrower after the receiver's appointment

10.157 Once a receiver has been appointed, any power of leasing under section 99(1) of the Law of Property Act 1925 that the borrower has is ended.[131] Moreover, it seems very likely that the effect of the appointment of a receiver with a right of possession prevents the borrower from creating new occupancy rights, whether tenancies, licences, or otherwise, which bind the receiver, at least once the receiver has taken possession.[132]

10.158 If the receiver can terminate the rights of occupancy created by the borrower because the borrower could, then he can do so in the borrower's name and take possession.

10.159 However, even if he cannot do so, because the borrower could not terminate the rights, if it is right that the borrower could not create rights binding the receiver, the receiver can take possession against the occupants as trespassers against him.

---

[128] See para 5.23. It is arguable that because of the deemed agency, the borrower has agreed to have his name used for acts, and those acts are valid, though the borrower could not do them, because the receiver has power to do them.

[129] See para 14.62. See, however, fn 149. If the argument from *Re Sartoris* [1892] 1 Ch 11 discussed there were right, and the receiver could not claim in his own name because he had no estate in land even if he has a right to possession, then he could not issue a possession claim against occupiers in his own name, though he could it seems obtain an injunction requiring them to leave.

[130] Although, presumably, he could then nominally put the borrower into possession, since he is the borrower's deemed agent.

[131] Law of Property Act 1925, s 99(19).

[132] See in relation to the extent of the displacement of the borrower's powers by the appointment of a receiver, the cases at paras 6.144–6.155, though none address the question of possession. For example *Gomba Holdings UK Ltd v Homan* [1986] 1 WLR 1301 at 1307: '[the borrower] has during the currency of the receivership no powers over assets in the possession or control of the receiver'. It is unclear whether the receiver would have had to have taken possession against the borrower, rather than against occupiers in the borrower's name, for the receivership to prevent the borrower creating rights binding the receiver. Since the borrower has given his right of possession to the receiver, it seems likely that the borrower could not say he could create new rights binding on the receiver whether or not the receiver has taken possession against the borrower, or indeed has taken possession at all, just as if the borrower had granted the receiver a tenancy and then, before the receiver took possession, sought to create a second tenancy.

Occupiers whose rights the lender could terminate

10.160   What is envisaged here is that the lender is bound by occupiers' rights, but could terminate them, i.e. either the rights pre-dated the mortgage, or the mortgage took subject to them, or the borrower has power to create new interests binding the lender,[133] or the lender has recognised the borrower's occupiers' rights so as to bind it,[134] or has granted new occupiers' rights which bind it alone.[135]

10.161   It is only in the last of these cases that there could be any need to rely on the lender's right of possession, rather than to evict the occupiers in the borrower's name.

Occupiers whose rights do not bind the lender

10.162   What is envisaged in this section is that the borrower has granted a third party a right to occupy which is not binding on the lender.[136]

10.163   For example, when a mortgage prohibits the grant of a lease by the borrower, and the borrower grants such a lease, that lease does not bind the lender.[137] Nor will leases granted after the appointment of the receiver bind the lender,[138] unless the mortgage deed makes contrary provision.

10.164   Similarly, a licence granted by the borrower contrary to the mortgage covenants could not bind the lender. An occupier may have a beneficial interest in the mortgaged property, but if that interest arises after the mortgage and without the consent of the lender, then the beneficial interest will not bind the lender.

10.165   If the borrower grants a lease or another interest or right which does not bind the lender, he binds no more than his equity of redemption with that right. He cannot give what he does not have, and he does not have an estate unburdened by the mortgage. The lender is free of the lease or other interest. That is why the lender can treat the new lessee, or occupant with another interest, as a trespasser.

10.166   If the receiver has a coterminous right to possession, he, too, can evict the occupier as a trespasser, whether or not the borrower could have done so. The receiver does not need to terminate the tenancy or licence or other right

---

[133]   For example under Law of Property Act 1925, s 99: see paras 2.63–2.72.

[134]   See Chapter 2 for example in relation to tenancies as in para.2.106(c), and see the following paragraphs for the position with other occupiers.

[135]   This would be unusual, and would likely have put the lender into possession.

[136]   For example, if the borrower's right of leasing is excluded or limited by the mortgage deed, or has ceased to be exercisable, under Law of Property Act 1925, s 99(19), by reason of the appointment of a receiver. See the discussion at para 2.69 and paras 9.141–9.156.

[137]   *Berkshire Capital Funding Ltd v Street* (2000) 32 HLR 373, CA. See paras 2.31–2.32.

[138]   Law of Property Act 1925, s 99(19). See para 2.69 for a further discussion.

granted by the borrower if he can rely on the lender's right to possession against that individual as a trespasser.

Statutory protection of unauthorised tenants

10.167 Statutory protection has, however, been given to some occupiers, which mitigates the harshness of the lender's power to evict them as trespassers.

10.168 On a mortgage possession claim, the Mortgage Repossessions (Protection of Tenants etc) Act 2010 gives a court jurisdiction, on the application of an unauthorised tenant, 'to postpone the date for delivery of possession for a period not exceeding two months'.[139]

10.169 An unauthorised tenancy is an assured tenancy under the Housing Act 1988 or a protected or statutory tenancy under the Rent Act 1977, but to which the mortgagee's interest is not subject.[140] Thus, it is a tenancy created by the borrower in breach of tenancy, or after the borrower's power, whilst in possession, to lease the land under section 99 of the Law of Property Act 1925 has been ended by the lender taking possession for example, or by the appointment of a receiver.[141]

10.170 The court, exercising the jurisdiction, must have regard to the circumstances of the tenant, and any outstanding breach by the tenant of a term of the tenancy.[142] The postponement may be conditional on the tenant making payment to the mortgagee in respect of the occupation.[143]

10.171 If the power has not been exercised when the court made the possession order,[144] the court can 'stay or suspend execution of the order for a period not exceeding two months', when the unauthorised tenant has asked the lender to give an undertaking in writing it will not enforce and the lender has not done so.[145]

10.172 The possession order may only be executed if the lender gave notice at the property in a form prescribed under the Dwelling Houses (Execution of Possession Orders by Mortgagees) Regulations 2010,[146] addressed to the tenant by name, if known, or to 'the Tenant or Occupier', by first class or registered post, or by leaving notice at the property in an envelope so addressed, or affixing and displaying it in a prominent place where its contents can be read by

---

[139] Mortgage Repossessions (Protection of Tenants etc) Act 2010, s 1(2).

[140] Mortgage Repossessions (Protection of Tenants etc) Act 2010, s 1(8).

[141] For example, if a receiver is appointed, but the borrower grants a new tenancy, rather than allowing the receiver to exercise any powers he has to do so.

[142] Mortgage Repossessions (Protection of Tenants etc) Act 2010, s 1(5).

[143] Mortgage Repossessions (Protection of Tenants etc) Act 2010, s 1(6).

[144] Mortgage Repossessions (Protection of Tenants etc) Act 2010, s 1(3).

[145] Mortgage Repossessions (Protection of Tenants etc) Act 2010, s 1(4).

[146] SI 2010/1809.

a person entering the property, or by personal service. Execution cannot be less than 14 days after notice was given.

10.173 The jurisdiction arises when a 'mortgagee under a mortgage of land which consists of or includes a dwelling-house brings an action ... in which the mortgagee claims possession of the mortgaged property'[147] and 'there is an unauthorised tenancy of all or part of the property'.[148]

10.174 Does the Mortgage Repossessions (Protection of Tenants etc) Act 2010 affect receivers, if taking possession against a borrower's tenant as a trespasser? Under section 3(5), '"mortgagee" includes any person deriving title under the original mortgagee'. The same arguments discussed in relation to section 36 of the Administration of Justice Act 1970 apply. It seems likely that the Act will apply to a receiver's claim against an unauthorised tenant. However, the matter is arguable.

The borrower

10.175 One of the most difficult conceptual questions about possession and receivers is whether a receiver with a right of possession granted by the mortgage conditions and his appointment can evict the borrower, if the borrower is in possession of the mortgaged property.

10.176 It might be thought that this is a rare occurrence, because, for example, in the residential market, receivers are rarely appointed when the mortgage is for owner occupation. However, problems arise where the borrower goes into occupation of, for example, a buy-to-let property, or remains in occupation of commercial property, or a property in course of development. Since receivership is usually available in the mortgage conditions even in owner-occupier mortgages, it is an option also worth considering in those cases.

10.177 The conceptual difficulty is that because a receiver is the deemed agent of the borrower, it seems very odd to suggest that he can take possession against his apparent principal. That conceptual difficulty is certainly a potential practical bar to convincing a court, in particular on a first possession hearing, that a possession order can be made.

10.178 Nevertheless, it is the thesis of this book that a receiver with suitable powers can obtain possession from the borrower.[149] It would be odd if it were

---

[147] Mortgage Repossessions (Protection of Tenants etc) Act 2010, s 1(1)(a).

[148] Mortgage Repossessions (Protection of Tenants etc) Act 2010, s 1(b).

[149] There is no reported decision on this issue, although both authors have separately successfully argued the point in the county court, and in *Pratchett v Drew* [1924] 1 Ch 280, the court made an order for possession against the borrower in an action by a court-appointed receiver. However, in *Patmore v Bean*, 2002, unreported, ChD, it was successfully argued that the receiver had no right to possession against the borrower, and the claim would have to be brought by the lender. It appears from counsel who acted in that case that reliance was put on *Re Sartoris* [1892] 1 Ch 11 where a receiving order was made under the then insolvency statutes, and it was said that the debtor's property did not pass to the receiver though he had a

not so, yet the receiver could evict occupiers when the borrower did not want to, because the latter shows that the receiver, not the borrower, is in control, and in that sense in possession as against the borrower.

The right to possession

10.179 There are a number of arguments why the receiver can take possession against the borrower. The first is the simplest. The borrower in the mortgage conditions agreed that the receiver would be given the right of possession over the property once appointed. A right of possession is a right to control the property to the exclusion of others. That includes the borrower. The receiver can take possession against the borrower.

10.180 The receiver's powers cannot be understood simply as agency powers, which cannot be exercised against the principal, but as first powers given to the receiver, over which, secondly, the cloak of deemed agency is drawn.[150]

10.181 However, there is a potential theoretical bar to a receiver being granted a possession order against the borrower.

10.182 A receiver can obtain an injunction against a borrower whose acts interfere with the performance of his receivership. In *Bayly v Went*,[151] a receiver obtained an injunction against a borrower who distrained for arrears of rent. In so doing, the borrower interfered with the performance of the receivership, in this case, collecting the rent.

10.183 It is not much of a step to say that a receiver can get an injunction against the borrower requiring the borrower to leave the property if vacant possession is needed for the receiver to perform the receivership, for example, if

---

right to collect the income, so that it was only the debtor who could bring proceedings for recovery of his property against third parties. A receiver appointed by the court is not at liberty to bring an action in his own name because he too has no property vested in him, but he can injunct the debtor against getting in money that the receiver is entitled to receive. It is not obvious that a receiver given an express right of possession should be treated as having no right exercisable in his name. Of course, much may depend on the scope of the receiver's powers in any given case, but where the receiver has the power to bring possession proceedings, as opposed to simply proceedings to recover the monies owing, it is considered that the receiver does have the ability to bring possession proceedings in his own name against the borrower even though neither the borrower nor the lender's estate has vested in him. In *McDonald v McDonald* [2014] EWCA Civ 1049 the receivers served s 21 notices in their own names (at [9]), which, as counsel for the tenant argued, was only permissible if they were the landlord or derived title from him. The court found the receivers had authority to serve notice, which suggests they also would have had power to take possession in their own name. See paras 10.64–10.84. In *Jennings v Quinn* [2017] NICh 21, the court decided there was 'no serious issue to be tried concerning the entitlement of the [receivers] to possession' in an interim injunction based on their claim against the borrower in trespass.

[150] See Chapter 6, for example, at paras 6.221–6.228, and, in particular, *Sowman v David Samuel Trust Ltd (In Liquidation)* [1978] 1 WLR 22 at 30C.

[151] (1884) 51 LT 764.

he has a power of sale, or indeed needs vacant possession for letting to generate an income.

10.184   It does not immediately follow that a possession order would be made in the same circumstances, however, even though the practical outcome sought is the same.[152] The law surrounding possession claims comes from the much older action of ejectment, which was based on the fiction that the claimant, the title holder, had granted a lease to a fictional John Doe, John Doe had gone into physical possession and had then been ejected by a fictional Richard Roe. The claim between the claimant and the defendant was then about who had the better title to that estate. This was a device developed to allow claims by tenants to be put back into possession which they had not been able to make by other actions.[153]

10.185   The effect of this source of the law of possession claims is that a possession claim is a claim to be put back into possession of the estate from which the claimant has been ousted[154] by someone wrongfully in possession.

10.186   This suggests a difficulty with a claim by a receiver for possession against the borrower. It might well be said on a borrower's behalf that it is not wrong for the borrower to be in possession. He owns the property. The receiver is given a right to possession, but is that actually a right which is better than the borrower's right, rather than permission to exercise the borrower's right of possession on his behalf?[155]

10.187   This view, which is commonly held, seems contrary to the wording of most mortgage covenants which give the receiver a right to possession. Once the receiver has been appointed, he has the right to exercise the powers which have been given to him, and the borrower loses his right to do so.[156] The borrower does not retain his right to possession thereafter, save with the receiver's consent, just as the borrower cannot thereafter enter into contracts which are within the scope of the receiver's powers, without the receiver's consent. The receiver's right to possession is superior to the borrower's.

The lender's right to possession

10.188   The second argument applies where the receiver has the lender's right to possession. The lender's right can prevail against the borrower, even though the receiver is said to exercise the right as the borrower's deemed agent. A claim for possession by the receiver based on the lender's power would not face the arguments above, because the lender could take possession against the borrower

---

[152]   In many cases, it will be prudent to seek possession and an injunction in the alternative.

[153]   See *Megarry & Wade* at Ch 4.

[154]   *Secretary of State for the Environment, Food and Rural Affairs v Meier* [2009] UKSC 11, [2009] 1 WLR 2780 at [6] per Lord Rodger of Earlsferry.

[155]   Something the receiver would be doing if he was acting under a power of attorney from the borrower only.

[156]   See paras 6.144–6.155.

even though the borrower retained his estate. If the borrower is wrongfully in possession as against the lender, then he is wrongfully in possession against the receiver who has the lender's right of possession. The receiver seeking a possession order against the borrower is seeking what the lender seeks, when it seeks a possession order. The lender seeks possession of its estate, not the borrower's. Even once evicted, the borrower retains possession of his estate, since he is entitled to the equity of redemption. He was only entitled to physical possession of the land whilst the mortgage covenants postponed the lender's exercise of its right to possession.

10.189   However, if the receiver relies on the lender's right to possession, it is likely that section 36 of the Administration of Justice Act 1970 will apply.[157]

Claim in whose name

10.190   It is usual to suggest that the receiver should bring all proceedings in the borrower's name, because he is the borrower's deemed agent. If he does so against the borrower, the borrower appears to be suing himself. The effect of the receiver taking possession against the borrower, and possibly against occupiers whom the borrower could not evict, is that the receiver is put into possession himself (just as he can be liable on contracts himself), and he should sue for that possession in his own name.

10.191   This is not inconsistent with the deemed agency. In principle, an agent, given irrevocable powers by his principal to control his principal's estate, could sue his principal for an injunction to prevent him from interfering with those powers. He would sue his principal in his own name. That would not defeat the agency. It would be because the agent was suing his principal on the contract with him.

Occupiers whose rights the lender cannot terminate

10.192   What the receiver cannot do, even if he has a right of possession co-extensive with the lender's right, is to evict an occupier whose rights of occupation bind the lender and the borrower. The receiver cannot be given greater powers than the lender has, because his powers come out of the mortgage. The appointment of a receiver cannot be used to get past a difficulty faced by the lender, for example, an occupant with a beneficial interest in the property binding on the lender.

10.193   A lender will not be able to terminate the right of possession of an occupant with an estate giving him a right of possession whose estate ranks ahead of the lender's charge in priority. Thus, the receiver will not be able to take possession against such an occupant, nor resist the occupant's demand for possession from the receiver, if he is in occupation.

---

[157] See paras 10.142–10.148.

10.194 Thus, a prior lender will have a better right to possession than a receiver appointed under a subsequent mortgage because he has a better right to possession than the lender who appointed the receiver, and the receiver cannot have a better right than his appointing lender.

10.195 A freehold reversioner entitled to forfeit a mortgaged lease will have a better right to possession than the receiver, because he will have a better right to possession than the lender. The question of whether the receiver is entitled to apply for relief from forfeiture, other than as the agent of the borrower, is considered in Chapter 8.[158]

10.196 If the mortgaged property is held on trust, and a beneficiary's interest has priority over the lender's,[159] and if the beneficiary is entitled to occupy the mortgaged property, then the receiver will not be able to take possession from the beneficiary.

POSSESSION PROCEDURE

Introduction

10.197 This section sets out the basics of procedure for claims for possession. The law discussed is not specific to receivership, save where explicitly mentioned, but it is necessary to understand it if the taking of possession of the mortgaged property is contemplated.

10.198 At common law, possession can be taken by peaceable re-entry,[160] or by obtaining and enforcing a possession order from the court.

10.199 However, the usual route to regaining possession of property, in particular if there is any risk that the property (whether commercial or residential by use) is being used to live in, is via the court, rather than by simply changing the locks, for two reasons.

10.200 First, it is an offence, under section 6 of the Criminal Law Act 1977, 'without lawful authority' to use or threaten:

> violence for the purpose of securing entry into any premises ... provided there is someone present on those premises at the time who is opposed to the entry which the violence is intended to secure, and the person using or threatening the violence knows that that is the case.

10.201 Secondly, in the residential case, two statutes make it a risk to take possession without a court order.

---

[158] See paras 8.180–8.182.

[159] See paras 8.149–8.151.

[160] Changing the locks.

10.202 The Protection from Eviction Act 1977 also makes any person guilty of an offence if he unlawfully deprives a residential occupier of his occupation or attempts to do so, without belief and reasonable cause to believe that the residential occupier had ceased to reside in the premises.[161]

10.203 It is also an offence to interfere with the peace and comfort of a residential occupier, or to persistently withdraw or withhold services reasonably required for occupation of the premises as a residence, if done with an intent to cause the residential occupier to give up occupation or to refrain from exercising rights or remedies in respect of the premises.[162] Section 1(3A) of the Protection from Eviction Act 1977 creates a similar offence for similar acts by the landlord, or an agent of his. It is clear that these offences are apt to capture acts if done by receivers.

10.204 Moreover, section 2 of the Protection from Eviction Act 1977 makes it unlawful to enforce a right of re-entry or forfeiture in respect of premises let as a dwelling otherwise than by proceedings in court while any person is lawfully residing in the premises or part of them. That limitation is not dependent on who is bringing the proceedings and hence includes receivers whether acting as deemed agent of the borrower or properly on their own account.

10.205 It is for this reason that possession is often sought through the courts, save where the property is known to be empty, because eviction by a county court bailiff, or a sheriff (if enforcement is via the High Court), of a warrant or writ of possession enforcing a possession order avoids the risk of these offences.

10.206 Secondly, under the CCA 1974, enforcement of a land mortgage securing a regulated agreement, regulated mortgage contract or consumer credit agreement which but for exemption would be a regulated agreement,[163] is enforceable on the order of the court only. It seems unlikely that 'enforcement' includes acts of a receiver once he has been appointed.[164] Surprisingly, however, there is little case law on this provision and it is little relied on in court,[165] so that the uncertainty surrounding it, added to the Protection from Eviction Act 1977 provisions, suggests that court proceedings for possession are advisable in the residential context.

---

[161] Protection from Eviction Act 1977, s 1(2).

[162] Protection from Eviction Act 1977, s 1(3).

[163] See Chapter 3 for a discussion of the types of mortgages which are regulated in one of these ways. Each involves an element of intended residential use of land.

[164] Although his appointment would likely be enforcement. See para 3.90 and para 4.4. The reason why exercise of the receiver of his powers would not be enforcement would be the court order on appointment would, usually, confirm that the receiver had his powers and was entitled to use them. If each act of the receiver required a separate court order, costs would escalate, and the receivership would be impractical.

[165] In part because, historically, the class of mortgages to which CCA 1974, s 126 applied was limited. It has been extended more recently, and hence more case law may result in the future.

10.207 There are cases when a court claim is not required by statute, in particular when the mortgaged property is empty.[166] The only reasons then to bring proceedings for possession rather than taking possession without a court order is to test whether the right to possession has arisen and to avoid any argument about the effect of section 126 of the CCA 1974.

10.208 If proceedings are issued and a possession order made, then eviction by enforcement of that order, provided it remains in force, is not a wrong, even if, subsequently, the order is overturned, for example on appeal.

10.209 Conversely, if possession is taken without the benefit of a court order, the occupant may then claim an injunction requiring him to be put back in, on the basis that the receiver (or the borrower as his deemed principal) did not have the right to possession against him. He may also claim damages for loss, which if the property is commercial, may include loss of business.

10.210 It may be appropriate, thus, to issue a possession claim if the question of the receiver's right to possession against the occupier is in any way contentious.

Possession orders versus injunctions

10.211 The court has a specific remedy when a claim is for possession: a possession order, sought in a possession claim. However, there are situations in which a possession order is not available, for example, when trespassers on one piece of land threaten to occupy another, neighbouring piece of land on eviction. In that case, an injunction prohibiting the occupation of the second piece of land should be sought.[167]

10.212 The distinction between a possession order and an injunction is technical in that a possession order is an order requiring someone to be put into control of an estate in land. It is not just an order requiring occupation of land to be given up by one person to another. The claimant must have an immediate right to possession, and hence to that control. Thus a possession order may not be available to a particular claimant.

10.213 The practical difference, however, is enforcement.

10.214 A possession order is an order '*in personam*',[168] i.e. it is made against the persons named as defendant only, rather than against the world at large. It is

---

[166] See *Ropaigealach v Barclays Bank Plc* [1999] 3 WLR 17 in which the mortgage took possession without proceedings. In that case CCA 1974, s 126 did not apply since the mortgage was not regulated.

[167] *Secretary of State for the Environment, Food and Rural Affairs v Meier* [2009] UKSC 11, [2009] 1 WLR 2780, which says that a possession order is not available in relation to land which trespassers are threatening to occupy, but have not yet occupied. Such a claim would usually be made under CPR, Pt 7, with perhaps an interim injunction sought prior to trial if the removal of the occupiers was urgent.

[168] *Secretary of State for the Environment, Food and Rural Affairs v Meier* [2009] UKSC 11, [2009] 1 WLR 2780 at [6].

available when the claimant proves a better right to possession against particular defendants who, in occupying the claimant's land, have ousted him from it.

10.215 Despite being an order *in personam*, a possession order is enforced by the county court bailiff or a High Court sheriff by eviction of anyone on the property at the date of the eviction.[169] Someone on the property who was not named in the litigation may apply to court before the eviction to prevent enforcement against him, or after eviction, to be let back in, if he has a better right to possession than the claimant.[170]

10.216 An injunction is usually enforced, on breach by the defendant, by committal for contempt of court, under Part 81 of the CPR, and hence, ultimately, by fine or imprisonment.[171]

10.217 Thus, a possession order results in the return of possession. An injunction is effective indirectly by the threat of criminal sanction, and, if the defendant is imprisoned and no one else is on the land, by giving an opportunity to the claimant to retake possession without, in the case of residential property, risking criminal sanction.

CPR, Part 55

10.218 The relevant part of the CPR for possession claims is Part 55.[172] Most possession claims are and must be issued in the county court. There are specific court forms for the claim form.[173]

10.219 Claims against trespassers, and where the property is let on a tenancy, have particular requirements for inclusion in the particulars of claim.[174] There is a specific court form for the particulars of claim for rented residential premises,[175] and for a claim against trespassers.[176]

---

[169] *Secretary of State for the Environment, Food and Rural Affairs v Meier* [2009] UKSC 11, [2009] 1 WLR 2780 at [6], citing *R v Wandsworth County Court, ex parte Wandsworth London Borough Council* [1975] 1 WLR 1314.

[170] *Secretary of State for the Environment, Food and Rural Affairs v Meier* [2009] UKSC 11, [2009] 1 WLR 2780 at [6].

[171] A mandatory injunction, requiring the defendant to do something, can also be enforced by an order under CPR, r 70.2A permitting someone else to take the step at the cost of the defendant.

[172] CPR, r 55.3. The CPR can be seen at www.justice.gov.uk/courts/procedure-rules/civil.

[173] Form N5 (general) and Form N5B (accelerated possession claim for possession of an assured shorthold tenancy on service of a s 21 notice). For copies, see the HM Courts & Tribunals Service website at https://hmctsformfinder. justice.gov.uk/HMCTS/FormFinder.do.

[174] See CPR, PD 55A, para 2.1 for general requirements as to the particulars of claim, paras 2.2–2.4B, for requirements for a claim where the property is let on a tenancy, and para 2.6 for a claim against trespassers. There are specific court forms for the claim form.

[175] Form N119.

[176] Form N121.

10.220 Usually,[177] when a court issues a possession claim, it will list a first, short[178] hearing at which it may: (a) make a possession order, if satisfied that the claim is made out and there is no defence; (b) dismiss the claim, if satisfied that the claim must fail, though that outcome is rare at the first hearing; or (c) give case management directions, for example, simply adjourning for a further short hearing of the claim, or longer directions towards a trial. The last of these options will be appropriate either if there simply is no time to deal with the issues raised, or if 'the claim is genuinely disputed on grounds which appear to be substantial',[179] i.e. where a defence is raised.

10.221 Under rule 55.7 of the CPR, if the defendant does not file a defence, 'he may take part in any hearing but the court may take his failure to do so into account when deciding what order to make about costs'. In practice, defendants usually fail to file a defence by the first hearing. If they can articulate a defence with realistic prospects of success, the court will likely give directions for a defence to be filed and re-list for a case management conference thereafter. It is common practice in those circumstances to ask the court to record in the order that the court will consider the making of a possession order at that case management conference if no defence has been filed by the date the court has allowed.

10.222 Certain housing statutes, regulating the taking of possession in certain circumstances for certain types of residential and other tenancies, give the court a jurisdiction to make a possession order only if it is reasonable to make it.[180] For example, tenancies protected under the Rent Act 1977 where possession is on one of the grounds specified in section 98(1); secure tenancies from local authorities and similar, under the Housing Act 1985; and assured and assured shorthold tenancies under the Housing Act 1988 where the grounds for possession are those in Schedule 2, Part II.

10.223 If the court makes a possession order it may have a discretion as to the period between the date of the order and the date on which the order requires possession to be given up to the claimant. The extent of the discretion is different for different categories of occupier:

(a) If the occupier is a trespasser who entered without any right to occupy the property,[181] then the court has no discretion and must order possession forthwith.[182]

---

[177] Save in accelerated possession claims for possession of assured shorthold tenancies on expiry of a s 21 notice under the Housing Act 1988.

[178] Ten minutes. If more time is likely to be needed, for example, on a forfeiture claim, where 30 minutes is often more appropriate, this should be requested at issue of the claim.

[179] CPR, r 55.8(2).

[180] This is the exception under Law of Property Act 1925, s 89(2)(c).

[181] If the occupier entered with permission but remained in occupation after that right ended, for example holding over after the end of a tenancy, then the court has a discretion, though that discretion is now limited by Housing Act 1980, s 89(1), as to which, see below.

[182] *McPhail v Persons Unknown* [1973] Ch 447.

(b) By section 89(1) of the Housing Act 1980, on the making of a possession order of any land not falling within one of the exceptions in section 89(2),[183] then the court has a discretion as to the period for possession, though that period is limited by section 81(1), which limits the date for possession to no later than 14 days after the making of the order, unless there appears to the court that exceptional hardship would be caused by requiring possession to be given up by that date. The maximum period the court can allow is 6 weeks after the making of the order.

(c) If the order is made on a claim by a lender for mortgage possession, then section 89(1) of the Housing Act 1980 does not apply.[184] The time period for possession is regulated by the mortgage conditions, unless the mortgage is of land consisting of or including a dwelling-house, in which case the court has a jurisdiction to adjourn the claim, or postpone or suspend the possession order, for example, on terms as to repayment of arrears, under section 36 of the Administration of Justice Act 1970, and section 8 of the Administration of Justice Act 1973.[185]

(d) If the order is made on forfeiture of a lease,[186] for arrears of rent alone, then under section 138 of the County Courts Act 1984, the court must give the lessee at least 28 days to pay the arrears and before possession must be given up. The court can give more time than that and extend the time period on subsequent applications. If the lessee complies, he will have relief from forfeiture and the lease will continue. If forfeiture is for breach of lease including something other than non-payment of rent, and the lessee seeks relief from forfeiture, then the court has a discretion as to the terms of relief, and can extend the time for possession, under section 146 of the Law of Property Act 1925.

10.224 A claimant in a possession claim can, in addition, seek a money judgment for any arrears of rent or licence fee, where applicable, for the period up to termination of any lease or licence, and use and occupation (or mesne profits), i.e. damages for trespass, until possession is returned.

10.225 Since the receiver is, subject to his precise appointment, entitled to the income from the mortgaged property, he should be entitled to sue for the same. Usually, he will be entitled to collect arrears, or damages, which accrued before his appointment, unless excluded on the wording of the mortgage conditions and

---

[183] The exceptions are: (a) where the claim is made by a lender; (b) if the order is made on forfeiture; (c) if the court could only make the possession order if it was reasonable to do so. See Rent Act tenancies at para A.45 and assured tenancies at para A.57, for example; (d) where the order relates to a dwelling-house which is subject of a restricted contract under Rent Act 1977, s 19; and (e) where the order is made on termination of a rental purchase agreement of a dwelling-house within the meaning of Housing Act 1980, s 88.

[184] This is the exception under Housing Act 1980, s 89(2)(a). In the authors' view, this will apply whenever the receiver relies on the lender's right of possession, for the reasons set out at paras 10.143–10.147 and 10.149–10.150.

[185] It is not thought that these Acts apply on a receiver's possession claim when the receiver relies on the borrower's right of possession, but see the discussion at para 10.148 and fn 119.

[186] This is the exception under Law of Property Act 1925, s 89(2)(b).

his appointment.[187] He would, of course, have to account for any sums received in his receivership.

10.226 It is usual to seek a judgment that the defendant pay the costs of the claim, if it is successful. Part 45 of the CPR imposes a fixed costs regime on possession claims where: (a) the defendant gives up possession and pays any sum claimed and the fixed commencement costs, without defending the claim;[188] (b) one of the grounds for possession is arrears of rent, and a possession order is made at the first, fixed hearing date, and the defendant has neither delivered a defence or counterclaim nor otherwise denied liability, or has delivered a defence limited to specifying proposals for payment of arrears; or (c) the claim is an accelerated possession claim for possession of a property let on an assured shorthold tenancy based on expiry of a notice under section 21 of the Housing Act 1988, and the defendant has not delivered a defence or counterclaim or otherwise limited liability. The fixed costs are low; they are limited to the issue fee and something in the order of a couple of hundred pounds.[189]

10.227 The court has a discretion to order payment of costs as incurred, rather than fixed costs. It is most likely to do so in tenancy/licence claims if there is a provision in the tenancy or licence requiring payment by the defendant of litigation costs for possession claims.[190] Otherwise, the court is highly likely to award fixed costs if possession is given at the first hearing.

Specific procedure for claims against trespassers

10.228 In the context of the CPR, 'a possession claim against trespassers' means:

> a claim for the recovery of land which the claimant alleges is occupied only by a person or persons who entered or remained on the land without the consent of a person entitled to possession of that land but does not include a claim against a tenant or sub-tenant whether his tenancy has been terminated or not.[191]

10.229 A special procedure for possession claims against trespassers falling within that definition is provided. Possession claims against other sorts of trespassers[192] are governed by the standard possession procedure described above.[193]

---

[187] See the discussion at para 9.66.

[188] CPR, r 45.1(2)(c).

[189] See CPR, Pt 45. They are varied from time to time.

[190] See *Church Commissioners for England v Ibrahim* [1997] 1 EGLR 13; *Chaplair v Kumari* [2015] EWCA Civ 798, [2015] CP Rep 46.

[191] CPR, r 55.1(b).

[192] Tenants who hold over after the termination of the tenancy. They are trespassers as against their landlord, within the meaning of that tort, but not within the meaning used in the CPR.

[193] See paras 10.218 *et seq*.

10.230   The special procedure does not apply where the person occupying was the borrower's tenant.

10.231   The special procedure also does not apply unless the person entered or remained on the land 'without the consent of a person entitled to possession'. Where the person entered before the receiver was appointed, without the borrower's consent, it is clear that the special procedure is available.

10.232   It is similarly available if the occupier entered after the receiver was appointed without his consent. If the receiver has the right to possession it is he, not the borrower, who is entitled to let people into possession.[194]

10.233   If the occupier initially had the borrower's consent to enter yet remained there without the receiver's consent,[195] then provided the receiver is a person entitled to possession, the special procedure is available. It is likely that the receiver will fall within the definition of a person entitled to possession for these purposes.

10.234   There are specific procedural requirements for trespass claims under Part 55 of the CPR. Often, trespassers in possession claims take technical points about non-compliance with the CPR in order to delay the making of a possession order, hence these requirements should be complied with. For example, there are requirements as to what must be set out in the particulars of claim.[196]

10.235   Similarly, there are requirements as to service of the claim where the names of the trespassers are not known and they are sued as 'persons unknown'. Under rule 55.6 of the CPR, service is by attaching copies of the claim form, particulars of claim and any witness statements, plus the response pack required by the CPR, to the main door or some other part of the land so they are clearly visible. In addition, the person serving should if practicable insert copies in a sealed transparent envelope addressed to 'the occupiers' through any letterbox, or place stakes in the land in places where they are clearly visible and attach to each stake copies of the same documents in a sealed transparent envelope addressed to 'the occupiers'.

10.236   Rule 55.5(2) of the CPR requires service in the case of residential land not less than 5 days before the hearing, and in the case of other land, not less than 2 days, unless time is abridged.[197] These periods are measured in clear days

---

[194]   See Chapter 6.

[195]   Assuming the receiver was not bound by the right so need not himself terminate it. The obvious example is where the receiver has the lender's right to possession and the lender is not bound by the right. If the receiver has the borrower's right to possession, the occupier will remain on the premises with consent until the right is terminated by the receiver, and will not be a trespasser in the sense of the CPR.

[196]   CPR, r 55.4 and PD 55A, in particular para 2.6.

[197]   Under CPR, r 3.1(2)(a). An application should be made for leave to serve short before the service is effected. A court may be reluctant to abridge unless there is no prejudice to the defendant.

(i.e. excluding the date of service and the date of the hearing), and weekends and bank holidays do not count.[198] Service is deemed to occur on the second business day after delivery.[199] It is not uncommon for courts to omit to factor deemed service in when fixing the hearing date, and to issue the claim with a date for hearing which does not allow time for service to occur in accordance with the rules.

10.237   The defendants in a possession claim against trespassers need not file a defence.[200]

10.238   A claimant in a possession claim based on trespass can in addition seek a money judgment for use and occupation of the property, i.e. damages for trespass. Since the receiver is, subject to his precise appointment, entitled to the income from the mortgaged property, he should be entitled to include a claim for the same.[201] He would, of course, have to account for any sums received in his receivership.[202]

10.239   In practice, in most possession claims against trespassers, the trespassers either do not identify themselves in the court proceedings, or are unlikely to have either means to pay a money judgment for damages, or indeed costs, or any property against which any such judgment can be enforced.

IPOs

10.240   If possession is sought urgently, there are two possibilities: an application to abridge time for the main hearing, or (where it is available) the IPO procedure.[203]

10.241   The IPO procedure is available for use where:[204]

(a)   the only claim is a possession claim against trespassers for the recovery of premises;

(b)   the claimant has an immediate right to possession of the premises; and has had such a right throughout the period of alleged unlawful occupation; and

(c)   the claim is made within 28 days of the date on which the claimant knew or ought reasonably to have known that the defendant (or any of them) was in occupation.

---

[198]   CPR, rr 2.8(2)–(4).

[199]   CPR, r 6.14.

[200]   CPR, r 55.7(2).

[201]   As the borrower's deemed agent, or in the name of the borrower or the lender under the statutory power: see Law of Property Act 1925, s 109(2) and (3), and paras 9.91–9.94.

[202]   See Chapter 12.

[203]   The relevant provisions of the CPR are rr 55.20–55.28 and PD 55A, paras 9.1 and 9.2. The relevant forms for completion by the claimant are Form N5 (claim form), Form N121 (Particulars of Claim against trespassers), Form N130 (application notice), Form N133 (defendant's witness statement). For copies, see the HM Courts & Tribunals Service website at https://hmctsformfinder.justice.gov.uk/HMCTS/FormFinder.do.

[204]   CPR, r 55.21(1).

10.242　If the receiver is claiming against possession against trespassers by relying on his deemed agency from the borrower and the borrower's immediate right to possession, then it is likely the borrower must have had an immediate right to possession throughout the period of alleged unlawful occupation, and the procedure will be precluded if either the borrower or the receiver knew or ought reasonably to have known of the possession. Thus, if the borrower knew or ought to have known of the trespass earlier than the receiver knew or ought to have known of it, the trespassers might well be able to argue that rule 55.21(1)(c) of the CPR has not been fulfilled.

10.243　If, as discussed above, a receiver can make a claim in trespass on his own account, then the knowledge in question is his own, not the borrower's, and the 28-day time period would run from that date even if the borrower knew of the trespass first.

10.244　Such a claim will, however, face difficulties if there were trespassers in occupation of the premises before the receiver was appointed, because the receiver as claimant will not be able to say that he has had an immediate right to possession throughout the period of alleged unlawful occupation.

10.245　Nor will the receiver be able to obtain an IPO if the borrower let the trespassers in when he had an immediate right to possession of the property. An IPO is not available against a person who entered with the consent of a person who, at the time, the consent was given, had an immediate right to possession of the premises.[205]

10.246　In either such case, the receiver will not be entitled to an IPO, and the matter will be considered by the court as a standard trespass claim.[206] The trespassers will remain in occupation until the trespass claim is heard, and a standard possession order made.

10.247　In brief, the IPO procedure is as follows.

10.248　The claimant must serve on the defendant the claim form, application notice with written evidence in support, and a blank form for the defendant's witness statement within 24 hours of issue of the application.[207]

10.249　The first hearing of an IPO is listed quickly, in comparison to other possession claims, though not less than 3 days after the date of issue.[208] At the first hearing, if the court is satisfied that the conditions in rule 55.21(1) of the

---

[205] CPR, r 55.21(2). See para 10.231. It is also questionable whether the court would permit an IPO if the borrower let the occupiers into possession during the currency of the receivership even though it is the receiver who has the right to possession, once appointed, not the borrower.

[206] CPR, r 55.25(5).

[207] CPR, r 55.23(1).

[208] CPR, r 55.22(6). Again, this is a period of clear days. In principle, the time period could be abridged under r 3.1(2)(a). Since the defendants are given very little time to prepare for the hearing, the court is unlikely to abridge time save in special circumstances.

CPR are fulfilled,[209] and the claimant has filed a certificate of service or otherwise proved service[210] and given adequate undertakings including[211] to reinstate the defendant and pay damages if the court so orders,[212] it will make an IPO. That order requires the defendant to vacate the premises within 24 hours of service of the order on it.[213]

10.250   The matter is then reconsidered at a hearing of the claim for possession, which will be not less than 7 days after the date on which the IPO was made.[214] The IPO expires on that second hearing date.[215] At the second hearing, the court may make a final possession order, or dismiss the claim, or give directions for the claim for possession to continue to trial as if a standard possession claim, or enforce the claimant's undertakings.[216]

The borrower as a third party to a possession claim

10.251   When a receiver makes a claim for possession against a borrower's tenant or licensee, it is not uncommon for the borrower to seek to defend that claim himself, or seek to influence the defence of the tenant, especially if he resists the validity of the appointment of the receiver. Issues as to the right of the receiver to take possession are often introduced into litigation in this way.

10.252   Although the claim for possession is not against the borrower, since he is not in possession of the property in this scenario, the court does have power to join him as a defendant at any time.[217]

10.253   It may also do so if an order is made, and the borrower applies to set it aside, under rule 40.9 of the CPR which allows a person who is not a party to a claim but is 'directly affected by a judgment' to apply to have it set aside or varied. The answer to the question of whether the borrower is 'directly affected' will depend on the particular facts in the case.

10.254   A borrower is not directly affected by a possession order against a tenant in the sense that he is not himself dispossessed by that order. However, the effect is to prevent the borrower from collecting rent from that tenant. If the borrower's case is that the receiver is not validly appointed, then that might well be enough for an application under rule 40.9 of the CPR.

---

[209]   CPR, r 55.25(2)(b)(i).

[210]   CPR, r 55.25(2)(a).

[211]   See CPR, r 55.25(1) for the full text of the required undertakings.

[212]   CPR, r 55.25(b)(ii).

[213]   CPR, r 55.25(3).

[214]   CPR, r 55.25(4).

[215]   CPR, r 55.27(2).

[216]   CPR, r 55.27(3).

[217]   CPR, r 19.2 gives the court the power to add a new party if it is desirable so that all the matters in dispute in the proceedings can be resolved, or there is an issue involving the new party and an existing party which is connected to the matters in dispute in the proceedings, and it is desirable to add the new party so that the court can resolve that issue.

10.255 A borrower who does not question the appointment of the receiver so admits that the rent from his tenant is to be collected by the receiver, but does say he has no right to possession, may still be directly affected by the judgment if the effect is that no rent will be paid (and the property not likely sold).

10.256 Alternatively, the borrower could apply to be added as a party, or the receiver could so apply, under rule 19.2 of the CPR on the basis that it is desirable to add him so that the court can resolve all the matters in dispute in the proceedings,[218] or there is an issue involving the borrower and an existing party, the receiver, which is connected to the matters in dispute and it is desirable to add the new party so that the court can resolve that issue.[219]

10.257 Despite the additional complexity in the litigation introduced by the joinder of the borrower, there may be a benefit because the borrower will be bound by any decision by the court, for example, on the validity of the appointment of the receiver, or his right to possession. If the borrower is likely to be a serial resistor of the receiver's actions, this may well be of assistance beyond eviction of the particular occupier against whom the receiver started the claim.

DUTIES

10.258 Just as with any other receivership power, the receiver must exercise his right to possession in accordance with his duties.[220]

10.259 The key issues to consider when a receiver is deciding whether to evict occupiers will likely depend on the receiver's strategy for fulfilling his primary duty to pay down the debt. If sale with vacant possession is likely to pay the debt off entirely, then it does not seem likely that it would be in breach of duty for the receiver to evict the current occupants to improve the prospects of that outcome.

10.260 If, however, sale is not a likely outcome, and the occupants are paying market rent, then it is harder to see why eviction would be an appropriate exercise of the receiver's powers. It seems likely that eviction would simply increase costs and might lose the income stream already available from the mortgaged property, with increased losses faced by the borrower.

10.261 Borrowers often complain that a receiver has evicted his rent-paying tenants. The effect of the eviction on the borrower is not irrelevant to the receiver's decision to do so, but the extent of that relevance should not be exaggerated. The receiver's primary duty is to the lender, and if the receiver considers that obtaining possession from the tenants will, overall, enable him to

---

[218] CPR, r 19.2(2)(a).

[219] CPR, r 19.2(2)(b).

[220] See para 6.64 *et seq.*

pay down the debt more effectively, the receiver will not be in breach of duty in evicting them.

10.262 However, a receiver who evicted paying occupiers, when there is no plan in place with prospects of obtaining a better return from the property, could be in breach both of his duty to the lender, and his secondary duties to those interested in the equity of redemption.

10.263 A receiver owes no duty to the borrower to notify him of the receiver's intention to seek possession from the borrower's tenants.[221]

10.264 The other issues which specifically arise in relation to possession, when considering the receiver's duties, are whether a breach of those duties could arise where:

(a) the receiver acted in the borrower's name so as to put the borrower in breach of statute, for example, by taking possession from a residential occupier without court proceedings;[222] or

(b) if the receiver waived the right to forfeit a lease, thus preventing the borrower from obtaining his estate unencumbered.

10.265 It is considered that the issues around waiver of the right to forfeit are similar to those considered above: if the receiver's acts are consistent with the discharge of his primary duty, the borrower will not be able to complain. On the other hand, if the receiver waives the right to forfeit inadvertently, in circumstances where keeping the tenancy on foot was not the best way to pay off the debt, the receiver is likely to be in breach.

10.266 It is more difficult to see that the receiver's duties would ever require him to act so as to breach a statutory requirement, and this should be avoided.

THE RECEIVER IN POSSESSION

10.267 If a receiver has taken possession against an occupant who the borrower could have evicted, and done so in the name of the borrower, then he is not in possession. The borrower remains in possession, though it is the receiver who has the control by reason of the deemed agency.

10.268 If, however, the receiver has taken possession against an occupant who the borrower could not have evicted, then it might be concluded that he has put himself into possession.[223] Similarly, if he takes possession against the borrower, then it might be said that he has put himself into possession.

---

[221] *JL Homes v Mortgage Express and Diakiw and Heap* [2013] EWHC 3928 (Ch).

[222] Protection from Eviction Act 1977, s 3, where the obligation is on the 'owner' of the property.

[223] Because he had dispossessed the borrower by evicting his occupiers, and occupied the property himself as principal. See *Richards v Overseers of Kidderminster* [1896] 2 Ch 212, though see

10.269 It is unlikely that that makes the receiver personally liable on any freehold or leasehold covenants.[224] The lender would not be liable on the leasehold covenants, since the mortgage is a sub-demise of the borrower's leasehold term, and a sub-lessee would not be liable to the landlord.

10.270 This raises issues about the extent to which the receiver is to be treated or can act as if, for example, he were the leaseholder. This is discussed above.[225]

10.271 It also raises questions about the extent to which the receiver may become liable for rates, and under other statutes which impose liability on the occupier. This is discussed above.[226]

---

also *Rees v Boston BC* [2001] EWCA Civ 1934, [2002] 1 WLR 1304 at [64], which suggests that since the act would be within the scope of the receiver's authority as deemed agent even that would not be enough to put the receiver in possession.

[224] Save as discussed above and at paras 8.201–8.206.

[225] See paras 8.188–8.191, for example.

[226] See paras 8.218–8.223.

Chapter 11

Sale and the Receiver

INTRODUCTION

11.1　This chapter is about sale of the mortgaged property when a receiver has been appointed. Despite the historical association between receivership and collection of income, lenders often appoint receivers with the intention that the receivers will get possession of the property and sell it, or get possession so that the lender can sell without the lender having to take possession proceedings.

11.2　Anyone who has ever bought or sold their own mortgaged house will have some understanding of how such a sale works. Typically, the owner sells in his own name, using the purchase money from the buyer to pay off the mortgage so that he can sell free of it. When a lender sells as mortgagee, the process is different. Although the lender does not have the borrower's estate, it has the power to sell that estate, free not only of the charge, but of the equity of redemption, and thus the charges and interest over which the mortgage has priority.[1]

11.3　Where a receiver is involved, it is necessary first to establish whether the receiver is exercising the borrower's power of sale, or the lender's. A receiver can act in a number of different capacities, depending on the terms of the mortgage conditions and his appointment, and whether other powers have been given to him:

(a)　he can act as the borrower's agent using the borrower's power of sale, if granted to him in the mortgage conditions;
(b)　he can act under a separate power of attorney from the borrower; or
(c)　he can use a lender's express power of sale, if the mortgage conditions so provide, to sell in the name of the borrower or the lender.[2]

11.4　Which of these he has, and which he uses, will affect the sale: whether he has an ability to sell so that the sale overreaches later charges and interests as the lender's sale would do, or whether he must obtain the discharge of the mortgage under which he was appointed, and must redeem or sell subject to any later charges or interests not binding on the lender, because he sells only as the

---

[1]　See para 2.136.
[2]　See para 2.129.

borrower could.[3] The necessary conveyancing steps likewise depend on the power of sale the receiver is exercising.[4]

11.5   Thus, this chapter first considers when the receiver will have the different powers to sell; it then discusses the exercise of each of those different powers; and, lastly, some general points about sale, including a consideration of the receiver's duties on sale, are discussed.

THE RECEIVER'S POWER OF SALE IN THE MORTGAGE CONDITIONS

11.6   The first question for any receiver considering whether to sell the mortgaged property is whether he has the power to do so, and, if so, whether that power is the borrower's, so that he will sell subject to the mortgage and any interests in the property which bind the borrower, or whether that power is the lender's so that he can sell free of the mortgage and of interests over which the mortgage has priority. The latter is more powerful.

11.7   Since the statutory powers of receivership are limited principally to receipt of income,[5] if the receiver is to have a power of sale, of whichever kind, he must be given it in the mortgage conditions.

11.8   Some mortgage conditions are drafted quite clearly to give a receiver the lender's power of sale to be exercised by the receiver as the deemed agent of the borrower. For example, the then GMAC mortgage conditions set out in *Horsham Properties Group Ltd v Clark*[6] included within the powers of the receivers not only an express power of sale,[7] but also a power 'to exercise all powers which the [lender] has by statute or under this mortgage', with both powers expressed as given to the receivers to exercise as the agents of the borrower.[8]

---

[3]   See *In Re White Rose Cottage* [1964] Ch 940 at 951 for a description of the difference between a power of sale as the borrower could sell, and the lender's power of sale.

[4]   The different regimes which govern use and distribution of the proceeds of a sale by a receiver depending on whether the sale is under the delegated power of the lender, or is a sale in the name of the borrower, are considered in Chapter 12.

[5]   Law of Property Act 1925, s 109(3). See para 9.45.

[6]   [2008] EWHC 2327 (Ch), [2009] 1 WLR 1255 at [20].

[7]   Presumably, a power of sale given by the borrower to the receiver, and thus a power to sell in the borrower's name and subject to any interests affecting the borrower's estate, and to the mortgage.

[8]   In *Horsham Properties Group Ltd v Clark* [2008] EWHC 2327 (Ch), [2009] 1 WLR 1255, sale was effected by the receivers under their power of sale, seemingly without thought being given to which power was being engaged. This appears to have continued in court: at [5] of the decision it is said that the receivers transferred as agents for the lender, GMAC, but there is no discussion of how that conclusion had been reached, given that the receivers were expressly the agent of the borrower. However, at [32] Briggs J said that the receivers had no statutory power of sale conferred by the Law of Property Act 1925, which was part of his reasoning that Human Rights Act 1998, Sch 1, First Protocol, Art 1 was not engaged, as the sale of the property did not involve the state. Since the terms of the mortgage purported to give the receivers the

11.9 Other examples of powers are less explicit about whose power the receiver is being given. For example, in *Phoenix Properties Ltd v Wimpole Street Nominees Ltd*,[9] the receiver's power was 'to sell or concur in selling ... any of the property hereby charged by the' borrower.[10] That power was 'a very different kind of power of sale than that conferred by statute on the mortgagee'[11] and appears to have been understood by Mummery J as the borrower's power of sale.[12]

11.10 Care is thus needed in determining the nature of a power of sale given to the receiver in the mortgage conditions. A power to sell the mortgaged property, where no reference is made to the lender's powers, is likely to be construed as a power to sell as the borrower could sell, subject to all interests binding him, unless there is something in the context to suggest that it was intended that the lender should have an express power of sale capable of delegation.

THE RECEIVER WITH THE BORROWER'S POWER OF SALE

11.11 This section discusses exercise of the borrower's power of sale by the receiver. First, how the power arises is considered, then issues relating to entry into a contract for sale, and, lastly, the transfer and registration requirements.

How the power arises

11.12 It is common for mortgage conditions to give the receiver an express power of sale.[13] Often, on the true construction of the mortgage, this will be the borrower's power of sale, which will vest in the receiver automatically on his appointment (if not excluded by the lender when making the appointment).

11.13 The borrower has a power of sale by reason of his ownership of (and registration as owner of) the legal estate. As any other owner of property can, the borrower is able to give third parties a power to dispose of it.[14] This means

---

lender's statutory powers, it is not obvious that that statement is correct (though an exercise of a statutory power given to receivers under private law would not likely engage the Human Rights Act 1998 in any event).

[9] [1992] BCLC 737.

[10] [1992] BCLC 737 at 741d.

[11] [1992] DCLC 737 at 743f.

[12] He describes it as 'sale on behalf of the mortgagor': [1992] BCLC 737 at 743g, and indeed the lender released its charge which would have been unnecessary if the power of sale was the lender's.

[13] See paras 11.6–11.9 for a discussion of express powers of sale in the mortgage conditions, and examples of powers at para 5.25.

[14] It is inherent in the ownership of a freehold or leasehold estate that the owner has a power to sell or otherwise deal with it. The owner can give a power to sell or deal with the estate to someone else, who can exercise it even though that person is not the owner. That is the nature of a power: 'a power of appointment is a power of disposition given to a person over property not his own by someone who directs the mode in which that power shall be exercised by a

that the borrower can give a receiver such a power so that he can convey good title to a purchaser.[15] A receiver is appointed by the lender after the grant of the mortgage. However, whomever the lender appoints as receiver, that receiver is entitled to exercise the receiver's power of sale in the mortgage conditions.[16]

11.14 In general, the terms of the mortgage will also make the receiver, exercising the power of sale, the borrower's deemed agent. The effect of such a provision is that the borrower will be bound by other terms in the sale contract, not just the promise to convey the property, provided that contracting with such terms is within the receiver's powers.[17]

11.15 An issue arises, however, when the borrower's estate is held on trust, either because of an express trust, or because there is a beneficial interest by reason of a resulting or constructive trust. For example, the problem always arises where there is more than one person on the title, so that there are joint registered proprietors.[18]

11.16 Registered proprietors of an estate in land have owner's powers to deal with it, for example by mortgaging it or selling it.[19] However, when an estate in land is held on trust, so that the registered proprietors are the trustees, then those proprietors when they decide to mortgage, or lease, or sell the property, are exercising powers as trustees. The problem is that, as a matter of trust law, trustees have a limited power to delegate their own trust powers.

11.17 If there is a trust of the borrower's estate at the date of the mortgage and the date of the appointment of the receiver,[20] then the delegation of the borrower's power of sale to the receiver was the delegation of a power by a

---

particular instrument': *Freme v Clement* (1881) Ch D 499 at 504. However, note the complication where the borrower holds the property on trust, discussed below.

[15] *Phoenix Properties Ltd v Wimpole St Nominees* [1992] 1 BCLC 737 at 743h.

[16] As a general rule, if a power is conferred not on a named individual, but by a class of persons described by an office, for example, as in mortgage covenants, a receiver, then the power can be exercised by anyone holding the office. See G Thomas, *Thomas on Powers* (Oxford University Press, 2nd edn, 2012) (*Thomas on Powers*) at para 7.81. See also *Phoenix Properties Ltd v Wimpole Street Nominees Ltd* [1992] BCLC 737 at 742c: since the mortgage is made by deed, a power of attorney in the mortgage conditions is validly made by deed even though the specific receiver has not been so appointed. Moreover, a reference to the receivers in a contract of sale entered into by them was apt to include receivers subsequently appointed by the same lender in their place so that the second receivers could serve notice to complete: *TBAC Investments Ltd v Valmar Works Ltd* [2015] EWHC 1213 (Ch) (under appeal).

[17] Which is likely unless the receiver used very unusual terms.

[18] Since either the joint proprietors hold on trust for themselves as joint tenants in equity, or as tenants in common (in undivided shares), or for beneficiaries including a third party. See para 8.113 *et seq* for further discussion of trusts.

[19] Land Registration Act 2002, ss 23 and 24(a).

[20] If the receiver's appointment pre-dated the trust, then the borrower would have delegated his power prior to the trust arising, and trustee issues should not arise. If there was a trust in place when the mortgage was executed or when the receiver was appointed, but not on both dates, it is unclear whether the delegation would be caught by the trust rules.

trustee. It is thus a question of trust law whether such a delegation was possible.[21]

11.18 Were the trustees authorised, under the terms of the trust, to delegate their power of sale in these circumstances?

11.19 Where it is practically necessary and/or in accordance with common practice for a legal owner to delegate a particular type of decision to an agent, the trustee will have the power to make such a delegation.[22] Trustees have power to enter into a mortgage.[23] Given that a term requiring the borrower to delegate his power of sale to the receiver is standard in the market place, it is likely that the trustees will have power to delegate the power of sale to the receiver in the event of mortgage default.

11.20 An alternative approach is suggested by the Land Registry. Paragraph 4.1 of Land Registry Practice Guide 36A suggests that where there is a trust of land, the borrower could delegate the power of sale to one or more receivers, under section 11 of the Trustee Act 2000.[24]

11.21 Certainly, the mere signing of a contract for sale, or the execution of a transfer by a receiver for trustees, are delegable acts, since both are simply administrative acts. Section 11 of the Trustee Act 2000 would permit the delegation. However, it is less clear that section 11 would allow delegation of the decision to sell, to whom, and on what terms.

11.22 The difficulty with section 11 of the Trustee Act 2000 is that it does not allow delegation of functions relating to whether or in what way any assets of the trust should be distributed.[25] If this expression includes the decision to sell,[26] then the trustees are not entitled to delegate their power of sale to the receiver, nor give him a power of attorney permitting him to make decisions as to sale. However, by section 24, if a trustee purports to authorise a person to exercise a function of theirs as an agent when he was not able to do so, the authorisation is not invalidated. Notwithstanding section 11, it is likely that the receiver would have the power to sell the property in the borrower's name.[27]

---

[21] See para 8.129–8.139 for a detailed discussion of trustee powers to delegate in the context of receivership.

[22] *Speight v Gaunt* (1883) 9 App Cas 1.

[23] Trustees of land have a power to mortgage since they have all the powers of an absolute owner of the land: Trusts of Land and Appointment of Trustees Act 1996, s 6(1). However, s 6(6) prevents exercise of the powers under s 6(1) in contravention of any other enactment.

[24] See paras 8.133–8.137 for a discussion.

[25] Trustee Act 2000, s 11(2)(a).

[26] As suggested in *Thomas on Powers* at para 6.16.

[27] The borrower might be liable to the beneficiaries if they suffer loss as a result of an unlawful delegation to the receiver, as suggested in *Thomas on Powers* at para 6.44. It seems that the answer to the issue is that the delegation is wrongful but not void, contrary to the position under the previous law: *Re Boulton's Settlement Trust* [1928] Ch 703; *Walia v Michael Naughton Ltd* [1985] 1 WLR 1115.

11.23 Land Registry Practice Guide 36A gives detailed commentary on trust issues in relation to transfers executed by receivers under a power of sale, and under a separate power of attorney, but does not expressly address this issue and does not suggest that a transfer by the receiver where there is a trust is void.[28]

The contract

11.24 The receiver should contract in the borrower's name.

Terms of the contract

11.25 Although the receiver does not have the benefit of section 101(1)(i) and (2) of the Law of Property Act 1925, which add to the lender's statutory power of sale a wide discretion as to the terms of sale and transfer, a receiver with a power of sale is likely to be found to have an incidental power to decide the terms of that sale.[29] He should exercise those powers in accordance with his duties.[30] For a standard sale, it is likely that use of standard conditions will be appropriate.

11.26 Typically, the purchaser will want vacant possession of the property on completion and to take it free of incumbrances. If a receiver cannot deliver vacant possession and a clean title, it is likely to have a significant impact on the price which he obtains. There are three particular issues which the receiver may encounter.

11.27 First, a transfer by the receiver under the borrower's power of sale will be subject to any rights which bind the borrower. This is a particular problem if, for example, the borrower has let the property in breach of mortgage, or there are beneficial interests.

---

[28] It appears that the Land Registry has required receivers to give evidence that the delegation of the power of sale or a power of attorney was compliant with Trustee Delegation Act 1999, s 1, i.e. that the borrowers had a beneficial interest in the property at the date of the transfer. In those circumstances, a power of sale could be validly delegated. Since receivers usually could do no such thing, this made transfers by receivers under the borrower's power of sale, or a power of attorney, difficult. If the Land Registry had such a requirement, then a sale by the lender under its power of sale would be preferable. Land Registry Practice Guide 36A does not suggest there is currently any such requirement either when the receiver executes under a power of sale or under a power of attorney. However, Land Registry Practice Guide 9, on execution under a power of attorney, at para 4 suggests that the Land Registry requires a written statement by the attorney within 3 months of the date of the transfer that the donor had a beneficial interest in the property, or other evidence that the donor of the power of attorney had a beneficial interest at the relevant time, in the absence of which, execution by the donor would be required. At para 7.2 it also appears to require such evidence. It is unclear why this is not expressly required in Land Registry Practice Guide 36A.

[29] *McDonald v McDonald* [2014] EWCA Civ 1049 at [65] (appealed to the Supreme Court on other issues); *M Wheeler & Co Ltd v Warren* [1928] Ch 840 as to the receiver's incidental powers.

[30] See para 6.64 *et seq* and paras 11.174–11.178.

11.28 If the receiver has a sufficient right to possession,[31] he will be able to take possession from any occupants. That may involve ending some of the occupant's rights. For example, where the borrower has granted assured shorthold tenancies which are terminable by the borrower, the receiver will be able to terminate them and gain possession.[32]

11.29 If, however, the receiver takes possession against an occupant as a trespasser, because he has the lender's right to possession, then that will not end the occupant's rights against the borrower, and sale under the borrower's power of sale will not be free of them.[33]

11.30 In those circumstances, a transfer under the lender's power of sale, either by the lender, or by a power of attorney given to the receiver by the lender to act in the lender's name and as its agent, in executing the transfer, is preferable because the transfer will be free of interests which bind the borrower and not the lender. Indeed, a transfer under the lender's power of sale is often a safer route because it ensures that every interest capable of being overreached on such a sale is overreached.

11.31 Secondly, there may be issues about the borrower giving up possession on completion. Although the purchaser will be able to sue the borrower for possession (because the borrower is, by the contract, promising to give vacant possession), in practice, many purchasers may require the receiver to obtain possession from the borrower in advance if there is any doubt about the borrower's willingness to vacate, or a substantial price reduction. The receiver's ability to obtain possession from the borrower is discussed in Chapter 10.[34]

11.32 The third issue as to vacant possession is where the borrower's chattels, or those of an occupant, are left in the property. Unless the mortgage is extensively drawn, those chattels will not form part of the security and cannot be sold under the power of sale. Moreover, on a contract which requires vacant

---

[31] The lender's right. See para 10.22 *et seq.* The receiver with the lender's right will be able to take possession from any occupant whose right does not bind the lender.

[32] See Chapter 10.

[33] It will not end the occupant's rights because the reason the lender, and hence the receiver, can take possession is that the occupier's interest does not bind it. The occupant's rights as against the borrower are unchanged by possession being taken. For example, if the occupier is the borrower's tenant, the taking of possession under a lender's power does not terminate the tenancy either at common law or, if applicable, under the Housing Act 1988 or other such statutes. The occupier could sue the borrower for possession if the borrower returned to possession. Unless the buyer of the mortgaged property took free of the occupier's interest, the occupier could sue the buyer for possession after completion. That is why sale under the lender's power of sale which would overreach the occupier's interest so that it would be certain that the buyer took free of it may be advisable.

[34] At paras 10.175–10.191.

possession to be given to the purchaser on completion, the presence of chattels at completion can amount to a breach of a covenant to give vacant possession.[35]

11.33 Although the breach will be the borrower's, since the contract will be in his name,[36] such an issue may well delay completion of the sale and increase costs. It may thus be preferable for the receiver to resolve any problem before completion.

11.34 There are two ways in which he can do so. First, if the receiver has a right to possession of the mortgaged property (before sale) then that is a right to vacant possession so the receiver may seek an order requiring the borrower or occupant to remove all of the chattels.[37] In any event, the receiver will be a bailee of the chattels, with limited duties to preserve them, and may make use of the procedure under the Torts (Interference with Goods) Act 1977, which permits their sale if the owner does not remove them on statutory notice.[38]

11.35 If the receiver does not have a right of possession, then the lender will have to use its rights to ensure removal of the chattels and to ensure that the mortgaged property is empty and vacant possession can be given at sale.

The effect of the contract on the purchaser

11.36 Unlike exercise of the lender's power of sale, the purchaser will not have the benefit of section 104(2) of the Law of Property Act 1925.[39] Thus, the purchaser will wish to see that the lender's power to appoint the receiver has arisen, including any requirements as to notice of any breach.[40]

The effect of the contract on the borrower

11.37 Since the contract will be in the borrower's name, it will bind him, and the buyer will be able to sue him for a failure to complete and any other breaches.

11.38 It is also difficult to see why a court would or could prevent entry into a contract or its completion by injunction against the receiver, assuming the

---

[35] If the chattels are such an impediment as substantially to interfere with the enjoyment of the right of possession of a part of the property: *Cumberland Consolidated Holdings Ltd v Ireland* [1946] KB 264.

[36] See para 8.207.

[37] An injunction, a breach of which is a contempt. Since actual removal is what is sought, an order under CPR, r 70.2A, allowing the receiver to remove the chattels at the borrower's cost, if the borrower fails to do so, may be appropriate. Alternatively, any money judgment might in principle be enforced by sale of the chattels under the appropriate court procedure on enforcement. Reference should be made to the CPR.

[38] It is possible that the costs of removal and storage, etc could be added to the mortgage debt on suitable mortgage conditions. This is more likely to be possible if possession is taken by the lender, than a receiver, though insofar as dealing with the chattels was an expense of the receivership, the cost of so doing would be payable out of the income of the property or on sale.

[39] See para 2.139.

[40] As per Law of Property Act 1925, s 103, if the receivership were statutorily based.

receiver were acting in good faith and not in breach of duty to the borrower.[41] After all, a receiver validly exercising a power of sale is doing no wrong to the borrower,[42] so that a claim for an injunction would have no basis.

11.39 Even if the claim was based on bad faith or a breach of duty, at an interim injunction application, a court might well prefer to allow the receiver to proceed, since he is more likely to have money to pay any damages to the borrower, if there were such a breach, than the borrower to him.[43]

11.40 Entry into a contract by a receiver does not suspend the equity of redemption, unlike a contract made under the lender's power of sale.[44] Presumably the point is that the lender's sale will overreach the mortgage itself, but a sale by the borrower is only ever of the equity of redemption unless the borrower redeems the mortgage as part of that sale.[45]

11.41 It follows that the court has jurisdiction to consider making an order under section 91 of the Law of Property Act 1925 directing a sale of the mortgaged property by the borrower, notwithstanding the receiver's contract.[46]

11.42 Despite this decision that the equity of redemption is not suspended, the case law strongly suggests that the borrower's power to sell ends when the receiver is appointed.[47] If the borrower purports to sell after the receiver has

---

[41] If, however, the borrower alleged the receiver was in breach of duty, for example, by selling at an undervalue, the position might be different. See para 6.118 and para 14.112 for example. But see for example *Lederer v Allsop LLP*; *sub nom Lederer v Kisby* [2018] EWHC 754 (Ch), in which an interim injunction based on a claim of invalid appointment restraining a receiver's sale was discharged. The prevention of sale simply increased the costs of management of the deteriorating property, and the borrower could not give a good cross-undertaking.

[42] Indeed the receiver could injunct the borrower to prevent him entering into a contract if that was an interference with the receivership. See para 6.144.

[43] Assuming a valid appointment.

[44] In *National Westminster Bank Plc v Hunter* [2011] EWHC 3170 (Ch) at [9], Morgan J decided that the principle in *Property & Bloodstock Ltd v Emerton* [1968] Ch 94, that a contract by the lender suspends the equity of redemption so that the borrower cannot prevent completion by redemption of the mortgage does not apply where the contract is by the receiver exercising the borrower's power of sale.

[45] There is an argument that, in an appropriate case, this might be revisited. The reason given in *Lord Waring v London Manchester Assurance Co Ltd* [1935] Ch 310 relied on in *Property & Bloodstock Ltd v Emerton* [1968] Ch 94, for suspension of the equity of redemption on a contract under the lender's power of sale was that the statutory powers at Law of Property Act 1925, s 101(1)(i) gave the lender a power to bind the borrower, so that when the lender contracted to sell, that contract bound the borrower and the court would not grant an injunction against completion of the sale unless the contract was entered into in bad faith. The equity of redemption is extinguished on completion. On that explanation, it is hard to see why a contract by a receiver with an express borrower's power of sale would not have the same effect. The reason for the suspension is that equity will no longer intervene to allow redemption. That seems as likely conclusion in a sale by the receiver under the borrower's power of sale, as it is when the sale is under the lender's power. Indeed, if it is right, as per the cases in paras 6.144–6.155, that the borrower cannot exercise receiver's powers once the receiver has been appointed, then the precise effect is that the borrower cannot sell if the receiver has the power of sale.

[46] It would be unusual for the court to so order in those circumstances. See paras 2.60 and 2.61.

[47] See paras 6.144–6.155. The apparent reason for the confusion is that the borrower is deemed to have owner's powers as registered proprietor under Land Registration 2002, s 24.

been appointed, the receiver is likely to be able to restrain completion by injunction, if he has good reason to do so.[48] If completion takes place and the transfer is registered, the borrower's estate will be deemed to be vested in the purchaser,[49] but the mortgage will remain unless it is discharged.[50]

11.43 If the borrower has already contracted before the receiver is appointed, how does this affect the receiver's ability to sell?[51]

11.44 The borrower's contract is not ended by the appointment of the receiver and can be enforced against the borrower via an order for damages or, in principle, specific performance. The borrower has divested himself of the power to complete it because he has given that power to the receiver,[52] but nevertheless if the borrower were to complete, and the transfer were registered, the purchaser would be deemed the owner.[53]

11.45 As a general principle, the receiver need not perform the borrower's contracts.[54] It is less clear whether this is the case where the contract is for sale of the property, since it is more common for the remedy of specific performance to be available to a purchaser of land than for many other contracts because land is unique, so that damages are less often an adequate remedy.[55] The mere appointment of a receiver is not enough to prevent such an order being made.[56]

11.46 An order for specific performance of a contract will not be made when there has been delay, or the grant of the remedy would cause hardship, or it is

---

[48] For example if he would not be in breach of duty in preventing completion, or completing the contract himself. The most likely circumstances when the receiver will be able to resist sale are when the sale price is below market value, or will not redeem the mortgage.

[49] Land Registration Act 2002, s 58.

[50] Assuming it is registered: Land Registration Act 2002, s 29. In practice, there will usually be a restriction on the title of the borrower's estate to prevent registration without the consent of the lender. Thus registration will unlikely be possible. The lender will still be able to sell free of the interest of the borrower's purchaser. That interest will remain in equity only, whilst unregistered, and is in any event later in priority to the mortgage. Even if the purchaser's interest is completed by registration, where there is no restriction for example, it will be subject to the undischarged mortgage, and hence the lender will be able to sell.

[51] See also the discussion at paras 8.19–8.34.

[52] See paras 6.144–6.155.

[53] Land Registration Act 2002, s 58. The purchaser will take the estate subject to the mortgage assuming it is registered, by reason of s 29. See above.

[54] *Airlines Airspaces v Handley Page* [1970] 1 Ch 193. See para 8.7.

[55] A court considering a claim for specific performance will first consider whether damages are an adequate remedy for the claim. If they are, an order for specific performance will not be made. Thus it is a threshold requirement for an order for specific performance to be made that damages are not an adequate remedy. However, even if that threshold is passed, since the remedy is equitable, the court need not make an order for specific performance. Damages are more likely to be an adequate remedy if the property is being bought for a generic purpose, for example where it is a freehold reversion and hence bought for the income stream not the specific property, or one of a number of properties used for buy-to-let purposes where there is a good market in such properties. Conversely, damages are not likely to be an adequate remedy if the property is being bought for the buyer to live in, or to run a specific commercial operation in.

[56] *Freevale Ltd v Metrostore (Holdings) Ltd* [1984] 1 Ch 199. But see paras 8.10–8.18.

impossible. It is these last two that are most likely to assist the receiver in resisting a claim by the borrower's purchaser for specific performance against the borrower:[57] if the sale would not redeem the mortgage and hence would leave the borrower in hardship, or would be impossible to complete because the mortgage would not be redeemed, or because the receiver, not the borrower, had the power to sell[58] and was in no breach of duty in refusing to do so because the sale was not at market value. In those circumstances, it is likely that an order for specific performance against the borrower would not be made.

11.47 If the receiver is aware that the borrower is planning to complete a prior contract and he has a good reason for seeking to prevent it, for example, because market value is not being obtained, he can seek an injunction seeking to restrain completion: an attempt by the borrower to complete his sale is likely an interference with the receivership, capable of prevention by injunction.[59] An order is likely for similar reasons to those why an order for specific performance would not be made.

11.48 Moreover, the receiver can enter into a contract with a different buyer, despite the existence of a pre-existing contract by the borrower.[60] His ability to complete that contract free of the existing borrower's contract will depend on the effect of section 29 of the Land Registration Act 2002.

11.49 If the borrower's prior contract is protected by notice, or is an overriding interest, or whilst the purchaser has a priority search, the receiver will not be able to sell free of it by using the borrower's power of sale. Transfer under the receiver's contract, if completed, will be subject to the earlier contract if it is protected by notice or as an overriding interest.[61] Thus, transfer under the receiver's contract may need to be under the lender's power of sale, so that it can be free of any such interest created by the borrower.[62]

---

[57] The only way in which a claim could be made by the purchaser against the receiver, to force him to complete the contract, was if the purchaser could argue he had an interest in the equity of redemption, and hence the receiver had a duty to him. In that case, a claim would be defeated if the receiver, in refusing to complete, was acting in good faith and not in breach of his duty, for example, because the sale would not redeem the mortgage debt and/or was not at market value. Otherwise, the receiver owes no duty to the purchaser and is not in any contractual relationship with him.

[58] Although that seems a reason arising just out of the existence of the receivership, without more, and hence contrary to the position suggested in *Freevale Ltd v Metrostore (Holdings) Ltd* [1984] 1 Ch 199 (where it was not argued).

[59] See para 6.144.

[60] After all, the borrower could contract more than once. See the discussion at paras 8.19–8.34.

[61] Under Land Registration Act 2002, s 29(1) and Sch 3. If the borrower's contract does bind the receiver's buyer on registration, the borrower's buyer would be able to call for specific performance of his contract as against the receiver's buyer. It would not necessarily follow that he would get such an order. That would depend on whether the receiver's buyer could make out one of the bars to such an order as to which see below.

[62] Use of the lender's power of sale, which is considered at para 11.87 *et seq*, would enable the receiver's purchaser to take free of the prior contract.

11.50 Likewise, if the borrower completed his contract but it was not registered,[63] then that transfer would operate in equity only. It would bind the receiver's purchaser on completion and registration of the receiver's contract only if protected by notice on the register, or as an overriding interest. It, too, could be defeated by a transfer under the lender's power of sale.

11.51 If two contracts are in existence, there is likely to be a risk of a battle of completion, and one or other of the receiver or the borrower, or indeed the purchasers, may seek an injunction to prevent completion of the other contract.

11.52 As between the borrower and the receiver, the receiver is highly likely to have the better argument, provided he entered into his contract in good faith without a breach of duty.[64] The receiver will have a power of sale and likely a power of attorney from the borrower. The borrower can no longer exercise the powers he gave to the receiver, including the power to execute a transfer.[65]

11.53 If, as is likely, the purchasers are involved, the question of whether to prevent completion of one contract, or give specific performance of the other, will depend on considerations common when a court is asked to exercise an equitable discretion. Thus relevant factors will be the order in which the contracts were entered into, delay in completion in either case, the effect on each party if a contract is not completed, and the practical possibility of completion by registration free of the mortgage under each of the contracts. A bar to registration because the lender will not release the charge or give consent under the restriction may well be a bar to the making of an injunction or an order for specific performance.[66]

Transfer and registration

11.54 First, a point common to all sales: any sale of the borrower's estate will require completion by registration.[67] Any application to change the register, including by registering a transfer, is made by Form AP1, to which must be attached the relevant transfer and any other documents required by the Land Registry.

---

[63] For example, because this was prevented by the lender's restriction on the title.

[64] If, knowing of the first contract, he entered into the second at a purchase price which would achieve less in proceeds of sale, a claim by the borrower based on breach of duty might well succeed.

[65] See paras 6.144–6.155, but note the difficulty that the borrower retains owner's powers which include powers to transfer property, under Land Registration Act 2002, ss 23 and 24, and see *Freevale Ltd v Metrostore (Holdings) Ltd* [1984] 1 Ch 199 and *Telemetrix Plc v Modern Engineers of Bristol (Holdings) Plc* (1985) 1 BCC 99417, which suggest to the contrary. See paras 8.10–8.18 where this is further discussed.

[66] See the more detailed discussion in Chapter 8, fn 26 and at para 8.16(a).

[67] If the borrower's estate were unregistered, a disposition on sale would trigger first registration: Land Registration Act 2002, s 4(1)(a). If it is already registered, a disposition on sale will require completion by registration: s 27(2)(a). A failure to register will prevent the disposition operating a law (ss 47(1) and 27(1)), so that it will have effect in equity only and be much more vulnerable.

11.55 Land Registry Practice Guide 36A[68] sets out what the Land Registry will require if a transfer by the receiver is to be registered and the effect.

11.56 The Land Registry requires evidence of the identities of the parties to a transfer[69] when there is an application for that transfer to be registered. The usual method of proving identity, and by far the easier,[70] is for identity to be proved by the conveyancers[71] for the parties to the transaction, in panels 12 to 14 of Form AP1. The reason is that conveyancers, who are members of a regulated profession, should themselves take steps to satisfy themselves of the identities of the parties at the beginning of their instruction.[72]

11.57 If the receiver exercises the borrower's power of sale, the requirements of the transfer, the application to register it and the effect of that registration are those of a sale by the borrower.

11.58 The Land Registry will require to be produced with the AP1 the mortgage and mortgage conditions[73] or certified copies, evidence that the power of appointment of the receiver has arisen[74] and a certified copy of the instrument of appointment of the receiver. This is so that the Registrar can satisfy itself that the power to appoint a receiver has arisen,[75] and the receiver has been appointed. If more than one receiver has been appointed, then the Registrar will need to be satisfied by the deed of appointment whether they have power to act jointly and/or severally.[76]

---

[68] 'Receivers appointed under the provisions of the Law of Property Act 1925'. Transfer and completion of property sales is a topic of some complexity. Recourse should be had more generally to practitioners' texts, and to the Land Registry Practice Guides.

[69] The buyer, and likely the receivers not the borrower, though the guidance does not make this clear. The requirements as to proof of receivership suggest that it is the receiver's identity which must be certified. After all, even if the borrower were dead or lost, the power to appoint a receiver with the express and statutory powers would remain, so the identity of the borrower does not seem as important.

[70] Otherwise, identity must be proved directly to the Land Registry.

[71] Defined by reference to the Legal Services Act 2007 in Land Registration Rules 2003 (SI 2003/1417), r 217A.

[72] See Land Registry Practice Guide 67 (evidence of identity; conveyancers) for further details.

[73] If it does not already have copies from registration of the mortgage. The Registrar will check proper execution of the mortgage, and that the mortgage conditions allow appointment of a receiver with a power of sale. He will also check registration of the mortgage at Companies House under the Companies Act 1985 or 2006, where those apply to company borrowers: Land Registry Practice Guide 36A, para 7.

[74] Usually a certificate from the lender.

[75] The Registrar will not enquire whether the power has become exercisable, i.e. whether the requirements of Law of Property Act 1925, s 103 (and see s 109(1)) or similar conditions precedent to appointment in the mortgage conditions have been fulfilled. See Land Registry Practice Guide 36A, para 2.2. The reason is that a purchaser will not need to satisfy himself of exercisability, but that the power has arisen only: s 104(2).

[76] Since this effects for example execution of the transfer deed. If the power is to act jointly only, both must take each step in the receivership, and both must execute the transfer. If the power is joint and several, then each could act alone.

11.59 Paragraph 2.2 of Land Registry Practice Guide 36A requires the receiver to disclose to the Registrar 'any challenge to the validity of the mortgage … (which will affect the power to appoint) which is within the actual knowledge of the … receiver …' both at the date of the Form AP1, and later.[77]

The transfer

11.60   The form of transfer must be by Form TR1 (if all of the registered estate is to be transferred), or Form TP1 (if part only of the registered estate is to be transferred). These are the forms of transfer the borrower would use.

11.61 Paragraph 5 of Land Registry Practice Guide 36A suggests signature may be by the receiver expressed as execution 'on behalf of the borrower'.[78] The section in the transfer for execution should be in the following form:

> signed as a deed by [name of borrower] by [AB] its receiver pursuant to powers granted to him/her by clause XXXX of a mortgage dated [date] in favour of [name of lender] in the presence of [signature, name and address of witness]. Signed [name of borrower by name of receiver] his receiver.[79]

11.62 Alternatively, where the borrower is a company, the transfer can also be made, at the direction of the receiver, by being sealed by the company using its common seal in the presence of the duly authorised officers of the company, or signed as a deed by a director or secretary of the company.[80]

---

[77] Presumably, this is simply an instance of Land Registration Act 2002, s 71, which imposes a duty to provide the Registrar with information about overriding interests under Sch 1 (on first registration) and Sch 3 (on a registrable disposition of registered land). The intention is to allow the Registrar to service notices on, for example, the borrower, to allow him to object to the registration of the transfer, and reduce the possibility of a later application for alteration of the register on the basis that the receiver did not have any power to give good title, and with the risk to completeness of the register, and that the Registry would become liable for the payment of an indemnity under s 103 and Sch 8. If there were such an objection, it would be determined by the First-tier Tribunal (Property Chamber). For more information on objections and indemnities and when they are payable, see any practitioner's text on registration.

[78] This is described as execution on behalf of the borrower, and not under a power of attorney. It is unclear what difference the form of signature could make. The receiver does not need a power of attorney to execute the transfer: see Land Registry Practice Guide 36A, para 2.3: the receiver's power:

> to sell the mortgaged property and execute a conveyance or transfer of it in the name of the borrower … is itself a power of attorney in favour of the receiver, whether or not it is expressed as such, and whether or not the mortgage also contains a specific power of attorney in favour of the receiver. The receiver does not need to execute a transfer as attorney; it is sufficient if they are expressed to execute it on behalf of the borrower …

[79] Land Registry Practice Guide 36A, para 5. Land Registry Practice Guide 8: execution of deeds, at para 7.3. It is unclear why the receiver cannot just sign in his own name since he has the power of sale.

[80] Land Registry Practice Guide 36A, para 5.

Restrictions on registration

11.63 A sale under a receiver's power of sale given by the borrower is a sale subject to the interests which bind the borrower. For that reason, the receiver must ensure compliance with any restrictions on the register of title which would otherwise prevent registration of the transfer executed by the receiver under his power of sale.

11.64 Since the sale is not free of the mortgage under which the power of sale arises, if there is a restriction for the benefit of the lender, then consent to registration must be obtained from the lender. As a matter of practicality, that should not be difficult to obtain. The sale will either be at a price sufficient to redeem the mortgage, or the receiver will, prior to contracting, or prior to executing the transfer, ensure that sale at a lower price than the redemption figure will not prevent the lender releasing the restriction.

11.65 More difficult will be compliance with any restrictions for the benefit of subsequent mortgages with later priority than the mortgage under which the receiver was appointed. Such a restriction[81] will catch a sale by the receiver under a power of sale from the borrower, because the sale will be treated as if by the registered proprietor.[82] The receiver is unlikely to be able to obtain the necessary consent to registration of a transfer unless the subsequent mortgage can be redeemed out of the proceeds of sale.

11.66 If sale is likely to be at too low a price for such redemption, then it is likely to be preferable to pursue sale under the lender's power of sale, either by the lender executing a Form TR2 or a Form TP2, or by the receiver so executing on the lender's behalf under a power of attorney from the lender. In that case, the restriction for the benefit of the subsequent mortgage will not prevent registration of the transfer.

11.67 Likewise, if a receiver sells under a power of sale from the borrower, any trust related restriction will need to be complied with. This can cause particular issues.[83]

11.68 The first issue is satisfaction of a Form A restriction.[84]

11.69 If the borrower, i.e. the registered proprietor of the freehold or leasehold estate that the receiver is selling, is two people, then a transfer by the two

---

[81] Most lenders will enter a restriction on the borrower's title to prevent sale without the lender's consent. The standard mortgage restriction permits a transfer for example by a prior mortgagee under its power of sale without the consent of the later lender: for example Form L 'no disposition of the registered estate by the proprietor of the registered estate is to be registered without a certificate signed by the lender or his conveyancer'. See Land Registry Practice Guide 19 and para 7.12.

[82] The receiver's power of sale does not entitle him to do what the borrower could not do.

[83] See paras 8.129–8.138 for delegation of trustee powers.

[84] See Chapter 8, fn 124 and para 8.114 for a discussion.

borrowers together[85] would not be caught by the Form A restriction since that affects a transfer by a sole proprietor. Paragraph 3.1 of Land Registry guide 36A suggests that in these circumstances, the two borrowers together could delegate the power of sale to one or more receivers, under section 11 of the Trustee Act 2000,[86] and that sale and execution of a transfer by even a sole receiver so appointed would be sufficient to satisfy the Form A restriction.

11.70 However, the beneficial interests under the trust would not be overreached by a transfer by a single receiver appointed in respect of joint borrowers. Although the transfer would be registered, the Form A restriction would remain. The purchaser or the receiver would have to apply separately for cancellation of the restriction with evidence that there was no third party beneficial interest to be overreached,[87] or that any beneficial interest there was lost priority on the transfer under section 29(2) of the Land Registration Act 2002 because the third party beneficiary was not in actual occupation and hence not protected by Schedule 3, paragraph 2.

11.71 Two receivers would have to be appointed for overreaching. The view expressed in paragraph 3.2.1.1 of Land Registry Practice Guidance 36A is that there must be at least two receivers, to satisfy sections 2(1)(ii) and 27 of the Law of Property Act 1925, and hence for the beneficial interests to be overreached. The reason is that section 7(1) of the Trustee Delegation Act 1999 prevents satisfaction of section 2(1)(ii) of the Law of Property Act 1925 by a single attorney acting for two or more trustees, not acting together with any other person or persons.[88]

11.72 In these circumstances, the Registrar should be satisfied that there has been overreaching and thus cancel the Form A restriction.

11.73 If there is only a single registered owner (a single borrower), then the Land Registry guidance is that even if two receivers are appointed, the Form A restriction will not be satisfied, and the transfer cannot be registered.[89] The only

---

[85] As necessary, since joint legal owners have to act jointly, and hence must both execute a transfer and accept the purchase money.

[86] But see discussion at paras 8.133–8.137 as to why such a delegation may be problematic.

[87] Because the Form A restriction was entered when there was a trust which had subsequently ended without its cancellation, or if the only beneficiaries were the registered proprietors who thus conveyed both their legal and beneficial interests on the transfer by the receiver, their deemed agent.

[88] Trustee Delegation Act 1999, s 7(2). A receiver appointed under Trustee Act 2000, s 11 by two trustees to execute a transfer and receive the purchase money, would, it is suggested in Land Registry Practice Guide 36A, para 3.2.1.1, be subject to the restriction in Trustee Delegation Act 1999, s 7 by reason of Trustee Act 2000, s 13(1) since the powers under the Trustee Act 2000 are 'subject to any restriction or exclusion imposed by … any enactment…': Trustee Act 2000, s 26(b).

[89] See Land Registry Practice Guide 36A, para 3.1. If the receiver is given a power of sale, though he is the deemed agent of the borrower, it is not right that he stands only in the shoes of the borrower. However, since Form A is designed to ensure overreaching of beneficial interests under Law of Property Act 1925, s 2(1)(ii) and (2), and that requires sale by two or more individual trustees, a sale by a receiver, unless viewed as an agent of the borrower, could never it appears overreach beneficial interests on sale.

practical solution to a problem such as this is a sale by the lender under the lender's power of sale, since that will not require compliance with the Form A restriction.[90]

11.74 If there is a restriction in Form B,[91] or a restriction requiring a beneficiary's consent to the registration,[92] the receiver is likely likewise to have difficulties in obtaining consent and will only be able to have the transfer registered if he were to make a successful application to the Land Registry to cancel the restriction on the basis that the estate is not subject to the trust of land despite the restriction.

Effect on other interests

11.75 If sale is under a receiver's power of sale given by the borrower, not the lender, then that sale will not be free of the mortgage, nor of any charges or interests whether they are earlier or later in priority to the mortgage.

11.76 Thus the lender will need to discharge the mortgage and any later mortgages or charges will likewise need to be discharged if sale is to be free of them.

11.77 Thus the purchaser will take subject to[93] any registered charge which is not discharged on sale, any interest protected by notice on the register, unless a successful application is made to cancel it, and the unregistered interest of anyone protected under Schedule 3 to the Land Registration Act 2002.[94]

11.78 In particular, if the borrower's estate is subject to a trust, with someone else having a beneficial interest in the estate, then on registration of a conveyance by the receiver, the purchaser will only take free of that beneficial interest under section 29(1) of the Land Registration Act 2002 if it is not protected by reason of Schedule 3, paragraph 2.[95] This is a particular risk if possession of the mortgaged property has not been obtained.

---

[90] Save for in the exceptional case that the restriction expressly captures a sale by the lender under its power of sale. The alternative is appointment of new trustees by the court under Trustee Act 1925, s 41(1) on the basis that it is expedient to do so, and inexpedient difficult or impracticable to do so without the assistance of the court. That is likely to be an expensive and uncertain route.

[91] No disposition by the proprietors of the registered estate is to be registered unless one or more of them makes a statutory declaration or statement of truth, or their conveyance gives a certificate, that the disposition is in accordance with the trust deed. See Land Registry Practice Guide 19, and para 7.2.

[92] A Form N restriction: see Land Registry Practice Guide 19, para 7.14.

[93] See Land Registration Act 2002, s 29.

[94] In particular, under Land Registration Act 2002, Sch 3, para 2, an interest belonging at the time of the disposition to a person in actual occupation.

[95] Protection of an interest belonging at the time of the disposition to a person in actual occupation. But see the discussion of overreaching above.

SALE UNDER A POWER OF ATTORNEY

11.79 Mortgage conditions often give the receiver a power of attorney[96] which allows the receiver to enter into a contract in the borrower's name and to execute a transfer as his attorney.

11.80 A sale or transfer under a power of attorney has the same effect as a sale under the borrower's power of sale delegated to the receiver,[97] but a power of attorney is legally a little different,[98] and the Land Registry requires a different form of execution by a receiver acting under his power of attorney to one exercising a power of sale and requires additional evidence of the validity of the power.

11.81 Land Registry Practice Guide 8 sets out the forms of execution appropriate for execution under a power of attorney.[99]

11.82 Land Registry Practice Guides 9 and 36A set out some additional evidence required on an application for registration, if the transfer was executed under a power of attorney.[100]

11.83 First, the Registrar will want evidence of the power of attorney. In the case of a receiver, the mortgage conditions and the appointment should suffice.[101]

11.84 Secondly, the Registrar will require evidence of non-revocation of the power of attorney if the transfer post-dates the power of attorney by more than

---

[96] A power of attorney at common law does not need compliance with the requirements as to form in Powers of Attorney Act 1971, s 10 and Sch 1 (in particular, the requirement there that a power of attorney must be said to be made under the Act). The Act did not displace the common law rules. The power must be made by deed, but a mortgage deed referring to mortgage conditions containing the power, and the subsequent appointment of the receiver, will suffice: *Phoenix Properties Ltd v Wimpole Street Nominees Ltd* [1992] BCLC 737 at 742c.

[97] Indeed, Land Registry Practice Guide 36A, paras 2.3 and 5 say that the power of sale is itself a power of attorney. It is unclear why two separate powers are needed. The Land Registry will treat a disposition as under the power of sale, not a power of attorney: para 5. The only reason appears to be that execution under a power of attorney is more easily understood by judges. See for example *Phoenix Properties Ltd v Wimpole Street Nominees Ltd* [1992] BCLC 737, in which Mummery J found a sale by a receiver valid because of the power of attorney, without explaining why the express power of sale was not sufficient.

[98] See the discussion at paras 6.229–6.243. A power of attorney is a true agency, though the normal agency duties may not apply because the power is analysed as a security for the lender's proprietary interest, but see para 6.238 for difficulties with this analysis.

[99] See Land Registry Practice Guide 8, para 9.5.1. These are not required for execution under the borrower's power of sale.

[100] As noted in Land Registry Practice Guide 36A, para 5, the power of sale is itself a power of attorney, but where the transfer is executed under a power of sale, the Registrar does not require this additional information. If a receiver with the borrower's power of sale executes under a power of attorney, he will in addition have to provide the documents referred to at para 11.55. Were the transfer executed by a receiver where sale is under the lender's power of sale, then the documents referred to at para 11.119 will also be required.

[101] See Land Registry Practice Guide 9, para 6.

12 months.[102] Evidence is by a statutory declaration or statement of truth from the purchaser that at execution of the transfer he did not know of any revocation, or of any bankruptcy, death or mental incapacity of the individual borrower, or winding-up of the company which could revoke the power. A certificate by the conveyance certifying the same will suffice. Clearly, if this cannot be provided, the transfer should be executed under the receiver's power of sale, or the lender's instead.[103]

11.85 In addition, where the property is trust property (including co-owned property) the Land Registry requires evidence that the power of attorney was compliant with section 1 of the Trustee Delegation Act 1999, i.e. that the borrowers had a beneficial interest in the property at the date of the transfer.[104] Receivers will often be in difficulty in providing such evidence.

11.86 If the receiver can execute as the borrower's agent, it is hard to see why execution under a power of attorney would be preferable.[105] Indeed, execution under a power of attorney may be more problematic, for example if the borrower is insolvent, and, if a company, has been wound up. It is clear the ability to execute under the borrower's power of sale survives such an event.[106] It is less clear that a power of attorney does unless properly construed it is irrevocable.[107]

THE RECEIVER EXERCISING THE LENDER'S POWER OF SALE

11.87 This section discusses the extent to which a receiver can exercise the lender's power of sale. The lender's power of sale is discussed in Chapter 2.[108]

---

[102] See Land Registry Practice Guide 9, para 5. Since Powers of Attorney Act 1971, s 5 protects someone dealing with an attorney whose power has been revoked provided he does not have knowledge of the revocation, the Registrar usually does not require any such evidence in general use of a power of attorney, though it appears he always does so where such a power is used in receivership. See s 5(4) for the conclusive presumption where the transaction was within 12 months of the date the power came into operation, and the person dealing with the attorney makes a statutory declaration as to his lack of knowledge of revocation within 3 months of the transaction.

[103] The Land Registry seeks no such evidence if the receiver exercises the borrower's power of sale.

[104] Land Registry Practice Guide 9, para 4.

[105] The Land Registry will treat a disposition as under the power of sale, not a power of attorney: Land Registry Practice Guide 36A, para 5. The only reason appears to be that execution under a power of attorney is more easily understood by judges. See, for example, *Phoenix Properties Ltd v Wimpole Street Nominees Ltd* [1992] BCLC 737, in which Mummery J found a sale by a receiver valid because of the power of attorney, without explaining why the express power of sale was not sufficient.

[106] See para 6.174.

[107] See para 6.238. The difficulty with irrevocability of a power of attorney to a receiver is that the receiver has no proprietary interest for which the power is a security, unlike the lender. But at common law, the irrevocability requirement did not require the attorney to have the interest: see para 6.239.

[108] See paras 2.121–2.140.

The key to it is that the lender, once the power of sale is exercisable, can sell the mortgaged property free of any interest later in priority to the mortgage, and in the name of the borrower.[109]

11.88 The first issue is whether the power of sale can be delegated by the lender to the receiver to be exercised by the receiver acting as the deemed agent of the borrower.

11.89 Next, entry into a contract by the receiver under such a delegated power is discussed, both the formal requirements and the effect on the borrower. Lastly, issues arising out of execution of the transfer and the application to register it are set out. These issues include the form of execution, the documents required by the Land Registry on an application to register and the effect on other interests in the borrower's estate.

Delegation of the power

The ability to delegate

11.90 The purpose of receivership is to allow steps to be taken to pay down the mortgage without the lender having to risk the potential liabilities of a mortgagee. Receivership is a device which, via the deemed agency of the receiver, prevents the borrower or a third party from suing the lender for a wrong by the receiver. It would thus be useful to the lender if a receiver could be given the lender's power of sale so that he could exercise it as the deemed agent of the borrower.

11.91 Indeed, some mortgage conditions are drafted to give a receiver the lender's power of sale to be exercised by the receiver as the deemed agent of the borrower. For example, the then GMAC mortgage conditions set out in *Horsham Properties Group Ltd v Clark*[110] appear to delegate the lender's power of sale to the receiver.[111] In *Horsham*, sale was effected by the receivers under their power of sale.[112]

11.92 The starting point in considering whether the lender's power of sale is delegable is discussion of delegability of powers more generally. An absolute

---

[109] Law of Property Act 1925, ss 88, 89 and 104. See paras 2.129 and 2.136.

[110] [2008] EWHC 2327 (Ch), [2009] 1 WLR 1255 at [20].

[111] See above.

[112] *Horsham Properties Group Ltd v Clark* [2008] EWHC 2327 (Ch), [2009] 1 WLR 1255 at [5] states that the receivers transferred as agents for GMAC, but there is no discussion of why that was given that the receivers were expressly the agent of the borrower. At [32], Briggs J said that the receivers had no statutory power of sale conferred by the Law of Property Act 1925, which was part of his reasoning that Human Rights Act 1998, Sch 1, First Protocol, Art 1 was not engaged as the sale of the property did not involve the state. Since the receivers had been given the lender's statutory powers, that statement does not seem quite right, though an exercise of a statutory power given to receivers under private law would not likely engage the Human Rights Act 1998 in any event.

owner of an estate in land can always delegate his powers. Thus, the borrower can give the lender, or the receiver, powers in the mortgage conditions. Likewise on the establishment of a trust, the trustees can be given powers.

11.93 Many powers, once created, cannot by their nature, be delegated.[113] That general principle does not apply if, as a matter of construction of the instrument conferring the power, it was intended that the power should be delegable.[114]

11.94 There are, however, various presumptions which apply:

(a) If the power is a special power, to dispose of the property to someone within an identified class of persons, then it is unlikely to be delegable.
(b) If, however, the power is a general power (to dispose to anyone), or a hybrid power (to dispose to anyone other than identified individuals), then it is likely to be delegable.
(c) If the power is conferred in circumstances which suggest that confidence is being reposed in the particular donee, then it will not be delegable.[115]
(d) If the power is delegated to the donee for the donee's own benefit, then it is likely to be delegable.[116]

11.95 It is of little doubt[117] that a lender can by power of attorney appoint a receiver, or indeed any other person, to sign a contract of sale the lender has decided to enter into, or likewise execute a conveyance, on the lender's behalf even if that sale or conveyance is in the exercise of the lender's statutory or express power of sale. That signature or execution is not a discretionary act; the lender has made the decision to sell.[118]

11.96 Can the lender go further and delegate its decision of whether to sell?

11.97 In order to answer this question, it is necessary to identify the instrument which creates the power. If the lender's only power of sale is the statutory power under section 101(1)(i) of the Law of Property Act 1925, though this is

---

[113] Prior to the Trustee Act 2000, many trustee powers could not be delegated to non-trustees, though the Act has extended the ability so to delegate.

[114] *Tasarruf Mevduati Sigorta Fonu v Merrill Lynch Bank and Trust Co (Cayman) Ltd* [2011] UKPC 17, [2012] 1 WLR 1721, especially at 52–53.

[115] For an example, see *Re Crunden and Meux's contract* [1909] 1 Ch 690. Trustee powers are an example.

[116] *Tasarruf Mevduati Sigorta Fonu v Merrill Lynch Bank and Trust Co (Cayman) Ltd* [2011] UKPC 17, [2012] 1 WLR 1721, especially at 52–53.

[117] Although the possibility is not mentioned in the relevant Land Registry Practice Guide 75, see especially para 2.1.

[118] Just as a trustees can execute a deed by an attorney. A trustee can delegate his decision to sell in only limited circumstances however, since that decision is discretionary. See *Thomas on Powers* at Ch 6.

capable of variation and extension by the mortgage terms,[119] the power cannot be delegated by the lender to a receiver.[120]

11.98 However, if, on the true construction of the mortgage terms: (a) a separate power of sale is given to the lender, and (b) that power is delegable to the receiver, then there is, in the authors' view, no reason why this delegation should not be effective.[121] *Phoenix Properties Ltd v Wimpole Street Nominees Ltd*[122] does not deal with the question of whether an express power of sale can be delegated to the receiver in the mortgage conditions as a fixed charge power.[123]

11.99 It is likely to be necessary for the mortgage terms to spell out that something other than an extension of the statutory power is intended, and that a different result, as regards the ability to delegate, is intended. If this were done, the following arguments could be deployed to uphold the validity of the delegation:

---

[119] Law of Property Act 1925, s 101(3).

[120] *Phoenix Properties Ltd v Wimpole Street Nominees Ltd* [1992] BCLC 737 especially at 743f. The argument run was that that power of sale was a variation or extension of the lender's statutory power of sale, and hence the receiver could exercise that power. That argument failed. The reason given by Mummery J was that some of the statutory powers of a lender were expressly made delegable in the Law of Property Act 1925: the power of leasing under s 99(19), for example. The lender's statutory power of sale was not. The reference in s 101(3) to express variation or extension of the s 101(1) powers, and hence of the statutory power of sale, could not include a variation or extension to allow a receiver to exercise that power. Strictly, the decision to this effect is *obiter* because the decision was that sale was effected under the receiver's power of attorney, and may properly be confined to the proposition that the lender's statutory power of sale is not delegable within s 109(3) so as to pick up the deemed agency in s 109(2), rather than not delegable at all. Moreover, the statutory power itself has the indicia of a delegable power since it can be exercised by 'any person for the time being entitled to receive and give a discharge for the mortgage money' (s 106(1)) so that sale by the mortgagee under the statutory power does not appear even to be limited to the original lender nor someone deriving title under him. Although the authors consider it possible to argue, in an appropriate case that the comments are wrong, this book is written on the basis that the view there expressed is correct. No case contradicts *Phoenix*, though it appears the receiver sold under the delegated lender's statutory power of sale in *In Re GL Saunders Ltd (In Liquidation)* [1986] 1 WLR 215.

[121] In *In Re B Johnson & Co (Builders) Ltd* [1955] Ch 634 at 662, Jenkins LJ discussing the receiver's duties on sale said: 'his power of sale is, in effect, that of the mortgagee'. Note that such an express lender's power of sale will have the statutory effect of over-reaching under Law of Property Act 1925, ss 88 and 89.

[122] [1992] BCLC 737.

[123] The effect of the decision in *Phoenix v Wimpole Street Nominees Ltd* [1992] BCLC 737 is that the lender's statutory power of sale cannot be a power given to an LPA receiver. See the discussion at paras 9.138–9.139. The court construed the mortgage conditions as conferring only the borrower's power of sale (see paras 11.97–11.98), so no consideration was given to a lender's express power of sale. As a matter of practicality, the authors understand from other practitioners that the Land Registry does accept transfers executed by the receiver under a delegated lender's power of sale, provided the mortgage conditions are clear that that power has been so delegated. If there is any doubt, it is safer to have the receiver execute the contract for sale, for that contract expressly to provide that execution of the transfer by the lender will be permitted on completion, and for the lender to execute the transfer under its power of sale. See the section on this hybrid method at para 11.161 *et seq*.

(a)   the power is not a special power;

(b)   assuming that the terms provided for any assignee of the mortgage to have the power of sale, then it would be clear that the identity of the original lender was not important;

(c)   the power is conferred for the benefit of the lender.

11.100   Although the lender would owe no duty to the borrower in the receiver's exercise of the power of sale,[124] if the receiver was the deemed agent of the borrower under the mortgage conditions, the receiver would owe the borrower a like duty, so that the borrower would have like protection.

11.101   However, the Land Registry guidance makes no mention of this possibility either in the guidance about the exercise of the lender's power of sale,[125] or the guidance about LPA receivers.[126] This issue of whether the lender's power of sale is delegable to the receiver such that in exercising it he acts as the borrower's agent is far from free of doubt. There is little commentary or case law about it.

11.102   Nonetheless, the authors' view is that there is no reason why the lender should not be able to delegate an express power of sale if the terms of the mortgage so provide.

Manner of delegation

11.103   The next question is how that delegation might occur. It follows from the above that a delegation can only be effective if in the mortgage conditions a separate power of sale was conferred on the lender, which was intended to be delegable. If the mortgage conditions give the lender a power of sale and express the receiver to have that power of sale, then it will be delegable, since it would clearly be intended to be so.

11.104   Conversely, if there is nothing in the mortgage conditions to this effect, the lender does not have power to delegate its statutory power of sale.

11.105   However, if the mortgage conditions do create a separate, express delegable power of sale, then, unless there is anything in the mortgage conditions to the contrary, the delegation can occur automatically on appointment (if the mortgage conditions so provide), by an express delegation in the appointment, or by an express delegation at some later time.

---

[124]   Conversely, delegation of its power of sale by the lender to a third party acting as the lender's agent would not absolve the lender of its duties.

[125]   See Land Registry Practice Guide 75, especially para 2.1

[126]   See Land Registry Practice Guide 36A, especially para 6.

Effect of delegation

11.106   If the receiver is able to exercise the lender's power of sale, the sale will be free of any interests later in priority than the mortgage,[127] even though the borrower could not sell free of them.

11.107   However, if the receiver is able to contract in the name of the borrower and/or the receiver's acts are deemed to be as agent for the borrower, it will be the borrower who is contractually liable to the third party purchaser on the contract and not the lender. The effect of the delegation, and the deemed agency, would be to make the borrower liable to third parties, and without recourse to the lender, in relation to any sale by the receiver under the power. However, the basis of that liability would be the borrower's agreement to the mortgage conditions when he entered into the mortgage.

11.108   Where the terms of the mortgage do provide for the receiver to contract in the borrower's name or as the borrower's deemed agent, there may be a suggestion that it is, nonetheless, impossible for the receiver to be given power to do something in the borrower's name and on his behalf which the borrower could not himself do. That is to misunderstand receivership, which is designed to give the receiver powers both of the borrower and of the lender, but to prevent the borrower or third parties from suing the lender for any act of the receiver. The deemed agency protects the lender from having liability for the receiver's acts. It does not limit the receiver's powers.[128]

11.109   Indeed, that this is the case is clear from section 109(3) of the Law of Property Act 1925, which gives the receiver power to demand and recover income in either the borrower's or the lender's name. Such an ability to act in the lender's name would be meaningless if the receiver could not take a step which was the lender's, that is, if the receiver could only do what the borrower could do.[129] Moreover, the lender can delegate some of its powers under the Act to the receiver, under section 109(3),[130] but that does not prevent the deemed agency in section 109(2).

The contract

11.110   If the lender's express power of sale entitles it to sell in the name of the borrower,[131] or as deemed agent of the borrower, as a matter of principle, the

---

[127]   Because the lender can so sell: Law of Property Act 1925, ss 88 and 89.

[128]   See Chapter 5.

[129]   This is a point made in *Lever Finance v Needleman's Trustee* [1956] Ch 375 at 382: 'in my judgment a receiver under the Act is such an agent [of the borrower], and, although he may use the mortgagee's name for certain purposes, he is not, by virtue of the statute, the mortgagee's agent'.

[130]   Specific powers described as delegable in the Law of Property Act 1925 are the lender's power of leasing at s 99(19), and of accepting surrenders, at s 100(13).

[131]   As per Law of Property Act 1925, ss 88 and 89.

receiver can and should[132] contract for that sale in the borrower's name,[133] and subsequently convey the mortgaged property in the borrower's name.

11.111 Entry into the contract will suspend the equity of redemption, and it is unlikely that a court would prevent completion of the contract unless the contract were entered into before the power of sale had arisen,[134] or the contract was entered into in bad faith, as set out above.[135]

Transfer and registration

11.112 Completion by registration of a sale of an estate in land is a topic of some complexity.[136] This section considers aspects specific to receivership when the sale is under the lender's power of sale and assumes that the land and the charge are registered.

The transfer and registration

11.113 A transfer of a freehold or leasehold title under the lender's power of sale must be by deed, made on a Form TR2 (for the transfer of the whole of the title) or a Form TP2 (for the transfer of part only of the title). These forms are specific to sale under a power of sale by a chargee.

11.114 The first question is who to name as the transferee. In principle, it ought to be possible for the borrower to be named as the transferee.[137]

11.115 In many cases, is likely to be more straightforward to name the lender in the Form TR2 or Form TP2.[138] However, it should be noted that if the transfer is in the name of the lender, the lender risks being found liable to the borrower if the transaction was not at the best price reasonably obtainable.[139]

11.116 The next question is whether the receiver can execute the Form TR2 or Form TP2. Paragraph 2.1 of Land Registry Practice Guide 75 says that the transfer 'must be executed[140] by the chargee'. It makes no reference to the

---

[132] To avoid any liability on the lender. The lender will have given no authority for its name to be used.

[133] In principle, the receiver as someone with a power of sale, should be able to contract in his own name. Since that could give him direct liability to the purchaser, it is unlikely he would want to.

[134] In which case, on most mortgage conditions, the receiver could not have been appointed validly.

[135] See para 11.38

[136] Reference should be made to any practitioner's text on this area and to Land Registry Practice Guides.

[137] By reason of Law of Property Act 1925, ss 88 and 89.

[138] Generally, on the true construction of the mortgage conditions, the receiver with the lender's power of sale would have a power of attorney to convey in the lender's name even without an express or separate power of attorney being required.

[139] *Re Stickley*, 1 May 2013, unreported.

[140] Execution as a deed requires that the instrument must make clear on its face that it is intended by the parties to it to be a deed, by description as a deed, or as executed and signed as a deed, or otherwise, and valid execution as a deed (Law of Property (Miscellaneous Provisions) Act

possibility of a sale by a receiver in the borrower's name under the lender's power of sale, nor indeed to anyone else having power to execute on the lender's behalf, for example under a power of attorney. Nor does Land Registry Practice Guide 36A.[141]

11.117   In principle, on the assumption that it is correct that a receiver can exercise a lender's power of sale, it should be possible to prove that power to the Land Registry by production of the mortgage conditions and the appointment of the receiver. In principle, the receiver with the power of sale ought to be able to execute the transfer himself, without a power of attorney from the lender or the borrower.

11.118   However, it is possible that the Land Registry would refuse to register a transfer so executed under such a power, and the availability of this route would need to be tested by litigation.[142] It is likely to be more straightforward to obtain a power of attorney from the lender to exercise the power in its name,[143] unless there are considerable risks on the sale which the lender seeks to avoid.[144] Indeed, sometimes receivers under their receivership powers will enter into a contract which expressly provides that the lender will execute the transfer, no doubt to avoid the issues of who should execute the transfer.

1989, s 1(2). Execution requires both signature and delivery (s 1(3(b)), where the latter is an acknowledgment by words or conduct of an intention to be bound and no longer requires a formal giving of the deed to the other party. Signature by an individual must be in the presence of an attesting witness to the signature (s 1(3)(a)(i)) or at the party's direction and in the presence of two attesting witnesses to the signature (s 1(3)(a)(ii)). Signature by a company incorporated in England and Wales is governed by the Companies Act 2006. Signature can be by affixing the common seal in the presence of the company secretary and a director, or in the presence of two directors, who attest the sealing by countersigning, and describing their offices: s 44(1)(a), or by signature on behalf of the company by two authorized signatories or a director in the presence of a witness attesting the signature: s 44(2). Authorised signatories include directors and the secretary: s 44(3).

[141] Although in Land Registry Practice Guide 36A, para 1, it notes the difficulty of this area 'particularly as regards the nature of receivership and delegation of powers to the receiver' and describes itself as 'not a definitive statement of the law'.

[142] For example, against the Registrar. As a matter of practicality, the authors understand from other practitioners that the Land Registry does accept transfers executed by the receiver under a delegated lender's power of sale, provided the mortgage conditions are clear that that power has been so delegated. If there is any doubt, it is safer to have the receiver execute the contract for sale, for that contract expressly to provide that execution of the transfer by the lender will be permitted on completion, and for the lender to execute the transfer under its power of sale. See the section on this hybrid method at para 11.161 *et seq.*

[143] The transfer would still need to be in the Form TR2 or Form TP2. See the discussion at para 11.82 of the evidence needed for registration of a transfer executed under a power of attorney. See fns 100 and 102 and Land Registry Practice Guide 36A, para 2.3. It seems likely that the appointment of a receiver with the lender's power of sale under the mortgage conditions would have a power of attorney to execute for the lender even without an express power of attorney.

[144] If there were such risks, and the receiver was to sell in his own name under a receivership power, a receiver would either want insurance covering these risks, or an indemnity from the lender as to his potential liabilities for breach of duty to the borrower. The latter would reduce the benefit of sale by the receiver. This may explain why there are so few cases about receivers selling with the lender's power of sale.

11.119 The transfer must be completed by registration to take effect in law.[145] It is therefore important to consider what documents the Land Registry will require to see in order to effect the registration. Guidance about this is set out in Land Registry Practice Guide 75.

11.120 The Registrar will presume the power of sale has arisen, provided the transfer has been made at least one month after the mortgage or charge was entered into, otherwise he will require evidence that the power of sale had arisen.[146]

11.121 The lender's power of sale is exercisable whether or not the mortgage has been registered.[147] The Land Registry does, however, require more documents to be provided in this event. A certified copy of the charge must be provided, together with a certificate by the lender named on the charge confirming that it remains the owner entitled to exercise the power of sale, or documentary evidence of the transfer of the ownership of the charge.

Removal of entries on the register

11.122 If the lender's power is being exercised, no separate discharge by the lender is required by the Land Registry, and on registration of the transfer, the charge will be released and its entry removed from the register. Likewise, any restriction in favour of the lender will be removed on a sale under the lender's power.[148]

11.123 If sale is under the lender's power of sale, delegated to the receiver, then that sale will be free of any charges and interests later in priority.[149]

11.124 This is true whether or not the mortgage under which the power of sale arises is registered, though more interests are likely to have priority over an unregistered mortgage. This section first considers removal of entries on the register where the mortgage under which the power of sale arises is registered and then, briefly, where the mortgage is unregistered.

11.125 The principle of which entries the Registrar will cancel, on registering a transfer made under the lender's power of sale, is easy to state: the Registrar will cancel entries for other interests if satisfied that the interest has been overridden by the exercise of the power of sale, i.e. that the interest is later in priority to the mortgage.

---

[145] Land Registration Act 2002, s 27.

[146] Land Registry Practice Guide 75, para 1.

[147] *Swift 1st Ltd v Colin* [2011] EWHC 2410 (Ch), [2012] Ch 206. See the discussion at Chapter 2, fn 171.

[148] It is likely that the lender would have to agree to the lifting of the restriction, since a lender's restriction on title often requires the lender's consent for there to be a disposition.

[149] Law of Property Act, ss 88, 89 and 104(1).

11.126 Entries for any registered mortgage or charge, or lease, or interest protected by notice[150] later in date than the registration date of the mortgage or charge under which the power of sale was exercised will be removed when the transfer under the power of sale is registered.

11.127 If there are interests earlier in priority to the mortgage under which the power of sale has been exercised, then sale will be subject to those interests. Thus, if there is a mortgage or charge with an earlier entry on the register of the borrower's title, then sale will be subject to that mortgage or charge, and the entry will remain when the transfer is registered, unless there is a successful separate application for its removal (as a result of it being discharged from the proceeds).

11.128 The rules of registration make it a little more complicated to say whether a particular entry will be removed automatically, or will require an application for removal. The question of whether an interest protected by an entry is earlier or later in priority than a mortgage registered on a particular date, under which the power of sale has been exercised, depends on whether the interest is protected by registration, or by the entry of a notice on the register, and the changing Land Registry practice as to how information about an interest is recorded on the register.

11.129 This chapter considers Land Registry practice in relation to the more common interests. Reference should be made to Land Registry Practice Guides and to practitioner's texts.

Other mortgages and charges

11.130 The priority of registered mortgages and charges on the register is shown by their order of appearance on the charges section of the register,[151] unless an entry says otherwise.[152]

11.131 Registered proprietors of mortgages prevent transfers[153] by the borrower of his estate by entry of a restriction on the register requiring the

---

[150] Agreed or unilateral notices can be used to protect certain types of interest. The presence of a notice on the register does not guarantee the existence of the interest described in the notice, but protects its priority on transfers for valuable consideration, if the interest does exist. Interests which can be protected include the benefit of a contract for sale, or other agreements about ownership for example boundary agreements, charging orders made by court order under the Charging Orders Act 1979, home rights under the Family Law Act 1996, orders under the Access to Neighbouring Land Act 1992, notices exercising rights under the Leasehold Reform Act 1967 and the Leasehold Reform, Housing and Urban Development Act 1993. Beneficial interests under trusts are not supposed to be capable of protection by notice.

[151] Land Registration Act 2002, s 48 and Land Registration Rules 2003 (SI 2003/1417), r 101.

[152] For example, if there has been a priority agreement, so that on a mortgage registered later, it is agreed by the lenders that that later mortgage is to have priority to some extent over an earlier mortgage, then that will need to be recorded: Land Registration Rules 2003 (SI 2003/1417), r 102.

[153] Automatic transfers on death or bankruptcy do not require to be registered: Land Registration Act 2002, s 27(5), and take effect subject to the pre-existing interests both legal and equitable.

lender's consent before registration of the transfer.[154] If there is more than one registered mortgage, the restriction for the later mortgage has effect to prevent a transfer without consent only if the transfer is not by the earlier lender.[155]

11.132 Thus, on a sale under a lender's power of sale, the Registrar will check whether any restriction in favour of any lender bites. If the only restriction is for a mortgage later in priority and requires no consent to registration of the transfer in question, then that restriction will not bite, and the transfer can be registered. The restriction will be removed.

11.133 If there is a restriction on the title which bites, for example, preventing registration of a disposition without the consent of a prior mortgagee, then that consent will be required if the transfer is to be registered. Consent will rarely be given without sufficient money on the sale to redeem the prior mortgage.[156]

11.134 If a charge is unregistered, but the subject of a notice entered on the register after the date of the registration of the mortgage under which the power of sale has been exercised,[157] then usually that notice will be cancelled.[158]

Estate contracts

11.135 It is not uncommon for someone with the benefit of a contract for the sale or disposition of land to protect it by notice[159] pending completion, for

---

On a transfer by the borrower, the transferee would take subject to the registered mortgage. The effect would be to leave the debt with the borrower, but the proprietary remedies would be enforceable against the transferee. Lenders usually prefer to prevent such transfers, in part so that any sale can be controlled, and any proceeds of sale can be used to repay the mortgage debt. That is achieved by the restriction.

[154] The standard restriction permits a transfer for example by a prior mortgagee under its power of sale without the consent of the later lender: for example Form L 'no disposition of the registered estate by the proprietor of the registered estate is to be registered without a certificate signed by the lender or his conveyancer'. See Land Registry Practice Guide 19 and para 7.12.

[155] For example, 'no disposition of the registered estate by the proprietor of the registered estate, or by the proprietor of any registered charge, not being a charge registered before the entry of this restriction, is to be registered without a certificate signed by the lender or his conveyancer'. See Land Registry Practice Guide 19 and para 7.12.

[156] Land Registry Practice Guide 75, para 2.2.2 says 'you will have to lodge a discharge from the lender for the charge or confirm that the transfer is being made subject to the other charge'.

[157] If there is a restriction preventing a disposition without the consent of the proprietor of a registered mortgage or charge, and consent cannot be obtained for a second mortgage or charge to be registered, then that later charge is often protected by a notice on the title.

[158] If a charge is protected by an agreed notice later in date to the date of the mortgage under which the power of sale has been exercised, the Land Registry will check if there was an earlier unilateral notice subsequently changed to an agreed notice, since that might indicate that the charge was earlier in priority to the mortgage.

[159] Agreed or unilateral.

example, if the borrower enters into a contract for sale.[160] The entry will usually give the date of the contract.

11.136   If the contract post-dates the mortgage, then the contract could only be of the borrower's equity of redemption and would not bind the lender exercising its power of sale.[161] The Registrar will remove the notice when registering the transfer by the lender.

11.137   This is unless the lender has consented to the contract. For example, if the borrower enters into a contract for the grant of a lease, after the date of the mortgage, but under his power of leasing,[162] or with the consent of the lender, and that contract is protected by notice, then the contract will bind the lender, and the lender's power of sale cannot be exercised free of it. The notice will not be removed on registration of the transfer.[163]

11.138   If the contract pre-dates the mortgage, and notice was entered before registration of the mortgage, then the lender will take subject to the contract.[164] That notice will remain on the register on registration of the transfer. If the notice is to be removed, there will have to be a successful application for its removal.[165]

11.139   More difficult are cases where the contract pre-dates the mortgage, but the notice post-dates its registration. In that case, the benefit of the contract would only be protected, at registration of the mortgage, if it fell within one of the paragraphs of Schedule 3 to the Land Registration Act 2002,[166] the most likely of which would be paragraph 2, an interest belonging at the time of disposition to a person in actual occupation.[167] If it is unclear whether the

---

[160]   If a contract is entered into by a prior lender under its power of sale, then since the equity of redemption is suspended by that contract, in principle a lender under a later mortgage could not sell the mortgaged estate, but only his own charge. An entry protecting the sale by the prior lender would be unusual, but whatever the date of the contract or its registration, it should indicate to the Registrar that the sale by the later lender cannot be registered as a sale of the mortgaged estate.

[161]   *Duke v Robson* [1973] 1 WLR 267.

[162]   Under Law of Property Act 1925, s 99. See para 2.64.

[163]   Land Registry practice is to require the lender, on registration of the transfer under its power of sale, to provide a written signed statement from an authorised officer or the conveyance, confirming that the lender was not party to the contract. See Land Registry Practice Guide 75, para 2.2.5.2. It is unlikely that a receiver, even with the power of sale, could do this, since the consent, or lack of it, to the contract would have to be the lender's.

[164]   Land Registration Act 2002, s 29.

[165]   An application for removal of an agreed notice must be in Form CN1. An application for removal of a unilateral notice must be in Form UN4. See Land Registry Practice Guide 75, para 2.2.4.

[166]   Land Registration Act 2002, s 29(2).

[167]   The risk of a lender being bound by the interest of a person in actual occupation suggests best practice, on the grant of a mortgage, for the lender to enquire into occupiers, and of them, as to whether they have any interest (since a failure of such a person to disclose the right would prevent his interest binding due to Land Registration Act 2002, Sch 3, para 2(b)), and require any such person to enter into a deed postponing the priority of his interest to the mortgage.

interest protected by the notice is binding on the mortgage, then the Land Registry may require a separate application for the removal of the notice.

Trusts

11.140   If the borrower's estate is subject to a trust, with someone else having a beneficial interest in it, but that beneficial interest is not binding on the lender, then on registration of the transfer pursuant to the lender's power of sale, the purchaser will take free of that beneficial interest under section 104(1) of the Law of Property Act 1925.[168]

11.141   Beneficial interests in property under a trust are not capable of protection by registration or by notice on a registered title.[169] If there is any protection of a beneficial interest under a trust, it will be by restriction.

11.142   There are two common restrictions where there is a trust of land. The first is Form A.[170] This is designed to ensure that any beneficial interests are overreached[171] and, hence, that the purchaser takes free of any such interests, by requiring a sale by and the purchase money paid to two registered proprietors, or a trust corporation. The Land Registry enters such a restriction whenever aware that the property is held on trust.[172] Such a restriction will not prevent a transfer in exercise of the lender's power of sale. The restriction will be cancelled automatically on the registration of the transfer.

11.143   The second common restriction is in Form B.[173] Such a restriction will also not prevent registration of a transfer in exercise of the lender's power of sale and will be cancelled, unless the form of restriction expressly prevents registration of a transfer by exercise of the lender's power of sale.[174]

Other restrictions

11.144   Interests in registered estates are often protected by restrictions on registration, so that the estate cannot be transferred in law without, for example,

---

[168]   It appears that the same effect will be obtained by overreaching, whether or not the mortgage is subject to the beneficial interest, by reason of Law of Property Act 1925, s 2(1)(iii). See the discussion at paras 2.136 and 2.137 and their footnotes.

[169]   Land Registration Act 2002, s 33.

[170]   No disposition by a sole proprietor of the registered estate (except a trust corporation) under which the capital money arises is to be registered unless authorised by the order of the court. See Land Registry Practice Guide 19 and para 7.1.

[171]   Under Law of Property Act 1925, ss 2(1)(ii), (2) and 27.

[172]   For example, where a trust is declared in the transfer deed on a purchase of the estate.

[173]   No disposition by the proprietors of the registered estate is to be registered unless one or more of them makes a statutory declaration or statement of truth, or their conveyance gives a certificate, that the disposition is in accordance with the trust deed. See Land Registry Practice Guide 19 and para 7.2. A Form N restriction, which requires the consent of the beneficiary, is also common. See para 7.14.

[174]   This would be rare, since few lenders would lend on terms that the power of sale would not be exercisable without the beneficiaries' consent.

the written consent of some person.[175] Above, restrictions commonly entered to protect mortgages and beneficial interests have been considered.

11.145   There are many standard forms of restriction, designed to protect various interests, for example, an overage agreement, or a charging order on a beneficial share in the estate, or the trustee in bankruptcy's beneficial share in a property.

11.146   There are also restrictions which protect the requirement of consent on a transfer, even though no property interest is protected. For example, where there is a named management company as a party to a lease, and the lease contains a covenant requiring the management company to give consent to a transfer of the lease, there may be a restriction on the leasehold title requiring evidence that such consent has been obtained.[176]

11.147   Two questions arise in relation to a transfer under the lender's power of sale. The first is whether the restriction will prevent registration. That will depend on whether the restriction is directed towards dispositions under the lender's power of sale[177] and when the restriction was entered. If it was entered after registration of the charge and without the lender's consent, it cannot usually affect registration of a transfer under the power of sale.

11.148   The second question is whether the restriction should be cancelled on registration of the transfer under the lender's power of sale. That will depend on whether whatever it is protecting is overreached by the sale, or not.[178] For example, a restriction protecting a trustee in bankruptcy's beneficial interest will be cancelled if the transfer overreached any beneficial interests because the purchaser will take free of that interest.

11.149   A restriction protecting a management company under a lease will likely not be cancelled since the purchaser of the leasehold estate will be subject to the covenant requiring the management company's consent.[179]

---

[175] If a conveyance of an estate which is required to be completed by registration, as a sale would be, is not completed by registration then it takes effect in equity only, and the equitable assignee takes subject to any pre-existing interest or charge.

[176] This will likely require compliance on a transfer under the lender's power of sale.

[177] Standard Form A and Form B restrictions are usually limited to preventing registration of transfers by the registered proprietor of the estate, not dispositions under the lender's power of sale, though they can be more extensively drafted.

[178] This may not simply be dependent on the date of the restriction. A restriction entered after the mortgage was registered may protect an interest which arose before the mortgage and whose priority was protected, for example, under Land Registration Act 2002, Sch 3, when the mortgage was granted and registered.

[179] Under Landlord and Tenant (Covenants) Act 1995, ss 3 and 28(6), if the lease was granted on or after 1 January 1996. For a lease predating the coming into force of that Act, it is much less obvious how covenants in leases with a management company, which is a third party to the lease but has no estate in the land, bind assignees. It is possible analysis as a rentcharge assists.

Other interests

11.150   If the borrower granted a lease after the mortgage, and without a power of leasing, that lease will not bind the lender. The Land Registry will register it, however, and will not automatically remove the entry noting it on the charges register for the borrower's estate, or close the leasehold title, on registration of a transfer under the lender's power of sale. A separate application for closure would need to be made, with evidence that the borrower's power of leasing[180] had been excluded by the mortgage conditions or any power of leasing did not permit the grant of that lease, and that the lender had not consented to the grant of the lease.

11.151   One example of a change in Land Registry practice which affects whether an entry would be removed on the registration of a transfer in exercise of a lender's power of sale is the change in practice on noting easements granted by the borrower after the grant of the mortgage.

11.152   An easement cannot be granted by a borrower over his estate so as to bind the lender without the lender's consent.[181] Prior to 11 April 2005, the Land Registry would not register easements granted by a borrower without evidence of the lender's consent. If an easement is registered on the borrower's title, granted post the mortgage but prior to 11 April 2005, then the sale under the lender's power of sale could not take free of that easement.

11.153   Land Registry practice after that date has been to register the easement on the borrower's estate[182] but note the lack of evidence of the lender's consent. On registration of a sale under the lender's power of sale, the Registrar will serve notice of an application for cancellation on the registered owner of the dominant tenement, so that they can object, for example, on the basis that the lender did consent. If there is no successful objection, the entry for the easement can be removed.

11.154   If there is no such note, for an easement granted post that date, then the entry cannot be removed because, due to Land Registry practice, it appears the lender consented to the grant of the easement. A separate application to cancel the entry will be needed if this is not so.

11.155   The Land Registry has a similar practice in relation to variations of leases. If the borrower's estate is leasehold, and he agrees a variation of the lease with his landlord, by deed and applies to register it, then the Land Registry will note that variation in the Register. If there is no evidence of consent by the lender, however, the Land Registry will note that. On a sale under the lender's power of sale, the lease sold would be the unvaried lease.

---

[180]   Under Law of Property Act 1925, s 99.

[181]   If one thinks of the mortgage as a lease, the easement is granted out of the borrower's reversionary interest on that lease, only, if he does not have the lender's consent. The borrower does not have a statutory right to create such an interest, unlike leasing, for example.

[182]   Which will be the servient tenement for the easement.

11.156   The Land Registry will cancel a notice under the Family Law Act 1996 protecting home rights, if its date post-dates the mortgage. If it pre-dates the mortgage and any rights were not expressly postponed, so that the lender took subject to it, the lender will have to make an application under the Act for its discharge.[183]

11.157   Notices protecting other rights, whatever the date of the notice, will not be cancelled automatically on registration of the transfer made under the power of sale, and will require a separate application for their cancellation.

When the mortgage is not registered

11.158   If the mortgage is not registered, then on registration of the transfer under the lender's power of sale, the Land Registry will only cancel entries when it is clear that the mortgage had priority to the interest protected by that entry.

11.159   So, for example, a Form A restriction applying to dispositions by a registered proprietor will be cancelled because any beneficial interests will be overreached by the transfer in exercise of the lender's power of sale.

11.160   The question of priority will be much less clear for other entries. In those cases, separate applications to cancel the entries will have to be made, with evidence of the priority of the mortgage over the interests which are the subject of the relevant entries.

A HYBRID: CONTRACT UNDER BORROWER'S POWER WITH CONVEYANCE BY LENDER

11.161   The authors understand that, in practice, it is common for the receiver to contract, using the borrower's power of sale, on terms which provide for the lender to effect the conveyance.

11.162   The receiver ought not to contract on such terms unless he has some legally binding commitment from the lender to effect the conveyance. Otherwise, he will be putting the borrower at risk of committing a breach of contract.

11.163   The effect of such a contract is that the third party will get the benefit of a conveyance by the lender, so as to overreach subsequent interests, and the benefit of contractual liability as against the borrower (but not the lender) if, for example, vacant possession is not delivered and costs are incurred in removing rubbish.

---

[183]   This is discussed at paras 8.156–8.166.

11.164   However, the lender will undertake a potential liability to the borrower in these circumstances: if the sale is not at the best price reasonably obtainable, the borrower will potentially have a cause of action against the lender.[184]

THE BORROWER'S DEATH OR INSOLVENCY AND SALE

11.165   If the borrower is a company, and is wound up, the winding up does not end the receivership; nor does it end either the lender's or the receiver's power of sale.[185] The receiver does not need leave under section 127 of the Insolvency Act 1986 to effect a sale.[186]

11.166   By analogy, it seems unlikely that the death of an individual borrower, or his bankruptcy will affect the receiver's ability to sell the property.[187]

11.167   The receiver's deemed agency ends.[188] Nonetheless, the transfer can still be executed in the borrower's name.[189]

11.168   Paragraph 3.3 of Land Registry Practice Guide 36A suggests that the sale, and execution of the transfer, can be in the name of the borrower and on its behalf.[190]

11.169   It is less clear whether the receiver's power of attorney continues. If it were an irrevocable power of attorney, it too, would survive. However, irrevocability, under section 4(1) of the Powers of Attorney Act 1971, must be granted to secure a proprietary interest in the donee of the power, and a receiver

---

[184]   *Re Stickley*, 1 May 2013, unreported.

[185]   In both cases, this is provided the mortgage was made before the commencement of the winding up. Otherwise the mortgage would be void: Insolvency Act 1986, s 127. The receivership and the lender's power of sale survive even if the mortgaged property is disclaimed on the insolvency: see *Scmlla Properties Ltd v Gesso Properties (BVI) Ltd* [1995] BCC 793. On a sale under the lender's power of sale of disclaimed property, the Land Registry will cancel any notice of disclaimer: Land Registry Practice Guide 75, para 1.

[186]   Land Registry Practice Guide 36A, para 3.3.

[187]   Land Registry will accept transfers executed by the receiver as valid in these circumstances: Land Registry Practice Guide 36A, para 3.3

[188]   *Gaskell v Gosling* [1896] 1 QB 669; *Thomas v Todd* [1926] 2 KB 511 at 516; *Gough's Garages Ltd v Pugsley* [1930] 1 KB 615 at 626; *Sowman v David Samuel Trust Ltd (In Liquidation)* [1978] 1 WLR 22. See para 6.170 *et seq* for a further discussion of the effect of insolvency on the power to appoint a receiver.

[189]   *Sowman v David Samuel Trust Ltd (In Liquidation)* [1978] 1 WLR 22.

[190]   A sale by the receiver in the name of the borrower company after winding up was valid in *Sowman v David Samuel Trust Ltd (In Liquidation)* [1978] 1 WLR 22. If it is correct that on the death or bankruptcy of an individual the receiver becomes the deemed agent of the executor or administrator, and on the bankruptcy, of the trustee in bankruptcy, in whom the mortgaged property automatically vests, then the transfer can be executed in the name of the executor or administrator, or in the name of the trustee in bankruptcy. See para 6.201 *et seq* (death) and para 6.212 *et seq* (bankruptcy).

has no such interest.[191] The Land Registry takes the view that the power of attorney does not survive, so will not accept a transfer executed under a power of attorney after liquidation.[192]

11.170   On an application to register a transfer made post the insolvency of the borrower, the Registrar will be concerned about the possibility of the liquidator or trustee in bankruptcy taking action which invalidates the mortgage, for example, were it a transaction at an undervalue.[193] For this reason, the applicant registering the transfer must disclose any challenge to the validity of the mortgage of which he is aware.

RESTRICTIONS ON SALE

11.171   Whatever power of sale the receiver has, he will need to be aware of any restrictions on sale of the mortgaged property.

11.172   For example, if the mortgaged property is leasehold, then compliance with any restrictions on assignment will be needed.

11.173   If the mortgaged property is a leasehold reversion of residential property, the receiver will need to comply with the Landlord and Tenant Act 1987. The Act[194] precludes a landlord from selling the property (or making any other relevant disposal)[195] without giving the tenants a right of first refusal. A mortgagee exercising its power of sale is under the same duty.[196] A receiver must therefore comply with this requirement, whenever he sells the property, whether he sells with the borrower's power of sale, or the lender's.

THE RECEIVER'S DUTIES ON SALE

11.174   The receiver owes duties imposed by equity, first, to pay down the loan, and, secondly, to those persons with an interest in the equity of redemption.[197] Where the receiver has a power of sale, those duties are not, in principle,

---

[191]   See para 6.239 and the suggestion there that at common law the power can be irrevocable even if it is not the attorney that has the interest. Land Registry Practice Guide 36A, para 3.3 says that the power of attorney will not survive.

[192]   Land Registry Practice Guide 36A, para 3.3.

[193]   See Land Registry Practice Guide 36A, para 3.3, and Insolvency Act 1986, ss 238–241, 244, 255, 339, 340, 342, 343 and 423. Reference should be made to any practitioner's text on insolvency.

[194]   This applies to premises if they contain two or more flats held by qualifying tenants and the number of flats held by such tenants exceeds 50% of the total number of flats in the buildings; and any non-residential parts of the building occupy less than 50% of the internal floor area, disregarding any common parts. Assured and assured shorthold tenants are not qualifying tenants (although their landlord, if holding a leasehold estate, could be).

[195]   Landlord and Tenant Act 1987, s 4 defines relevant disposals.

[196]   Landlord and Tenant Act 1987, s 4(1A).

[197]   See para 6.64 *et seq*.

different depending on whether the receiver has the borrower's power of sale or the lender's,[198] though no doubt a receiver with the borrower's power of sale only in exercising it must consider whether he will be able to sell free of the mortgage.

11.175 Whichever the receiver's power of sale, he need not decide to sell the property even if appointed with a power to do so,[199] but if he does he must use reasonable care in selling the property to obtain a proper price,[200] that is 'the best price reasonable obtainable at the time'.[201] The court, when deciding whether that duty has been breached must look at the facts broadly. The receiver 'will not be adjudged to be in default unless he is plainly on the wrong side of the line'.[202]

11.176 He can choose when to sell even if the date is disadvantageous to the borrower and waiting would increase the price.[203] Thus, the borrower cannot restrain properly appointed receivers by injunction from selling at a time of the receivers' choosing unless a valid tender of the sum needed to redeem the loan in full had been made,[204] or the receivers were not acting properly.[205] A receiver also has considerable latitude in choosing the method of sale, though the property must be properly marketed once this has been chosen.[206] The receiver can have regard to the principal duty of repayment of the mortgage debt when deciding on timing and method of sale, resolving doubts in the favour of that

---

[198] Just as the duties on the lender exercising his power of sale are the same whether the lender's power is statutory or express: *Yorkshire Bank Plc v Hall* [1999] 1 WLR 1713 at 1728.

[199] Although, presumably, he must consider the possibility of sale, and his decision must be taken in good faith and with due diligence. A receiver, like a lender, cannot simply ignore it if a short delay might lead to an increased price: see *Meftah v Lloyds TSB Bank Plc* [2001] 2 All ER (Comm) 741 at 744 ([9](h)). Presumably, this is an example of a receiver's general duty to consider whether to use his powers. See Chapter 6, fn 105. See also *Lloyds Bank Plc v Cassidy* [2002] EWCA Civ 1606, [2002] BPIR 424 at [41] per Mance LJ, suggesting this as an area of law needing further examination. For recent examples of cases where breach of duty on sale was claimed, and failed, see *Ahmad v Bank of Scotland Plc* [2016] EWCA Civ 602 and *Centenary Homes Ltd v Gershinson*, 19 September 2017, unreported, QBD.

[200] *Medforth v Blake* [2000] Ch 86 at 112F, which has a good summary of the duties on a receiver. Once the decision to sell has been made, it is unclear whether the receiver has a duty to take into account a reasonable proposal from the borrower as to sale: *Lloyd Bank Plc v Cassidy* [2002] EWCA Civ 1606 at [41]. 'Once a mortgagee or receiver has decided to sell, he or she cannot, presumably, avoid liability if he or she fails to accept or follow up an obviously favourable proposal'.

[201] *Mortgage Express v Trevor Mardner* [2004] EWCA Civ 1859 at [5]–[9].

[202] *Cuckmere Brick Co Ltd v Mutual Finance Ltd* [1971] 1 Ch 949 at 969, in relation to the lender's duties.

[203] *Bell v Long* [2008] EWHC 1273 (Ch), [2008] 2 BCLC 706 at [12] (since sale of a portfolio at a discount guaranteed a disposal, so that there was no obligation to wait longer for an uncertain future sale at a greater price), and *Gomba Holdings UK Ltd v Homan* [1986] 1 WLR 1301 at 1304F. This is just like the position for the lender who need not wait to sell at a better time for the borrower: *Cuckmere Brick Co Ltd v Mutual Finance Ltd* [1971] 2 All ER 633 at 646–647; *Tse Kwong Lam v Wong Chit Sen* [1983] 3 All ER 54 at 59.

[204] *Gomba Holdings UK Ltd v Homan* [1986] 1 WLR 1301 at 1304F.

[205] *Watts v Midland Bank Plc* (1986) 2 BCC 98961 at 98967, col 1.

[206] *Bell v Long* [2008] EWHC 1273 (Ch), [2008] 2 BCLC 706 at [17].

principal duty, rather than the borrower, provided the decision is a genuine one, i.e. has been taken in good faith.[207]

11.177   When the lender exercises the power of sale, then he has an equitable duty to all the people interested in the equity of redemption 'to take proper precautions to obtain "the fair" or "the true market" value of or the "proper price" for the mortgaged property at the date of the sale'.[208] He has similar duties if he takes possession. He need not improve the property, by repairing it or getting planning permission, but he cannot sell 'hastily at a knock-down price sufficient to pay off his debt'.[209]

11.178   The receiver's duties are similar. The receiver must take proper precautions to obtain the proper price at the date of sale, though in considering offers he is entitled to balance the certainty of a sale at a lower offer against a speculative higher offer and the intended dates of completion on different offers to buy.[210] Just like the lender, the receiver exercising a power of sale need not spend money to increase its value, for example by carrying out repair works,[211] or by seeking planning permission, but may sell it in the condition it is in, without a breach of duty.[212] He should advertise the benefit of planning permission when marketing the property, however, if the property has it, and assuming it increases the value.[213]

---

[207] *Bell v Long* [2008] EWHC 1273 (Ch) at [17].

[208] *Silven Properties Ltd v Royal Bank of Scotland Plc* [2003] EWCA Civ 1409, [2004] 1 WLR 997 at [19].

[209] *Palk v Mortgage Services Funding Plc* [1993] Ch 330 at 337–338.

[210] *Meftah v Lloyds TSB Bank Plc* [2001] 2 All ER (Comm) 741 at 744 ([9](f)); *National Westminster Bank Plc v Hunter* [2011] EWHC 3170 (Ch) at [62]–[63].

[211] *Meftah v Lloyds TSB Bank Plc* [2001] 2 All ER (Comm) 741 at 744 ([100]).

[212] *Silven Properties Ltd v Royal Bank of Scotland Plc* [2003] EWCA Civ 1409, [2004] 1 WLR 997 at [28]; *Garland v Ralph Pay & Ransom* [1984] 2 EGLR 147 at 151; *Routestone Ltd v Minories Finance Ltd* [1997] BCC 180 at 195C–D; *Bell v Long* [2008] EWHC 1273 (Ch) at [12].

[213] *Cuckmere Brick Co Ltd v Mutual Finance Ltd* [1971] 1 Ch 949 in relation to the lender's duties.

Chapter 12

Use and Distribution of Funds Collected

12.1   This chapter explains what a receiver must do with monies coming into his hands.

12.2   As set out in Chapter 5, a receiver may derive his powers from more than one source. The receiver's obligations in respect of monies received may well depend on the source of the power which led to him receiving the money and the type of funds received. The various possibilities are considered in turn in this chapter.

INCOME

12.3   Any income[1] collected in exercise of the statutory powers[2] is[3] to be distributed as follows:[4]

(a)   in discharge of all rents, taxes, rates and outgoings whatever affecting the mortgaged property;

(b)   in keeping down all annual sums or other payments, and the interest on all principal sums, having priority to the mortgage under which the receiver was appointed;

(c)   in paying the receiver's commission, insurance policies and doing any necessary or proper repairs directed in writing by the lender;

(d)   in payment of the interest accruing due in respect of any principal money due under the mortgage; and

(e)   in or towards discharge of the principal money if so directed in writing by the lender;

(f)   the residue is to be paid to the person who, but for the possession of the receiver, would have been entitled to receive the income of which the receiver has been appointed, or who is otherwise entitled to the mortgaged property.

12.4   What is and is not included in each category is considered in detail below. A few general points need explaining first.

---

[1]   There is no comprehensive definition of income. It is defined, in Law of Property Act 1925, s 205(1)(xix), to include rents and profits.

[2]   I.e. the powers of an LPA receiver. See Chapter 9 for an explanation of what the statutory powers are.

[3]   Absent any agreement between the lender and the borrower to alter the statutory regime: *Marshall v Cottingham* [1982] 1 Ch 82.

[4]   Law of Property Act 1925, s 109(8).

12.5 First, the statute creates an obligation on the receiver to the lender and to the borrower[5] to pay out monies received as set out above. The receiver does not have a discretion as to which items to pay.[6]

12.6 However, the statute does not create any obligation enforceable by third parties, such as the local authority[7] or utility suppliers. So if all potential payees agree[8] that a particular debt need not be paid because there will be no adverse consequence if it is not, or that the order of priority should be changed,[9] no party will later be able to resile from the agreement.[10] The receiver can safely act in accordance with it. It is thought that the lender and the borrower could not prejudice the receiver's priority in respect of his commission without his agreement, unless this is done before he is appointed.

12.7 Secondly, it is unclear whether the receiver should distribute in full on each receipt by reference to the liabilities which have then fallen due, or whether he should hold back monies from those in inferior categories until he is satisfied that he will have enough money to pay the creditors in earlier categories in full for everything that they will be entitled to during the entire receivership. It is considered that the latter construction is more likely to find favour. It is unlikely that Parliament intended that the receiver should be

---

5   And to others potentially entitled to payment under the statutory regime, including chargees with charges later in priority to the mortgage under which the receiver is appointed: *Yourell v Hibernian Bank Ltd* [1918] AC 372 at 386; *Re Kentish Homes Ltd* [1993] BCC 212 at 220. Presumably, the duty is also owed to chargees with charges with priority over the mortgage since payments to them are specifically named. See also para 6.66, which discusses whether a receiver has duties to prior chargees.

6   The contrary appears to be suggested in *In Re John Willment (Ashford) Ltd* [1980] 1 WLR 73 (and some subsequent cases), but on a careful reading of the case it is clear that the judge was saying no more and no less than what is said here as to the scope of the receiver's obligations. It is not right to say that a discretion exists.

     If the receiver does not pay in accordance with the statutory provisions, he can be sued by the lender or the borrower (or, presumably, any other potential payee) for breach of statutory duty if they suffer loss as a result: *Leicester Permanent Building Society v Butt* [1943] Ch 308 (lender claim against receiver); *Re Kentish Homes Ltd* [1993] BCC 212 (overruled on other grounds in *Re Toshuko Finance UK Plc* [2000] 1 BCLC 683). Any potential payee could obtain an injunction against the receiver to enforce such obligations.

     Furthermore, if the receiver wrongly makes a payment and there is insufficient to pay the lender what is owed under the charge, the lender can also sue the borrower because the receiver is deemed to be his agent, unless the mortgage deed provides otherwise: *White v Metcalf* [1903] 2 Ch 567 at 571; Law of Property Act 1925, s 109(2) as to the statutory agency, which is considered in detail in Chapter 6.

7   *Liverpool Corp v Hope* [1938] 1 KB 751.

8   An agreement can be inferred from conduct, or can arise if one party is estopped from denying that it had agreed to alter the statutory regime: *Yourell v Hibernian Bank Ltd* [1918] AC 372. In the absence of an express agreement, some receivers will take a view as to whether not paying a particular debt is likely to lead to any claim by the lender or the borrower. However, this is a risky strategy.

9   *Yourell v Hibernian Bank Ltd* [1918] AC 372.

10   If there had been some fraud, misrepresentation or undue influence which entitled one party to have the agreement set aside, that would not entitle that party to complain, as against the receiver, that he had acted in accordance with it – unless he were himself involved in the fraud, misrepresentation or undue influence.

obliged, in the event of a large receipt early on in the receivership, to pay monies over to the borrower, even if it was clear that there would be no surplus by the end of the receivership. Receivers should therefore only distribute income receipts when they are in a position to assess all the claims that they are likely to face during the receivership, and all the income that they are likely to receive.

12.8   Thirdly, if the receiver does not have enough money to pay everyone in a particular category, it is considered that he should pay them pro rata. The only exception to this is the category of prior charges. It is thought (although not spelt out in the legislation) that the receiver should pay prior charges in the order of priority.

12.9   Fourthly, it is important that the receiver checks that any payment is, in law, due from the borrower before it is made. So if, for example, payment of an invoice in respect of service charges is sought, the receiver should check that the contractual machinery in the lease has been correctly operated before any payment is made. Similarly, the receiver is not obliged or entitled to pay statute-barred claims.[11]

12.10   Lastly, it is important to note that the receiver is obliged (in the sense set out above) to pay arrears existing at the date the receivership commences, as well as sums falling due afterwards, at least as regards rents, taxes, rates and outgoings.[12]

12.11   If the receiver has additional powers[13] that result in him collecting money in the nature of income,[14] the mortgage must be construed to ascertain the parties' intention as to how that income is to be distributed.[15]

Rents, taxes, rates and outgoings

12.12   Rents are payable where the mortgaged property is leasehold. Rents are relatively straightforward. It is considered likely that 'rents' will be interpreted as those items reserved as rent in the lease. This means that it is necessary to

---

[11]   *Hibernian Bank v Yourell (No 2)* [1919] 1 IrR 310.

[12]   This appears to have been assumed in *Liverpool Corp v Hope* [1938] 1 KB 751. The wording of Law of Property Act 1925, s 109(8) suggests that there may be a distinction between rents, taxes, rates and outgoings on the one hand, and the other categories: in particular as regards sums due to prior mortgagees ('keeping down') and interest due to the appointing lender ('accruing due'), but note that in *National Bank v Kenny* [1898] 1 IR 197, it was held that interest which had already accrued should be paid.

[13]   Deriving from the mortgage, as a fixed charge receiver.

[14]   The receiver's duties as regards the proceeds of sale are considered at para 12.69 *et seq*.

[15]   In *In Re Hale* [1899] 2 Ch 107, especially at 118, the receiver was given the power to carry on the business, in addition to the statutory powers. The court held that payment of the business debts was authorised, in priority to the payments due under the statutory regime – presumably, on the basis that this is what the parties must have intended. However, in other cases, the right construction may be that the parties intended the statutory regime to apply to both statutory and additional powers which generate income.

check the terms of the lease in each case to see what is and what is not reserved as rent. Note that this could include a turnover rent, and payments due in respect of insurance and service charges (which would, in any event, be payable as 'outgoings' affecting the property).

12.13 Outgoings would also include water and sewage and utility bills (but whether this includes telephone and internet charges may, perhaps, be open to some debate, depending on the nature of the property). However, the receiver should consider whether continued supplies are required. If they are not, he should consider terminating the supplies, taking into account the time and cost which will be involved in reconnecting the supply.

12.14 The receiver will also have to consider whether to leave each existing utility contract in place (and simply change the billing address to his own), to enter into a new contract in his own name or to allow the supply to be made under a deemed contract.[16] Key factors are likely to be:

(a)   whether the existing tariff is competitive, and the tariffs that would apply if a new contract or a deemed contract arose;
(b)   whether there are arrears on the account, and, if so:

  (i)   whether the lender and borrower are suggesting that these arrears should not be paid by the receiver; and
  (ii) whether the existing supplier is suggesting that it will not continue to supply unless the arrears are cleared;

(c)   whether the lender is willing to indemnify the receiver (and provide any deposit required) if he enters into a new contract in his own name.[17]

12.15 It is likely that outgoings will also include other expenses relating to the property, even if these are of a capital nature, such as the costs of complying with a planning enforcement notice.[18] For the same reason, it is considered that the costs of resisting a claim to enfranchisement by a tenant of the borrower could also fall within 'outgoings', but, in the absence of authority, it would be

---

[16]   Utilities Act 2000, Sch 4, para 3.

[17]   If the contract remains in the borrower's name, the receiver could not be sued by the provider. If the receiver wishes to avoid the arrears, it is likely that the utility company will require him to contract personally rather than as agent of the borrower, since otherwise the receiver will be having his cake and eating it. If the receiver enters into a new contract, he will have a direct contractual relationship with the provider, and will himself be liable on the contract. A deemed contract is made with the occupier (or the owner if the premises are unoccupied), so, although there is no authority on the question, it is likely that the borrower will be liable on the deemed contract, not the receiver: see the position in relation to non-domestic rates, discussed at para 12.16, by analogy.

[18]   In *Crosse v Raw* (1873–74) LR 9 Ex 209, a lessees' covenant to pay 'outgoings' was held to require the lessee to pay the cost of connecting the house to a sewer under Sanitation Act 1866, s 10; in *Aldridge v Ferne* (1886) 17 QBD 212, a lessees covenant to pay 'outgoings' required him to pay the owner's proportion of paving the street under the Metropolis Local Management Act 1862; see also *Greaves v Whitmarsh, Watson & Co Ltd* [1906] 2 KB 340.

wise to secure the agreement of the lender, the borrower and any prior incumbrancer that these costs should be treated as outgoings.

12.16 If the borrower is liable to pay non-domestic rates or council tax in respect of the property, the receiver should discharge that liability.[19]

12.17 However, the position in relation to the various taxes for which a borrower might be liable is less straightforward. The first thing to stress is that only taxes which 'affect the mortgaged property' need to be considered.[20] Income tax and corporation tax do not affect the property and should not be paid by a receiver appointed under the statutory powers (even if he were, in fact, able to ascertain the borrower's overall income and liability to tax).

12.18 VAT is a tax affecting the mortgaged property for the purposes of section 109(8) of the Law of Property Act 1925.[21]

12.19 Receivers are therefore liable to collect and pay VAT, if the borrower is liable to do so.[22] That turns on whether an election to tax has been made (since property income is exempt unless such an election is made). This can be ascertained by the receiver, provided he has the borrower's VAT number, by enquiry of the tax office.[23]

12.20 If the receiver is liable to pay the VAT, HMRC will allow him to set off as input tax the amount that the borrower itself could have claimed as input tax.[24] Form VAT 833 should be used by the receiver.[25] However, the obligation to file the return remains the borrower's, and it is the borrower who must reclaim any overpayment.[26]

---

[19] *Re Kentish Homes Ltd* [1993] BCC 212 (overruled on other grounds in *Re Toshuko Finance UK Plc* [2000] 1 BCB 683). See also *In Re Emmadart* [1979] 1 Ch 540, where the receiver wound the company up in order to bring the liability to pay rates to an end.

The question of whether the receiver has a personal liability to the local authority to pay the rates is a different question: see para 6.55 *et seq*. The receiver is only liable (in place of the borrower) for non-domestic rates if the receiver has taken possession in his own right (i.e. not as agent for the borrower): *Ratford v Northavon DC* [1987] QB 357. If the property is unoccupied, the key question is whether the receiver is the person 'entitled to possession' immediately: *Brown v City of London Corp* [1996] 1 WLR 1070. The position does not change if the borrower goes into liquidation: *Rees v Boston BC* [2001] EWCA Civ 1934, [2002] 1 WLR 1304.

The receiver is unlikely to be liable for council tax, because the liability to pay falls on the 'resident', and if there is none, the owner.

[20] Law of Property Act 1925, s 109(8).

[21] *Sargent v Customs and Excise Commissioners* [1994] 1 WLR 235.

[22] VAT Notice 742, paras 9.3 and 9.4.

[23] VAT Notice 700/56, para 17.2.

[24] VAT Notice 700/56, para 17.3.

[25] VAT Notice 700/56, para 17.3.

[26] VAT Notice 700/56, para 17.3.

Sums due to those with priority

12.21 Next, the receiver should make any payments falling due under arrangements, generally charges, which have priority to the charge under which he was appointed.[27]

12.22 In order to ascertain whether any such charges exist, the receiver must obtain office copy entries. He must check the date on which 'his' charge was registered and whether there is any note on the register altering priorities. If there is no such note, then 'his' charge will have priority over:

(a) any legal or equitable charges granted after the date on which 'his' charge was registered;

(b) a legal or equitable charge granted before 'his' charge, but which was not registered before his charge was registered;[28]

(c) a legal charge granted in the period between the grant of 'his' charge and registration of it, which was not registered before 'his' charge was registered;[29]

(d) an equitable charge granted in the period between the grant of his charge and registration of it, even if it (the equitable charge) was registered before 'his' charge was registered.[30]

12.23 Conversely, the following will have priority over 'his' charge:

(a) a legal or equitable charge granted and registered before 'his' charge was granted;[31]

(b) a legal or equitable charge granted before 'his' charge, which was registered after 'his' charge was granted, but before 'his' charge was registered; and

(c) a legal charge granted after 'his' charge was granted, but registered before 'his' charge was registered.[32]

12.24 Once the receiver has identified that there is a charge[33] with priority over that under which he was appointed, he then needs to see the terms of the charge and ascertain what sums are then due under it.

---

[27] The wording of Law of Property Act 1925, s 109(8)(ii) is 'in keeping down all annual sums or other payments ... having priority to the mortgage in right where of he is receiver', which would include payments due to persons other than prior chargees. For example, presumably, this includes payments falling due under a trust for securing money, liens, annuities and other capital or annual sums within the meaning in s 205(1)(vii). The existence of any obligation may be more difficult to ascertain than the existence of a registered charge.

[28] Land Registration Act 2002, s 29.

[29] Land Registration Act 2002, s 28. This will only arise if 'his' charge was not registered in a priority search period for the earlier charge.

[30] An equitable charge is not a registrable disposition, so the equitable chargee does not get the benefit of Land Registration Act 2002, s 29.

[31] Land Registration Act 2002, s 28. In unregistered land, the rule on priorities is that the first in time wins.

[32] Land Registration Act 2002, s 29.

[33] Or other interest.

Remuneration, insurance and repairs

Remuneration

12.25 The default position is that the receiver is entitled to be remunerated by the retention of 5% of the gross amount of all monies received by him for his remuneration and expenses.[34] That remuneration covers both his time and any costs and expenses he incurs – save those which are separately dealt with, such as rents, rates, taxes, outgoings, insurance and the cost of repairs.[35] It follows that if his expenses (within the statutory definition) are high, he may have little or no remuneration.

12.26 There are five ways in which that default position can be changed.

12.27 First, if a lower rate is specified in the appointment, that rate will apply.

12.28 Secondly, if no rate is specified in the appointment,[36] the court has power to allow a higher rate, on application by the receiver.[37] Such applications are rare, and it is unclear to what extent the court will be prepared to depart from the statutory regime. If the receiver accepts an appointment without giving any consideration to whether the statutory regime is adequate, it is not anticipated that the court will be receptive to the application. However, if the receiver did consider the matter at the outset, but some radical change of circumstance since the appointment has occurred so that it is now inadequate, it is perhaps more likely that the court would order higher remuneration.

12.29 Thirdly, if the terms of the mortgage provide for some other charging regime, the agreed terms will apply. Many mortgages make express provision for all the receiver's expenses to be paid.

12.30 Often, the mortgage also provides that the receiver can charge remuneration at his standard rate, or for the lender to have power to agree the receiver's remuneration. Generally, receivers seek remuneration on a time basis.[38]

---

[34] Law of Property Act 1925, s 109(6). This applies (unless the default position is modified: see para 12.26 *et seq*) even if the receiver's powers go beyond the power to collect income: *Marshall v Cottingham* [1982] 1 Ch 82.

[35] Note also that the mortgage may modify what is to be included as receivers' expenses (even if it does not affect a more radical change to the remuneration regime): *Marshall v Cottingham* [1982] 1 Ch 82, where the mortgage made specific provision for the costs of sale.

[36] Note that if a charging regime is specified in the mortgage, and the appointment is made by reference to the terms of the mortgage, the terms of the mortgage will be 'specified in the appointment'.

[37] Law of Property Act 1925, s 109(6). Note that if an application is made, the receiver is at risk that the court will conclude that a lower rate is appropriate. The application should be made 'by summons in chambers' per Law of Property Act 1925, s 203(2)(a); now, unless there are already proceedings on foot (in which case, the receiver should apply within those proceedings by filing and serving an application notice), by claim form under CPR, Pt 8. See Insolvency Practice Direction, Pt 6, for factors that may be relevant.

[38] And an indemnity against all costs and expenses.

12.31 Agreeing to accept a percentage of receipts leaves a receiver exposed (even if his expenses are paid on top), particularly in the case where a sale of the security is anticipated, but the conveyance is ultimately made by the lender under its power of sale. In this situation, there is a good argument that the sale proceeds are not 'received by him', so he would not be entitled to his percentage of that sum. The receiver is similarly exposed if his appointment is terminated before the sale. In either of these situations, the receiver is thrown back on arguments about implied terms if he has agreed to accept a percentage of receipts.

12.32 Where there is no express term in the mortgage for remuneration beyond the statutory regime, it is unlikely that such a term will be implied into the mortgage. Statute provides for some remuneration, albeit on a basis which may not reflect the amount of work in fact carried out, so the contract is not commercially incoherent without the proposed implied term.[39]

12.33 If the terms of the appointment provide for some other charging regime, those terms will be effective as between lender and receiver,[40] but the receiver will not be entitled to deduct remuneration beyond that to which he is entitled on the basis set out under the LPA from his receipts. However, since the lender will not be able to add costs to the mortgage account beyond those authorised in the mortgage conditions or ordered by the court,[41] it will be rare for the lender to provide in the appointment for a different charging regime. Moreover, it is most unlikely that any term for additional payment will be implied into the appointment.[42]

12.34 If the mortgage terms do not deal with remuneration, and the receiver is not content with the basic 5% of gross receipts, a better course might be for the appointment to remain silent as to the receiver's remuneration, so that the receiver can make an application for the court to fix his remuneration at a higher rate. There does not seem to be any reason why the application cannot be made at the outset of the appointment (or for the lender and the receiver to agree that if acceptable terms as to remuneration are not obtained from the court, the receiver shall be entitled to resign forthwith). If the court does agree a higher remuneration is appropriate, the lender will be able to add the remuneration to the mortgage account, since the borrower has agreed to the possibility of a higher rate being approved by the court: this is inherent in section 109(6) of the Law of Property Act 1925.

---

[39] The test for the implication of terms was clarified in *Marks & Spencer Plc v BNP Paribas* [2015] UKSC 72, [2016] AC 742. In *Deyes v Wood* [1911] 1 KB 806, the court appears (at 814) to have suggested that a term for payment of reasonable remuneration should be implied. It is considered unlikely that this result would be reached today.

[40] The question of whether the lender could sue the receiver for this remuneration is considered at para 7.28 *et seq.*

[41] *Vedalease Ltd v Averti Developments Ltd* [2007] 2 EGLR 125.

[42] A term might be implied if there was a course of dealing between the lender and the receiver to pay on a basis other than as set out in the lender's standard mortgage terms.

12.35 Fifthly, the receiver may forfeit his right to remuneration if he is in breach of his duties owed to the lender. This will only occur if the breach is so serious that it amounts to a repudiation of the contract.

12.36 A question may arise as to whether the same rate applies where the receiver is exercising powers beyond those of an LPA receiver and, in particular, if he is exercising a lender delegated power. If, as is usual, the mortgage conditions provide for the receiver to exercise lender delegated powers as the borrower's deemed agent, then it is likely the conditions will be construed so that the same remuneration regime also applies in respect of these powers.[43]

Company borrower

12.37 Statute provides for the receiver's remuneration to be a charge over any property of the company.[44] This can be important if the receivership is terminated before the receiver has been paid.[45]

12.38 If a company is in liquidation, the court has power to vary the remuneration provisions[46] in the statute and/or the mortgage on an application made by the liquidator.[47] Multiple orders can be made, and the first can be retrospective.[48] Such an order can be made even if the receivership has terminated, and even if the receiver has died. Furthermore, if there are special circumstances, the order can require the receiver or his personal representatives to disgorge remuneration already paid or retained by them.[49]

12.39 On its face, this appears to be a very wide power. Regardless of what has been agreed in the mortgage or at the time the appointment is accepted, the court can, if the borrower goes into liquidation at any time,[50] re-open the remuneration. However, although there is an unfettered discretion as to whether to interfere at all, and, if so, as to the amount, the court will not interfere unless the remuneration can clearly be seen to be excessive.[51] The power is rarely used.

---

[43] Where the mortgage does not, on its true construction, authorise the delegation of powers by the lender, there will be no right, as against the borrower, to retain any remuneration in respect of this work from the income: *Vedalease Ltd v Averti Developments Ltd* [2007] 2 EGLR 125.

[44] Insolvency Act 1986, s 37.

[45] Termination is dealt with in Chapter 13.

[46] The court does not have any power to interfere in relation to the receivers' disbursements: *Re Potters Oils Ltd* [1986] 1 WLR 201.

[47] Insolvency Act 1986, s 36. This applies to a fixed charge receiver: s 29. Reference should be made to any practitioner's text on insolvency for the procedural requirements on such an application, which are beyond the remit of this book.

[48] Insolvency Act 1986, s 36.

[49] Insolvency Act 1986, s 36.

[50] There is no express long stop in the statute. However, it is considered that a liquidator could not take action to recover sums already in the receiver's hands more than 6 years after he was appointed (which is when his cause of action would accrue): Limitation Act 1980, s 9.

[51] *Re Potters Oils Ltd* [1986] 1 WLR 201; *Munns v Perkins* [2002] BPIR 120.

12.40 It is unclear whether an application under this section can be founded on a complaint about the adequacy of the work done by the receivers.[52]

Challenges to the receiver's remuneration

12.41 If the receiver seeks to retain more than the terms of the mortgage (or the statute) permit, the borrower will be able to challenge the receiver's accounts.

12.42 However, if the receiver is seeking to retain remuneration in line with the terms which were agreed in the mortgage, or in default, as set out in statute, the borrower cannot challenge the receiver's remuneration.

12.43 The borrower can, however, always challenge whether particular items fall within the scope of the entitlement to remuneration.[53]

12.44 Even if the language of the mortgage is very wide, some limits will be implied. For example, if the mortgage gives the lender the right to appoint a receiver 'on such terms as to remuneration or otherwise' as the lender sees fit, that power must be exercised in good faith.[54] Similarly, a clause which entitles the receiver to all costs, charges and expenses on a full indemnity basis is likely to be interpreted as limited to those costs which were reasonably and properly incurred and reasonable in amount.[55]

12.45 A borrower wishing to challenge the remuneration (or any other deduction the receiver has made) must assert that the receivers have acted in breach of statutory duty in paying themselves more than they were entitled to on the true construction of the mortgage deed. The claim should be brought under Part 7 or Part 8 of the CPR, depending on whether disputes of fact are anticipated.

Insurance

12.46 A receiver must determine what powers he has to insure the property, immediately after he is appointed.

12.47 There is a statutory power and duty to insure against loss or damage by fire, but this only arises if:

---

[52] *Re Delberry Ltd* [2008] EWHC 925 (Ch), [2008] BCC 653.

[53] *Rottenberg v Monjack* [1992] BCC 688.

[54] *Re Potters Oils Ltd (no 2)* [1986] 1 WLR 201.

[55] *Gomba Holdings (UK) Ltd v Minories Finance Ltd* [1993] Ch 171, in which the mortgage terms obliged the borrower to pay on demand and on a full indemnity basis all costs, charges and expenses of any receiver appointed. The clause was construed so as to exclude any charges which had not been reasonably incurred or were unreasonable in amount.

(a) the lender could have insured against fire;[56] and

(b) the lender directed the receiver, in writing, to effect the insurance.[57]

12.48 The amount of the insurance must not exceed the amount specified in the mortgage deed, or if no amount is specified, two-thirds of the amount that would be required to restore the property in the event of a total destruction.[58]

12.49 The mortgage deed may confer additional powers to insure on the receiver. Alternatively, the mortgage deed may confer additional powers to insure on the lender, and the lender may have delegated those powers to the receiver in the appointment.

12.50 Having determined the scope of his power to insure, the receiver should put in place appropriate insurance cover as soon as he has the money to do so. Indeed, the receiver risks a finding that he has breached his duty of care if he does not seek funding from the lender for the insurance premium as soon as he is appointed.

12.51 The borrower may already have an insurance policy in place when the receiver is appointed. However, it is risky for the receiver to rely on this, for many reasons: cover may be inadequate; insurers may be able to avoid the policy because of some material non-disclosure when the policy was taken out; the borrower may cancel the policy; or insurers may not be prepared to pay the proceeds to the receiver in the event of a claim. It is therefore not advisable for receivers to rely on the borrower's own policy.[59] Once the receivers have put their own policy in place, they should inform the borrower so that he can cancel his policy.

12.52 In reality, insurers are unlikely to offer terms for insurance against fire only, so in order to comply with any duty to insure against fire, a wider insurance is likely to be obtained. It is considered that the whole of the premium for this insurance would fall within the insurance costs which the receiver is entitled and obliged to discharge ahead of paying the appointing lender.

---

[56] Law of Property Act 1925, s 101(1)(ii) confers such a power on lenders, unless the terms of the mortgage disapply it. Section 108(2) excludes the power to insure:

   (i) where there is a declaration in the mortgage deed that no insurance is required;

   (ii) where an insurance is kept up by or on behalf of the borrower in accordance with the mortgage deed;

   (iii) where the mortgage deed contains no stipulation respecting insurance, and an insurance is kept up by or on behalf of the mortgagor with the consent of the mortgagee to the amount to which the mortgagee is authorised to insure.

[57] Law of Property Act 1925, s 109(7).

[58] Law of Property Act 1925, s 108(1).

[59] The position may be different in relation to life insurance, where the receiver would not, in practice, have the information to take out the policy. If the mortgage requires life insurance to be in place, the receiver could pay the premiums on the borrower's pre-existing policy and include them in this category.

12.53 In addition, the receiver may also have to take steps to make the risk more attractive to insurers in order to persuade them to cover it. Such steps might include the employment of a security guard. These costs would not appear to fall within this category (though would, presumably, be outgoings).

12.54 If grounds for making a claim under the insurance policy exist, the receiver owes a duty to the person(s) interested in the equity of redemption[60] to make the claim. The duty is an equitable duty of care. If the duty is breached, *prima facie*, the person interested in the equity of redemption can claim damages.

12.55 In order to quantify his loss, it is important to consider what different position he would have been in, if a claim had been made. It is therefore necessary to consider whether the claim would have been successful and what the receiver would have done with the money if it had been.[61]

12.56 The statute specifically exempts insurance monies[62] from the statutory regime applicable to distribution of other monies received by the receivers.[63] Instead, it provides that where the insurance effected is insurance against fire under the Law of Property Act 1925, or is an insurance which the borrower is obliged to maintain under the mortgage deed,[64] the lender can elect whether the money should be applied to making good the loss or damage which led to the claim, or be applied in or towards the discharge of the mortgage money.[65] The lender's rights under this section will trump the rights of someone with the benefit of a third party debt order.[66]

Repairs

12.57 It is important to stress that the receiver can only use the income to pay for repairs: (a) which are necessary or proper; and (b) which he has been

---

[60]   See para 6.69 *et seq*. The borrower unless insolvent; but if the borrower is bankrupt, to the trustee in bankruptcy: *Purewal v Countrywide Residential Lettings Ltd* [2015] EWCA Civ 1122, [2016] 4 WLR 31. Also, subsequent chargees.

[61]   Although there was a suggestion (*obiter*) in *Purewal v Countrywide Residential Lettings Ltd* [2015] EWCA Civ 1122, [2016] 4 WLR 31 at [22] that the question is simply one of 'but for' causation, it is considered that the better analysis is that the claim is a loss of a chance claim. In a case where a breach of duty is established, the court will assess the likelihood of the claim having been successful, and the lender directing the receiver to carry out the works, and will award as damages that proportion of the damages that would have been payable if it were clear that the claim would be met and the repairs would be done.

[62]   I.e. the proceeds of an insurance claim.

[63]   Law of Property Act 1925, s 109(8).

[64]   In *Sinnott v Bowden* [1912] 2 Ch 414, the borrower had insurance in place when the mortgage was executed. The mortgage contained a covenant to insure. The policy was renewed on expiry. The court held that this was an insurance policy 'effected under the mortgage deed'. Query what would have been the outcome if the claim had arisen before the policy had renewed.

[65]   Law of Property Act 1925, s 108(3) and (4).

[66]   *Sinnott v Bowden* [1912] 2 Ch 414.

directed in writing by the mortgagee to carry out.[67] This means that he cannot pay for repairs executed before the receivership is commenced.

12.58 That does not mean that the receiver should simply sit back and allow the property to fall apart around him. He owes a duty to the borrower to seek the lender's authorisation to carry out repairs which are necessary[68] and should consider whether it would be proper to seek authorisation to carry out any other repairs which are not essential.

Interest and principal

12.59 The receiver must pay interest accruing in respect of the principal money due under the mortgage under which he was appointed, including arrears of interest due at the date of the appointment (other than statute-barred arrears).[69] He must also pay interest which accrues due after his appointment.

12.60 If income tax is deductible from mortgage interest payments,[70] then the receiver should make the appropriate reduction and pay the tax over to the borrower.[71]

12.61 As regards the principal due under the mortgage, he must only pay this to the lender if directed to do so in writing by the lender.[72] Typically, the lender will expect that any surplus will be used to pay down the principal rather than being passed to the borrower as residue, but receivers must ensure that an appropriate direction, in writing, is given by the lender.

Residue

12.62 The residue is payable to the person who, but for the possession[73] of the receiver, would have been entitled to receive the income, or who is otherwise entitled to the mortgaged property.[74]

---

[67] Law of Property Act 1925, s 109(8); *White v Metcalf* [1903] 2 Ch 567. The receiver's failure to seek authority meant the receiver was unable to recover the costs.

[68] See para 6.91.

[69] Note that the position is different where the receiver exercises the lender's power of sale: see para 12.83.

[70] This might arise if the borrower is a company within the corporation tax loan relationship or an individual carrying on a letting business or a trade for the purposes of which the interest is incurred. There are also some other specific reliefs. Reference should be made to any practitioner's text on tax law, which is beyond the remit of this book.

[71] It is thought that this applies even where the borrower had an obligation (as opposed to an entitlement) to deduct basic rate tax at source and account for that money to HMRC, since it remains the borrower's liability to pay its income tax.

[72] Law of Property Act 1925, s 109(8).

[73] 'Possession' includes receipt of the rents and profits and hence is an apt expression even if the receiver is not in possession of the mortgaged property in the sense of occupation: Law of Property Act 1925, s 205(1)(xix).

[74] Law of Property Act 1925, s 109(8).

12.63 If there is a lender in possession, the residue should be paid to the lender. This means that if the appointing lender is in possession, it will be entitled to monies towards its principal debt even if it does not give notice in writing so as to get it under section 109(8)(v) of the Law of Property Act 1925.

12.64 If the lender is not in possession and has not been paid out under section 109(8)(v) of the Law of Property Act 1925, there is then a question as to whether the lender is 'the person who … is otherwise entitled to the mortgaged property'. It is thought that it cannot have been intended that the appointing lender should fall within this definition, for this would render section 109(8)(v), and its requirement for written notice, redundant.[75]

12.65 However, if the appointing lender is not 'otherwise entitled to the mortgaged property' if he is not in possession, it is difficult to see how subsequent incumbrancers (who are not in possession) can fall within that wording so that they would be entitled to the residue. It would be curious if it were intended that any residue were to be paid over to the borrower disregarding any subsequent charges, and to interpret these words as excluding subsequent incumbrancers would be inconsistent with the way in which similar words have been interpreted, in cases considering the same wording in another section of the Law of Property Act 1925.[76] The position should therefore be regarded as unclear where there is a subsequent incumbrancer.

12.66 A possible solution is for the subsequent incumbrancer to appoint the receivers to act as its receivers also, so that they would be entitled to receive the income but for the possession of the receiver. This would appear to solve the difficulty, but could only occur if both lenders consented.

12.67 If there is no subsequent incumbrancer, it is clear that the payment should be made to the borrower, or his representative. This means, if the borrower is dead, payment should be made to his personal representative; similarly, if the borrower is bankrupt, the payment should be made to the trustee in bankruptcy.[77] If the borrower is a company in liquidation, the payment should be made to the liquidator.[78]

12.68 If there is a dispute as to who is entitled to the residue, the receiver can make a stakeholder application to the court.[79] However, if the receiver knows

---

[75] If this is right, it seems to suggest that the receiver has a duty to seek the lender's instructions as to whether to discharge the principal, so that the lender does not lose the chance to have the principal discharged or reduced before the money passes out of the receiver's control.

[76] *Re Thomson's Mortgage Trusts* [1920] 1 Ch 508, where it was held that a subsequent chargee was 'the person entitled to the mortgaged property' where a prior chargee had exercised a power of sale, under Law of Property Act 1925, s 105. Although the judge expressed some doubt in *Re Thomson*, it is considered that the case was correctly decided under s 105: see para 12.84 *et seq*.

[77] Insolvency Act 1986, s 306; *Purewal v Countrywide Residential Lettings Ltd* [2015] EWCA Civ 1122, [2016] 4 WLR 31.

[78] *Re G L Saunders Ltd* [1986] 1 WLR 215.

[79] CPR, Pt 86. See para 14.11 *et seq*.

who he should pay, but cannot trace that person, it is uncertain whether the receiver can apply to the court.[80] If he does not (or cannot), he should simply hold the monies until the limitation period has expired.[81]

THE BORROWER'S POWER OF SALE

12.69 If the receiver sells in exercise of the borrower's right to sell, the principles to be applied in establishing who is entitled to the proceeds are not necessarily the same as the regime set out above for income. Although the regime discussed above appears, on its face, to apply[82] to 'all money received' by the receiver,[83] strictly, the statutory regime only applies to monies arising as a result of the exercise of the statutory powers. Where other powers are conferred by the mortgage, the mortgage must be construed to see what regime the parties should be taken to have intended would apply to the proceeds of sale.[84]

12.70 Often, the parties will be taken to have intended that the 'income' regime specified above[85] should apply to any monies received by the receiver, even if the monies were received by exercising powers other than those conferred on the receiver by statute.[86] However, where the terms of the mortgage make some other provision, those terms will apply.

12.71 Where the statutory regime is applied, a difficulty arises about the costs of sale. These do not appear to be included in any of the categories.[87] It will

---

[80] It has been suggested that the receiver can apply to the court and/or pay into court on the basis that the receiver holds the proceeds on trust (i.e. under CPR, Pt 64). The cases discussed at para 12.5 suggest that the cause of action against a receiver who does not pay what he should is for breach of statutory duty, not breach of trust. Furthermore, Law of Property Act 1925, s 109 does not contain any reference to the receiver holding the property on trust; cf Law of Property Act 1925, s 105 which expressly provides that the mortgagee holds the proceeds on trust if it sells. However, in *Banner v Berridge* (1881) 18 Ch D 254, the court suggested that a constructive trust might arise where a mortgagee received proceeds and there was no express imposition of a trust. There is therefore an argument that the receiver holds as a constructive trustee.

[81] Limitation Act 1980, s 9 provides for a 6-year period for actions to recover any sum recoverable by virtue of an enactment.

[82] In default of any other agreement in the mortgage

[83] Law of Property Act 1925, s 109(8).

[84] In practice, the receiver will have to discharge registered prior charges and the mortgage under which he is appointed for sale free of them, and, if they are the subject of restrictions on the title, for registration of the transfer.

[85] See para 12.3 *et seq.*

[86] Save those arising under lender delegated powers where the lender was under different obligations: see para 12.74 *et seq.*

[87] In *Marshall v Cottingham* [1982] 1 Ch 82, at 89, the Court had to consider a mortgage which expressly stated that the costs of sale were to be paid first and then the proceeds of sale were to be applied per Law of Property Act 1925, s 109(8). Megarry V-C considered (*obiter*) where costs of sale could be accommodated within the 'income' regime set out in Law of Property Act 1925, s 109(8). He indicated that he did not consider such costs would naturally fall within

therefore be necessary to establish that it is appropriate to imply a term that the parties must have intended that these should be deductible from the proceeds of sale if they are not to come out of the receiver's commission.

12.72 The borrower may have a liability for CGT by reason of the sale. This is a personal liability of the borrower and not a liability which the receiver should treat as charged on the property. In those circumstances, it is considered unlikely that the court would imply a term requiring the receiver to pay any CGT before passing the residue to the borrower. In practice, of course, the receiver may not know what the borrower had paid for the property, so it is unlikely that the parties would have intended him to make the return and pay the tax.

THE LENDER'S POWER OF SALE

12.73 As already noted, the income regime discussed above appears, on its face, to apply[88] to 'all money received' by the receiver.[89] Another issue therefore arises about whether it applies to the proceeds of sale of the property if the receiver exercises the lender's power of sale.[90]

12.74 If the lender were to sell itself, a slightly different statutory regime[91] would apply to the proceeds. The lender must first discharge any prior incumbrances. Then, he holds the remainder of the proceeds on trust to be applied in the following order:

(a) all costs, charges and expenses properly incurred by him as incident to the sale or any attempted sale;

(b) the mortgage money, interest and costs and any other monies due under the mortgage;

(c) the residue is to be paid to the person entitled to the mortgaged property, or authorised to give receipts for the proceeds of the sale thereof.

12.75 The better view is that the lender regime described in the previous paragraph applies where the receiver is exercising the lender's power of sale, and not the regime described above under the heading 'Income'.[92] A lender cannot delegate any power to the receiver beyond the power which it, itself, had.

'outgoings', and concluded that they might therefore fall within the costs which the receiver was to bear himself out of his 5% commission.

[88] In default of any other agreement in the mortgage.

[89] Law of Property Act 1925, s 109(8).

[90] The extent to which the receiver can exercise the lender's power of sale is discussed in detail at para 11.87 *et seq.*

[91] Law of Property Act 1925, s 105.

[92] See para 12.3 *et seq.* In *Re G L Saunders Ltd* [1986] 1 WLR 215, the court proceeded on the basis that Law of Property Act 1925, s 105 applied, but it is not clear if there was any argument about this. Since there were no subsequent incumbrancers, it would not have made a difference to the outcome if the, s 109 regime had been applied instead.

The lender's power of sale is impressed with a statutory trust which governs what must be done with the proceeds.

12.76 Furthermore, the 'income' regime discussed in the previous section does not obviously make any provision for the costs of sale,[93] so where there is an alternative scheme which does make provision for the costs of sale, it is more likely that the parties would have intended it to apply.

Prior incumbrance

12.77 This phrase in section 105 of the Law of Property Act 1925 means an incumbrance which has priority over the appointing lender's mortgage.[94] Often, this will be a prior charge, but not inevitably so.[95]

12.78 As regards charges, in practice, the conveyancing solicitor for the receiver will have to undertake to discharge such charges from the proceeds of sale, so that sale can be free of them, so the receiver will have little choice in practice but to pay off such charges.

12.79 However, if discharge of the prior incumbrance did not happen, the incumbrancer with priority would have a cause of action for breach of trust. The proper defendant would be determined by considering whether the receiver acted as deemed agent of the borrower, on his own account as donee of a power from the lender, or as the lender's agent.[96]

Costs, charges and expenses incidental to the sale

12.80 As well as covering the obvious legal and agent's fees involved in effecting the sale, the statutory language is likely to be construed as wide enough to cover the costs properly incurred in holding and preparing the property for sale.[97] *Prima facie*, this could cover rents, taxes, rates and outgoings,[98] insurance premiums,[99] receiver's remuneration and expenses[100] and

---

[93] See para 12.71.

[94] See paras 12.22–12.23 for an explanation as to which mortgages will and will not have priority.

[95] 'Prior incumbrance' is not limited to mortgages. See Law of Property Act 1925, s 205(1)(vii). It appears to include a co-owner in equity whose beneficial interest takes priority over the mortgage. Section 105 follows s 104(1), which allows sale of the mortgaged property freed from 'all estates, interests, and rights to which the mortgage has priority' so that it is tempting to assume 'incumbrance' in s 105 includes the same list. It is usually assumed that such a person should be paid out of the proceeds of sale in advance of repayment of the secured sum since otherwise that person would be forced to pay a debt for which they were not liable to redeem a mortgage they took free of. See for example *Barclays Bank Plc v Burgess* [2002] EWCA Civ 291.

[96] See para 7.58 *et seq*. See *American Express v Hurley* [1985] 3 All ER 564 for an example of such a claim where the receiver was held to be acting as the lender's agent.

[97] See, by analogy, *McHugh v Union Bank of Canada* [1913] AC 299 at 312.

[98] See para 12.12 *et seq*.

[99] See para 12.46 *et seq*.

[100] See para 12.25 *et seq*.

the cost of any repairs[101] not paid for out of the income – though in each case it would be necessary to show that it was proper for the expense to be incurred.

12.81 The lender has no obligation to pay CGT on the disposal.[102] The borrower remains liable to account for any CGT arising. The receiver should not, therefore, deduct any sums in respect of any CGT liability.

12.82 However, if the disposal attracts a liability to pay VAT (i.e. if the disposal does not fall within the 'transfer as a going concern' regime),[103] the receiver should deduct the VAT and account for it.[104]

The mortgage money

12.83 If the lender exercises his power of sale, he is entitled to retain statute-barred interest arrears from the proceeds.[105] It is considered that if the receiver is exercising the lender's power of sale, the lender's position should be the same: the receiver should pay even statute-barred arrears to the lender out of the proceeds.

Residue

12.84 Any residue should be paid over to the incumbrancer next in line.[106] It is a matter for that chargee to pay himself what is properly owing (and he, too, is entitled to retain statute-barred interest)[107] and then pass the rest to the incumbrancer next in line, and so on. The appointing lender does not have to work out how much each subsequent incumbrancer is owed, and neither does the receiver.[108]

12.85 If there are no subsequent incumbrancers, then the residue must be paid to the borrower, unless the borrower is bankrupt (when it should be paid to the

---

[101] Note that it is possible to include repairs and improvement works which the receiver has carried out even though they would not fall within the repairs which the receiver would be entitled to pay for out of income. The test is simply whether it was proper for the lender to spend the monies in order to realise the security. Any decision to undertake substantial works should be considered carefully.

[102] Taxation of Chargeable Gains Act 1992, s 26(2).

[103] VAT Notice 742A, para 11 describes this in more detail. Specialist advice should be sought in cases of any doubt.

[104] VAT Notice 742, para 9.2; VAT Notice 700/56, para 17.3.

[105] *Edmunds v Waugh* (1865–66) LR 1 Eq 418. Similarly, on discharge of the mortgage, the lender is entitled to his costs reasonably and properly incurred of any claim by it against the borrower or against a third party impugning title, even though there is no covenant in the mortgage for the lender to pay such costs. However, most mortgages have express costs clauses which allow recovery of costs as a debt against the borrower.

[106] *Re Thomson's Mortgage Trusts* [1920] 1 Ch 508; unless his title has been extinguished under the Limitation Act 1980: see para 12.86.

[107] *Re Thomson's Mortgage Trusts* [1920] 1 Ch 508. He will likewise be entitled to costs.

[108] Although the judge expressed doubt about this in *Re Thomson's Mortgage Trusts* [1920] 1 Ch 508.

trustee in bankruptcy),[109] or in liquidation (when it should be paid to the liquidator).[110]

12.86 If the mortgagor and any subsequent incumbrancers are statute-barred from redeeming, because their title has been extinguished,[111] the whole of the proceeds can be retained by the lender.[112]

12.87 If the receiver pays the wrong person, he (or his principal if he is acting as agent or deemed agent) commits a breach of trust. This is the case even if neither the receiver nor the principal knew of the claim nor that the person appearing to be next in line had no valid claim, and even if there was nothing on the register to suggest this. The breach is actionable, in the case of a failure to pay a subsequent chargee, by the subsequent chargee.[113]

12.88 However, if the receiver (and/or his principal, if any) acted honestly and reasonably and ought fairly to be excused for the breach of trust, the court can relieve him from liability.[114] It is to be noted that acting honestly alone is not enough. So, if, for example, the receiver (and/or his principal) is given notice of a subsequent equitable charge which does not appear on the register, but has forgotten about it by the time of the sale, relief is unlikely to be given.[115] Likewise, if no one checks at Land Registry whether any subsequent charges exist, it is inconceivable that relief would be given, even if all involved were completely honest.

---

[109] Insolvency Act 1986, s 306; *Purewal v Countrywide Residential Lettings Ltd* [2015] EWCA Civ 1122, [2016] 4 WLR 31.

[110] *Re G L Saunders* [1986] 1 WLR 215.

[111] Limitation Act 1980, s 17.

[112] *Young v Clarey* [1948] 1 Ch 191, where the lender had been in possession for more than 12 years, without receiving any payment and without making any acknowledgment sufficient to start time running again. See also *C & M Matthews Ltd v Marsden Building Society* [1951] 1 Ch 758, where the court rejected a claim by a second mortgagee, who was precluded from bringing any action on the loan by the Moneylenders Act 1927, to the residue. However, the court did suggest that the borrower might not be able to obtain an order for payment out of the residue without agreeing to discharge the second mortgagee's debt, because the Moneylenders Act 1927 merely precluded bringing any action to enforce it, rather than extinguishing the debt. Cf Limitation Act 1980, s 17.

[113] *West London Commercial Bank v Reliance Permanent Building Society* (1885) 29 Ch D 954.

[114] Trustee Act 1925, s 61; *Re Allsop* [1914] 1 Ch 1.

[115] The issue did not arise in *West London Commercial Bank v Reliance Permanent Building Society* (1885) 29 Ch D 954, but it is considered that the same result would be achieved, if those facts occurred now, and an application were made under the Trustee Act 1925, s 61.

Chapter 13

Termination

13.1   This chapter addresses the different ways in which a receivership can be terminated and the consequences of termination.

MODES OF TERMINATION

Completion of the receivership

13.2   Typically, a receivership comes to an end when the receivers sell the security and pay over the proceeds of sale to the lender to pay the mortgage debt.

13.3   If the proceeds are sufficient to pay off the debt in full,[1] the receiver becomes *functus officio*,[2] which means that, having fulfilled his role, he no longer has authority to act, save to complete the necessary administrative tasks to conclude the receivership.[3]

13.4   Similarly, if the debt[4] is paid off in full from some other source, for example, if the borrower refinances, the receivership is complete, and the receiver becomes *functus*.

---

[1]   Having paid any other liabilities with priority first: see Chapter 12. If contingent liabilities remain, the receiver does not become *functus*.

[2]   The reason is that on receipt of all of the mortgage debt, the mortgage is discharged, ending all rights and obligations between the borrower and the lender. See *Gomba Holdings v Homan* (1986) 2 BCC 99 at 102: 'Until actual redemption or at least a valid tender of the redemption price, these powers [receivership] continue to exist'. Redemption is discussed at para 2.53 *et seq*.

[3]   See para 13.35 *et seq*. In *Rottenberg v Monjack* [1992] BCC 688, the court appears to have accepted that administrative receivers who had paid the debt off in full, but who had not paid themselves the remuneration to which they were entitled, remained in office, but query whether this is correct, unless the remuneration forms part of the debt. It is plainly wise to pay out the remuneration before (or as part of) discharging the debt in full, so that no question of whether the receivership has been terminated before the remuneration is paid can arise. In *Rottenberg*, the court also indicated (at 694A) that holding sufficient monies to pay off the debts and the remuneration would also bring the receivership to an end, but query if that is right, since it would suggest that the receiver's duties in using the money would end. Presumably, what was meant is that the receiver would no longer have any powers other than those needed to distribute the sums held in accordance with his duties.

[4]   I.e. the complete amount owing to the lender, not the arrears.

13.5   Any termination of the receiver's authority in the above circumstances would be automatic. It would not depend on any act of the parties. In practice, the receiver will seek a release from the lender and, typically, an indemnity against any future claims, if this was not provided on appointment.

13.6   It should be noted that if the borrower clears only the arrears not the total mortgage debt (or only remedies the default which gave rise to the power to appoint the receiver arising), this does not bring the appointment to an end.[5] The significance of the breach of covenant, for example arrears on the mortgage, is that it satisfies a condition precedent to the right to appoint a receiver. It is not the case that there must continue to be arrears for the appointment to continue.[6]

13.7   If the property is worth less than the debt, it may be sold free of the charge, with the lender's consent. In that situation, although the charge is released by the lender (so that the purchaser takes free of it), the lender retains his contractual remedies under the mortgage.[7] The shortfall will remain as a debt between the lender and the borrower, and the lender will have only personal remedies.[8] It is thought that the better view is that the receivership will not then end but the receiver's powers will be limited to collecting income due to the borrower prior to the sale.[9]

---

[5]   *Jumani v Mortgage Express* [2013] EWHC 1571 (Ch); cf where the borrower asserts that there were no arrears at the time the purported appointment was made, so that it is invalid. See para 4.36 *et seq*.

[6]   Borrowers often suggest otherwise, perhaps by comparison with forfeiture in landlord and tenant law. In forfeiture, the landlord can end the lease by the right to forfeit. Conversely, the lender in exercising a remedy does not choose to end the mortgage. The breach is the condition precedent to exercise of the remedy, and once there has been any breach, the starting point the remedy is available. In other contexts (e.g. forfeiture, or a lender's possession claim), paying off the arrears or remedying the default can preclude the lender from obtaining its remedy to which it would otherwise be entitled. This is because statute has intervened (e.g. the automatic relief from forfeiture provided under County Courts Act 1984, s 138 (discussed at para A.29) and the provisions of the Administration of Justice Acts (discussed at para 2.104). However, there is no such statutory provision here. Equity does retain a general discretion to grant relief when a mortgagee is seeking to exercise remedies due to non-payment under a mortgage: see *Union Eagle Ltd v Golden Achievement Ltd* [1997] 2 WLR 341 at 519. This might be prayed in aid by a borrower in an attempt to remove a receiver if he has cleared the arrears, but the authors are not aware that this has ever been done. It is thought that equity's willingness to intervene will depend on whether the receiver is merely collecting income (when an intervention is unlikely) or is seeking to sell the property (when it is more likely that equity will intervene). Otherwise, the lender will be able to enforce the remedy to which he is entitled as a matter of contract with the borrower, unless he is prevented from doing so by representation or conduct so as to estop him, the argument in *Jumani v Mortgage Express* [2013] EWHC 1571 (Ch).

[7]   The lender should release the charge and retain the contractual debt, rather than discharging the mortgage, since the latter ends all rights and remedies, with the lender usually giving receipt for repayment of the whole of the mortgage debt.

[8]   The proprietary remedies over the property will end because the sale will be free of the mortgage.

[9]   Assuming this right has not passed, under the terms of the contract, to the purchaser. It is thought that the receiver would have to be party to the contract with the purchaser, and agree this expressly, for this to occur, save where the property was let under a tenancy which is not a new tenancy for the purposes of the Landlord and Tenant (Covenants) Act 1995.

13.8   The reason is that once the charge is released, the purchaser takes free of the mortgage, and hence proprietary remedies cannot be exercised against the purchaser. New income from the property could not be collected. However, the rights and obligations under the mortgage would continue between borrower and lender. The borrower would remain liable for the shortfall as a personal debt. The receiver would be entitled to collect any pre-existing income due to the borrower. On this analysis, the receiver would have authority to continue to act on behalf of the borrower in pursuing insurance claims, or legal claims, or otherwise taking steps to attempt to clear the shortfall from income from the property due to the borrower.

Resignation during the receivership

13.9   A receiver can only resign during the receivership if, on their true construction, the terms of the appointment permit this, or the lender consents. The receiver must comply with the terms of the appointment as regards any pre-conditions or formalities for terminating. If none are specified, the receiver should give notice in writing to the lender to effect the resignation.

13.10   If two or more receivers are appointed, whether one alone can resign is a matter of construction of the appointment. If the receivers are appointed jointly, then, absent some specific terms in the appointment, it is likely to be construed so that one of two joint receivers cannot resign.[10] However, if the receivers are appointed to act jointly or severally, the starting point in construing the terms will be that one of them can resign alone with the other remaining appointed.

13.11   If the terms do not entitle the receiver to resign, in practice the lender is unlikely to stand in his way, provided that the receiver agrees to indemnify the lender against any additional costs it incurs. For, if the lender sought specific performance of the receiver's obligations, the court would be unlikely to make the order. The court will not order specific performance of contracts for personal service.[11]

13.12   If a person appointed receiver over a company's property[12] becomes bankrupt, or a disqualification order is made against him and he does not obtain leave to continue acting, he should resign.[13] The bankruptcy/disqualification order will not automatically terminate the appointment.

---

[10]   An analogy can be drawn with the position of joint tenants. One joint tenant cannot alone exercise a contractual option to determine a tenancy: *Hounslow LBC v Pilling* [1993] 2 EGLR 59.

[11]   However, the court will order specific performance of purely administrative tasks, so as to ensure an orderly handover.

[12]   Members of Nara are obliged by their Code of Practice to resign an appointment over an individual borrower's property in these circumstances as well. In addition, they are obliged to resign any appointment if they become mentally ill. Further circumstances in which the receiver should consider resigning are also specified.

[13]   Insolvency Act 1986, s 31; Company Directors' Disqualification Act 1986, ss 1 and 22; Companies Act 2006, s 1170A.

Dismissal by lender

13.13 The lender can dismiss the receiver at any time during the receivership, by writing under his own hand.[14]

13.14 The removal will take effect when the lender communicates to the receiver that he has been dismissed,[15] unless the lender indicates that he wishes the receivership to terminate at some future date. This is sometimes more practical than an instant dismissal, because the receiver has time to wind down the receivership.

13.15 If two or more receivers are appointed jointly, then, absent some specific terms in the appointment, it is thought that the lender cannot dismiss one of them.[16] However, if the receivers are appointed to act jointly or severally, the starting point will be that the lender can dismiss one of them alone.

By prior chargee

13.16 A prior chargee retains the right to appoint a receiver at any time after the power has arisen under the terms of the prior charge. If he chooses to appoint a different receiver, the receiver appointed under the later mortgage must stand aside so that the prior chargee's receiver can take control of the income. However, it is unlikely that this terminates the receivership itself, merely the receiver's ability to exercise his powers for the time being. If the prior chargee were to terminate the receivership, then the original receiver would, it is thought, be able to resume control without the need for re-appointment.[17]

Death of the receiver

13.17 If a sole receiver dies, the receivership automatically terminates.

13.18 If one of two joint receivers dies, the remaining receiver becomes a sole receiver – unless there is anything in the terms of the appointment to the contrary. Of course, in practice, the parties may agree that the remaining receiver should resign so that he can be re-appointed with a replacement co-receiver. If that does not happen, the surviving receiver can and must continue to act alone.

---

[14]   Law of Property Act 1925, s 109(5). If the contrary is suggested by the terms of the appointment, the dismissal would be effective, but the receiver would have a damages claim against the lender.

   See para 4.83 *et seq* for the meaning of 'by writing under his own hand'.

[15]   *Windsor Refrigerator Co v Branch Nominees* [1961] Ch 375 at 398–399.

[16]   An analogy can be drawn with the position of joint tenants. One joint tenant cannot alone exercise a contractual option to determine a tenancy: *Hounslow LBC v Pilling* [1993] 2 EGLR 59.

[17]   This situation occurred in *Downsview Nominees Ltd v First City Corp Ltd* [1993] AC 295. The original receivers did stand aside, but the conduct of the receivers appointed by the first chargee led to them being liable in damages to the second chargee.

Borrower status

Death

13.19 The death of a sole borrower has no impact on the continuation of the receivership.[18] The receiver becomes the agent of the personal representatives.[19]

13.20 On the death of one of two joint borrowers who own the mortgaged property as joint tenants at law, the surviving borrower becomes the sole legal proprietor of the mortgaged property. The receiver will remain appointed, as that borrower's deemed agent. The reason is that multiple owners of property, at law, are considered as if one. Thus the agency of the receiver to the two borrowers, whilst both were alive, simply becomes the agency of the sole survivor.

Individual insolvency

13.21 The borrower's bankruptcy does not terminate the receivership. However, it does change the receiver's status.[20]

13.22 Entry into an IVA does not terminate a receivership or the receiver's powers.[21]

Company borrower

13.23 Liquidation does not terminate the receivership either. However, the receiver's ability to act as the borrower's deemed agent thereafter is limited. That limitation is discussed above.[22]

13.24 If the borrower goes into administration, the receivership is not automatically terminated.[23] However, the administrators can require the receivers to vacate office.[24] If the receivers are not required to vacate, they will need the administrator's consent to exercise any management power, or take any steps to enforce the security.[25] However, it is thought that if consent is given, they will exercise those management powers as agent for the company.

13.25 The court has power to order an administrator to dispose of property which is subject to a security as if it were not subject to the security.[26] If this

---

18 For authority for the proposition that death prior to an appointment being made does not preclude it, see para 4.34.

19 See para 6.198 *et seq*.

20 See para 6.213 *et seq*, where the question of whether the receivers become the deemed agent of the trustee in bankruptcy is discussed.

21 See para para 6.208 *et seq*.

22 See para para 6.165 *et seq*.

23 *In Re Fivestar Properties Ltd* [2015] EWHC 2782 (Ch), [2016] 1 WLR 1104 at [4].

24 Insolvency Act 1986, Sch B1, para 41(2). If the decision to do so is irrational or in bad faith, the court will likely grant permission for receivers to be re-appointed: *Promontoria (Chestnut) Ltd v Craig* [2017] EWHC 2405 (Ch).

25 Insolvency Act 1986, Sch B1, paras 64 and 43(2). A management power is defined as 'a power which could be exercised so as to interfere with the exercise of the administrator's powers'.

26 Insolvency Act 1986, Sch B1, para 71.

occurs, the receiver will lose his powers over the property, but will (probably) retain his powers over income due to the borrower before the sale,[27] save where these powers are management powers. It does not appear that this power has, to date, been exercised against an arm's length lender,[28] without its consent.[29]

13.26 A CVA does not end the receivership either; nor, probably, does it affect the receiver's deemed agency.[30]

13.27 The dissolution of the company does not terminate the receiver's appointment.[31] However, the receiver can no longer act as the company's deemed agent.[32]

Court proceedings

13.28 A borrower may assert that the charge is void or voidable, because of something that went wrong at the time it was executed.

13.29 Where the borrower alleges that the mortgage is void, the first matter to consider is whether the receiver was ever validly appointed at all. This is considered in Chapter 4.

13.30 If the only reason that the appointment was valid was because the mortgage was registered,[33] then if the register is rectified to remove the charge,[34] the receivership will come to an end automatically.[35]

---

[27] See para 13.7.

[28] It was exercised against directors who had security over the company's property in *O'Connell v Rollings* [2014] EWCA Civ 639.

[29] The secured creditors did consent in *Re Phones 4u Ltd (in administration)* [2014] EWHC 3571 (Ch).

[30] See para 6.179 *et seq*.

[31] *In Re Fivestar Properties Ltd* [2015] EWHC 2782 (Ch), [2016] 1 WLR 1104 at [25].

[32] See para 6.189.

[33] An LPA receiver can only be appointed where the mortgage was by deed: Law of Property Act 1925, s 101. If the signature of one or more of the borrowers was forged, or there were some defect in the execution of the mortgage, then the lender has no valid deed and no right to appoint an LPA receiver. However, registration would give the lender the same rights as if it had a charge by deed by way of legal mortgage: Land Registration Act 2002, s 51. Therefore the original appointment was valid, but only because of the registration.

However, if, on the true construction of the mortgage terms, the parties intended that the lender should have a separate right to appoint a fixed charge receiver, which was to be exercisable even if there were some defect in execution of the legal charge, it is possible that the receiver could remain in office notwithstanding the rectification of the register: *Rushingdale v Byblos Bank* (1986) 2 BCC 99509 at 99515–6.

[34] This is the appropriate course of action for a borrower in these circumstances. For an example, where the borrowers relied on their own defective execution to seek rectification, see *Bank of Scotland v Waugh* [2014] EWHC 2117 (Ch). In that case it was said that the rectification took effect prospectively not retrospectively.

[35] Unless the lender can rely on rights of subrogation to an earlier, valid, charge: *Day v Tiuta* [2014] EWCA Civ 1246, [2015] 1 P & CR DG10.

13.31 So, too, if the mortgage (or the underlying transfer to the borrower) was voidable, or there is some other basis for setting it aside,[36] and the borrower succeeds in getting the mortgage, or transfer, set aside. The receivership will end automatically.[37]

13.32 In some cases, the lender will be able to rely on a valid contractual obligation, binding one or more of the borrowers, to perfect the security,[38] and may be able to re-appoint the receiver thereafter.

13.33 If a claim that the charge should be set aside is made, the court may be asked to remove the receiver (or at least restrict his powers) pending determination of the claim. On such an application, as with any other application for interim injunctive relief, the court will consider whether the party asserting that the charge should be set aside has raised a serious issue to be tried, whether the applicant has given an undertaking in damages to protect the position if at trial his claim fails, and, if so, the balance of convenience. Often, this will favour leaving the receiver in office until the claim is tried, where there is no doubt that the lender will be able to pay any damages ordered.

13.34 An interim injunction may also be sought pending trial if the borrower asserts that the receiver has been invalidly appointed, or the appointment is defective.[39] Again, the court must consider whether there is a serious issue to be tried, whether the applicant has given an undertaking in damages to protect the position if at trial his claim fails and, if so, the balance of convenience.[40]

AFTER TERMINATION

Administrative tasks

13.35 The receiver should notify interested parties that his receivership has terminated. This would include the borrower, other charge holders and any tenants.

13.36 The receiver must settle any outstanding invoices and cancel insurance policies and other contracts he has taken out. The receiver must prepare final

---

[36] The borrower may assert that the charge should be set aside because of misrepresentation, or if the lender was guilty of an abuse of confidence or undue influence. A liquidator/trustee in bankruptcy may also challenge the charge on the basis that it was a preference or a transaction at an undervalue: Insolvency Act 1986, ss 238, 239, 339 and 340. see *In Re Goldburg (No 2), ex parte Page* [1912] 1 KB 606. A spouse can make an application to set aside a transaction made with the intention of defeating any claim for financial relief: Matrimonial Causes Act 1973, s 37. A dependant can apply to set aside a transaction made less than 6 years before death which is not made for full consideration: Inheritance (Provision for Family and Dependents) Act 1975, s 10.

[37] Subject to any argument about subrogation: see para 4.9.

[38] See *Bank of Scotland v Waugh (No 2)* [2014] EWHC 2835 (Ch).

[39] See Chapter 4 for the bases on which such challenges can be brought.

[40] See *Rushingdale Ltd SA v Byblos Bank SAL* (1986) 2 BCC 99509 for an example of such an application.

accounts. Interested parties may want to verify that the receiver has correctly dealt with all income and that any payments out were made in accordance with the statutory priorities.[41]

Company borrower

13.37 The receiver's accounts must be filed at Companies House within a month.[42] If he does not comply, a daily default fine may be imposed.

13.38 The receiver must give notice to the Company Registrar that he has ceased to act.[43] If he does not, he commits an offence and is liable to a fine.[44]

Consequences of termination

13.39 Unless the receivership has been completed, it is likely that sums owed to the receiver by way of remuneration or expenses will be outstanding when the receivership terminates. How can the receiver ensure that he is paid those sums?

13.40 The receiver could sometimes sue the appointing lender in contract.[45] But that may be unattractive because of the costs and because it may lead to adverse publicity for the receiver and/or the lender, if, for example, the reasons why the receivership was terminated are ventilated in a public forum.

13.41 If it remains likely that the property will be sold in the not too distant future, the receiver may be content to receive payment from the proceeds of sale. In this situation, the receiver should take the following steps to protect his right to remuneration:

(a) Where the receiver's right to remuneration is protected by a charge,[46] he should register a notice against the property title.[47]
(b) Where there is no charge, the receiver should enter a restriction[48] against the property title.
(c) In either case, the receiver should also register a restriction[49] against the lender's registered charge. This is necessary, even if there is a charge against the land protecting the receiver's right, and a notice relating to it, because the lender is able to sell free of the receiver's charge, even if the

---

[41] Law of Property Act 1925, ss 105 and 109. See Chapter 12.

[42] Insolvency Act 1986, s 38.

[43] Companies Act 2006, s 859K(3).

[44] Companies Act 2006, s 859K(6) and (7).

[45] See para 7.29 *et seq*.

[46] Where the borrower is a company (and, arguably, in all cases: see para 8.203), the receiver's right to remuneration is charged on the property: Insolvency Act 1986, s 37(4). In addition, in some cases, the terms of the mortgage will create a charge.

[47] Land Registration Act 2002, s 32.

[48] In Forms N and T.

[49] In Form T.

notice is registered, if it sells as lender under its statutory powers.[50] The basis for this restriction is that it is necessary to prevent unlawfulness in relation to a disposition,[51] i.e. because there is a risk that the lender will not honour the statutory (or contractual) scheme when distributing the proceeds of sale.

13.42 The receiver will remain liable for any prior breaches of duty.

13.43 Other consequences depend on the circumstances in which the receivership terminated.

Replacement of receiver

13.44 If a new receiver is appointed[52] without undue delay,[53] the receivership is regarded as continuous.[54] In practice, this means that the borrower will not be able to treat the receivership as at an end until a reasonable time for a replacement receiver to be appointed has elapsed, unless it is clear that the lender does not intend to appoint a replacement.

13.45 If the receivership is continuous:

(a) the borrower cannot collect rent (or otherwise seek to exercise the receiver's powers) during the 'gap' between the termination of the first receiver's appointment and the appointment of his replacement;
(b) the receiver should continue to hold any money held by him until a replacement receiver is appointed, and then pay it over to the replacement receiver;
(c) contracts made by the original receivers as agents for the borrower can be enforced by the replacement receivers.[55]

No replacement

13.46 If no replacement receiver is appointed, or the gap between the end of one receiver's appointment and his replacement is too long, the borrower's power to deal with the property returns. He can collect rent, make contracts, grant leases[56] and otherwise manage the property.

---

[50] Law of Property Act 1925, s 104.

[51] Land Registration Act 2002, s 42(1)(a).

[52] Appointment is dealt with in Chapter 4.

[53] It was held in *Re White's Mortgage* [1943] Ch 16 that 14 months was too long. There is little other guidance in the authorities.

[54] *Re White's Mortgage* [1943] Ch 166.

[55] *TBAC Investments Ltd v Valmar Works* [2015] EWHC 1213 (Ch), unless, on the true construction of the contract, it required the borrower to act through the particular agents named in the contract.

[56] Under Law of Property Act 1925, s 99(1), provided that right has not been excluded by the mortgage conditions, and the lender is not in possession.

13.47 Any money standing to the credit of the receiver at a bank must be transmitted to the borrower.[57]

13.48 If the termination occurs because an underlying transaction is set aside under the insolvency legislation, and the receiver was appointed after the bankruptcy or winding up petition was presented, the receiver will have to account to the trustee/liquidator for all of the property which came into his hands.[58]

Consequences of continuing to act after termination

13.49 The consequences of the receiver continuing to act after the receivership has been terminated are the same as the consequences of acting when the appointment is invalid or defective.[59] In brief:

(a) the receiver's acts are tortious. He may be liable in trespass[60] or conversion. The borrower can seek possession from him, or an injunction preventing him from continuing to act;[61]
(b) the receiver is not entitled to remuneration, and any indemnity is likely to be construed as lasting only so long as he is properly acting; and
(c) third parties will be able to claim against the receiver for breach of warranty of authority.

---

[57] *Societe Coloniale Anversoise v London and Brazilian Bank Ltd* [1911] 2 KB 1024.
[58] *In Re Goldburg (No 2), ex parte Page* [1912] 1 KB 606.
[59] Considered in more detail at para 4.108 *et seq*.
[60] *In Re Goldburg (No 2), ex parte Page* [1912] 1 KB 606.
[61] *Rottenburg v Monjack* [1992] BCC 688.

Chapter 14

Litigation

GENERAL PRELIMINARIES

14.1   Before looking at the different sort of claims which a receiver can become involved in, there are some preliminary matters to consider.

Insurance

14.2   The first matter to check (particularly in a case where the receiver is to be defendant) is whether the claim falls within the scope of the receiver's professional indemnity (or other) insurance. If it does, he should notify his insurers of the claim before instructing solicitors or taking any other step. Typically, insurers will instruct solicitors, if this is necessary.[1]

Joint receivers

14.3   Where joint receivers are the potential claimants[2] and the receivers disagree as to whether a particular claim should be brought, and neither wishes to resign from the receivership, the lender may consider removing one or both of the receivers.

14.4   If that does not happen, the best course to resolve the dispute, if the borrower is a company, is to seek directions from the court as to whether or not the claim should be brought.[3] Where this procedure is not available, the receiver who wishes to bring the claim must consider whether he has power, acting alone, to do so. This turns on whether the receivers are appointed jointly, or jointly and severally.[4]

14.5   Where a claim is brought against the receivers because of acts carried out by only one of them, questions about the extent to which the other receiver is liable for his acts and the availability of an indemnity or contribution claim[5] might, in theory, arise. However, since joint receivers are almost invariably at

---

[1]   In some cases, the receiver will be able to share representation with the lender. See para 14.109.

[2]   Or the borrower is the potential claimant, but the receivers will run the litigation in the borrower's name, by reason of a receivership power to do so.

[3]   See para 14.11 *et seq.*

[4]   See para 4.72 *et seq.*

[5]   I.e. a claim by one receiver against the other. The question of the lender's liability to indemnify either or both of them is a separate question, considered at para 7.34.

the same firm (and may be covered by the same insurance policy), in practice, such questions are unlikely to arise.

The firm

14.6   Suppose receivers intend to issue a claim, or a claim against receivers is being considered by the borrower, the lender or a third party. Should the individual receivers be joined to the claim or the firm of which they are members/employees?

14.7   First, if the claim is the borrower's, then the receivers should usually bring it in the borrower's name, acting via his receivers. The receivers are appointed as individuals and should be referred to by name in the title to the claim ('borrower by his receivers A and B') and/or in the pleadings. A claim against the borrower should be brought against the borrower even though receivers have been appointed.

14.8   When the claim is by or against the receivers personally,[6] not the borrower, although firms are sometimes joined, in most cases, this will be wrong.[7] The receivers are appointed as individuals, and should sue/be sued as such.

14.9   However, if a claimant asserts that there is a cause of action against the firm itself, for example, because the firm is vicariously liable for the torts of its employees, the firm can be joined as well.[8]

14.10 Whether the firm could be vicariously liable for the receivers' acts despite their personal appointment as receivers (and if so, in what circumstances) has not been tested.[9] However, as a matter of general principle:

(a)   If the receiver is an employee of the firm, the firm could be vicariously liable for torts he commits within the course of his employment. Although the appointment is a personal one, it is thought that this would not preclude a claim against the firm, at least where the job which the employee has been hired to do includes acting as receiver and the firm is entitled[10] to recover his remuneration (and pays him a salary).

---

[6]   For example, a claim against the receivers by the borrower for breach of duty, or a claim by the receivers against the borrower for injunction preventing him interfering with the receivership.

[7]   *Jumani v Mortgage Express* [2013] EWHC 1571 (Ch) at [16]; *Centenary Homes Ltd v Gershinson*, 19 September 2017, unreported, Master Thornett.

[8]   It is hard to imagine a receivership claim which would be brought by the firm not the receivers, unless the receivers assigned their right to remuneration, for example, to their firm.

[9]   The firm was joined in *Purewal v Countrywide Residential Lettings Ltd* [2015] EWCA Civ 1122, [2016] 4 WLR 31, but does not appear to have argued that it was inappropriately joined, and the judgment does not contain any guidance as to when a firm might be vicariously liable.

[10] As between the employee and the firm.

(b)   Where the receiver is a partner in a partnership, similar principles apply.[11] Every partner is, by statute, an agent of the firm and his other partners for the purposes of the business of the partnership.[12] Further, if a partner commits a wrongful act or omission in the ordinary course of the business of the firm, the firm is liable for any loss and damage.[13] The better view, therefore, appears to be that the firm would be liable for the acts of one partner appointed as receiver, if the business of the partnership includes acting as fixed charge receivers.

(c)   If a partner misapplies monies received, the partnership will be liable.[14]

(d)   It is considered that a firm could not be liable on the basis that it has hired an incompetent person, because the lender makes a personal appointment.

RECEIVER'S APPLICATION FOR DIRECTIONS

Stakeholder application

14.11 If the receiver is aware that there is a dispute as to whether he should make a particular payment, before it is made, the receiver can make a stakeholder application under Part 86 of the CPR, for the court to determine who he should pay.

14.12 A claim form under Part 8 of the CPR, and witness statement, are required. The witness statement must state:

(a)   the receiver claims no interest in the subject matter other than for charges and costs;

(b)   the receiver does not collude with any of the claimants to the subject matter;

(c)   the receiver is willing to pay or transfer the subject matter into court or to dispose of it as the court may direct.

14.13 The respondents should be the persons likely to be (or who claim to be) affected by the determination – so, any third party who claims a payment, the lender and (if there is likely to be any surplus for the borrower), the borrower.

14.14 The respondents must file any evidence in response within 14 days of being served. Thereafter, a judge will consider the application and the evidence, and either determine the application summarily, or order a trial of any disputed issues.

---

11   *Dubai Aluminium Co Ltd v Salaam* [2002] UKHL 48, [2003] 2 AC 366.

12   Partnership Act 1890, s 5.

13   Partnership Act 1890, s 10.

14   Partnership Act 1890, s 11.

Applications available to the receiver of a company

14.15   Where the borrower is a company, there is an express statutory provision entitling the receiver[15] to seek directions from the court 'in relation to any particular matter arising in connection with the performance of the function of the receiver'.[16] It is thought that any receiver appointed over a company's property can seek directions under this provision, regardless of the terms of the mortgage or deed of appointment as to the powers the receiver is to have. The statutory power is conveyed on any receiver of company property.

14.16   The application should be made by application notice containing the prescribed information,[17] even if there are no existing proceedings,[18] with directions as to whether any statements of case are required being given later.[19] A witness statement in support will be required.[20]

14.17   The respondents should be anyone with an interest in the outcome.

Other applications by the receiver of an individual

14.18   Although there is no equivalent statutory provision to that in company receivership applying where the borrower is an individual, there is no reason why a receiver cannot issue proceedings seeking a declaration[21] from the court if he is aware that there is a dispute as to what he can and cannot do.[22]

---

[15]   Or the lender. But not the borrower: *SS Agri Power Ltd v Dorins* [2017] EWHC 3563 (Ch).

[16]   Insolvency Act 1986, s 35. For a case where such an application was made, see for example *Rees v Boston BC* [2001] EWCA Civ 1934, [2002] 1 WLR 1304, where the receivers sought directions as to their liability to pay rates. See also *In Re John Willment* [1980] 1 WLR 73 under Companies Act 1948, s 369; and *Rhodes v Allied Dunbar Pension Services Ltd* [1989] 1 WLR 800 under Companies Act 1985, s 492.

[17]   Insolvency Rules 2016, r 1.35. Form IAA should be used. For copies, see the HM Courts & Tribunals Service website at https://hmctsformfinder.justice.gov.uk/HMCTS/FormFinder.do.

[18]   In this event, instead of stating the case number of the existing proceedings, the application notice should make it clear that there are no existing proceedings.

[19]   Insolvency Rules 2016, r 12.11.

[20]   Insolvency Rules 2016, r 12.28.

[21]   In *Rhodes v Allied Dunbar Pension Services Ltd* [1989] 1 WLR 800, the receivers sought a declaration, as well as directions under the statutory provision.

[22]   Such a claim would usually be by the receiver personally, not on behalf of the borrower, and it is likely that a receiver has an incidental power to instruct solicitors to advise on the working of the receivership and his duties, and to bring litigation to determine such questions, so that the costs and expenses are recoverable, though the issue must be determined by reference to the wording of the mortgage covenants. For an example of a receiver instructing solicitors to advise on duties, see *Edenwest Ltd v CMS Cameron McKenna (A Firm)* [2012] EWHC 1258 (Ch). The solicitors could not be said to be retained by the borrower simply because the receivers had the power to act as the deemed agent of the borrower. Indeed, the solicitors would face conflicts of interest were it deemed to represent the borrower on such an instruction: at [67]. It would be rare for a receiver to have power to bring such a claim in the name of the borrower, since it is not usually the case that the receiver has the borrower's powers to question the operation of the mortgage, and hence of the receivership. See the discussion in *Newhart Developments Ltd v Cooperative Commercial Bank Ltd* [1978] 1 QB 814.

THE RECEIVER AS CLAIMANT IN HIS OWN RIGHT

14.19 Where the receiver has a cause of action in his own right,[23] no question of authority arises. If the receiver has a cause of action, he can litigate. He should be named as claimant.

Claims against the lender for remuneration/indemnity

14.20 A claim brought by a receiver against the lender, for example, for his remuneration or under an indemnity, is a good example of a claim arising out of the receivership but where the receiver is claimant in his own right. In such a case, the claim is for his own benefit. The circumstances in which such a claim will be possible are discussed in Chapter 7.[24]

14.21 Another claim which a receiver might make in his personal capacity is under an indemnity against the lender where another party has sued the receiver. Where a receiver has an indemnity from the lender for such losses, unless the terms of that indemnity provide otherwise, the receiver can sue the lender as soon as his liability to the third party has arisen. He does not need to make payment himself first.

14.22 If there is a dispute about the lender's obligation to indemnify the receiver against a claim brought against him, it will generally be wise to join the lender as a third party to that claim.

14.23 Multi-party litigation presents particular case management challenges. Careful thought needs to be given, in each case, to the most cost-effective way to manage the case. In some cases, it will be sensible to take the question of whether the lender is obliged to indemnify the receiver (in the event that the third party's claim is made out) as a preliminary issue, so that if the receiver is successful on that issue, he can then drop out of the picture leaving the lender to fight the third party. However, this route will be less attractive if the dispute between the receiver and the lender goes beyond a simple question of construction of the terms of appointment.

14.24 In general, no indemnity out of the receivership assets is available where the receiver is suing the lender. If the receiver wishes to bring such a claim, he must fund it himself.[25] Costs will typically follow the event.

---

[23] I.e. without needing to rely on his powers *qua* receiver. For claims which may be brought in the receiver's name in reliance on the receivership powers, for example, where the borrower is insolvent, see below.

[24] See para 7.28 *et seq*.

[25] Unless he has any relevant insurance.

Claims against the borrower

14.25 The receiver also has a right to bring some claims against the borrower in his own right and for his own benefit, for example a claim under the Occupiers Liability Act 1957 if the receiver is injured on the property, or, perhaps a *quantum meruit* claim against the borrower for remuneration in the event of a defective appointment.[26] Such claims should be brought in the receiver's name, and the receiver must fund this sort of claim himself, unless an indemnity from the lender is available.

14.26 However, other claims against borrowers involve the receiver relying on his receivership powers. The principles set out above do not apply to these claims. The relevant principles are considered below.[27]

Claims against third parties

14.27 In some circumstances,[28] the receiver will contract on his own behalf,[29] for example with utility suppliers, or with solicitors to provide advice to him as to how he should conduct the receivership.[30] Such contracts can plainly be enforced by the receiver, and only by the receiver.

14.28 The receiver will be the party to any claim to enforce such a contract and will be the person who retains solicitors to act in the claim. The receiver will have the liability for their fees, but, in this sort of claim, the receiver might, depending on the terms of his appointment, be entitled to recover his expenses from the income.[31]

CLAIMS WHERE THE RECEIVER RELIES ON RECEIVERSHIP POWERS

General principles

Capacity

14.29 There are three different types of claim which, in principle, the receiver might bring, relying on powers given to him in the receivership:

---

[26] For an example from Australia, see *Monks v Poynice* (1987) 8 NSWLR 662. See para 4.117.

[27] See para 14.61 *et seq*.

[28] See para 8.201 *et seq*.

[29] Although he may do so in exercise of his receivership powers.

[30] See *Edenwest Ltd v CMS Cameron McKenna (A Firm)* [2012] EWHC 1258 (Ch) for a case in which the receiver instructed solicitors for advice as to their duties in the receivership.

[31] This is most likely when the contract is entered into under receivership powers and for the benefit of the receivership albeit in the receiver's own name.

(a) a claim brought on behalf of the borrower against third parties;
(b) a claim brought as donee of a power; and
(c) a claim brought as agent of the lender.

These different types of claim are treated separately in the sections which follow.

14.30 It is necessary to determine in which capacity the receiver is acting in order to ascertain in whose name the claim should be brought, who is instructing the solicitors and is liable for their fees.

14.31 In many cases, the receiver could act in more than one capacity. In general, the receiver will seek to make the borrower liable if it is possible.

14.32 Accordingly, where: (a) the borrower has the cause of action; and (b) bringing the proceedings is within the scope of the deemed agency, then neither the borrower nor the third party can complain that the receiver cannot cause the borrower to bring the proceedings, and it is likely that it will be assumed that the receiver is, indeed, intending to act on behalf of the borrower in doing so.

14.33 However, where the borrower does not have a cause of action, the third party could complain if the proceedings were brought in the borrower's name.

14.34 For example, it is the thesis of Chapter 10 that a receiver who has the lender's power to take possession of the mortgaged property can take possession from occupiers against whom the borrower has no right of possession, and indeed from the borrower himself. If such a claim were brought in the borrower's name, the defendant might complain that the receivers' powers were limited to those which the borrower has. However, the defendant could not complain if the receiver was named as claimant.[32]

14.35 A similar issue arises where the deemed agency no longer has a principal, for example, arguably, on borrower insolvency and dissolution.[33] A claim brought in the name of the borrower seems difficult conceptually; a claim by the receiver in his own name exercising his powers would not seem difficult.

14.36 In those circumstances, the receiver will usually[34] litigate on his own account as the donee of a receivership power.

---

[32] See paras 10.151–10.156 for claims against the borrower's tenants, and para 10.178 especially fn 149 for claims against the borrower. In addition, there is an argument as to whether the receiver could exercise a power which the borrower could not in the borrower's name simply because of the deemed agency, and hence litigate in the borrower's name with cause of action based on his own powers. The borrower's lack of a cause of action will make such a claim difficult, and hence best avoided even were it theoretically possible. See para 5.23 and para 10.151 *et seq.*

[33] See para 6.160 *et seq.*

[34] But see *Gough's Garages v Pugsley* [1930] 1 KB 615, where the court accepted that a claim commenced by receivers in the borrower's name prior to the winding up of the borrower could continue thereafter.

14.37 If the receiver has been given a power by the lender, then any claim based on exercise of that power must be either in the lender's name, with the receiver acting as the lender's agent,[35] or by the receiver in his own name as the donee of the power.

14.38 In many cases, the receiver will not be acting as the lender's agent, even when exercising delegated powers falling outside the scope of the deemed agency.[36]

14.39 Furthermore, where the proceedings are possession proceedings, taking them in the lender's name will result in the lender going into possession, which is precisely the result which the lender is seeking to avoid by appointing a receiver.

14.40 In the circumstances, the better course seems to be for proceedings to be brought in the name of the receiver where they cannot be brought in the borrower's name and for the receiver to seek an indemnity from the lender in respect of his own costs and any liability to costs which he may incur.

Authority

14.41 Where the receiver wishes to rely on the powers in the mortgage to bring a claim, the extent of his powers under the mortgage needs to be checked.

14.42 An LPA receiver has power to sue for income.[37] Where the receiver has other powers, whether he will have a power to sue (or defend) is a question of construction of the mortgage deed and the deed or other documents by which they were appointed.

14.43 In addition to the powers a receiver is expressly given, the receiver will have power to do anything which is necessarily incidental to the exercise of his express powers.[38] It seems likely that incidental powers will extend to powers to litigate.[39]

14.44 In case of any doubt about the scope of his powers, the receiver should seek to negotiate the express authority of both the lender and the borrower to

---

[35] Where the lender has delegated to the receiver a power which is not within the receivership powers to use as the lender's agent.

[36] Where the power is within the scope of the deemed agency on behalf of the borrower on the terms of the mortgage, it is most unlikely that an agency on behalf of the lender arises. However, where the lender delegates a power to the receiver which falls outside the deemed agency on behalf of the borrower, it is a question of construction of the appointment and/or the document by which the power was conferred whether it was intended that the receiver could act as the lender's agent or has been given the power to exercise in his own name.

[37] Law of Property Act 1925, s 109(3). See para 9.47 *et seq*.

[38] See para 8.79.

[39] *M Wheeler & Co Ltd v Warren* [1928] Ch 840.

him bringing or defending the litigation. If this cannot be obtained, the receiver can seek directions or a declaration from the court.[40]

Duty to advance claim

14.45 If the receiver has power to sue, he must:

(a) consider whether to sue;[41] and
(b) exercise reasonable care in considering offers to settle. However, if the receiver acts on professional advice, and his decision is within the scope of reasonable professional judgment, no breach will be established.[42]

Claims brought on behalf of the borrower against third parties

Authority

14.46 The problem of authority is particularly acute where the receiver brings a claim in the borrower's name against third parties. Confirming that the receiver has the power to bring the claim is particularly important in this type of case. If receivers cause the borrower to bring a claim when they had no actual authority to do so:

(a) the solicitors cannot have actual authority to act on behalf of the borrower either;
(b) however, if the solicitors had ostensible authority to act on behalf of the borrower, the borrower will be bound by the proceedings, so the lack of actual authority would be of no significance to the third party;[43]
(c) a firm of solicitors can only have ostensible authority if the borrower has done something to convey to the third party that the solicitors had his authority to bring the proceedings, or the receiver had his authority to instruct solicitors on his behalf. This might arise, for example, if the receiver properly instructs solicitors to bring a claim, but his appointment is then terminated, without the other side's knowledge (or, presumably, the solicitors' knowledge). Another example might be if the solicitor is properly instructed to claim rent arrears, but is then asked to amend the claim to include a possession claim (the latter falling outside the receiver's authority). It should be noted that it has been held in another context that it is sufficient for ostensible authority can arise if the principal fails to take

---

[40] See para 14.11 *et seq.*

[41] See para 11.175. In *Purewal v Countrywide Residential Lettings* Ltd [2015] EWCA Civ 1122, [2016] 4 WLR 31, the court accepted that it would be a breach of duty not to claim on an insurance policy. Litigation is, of course, riskier and costlier than making a claim on an insurance policy, so receivers will not inevitably have to sue, if they have power to do so, but they must consider the question.

[42] *Ahmad v Bank of Scotland* [2016] EWCA Civ 602.

[43] *In Re The Sherlock Holmes International Society Ltd* [2016] EWHC 1392 (Ch).

any steps to prevent someone from continuing to hold himself out as his agent, when the principal knows that he is doing so;[44]

(d) if the solicitors did not have actual or ostensible authority, the borrower will not be bound by any findings in the proceedings, and will not be obliged to pay the third party's costs;

(e) there is a significant risk that a costs order will be made against the receiver in these circumstances.[45] Absent express agreement to indemnify in relation to any costs orders made in the litigation, any indemnity from the lender may be construed as being limited to the costs incurred whilst the receiver is acting within the scope of the receivers' authority. Thus, the receiver risks personal liability for costs;

(f) the solicitors will be held to have warranted that they had the authority of the borrower to bring the proceedings[46] (at least until there was any reason for the other party to doubt that this was so), and the firm is likely to be ordered to pay the other side's costs under the court's inherent jurisdiction to control its officers, provided that the third party would have received costs from the borrower if the warranty had been true.[47] Thus, the solicitors are at risk of liability for costs;

(g) the solicitors might also be liable for wasted costs, if their failure to confirm the receiver's authority to give instructions on behalf of the borrower was improper, unreasonable or negligent;[48]

(h) in a less clear case, the third party may have to bring a separate claim against the solicitors for damages for breach of warranty of authority. Liability for breach of warranty of authority is strict, so it is not necessary for the third party to prove that the solicitors should have known that the receiver did not have authority; and

(i) whether the solicitors can pass on this claim to the receivers, by arguing that the receivers warranted to them that they had authority to act for the borrower will depend on the circumstances. In most cases, since the solicitor will have the means of establishing whether the receiver does, in fact, have authority to act for the borrower, by obtaining a copy of the legal charge and the appointment, the receiver will not be held to have given any warranty as to their authority. However, if a receiver continued to instruct solicitors to act on behalf of the borrower after the receivership is terminated, the solicitors might have a claim against the receiver.

Funding

14.47 Once satisfied that there is authority, the next question which the receiver must consider is the liability for the solicitors' costs. If the receiver is instructing the solicitors on behalf of the borrower, the borrower will be liable, as a matter of contract, for the solicitors' costs. However, the receiver may be able to pay

---

44 *Freeman & Lockyer v Buckhurst Park Properties (Mangal) Ltd* [1964] 2 QB 480.

45 *Zoya Ltd v Sheikh Nasir Ahmed (trading as Property Mart) (No 2)* [2016] EWHC 2249 (Ch).

46 *Gwembe Valley Development Co Ltd v Koshy* [2000] BCC 1127.

47 *In Re The Sherlock Holmes International Society Ltd* [2016] EWHC 1392 (Ch).

48 *Zoya Ltd v Sheikh Nasir Ahmed (trading as Property Mart) (No 2)* [2016] EWHC 2249 (Ch).

the costs from the receipts as 'outgoings', depending on the nature of the claim.[49] If the receipts are not likely to cover the costs, or if there is any doubt about the entitlement to use the receipts for this purpose, the solicitors might well seek an indemnity from the lender before agreeing to act.[50]

Title of the action

14.48 The claimant should be described as:

[the Borrower] (acting by [the Receivers] as fixed charge receivers)

Pleading and evidencing the appointment of the receiver

14.49 It is considered that, in most cases, it will be unnecessary to plead or evidence the appointment of the receiver in a third party claim. The third party is simply meeting a claim brought by the borrower. Just as one would not normally plead or prove that the directors of a company are authorised to instruct solicitors on behalf of the company, unless that is put in issue, there is no need to plead and prove that the receiver has authority to cause the borrower to bring the claim.

14.50 However, if the third party does suggest that the receiver does not have authority to instruct solicitors to advance the claim, that issue will have to be dealt with. The third party will have to make an application for the determination of whether the receiver, and hence the solicitors, did have authority, which will be heard before any further steps are taken in the action.[51] The application ought to be made promptly. If it is not, the applicant may be deprived of some of its costs.[52]

14.51 If such an application is made:

(a) the borrower need not be served;
(b) the lender is entitled to intervene; and
(c) if a claim for costs is made against the solicitors, they must consider whether they require separate representation.[53]

---

[49] See para 12.15.

[50] In many cases, the lender will be able to add the expenses to the mortgage debt.

[51] *Gwembe Valley Development Co Ltd (in receivership) v Koshy* [2000] BCC 1127. The decision (though not the comments on procedure) was appealed successfully: 14 December 2000, unreported, CA. The court has wide powers under the CPR to correct errors of procedure (see especially CPR, r 3.10). Even under the old rules, at least in the county court, the judge would hear an objection that the receivers did not have authority to conduct the proceedings without an application: *Gough's Garages Ltd v Pugsley* [1930] 1 KB 615.

[52] *Gwembe Valley Development Co Ltd (in receivership) v Koshy* [2000] BCC 1127 at 1147. However, delay will not mean that an applicant is shut out from complaining that the action has been commenced without the borrower's authority.

[53] In *Gwembe Valley Development Co Ltd (in receivership) v Koshy* [2000] BCC 1127, the solicitors who had acted for the borrower on the instructions of the receivers acted for the lender and for itself on the strike out application. However, they instructed separate counsel to act for

14.52 Evidence to prove each of the following will be needed if, and to the extent that, the authority of the receiver to bring the litigation is put in issue:

(a) The appointing lender is registered as proprietor of a registered charge, or was otherwise entitled to appoint the receiver.[54]

(b) Any statutory or contractual preconditions to appointment were met.[55] Note that this means that the mortgage terms need to be proved, so a copy of the mortgage, including the applicable mortgage conditions, must be produced.

(c) A copy of the document which effected the appointment must also be produced. This will set out the terms of the appointment and by whom the appointment was made.

(d) If the statutory power (in section 109 of the Law of Property Act 1925) is relied on, that the appointment was made 'by writing under his [the appointor's] own hand'.[56] A company lender must have either:

    (i) validly executed a power of attorney by deed entitling one or more named attorneys to appoint receivers on its behalf, and the attorney must have made the appointment as such;[57] or

    (ii) executed the appointment itself in accordance with the formalities in section 44 of the Companies Act 2006.

(e) Any other formalities stipulated in the statute or mortgage deed were complied with.

(f) Notice of the appointment was served on the receiver, and the receiver accepted the appointment within time.[58]

Injunctions and cross-undertakings

14.53 A receiver, in the name of the borrower, may wish to seek an interim injunction, for example, to prevent damage by a trespasser to the mortgaged property, or works by a neighbour to the party wall, or similar.

14.54 The principles applied by the court in determining whether to grant such an application are: (a) whether there is a serious issue to be tried; (b) whether damages are an adequate remedy for the claimant; (c) whether the claimant has given a cross-undertaking in damages to pay any losses to the defendant

---

themselves because of a potential conflict: at 1129. See *Edenwest Ltd v CMS Cameron McKenna (A Firm)* [2012] EWHC 1258 (Ch) at [67] for further discussion of possible conflicts of interest when a solicitor is instructed by a receiver in the name of the borrower.

[54] See para 4.11.

[55] See para 4.5 *et seq*.

[56] See the discussion at para 4.83 *et seq* of the meaning of this.

[57] It is necessary to do more than produce the power of attorney and the deed of appointment. In *Smith and Hughes v Black* [2017] NICA 56, the receivers' claim failed because they did not prove the identity of the persons who executed the power of attorney, and that they were duly authorised by the lender to do so.

[58] See para 4.93 *et seq*.

resulting from the interim injunction being granted if the claim fails at trial; and (d) where the balance of convenience lies. Their application, and the evidence required on such an application, will depend on the particular claim brought.

14.55 The borrower is not relieved of the obligation to offer a cross-undertaking because receivers have been appointed and are running the proceedings.[59]

14.56 If the only funds that the borrower has to meet the cross-undertaking are from income from the mortgaged property (e.g. from the occupants) which the receiver will be collecting, it is necessary to consider whether the receiver should also be required to give a cross-undertaking, limited to the funds that come into his hands *qua* receiver.[60] It is considered that if the receiver has power to litigate, he will have power to give and honour such an undertaking, even though it will involve the receiver in distributing income other than in accordance with the statutory regime.

14.57 If either or both of those cross-undertakings are not sufficient to protect the third party against suffering irrecoverable losses in the event it turns out that the interim injunction was wrongly granted, the interim injunction is unlikely to be granted without more. In such circumstances, the receiver may approach the lender to see whether it wishes to provide some security for the cross-undertaking.

Costs

14.58 If the proceedings are not successful, the defendant will generally obtain a costs order against the borrower. If a defendant is concerned about his ability to enforce a costs order against the borrower, he should make an application for security for costs at an early stage.[61]

---

[59] In *Bower Terrace Student Accommodation Ltd v Space Student Living Ltd* [2012] EWHC 2206 (Ch), the receivers initially offered a more limited undertaking, but when the third party objected that there was no reason of principle why a full cross-undertaking should not be given, offered a full cross-undertaking in damages. The judge noted the receivers' willingness to give a full cross-undertaking in damages as one of the factors to be taken into account in assessing the balance of convenience (at [65]). A receiver with sufficient powers will be able to give such an undertaking in the borrower's name.

[60] An undertaking in the following terms was described in *Maloney v Filtons Ltd* [2012] EWHC 1136 (Ch) at [21] as the 'usual receiver's cross-undertaking':

If the court later finds that this order has caused loss to the Defendants and decides that the Defendants should be compensated for that loss, the Claimants will comply with any order the court may make, up to a limit of the value of the assets under their control in the receivership and with any liability under this undertaking to be discharged from those assets.

The receivers were named as claimants in that action, although it is not clear why.

[61] Where this is available. See CPR, r 25.13(2) which allows a court to give an order for security for costs in only limited circumstances. An application for security for costs is likely to be particularly difficult against an individual borrower.

14.59 The defendant will not normally obtain a third party costs order that the receiver should pay the costs,[62] nor will he normally obtain a third party costs order against the lender. However, if the lender funds the proceedings, a different result might occur.[63]

14.60 In addition, if the receiver continues litigation in the name of the borrower after the borrower has become insolvent, the receiver is at risk of a third party costs order[64] at least where he will be indemnified by the lender.[65] The receiver may wish to apply to be substituted as claimant and continue the claim in his own name under his powers. If he does so, he will become liable personally for the costs post that substitution. [66]

Claims brought by the receiver in his own name as donee of a power

14.61 An obvious example of such a claim is the claim that the receiver will need to bring if the borrower impedes the receivership, for example, if the borrower endeavours to continue to collect rents from the occupants of the mortgaged property after the appointment of the receiver. In these circumstances, the receiver could seek an injunction, both on an interim and on a final basis, to restrain the borrower from acting in this way.[67] A claim for possession against the borrower also falls into this category.[68]

14.62 The receiver may also need to act in his own name using a receivership power if he cannot use the borrower's name, because the deemed agency has come to an end either because of the borrower's insolvency,[69] or because the action is not one the borrower could take. For example, the receiver may have a right of possession co-extensive with the lender's right and seek possession from occupiers whom the borrower could not evict.[70]

---

[62] *Mills v Birchall and Gilbertson* [2008] EWCA Civ 385, [2008] 1 WLR 1829 in which a third party costs order under CPR, r 46.2 was sought against the receivers. The receiver is not a real party just because he may benefit from the litigation because of fees ([79]).

[63] *Mills v Birchall and Gilbertson* [2008] EWCA Civ 385, [2008] 1 WLR 1829 at [80]. This is because of the test for making a third party costs order.

[64] Under Senior Courts Act 1981, s 51. The procedure is set out in CPR, r 46.2.

[65] *Bacal Contracting Ltd v Modern Engineering (Bristol) Ltd* [1980] 2 All ER 655.

[66] Note that a claim against the borrower would continue against him, and be dealt with under the Insolvency Act 1986. The receiver usually could not be substituted as defendant since his powers would not put him into the borrower's shoes in that sense. For example, if the claim were by a lessee of the mortgaged property against the borrower as landlord, the receiver's powers over the mortgaged property would not make him the landlord on the borrower's insolvency. Adverse claims are dealt with at para 14.85 *et seq.*

[67] These claims are discussed in detail at para 6.144 *et seq.*

[68] These claims are discussed in detail at para 10.75 *et seq.*

[69] See para 6.160 *et seq.*

[70] See above and para 10.151 *et seq.*

14.63 The receiver may also need to act in his own name because the power on which he relies was not given to him by statute or the mortgage conditions, nor is a lender-delegated power to lease,[71] but by the lender to exercise in the receiver's own name.[72]

14.64 These claims should be brought in the receiver's own name.

Funding

14.65 The receiver instructs the solicitor in his own right on such a claim and will be liable to pay the solicitor's bills[73] and any costs orders made in the defendant's favour. How will he do this?

14.66 Often, when the receiver is relying on his powers *qua* receiver to bring or defend a claim, he will be entitled to an indemnity out of the assets in the receivership against his expenses.[74] If the assets he collects in the receivership are sufficient, and provided that the amount he is entitled to take is not capped,[75] he will be able to recoup the costs from the recoveries under the indemnity.

14.67 However, in general, no such indemnity will be available where:

(a) he has been negligent or otherwise breached his duties; or
(b) he is acting outside his powers.

14.68 Equally, if the assets are not sufficient, the receiver will be in difficulties. He will want an indemnity from the lender before his exposure exceeds the figure he can meet.

Title of the action

14.69 The claimant should be described as:

[name of receiver] as fixed charge receiver for [name of borrower]

---

[71] Which he likely can exercise in the borrower's name: see para 9.146.

[72] Not as agent of the lender.

[73] Insolvency Act 1986, s 37, discussed at para 8.201. The solicitor is unlikely to agree any attempt to exclude personal liability (unless the solicitor has some other security for the fees). Furthermore, where the borrower is an individual, a prudent solicitor will require the receiver to agree, expressly, that the receiver will have personal liability.

[74] See para 12.30. However, if the receiver relies on a lender delegated power which goes beyond the receivership powers expressly granted in the mortgage deed, there is a good argument that he cannot use the receipts to pay the fees. Whether the lender is obliged to indemnify him is considered at para 7.33 *et seq.*

[75] By Law of Property Act 1925, s 109(6) (or any contractual term): see para 12.25 *et seq.*

Pleading and evidencing the appointment of the receiver

14.70 Where the receiver himself is making the claim, it is necessary to plead and prove that the receiver has the power to bring the claim. The matters set out above[76] should be pleaded and proved.

14.71 In addition, where the receiver is relying on a lender's power, the claim should plead the delegation of the power (if this was done separately from the appointment) and that the right to exercise that power has arisen. For example, if the receiver in the mortgage conditions was given the lender's power of sale, and that power is only exercisable when arrears have arisen, or on breach of the mortgage, then those arrears or breach should be pleaded. The requirement is similar if the receiver has been given a right of possession co-extensive with the lender's right, and that right is exercisable only on arrears or breach. Since exercise of the lender's power to appoint a receiver and its power of sale and right to possession are often all subject to the same pre-conditions, this pleading will add little to pleading the valid appointment of the receiver.

Injunctions and cross-undertakings

14.72 The receiver, acting in his own name as donee of a power, may wish to obtain an interim injunction, prior to trial.

14.73 If the receiver seeks an injunction, the receiver will have to give a cross-undertaking. Usually,[77] an undertaking in the following form is appropriate:

> If the court later finds that this order has caused loss to the defendants and decides that the defendants should be compensated for that loss, the claimants will comply with any order the court may make, up to a limit of the value of the assets under their control in the receivership and with any liability under this undertaking to be discharged from those assets.[78]

14.74 If the receipts will not, in fact, provide the third party with adequate security, the receiver will have to consider, with the lender, what additional undertaking could be offered.

---

[76] See para 14.52.

[77] However, where the receiver acts as done of a power from the lender which goes beyond the receivership powers expressly given in the mortgage deed, there is a good argument that it is inappropriate for him to use funds coming into his hands in the receivership for this purpose. Such an undertaking should not, therefore, be agreed in these circumstances without the consent of the lender, any prior chargees, the borrower and all those interested in the equity of redemption. In the circumstances, it is often simpler to give an ordinary cross-undertaking backed by a lender indemnity.

[78] An undertaking in that form was described in *Maloney v Filtons Ltd* [2012] EWHC 1136 (Ch) at [21] as the 'usual receiver's cross-undertaking'.

Claims brought by the receiver as lender's agent

14.75 The receiver is sometimes given separate powers by the lender in the appointment or afterwards,[79] which are not part of his receivership under statute or the mortgage conditions so that he cannot exercise them as deemed agent of the borrower.

14.76 The receiver may be given such lender's powers to exercise as the lender's agent. Alternatively, he may be given them in his own name, so as to avoid lender liability, rather than as the lender's agent.[80]

14.77 In either case, care should be taken to ensure that the receiver has authority to litigate in relation to the power.

Funding

14.78 If the receiver litigates by reason of lender's powers which he has been given to exercise as the lender's agent, then it is the lender who will be liable to any solicitors instructed by the receiver,[81] and the lender who will be at risk on costs.

14.79 The receiver cannot use his receivership receipts to pay costs up-front because his actions are not within the receivership.

Title of the action

14.80 The lender should be named as the claimant.

Pleading

14.81 The claim will have to plead that:

(a) the appointing lender is registered as proprietor of a registered charge, or is otherwise entitled to the relief sought;[82] and
(b) any statutory or contractual preconditions to exercise of the lender's power were met.[83]

14.82 As with a claim brought in the borrower's name, it is considered that there is no need for the pleading to recite how the receiver has the power to cause the proceedings to be brought in the lender's name. However, if this is put

---

[79] For example sale, if this is not in the mortgage conditions.

[80] This is not something the authors have seen in practice, though it seems perfectly possible. The receiver is unlikely to be content to litigate in his own name on this basis without a strong indemnity from the lender.

[81] Assuming the receiver has been given authority to instruct solicitors.

[82] See para 4.11.

[83] See para 4.5 *et seq.*

in issue by the defendant, then delegation of the power will need to be proved. Every step in the chain would need to be proved strictly.[84]

Injunctions and cross-undertakings

14.83 If an injunction is sought, and a cross-undertaking must be given, it will be the lender who must give it, if the receiver is acting as the lender's agent.

Winding up the borrower

14.84 In the past, companies in liquidation benefitted from an exemption from business rates. That meant that it might be advantageous for receivers to obtain an order for the winding up of the borrower. A receiver with power to take possession of the charged property and do all things incidental or conducive to that purpose has power (if the company could petition for its own winding up) to seek the winding up of the company, in the company's name.[85] However, the receiver only has power to do so if it is going to advance the purposes for which he was appointed. Now that there is no advantage in terms of rates liability, it is difficult to see why a fixed charge receiver would wish to wind up the borrower.

ADVERSE CLAIMS MADE BY THIRD PARTIES

14.85 Three different types of claim can be identified:

(a) Claims against the receiver personally where he is accused of a wrong during his receivership, which do not derive from the exercise by him of any receivership power, for example, where the receiver has committed a tort.
(b) Claims against the receiver personally, where he has acted on his own account (rather than as agent for the borrower, or lender) in exercising receivership powers. An example might be where he has contracted for utility supplies.
(c) Claims where the real defendant is the borrower because, for example, the complaint is that the borrower has breached a contract. The correct defendant is the borrower even if the receiver caused the borrower to breach the contract.

14.86 As before, it is important to ascertain which type of claim is in issue before the claim is commenced.

---

[84] See para 14.52.

[85] In *Re Emmadart Ltd* [1979] 1 Ch 540, the court held that a receiver appointed by the holder of a floating charge had power to petition, in the company's name, in order to avoid liability for rates. The receiver took steps to bring the petition to the attention of the directors and secretary. The court took into account that there was no opposition from these persons when considering whether to make the winding up order. It might, of course, be different if the directors opposed.

Parties

14.87 Plainly, if the third party asserts a cause of action against the receiver, the receiver should be joined to the claim as defendant.

14.88 If there is no cause of action against the receiver, for example, when the receiver's actions have caused the borrower to breach his contract, the receiver should not be joined.[86] In these circumstances, the third party's claim is against the borrower not the receiver,[87] and the defendant should simply be the borrower.

14.89 If a receiver is joined to proceedings, he should consider at the earliest opportunity whether the third party does, in fact, have a cause of action against him.[88]

14.90 In general:

(a) If the third party is complaining that the receiver is going to cause, or has caused, the borrower to breach its contract, the third party generally has no cause of action against the receiver.[89] The better course is to seek an injunction restraining the borrower, whether by its directors, servants, agents or receivers, from breaching the contract.[90]

(b) Similar principles apply if the allegation is that the receiver is going to cause the borrower to commit a breach of trust, or some statutory duty.

(c) However, if the receiver is acting outside his authority, or in bad faith, the third party may have a cause of action for inducing breach of contract/trust.[91]

(d) The receiver will be liable for any acts he has done on his own account (i.e. outside the scope of deemed agency) and for any contracts he has entered into on his own account.

---

[86] *Telemetrix Plc v Modern Engineers of Bristol (Holdings) Plc* (1985) 1 BCC 99417 at 99420. The conclusion in that case that there was a cause of action cannot stand with later cases, discussed at para 8.9, but the result is probably correct because the receivers did not complain that they had been wrongly joined until costs was being decided.

Although under CPR, r 19.2, a person can be joined as a party where it is desirable so the court can resolve all the matters in dispute in the proceedings, or there is an issue involving which is connected to the matters in dispute, and it is desirable to add him to the court can resolve that issue, it is rare to join a party against whom no cause of action is pleaded, since he can be summoned to give evidence without being a party, and his joinder as a party puts him at risk on costs.

[87] See para 8.9.

[88] For so long as the receiver is a party, he is at risk of a costs order against him. If he engages with the substance of the case rather than complaining that he has been wrongly joined, the court may well exercise its discretion to make a costs order against him, at least in relation to the period up until he complained that he should not have been joined.

[89] See para 8.9. For the receiver's liability on contracts made by him, see para 8.201 *et seq.*

[90] An order in similar terms was made in *Ash & Newman Ltd v Creative Devices Research Ltd* [1991] BCLC 403. But see the discussion at para 8.9 *et seq* as to whether and when the receiver could be prevented by such an injunction from causing the breach of contract.

[91] See para 8.9.

(e)   The receiver will be liable for torts he commits during the course of the receivership.[92]

(f)   If a third party seeks an account of the monies coming into the receiver's hands, the receiver is a proper party.[93]

14.91 If the receiver is not a proper party, he should seek the striking out of the claim against him at the earliest opportunity.

Service

14.92 It is important to serve the correct person. Personal service on the receiver will not be personal service on the borrower.[94] However, if the receiver is at the borrower's premises when a claim form is handed to him, the claim form will be deemed served on the borrower after 2 business days, if the borrower is a company or an individual being sued in the name of a business or a partnership.[95] Otherwise, the borrower must be served at his last known residence.

14.93 If the receiver is, properly, a party, and the claimant cannot effect personal service on the receiver, the receiver must be served at his usual or last known residence (unless the receiver has provided an address for service or a solicitor has been authorised to accept service).[96] Ascertaining the address may be problematical for third parties.

Representation and conflicts of interest

14.94 A solicitor who is approached to act must take care to identify who he is instructed by. In the vast majority of cases, the solicitor will be taken to have intended to contract with the named defendant. It is this person who will be liable to pay the solicitor's bills, and consideration should be given as to whether the named defendant has the means to do so.

14.95 If the named defendant is the borrower, the first thing which the solicitor must do is to ascertain whether the person who is giving the instructions on behalf of the borrower has authority to do so. The receiver will only have power

---

[92]   See para 8.214 *et seq.*

[93]   Note though that the circumstances in which a third party will be entitled to an account against a fixed charge receiver are limited. See para 14.52.

[94]   CPR, r 6.5 requires service on an individual defendant personally, or on a 'person holding a senior position within the company or corporation' where the defendant is a corporate body. A receiver is not within that definition.

   However, if the third party is suing on a contract made by the receiver and the borrower is out of the jurisdiction, the court may give permission to serve on the receiver: r 6.12.

[95]   CPR, rr 6.14, 6.9 and 7.5.

[96]   CPR, r 6.9.

to give instructions on behalf of the borrower if this power has been expressly or impliedly delegated to them by the mortgage deed.[97]

14.96 Then, if the receiver is joined, it may be necessary to consider whether the same solicitor can represent both the receiver and the borrower.[98] The solicitor will have to consider this on a case-by-case basis, but generally:

(a) there will be a conflict between the interests of the receiver and those of the borrower; but

(b) if the borrower has delegated his power to defend the litigation to the receiver, the receiver will be giving instructions on behalf of the borrower even if there is a separate solicitor, so there is no reason for him to decline to act for both, if the receiver is content that he should do so;[99]

(c) where the receiver is not giving instructions on behalf of the borrower, and there is a conflict, the same solicitor can only act if both the receiver and the borrower consent.

Evidence in opposition to an application for interim injunctions

14.97 On an application for an interim injunction within a claim, the court will consider: (a) whether there is a serious question to be tried (e.g. as to whether specific performance of a contract would be ordered at trial); (b) whether damages would be an adequate remedy; (c) whether the claimant has given an undertaking in damages for any losses by the defendant if the claim fails at trial; and (d) the balance of convenience.

14.98 Where the claim is a claim brought against the borrower because the receiver is intending to cause the borrower to breach a pre-existing contract with a third party, the need to show a serious issue to be tried will be a substantial hurdle for the third party: generally, unless an order for specific performance of the contract should be made, the receiver is entitled to cause the borrower to breach it. It is therefore unlikely that an interim injunction would be granted in this type of case,[100] unless there were a real argument that an order for specific performance would be granted in due course.

14.99 Where the court is concerned with a claim properly made against the receiver, it is less likely to be easy to oppose the grant of an interim injunction on the grounds that there is no serious issue to be tried.

---

[97] See paras 14.42–14.43.

[98] See *Edenwest Ltd v CMS Cameron McKenna (A Firm)* [2012] EWHC 1258 (Ch) at [67] for a brief discussion of conflicts of interest.

[99] Unless it is the receiver's position that he should not have been joined. In that case, the receiver will wish to make an application striking out the claim against him, and the solicitor can only properly act for both if they both consent.

[100] For example, an injunction was refused in *Airlines Airspares Ltd v Handley Page Ltd* [1970] 1 Ch 193, discussed at para 8.6 *et seq*.

14.100   If the third party gets over that first hurdle, the court will then consider the impact on the claimant if the interim injunctive relief is not given. In many cases where the borrower is the correct defendant, there will be a real concern about the borrower's ability to satisfy any damages award.[101] In a case where this is likely to be determinative, a receiver can ask the lender whether it wishes to provide some security that any award of damages will ultimately be met. This will rarely be attractive to a lender, but in a few cases it might be worth doing.

14.101   The other side of the coin is the loss that the defendant will suffer if the injunction is wrongly made. A receiver should provide evidence of what the effect of the injunction would be on the receivership, and quantify it (as best he can) so as to enable the court to consider whether the claimant will be likely to satisfy the cross-undertaking in damages. Evidence of the redemption figure on the mortgage, and the greater sums which can be realised if the injunction is refused and the receiver is able to continue with the aspect of the receivership which is the subject of the claim, will often be required.[102] The loss can include loss of the ability to bargain with the claimant to supply the same goods at a higher price.[103]

Costs

14.102   Typically, costs follow the event in contentious litigation. In a simple dispute between a third party and the borrower, if the borrower loses, generally a costs order would be made against the borrower in the third party's favour. If the borrower does not have the money to satisfy the order, the third party might try to seek an order that the receiver should pay the costs, if the receiver has been conducting the litigation on behalf of the borrower.[104] On any such application, the court will consider all of the circumstances, but it likely to have regard to:

(a)   whether the receiver has an indemnity from the lender which would cover his liability to pay the claimant's costs;

(b)   whether the lender has funded the borrower's litigation costs, or whether this has been funded from income in the receivership;

---

[101]   This is less of a concern where the receiver is, properly, named as the defendant, because the receiver is likely to be insured.

[102]   These will be the borrower's losses if the injunction will reduce the receivership assets available to repay the mortgage debt. Where the borrower is the defendant, this is straightforward. If the defendant is the receiver, it is less obvious that these losses fit the conventional formula, because they are not losses the receiver will suffer if the injunction is made. However, the conventional formula should be viewed as mere shorthand for the exercise which the court is undertaking, namely to weigh up whether more harm will be caused by the granting of the injunction than by its refusal.

[103]   *Land Rover Group Ltd v UPF (UK) Ltd* [2002] EWHC 3183 (QB), [2003] 2 BCLC 222.

[104]   Under Senior Courts Act 1981, s 51; CPR, r 46.2. In *Mills v Birchall and Gilbertson* [2008] EWCA Civ 1829, [2008] 1 WLR 1829 at [88], the Court of Appeal left open whether orders against a receiver should more readily be made when a receiver caused the company to defend litigation unsuccessfully, than when he caused it to institute unsuccessful proceedings, because a claimant is not able to apply for security for costs.

(c) who would have benefitted from the defence, if it had been successful;

(d) whether the borrower is in liquidation, so that the receiver cannot have been acting as his agent.

14.103 If the receiver is a party, then he can expect to recover his costs from the claimant if his defence is successful and to pay the claimant's costs if it is not. But that is only the starting point. If, for example, the receiver does not suggest that he has been wrongly joined until the end of the case, a costs order may be made against him.[105]

14.104 If the receiver is liable to pay costs, or does not recover his costs from the other party, he is generally entitled to recoup them from the assets within the receivership.[106]

ADVERSE CLAIMS BROUGHT BY THE BORROWER OR THE LENDER

14.105 In such claims, the receiver is always the proper defendant.

Claims by the borrower

14.106 By far the most common type of litigation involving receivers is claims brought against them by borrowers. Frequent complaints are:

(a) the appointment was invalid so the receiver is, or was, trespassing on the mortgaged property;[107]

(b) the receiver is not applying, or has not applied, the monies he has received correctly, or has produced inadequate accounts;[108]

(c) the price the receiver is proposing to accept, or has accepted, on the sale of the security is inadequate;[109]

---

[105] *Telemetrix Plc v Modern Engineers of Bristol (Holdings) Plc* (1985) 1 BCLC 99417.

[106] See para 12.29. Insofar as the lender pays his expenses, these will usually be expenses of the mortgage, under the mortgage conditions, and hence can be added to the mortgage debt. Reference should be made to any practitioner's text on mortgage law in relation to mortgage costs.

[107] For example *Windsor Refrigerator Co Ltd v Branch Nominees Ltd* [1961] 1 Ch 375; *RA Cripps & Son Ltd v Wickenden* [1973] 1 WLR 944; *Shamji and Others v Johnson Matthey Bankers Ltd* (1986) 2 BCC 98910; *Bank of Baroda v Panessar* [1987] 1 Ch 335; *Day v Tiuta* [2014] EWCA Civ 1246; *SS Agri Power Ltd v Dorins* [2017] EWHC 3563 (Ch), where an alternative case that the receiver was exceeding his powers was also run; *Sinha v Saluja* [2018] EWHC 707 (Ch).

[108] See Chapter 12 for the receiver's obligations as to the use of the money. In such circumstances, the borrower can claim an account: *Smiths Ltd v Middleton (No 1)* [1979] 3 All ER 842, and see the discussion in para 6.140.

[109] For example, *Ahmad v Bank of Scotland* [2016] EWCA Civ 602. The claim is based on breach of receiver's duty. See 11.174 *et seq*.

(d) the receiver is otherwise not acting in accordance with his duties,[110] or with some agreement made between the receiver (or the lender) and the borrower.[111]

14.107 If the borrower goes into liquidation, claims of this nature can also be brought by the liquidator. Such claims should still be brought by action and not by application in the winding up.[112]

Defences

14.108 Whether acting for the borrower or the receiver, it will be important to consider at an early stage (and preferably before the proceedings are issued) what defences may be open to the receiver.[113] In particular, the terms of the mortgage should be read carefully, to see whether any exclusion or limitation clause applies.[114] Where the borrower is raising issues which he has previously litigated, or which plainly do not give rise to a cause of action, the receiver may be able to strike the proceedings out as an abuse of process.[115]

Representation

14.109 Often, the lender is also a party to the claim. Indeed, in many cases, the lender has commenced an action against the borrower, and the borrower joins the receiver to his counterclaim. In many cases, it will be possible for the lender's lawyer to represent the receivers as well, but this requires careful consideration in each case. Where the lender and the receiver do not agree as to the consequences (between the receiver and the lender) if the borrower's contentions are made out, or if different allegations are made against the lender and the receiver,[116] separate representation is likely to be required. However, even if separately represented, it may be possible for the receiver to stand behind the lender's submissions on some points, in order to save costs.[117]

---

[110] See para 6.89 *et seq*.

[111] For example *Jumani v Mortgage Express* [2013] EWHC 1571 (Ch).

[112] *In Re Vimbos Ltd* [1900] 1 Ch 470.

[113] See para 6.126 on defences to claims for breach of duty.

[114] The fact that the receiver is not a party to the mortgage is unlikely to mean that he cannot rely on any applicable exclusion clause, by reason of the Contract (Rights of Third Parties) Act 1999.

[115] *JL Homes Ltd v Mortgage Express and Diakiw and Heap* [2013] EWHC 3928 (Ch).

[116] Typically, where there is an allegation that the receiver breached its duties to the borrower, for example, in *Ahmad v Bank of Scotland* [2016] EWCA Civ 602, where it was alleged that the receivers had sold the properties too cheaply. See also *Jumani v Mortgage Express* [2013] EWHC 1571 (Ch). In addition, it may be that the receiver who has breached his duty to the borrower has breached his duty to the lender. See *International Leisure Ltd v First National Trustee Ltd* [2012] EWHC 1971 (Ch), [2013] Ch 346 and the discussion at para 6.96 *et seq*.

[117] In *Day v Tiuta* [2014] EWCA Civ 1246, the lender applied for summary judgment of its claim that the receivers were validly appointed. The receivers were joined as defendants, but were not party to the application. Similarly, in *SS Agri Power Ltd v Dorins* [2017] EWHC 3563 (Ch), the receiver did not appear on an application seeking to restrain the receiver from acting where it was suggested that his appointment was in breach of an agreement not to enforce.

Third parties

14.110 If the receiver contends that, in the event he is liable to the borrower, some other party is liable to indemnify him, he will have to consider whether to join that party as a defendant to a Part 20 claim.[118] Typically, the receiver may have claims of this sort against the lender[119] and/or against any solicitor consulted by the receiver.[120] The receiver will not want to run the risk of inconsistent findings if he seeks to sue a third party in a separate claim, and will generally be well advised to join any potential third party to the borrower's claim unless the third party agrees to be bound by the findings of fact.

14.111 It is theoretically possible for a receiver to make a claim that the borrower has contributed to his own loss, but it is likely to be difficult to establish contributory negligence in practice.[121]

Interim injunctions

14.112 A borrower may well wish for interim relief, for example, to prevent the receiver selling the mortgaged property prior to a trial of the borrower's claim than he was invalidly appointed, or that his proposed sale is in breach of duty.

14.113 In order to obtain an interim injunction, the borrower will have to:

(a) show that there is a serious issue to be tried;

(b) demonstrate that damages will not be an adequate remedy and that the balance of convenience points towards the grant of interim relief; and

(c) give a cross-undertaking in damages and show that he is able to satisfy it.

14.114 Where the borrower is seeking to restrain a proposed distribution or sale, an interim injunction might lie;[122] but where the borrower seeks the

---

[118] See CPR, Pt 20.

[119] Under an express indemnity (as to which, see para 7.33 *et seq*) and/or under the Civil Liability (Contribution) Act 1978, if the lender is also liable to the borrower for the same damage.

[120] If the actions challenged by the borrower were done on legal advice.

[121] In *Knight v Lawrence* [1991] BCC 411, the receiver failed to serve rent review notices. The court rejected his contributory negligence plea, on the basis that he had plenty of time (3 months) to serve the notices after his appointment, and the borrower could not be expected to have served the notices before, or to intervene in the receiver's management afterwards. It might have been different if the receiver were appointed at the very end of the period for serving the trigger notice. No consideration was given in the case to the argument that since the receiver's duties are equitable, contributory negligence ought not to lie. See para 6.128 *et seq*.

[122] Particularly if the borrower is able to offer to service the ongoing mortgage instalments until trial: for an example from Northern Ireland, see *J&N Cowden LLP v Ulster Bank Ltd and Others* [2014] NIQB 138. Similarly, if there will be sufficient equity in the property at trial to repay the lender, even if the instalments are not met. However, where granting an injunction would result in the property remaining vacant until trial, deteriorating in condition and posing a risk to trespassers in the meanwhile, and there was a risk of negative equity, an injunction to restrain a sale was not granted: *Lederer v Allsop LLP*; *sub nom Lederer v Kisby* [2018] EWHC 754 (Ch).

removal of the receiver on the basis that his appointment is invalid, the court is more likely to order a speedy trial.[123]

Expert evidence

14.115   The court will receive expert evidence as to the normal practice of receivers, if the allegation is that the receiver fell below the standard to be expected of reasonably competent receivers.[124]

14.116   Expert valuation evidence may also be required to establish quantum, for the court must consider what different position the borrower would have been in had the receiver's breach of duty not occurred.

Costs

14.117   Typically, costs will follow the event. This means that a receiver is at risk of paying all the costs if a breach of duty is found, even if the damage that flows from it is significantly lower than the borrower is claiming. The receiver should always consider making an offer under Part 36 of the CPR.

14.118   Where an allegation against the receiver is made without any justification, an order that the borrower pays the receiver's costs on an indemnity basis might be appropriate.[125]

Claims by the lender

14.119   The lender can usually remove the receiver if he is unhappy with the way in which the receiver is conducting the receivership. It follows that the circumstances in which the lender will wish to bring a claim against the receiver will be limited. However, if, for example, the receiver misapplies monies he has received, such a claim could arise.[126]

---

[123]   See, for example, *Shamji and Others v Johnson Matthey Bankers Ltd* (1986) 2 BCC 98910, where the trial started just over a month after the writ was issued. See also *SS Agri Power Ltd v Dorins* [2017] EWHC 3563 (Ch). Of course, if the court is not satisfied that there is a serious question to be tried about whether the appointment was valid, the application will be dismissed: *Sinha v Saluja* [2018] EWHC 707 (Ch).

[124]   *Knight v Lawrence* [1991] BCC 411 at 418.

[125]   For an example of an allegation of negligence: *Bank of Baroda v Panessar* [1987] 1 Ch 335. In this case, it was also alleged that the receiver had not been validly appointed and had committed trespass and conversion. There was a reasonable argument as to whether the appointment was valid (albeit one that the borrower ultimately lost), but because the allegation of negligence should not have been made, the borrower was ordered to pay all of the receiver's costs on an indemnity basis. Although not spelt out in the judgment, the rationale for this might have been that but for the allegation of negligence, the receiver would not have required separate representation. Such an order will only be made if it is appropriate to do so under the CPR. Reference should be made to case law on when an indemnity costs order is appropriate.

[126]   For an example, see *Marshall v Cottingham* [1982] Ch 82.

14.120   Again, costs would generally follow the event.

14.121   Alternatively, where the borrower is a company, the lender can seek directions from the court.[127]

---

[127] This procedure is discussed at para 14.15.

Appendix

Termination of Leases

A.1   There are different kinds of tenancies[1] under which the borrower or receiver may have let the mortgaged property. There are also different types of statutory protection which arise in different circumstances depending on the nature of the landlord (here the borrower), the nature of the tenant and/or the nature of the tenant's occupation. Which kind of tenancy there is will affect whether termination is available and what steps are necessary for the tenancy to be terminated.

A.2   In this appendix, first, the different types of tenancy at common law are sketched, and their modes of termination at the instance of the landlord, if any, are addressed. Forfeiture of leases and surrender are then discussed.

A.3   Lastly, the various forms of statutory protection which affect the ability of a landlord to terminate are set out briefly. This is an area of law of some complexity. Reference should be made to any practitioner's text on landlord and tenant law for proper detail.

TYPES OF TENANCIES

A.4   At common law, the types of tenancy, or lease, on which the property may be let are:

(a)   A written or oral[2] fixed term tenancy: i.e. a tenancy for a term of years certain, which is a known fixed period of time, say 1 year, or 21 years or 99 years, or, for example, until the death of Prince Charles. The tenancy will end at the end of the term,[3] unless continued by statute, as sketched

---

[1]   Or leases; the two words are now used relatively interchangeably, though the estate in land is the tenancy, and the lease is the written document whose execution was the grant of the tenancy.

[2]   A lease is a conveyance of land and hence must be made by deed: Law of Property Act 1925, s 52(1), save where not required to be made in writing: s 52(2)(d). Such leases not required to be made in writing are those taking effect in possession for a term not exceeding 3 years at the best rent which can be reasonably obtained without taking a fine: s 54(2). Short leases can be created orally. A lease which is required to be made by deed but is created by contract complying with Law of Property (Miscellaneous Provisions) Act 1989, s 2 will take effect in equity only. An oral agreement to grant a lease of longer than 3 years will be of no effect unless a proprietary estoppel arises. The grant by deed of a lease for a term of years absolute of more than 7 years must be registered to take effect at law: Land Registration Act 2002, ss 4(1)(c) and 7(1) and (2)(b).

[3]   Ending subsidiary interests such as sub-leases and mortgages.

below. The lease may have an express break clause in it allowing the landlord[4] to terminate before the end of the term. If the break clause is exercised, the lease will be terminated early. The steps required are prescribed by the lease and must be followed precisely.

(b)   A written or oral[5] periodic tenancy: i.e. a rolling tenancy. The most common are from week to week, or month to month, or year to year. At common law, periodic tenancies continue until ended by one of the parties. At common law, they can be ended by either party by the service of a notice to quit expiring on the last day of one period or the first of the next. The amount of notice required depends on the period of the tenancy (save where the lease provides otherwise). Half a year's notice must be given for termination of a yearly tenancy. A month's notice must be given to terminate a monthly periodic tenancy, and a week's notice must be given to terminate a weekly periodic tenancy.

(c)   A written or oral tenancy at will: i.e. a tenancy at the will only of the parties, and is most commonly found when the landlord lets the tenant into the property before finalising the formalities of an intended lease, or when the tenant holds over the end of the contractual term but with the assent of the landlord.[6] Such a tenancy is terminable on reasonable notice by either party. What is reasonable depends on the circumstances, including the length of occupation.

(d)   A written or oral tenancy on sufferance: i.e. a tenancy which arises on the holding over by the tenant after the contractual term of a tenancy, where the landlord has neither assented nor dissented. The tenancy can be terminated by the landlord without notice. A claim for possession will suffice.

TYPES OF TERMINATION

A.5   In addition to the methods of termination discussed above, tenancies can also be brought to an end in a number of other ways, common to all leases. The most common are discussed briefly below.

A.6   Of these, forfeiture of leases is likely the most commonly encountered in receivership, in particular, where the mortgaged property is leasehold, since if the borrower is in arrears with the mortgage, he is likely in arrears with rent and/or service charges under his lease. It is thus discussed in more detail below.[7]

---

4   Or the tenant.

5   A periodic tenancy of period not exceeding 3 years can be made orally: Law of Property Act 1925, s 54(2).

6   Although the court sometimes decides that a periodic tenancy then arises.

7   See para 8.181 for a discussion of whether and when the receiver can seek relief from forfeiture of the mortgaged property, and paras 10.105–10.111 as to whether and when the receiver can forfeit a lease out of the mortgaged property.

Surrender

A.7   Surrender[8] is a consensual act in which the landlord and tenant agree to the lease coming to an end.

A.8   Surrender is a disposition of land. Hence the surrender should be by deed,[9] save that surrender by operation of law is possible without deed or even writing if the conduct of the landlord and the tenant unequivocally amounts to acceptance that the tenancy has ended,[10] for example where the tenant returns possession to the landlord, perhaps by returning the keys, and the landlord accepts for example by re-letting the premises, or where the landlord grants a new lease to the tenant as a replacement for the old one.[11]

A.9   Surrender does not end subsidiary interests[12] such as sub-leases[13] and mortgages,[14] though the exact relationship between the old landlord and the person with the subsidiary interest is a subject of case law dispute.[15]

Merger

A.10   When the leaseholder acquires his immediate reversion, or the landlord acquires the lease, then at common law the leasehold merged[16] with the reversion so that it is unencumbered and the covenants cease, because someone could not be both landlord and tenant, and hence covenant with himself. A sub-lease would continue despite a merger.[17]

A.11   In equity, however, merger only occurs if that is the intention of the parties. Merger is not presumed. The equitable rule prevails. Hence, merger is now rare.

---

[8]   See paras 9.157–9.163 for the receiver's power of accepting surrenders.

[9]   Law of Property Act 1925, s 52(1).

[10]   Surrender by operation of law operates by estoppel, not intention. The parties act in such a way that they are estopped from denying that there has been a surrender.

[11]   This is what happens when a new lease is granted by reason of a statutory right, for example, under the Leasehold Reform, Housing and Urban Development Act 1993.

[12]   Law of Property Act 1925, s 139.

[13]   *Mellor v Watkins* (1873–74) LR 9 QB 400.

[14]   *ES Schwab & Co Ltd v McCarthy* (1976) 31 P & CR 196.

[15]   *Plummer v David* [1920] 1 KB 326; *Electricity Supply Nominees v Thorn EMI Retail* [1991] 2 EGLR 46.

[16]   Provided the person held the two interests in the same capacity. Thus, if a leaseholder becomes the executor of his landlord, the estates will not merge.

[17]   Law of Property Act 1925, s 139.

Forfeiture

A.12   Forfeiture[18] occurs when the landlord elects to bring the lease to an end when the tenant has breached one of his obligations in it, for example, not paying rent, or not repairing (when it is the tenant who has the obligation to repair), or making structural alterations without consent (where the tenant is obliged to seek the landlord's consent). The right is called the right to forfeit or the right of re-entry.

A.13   For forfeiture to be available, the lease must contain a forfeiture clause setting out when the right arises and for which breaches. Occasionally, leases are silent as to forfeiture, for example when the tenancy is oral. It is reasonably possible to imply a right to forfeit for breach of an obligation central to the landlord and tenant relationship, in particular non-payment of rent.

Actions constituting forfeiture

A.14   When there is a breach of covenant, the landlord must elect whether or not to forfeit. The action he must take to forfeit is either peaceable re-entry, i.e. going into the property and re-taking possession by changing the locks or otherwise securing it, or by issuing a possession claim.

A.15   In the case of premises let as a dwelling, it is unlawful to enforce a right of re-entry without taking court proceedings while any person is lawfully residing in the dwelling.[19]

Waiver of the right to forfeit

A.16   A landlord may lose the right to forfeit for a particular breach of lease by waiving that breach. This occurs if knowing the facts upon which the right has arisen, he acts unequivocally so as to recognise the continued existence of the lease.

A.17   For example, if the landlord knows that the tenant has altered the property without consent, in a situation where the lease required the landlord to give consent first, but then demands and accepts rent which next falls due, then he will have waived the right to forfeit for that breach.

A.18   Acceptance of rent falling due after knowledge of the breach is the epitome of an act recognising the continuation of a lease. There is some dispute as to what other acts would be waiver; see, for example, the discussion in *Yorkshire Metropolitan Properties Ltd v Co-operative Retail Services Ltd*,[20] in

---

[18]   See para 8.181 for a discussion of whether and when the receiver can seek relief from forfeiture of the mortgaged property, and paras 10.105–10.111 as to whether and when the receiver can forfeit a lease out of the mortgaged property.

[19]   Protection from Eviction Act 1977, s 2. See the discussion at paras 10.198–10.210 as to the decision whether to take possession though the courts versus without a court order.

[20]   [2001] L&TR 26.

which an agent's service charge demand did not waive when the landlord had been clear in correspondence that it intended to forfeit.

A.19   Great care must be taken to avoid waiver since the tenant will likely rely on any act of the landlord which relies on the covenants in the lease, for example demanding entry under an access provision in the lease.

A.20   Breaches of covenant divide into 'once and for all breaches' and 'continuing breaches'. A once and for all breach is one that arises once. If it is waived, then the right to forfeit is entirely lost. Non-payment of rent is a once and for all breach for each instalment of rent due under the lease. Carrying out alterations without consent is also a once and for all breach. A continuing breach is one, if not remedied, is a breach which arises every day afresh. For example, a breach of a repairing covenant arises afresh every day until the repairs are carried out. Thus, a waiver of the right to forfeit which arises on day one is not fatal because the breach arises again on day two, if not remedied.

Notices under Law of Property Act 1925, section 146 for breaches other than rent

A.21   Where the breach is non-payment of rent, the landlord may immediately forfeit the lease. For other breaches, however, he must first serve a notice under section 146 of the Law of Property Act 1925 specifying the breach complained of, if the breach is capable of remedy requiring the lessee to remedy it, and requiring the lessee to compensate him in money for the breach. The landlord can only then forfeit if the lessee fails to remedy the breach (if capable of remedy) and to make reasonable compensation to the landlord's satisfaction within a reasonable time. If the tenant satisfies these requirements, the lease continues.

Forfeiture of leases of premises let as a dwelling

A.22   In the case of premises let as a dwelling, the landlord cannot serve a valid notice under section 146 of the Law of Property Act 1925, let alone forfeit, for a failure by his tenant to pay a service charge[21] or an administration charge[22] without it having first been 'finally determined'[23] by a court,[24] a First-tier Tribunal (Property Chamber), or an arbitral tribunal, that the amount of the service charge or administration charge is payable by the tenant, unless the tenant has admitted that it is so payable.[25] Once the determination has been

---

[21]   Defined in Landlord and Tenant Act 1985, s 18.

[22]   Defined in Commonhold and Leasehold Reform Act 2002, Sch 11, para 1.

[23]   See Housing Act 1996, s 81(3A) for the meaning of 'finally determined'. The time period for appeal must pass even if no appeal is made.

[24]   A default judgment is likely sufficient: *Church Commissioners for England v Koyale Enterprises* [2012] 2 EGLR 42.

[25]   Housing Act 1996, s 81.

obtained, there are time limits that must pass before a section 146 notice can be served.[26]

A.23   There is nothing in the wording of section 81 of the Housing Act 1996 specifying who the parties to the proceedings resulting in the determination must be. Clearly, the tenant must be a party, to be bound.

A.24   In the case of a long lease[27] of a dwelling, the landlord cannot forfeit for breach of any covenant other than non-payment of rent or service charges, without it having been 'finally determined'[28] by a court, or the First-tier Tribunal (Property Chamber), or an arbitral tribunal, that the breach has occurred, or the tenant has admitted the breach.[29]

A.25   There is nothing in the wording of section 168 of the Commonhold and Leasehold Reform Act 2002 specifying who the parties to the proceedings resulting in the determination must be.

A.26   Lastly, a landlord under a long lease of a dwelling may not forfeit for non-payment of an amount consisting of rent, service charges or administration charges, or a combination of them, unless the amount exceeds the prescribed sum, or consists of or includes an amount which has been payable for more than a prescribed period.[30]

A.27   Even if the rent is unpaid at the required level or for the required period, care should be taken to check that the tenant is liable for it before issuing a possession claim. Ground rent is not payable by a tenant under a long lease unless demanded in a prescribed form with prescribed information.[31]

Relief from forfeiture

A.28   Whatever the basis of the claim for forfeiture, the tenant has an opportunity to seek relief from forfeiture from the court so that the lease will continue. Usually, the court orders relief on terms that the tenant remedy the breach in some way, and pays costs.

---

[26]   *Freeholder of 69 Marina v Oram* [2011] EWCA Civ 1258 decided that after a Housing Act 1996, s 81 determination had been obtained, a s 146 notice must be served, even if the service charge or administration charge in question had been reserved as rent. This is contrary to *Escalus Properties Ltd v Robinson* [1996] QB 231, which had previously been followed.

[27]   'Long lease' includes various categories of lease, though the standard lease caught is a lease of at least a 21-year term. See Commonhold and Leasehold Reform Act 2002, s 76 and s 77, and s 169(4).

[28]   See Commonhold and Leasehold Reform Act 2002, s 169(2) for the meaning of this. The period for an appeal must pass, even if the decision is not appealed.

[29]   Commonhold and Leasehold Reform Act 2002, s 168.

[30]   Commonhold and Leasehold Reform Act 2002, s 167. At present, the prescribed sum is £350, and the prescribed period is 3 years.

[31]   Commonhold and Leasehold Reform Act 2002, s 166, and see Landlord and Tenant (Notice of Rent) (England) Regulations 2004, and Landlord and Tenant (Notice of Rent) (Wales) Regulations 2005 for the forms of rent demand.

A.29 Where forfeiture is for non-payment of rent alone, and a claim for possession made by the 'lessor' in the county court, relief is automatic if the tenant pays the arrears and any costs before the first possession hearing.[32] If this has not been done, then the court must make a possession order giving relief conditional on the tenant paying the arrears and costs within a specified time period which is not to be less than 28 days.[33] The tenant can apply for more time if necessary,[34] up to execution of the possession order.

A.30 If forfeiture was by peaceable re-entry, the tenant may apply at time within 6 months for relief, and the county court may grant such relief as the High Court could have granted.[35]

A.31 Relief is also available in the High Court under section 38 of the Senior Courts Act 1981 in an action for forfeiture for non-payment of rent, or, more generally, within the High Court's inherent jurisdiction.

A.32 For breaches of other covenants than non-payment of rent alone, relief is available under section 146(2) of the Law of Property Act 1925, whether forfeiture was by peaceable re-entry or possession proceedings.

Disclaimer

A.33 Disclaimer is a statutory right given to trustees in bankruptcy, and to company liquidators, and separately to the Crown, in certain circumstances to refuse to be bound by a freehold or a lease that has become vested in them. It is available in two situations.

A.34 First, if a company leaseholder is being wound up, the liquidator can disclaim company property if it is onerous.[36] Likewise, where an individual leaseholder is bankrupt, and his property vests in his trustee in bankruptcy, the trustee can disclaim onerous property.[37]

A.35 In either case, the disclaimer determines the rights, interest and liabilities of the individual/company, but does not, except so far as necessary for the purpose of releasing the individual/company from any liability, affect the rights or liabilities of any other person.[38] Thus subsidiary interests such as leases, sub-leases and mortgages continue, but in a shadowy form since, with leases, there

---

[32] County Courts Act 1984, s 138(2).

[33] County Courts Act 1984, s 138(3).

[34] County Courts Act 1984, s 138(4).

[35] County Courts Act 1984, s 139(2).

[36] Insolvency Act 1986, Pt IV, Ch VIII, s 178. An onerous contract is one which is unprofitable, unsaleable or not readily able to be sold, or giving rise to a liability: s 178(3).

[37] Insolvency Act 1986, Pt IX, Ch IV, s 315.

[38] Insolvency Act 1986, Pt IV, Ch VIII, s 178 (company); s 315(3) (individual).

is no longer a landlord, and in the case of a mortgage, the borrower no longer has an interest.[39]

A.36   Where the disclaimed property is leasehold, the disclaimer does not take effect until a copy has been served on all interested persons, underlessees and the mortgagee, and then only if an application for a vesting order has not been made within 14 days of service of the last such notice, or an application has been made but the court orders disclaimer rather than a vesting order.[40] It is thus important that a vesting order is sought.[41]

A.37   Secondly, on the dissolution of a company, for example, on the conclusion of a winding up, or the striking off of a company from the company register for example for non-filing of accounts,[42] any remaining company property[43] vests in the Crown[44] *bona vacantia*.[45] The Crown will rarely want any liability on it from that property. It can thus disclaim it.[46]

A.38   The effect is to terminate the company's rights, interests and liabilities,[47] but not, except so far as is necessary for the purposes of releasing the company from any liability, to affect the rights or liabilities of any other person.[48] Thus any underleases and any mortgage continue, albeit in an odd way given that the lease has become shadowy because of the disclaimer, so that there is no landlord/borrower interest. Such underlessees, or the lender,[49] can apply to the court for an order vesting the disclaimed property in them.[50]

STATUTORY CONTINUATION OF TENANCIES

A.39   In numerous circumstances, statute imposes limits on termination of tenancies. This section sets out in brief some key examples.

---

[39]   Thus, the lender can sell the disclaimed property under his power of sale, and revive it in the purchaser: *Scmlla Properties Ltd v Gesso Properties (BV) Ltd* [1995] BCC 793 a case on disclaimer of a freehold.

[40]   Insolvency Act 1986, s 179 (company), s 317 (individual); and see s 318 in relation to dwelling-houses where service on occupiers is required.

[41]   On an application under Insolvency Act 1986, s 181 (company), s 320 (individual). Note that the vesting order will usually make the person in whom the disclaimed property is vested directly liable on the leasehold covenants: s 182 (company), s 321 (individual).

[42]   Companies Act 2006, Pt 31 for example, s 1000.

[43]   Save if held by the company on trust for another: *Re Strathblane Estates* [1948] Ch 228.

[44]   Or the Duchy of Lancaster, or the Duke of Cornwall, depending on its location.

[45]   Companies Act 2006, s 1012.

[46]   See Companies Act 2006, Pt 31, Ch 2. Notice on underlessees and the lender is necessary: s 1016(1).

[47]   Companies Act 2006, s 1015.

[48]   Companies Act 2006, s 1015(2).

[49]   See Companies Act 2006, s 1017(1) for the categories of people who can apply.

[50]   Companies Act 2006, ss 1017(2), and 1018 in relation to applications by underlessees and mortgagees.

Business tenancies

A.40   Business tenancies are regulated by Part II of the Landlord and Tenant Act 1954, which applies to 'any tenancy where the property comprised in the tenancy is or includes premises which are occupied by the tenant and are so occupied for the purposes of a business carried on by him or for those and other purposes'.[51]

A.41   A common law notice to quit cannot be served validly so as to end the lease. Nor does the lease simply end at the contractual term date. If the business occupation is continuing at the notice date in a notice to quit or the contractual term date, then the lease is continued by section 24 of the Landlord and Tenant Act 1954.

A.42   The Landlord and Tenant Act 1954 sets out a statutory regime of notices[52] which can be served to terminate the tenancy, but give the tenant a right to request a new tenancy, via an application to the court if necessary, and only limited grounds of opposition for the landlord.

Rent Act tenancies

A.43   There is considerable regulation of residential tenancies, beyond that set out above in the section on forfeiture.

A.44   A lease granted before 15 January 1989[53] under which a dwelling-house is let as separate dwelling is a protected tenancy under section 1 of the Rent Act 1977 unless it falls into one of the exceptions at sections 4 to 16.[54] At the end of the contractual term, or if a break clause is exercised, or a notice to quit served to terminate a contractual periodic tenancy, the tenancy will continue as a statutory tenancy 'if and so long as [the tenant] occupies the dwelling-house as his residence'.[55]

A.45   The Rent Act 1977 prevents the court from making a possession order[56] of a dwelling-house let on a protected or statutory tenancy unless the court considers it reasonable to make a possession order and either the court is satisfied that suitable alternative accommodation is available for the tenant, or one of the cases in Schedule 15, Part I is made out. These include grounds such as non-payment of rent, nuisance and deterioration of the dwelling-house due to acts of waste and neglect or default by the tenant.

---

[51]   Landlord and Tenant Act 1954, s 23.

[52]   Landlord and Tenant Act 1954, s 25 and s 26 notices.

[53]   When the Housing Act 1988 came into force and prevented new Rent Act tenancies from being granted save in exceptional circumstances.

[54]   For example, tenancies with high rateable values, if granted before 1 April 1990, or at high rent – £25,000 pa or over – if granted thereafter, or at low rent – £1,000 or less pa in Greater London, or £250 or less pa elsewhere.

[55]   Rent Act 1977, s 2(1)(a).

[56]   Rent Act 1977, s 98.

A.46   Schedule 15, Part II of the Rent Act 1977 sets out grounds for possession on which the court must make a possession order, and reasonableness need not be considered. These include where the landlord occupied the dwelling-house as his residence prior to letting it, and gave notice in writing[57] beforehand that he might recover possession on this ground (case 11).[58] One of the requirements for the making of a possession order[59] is satisfaction of one of a number of conditions in Part V of the Schedule including at 2(e), that the dwelling-house is subject to a mortgage, granted by deed before the tenancy, and the lender is entitled to exercise a power of sale and requires to dispose of the dwelling-house with vacant possession.

A.47   There are considerable difficulties in obtaining and executing a possession order in relation to a tenancy protected by the Rent Act 1977. The requirement for reasonableness in relation to the Schedule 15, Part I grounds, and the court's extended discretion to adjourn, stay or suspend execution, or postpone the date of possession where possession is sought on Part I grounds,[60] results in numerous hearings in which the court gives the tenant opportunities to remedy any wrong on which possession was sought.

Assured tenancies

A.48   Since 15 January 1989, it has not been possible to create any new Rent Act 1977 tenancies, save in very limited circumstances. That is because the Housing Act 1988 commenced on that date, introduced assured tenancies, and prohibited the granting of new Rent Act tenancies.

A.49   Under section 1(1) of the Housing Act 1988, any tenancy granted on or after 15 January 1989 under which a dwelling-house is let as a separate dwelling is assured if and so long as the tenant is an individual, and occupies the dwelling-house as his only or principal home.

A.50   There are a number of exceptions to assured status, set out in Schedule 1 to the Housing Act 1988. These include tenancies at low rent, i.e. for a tenancy entered into on or after 1 April 1990, at a rent of £1,000 pa in Greater London, or £250 pa elsewhere.[61] Tenancies at high rents – £100,000 pa – are also excluded.[62]

---

[57]   The court can dispense with notice if of the opinion that it is just and equitable to make an order for possession.

[58]   Full details of the requirements are set out in the Rent Act 1977.

[59]   It is also a requirement for case 12 (landlord intending to occupy on retirement) and case 20 (letting by owned when a member of the regular armed forces).

[60]   Rent Act 1977, s 100.

[61]   Housing Act 1988, Sch 1, para 3A. It is this low rent exception that prevents owner-occupied long residential leases from being assured. Conversely, shared ownership leases are often assured.

[62]   Housing Act 1988, Sch 1, para 2(1).

A.51 Under section 5(1) of the Housing Act 1988, an assured tenancy cannot be brought to an end by a landlord except by obtaining a possession order from the court, and the execution of the order.

A.52 If a fixed-term assured tenancy expires by effluxion of time, or contains a landlord break clause which the landlord operates, then a statutory periodic tenancy arises[63] immediately,[64] on like terms,[65] unless the tenant is then entitled to a possession of the same or substantially the same dwelling-house by grant of another tenancy,[66] i.e. if a new contractual tenancy is granted.

A.53 The period is 'the same as those for which rent was last payable under the fixed term tenancy'.[67] If the rent was payable weekly, a statutory weekly-periodic tenancy arises. If the rent was payable monthly, a statutory monthly-periodic tenancy arises. In all such cases, the day of the first period is the first day after the term date of the contractual tenancy.

A.54 Notices to quit are of no effect in relation to a contractual periodic assured tenancy.[68] Nor can an assured tenancy be terminated by forfeiture.[69] It follows that relief from forfeiture is not available.[70]

A.55 An assured tenancy can only be terminated by a landlord by serving a section 8 notice[71] on one of the grounds for possession in Schedule 2 to the Housing Act 1988, issuing possession proceedings, obtaining a possession order, and executing it.

A.56 The Schedule 2 grounds divide into two kinds, those in Part I, the mandatory grounds, and those in Part II, the discretionary grounds.

A.57 The key difference is that if the court is satisfied on any of the Part I grounds, then it 'shall' make an order for possession.[72] This gives considerable certainty. If the court makes a possession order on a mandatory ground, then it cannot postpone, whether by the order, or any variation, suspension or stay of execution, to a date later than 14 days after the making of the order, unless it

---

[63] Housing Act 1988, s 5(2).

[64] Housing Act 1988, s 5(3)(a).

[65] Housing Act 1988, s 5(3)(b), (c) and (e).

[66] Housing Act 1988, s 5(4).

[67] Housing Act 1988, s 5(3)(d).

[68] Housing Act 1988, s 5(1).

[69] See *Artesian Residential Investments Ltd v Beck* [1999] 2 EGLR 30, CA, overruled in *Knowlsey Housing Trust v White* [2008] UKHL 70, [2009] AC 636 on another point. See also Housing Act 1988, s 45(4), which excludes re-entry and forfeiture from the meaning of s 5(1)(c).

[70] This is particularly problematic for mortgagees of shared ownership leases, which have rents above the low rent exception, if a ground 8 mandatory possession order is made and executed for the tenant's non-payment of rent: *Richardson v Midland Heart Ltd* [2008] L&TR 31.

[71] Possession on valid service of a s 21 notice, where an assured tenancy is an assured shorthold tenancy, is discussed below.

[72] Housing Act 1988, s 7(3).

appears to the court that exceptional hardship would be caused by requiring possession to be given up by that date.[73] The maximum postponement in any event, for a mandatory possession order, is 6 weeks from the making of the order.[74]

A.58 Conversely, on a claim for possession on a Part II discretionary ground, even if the court is satisfied that the ground is established, it may make an order 'if it considers it reasonable to do so'.[75] Section 89(1) of the Housing Act 1980 does not apply.[76] Thus, the process of obtaining possession on a Part II ground is often much slower and more difficult. The tenant often makes numerous applications to suspend the possession order, or a warrant of possession, once issued.

A.59 A notice under section 8 of the Housing Act 1988 must be served before the issue of a possession claim, save, in relation to grounds 7A, 7B or 8 only, and the court considers it just and equitable to dispense with notice.[77] Section 8 sets out various requirements as to form and content of the notice.[78] It is intended that the tenant will have both the text of the grounds relied on and particulars of the facts relied on to allow him to know why it is said the ground is made out. Section 8 also sets out required time periods between service of the notice and issue of the claim. In the case of a claim on ground 8, for example, 2 weeks are required from service of the notice.[79]

A.60 The Part I grounds include ground 2: where the dwelling-house is subject to a mortgage granted before the beginning of a tenancy, the lender is entitled to exercise a power of sale, requires possession to sell with vacant possession, and notice in writing was given to the tenant before the beginning of the tenancy that possession might be sought on this ground. There is no further definition of 'mortgagee' that suggests whether it includes 'receiver'. Nor, however, does it appear the claim on this ground must be brought by the lender.

A.61 It also includes ground 8, one of the most common grounds on which possession is sought, when there are rent arrears. For a claim to succeed, assuming a tenancy where rent is payable monthly, then both at the date of the service of the section 8 notice and at the date of the possession hearing at least 2 months' rent is unpaid. There are similar requirements where rent is payable by reference to different periods.

---

[73] Housing Act 1980, s 89(1).

[74] Housing Act 1980, s 89(1) does not apply to possession claims by mortgagees: s 89(2)(a). 'Mortgagee' is not further defined. It is unclear whether this could include a possession claim by a receiver. See the discussion at paras 10.10.149–10.150.

[75] Housing Act 1988, s 7(4).

[76] Housing Act 1980, s 89(2)(c).

[77] Housing Act 1988, s 8(1).

[78] The form of the notice can be found at Assured Tenancies and Agricultural Occupancies (Forms) (England) Regulations 2015 (SI 2015/620), Form No 3.

[79] Housing Act 1988, s 8(4B).

A.62   The Part II grounds include grounds 10 (some rent is unpaid on the date of claim, and at the date of service of the s. 8 notice) and 11 (persistent delay in paying rent), which are discretionary grounds where rent is unpaid, but ground 8 cannot be made out, and ground 12, breach of any other obligation under the tenancy than one relating to payment of rent.

Assured shorthold tenancies

A.63   Tenancies protected under the Housing Act 1988 are assured tenancies, but that includes a sub-category, assured shorthold tenancies. The significant difference is that an assured shorthold tenancy can be terminated by service of a section 21 notice and court proceedings. This is a no-fault ground of possession, akin to a notice to quit at common law.

A.64   Prior to 23 August 1996, when section 96 of the Housing Act 1996 came into force,[80] an assured shorthold tenancy could only be created if prescribed notices were served prior to before the tenancy was entered into. After that date, all assured tenancies entered into (apart from those continuing pre-1996 tenancies) have been assured shorthold tenancies. Most short-term tenancies protected by the Housing Act 1988 are now assured shorthold.

A.65   A possession order in relation to a fixed term tenancy can be sought under section 21 of the Housing Act 1988 if the contractual tenancy has come to an end (by effluxion of time, or service of notice exercising any break clause) and the landlord has served a section 21 notice giving the tenant not less than 2 months' notice stating that he requires possession.

A.66   A possession order in relation to a periodic tenancy[81] can be sought under section 21 of the Housing Act 1988 if the landlord has given the tenant not less than 2 months' notice in writing stating that after a date specified, being the last day of a period of the tenancy, possession is required.[82] In England, this requirement that the notice specify the last day of a period has been omitted for notices served after 1 October 2015.[83]

A.67   Since 1 October 2015, the form of section 21 notice that must be used in England can be found in the schedule to the Assured Shorthold Tenancy Notices and Prescribed Requirements (England) Regulations 2015.[84] The form requires signature by someone acting for the landlord, though there is no express statutory requirement for a signature save by the implication from the form of the notice in the Regulations.

---

[80]   Housing Act 1988, s 19A.

[81]   Provided the tenancy started as a fixed term tenancy, so that it is a statutory periodic in force, a notice satisfying Housing Act 1988, s 21(1) is sufficient, and hence the requirement that the notice specify the last date of a period can be avoided: *Taylor v Spencer* [2013] EWCA Civ 1600, [2014] HLR 113.

[82]   Housing Act 1988, s 21(4).

[83]   Housing Act 1988, s 21(4ZA).

[84]   SI 2015/1646.

A.68 The Assured Shorthold Tenancy Notices and Prescribed Requirements (England) Regulations 2015 have also set out prescribed requirements under section 21A of the Housing Act 1988.[85] The prescribed requirements are to provide an energy performance certificate to a tenant free of charge, and a requirement to provide a tenant with a gas safety certificate.[86] A section 21 notice may not be given when the landlord is in breach of either of these prescribed requirements.[87]

A.69 The Assured Shorthold Tenancy Notices and Prescribed Requirements (England) Regulations 2015 also set out prescribed information that the landlord must provide the tenant. The prescribed information is a document entitled 'How to rent: the checklist for renting in England' published by the Department for Communities and Local Government.[88] A failure to do so prevents a valid notice under section 21 of the Housing Act 1988 from being given.[89]

A.70 There are other statutory restrictions on service of valid notices under section 21 of the Housing Act 1988.

A.71 First, section 33 of the Deregulation Act 2015, which is intended to prevent 'retaliatory evictions'.[90] Since 1 October 2015, no notice under section 21 of the Housing Act 1988 may be given within 6 months of service of a relevant notice, i.e. an improvement notice relating to a category 1 or 2 hazard, or a notice requiring emergency remedial action, all within the meaning of the Housing Act 2004.[91]

A.72 Nor can a valid notice under section 21 of the Housing Act 1988 be given if, before it was given, the tenant made a complaint in writing to the landlord regarding the condition of the dwelling-house, and the landlord did not provide a response within 14 days, or did not provide an adequate response describing the action the landlord proposes to take, and a reasonable timescale, or served a section 21 notice, the tenant complained to the relevant local housing authority, and the authority served a relevant notice.[92]

---

[85] Various amendments to the Housing Act 1988, including the introduction of s 21A and s 21B, were made by the Deregulation Act 2015: see ss 33–41 of that Act. They apply only to assured shorthold tenancies granted on or after the date each provision was brought into force, usually 1 October 2015, until 3 years from that date when they apply to all assured shorthold tenancies whenever granted: s 41.

[86] Assured Shorthold Tenancy Notices and Prescribed Requirements (England) Regulations 2015, reg 2.

[87] Housing Act 1988, s 21A(1), though note the limits to its application for older tenancies until the elapse of 3 years from 1 July 2015, the date the provision came into force: fn 85.

[88] Assured Shorthold Tenancy Notices and Prescribed Requirements (England) Regulations 2015, reg 3(2).

[89] Housing Act 1988, s 21B(3).

[90] See Deregulation Act 2015, s 41 for the limit of applicability.

[91] Deregulation Act 2015, s 33(13).

[92] Deregulation Act 2015, 33(2).

A.73 These provisions under section 33 of the Deregulation Act 2015 are subject to limitations in section 34, in particular neither section 33(1) nor section 33(2) applies where the house is subject to a mortgage granted before the beginning of the tenancy, the lender is entitled to exercise a power of sale, and at the time of service of the notice under section 21 of the Housing Act 1988, the lender requires possession for sale with vacant possession.[93] Moreover, 'mortgagee' includes a receiver appointed by the lender under the terms of the charge of the Law of Property Act 1925.

A.74 The Housing Act 2004 also limits the validity of notices under section 21 of the Housing Act 1988. No section 21 notice may be given in relation to a tenancy of part of an unlicensed houses in multiple occupation.[94] Nor can a section 21 notice be served in relation to a tenancy of whole or part of an unlicensed house.[95]

A.75 The Housing Act 2004 also includes requirements as to tenancy deposit schemes for assured shorthold tenancies.[96] A tenancy deposit[97] must be dealt with in accordance with an authorised scheme from the time it is received.[98] Moreover:

(a) the initial requirements of the scheme must be complied with by the landlord within 30 days of receipt.[99] The initial requirements are what is imposed by the scheme;[100]

(b) the landlord must give the tenant information about the authorised scheme, compliance with the initial requirements, and the operation of provisions of the Housing Act 2004 as may be prescribed,[101] in the prescribed form, and within 30 days of receipt.[102]

A.76 The prescribed information is set out in the Housing (Tenancy Deposits) (Prescribed Information) Order 2007.[103] That was amended, so that the current version has been in force since 26 March 2015, but is to be treated as having had effect since 6 April 2007.[104]

---

[93] Deregulation Act 2015, s 34(7).

[94] Housing Act 2004, s 75(1).

[95] Housing Act 2004, s 98(1).

[96] Housing Act 2004, ss 212–215C. Tenancy deposit requirements were originally brought into force on 6 April 2007, but the provisions are much amended. The schemes are custodial – the money is paid to the scheme – or insurance – the landlord retains the deposit but it is insured.

[97] Money intended to be held by the landlord or otherwise as security for the performance of tenant obligations or the discharge of tenant liability arising under or in connection with the tenancy: Housing Act 2004, s 212(8).

[98] Housing Act 2004, s 213(1).

[99] Housing Act 2004, s 213(3).

[100] Housing Act 2004, s 213(4).

[101] Housing Act 2004, s 214(5).

[102] Housing Act 2004, s 213(6).

[103] SI 2007/797.

[104] SI 2007/797, art 3(1). There are transitional provisions in art 3. In addition, Housing Act 2004, s 215A(3) gave a 90-day period from 26 March 2015 for compliance with s 213 as amended from that date. Receivers may well find that s 213 compliance is lacking.

A.77   There are two sanctions for non-compliance with these requirements. The first, in section 214 of the Housing Act 2004, allows the tenant to apply to court on the grounds of non-compliance with section 213(3) or (6) or an inability to obtain confirmation from the scheme administrator for the scheme notified to him by the landlord, that the deposit is being held.[105]

A.78   If the application succeeds, the court must order the repayment of the deposit by the person who appears to be holding it, or the payment of it into a scheme, within 14 days, and it must order the landlord[106] to pay the tenant a sum between the amount of the deposit and three times the amount of the deposit within 14 days.

A.79   The second sanction is that no valid notice under section 21 of the Housing Act 1988 can be served where a tenancy deposit has been paid when:

(a)   it is not being held in accordance with an authorised scheme;[107]
(b)   section 213(3) has not been complied with, i.e. compliance with the initial requirements within 30 days;[108]
(c)   section 213(6) has not been complied with, i.e. provision of prescribed information within 30 days, save that once the prescribed information has been provided, this prohibition on service of a section 21 notice is lifted.[109]

A.80   However, the prohibition on service of a notice under section 21 of the Housing Act 1988 can be lifted by returning the deposit in full, or with agreed deductions only, or if a section 214 application has been made, determined by the court, withdrawn, or settled.[110] Tenants sometimes refuse to accept repayment. It seems likely, however, that a court would not permit the effect of section 215(2A) being prevented in this way.

Other statutory regulated tenancies

A.81   Business tenancies, Rent Act tenancies and assured and assured shorthold tenancies are far from all of the types of statutorily regulated tenancies. For example, the Housing Act 1985 regulates secure tenancies, tenancies of dwelling-houses let by local authorities, and certain housing associations and similar social landlords to individuals, where the individual occupies the dwelling-house as his only or principal home.

---

[105]   Housing Act 2004, s 214(1).
[106]   Which may include any person acting on his behalf: Housing Act 2004, s 212(9)(a).
[107]   Housing Act 2004, s 215(1).
[108]   Housing Act 2004, s 215(1A).
[109]   Housing Act 2004, s 215(2).
[110]   Housing Act 2004, s 215(2A).

A.82 There is statutory regulation of lettings of agricultural land under the Agricultural Holdings Act 1986 and the Agricultural Tenancies Act 1995, for example.

A.83 In each case, there is a particular scheme of grounds for possession, and jurisdiction on the court to grant possession orders. Reference should be made to practitioners' texts in these areas for details.

Index

References are to paragraph numbers.